S0-BDM-821

MODEL VOICES:
Finding a Writing Voice

MODEL VOICES:
Finding a Writing Voice

Jeffrey Sommers

Miami University–Middletown

McGraw-Hill Book Company

New York St. Louis San Francisco Auckland Bogotá Caracas
Colorado Springs Hamburg Lisbon London Madrid Mexico
Milan Montreal New Delhi Oklahoma City Panama Paris
San Juan São Paulo Singapore Sydney Tokyo Toronto

This book was set in Plantin by the College Composition Unit
in cooperation with General Graphic Services, Inc.
The editors were Susan D. Hurtt and Bernadette Boylan;
the production supervisor was Friederich W. Schulte.
The cover was designed by Joan E. O'Connor.
Cover illustration by Cathy Hull.
R. R. Donnelley & Sons Company was printer and binder.

See acknowledgments on pages 517–521.
Copyrights included on this page by reference.

Model Voices: Finding a Writing Voice

Copyright © 1989 by McGraw-Hill, Inc. All rights reserved.
Printed in the United States of America. Except as permitted under the
United States Copyright Act of 1976, no part of this publication may be
reproduced or distributed in any form or by any means, or stored in a data
base or retrieval system, without the prior written permission of the publisher.

1 2 3 4 5 6 7 8 9 0 D O C D O C 8 9 4 3 2 1 0 9

ISBN 0-07-059668-9

Library of Congress Cataloging-in-Publication Data

Sommers, Jeffrey.
   Model voices: finding a writing voice / by Jeffrey Sommers.
      p. cm.
   Includes index.
   ISBN 0-07-059668-9   ISBN 0-07-059669-7 (instructor's manual)
   1. College readers.   2. English language—Rhetoric.   I. Title.
PE1417.S617   1989
808'.0427—dc19   88-8545

To Mom and Dad who saved
my very first "book"
—here's my second.

To Sam and Ben:
May writing always bring you joy.

And mostly for Lynn:
I.A.I.L.Y. yja

Contents

CHAPTER FOUR
The Sarcastic Voice   81

CHAPTER SIX

The Angry Voice   145

CHAPTER SEVEN

The Persuasive Voice   166

CHAPTER NINE
The Meditative Voice   251

SECTION IV
The Voice of Authority   285

CHAPTER TEN
The Voice of Firsthand Experience:
Narration and Description   291

CHAPTER ELEVEN
The Voice of Firsthand Experience: Exposition   335

CHAPTER TWELVE
The Interview Voice   382

CHAPTER THIRTEEN
The Research Voice   428

SECTION V
Other Voices   473

Contents
by Subject

Contents by Mode
of Discourse

Preface

Model Voices: Finding a Writing Voice offers a fresh idea in college readers. Unlike most of its competitors, which are either organized according to the mode of development used in the anthologized selections or according to topics covered by those essays, *Model Voices* offers readings organized by the dominant voice in each. The value of the book's approach is that it allows instructors to teach their students the significance of understanding the rhetorical situation in which all writing occurs. Writers, at some point in the writing process, need to increase their awareness of their audience of readers, their purpose in addressing these readers, and their own attitudes toward the subject about which they are writing. *Model Voices* asks students to read and listen to familiar voices, such as comic voices, angry voices, persuasive voices, and authoritative voices, in lively and varied essays—a number of them written by students just like themselves.

Students will recognize that they hear these voices in their daily reading—they are not artificial categories created by English teachers. These voices serve as excellent models of how writing sounds. The value to the students is that by emulating a number of such voices, they will learn more about the importance of audience, purpose, and their own attitudes toward their subject matter as they move on from emulation to creating their own voices. In other words, as the students attempt to emulate these model voices, they learn about the importance of the rhetorical situation faced by all writers.

By working through the book, the students discover not only that they can create a variety of voices, some more comfortable than others, but also that they can discover the appropriate voice through writing itself. Thus, *Model Voices* encourages students to learn more about themselves as writers through writing in a variety of personas. Students exercise their own creativity as writers and gradually begin to apply the lessons they have learned about audience, purpose, and attitude so that their writing begins to develop its own authentic voice. While so many essay anthologies ask student/writers to mimic modes of organization, an activity that does not reflect how actual writers really write because it puts the form of the writing ahead of the development of meaning, *Model Voices* encourages students to experiment as they seek to find their own voices.

Model Voices is solidly grounded in recent composing theory. It emphasizes the writing process in action and acknowledges at all points that writing is not only a means of communicating but that it is also a means of learning. Students get to see a number of essays in draft form as well as in final published form. The introductions to each section of the book not only explain the voice to be studied, but also, in a friendly, informal way, illustrate a writer's voice in action, demonstrating that when teachers themselves write, they too confront the very same problems in creating a voice that the students confront.

The book is sequenced so that misconceptions about college writing are broken down immediately. In the opening section on the humorous voice, students can see—and hear—that good writing need not be ponderous and pedantic. The book leads through increasingly hostile forms of humor and sarcasm to the measured and logical voice of persuasion. It then approaches sophisticated personal voices that appeal to the mind and heart and finishes, with its longest section, on the voice of authority. This section includes useful discussions on research techniques, both formal and informal. The text concludes with a selection of voices frequently encountered by students in their daily reading: letters, diaries, public addresses, sermons.

Throughout the book, reading selections are preceded by several "Questions about Ideas" that preview the essays and suggest to the students important issues to be aware of in the selections to follow. Each essay then is followed by questions about the rhetorical situation—questions focused on the authors' choices in dealing with their intended audiences and purposes as well as with their apparent attitude toward their material—and questions about the voice itself—questions that focus on the writing decisions made by the writers, such as diction and organization, that have created the essay's voice. Every selection is followed by several suggested topics to write about, each with a suggested audience and purpose, in keeping with the book's emphasis on the rhetorical situation that informs all writing.

Even for more traditionally oriented composition classes, *Model Voices* should prove useful. There are alternate tables of contents according to topic and rhetorical mode. But the book includes more student writing, a greater variety of types of writing, and more writing in progress than do most of its traditional competitors.

While it is my name alone that appears on the cover of *Model Voices*, I am certainly grateful to a number of people without whose insight, advice, and encouragement, this book would not have come into existence. I wish to thank a number of colleagues in the profession who have read and commented upon earlier versions of *Model Voices:* Barbara Daniel, Pennsylvania State University; Loris Galford, McNeese State University; Jake Gaskins, Southeast Missouri State University; Stan Kozikowski, Bryant College; Arthur Palacas, University of Akron; Larry Perkins, Jefferson Community College; Joyce Schenck, El Camino College; Dora Tippens, McHenry County College; and Sheila Webster-Jain, University of Maryland. I also wish to thank the people at McGraw-Hill who proved so very helpful to me in writing this book: Emily Barrosse, Bernadette Boylan, Sue Hurtt, Bill Mullaney, and Kathy O'Rourke. Certainly, while I could thank a long list of my colleagues at Miami University, I would rather thank them collectively for making Miami such a nurturing place to teach and write for those of us interested in the teaching of writing. And, of course, this book would not exist at all without the inspiration and challenge provided by the students I have taught at all three campuses at Miami, a number of whom, I am glad to say, are represented by their writing in this book.

Finally, I must thank my family for their patience with a father and husband who seemed at times to be living in a separate world with his Macintosh computer. It's their support and encouragement that gave me the persistence to survive in that world and that gave me a better world to which to return.

Jeffrey Sommers

MODEL VOICES:
Finding a Writing Voice

1

Rhetorical Situations and Voice

Imagine yourself in this situation: you are pledging the most prestigious fraternity/sorority on campus, the venerable I Ata Potata House. The pledgemaster informs you that I Ata Potata has agreed to participate in the annual Sorority-Fraternity Pledge Follies to be performed at the campus conference center the following night. Your job, as determined by your pledgemaster, is to play the role of the Giant Chicken in the skit being put on by I Ata Potata. After constructing a suitable costume by the next night, you must show up at the University's Conference Center promptly at 7 P.M.

"When do I rehearse?" you ask nervously, since you don't see yourself as an accomplished comedy performer.

"That's the great part about the skit," the pledgemaster assures you. "No rehearsal is necessary! Just stand there in your funny suit, and the other performers will do their stuff. Don't worry about it. You'll be great! That's why we picked you. Remember—7 P.M., chicken suit. Be there!" And with a cheery wave, the pledgemaster leaves you to your fate.

Being a dutiful pledge, and a rather resourceful person, you manage to put together the necessary costume on short notice, and you show up at the conference center at 7 P.M., still quite nervous but prepared to give your best impression of a giant fowl. You arrive backstage, where the helpful pledgemaster congratulates you on your outfit and then, without warning, shoves you through the curtain onto the stage.

Wait a minute! Where's the sketch? Where are the other performers? There's no one on stage with you except for a distinguished-looking woman standing at a podium. She is looking at you. Oh no! It's the president of the university, and the auditorium is full of people dressed formally and sitting at dinner tables. Now what?

Have you ever been in such a preposterous situation? Of course not, but imagine for a moment that you have. What if you decided to write to

1

your best friend, who attends a different college, telling her about your adventure? One of my students decided that that letter might sound like this:

Dear Terri,

I know you are anxious to hear about my big night Friday! It sure was big! Bigger than I would have imagined!

Do you remember my being asked to pledge one of the sororities? I had to participate in the Pledge Follies as a huge chicken. I decided to make a round cage of chicken wire and put straps on it to slip over my shoulders. I used bright yellow and orange tissue paper to stuff in the wire. Some of the girls here helped me make a head of cardboard and we covered it with red felt. The most beautiful part of the costume was the tail! We "borrowed" some plumes from the planter in the main lobby and tied them to the rear.

To finish off my chicken suit, I wore red wool kneesocks and a pair of size 11 gym shoes that we painted yellow. If I do say so myself, I was a gorgeous chick!

Everyone was so helpful in getting me to the hall on time. I was so excited too. When I got backstage, though, there weren't any other girls in costume. Everyone kept saying, "Shhh!" and giggling. I was puzzled, but they assured me they just didn't want to disturb the act ahead of me.

Then it happened! They pushed me through the curtain and onto the stage! You'll never believe it! You know who was there? President Peters herself! There were no Pledge Follies, oh no. Only a dining hall of hungry people waiting for President Peters to finish her speech so they could eat! I was had!

My mind raced as I wondered what to do next. What would you do if you were on stage in a yellow chicken suit with size 11 sneaks on standing in front of the President of the University? The only decent thing to do was to let out a big "cock-a-doodle-doo!" and run off the stage, plumes trailing behind, and shouting, "No chicken for dinner tonight!"

It was great fun, even though the "yolk was on me." Hey, did you put these guys up to this? That would be just like you!

More news later.

See ya,

Vikki

P.S. Just wait until I'm in the sorority next year. The freshmen won't have a chance!

Now imagine that you are writing a letter home to your parents discussing the same events. Vikki decided that such a letter might sound like this instead:

Dear Mom and Dad,

Hi! How is everyone at home? I'm doing fine here. I've only been here a few days and already I'm learning a lot.

At dinner last night we had a real treat. President Peters was addressing those assembled for dinner when all of a sudden this huge yellow and orange chicken came stumbling on stage. It was the funniest creature you've ever seen! It had a big red head, yellow and orange tissue body, red legs, great big yellow feet, and this magnificent tail of feathers!

That poor chicken! Someone really pulled a joke on it! It just stood there in a dazed silence looking at President Peters. Then suddenly it let out a loud "cock-a-doodle-doo!" and ran through the dining hall, yelling, "No chicken for dinner tonight!" You should've seen the President. Shaking her head, she grinned and finished her speech. All the kids got a big kick out of the whole incident. I especially found it funny.

Remember teaching us kids the importance of being good sports? That's the lesson I learned this week. Could you store a yellow and orange chicken suit in the attic? I may need it again sometime.

Much love,

Vikki

Two letters on the same subject, yet they sound different. Why? Because the rhetorical situation of each one is different. Rhetoric is the art of communicating with an audience, an art with its roots in the days of the ancient Greeks. Nowadays we commonly understand "rhetoric" to apply not only to the spoken language but to writing also, and a rhetorical situation is the set of circumstances surrounding a piece of writing. To whom is the writing addressed? Why address those readers? What will those readers "get out of" the writing? These are a few of the questions writers need to answer as they attempt to produce an effective piece of writing.

TWO DIFFERENT VOICES

Let's take a closer look at Vikki's two letters. In her first letter she is writing to a friend. Why? Well, she wishes to tell Terri about her strange experience, but she also, it seems, wishes to show herself in the best possible light. Evidently Vikki wants Terri to see her as a rather resourceful person who has turned a potentially embarrassing personal disaster into something of a comic triumph through quick thinking. So she describes in detail how she put her costume together, how ignorant she was of the trick being played on her, how confused she was at the moment when she realized what was going on. Then she solves her problem, and even makes a few jokes at the end of the letter. Her postscript too is light-hearted. So Vikki comes across as the winner in the entire episode, a good-natured, quick-witted sorority woman. She, of course, could have written an angry letter complaining about the mental cruelty to which she had been subjected as well as voicing her fears that the university would take punitive action against her, but she has chosen to define her rhetorical situation differently.

In her letter home, however, we hear a different Vikki. She seems to understand that her parents will be less likely than Terri to see the great humor in their daughter's being humiliated in public. (Parents, of course, are like that, as we know.) So Vikki strikes upon a brilliant new strategy: she tells the same story—notice that she has not changed the facts at all—but now she no longer claims credit for her own quick thinking. In fact, she narrates the story in the third person so that, while her presence at the incident is clear, her role in it remains unclear until the end of the letter. Perhaps her most effective strategy is brought into play when she asks the question at the beginning of the final paragraph: "Remember teaching us kids the importance of being good sports?" Fair or unfair, she has cleverly disarmed her parents' objections to her behavior by quoting their own advice back to them. (The question of Vikki's honesty or lack of honesty is an interesting one to discuss.) In fact, it is now their turn to be good sports about Vikki's behavior. She never confesses outright to being the chicken, but it is clear enough that the poultry and she are one and the same.

Vikki has understood that her different readers and her changed purpose in writing must inevitably produce two different letters. Imagine if Vikki now had to write a letter to the president of the university. What purpose might such a letter have? It might be an apology, reminding the president of what pledging a sorority is like and assuring her that Vikki's behavior was not intended maliciously. Or the letter might take the form of a scathing indictment of the entire pledging system, which places naive first-year students in such mortifying situations. The point is that this third letter would inevitably have to take a different form; it would certainly sound different from the other two, and not only because of a change in Vikki's purpose but also because she and the president are neither close friends nor relatives. In other words, the letter's voice would be different.

THE VOICE OF THE WRITER

This book is concerned with the voice of the writer, with your voice as you write. When you speak, of course, you use your voice. But voice means something else in writing, something more than the sounds represented by the words that you put on paper. Speaking vending machines and automated telephone information systems use voices to speak, yet these voices somehow never sound quite human to us. They lack personality; they lack life. When we speak of voice in writing, we are speaking of the personality of the writer, the life that should be audible in the writer's words.

One of the greatest and most persistent problems I have seen in my years of teaching writing courses is that much of the writing I read seems to have no voice. It seems to be the written equivalent of the talking vending machine. Why should that be? I believe that when a writer does not understand fully or does not pay enough attention to the rhetorical situation of the piece of writing, it becomes more likely that that writer will produce a piece of writing with little or no life, no voice. Such writing almost sounds canned. When all the essays in a class sound as if the same person wrote them, then the writing is not going to be very lively, or, to be candid about it, very readable.

So how can a writer, especially one who may not have had vast experience in writing, start to develop his own voice? By understanding the dynamics of the rhetorical situation, the writer can find an individual voice. But there is more than one way to learn about rhetorical situations, and this book will be employing a time-honored approach: imitation. In this book you will be asked to imitate models of different voices, but first it is important to sketch out in some detail the factors of which any rhetorical situation is comprised. As a writer, you will need to be aware of several important factors if you are going to understand the rhetorical situation in which you find yourself:

1. You should be aware of who you are as a writer.
2. You should be aware of who your readers are.
3. You should be aware of why you are addressing these readers.
4. You should be aware of what your relationship to your subject matter is.

I want to be clear, however, that I am not saying that all writers always understand these factors fully as they begin to write. Quite often, writers will only have a tentative feeling about these factors in the writing situation, but the very act of writing helps those feelings grow into greater awareness. As you write, you need to become increasingly aware of your own role as a writer, of your readers, of your reason for writing to those readers, and of your own attitudes about your subjects. Let me be more specific.

You should be aware of who you are as a writer. From one piece of writing to another, your role as a writer can vary. How much knowledge will you demonstrate about your subject? In other words, will you sound like an expert? That is the role I am adopting here. But at other times, I adopt other roles. I might write an exploratory sort of essay in which I confess to my confusion about some subject and try to work out my ideas as I write. Of course, to write effectively, writers need to have a great deal of knowledge about their subject, but it is quite possible to play different roles when writing down these ideas.

Another consideration about your role as a writer is to know what distance you plan to establish between yourself and your reader. If you are writing a brief note to place on the refrigerator with a magnetized ceramic slice of pepperoni pizza, then you are likely to write in a very

informal, casual, conversational way, almost as if you and your reader
were in the room together, standing next to one another. But if you are
writing a research paper in a social science course, the distance between you and your reader is much more likely to be greater. You will
sound far more formal; you will avoid slang, you may even avoid using
the first person in your writing. The distance between you and your
reader may resemble the distance between a professor standing at the
podium in a large lecture hall and the hundreds of students assembled
there to hear the lecture. Every piece of writing establishes a distance
between writer and reader simply because the reader *is not* the same
person as the writer.

You should be aware of who your readers are. A colleague of mine likes to
tell the story of how her brother, a music professor, once delivered his
entire lecture in Spanish, as a joke. Of course, his students did not understand much of what they had heard (and unfortunately did not
complain to him!). But imagine if the music professor went to teach in
Mexico City, assumed that his students were all native Spanish speakers, and delivered the same lecture in Spanish, only to discover later that
he had been instructing a group of American students who had simply
chosen to attend a foreign university. Here there would be no joke. He
would have utterly failed to convey much of anything to his audience.

I think you can usually assume that your readers can read English! But in order to write effectively, you will need to know more
than that about your readers. And you need to remember that every
piece of writing you compose *will* have a reader. Even diary entries
have a reader—you. That note on the refrigerator door has an intended
reader. It would make little sense for me to write a note saying "Went
to the store to buy a six-pack. Be back for dinner. Jeff" and then toss
it out the car window as I drove to the store. But what do you need to
know about your readers? It would help to know how much knowledge
they have about your subject. Will you need to define terms like "rhetorical situation" and "voice" as I felt I needed to? Can you use technical jargon? You do not want to waste your readers' time explaining
things they will already know, but neither do you want to leave them
in the dark about important information.

You must also know something about your audience's attitudes.
How does the audience feel about the ideas you are describing or explaining? Vikki knew that her parents' attitude toward her sorority prank
might not be entirely positive, so she worked to change that attitude. The
more your audience's attitudes toward a subject differ from your own, the
harder you will have to work to make them see what you mean.

Finally, you ought to know something about what your readers
need in your piece of writing. To some extent this idea overlaps with
knowing how much your readers know and with knowing what their

attitudes are, but here I mean that you must be concerned in particular with understanding what information you simply must provide to your readers if your writing is to be clear and effective. Vikki understands that her parents need to know, above all else, that she is doing well, so she says clearly in her opening paragraph that she is fine.

By understanding as much as possible about your readers, you can begin to write more effectively. Sometimes it is useful to try to analyze your potential readers from the very start of planning a piece of writing, while there will be other times when you simply start writing and concern yourself with your readers only much later on, as you revise the draft you have written. But at whatever point in the writing process you start to think about your readers, try to determine as much as you can about them: their age, their gender, their educational backgrounds, their interests, even where they live (rural or urban, local or regional or national). Learn what you can about your readers because a change in readers will probably necessitate some change in your writing voice.

You should be aware of why you are addressing these readers. In other words, all writing has a purpose. Rather, all effective writing has a purpose, and experienced writers make sure that they understand that purpose as best they can when writing. The note on the refrigerator, the two letters Vikki wrote, that social science research paper—all have purposes. Freshman English is a strange course in that all of your writing has, in a sense, the same purpose: to satisfy the course requirements so that you can earn college credits and possibly a high grade. That is not the kind of writing purpose I have in mind, however. I am not under any compulsion to write notes for my refrigerator door ("In the next six weeks, you will write fifteen notes for the refrigerator door and take thirteen phone messages on the pad next to the wall phone" would be a rather ridiculous "assignment" for my wife to give me). I write the notes when I need to.

In your writing during this course, you must also attempt to find a reason, a purpose for what you are writing. This book will offer you some suggestions, or perhaps your instructor will, but all writers write to readers for a purpose. There may be another purpose "outside" the writing, such as obtaining college credit or earning money from the writing, but the individual piece of writing needs to have a purpose itself, a purpose best defined in terms of the intended reader. Vikki wants Terri to be impressed with her, and she wants her parents to be understanding of her, while I want my wife to know that I will return with the diet cola. Your social science research paper may be designed to inform other students of the growing prevalence of suicide among teenagers and may also offer suggestions for ways to identify suicidal-friends and get them needed assistance.

You may write to amuse or to entertain or to inform or to per-

suade. You may want to convince an employer to grant you an interview for a high-paying position with a prestigious business firm, or you
may wish to convince your hometown sweetheart that you do indeed
still feel the same way that you did at the end of the summer. You may
wish to convince the readers of the campus newspaper that they need
to become involved in protesting apartheid in South Africa, or you
may try to get those same readers to calm down and listen to one another in a civil manner when discussing apartheid. And sometimes you
will be trying to amuse, entertain, and persuade all at the same time.
Just as your roles in your writing and your readers change from one
piece of writing to another, so too will your purposes.

   For example, I am trying in this opening chapter to make you see
some of the principles upon which my book is based so that you can
use it effectively. I also want to keep you interested because I know
that even a great book serves little purpose if it remains unread. But
months ago, I had to write to my publishers about many of the same
ideas in order to convince them that my book is clear, important, and
useful, or else the book would never even have gotten to *be* a book in
the first place. Same material, different audiences, different purposes—therefore, different voices.

You should be aware of what your relationship to your subject matter
is. The writer's attitude toward her subject matter and audience can
be called her tone. The tone of the writer's voice is its sound. And that
tone can be ironic, bitter, witty, modest, resigned, cheerful, enthusiastic, earnest, angry, astonished, solemn, nostalgic, indignant, wistful,
sarcastic, and on and on. Look at the three cartoons below. Each one
has the same caption: "Come on!" Yet, if you try saying these captions
aloud, the tone of each will be different.

Come on!

Come on!

Come on!

While the talking vending machine seems to lack any human tone, your speaking voice always has tone; if it doesn't, we would describe it as a monotone, and your friends would start asking you if you were feeling all right. As you speak, you use different inflections, facial expressions, hand and arm gestures, pauses, volume to create the tone you want. You would not sound the same explaining the chicken suit episode to your friend on the phone as you would explaining to the president in her office.

Writers, however, cannot rely upon facial expressions, gestures, volume, and so forth to create an effective tone. Instead, writers rely upon words, sentences, paragraphs, and punctuation to create voice. Read the following two passages about the same subject, the platypus. Then, before you read what I have to say about the two passages, try answering the questions that follow them.

Passage 1

In 1800, a stuffed animal arrived in England from the newly discovered continent of Australia.

The continent had already been the source of plants and animals never seen before—but this one was ridiculous. It was nearly two feet long, and had a dense coating of hair. It also had a flat rubbery bill, webbed feet, a broad flat tail, and a spur on each hind ankle that was clearly intended to secrete poison. What's more, under the tail was a single opening.

Zoologists stared at the thing in disbelief. Hair like a mammal! Bill and feet like an aquatic bird! Poison spurs like a snake! A single opening in the rear as though it laid eggs!

There was an explosion of anger. The thing was a hoax. Some unfunny jokester in Australia, taking advantage of the distance and strangeness of the continent, had stitched together parts of widely different creatures and was intent on making fools of innocent zoologists in England.

Yet the skin seemed to hang together. There were no signs of artificial joining. Was it or was it not a hoax? And if it wasn't a hoax, was it a mammal with reptilian characteristics, or a reptile with mammalian characteristics, or was it partly bird, or *what?* ("What Do You Call a Platypus?" by Isaac Asimov)

Passage 2

At the end of the eighteenth century, the skin of an altogether astounding animal arrived in London. It had come from the newly established colony in Australia. The creature to which it had belonged was about the size of a rabbit, with fur as thick and fine as an otter's. Its feet were webbed and clawed; its rear vent was a single one combining both excretory and reproductive functions, a cloaca like that of a reptile; and most outlandish of all, it had a large flat beak like a duck. It was so bizarre that some people in London dismissed it as another of those faked monsters that were confected in the Far East from bits and pieces of dissimilar creatures and then sold to gullible travellers as mermaids, sea dragons, and other wonders. But careful examination of the skin showed no sign of fakery. The strange bill which seemed to fit so awkwardly on to the furry head, with a flap-like cuff at the junction, did truly belong. The animal, however improbable it might seem, was a real one.

When complete specimens became available, it was seen that the bill was not hard and bird-like as it had first seemed when the only evidence was a dried skin. In life it was pliable and leathery so the resemblance to a bird could be discounted. The fur was much more significant. Hair or fur is the hallmark of a mammal, just as feathers

are of birds. It was clear, therefore, that this mystery animal must be
a member of that great group which contains creatures as diverse as
shrews, lions, elephants, and men. The function of a mammal's hairy
coat is to insulate the body and enable it to maintain a high
temperature, so it followed that this new creature must also be warm-
blooded. And, presumably, it also possessed a third characteristic
of mammals and the one that gives the group its name, a mamma, a
breast, with which to suckle its young. (*Life on Earth* by David
Attenborough)

QUESTIONS

1. What adjectives would you use to describe the voice in Asimov's piece?
   What adjectives best describe the voice in Attenborough's piece?
2. How do Asimov and Attenborough use word choice to create voice?
   What is noticeable about the diction (word choice) in the two passages—
   are the words long, short, simple, complex, ordinary, unusual, formal,
   informal? How are the two passages different in diction? (See if you can
   find both writers describing precisely the same thing but with different
   words.)
3. How do Asimov and Attenborough use sentences to create voice? In
   other words, what is noticeable about their sentences? Are they long,
   short, simple, complex? What sort of rhythms do they create? Does either writer make use of figurative language (poetic comparisons) in his
   sentences? How are the two passages different in their use of sentences?
4. How do Asimov and Attenborough use paragraphs to create voice? What
   is noticeable about their paragraphs—are they long, short, simple, or
   complex in structure? Are they full of concrete details? Do they make use
   of topic sentences (sentences that announce the central idea of a paragraph)? How are the two passages different in their use of paragraphs?
5. Is there anything out of the ordinary or noticeable in the two writers' use
   of punctuation—anything that contributes to the sound of the voice in
   the passages?
6. Which of the two passages is the one you prefer? Why?
7. Which of the two passages is the better piece of writing? Why?

SAME SUBJECT, DIFFERENT VOICE

You probably noticed that Asimov's vocabulary is simple, familiar, casual, at
times almost slanglike ("jokester"). What Asimov calls a "thing," Attenborough calls a "creature." Asimov calls the platypus "ridiculous," while Attenborough terms it "astounding." Attenborough's sentences tend to be
longer than Asimov's; in fact, in ¶3, Asimov has only one complete sentence,

while the remaining four "sentences" are actually sentence fragments. Asimov's excerpt covers about the same amount of space on the page as does Attenborough's, yet his is five paragraphs long, and Attenborough's is only two. And notice also Asimov's punctuation: he relies on exclamation points, question marks, dashes, underlining.

What is the total effect? Asimov's selection to me sounds excited, lively, almost astonished; it sees the humor in the situation and leaves me slightly breathless. Attenborough's selection is more sedate; it is interesting and thorough, and it makes me think. Both men have covered fundamentally the same ground, so why should these two excerpts be so different in tone? I would suggest that the different tone is a product of other differences in the rhetorical situation, the factors I have discussed earlier. I suspect that each man is writing to a different audience and for a different purpose.

Usually, I ask my classes which passage they prefer, and most classes choose Asimov's. However, when I ask them which is the better piece of writing, they usually say Attenborough's. Why? The students enjoy reading Asimov's piece. Because the subject sounds unpromising to them, especially the nonscience majors who form a majority of the class, they are pleasantly surprised when Asimov makes the discussion of a scientific subject so lively and interesting. Yet they are convinced that good writing must be serious and formal, and thus they point to Attenborough's passage as the better-written one.

Which actually is the better piece of writing? How can we say without knowing *why* and *to whom* each one was written? Suppose you were the editor of *TV Week*, a magazine that previews upcoming TV shows of interest for its readers. The educational channel has an hour-long documentary on the platypus coming up shortly, and you feel that it would be useful to run a short article to help prepare your readers for the TV documentary. You ask Isaac Asimov and David Attenborough to write you such an article. A week goes by, and you receive the two passages we have just read. Which one will you choose? Your magazine's readers are not scientists, at least most of them are not, and they do not customarily find articles on science in your magazine. Which of the two passages will capture and hold their attention? Asimov's undoubtedly. (So you are forced to send a note back to Attenborough: "Dear Dave. Loved your platypus piece. But I need something with more pizzazz, more glitz. Sorry! Let's do lunch. Ciao.")

Or maybe you are an editor at McGraw-Hill, and you are planning a new introductory textbook for a general science course. You contact Isaac Asimov and David Attenborough and ask each of them to contribute an article on the intriguing history of the platypus to your textbook. Here come the same two passages in the following week's mail. Now which is the better one? The audience is different and the purpose has changed, and now Attenborough's tone is probably the more appropriate one.

WRITING AND SPEAKING

Does all of this sound too complicated to put into practice in your own writing? Although it is complicated, and most writers struggle with audience, purpose, and tone throughout their writing careers, it is not at all impossible to improve as a writer by understanding these concepts. In fact, quite the contrary is true, for you already understand the basic principles of rhetorical situations in your own lives. Do you speak to your professor the same way that you speak to your friends? Do you speak to the professor the same way in class that you do in her office? Or in the university bookstore if you bump into her there? Of course not. You change the way you speak to suit the situation. And through practice you will be better able to understand the dynamics of the rhetorical situation in your writing also and will thus be better able to create an appropriate voice for your writing. That's where this book will prove helpful. This book is organized according to the dominant voice in the reading. So, for instance, all of the selections in the next section will have a humorous voice. Later on you will be reading other voices, such as those I call in this book the persuasive voice and the voice of experience. The reason why this textbook has been organized in this fashion can be graphically explained in the form of an equation:

Awareness of audience +

understanding of purpose +

attitude toward subject = voice

In arithmetic the commutative property states that addition, for instance, can be performed in either direction with the same results. So $2 + 3 = 3 + 2$ and it doesn't matter if you add from right to left or left to right. So it is with the equation above. I have tried in this chapter to explain the significance of audience, purpose, attitude as if we were reading from left to right in my equation. In the rest of the book I want you to observe the significance of voice, or rather, I want you to *hear* the different voices and then try them out on your own. Being a writer is to some degree like being an actor in that accomplished actors can play more than one role. Just as actors practice for different parts by playing different roles in workshops and at rehearsals, so too, I think, writers can practice and rehearse sounding different. This book will not ask you to try to write like Mark Twain or Jonathan Swift or James Thurber; that is not the kind of imitation I have in mind. Instead, I will ask you to sound like or emulate the voices of these writers. You will read several humorous essays and consider what they have in common that makes them sound somewhat alike. Then you can try to duplicate the sound of that voice. I am convinced through experience with my own students that you can do this.

But—and this is equally important—I am convinced that you will gain an even better understanding of the significance of audience and purpose. My hope is that through the experimentation that you do with the various voices in this textbook, you will discover a voice of your own that works for you. How can imitating other voices lead you to your own unique or distinctive voice? Because this book will ask you to sound so different from one piece of writing to another, you should be able to demonstrate to yourself that you do indeed have the power to be who you want to be when you write. I write humorously, seriously, angrily, sarcastically, lovingly at different times to suit my rhetorical situation. In all those writings I still sound like me, but I sound like the me that seems most appropriate to the situation.

A PREVIEW OF WHAT LIES AHEAD

In the remaining chapters of this book, then, what will you find? There are four major sections in the book, each divided into smaller chapters. In each section of the book you will find an explanation of the type of voice you are about to read, identifying its noteworthy features, and connecting that voice with the voices that you have already heard and those you will hear later on. Each reading selection will be followed by questions and suggestions for writing in that voice. Remember that the topics, audience, and purposes are merely suggestions. It will be your task to make the writing interesting and meaningful to both your readers and yourself. Don't be afraid to experiment as you try to find an audience and purpose that work for you. The final section of the book offers a variety of additional readings.

I think that by the time you have finished this book and its suggested writing, you will be pleased at how much you understand about writing effectively, and I suspect that you will have surprised yourself with the degree of your versatility as a writer. Most of all, I think you will find that creating your own voice in your writing is quite possible and that when you do so, the writing becomes better for your readers and also better for you as a writer.

SECTION ONE

The Humorous Voice

THE GREAT PHILOSOPHER

Must all effective writing be serious, solemn, sober? Many inexperienced writers seem to think so. No sooner do they start writing than they adopt the pose, usually a quite uncomfortable pose, of The Great Philosopher Pronouncing Great Truths and writing essays about Religion, Prejudice, Our World Economy. The problem with adopting The Great Philosopher pose is that it often leads to dead writing, to the kind of voiceless writing I was discussing in the introductory chapter of this book. Why should that be? Unfortunately, when inexperienced writers attempt the Great Philosopher pose, they begin to rely upon general statements to make their points, frequently piling up one abstraction upon another, one generalization after another. The reader too often remains uninvolved and unimpressed.

Of course, there is a place for writing about great truths. My point, however, is that there are other sorts of truths to write about also, smaller aspects of our lives about which both the reader and writer can communicate in a significant way. Humor is one effective method of exploring these smaller aspects of our lives. Mark Twain is generally acknowledged to be one of the greatest of American writers; his was primarily a comic genius. Charles Dickens is arguably the greatest novelist in the English language, and he too was basically a comic writer. In other words, writing can be humorous and still be good.

CAN HUMOR BE SERIOUS?

Perhaps there is a confusion about the terms "humorous" and "serious" that needs to be dispelled. The humorous writing that you will be

15

reading in this section of the book is at times, perhaps even most of the time, also serious. The writer's purpose is often to make a serious point about the subject. In its effect, however, the writing is comic in that the writers use humor as the vehicle for making the serious point that they have in mind. Humorous writing can seek to provoke a laugh or a grin; it can hope for a smile or a smirk or perhaps merely a nod of the head as readers acknowledge having recognized their own foibles in the piece of writing. Some of the essays that you will read in this section of the book will be funny and will make you laugh—inwardly perhaps, or even out loud—but others will simply elicit that knowing nod of the head. Some of the essays will amuse you and entertain you for the moments that you are reading them, but others will get you to think about the ideas in the essay in a serious manner that may surprise you given that the essay seemed so amusing. In some of the essays, the humor will be "low" humor, the broad slapstick of farce, while in others the humor will be a bitter, sharp-edged wit almost bordering on anger. The essays will not demonstrate the very same voice, but they will all share one objective: they will all attempt, in one way or another, to appeal to your sense of humor. Lacking a sense of humor, a reader will simply miss out on much of what these essays have to offer.

Why start this book with humorous writing? Many of my students over the years have objected that they cannot write humorously; colleagues of mine have insisted that good humorous writing is too difficult to achieve. To my students, I usually say, "You'll be surprised at how well you can write this way." To my colleagues, I say, "You may be right, but the effort itself is worthwhile." I want you to see that good writing is not always sermonlike, that it does not always make pronouncements about issues of cosmic (or even national) significance. Yet be sure to remember that "humorous" need not mean "frivolous" and that you *may* choose to make an important point about an issue of national significance by using humor. Social commentators such as Will Rogers have long used humor to make serious points.

THREE HUMOROUS VOICES

In this first section of *Model Voices*, you will find essays in three different humorous voices: the comic voice, the satirical voice, and the sarcastic voice. You will find that at times you disagree with my placement of a particular essay because you would have called the voice satirical rather than sarcastic. That's fine, because in truth none of these writers set out to write in the "comic voice," or in the "sarcastic voice." They determined that in order to achieve their purpose for their piece of writing, given their selected audience, the best attitude to take toward that material was a humorous one. Only later on will readers, such as you and I, attempt to classify what the writers have done. The question that the writers want answered is, "Did my writing achieve its purpose?"—not "Did you hear the comic voice in my prose?"

But in general I think each essay is placed in the section with those other essays with which it shares the most in terms of the type of humorous voice created. Although I will explain each voice more fully later, let me now suggest several significant differences among the comic, satiric, and sarcastic voices.

Perhaps the cartoons on page 18 can illustrate the differences I have in mind.

In Cartoon 1, we see the comic voice, the least hostile of the three, with the humor gentle and often whimsical. We are asked to laugh or smile along with the writer as he observes the idiosyncrasies of human beings, our society, our culture, our habits. The humor is like that of one friend nudging the other with an elbow while making a wisecrack.

In Cartoon 2, we see the satiric voice, which ridicules the pretensions of human beings in hopes of bringing about an improvement in human behavior but does so without the rancor of sarcasm or the good-hearted cheer of the comic voice. The satiric voice sticks pins in our inflated pride, while the comic voice gently nudges us with an elbow.

In Cartoon 3, we see the sarcastic voice, a voice that employs hostile humor, humor that is often bitter and derisive. The sarcastic voice may well observe the very same idiosyncrasies of human beings, but it is far less understanding of them, criticizing them harshly. The sarcastic voice bludgeons us over the head, although still in a humorous way.

WHAT YOU WILL LEARN

Such distinctions may still seem fuzzy and are, I admit, not very precise. Later I will explain more fully what the distinctive features of each voice are and ask you to read several examples of each that should illustrate my points. For right now, I would like to conclude this introductory comment by reminding you of the purpose of this section, in fact of all the sections of the book: by listening to the voices in the writing and then by attempting to model your writing after one of those voices, you will learn more about the rhetorical situations that underlie all writing. To be more specific, I think that reading and writing in the humorous voice will help you in several ways:

You will gain an increased awareness of audience

It is impossible to write humorously without thinking about your
audience. Stand-up comics, comedy scriptwriters, comic newspaper
columnists, talk show hosts—all share the desire to amuse their audiences.
Thus, as they write their comedy monologues or scripts or newspaper
columns, they are constantly thinking "Will this make them smile? Will
they laugh at this line?" As you attempt to write a humorous paper, you
too will have to be similarly concerned. As a humorous writer, you cannot
afford to forget your audience or else you run the risk of not being
humorous at all.

You will see the need to be specific in your writing

Although humorous writing is not exclusively restricted to joke telling, it
might be helpful to think of any joke you have ever heard or told. Jokes
are always specific about details. The comedian does not say, "A man goes
to the doctor and complains about his head." Instead he says, "A man
with a parrot on his head goes to a psychiatrist and says, 'Doc, I've got a
parrot on my head.'" Your humorous sketch of your eccentric Uncle
Charlie will not amuse your readers if you write, "Uncle Charlie always
wore outrageous clothes and did outlandish things." You will amuse your
readers only if you go on to describe Uncle Charlie's usual business outfit
of striped golf knickers, a red and blue University of Pennsylvania
sweatshirt, and a top hat or if you tell the story of how after he had been
pulled over by a state trooper and asked, "Sir, do you understand what
that double yellow line in the center of the road is for?" Uncle Charlie
answered, "Bicycles?" Being specific is a necessity to all good writing, as
you will see again and again throughout your reading in this book. But
here in the section on the humorous voice, you can begin to observe just
how very essential using specific details can be.

You will see that there are many ways to write about the things that you know and care about

Many of my students have complained to me over the years that they
really have nothing to write about, that they do not know enough about
anything interesting, that their lives are too ordinary. I really do not agree,
but for the sake of argument, let's say that I do. Humorous writing
provides a solution to this problem of having nothing to write about, for
humorous writing quite often focuses on the very ordinary. By writing
humorously, you can present your "ordinary, dull" information in a new
and interesting way. You may be selling old wine, but at least you will be
putting it in new bottles. That is a worthwhile achievement because if the

humorous approach provides you with a means of becoming more interested yourself in your subject, the odds improve that your writing about that subject will be more interesting to your readers also. There is more than one way to eat an Oreo cookie, and there are more voices available to you than that of The Great Philosopher Pronouncing Great Truths.

Humorous writing can also help you understand more about the need to organize your writing and about the ethical responsibilities of the writer, but the proper time to investigate those concepts will be later, after you have read some of the selections in the next chapters. So, go ahead, read some of the humorous writing to follow. As The Great Philosopher once declaimed, "Go ahead, laugh. It couldn't hurt."

2

The Comic Voice

The word "comic" may suggest to you a red-haired woman with a loud brash voice speaking a mile a minute. Or maybe you think of a younger man in a checked suit too small for him who seems to be a bratty eight-year-old child trapped in a man's body. Or maybe you think of a middle-aged man with a large cigar and a rubbery face who tells stories about his childhood and about being a father. What all these "comics"—Bette Midler, Peewee Herman, Bill Cosby—have in common is that they are all trying to amuse their audiences. And they all rely upon some of the same techniques, even though each has a distinctive voice. While several of these comedians border on being sarcastic in their humor, for the most part they ask us to laugh along *with* them rather than asking us to laugh *at* someone else. They tend to include themselves and us as one group of people with similar interests, and then they ask us to laugh at ourselves.

How do they go about provoking laughter? Of course, as performers they have available to them hand gestures, facial expressions, vocal inflections, even costumes—which we as writers certainly do not. However, all of their humor begins as writing, either written by the performers themselves or by comedy writers. And these comedy writers rely upon certain devices and approaches that anyone can use.

TECHNIQUES USED TO CREATE A COMIC VOICE

What are some of the techniques that writers use when they wish to create a comic voice? Four of the most familiar approaches are *exaggeration, oversimplification, surprise,* and *repetition.* Each deserves a closer look.

Exaggeration works to create humor by taking something familiar and making it ridiculous. In an essay about the pitfalls of shaving, Tim Verquer, a college freshman, wrote the following paragraph:

Then we have shaving cream for certain kinds of skin. We have types

21

for regular skin, sensitive skin, dry skin, oily skin, dirty skin, extra sensitive skin and of course for super extra sensitive skin. We also have the different smelling types of shaving cream. We can get our shaving cream with the scent of spice, cinnamon, peppermint, spearmint, juicy fruit, sour green apple, or my favorite, the regular scent.

There is much truth to his comments, but there is also exaggeration, especially toward the end of his list of different scents.

Another method of exaggeration often employed by humor writers is the use of ridiculous numbers. Dave Barry writes, in his essay "For the Birds," "Zoologists tell us that there are more than 23,985,409,098,744,885,143 birds in the city of Lincoln, Nebraska, alone which is one of the many reasons not to go there." Here the exaggeration of the ridiculous number creates the humor.

One of the secrets to using exaggeration effectively is to know just how much to exaggerate. If Barry's number is much longer, it is possible that there will be no humor because the exaggeration will be so far out of touch with reality that no reader will identify with it. On the other hand, if Barry says that there are thousands of birds in Lincoln, he has not exaggerated enough, for what he is saying is too close to reality to be funny.

Oversimplification

Oversimplification is another tried and true technique of the humorous writer. By examining a complex issue or question and reducing its complexity to a level so simple that it clearly does an injustice to the original concept, the writer can amuse her reader. In one essay a student was reminiscing about his high school days and discussing how difficult most students found it to sit still during those tense final few minutes of class just before the bell would ring. He labeled this problem "The Ding-Dong Syndrome," a foolish name that oversimplifies the language used by scientists to describe important phenomena. Here are two of his proposed solutions to the problem: "1. Shorten all classes to thirty-five minutes thus eliminating the crucial last five minutes. 2. Have the bell ring for the entire period, stopping only at the end of the period." Of course, it is hard to imagine more simple-minded solutions than these. However, the writer blissfully ignored all of the consequences of his proposed solutions, and his foolishness made for humor.

It is easy to see the possibilities for oversimplification. By selecting a complex situation and reducing an analysis of its causes to a simple explanation, a writer can take a serious subject and make it the source of humor.

Oversimplifying may be nothing more than a variation on exaggerating, but it can work effectively in creating a comic voice. Usually the writer offers his suggestions sincerely, letting the reader understand just how simple-minded the suggestion has been. But even the oversimplification must be clever. The student writing about the class bells in high school could have simply proposed doing away with the bells. That's an oversimplified solution, but it's not funny. The oversimplification needs to be combined with exaggeration in order to create the necessary effect.

Surprise

And both exaggeration and oversimplification are often most effective when combined with *surprise*. Taking the reader down a familiar pathway to an unfamiliar destination—or down an exotic pathway to an ordinary and familiar destination—can also produce humor. The unexpected is often funny. So we laugh when the fellow in top hat and tails suddenly pushes a cream pie in the face of his business partner, or we laugh when the elegantly dressed woman slips on the banana peel, to use two familiar slapstick examples of surprise. Actually, all of the examples I have mentioned so far rely upon surprise, upon the unexpected. Who among us has ever really smelled juicy-fruit-scented shaving cream? Who among us really views "The Ding-Dong Syndrome" as a problem worthy of a medical-sounding name? Which of us has ever counted the number of birds in any single city, much less Lincoln, Nebraska, specifically?

I once worked for a magazine and was assigned a story about the garlic crop in Guatemala, which, I had been told, was going to be a fabulous source of income for that Central American country. The sources I consulted were wildly enthusiastic about the future of Guatemalan garlic, citing many experts about its nutritive and curative powers. I had a ton of information about the mythical potency of garlic. Yet I found the entire subject quite amusing, and so did my editor, who, in fact, expected me to write a humorous article. I did, but he was not pleased with my approach.

"When you have a ridiculous subject like this one," he advised me, "be sure you treat it as if you think it's serious. Let the humor assert itself. If you want to write about a serious subject and be funny, then write about it as if you think it's humorous."

His advice made sense, so I changed my article, and the essay turned out to be humorous even though I wrote about the garlic with a straight face. The element of surprise was at work. My readers found my discussion amusing because I unexpectedly did not seem to see the humor in the situation. So, in this case, I did not exaggerate nor did I oversimplify, but instead I merely reported, and that alone was surprising enough to be funny.

Now things are getting tricky, for I seem to be saying that you can sound serious and yet still be amusing, which would appear to be a contradiction. Remember, however, that you are always adopting a role when you write—that's what voice is all about—so that by sounding like a mock expert on some foolish subject, whether garlic in Guatemala or school bell schedules, you may well be provoking a humorous response from your readers by surprising them.

Once, in an essay I called "The New Four Food Groups," I poked fun

at junk food addicts like myself. My essay began, "Humanity has been limp-
ing along with the same dull four food groups we learned about in grade
school for far too long. Sure, dairy, meats, grains, and produce are nutri-
tious but they are not 'today.' Time has passed these snacks by. What we
need now is a new classification of food groups, one which reflects the 1980s
life-style." I continued to play mock expert by identifying the new food
groups as the pastry group, the chocolate group, the fruits and vegetables
group (offering caramel popcorn and fruit-flavored bubble gum as examples), and the carbonated beverage group. I treated a ridiculous subject in a
serious fashion, and it surprised my readers.

Repetition

Repetition figures in the comic voice as a matter of timing. Sometimes a joke
needs to be "set up"; the reader needs to be prepared for it. In other words,
quite often the comic writer will introduce an idea early in a piece of writing
and then build on that idea as the piece of writing continues, perhaps exaggerating more and more each time, making it funnier and funnier. A forget-
ful character who at first simply forgets where her car is parked at the mall,
eventually forgets where she lives, what her name is, and that she has a neck
(causing her head to roll off) as the essay progresses.

At other times the comic writer will introduce a detail and then return
to it again (and again) as a means of inducing the audience to laugh. So a
writer might be sketching in a comic encounter between a frustrated traveler
and an uncooperative cabdriver, referring to the cabdriver as "no paragon of
tact." Later in the piece he may refer to the cabbie simply as "Mr. Tact"
and continue to call him that throughout the essay. The final comment in
the essay may be yet one last joke about tactlessness. This type of repetition
is sometimes called a "running gag," for it runs throughout the piece. What
is being repeated, moreover, is generally exaggerated and frequently comes
as a surprise to the reader.

The comic voice, then, makes use of all of these techniques—*exaggeration, oversimplification, surprise, and repetition*—in very much the same way,
relying upon everyday events in our lives which the writers then distort,
change, magnify, and turn inside out to become something unfamiliar, unexpected, and eventually amusing.

Structure

The ways in which comic writers use these techniques are many and varied
but several structural approaches seem to work consistently:

Classification Placing ideas, objects, people into categories, attaching silly
names and describing each category can be an extremely effective

method of organizing a comic paper. "The New Four Food Groups" essay used this approach.

Cause and Effect Describing a problem and offering foolish explanations of its causes or foolish solutions to the problem also effectively organizes a comic essay. "The Ding-Dong Syndrome" essay used this method of organization.

Comparison/Contrast Comparing one situation with a similar situation and exaggerating one or the other or both can be an effective means of organizing a comic paper. The use of comparison can be more specific also, as in the use of exaggerated metaphors. See Lewis Grizzard's description in this chapter of how doctors view heart surgery ("Doctors, of course, enjoy seeing a man's heart being tugged and pulled like it was a strip steak about to be flung upon the grill....")

History/Definition Humorous writers fairly often explain their subjects by offering their own half-baked explanations of terms or their own off-the-wall historical narratives. If poets possess poetic license, then comic writers seem to possess a comic license to make up the facts. Note how Dave Barry offers a brief natural history of the evolution of birds in his "For the Birds." There is just enough zoological fact mixed into his historical narrative so that readers can find the humor in those portions which are exaggerated.

Of course, there are other tools available to the comic writer—the same tools available to all writers, really. Comic writers can tell stories, paint word pictures, create dialogue. Usually, however, they exaggerate, oversimplify, and surprise. Remember, as you read the following selection of comic essays, to look for those techniques at work, and remember that even comic essays can make a serious point. But most of all listen to the voices in these essays. This is writing with personality, writing that is alive, the kind of writing you yourself want to produce.

This Might Sting a Little
Lewis Grizzard

Lewis Grizzard is a nationally syndicated newspaper columnist originally from Moreland, Georgia, who has published a number of books of humorous writing. Grizzard's writing has been praised for its "sense of humor, common sense and appreciation of people." Perhaps the best introduction to Grizzard is to read the titles of his books: *Shoot Low Boys, They're Riding Shetland Ponies; If Love Were Oil, I'd Be About a Quart Low,* and *Elvis Is Dead, and I Don't Feel So Good Myself.*

"This Might Sting a Little" appears in his 1986 book, *They Tore Out My Heart and Stomped That Sucker Flat,* in which he recalls his experiences as a cardiac surgery patient.

QUESTIONS ABOUT IDEAS

1. What is the central theme of Grizzard's essay? How carefully does he stick to that theme?
2. Is the problem of communication between doctor and patient a significant one? Have you ever experienced any of the confusion Grizzard writes about?
3. To what extent do you think it is justifiable to cause pain to patients in the cause of attempting to cure them?
4. How familiar are the examples given by Grizzard? How accurate a picture of medical practice has he presented?

My doctor sent me to another doctor, and that doctor listened and felt   1
and poked and prodded and ordered more tests. I took the standard EKG and then I took something called an Echocardiogram where they send sound waves into your heart, and when they had done all that, they still didn't know much more than they had known before, so they scheduled me for a cardiac catheterization.

I didn't know what cardiac catheterization was, so I had to be a smart   2
aleck and ask.

"Before we perform the new heart surgery in this country," one of the   3
doctors explained, "we first put the patient through cardiac catheterization. It is the best diagnostic tool we have available to us.

"We will insert catheters—little tubes—into an artery and a vein, and   4
we will send them into your heart. We will inject dyes through the catheters so that we can take movies of the heart and of the arteries around your heart so that we can determine whether or not there is any blockage.

"This way, we can determine exactly what is your problem, we can see 5 exactly how your heart is functioning, and we can tell if there are any hidden problems we didn't already know about."

That didn't sound so terrible, but doctors tend to leave out details 6 when they are explaining things.

Friend of mine called me a few days before I was to have the catheter- 7 ization.

"Had it myself a couple of years ago," he said. 8

"How bad is it?" I asked. 9

"Not too bad," he said. "First, they whack open your arm and start 10 shoving all these tubes up in you. When they get the tubes in, they shoot in the dye.

"The doctor will say, 'This is going to burn a little.' What he doesn't 11 say is where it burns."

I never learn my lesson. I had to ask where it burns. 12

"Your testicles," he said. "The dye goes from your heart to your blad- 13 der and burns your testicles. You'll think your testicles are going to burn right off. But try not to think about it before you go in there."

As my wife was driving me to the hospital to have my catheterization, 14 she asked, "Something's been on your mind for days. What is it?"

I thought it best not to tell her. 15

Aside from the evening I was born, I had never been a hospital patient 16 before. First, they make you put on one of those silly gowns with no back. Those gowns have no backs so it is easier for the nurses to slip up behind you and give you a shot in your hip.

"This is going to make your mouth very dry," said the nurse as she 17 gave me a shot in my hip. A lot of things puzzle me about medicine. One is, if they want to make my mouth dry, then why do they give me a shot in my hip?

Next, you have to sign a release saying it is okay for your doctor to do 18 this cardiac catheterization thing to you.

"Just sign it," said the nurse. 19

"But I think I should read the release first," I said. 20

"Just sign it," said the nurse. 21

Like I said, I never learn. I read the release, all the way down to the 22 part where it said, in large letters, that cardiac catheterization includes "THE ULTIMATE RISK OF DEATH."

"Nobody said anything about dying from this," I said to the nurse. 23

"It's just a routine release," said the nurse. "I told you not to read it." 24

I asked for the number of the nearest cab service. 25

"You can't leave now," the nurse insisted. "I've already given you a 26 shot. What are you afraid of?"

"I'm afraid my testicles will get burned off and I will die," I said. 27

Before I could get out of my hospital gown and back into my clothes— 28
you wouldn't have much luck hailing a cab with a bare bottom, I decided—
they came to take me away for the catheterization.

They were bringing in another victim as I left the prep room. A nurse 29
handed him his release.

"Just sign it," I said to him.   30

"But shouldn't I read it first?" he asked.   31

"Not unless you think you can catch a cab half-naked," I said, as they 32
rolled me away.

The first thing I asked the doctor, once I had been strapped down on 33
the platform that poses for a bed in the catheterization room was, "How
much is this going to hurt?"

"You are hardly going to feel a thing," he answered.   34

The next thing I asked the doctor was, "Have you ever undergone this 35
procedure yourself?"

"No," he answered.   36

Just as I thought. He's going to cut open my arm on the other side of 37
my elbow, stick tubes into my heart, inject dyes that will burn my testicles,
and I am hardly going to feel a thing.

There is, in fact, this awesome communications gap between the med- 38
ical profession and its patients when it comes to pain.

I happen to be an expert on pain. I can get hurt pouring a glass of milk. 39

To me, pain is anything even slightly uncomfortable that is caused by 40
somebody other than myself poking, pricking, sticking, or jabbing me.

Pain to the medical profession probably would be something like cut- 41
ting off your left foot without first giving you an aspirin.

The next time you're having something done to your body by a doctor, 4:
ask him, "Is this going to hurt?"

He will likely answer, "It might sting a little."   4

Sting is a word they use a lot in medicine. *Sting,* to me, means a slight 4
pain, a level or two under a mosquito bite.

When a doctor says, "This might sting a little," he really means, 4
"Have you ever been bitten by a large animal with very sharp teeth?"

Here are some other phrases to be careful of the next time you go to ·
the doctor or spend any time in the hospital:

- "You might feel a little pressure here." This means the brakes on the delivery truck full of frozen pudding that is unloading in front of the hospital
  are about to give way and the truck, all ten tons of it, is going to roll over
  you. That's the "little pressure" you're going to feel.
- "This might pull a little." They used to say the very same thing to enemies
  of the state just before they put them on the rack. If a doctor says, "This

might pull a little," prepare for your kidneys to be yanked up to your throat. I'm no expert on the anatomy, but your kidneys have no business in your throat.

If you happen to be in the hospital or at your doctor's office and some- 47 body mentions something something "pulling a little," run as fast as you can for the nearest bus, even if you are half-naked.

- "I did this same thing to a seven-year-old boy this morning, and he didn't even whimper." Had the child been conscious, however...
- "Now, that wasn't so bad, was it?" Not if you're used to finishing third in ax fights, no.
- "Very few of my other patients ever complain about this procedure." That doesn't surprise me at all, Dr. Quincy.
- "This may tingle a bit when the needle goes through the nerve." Look around for a soft place to land.
- "I think the anesthetic has had plenty of time to take effect." Couldn't we wait just six more weeks to be sure?
- "If you will just relax, this will be over before you know it." Be especially careful of this one. The doctor is just trying to buy time before you start trying to hurt him back. What he really means is that the British fleet can turn around and sail all the way back from the Falkland Islands and this tube will still be stuck straight up Argentina.

I am strapped onto the bed. The room is out of the Mad Scientist. 48 I am wishing they had put me to sleep for this. They don't put you to sleep for catheterization because there are times when they want you to cough and hold your breath. All they can do, I suppose, is make your mouth dry.

"One thing before we start," said a nurse. "If your nose itches, don't 49 try to scratch it. We want you to lie still. If your nose itches, ask me and I will scratch it for you."

Why did she have to say that? My nose hadn't itched for years. As soon 50 as she said not to scratch my nose, it started itching. It itched during the entire two hours of the procedure.

You can get somebody to scratch your back. You can get somebody to 51 scratch your head. Your nose is something else. Only the person who owns the nose can adequately scratch it.

The catheterization. They deadened my right arm with shots of No- 52 vocain before making the incision. There are no nerves inside the heart, so there was no pain involved with the tubes. I felt the shots all the way down to my fingers.

The dye.   53

"This is going to burn a little," said the doctor.   54

"For God's sake, go easy, man," I said.   55

I thought about cursing, but there were ladies present. I made a hor- 56
rible face as the intensity of the heat from the dye reached its peak at the
precise point my friend had indicated.

"Your nose itch?" asked the nurse.   57

"It's not my nose, and it doesn't itch," I answered.   58

All this time, they are taking pictures of my heart and my arteries.   59

"If you look on the screen," said the doctor, "you can see what's hap-   60
pening."

Doctors, of course, enjoy seeing a man's heart being tugged and pulled   61
like it was a strip steak about to be flung upon the grill, but I close my eyes
even when I get a haircut. I didn't choose to see what was happening.

I must admit there was very little actual pain involved with the cathe-   62
terization, save the moment the doctor yanked the last tube down my arm
and out through the incision. It felt like he was bringing my entire shoulder
with it.

"Oops," said the doctor when I howled in anguish. "Oops" is not   63
something you want to hear a doctor say.

They rolled me out of the catheterization room and into another room   64
where the doctor took four stitches to close the incision in my arm. I had a
tremendous desire to use the restroom at this point. The dye *had* gone to my
bladder.

A nurse brought me a small, pitcher-like container. I was supposed to   65
hold it under the sheet and go to the bathroom in it.

Something I didn't know. It is impossible to go to the bathroom in a   66
small pitcher-like container while lying on your back while somebody is sewing up your arm and your nose itches.

The doctor finished my arm, and they put me in a wheelchair and took   67
me to my room. I was finally able to relieve myself, drink a cold glass of tea,
and fall into bed.

I spent the rest of the afternoon watching old movies on the television   68
above me and answering calls from wellwishers.

The doctor who had performed the cath came in after dinner.   69

"We'll look at the films together tomorrow," he said.   70

"I'd rather not, if you don't mind," I replied.   71

"You should look," he said.   72

I guess they teach that sort of thing in medical school—how to say a lot 73
by saying a little.

QUESTIONS ABOUT THE RHETORICAL SITUATION

1. How would you characterize Grizzard's attitude toward himself as a patient? Toward the medical staff? Toward the medical procedure itself?

2. How does Grizzard want his reader to respond to his story? How are we to view cardiac catheterization? Doctors? Nurses?
3. Grizzard makes a joke about "Dr. Quincy" and refers to the Falklands war as part of another joke. Clearly, he assumes that his readers are familiar with both references. Do you think that he has made a reasonable assumption? Can you describe the audience he appears to have in mind as he writes his essay?
4. Is there a serious point to Grizzard's reminiscence? If so, what is it?

QUESTIONS ABOUT THE ESSAY'S VOICE

1. Some of Grizzard's descriptions border on being in bad taste, yet they are not. How does he avoid becoming offensive to his reader?
2. Grizzard's topic is not one which most of us would ordinarily see as inherently funny. How does he make a potentially serious subject into a source of humor?
3. Grizzard mentions his fears of being burned and his dry mouth more than once. What other repetitions does he use? Why does he rely so heavily on repetition? What is the effect of such repetitions?
4. How is Grizzard's voice when he speaks, which is evident in his dialogue, similar to and different from his written voice in this essay?
5. At one point Grizzard compares being stung to being bitten by a "large animal with very sharp teeth." How funny is this comparison? Why would it have been more amusing if he had written "bitten by a lovesick grizzly bear with thirty-three razor-sharp incisors?" What other specific comparisons does Grizzard use to make his points clear? Which ones are amusing? Why?
6. Notice how short most of Grizzard's paragraphs are. What effect did such short paragraphs have on you as you read his essay?

TOPICS TO WRITE ABOUT

1. Write an essay poking fun at the language used by other workers: for example, auto mechanics, computer programmers, travel agents, English teachers. POTENTIAL AUDIENCES: the general public/the workers themselves. POTENTIAL PURPOSE: to point out how modern consumers' expectations of polite, helpful service have diminished/to inform these workers of your confusion when they converse with you.
2. Write a narrative about a frightening experience of your own, but make it amusing. POTENTIAL AUDIENCES: your classmates/your younger sibling. POTENTIAL PURPOSE: to amuse them or make them laugh/to reassure her that she is not the first person to experience this fear.

For the Birds

Dave Barry

Dave Barry is a nationally syndicated humor columnist for the Knight-Ridder
News Service. His syndicated column, which runs in the *Miami Herald*, generally takes a slightly wry look at modern life in America. Barry, who graduated from Haverford College in 1969, has published several collections of his
columns, including *Babies and Other Hazards of Sex*, *The Taming of the Screw*,
Bad Habits, and *Stay Fit and Healthy Until You're Dead*. "For the Birds" originally appeared in 1983.

QUESTIONS ABOUT IDEAS

1. Birds are a rather large subject. How does Barry manage to narrow down
   his topic in this essay?
2. What is it about birds which so fascinates many bird-watchers?
3. What other hobbies might be susceptible to similar treatment by Barry in
   his weekly column? Why?

Everybody should know something about birds, because birds are every- 1
where. Zoologists tell us that there are more than 23,985,409,098,744,885,143
birds in the city of Lincoln, Nebraska, alone which is one of the many reasons not to go there.

Now perhaps you get a bit nervous when you think about all those 2
birds out there. Perhaps you remember Alfred Hitchcock's famous movie,
The Birds, in which several million birds got together one afternoon and decided to peck a number of Californians to death. Well, you needn't worry.

First, any animal that attacks Californians is a friend of man. And sec- 3
ond, *The Birds* was just a movie; in real life, your chances of being pecked
to death by birds are no greater than your chances of finding a polite clerk at
the Bureau of Motor Vehicles.

There is an incredible range of birds, from the ostrich, which weighs 4
up to 600 pounds and stands up to nine feet tall, and can run 200 miles an
hour and crush a man's head as if it were a Ping-Pong ball; to the tiny bee
hummingbird, which is a mere 6.17 decahedrons long and can fly right into
your ear and hum its tiny wings so hard you think your brain is going to
vibrate into jelly, and you eventually go insane.

Birds, like most mammals, especially lawyers, evolved from reptiles. 5
The first bird appeared millions of years ago, during the Jurassic Period.
What happened was this reptile, inspired by some mysterious, wondrous in-

spiration to evolve, climbed up a Jurassic-Period tree and leaped from the topmost branch and thudded into the ground at 130 miles per hour.

Then other reptiles, inspired by the same urge as the first reptile but 6 even stupider, climbed up and began leaping from the branch. Soon the ground trembled with the thud of many reptile bodies, raining down on the Jurassic plain like some kind of scaly hailstorm.

This went on for a few thousand years, until one of the reptiles evolved 7 some feathers and discovered it could fly. As it soared skyward, the other species, who had grown very tired of being pelted by reptile bodies, let out a mighty cheer, which stopped a few seconds later when they were pelted by the first bird droppings.

Soon the birds had spread to the four corners of the earth, which is 8 where they are today. And wherever there are birds, there are also bird-watchers, in case the birds decide to try something. Birdwatchers are known technically as "birdwatchers," which comes from the Latin word for "orni-thologist." Birdwatchers divide birds into four main groups:

- Boring little brownish birds that are all over the place: Wrens, chickadees, sparrows, nutcrackers, spanners, catcalls, dogbirds, hamsterbirds, finches.
- Birds that can lift really heavy things, such as your car: Albatrosses, winches, pterodactyls, unusually large chickadees, elephant birds, emus.
- Birds with names that you are going to think I made up but didn't: Boo-bies, frigate birds, nightjars, frogmouths, oilbirds.
- Birds that make those jungle noises you always hear during night scenes in jungle movies: Parrots, cockatoos, pomegranates, macadams, cashews, bats.

Your avid birdwatchers spend lots of time creeping around with bin- 9 oculars, trying to identify new and unusual birds. The trouble is that most birds are of the little-and-brownish variety, all of which look exactly alike, and all of which are boring. So what birdwatchers do is make things up.

If you've ever spent any time at all with birdwatchers, you've probably 10 noticed that every now and then they'll whirl around, for no apparent rea-son, and claim that they've just seen some obscure, tiny bird roughly 6,500 feet away. They'll claim they can tell whether it was male or female, which in fact you can't tell about birds even when they're very close, what with all the feathers and everything.

I advise you to do what most people do when confronted with bird- 11 watchers, which is just humor them. If their lives are so dull and drab that they want to fill them with imaginary birds, why stand in the way? Here's how you should handle it:

BIRDWATCHER: Did you see that?
YOU: What?

BIRDWATCHER: Over there, by that mountain [he gestures to a mountain in the next state]. It's a male Malaysian sand-dredging coronet. Very, very rare in these parts.

YOU: Yes, I see it.

BIRDWATCHER: You do?

YOU: Certainly. It's just to the left of that female European furloughed pumpkinbird. See it?

BIRDWATCHER: Uh, yes, of course I see it.

YOU: Look, they're playing backgammon.

BIRDWATCHER: Um, so they are.

If you have a good imagination, you may come to really enjoy the bird-watching game, in which case you should join a birdwatching group. These groups meet regularly, and usually after a few minutes they're detecting obscure birds on the surface of Saturn. It's a peck of fun. 12

QUESTIONS ABOUT THE RHETORICAL SITUATION

1. Barry is a syndicated newspaper columnist. What does that tell you about his probable audience? How is his essay aimed appropriately at that audience?

2. What reaction is Barry seeking from his readers? How does his purpose justify his seemingly irrelevant digs at Lincoln, Nebraska; Californians; and lawyers?

3. Does Barry really know anything at all about his topic or does he make up everything as he goes along? Which parts of his essay do seem grounded in fact and which are merely imaginary? Is it fair to his readers to mix fact and fiction or to pass off fiction as fact in this manner? Why (or why not)?

QUESTIONS ABOUT THE ESSAY'S VOICE

1. Although Barry's title suggests that his subject is birds, he actually covers two major topics here. How successful is he in holding the two topics together? What efforts does he make to try to hold his essay together?

2. Barry relies upon many specific examples in his essay. Without rereading the essay, which of Barry's specific examples can you recall? Why does he use so many specific details?

3. Barry relies frequently on surprising his reader. For example, his comment about lawyers is unexpected. Where else in the essay has Barry surprised you? What is the effect of most of these surprises?

4. Does Barry seem angry in this essay? Is he hostile? Would you term his voice comic or is it harsher than that? Why? Why not?

5. Has Barry been fair to bird-watchers in his essay or is he being unfair? Would bird-watchers reading this essay become offended? Is Barry engaging in harmful stereotyping? How ethical is it for writers to stereotype groups of people?
6. How does Barry's essay about bird-watchers resemble Lewis Grizzard's essay about doctors in tone? Structure? Technique?
7. At one point in the essay, Barry wishes to discuss the great variety of birds. Which techniques for creating humor does he use in that section of the essay? What method of organization does he use? How successful is this section of his essay? Why?
8. Which of the many techniques for creating humor that Barry employs here works most effectively in your view? Why? Which jokes misfire here? Why?

TOPICS TO WRITE ABOUT

1. Write a comic essay about an offbeat (or even a familiar but often misunderstood) hobby: stamp collecting, gardening, beer can collecting, mountain climbing, folk dancing, hang gliding, needlepoint. If the hobby is offbeat, make it sound normal and usual; if the hobby is ordinary and everyday, make it sound exotic or dangerous. POTENTIAL AUDIENCES: would-be hobbyists/the actual hobbyists themselves. POTENTIAL PURPOSES: to offer a warning of sorts about the pitfalls of such a hobby/ to show them how their hobby appears to outsiders.
2. Create several amusing categories as a means of explaining some group of animals or objects. For instance, classify dogs or fish into categories or classify jewelry or the food in the cafeteria into categories. POTENTIAL AUDIENCE: senior citizens (try classifying punk clothing or hairstyles for this group). POTENTIAL PURPOSE: to explain a somewhat unfamiliar or bewildering phenomenon.

University Days
James Thurber

James Thurber (1894–1961) began his writing career in 1920 as a reporter on the *Columbus* (Ohio) *Evening Dispatch.* In 1927, Thurber began a long association with *The New Yorker* magazine after returning from Europe. Thurber's fame grew in the 1930s, not only because of his writing but perhaps just as much because of his cartoons. Perhaps most famous for his short story, "The

Secret Life of Walter Mitty," Thurber also published *The Years with Ross,* about his experiences at *The New Yorker.* In 1960 a Broadway show, *A Thurber Carnival,* based on his writing and cartoons was a moderate success. A television series based on Thurber's life, *My World and Welcome to It,* was also a success in the 1960s.

"University Days," taken from his collection of essays entitled *My Life and Hard Times* (1961), was originally published in 1933 and is based on Thurber's undergraduate days as a student at Ohio State University in Columbus.

QUESTIONS ABOUT IDEAS

1. How has life at the university changed over the past five decades? Which changes seem significant? Why?
2. How does James Thurber, college student, resemble James Thurber, professional writer, as described in the brief biographical sketch?
3. Thurber's account of university life accepts the role of intercollegiate athletics and military training on campus. What are the prevailing attitudes toward these two aspects of college life on your campus?
4. Thurber, after leaving Ohio State, became a professional writer and cartoonist. He may well have objected, during his "University Days," to taking courses outside his major areas of interest. What arguments could be made that these courses, such as botany, were important to his education?

I passed all the other courses that I took at the University, but I could   1
never pass botany. This was because all botany students had to spend several hours a week in a laboratory looking through a microscope. I never once saw a cell through a microscope. This used to enrage my instructor. He would wander around the laboratory pleased with the progress all the students were making in drawing the involved and, so I am told, interesting structure of flower cells, until he came to me. I would just be standing there. "I can't see anything," I would say. He would begin patiently enough, explaining how anybody can see through a microscope, but he would always end up in a fury, exclaiming that I could *too* see through a microscope but just pretended that I couldn't. "It takes away from the beauty of flowers anyway," I used to tell him. "We are not concerned with beauty in this course," he would say. "We are concerned solely with what I may call the *mechanics* of flars." "Well," I'd say, "I can't see anything." "Try it just once again," he'd say, and I would put my eye to the microscope and see nothing at all, except now and again a nebulous milky substance—a phenomenon of maladjustment. You were supposed to see a vivid, restless clockwork of sharply defined plant cells. "I see what looks like a lot of milk," I would tell him. This, he claimed, was the result of my not having adjusted the microscope properly,

so he would readjust it for me, or rather, for himself. And I would look again and see milk.

I finally took a deferred pass, as they called it, and waited a year and   2
tried again. (You had to pass one of the biological sciences or you couldn't graduate.) The professor had come back from vacation brown as a berry, bright-eyed, and eager to explain cell-structure again to his classes. "Well," he said to me, cheerily, when we met in the first laboratory hour of the se-mester, "we're going to see cells this time, aren't we?" "Yes, sir," I said. Students to right of me and to left of me and in front of me were seeing cells; what's more, they were quietly drawing pictures of them in their notebooks. Of course, I didn't see anything.

"We'll try it," the professor said to me, grimly, "with every adjust-   3
ment of the microscope known to man. As God is my witness, I'll arrange this glass so that you see cells through it or I'll give up teaching. In twenty-two years of botany, I—" He cut off abruptly for he was beginning to quiver all over, like Lionel Barrymore, and he genuinely wished to hold onto his temper; his scenes with me had taken a great deal out of him.

So we tried it with every adjustment of the microscope known to man.   4
With only one of them did I see anything but blackness or the familiar lac-teal opacity, and that time I saw, to my pleasure and amazement, a varie-gated constellation of flecks, specks, and dots. These I hastily drew. The instructor, noting my activity, came back from an adjoining desk, a smile on his lips and his eyebrows high in hope. He looked at my cell drawing. "What's that?" he demanded, with a hint of a squeal in his voice. "That's what I saw," I said. "You didn't, you didn't, you *did*n't!" he screamed, los-ing control of his temper instantly, and he bent over and squinted into the microscope. His head snapped up. "That's your eye!" he shouted. "You've fixed the lens so that it reflects! You've drawn your eye!"

Another course that I didn't like, but somehow managed to pass, was   5
economics. I went to that class straight from the botany class, which didn't help me any in understanding either subject. I used to get them mixed up. But not as mixed up as another student in my economics class who came there direct from a physics laboratory. He was a tackle on the football team, named Bolenciecwcz. At that time Ohio State University had one of the best football teams in the country, and Bolenciecwcz was one of its outstanding stars. In order to be eligible to play it was necessary for him to keep up in his studies, a very difficult matter, for while he was not dumber than an ox he was not any smarter. Most of his professors were lenient and helped him along. None gave him more hints, in answering questions, or asked him sim-pler ones than the economics professor, a thin, timid man named Bassum. One day when we were on the subject of transportation and distribution, it came Bolenciecwcz's turn to answer a question. "Name one means of trans-portation," the professor said to him. No light came into the big tackle's eyes. "Just any means of transportation," said the professor. Bolen-

ciecwcz sat staring at him. "That is," pursued the professor, "any medium, agency, or method of going from one place to another." Bolenciecwcz had the look of a man who is being led into a trap. "You may choose among steam, horse-drawn, or electrically propelled vehicles," said the instructor. "I might suggest the one which we commonly take in making long journeys across land." There was a profound silence in which everybody stirred uneasily, including Bolenciecwcz and Mr. Bassum. Mr. Bassum abruptly broke this silence in an amazing manner. "Choo-choo-choo," he said, in a low voice, and turned instantly scarlet. He glanced appealingly around the room. All of us, of course, shared Mr. Bassum's desire that Bolenciecwcz should stay abreast of the class in economics, for the Illinois game, one of the hardest and most important of the season, was only a week off. "Toot, toot, too-toooooot!" some student with a deep voice moaned, and we all looked encouragingly at Bolenciecwcz. Somebody else gave a fine imitation of a locomotive letting off steam. Mr. Bassum himself rounded off the little show. "Ding, dong, ding, dong," he said, hopefully. Bolenciecwcz was staring at the floor now, trying to think, his great brow furrowed, his huge hands rubbing together, his face red.

"How did you come to college this year, Mr. Bolenciecwcz?" asked the   6
professor. "*Chuf*fa, chuffa, *chuf*fa, chuffa."

"M'father sent me," said the football player.   7

"What on?" asked Bassum.   8

"I git an 'lowance," said the tackle, in a low, husky voice, obviously 9
embarrassed.

"No, no," said Bassum. "Name a means of transportation. What did   10
you *ride* here on?"

"Train," said Bolenciecwcz.   11

"Quite right," said the professor. "Now, Mr. Nugent, will you tell   12
us—"

If I went through anguish in botany and economics—for different rea- 13
sons—gymnasium work was even worse. I don't even like to think about it. They wouldn't let you play games or join in the exercises with your glasses on and I couldn't see with mine off. I bumped into professors, horizontal bars, agricultural students, and swinging iron rings. Not being able to see, I could take it but I couldn't dish it out. Also, in order to pass gymnasium (and you had to pass it to graduate) you had to learn to swim if you didn't know how. I didn't like the swimming pool, I didn't like swimming, and I didn't like the swimming instructor, and after all these years I still don't. I never swam but I passed my gym work anyway, by having another student give my gymnasium number (978) and swim across the pool in my place. He was a quiet, amiable blonde youth, number 473, and he would have seen through a microscope for me if we could have got away with it, but we couldn't get away with it. Another thing I didn't like about gymnasium was

that they made you strip the day you registered. It is impossible for me to be happy when I am stripped and being asked a lot of questions. Still, I did better than a lanky agricultural student who was cross-examined just before I was. They asked each student what college he was in—that is, whether Arts, Engineering, Commerce, or Agriculture. "What college are you in?" the instructor snapped at the youth in front of me. "Ohio State University," he said promptly.

It wasn't that agricultural student but it was another a whole lot like 14 him who decided to take up journalism, possibly on the ground that when farming went to hell he could fall back on newspaper work. He didn't realize, of course, that that would be very much like falling back full-length on a kit of carpenter's tools. Haskins didn't seem cut out for journalism, being too embarrassed to talk to anybody and unable to use a typewriter, but the editor of the college paper assigned him to the cow barns, the sheep house, the horse pavilion, and the animal husbandry department generally. This was a genuinely big "beat," for it took up five times as much ground and got ten times as great a legislative appropriation as the College of Liberal Arts. The agricultural student knew animals, but nevertheless his stories were dull and colorlessly written. He took all afternoon on each of them, on account of having to hunt for each letter on the typewriter. Once in a while he had to ask somebody to help him hunt. "C" and "L," in particular, were hard letters for him to find. His editor finally got pretty much annoyed at the farmer-journalist because his pieces were so uninteresting. "See here, Haskins," he snapped at him one day. "Why is it we never have anything hot from you on the horse pavilion? Here we have two hundred head of horses on this campus—more than any other university in the Western Conference except Purdue—and yet you never get any real low down on them. Now shoot over to the horse barns and dig up something lively." Haskins shambled out and came back in about an hour; he said he had something. "Well start it off snappily," said the editor. "Something people will read." Haskins set to work and in a couple of hours brought a sheet of typewritten paper to the desk; it was a two-hundred-word story about some disease that had broken out among the horses. Its opening sentence was simple but arresting. It read, "Who has noticed the sores on the tops of the horses in the animal husbandry building?"

Ohio State was a land grant university and therefore two years of mil- 15 itary drill was compulsory. We drilled with old Springfield rifles and studied the tactics of the Civil War even though the World War was going on at the time. At 11 o'clock each morning thousands of freshmen and sophomores used to deploy over the campus, moodily creeping up on the old chemistry building. It was good training for the kind of warfare that was waged at Shiloh, but it had no connection with what was going on in Europe. Some people used to think there was German money behind it, but they didn't dare say so or they would have been thrown in jail as German spies. It was a period of muddy thought and marked, I believe, the decline of higher education in the Middle West.

As a soldier I was never any good at all. Most of the cadets were glumly 16 indifferent soldiers, but I was no good at all. Once General Littlefield, who was commandant of the cadet corps, popped up in front of me during regiment drill and snapped, "You are the main trouble with the university!" I think he meant that my type was the main trouble with the university, but he may have meant me individually. I was mediocre at drill, certainly—that is, until my senior year. By that time I had drilled longer than anybody else in the Western Conference, having failed at military at the end of each preceding year so that I had to do it all over again. I was the only senior still in uniform. The uniform which, when new, had made me look like an interurban railway conductor, now that it had become faded and too tight made me look like Bert Williams in his bellboy act. This had a definitely bad effect on my morale. Even so, I had become by sheer practice little short of wonderful at squad maneuvers.

One day General Littlefield picked our company out of the whole regiment and tried to get it mixed up by putting it through one movement after 17 another as fast as we could execute them: squads right, squads left, squads on right into line, squads right about, squads left front into line, etc. In about three minutes one hundred and nine men were marching in one direction and I was marching away from them at an angle of forty degrees, all alone. "Company, halt!" shouted General Littlefield. "That man is the only man who has it right!" I was made a corporal for my achievement.

The next day General Littlefield summoned me to his office. He was 18 swatting flies when I went in. I was silent and he was silent too, for a long time. I don't think he remembered me or why he had sent for me, but he didn't want to admit it. He swatted some more flies, keeping his eyes on them narrowly before he let go with the swatter. "Button up your coat!" he snapped. Looking back on it now I can see that he meant me although he was looking at a fly, but I just stood there. Another fly came to rest on a paper in front of the general and began rubbing its hind legs together. The general lifted the swatter cautiously. I moved restlessly and the fly flew away. "You startled him!" barked General Littlefield, looking at me severely. I said I was sorry. "That won't help the situation!" snapped the general, with cold military logic. I didn't see what I could do except offer to chase some more flies toward his desk, but I didn't say anything. He stared out the window at the faraway figures of co-eds crossing the campus toward the library. Finally, he told me I could go. So I went. He either didn't know which cadet I was or else he forgot what he wanted to see me about. It may have been that he wished to apologize for having called me the main trouble with the university; or maybe he had decided to compliment me on my brilliant drilling of the day before and then at the last minute decided not to. I don't know. I don't think about it much any more.

QUESTIONS ABOUT THE RHETORICAL SITUATION

1. Thurber's anecdotes depict a number of his professors. What do these professors have in common? To what extent is Thurber critical or understanding of them? How does Thurber depict himself in these anecdotes? Do we laugh at the expense of Thurber and his teachers or along with them?
2. Thurber's essay was written in 1933. What clues are there to suggest that this essay was written many years ago? Can today's readers follow the essay despite its age? Why? Why not?
3. Thurber tells five anecdotes here and uses transitions to link the first four together. His final anecdote is not really connected very forcefully to the earlier ones. What is Thurber's main intention in writing this essay, given that it does not really hold together very tightly? Is he successful, or would his essay be improved if it had a more traditional introduction, body, and conclusion? Why or why not?

QUESTIONS ABOUT THE ESSAY'S VOICE

1. Thurber employs exaggeration much less frequently than some of the other humorous writers you have read (he does so at the conclusion of ¶15, to cite one example). He seems, instead, to rely upon understatement (such as his comments about the Illinois football game in ¶5). What is the effect of such understatement on the essay's voice?
2. How does Thurber rely upon surprise in this essay to create humor?
3. How is Thurber's voice different from Dave Barry's or Lewis Grizzard's in the two earlier selections in Chapter 2? How would you describe these three writers based on what you have read? What would each one look like? What would each one dress like? Point to the details in the writing that lead to your answers.
4. Thurber's essay is a series of anecdotes about his days at Ohio State as a student. The anecdote is an excellent means not only for providing specific illustrations of general ideas but also for creating humor (see *Readers' Digest*, for example, which makes heavy use of anecdotal humor). Which of Thurber's anecdotes seems the most amusing to you? Why? Do some of the anecdotes fail to be amusing? Why? What do the successful anecdotes have in common?

5. Is Thurber satirizing Bolenciecwcz, the football player, or Haskins, the farmer-journalist? Is his commentary about these students pointed or is it wry?

TOPICS TO WRITE ABOUT

1. Write an amusing essay about your high school days, your sleepaway camp days, your Little League days, or your Brownie days (or any set of experiences from your past), using anecdotes which reveal your personality at the time. POTENTIAL AUDIENCES: your parents (or your children)/ your old camp counselor (or Little League coach or homeroom teacher or troop leader). POTENTIAL PURPOSES: to remind them of "the good old days" (or to teach a lesson about growing)/to say thanks to an old friend.

2. Write an amusing essay that demonstrates how some aspect of life in the 1980s is different from the way it used to be in the 1960s (or 70s or 50s or 40s). For instance, discuss popular music or restaurants or TV shows or political candidates or growing up. POTENTIAL AUDIENCES: Pretend you are delivering your essay as a speech to a group of anthropologists./Write the paper addressed to a group of astronauts who have just returned after being out of touch with Earth for twenty years. POTENTIAL PURPOSES: to explain your own interpretation of changing times/to help them readjust to Earth.

Index: There Is No Index

Stephen Leacock

Stephen Leacock (1869–1944) retains his reputation as Canada's foremost humorist. Born in Great Britain, Leacock and his family emigrated to Canada when he was a boy. He graduated from the University of Toronto and began a career as an educator and scholar, serving as head of the Department of Economics and Political Science at McGill University. While pursuing academic and scholarly activities, Leacock also published extensively as a humorist, producing more than thirty books of satire and humor, including such titles as *Wet Wit and Dry Humor, Moonbeams from the Larger Lunacy,* and *Literary Lapses.*

"Index: There Is No Index" is a selection from *The Leacock Roundabout: A Treasury of the Best Works of Stephen Leacock,* published posthumously in 1946.

QUESTIONS ABOUT IDEAS

1. Have you ever considered the work that must go into creating an index for a book? How much truth do you suppose there is in Leacock's depiction of the "Index Problem"?
2. Do indexes serve useful purposes? Do readers use indexes properly? Does Leacock think so?
3. What kind of books are served well by having indexes? What kinds of books have no need of indexes? Does this book need an index? (It isn't going to get one!)

Readers of books, I mean worth-while readers, like those who read this ¹ volume, will understand how many difficulties centre around the making of an Index. Whether to have an Index at all? Whether to make it a great big one, or just a cute little Index on one page? Whether to have only proper names, or let it take in ideas—and so so. In short the thing reaches dimensions that may raise it to the rank of being called the Index Problem, if nothing is done about it.

Of course one has to have an Index. Authors themselves would prefer ² not to have any. Having none would save trouble and compel reviewers to read the whole book instead of just the Index. But the reader needs it. Otherwise he finds himself looking all through the book, forwards and then backwards, and then plunging in at random, in order to read out to a friend what it was that was so darned good about Talleyrand. He doesn't find it, because it was in another book.

So let us agree, there must be an Index. Now comes the trouble. What ³ is the real title or name of a thing or person that has three or four? Must you put everything three or four times over in the Index, under three or four names? No, just once, so it is commonly understood; and then for the other joint names, we put what is called a cross-reference, meaning, "See this" or "See that." It sounds good in theory, but in practice it leads to such results as—*Talleyrand, see Perigord*...and when you hunt this up, you find—*Perigord, Bishop of, see Talleyrand.* The same effect can be done flat out, with just two words, as *Lincoln, see Abraham...Abraham, see Lincoln.* But even that is not so bad because at least it's a closed circle. It comes to a full stop. But compare the effect, familiar to all research students, when the circle is not closed. Thus, instead of just seeing Lincoln, the unclosed circle runs like this, each item being hunted up alphabetically, one after the other—*Abraham, see Lincoln...Lincoln, see Civil War...Civil War, see United States...United States, see America...America, see American History...American History, see also Christopher Columbus, New England, Pocahontas, George Washington...* the thing will finally come to rest somehow or other with the dial pointing at *see Abraham Lincoln.*

But there is worse even than that. A certain kind of conscientious au- 4
thor enters only proper names, but he indexes them every time they come
into his book, no matter how they come in, and how unimportant is the context. Here is the result in the Index under the letter N:

Napoleon—17, 26, 41, 73, 109, 110, 156, 213, 270, 380, 460. You be- 5
gin to look them up. Here are the references:

Page 17—"wore his hair like Napoleon."
Page 26—"in the days of Napoleon."
Page 41—"as fat as Napoleon."
Page 73—"not so fat as Napoleon."
Page 109—"was a regular Napoleon at Ping-pong."
Page 110—"was not a Napoleon at Ping-pong."
Page 156—"Napoleon's hat."
Pages 213, 270, 380, 460, not investigated.

Equally well meant but perhaps even harder to bear is the peculiar 6
kind of index that appears in a biography. The name of the person under
treatment naturally runs through almost every page, and the conscientious
index-maker tries to keep pace with him. This means that many events of his
life get shifted out of their natural order. Here is the general effect:

John Smith: born.p.1: born again.p.1: father born.p.2: grandfather 7
born.p.3: mother born.p.4: mother's family leave Ireland.p.5: still leaving
it.p.6: school.p.7: more school.p.8: dies of pneumonia and enters
Harvard.p.9: eldest son born.p.10: marries.p.11: back at school.p.12:
dead.p.13: takes his degree.p.14:...

Suppose, then, you decide to get away from all these difficulties and 8
make a Perfect Index in which each item shall carry with it an explanation,
a sort of little epitome of what is to be found in the book. The reader consulting the volume can open the Index, look at a reference, and decide
whether or not he needs to turn the subject up in the full discussion in the
book. A really good Index will in most cases itself give the information
wanted. There you have, so to speak, the Perfect Index.

Why I know about this is because I am engaged at present in making 9
such an Index in connection with a book on gardening, which I am writing
just now. To illustrate what is meant, I may be permitted to quote the opening of the book, and its conversion into Index material:

As Abraham Lincoln used to say, when you want to do gardening,
you've got to take your coat off, a sentiment shared by his fellow
enthusiast, the exiled Napoleon, who, after conquering all Europe,
retaining only the sovereignty of the spade in his garden plot at St.
Helena, longed only for more fertilizer.

As arranged for the Index, the gist, or essential part of this sentence, 10
the nucleus, so to speak, appears thus:

Abraham Lincoln; habit of saying things, p.1; wants to do gardening, p.1; takes his coat off, p.1; his enthusiasm, p.1; compared with Napoleon, p.1.

Coat; taken off by Abraham Lincoln, p.1.

Gardening; Lincoln's views on, p.1; need of taking coat off, for, p.1; Napoleon's enthusiasm over, p.1; see also under spade, sovereignty, St. Helena.

Napoleon; his exile, p.1; conquers Europe, p.1; enthusiastic over gardening, p.1; compared with Lincoln; retains sovereignty of spade, p.1; plots at St. Helena, p.1; longs for fertilizer, p.1; see also Europe, St. Helena, fertilizer, seed catalogue, etc., etc....

That's as far as I've got with the sentence. I still have to write up *sov-* 11 *ereignty, spade, sentiment, share, St. Helena,* and everything after S. There's no doubt it's the right method, but it takes time somehow to get the essential nucleus of the gist, and express it. I see why it is easier to do the other thing. But then sin is always easier than righteousness. See also under Hell, road to, Pavement, and Intentions, good.

QUESTIONS ABOUT THE RHETORICAL SITUATION

1. Leacock's opening sentence identifies his audience. Why does he make a joke? How would writers who have already published their own books respond to this essay? Would their response be different from yours? How would people who don't read books with indexes respond to this essay?
2. Leacock was a scholar and college professor who published serious writing in his field of expertise. Do you think this essay reflects all of his views of book indexes? Why is he poking fun at indexes? What does his humorous voice say about his purpose in this essay?
3. To what extent has this essay changed your views of book indexes? Is there any serious point to the humor?

QUESTIONS ABOUT THE ESSAY'S VOICE

1. Leacock uses a familiar humorist's technique in identifying a problem (¶1). However, he really does not offer solutions to the problem. What does he do instead?
2. Leacock relies heavily upon repetition to create humor. Trace the references to Napoleon, Lincoln, and Talleyrand in this essay. How does Leacock build humor upon these repeated references?
3. Notice Leacock's use of capital letters. What is the purpose of his capi

talizing the words he capitalizes? How does this help make the essay's voice comic?

4. Leacock's essay makes extensive use of specific examples. How would the essay be affected if ¶7, for example, were not included?

5. How exaggerated are Leacock's examples of book index references? In ¶3, he writes that the situation he is describing is "familiar to all research students." How familiar are Leacock's examples?

6. To what is Leacock alluding in his essay's final paragraph? How has he prepared the reader for this final joke?

TOPICS TO WRITE ABOUT

1. Write an essay poking fun at the dictionary or at an encyclopedia or any reference text that has occasionally frustrated you. POTENTIAL AUDIENCES: students likely to use the same reference texts/your teacher. POTENTIAL PURPOSES: to describe to them the problems they are likely to face in using these reference texts/to convince the teacher that *you* have tried your best but the reference texts have let you down.

2. Write an essay describing your best efforts to prepare a bibliography or a lab report or a précis or a résumé or any other sort of required academic or business document. POTENTIAL AUDIENCES: your little brother or sister/as part of a time capsule to be buried for 100 years. POTENTIAL PURPOSES: to warn them about the horrors that await them in their future school or work endeavors/to explain to future citizens how primitive our society was.

Training for the Magic Kingdom
Jeff Sommers

Jeff Sommers is an Associate Professor of English at the Middletown Campus of Miami University of Ohio, where he has been teaching a variety of writing courses and literature courses since 1981. Sommers has published fiction and poetry in addition to scholarly work. His experience as a writing instructor includes teaching creative writing to students in elementary school and junior high school.

This essay, which is followed by a rough draft and planning notes used by the author in writing this final draft, is based on a family trip taken in 1981. Sommers reports that his two sons' usual response to his jokes consists of the comment "Oh, Dad" and a deep sigh.

QUESTIONS ABOUT IDEAS

1. Is it really important to make such extensive preparations before vacationing? How sensible are the suggestions made in this essay about such preparation?
2. How might the advice offered in this essay be applicable to other sorts of vacations such as sightseeing tours of foreign countries or American landmarks?
3. What do American theme amusement parks tell foreigners about us as a society? What other forms of American leisure activities are peculiarly twentieth-century American?

For all red-blooded American tourists, a trip to Disney World/EPCOT 1
(or Disneyland Tokyo for our friends in the Far East) can be a dream come true. But, as with any truly significant life activity, one would be a darn fool to simply pack up and jump into such a trip without being properly prepared. That, sad to say, was my family's mistake: we did not train for the trip effectively. It really isn't difficult to get ready for the big dream vacation, but it does take some willpower and advance planning. Let me show you.

Foolishly we spent what little time we did devote to training to pre- 2
paring a budget. My wife and I separately composed budgets which included room and board, admission to the theme park, gas money, souvenirs, etc. We compared budgets, revised budgets, merged budgets, and soon, at great psychic cost, we had a thing of beauty, that elusive grail which our government searches for every year: a balanced budget within our means.

But when we gaily rushed into Disney World that first December 3
morning, we had to scoot straight for the souvenir shops to buy Mickey Mouse mittens, Donald Duck sweatshirts, and Goofy woolen hats. The mercury was a surprising 33°, and we were freezing! We thus blew more than our entire souvenir budget in the opening ten minutes. Like the famous domino effect which brought America into Southeast Asia, our souvenir budget forced us to borrow from our gas budget which in turn forced us to borrow from our food budget which in turn....

Now I realize that to train properly for budgeting such a trip in the 4
future, I should plan to go to the new mall near our house with the entire family. There, in front of the entrance is a lovely, splashing fountain with sparkling lights of green and red and blue where children throw their parents' spare change and make wishes. We, however, will stand there and practice throwing singles and fives and even ten dollar bills into the fountain in order to cultivate the proper attitude toward money needed for a trip to Disney World: indifference.

Our second serious error in preparing for our trip had to do with 5
physical activity. In the weeks prior to the trip my sons continued their

usual activities: running around pointlessly (as four- and six-year-olds generally do), fleeing from bathtubs, and squirming in bed every night after being tucked in. My wife continued her jogging and aerobicise, and I pursued my usual exercise regimen of grading papers in an easy chair. Every once in a while we would eat a meal, wash up, even use the bathroom. What fools we were to think we were in proper shape for our trip! All of our pursuits proved to be so much valuable training time just frittered away.

The truly prepared Disney World traveler is the one who has practiced **6** standing motionless for hours on end. After all, that is what most of the time spent at the Magic Kingdom will be devoted to. I think I can grade papers while standing in one place; I know my boys can pose motionless in front of Scooby Doo and Gilligan TV re-runs for an hour if pressed. And speaking of pressing, my wife can easily stand at an ironing board for the latest Richard Chamberlain miniseries—the entire thing—if necessary. And that's precisely what we will do before we ever return to Orlando: practice standing still. Oh—and we will practice abstaining from food and drink and trips to the bathroom also. After two hours of waiting to ride the Space Mountain, only an undertrained weakling would leave the line to visit the restroom because one of the laws of physics which operate in Tomorrowland (and Fantasyland and Frontierland and all of the other lands) is that a place in line tends to stay motionless while you are in it but moves at the speed of light if you leave. In other words, there ain't gonna be any place left for you when you come back.

I hope such tips can make your vacation to Disney World a bit more **7** successful than ours was. Actually I think we Americans might learn a lesson from our counterparts in the east: practitioners of yoga already know the futility of material things, like cash, and have the infinite patience to stand statue-like indefinitely. In fact, maybe yoga meditation is the real answer to my training problems. OM. OM. OM. OM.

QUESTIONS ABOUT THE RHETORICAL SITUATION

1. I actually enjoyed my visit to Disney World quite a bit. In the essay I tried to be amusing about the trip, but I really did not intend to give a negative impression of the Magic Kingdom. How successful is the essay in this regard? Does it seem too critical of Disney World?

2. I assumed that my readers, college students taking a freshman writing course, had all been to at least one theme park, and that the problems I was discussing would be familiar. You are members of that same audience. Was my assumption a safe one to make? Is the essay more entertaining if you have been to Disney World or King's Dominion or Busch Gardens or another theme amusement park? Is the essay understandable if you have not?

3. I would describe my major purpose as being to entertain or amuse my readers. If the essay did not amuse you, where did it go wrong? I would not object if my readers found a serious point in the essay also. Did you?

QUESTIONS ABOUT THE ESSAY'S VOICE

1. The essay purports to be offering a solution to a problem. How serious is the problem? How serious are the solutions? How appropriate are the solutions for this essay?
2. In addition to having a few laughs at the expense of theme parks, the essay also pokes fun at several other subjects such as small boys, the federal government, non-physically active, balding college English professors (such as me). How do such comments affect the sound of the essay's voice? How do such comments make you react to the person telling you all of this?
3. What is the organizational logic behind this essay? How effective is this organization? Could the essay work as a process analysis? How? (See page 59, Chapter 3).

TOPICS TO WRITE ABOUT

1. Write a comic essay about a minor problem but make the problem seem highly significant. Offer solutions. (Remember the student's essay about the bells ringing to end high school classes.) POTENTIAL AUDIENCES: the unsuspecting public/a government agency which might be able to fund your proposed solutions. POTENTIAL PURPOSES: to "sound the alarm" on this "significant" problem/to convince the agency to fund your mock research.
2. Describe in exaggerated and amusing detail a trip you have taken. POTENTIAL AUDIENCES: Write the essay as a mock travel brochure for unsuspecting vacationers or for the travel section of your local newspaper's Sunday supplement. POTENTIAL PURPOSE: to entice the readers to take the same trip so that you don't feel like the only "sucker" gullible enough to travel there.

THE WRITING PROCESS: CUBING

I have included my short essay on Disney World because it will allow me to show you how voice grows out of an understanding of the rhetorical situation. Every semester, I and my students use a prewriting activity called *cubing* in class. Cubing is designed to generate ideas about a very general topic for later use in narrowing down the topic. At the time that this essay was written I had just recently returned from a family vacation to Disney World and chose to write about that trip.

Cubing is based on *free writing,* which means writing quickly without stopping to edit or change what is written. In cubing, the writer free writes six times on his chosen topic, each time looking at the topic in a slightly different manner for five minutes. When cubing, a writer continues to write for the entire five-minute interval; if he draws a blank, he simply repeats the last word he has written until a new idea comes to mind. Although some textbooks suggest that cubing is best when used with a concrete object, I have found that it can be used with any topic at all providing the writer uses imagination, and I advise my students to write silly things when they cannot find serious things to write because that silliness can sometimes be insightful. Here are the six sides of the cube which the class used:

1. Describe the topic.
2. Compare the topic.
3. Connect the topic.
4. Analyze the topic.
5. Apply the topic.
6. Argue for or against the topic.

In my first five minutes of free writing, I described the theme park. In the second section I tried to compare Disney World to several other experiences, ranging from a visit to another theme park to a battle. In the third section, I attempted to connect my experience at Disney World to other recollections. In the analysis section, the fourth paragraph, I tried to analyze the trip, or any trip to an amusement park; what makes a successful trip? In the fifth section, I was trying to find practical applications or uses for a trip to an amusement park. And finally I presented arguments in favor of vacationing at the park. Here is my unedited cubing exercise, exactly as it turned out when I did it in class with my students.

My Cubing Exercise

1. Disney World—I see the monorail high above me as I stand in the parking lot. The pylons—towers?—are on either side of me, maybe 30–40 feet apart. The track is above me about 25 feet high. To the left is the yawning rectangular opening from the hotel (Contempo). The monorail glides out like a snake/worm easing out of an apple and almost noiselessly glides over my head.

I also see the sculptured hedges—animals like hippos, rhinos, horses, pigs—as we drive into the complex. A wide expanse of green grass—a rolling lawn.

2. A Different Theme Park: cleaner, larger, more equitably priced—not geared to rip off the clientele at every stage [Note: These positive statements

refer to Disney World, not the other theme park.]

Catskill resorts—the hotels were cleaner, brighter [at D.W.]. The help was friendlier [at D.W.]. Families were truly made to feel welcome [at D.W.]. The food, however, was not as scrumptuous or delicious.

Museum—many Disney "artifacts"—characteristic (like a mausoleum to Walt himself).

Business trip—need to plan ahead for hotel, keep track of charged items.

Battle—must have a daily plan in oder to see the sights and ride the rides, must be supplied (bandaids, aspirin, warm clothing, etc.).

3. Reminds me of being a kid again

of hating to leave a place—of wanting the ball game we were playing to never end

of being in college—no newspapers—no attention paid to "off campus" at all

of staying at other scrumptuous hotels—Cobby Nob—the unlimited ice. The lack of chores to do, no cooking.

of being in college and having to budget for meals out

of being places with my parents

of taking Sam to the board walk in NJ—how utterly thrilled he was, of the joy in his face and of feeling the joy of seeing his happiness again

4. Analysis: What makes up a trip to Disneyland?—or what makes Disneyland? Planning—they must train their workers effectively,

Kids—you can't really enjoy D.W. unless you bring kids along

Adults who are still kids—you've got to be willing to be dumb and silly, to get "into it" or it doesn't work

No interest in money—you can't be counting pennies, altho you really have to—you've got to go with the flow! A balloon here, a souvenir mouse hat there, etc.

Good shoes—and strong legs and Dr. Scholl's pads

Strong bladder—don't lose your place in line (after an hour) to run to the bathroom

No BEER—see above

5. Applications—To take grumps to so as to liven them up

For business mtgs—a place to relax after?

For honeymoons—Why? Maybe for those who've lived together for years and don't need to spend the entire wk in the hotel room

For souvenir-hunting

For tax write-off—think of a reason to do research—collect and analyze instructions on hotel literature and menus—that's linguistics, right?

To pray at the feet of W.D.—it's a holy trip, like a pilgrimage, to a 20th century "holy" man, a visionary

To escape the world—you can and probably will. This is what it's all about.

6. Argue for—Sure it's expensive. Sure it's "manufactured" fun, not natural, organic fun but—   (a) You get what you pay for—the hotel and the park and all the facilities are clean, comfortable, convenient, abidingly pleasant. The food is tasty and well-prepared. The souvenirs are not deceptive—they look fake or real if they are fake or real.

      (b) It unites families—the parents don't have to pretend to be excited so jr. will be happy; the kids needn't be bored so M & D can have fun

      Do more describing now—of the attractions, of the kids, of the feeling of being there.

My Explanation

Before continuing, I should point out a few things about my cubing exercise. Notice that there are parts of it which do not make much sense to you (family names; "Cobby Nob," a family nickname for another hotel we had once visited), that grammar seems to have slipped from my mind (there are an awful lot of sentence fragments in the exercise as well as a very erratic use of punctuation), that spelling is inaccurate ("scrumptuous" and "altho" for instance).

    My goal in doing this exercise was not to produce a polished final draft of a paper about my trip but rather to try to determine just how I could go about developing an essay about my vacation experiences. Hence I did not pay much attention to style, grammar, spelling, even audience: you cannot understand parts of what I wrote because I wrote them to myself. And *I* understand what I meant, even several years after writing the exercise. I was not even consistent in referring to the amusement park, calling it Disney World at times and Disneyland at other times as if I had hopped 3,000 miles back and forth between Florida and California.

    So this exercise was no final draft. But could it lead to a first draft? That was the key question. I started sifting through what I had written to see what seemed interesting. I intended to write a short paper for use in my composition classes, so I knew that my audience would be first-year students at my university. I wanted to be sure to make the essay interesting to them, so that they would want to pay close attention to what I had written. Several possibilities seemed to exist:

- I could write about how Disney World brings out the child even in adult visitors (as I mentioned in ¶3, ¶4, ¶6).
- I could write a paper urging everyone to visit Disney World (I praise it in ¶2, ¶3, ¶5, ¶6).
- I could write a comparison/contrast essay comparing Disney World to the local theme park (see ¶2).

    And still other possibilities exist. However, I noticed something as I reread my exercise. Suddenly in ¶4 my voice changed, and I began to poke fun at the vacation in my comments about money and especially in my comments about Dr. Scholl's foot pads and beer. It struck me that I could develop that voice into an entire essay in which I described the humorous aspects of going to Disney World. I grew excited about this idea because I realized that by using humor I could make a potentially boring essay about my family's trip (be honest: how often have you been bored when your friends' recounted the events of their trip to Florida or somewhere else on vacation?) into something a bit fresher and more original.

My First Draft

Following these remarks, you will find my first draft of the Magic Kingdom essay. In it you will recognize, I think, both the final draft you have already read and the cubing exercise which I used to generate the essay in the first place. Both the money and physical activity sections of the first draft have their roots in the jokes about money and bladders in part 4 of the cubing exercise. My students helped me rewrite this paper in a revision workshop where two comments in particular surfaced repeatedly. Many students were puzzled by my reference to the Japanese in the opening line of the first draft, and quite a few students felt that ¶4 was not in a very effective order. By comparing the first draft to my final draft, you can see how I have attempted to make use of my readers' comments.

In preparing this book, I realized that my audience, while still college students, was now a national audience and no longer a local one. So while I have left references to Scooby Doo and Gilligan in the paper, I have changed my reference to a shopping mall in ¶4 from a specific example in the Cincinnati area to a more general phrasing so that readers outside the southwestern Ohio area would be able to follow the joke.

Here is the first draft of my essay:

Training for the Magic Kingdom

For all red-blooded Americans and Japanese a trip to Disney World/ EPCOT is a dream-come-true. But, as with any truly significant life activity, one would be a darn fool to simply pack up and jump into such a trip without first going into training. That, sadly to say, was my family's mistake: we did not prepare for the trip properly. It really isn't difficult to get ready for the big dream vacation, but it does take some willpower. Let me show you.

Foolishly we spent what little time we devoted to training to preparing a budget. My wife and I separately composed budgets which included room and board, admission to the theme parks, gas money, etc. We compared budgets, revised budgets, merged budgets, and soon, at great psychic cost, we had a thing of beauty, that elusive grail which our government searches for every spring and summer: a balanced budget within our means.

We gaily rushed into Disney World that first December morning and scooted straight for the souvenir shops to buy Mickey Mouse mittens, Donald Duck sweatshirts, and Goofy woolen hats. The mercury was just barely tipping 33° and we were freezing. We thus blew our entire souvenir budget in the opening ten minutes. I know now that to train properly for budgetting such a trip next time, I should go to Northgate Mall with the entire family. There, in front of the entrance to Pogue's, is a lovely, splashing fountain with sparkling lights of green and red and blue where children throw their parents' spare change and make wishes. We, however, will stand there and practice throwing singles and fives and even tens into the fountain in order to cultivate the proper attitude toward money needed for a trip to Disney World: indifference.

Our second serious error in preparing for our trip had to do with physical activity. In the weeks prior to the trip my sons continued their usual activities: running around pointlessly (as 4 and 6 year olds do), fleeing from bathtubs, and squirming in bed every night after being tucked in. My wife continued her jogging and aerobicise and I pursued my usual exercise activities of grading papers in an easy chair. What fools we were to think we were in proper shape! Every once in awhile we would eat a meal, wash up, even use the bathroom. All of these pursuits were valuable time frittered away.

The truly prepared Disney World traveler is the one who has practice standing motionless for hours on end. After all, that is what most of your trip to the Magic Kingdom will consist of. I think I can grade papers while standing in one place; I know my boys can stand motionless in front of Scooby Doo and Gilligan re-runs for an hour if pressed. And speaking of pressing, my wife can easily stand at an ironing board for an entire episode of Shogun if necessary. That's what we will do if ever we return to Orlando. Oh—and we will practice abstaining from food and drink and trips to the bathroom also. After two hours waiting to ride the Space Mountain only an undertrained weakling would leave the line to visit the restroom. Because one of the laws of physics operable in Tomorrowland (and all of the other lands) is that a place in line tends to stay motionless while you are in it but moves at the speed of light if you leave. In other words, there ain't gonna be any place left for you when you come back.

I hope that such tips can make your vacation to Disney World a bit more successful than ours. Actually I think I know why Japanese tourists enjoy Disney's Magic Kingdom so much: practitioners of yoga already know the futility of material things, like cash, and have the infinite patience to stand statue-like indefinitely. In fact, maybe yoga meditation is the real answer. OM, OM, OM, OM.

How I Began Writing This Essay

I did not set out to write an amusing paper when I first began this project. Instead I began with the idea that I wanted to write about a particularly enjoyable vacation I had taken, a trip still very fresh in my mind. I arrived at a comic voice quite unintentionally, but I saw its possibilities. It was a voice which would allow me to avoid becoming so bogged down in telling about my personal enjoyment of the trip that I might put my students to sleep. The comic voice seemed suitable for those readers, particularly since I assumed that most if not all of them had had similar experiences at the local theme park. I felt confident that making humorous observations about common experiences would keep my readers interested and amused. At other times, I have set out to write in the comic voice, as *Model Voices* is asking you to do now, and because I had done so in the past, when I found a new subject conducive to a comic approach, I knew how to create a comic voice again. So will you.

I know that I have written better essays than this one, and I have also certainly written more important essays than this one. But "Training for the Magic Kingdom" had modest goals—to interest and amuse my students—and I feel basically satisfied that I achieved those goals.

QUESTIONS TO CONSIDER

1. How would this essay need to be changed if it were to be read by an audience of senior citizens? An audience of fifth graders?
2. What other possible essays about Disney World can you see developing out of the cubing exercise reproduced on pages 50–52?
3. Could this same point about being properly prepared for a vacation trip be communicated to the same audience in an essay which has a serious voice instead? How would you change the essay to make it sound more serious? Would such changes make the essay more or less interesting reading?
4. Comparing the first draft (pages 53–54) with the final draft (pages 47–48), which changes seemed to you to be most effective in improving the essay? Which seemed least effective? Which ones might you make in a different way? Which changes might you simply undo, preferring the original version to the edited version?
5. Notice the changed conclusion. Yoga is widely practiced in India, an Eastern nation, at least from an American perspective, rather than in Japan. I have struggled with this conclusion. My students too have always had a problem with my conclusion, raising the objection that it shows too much disrespect for the religious beliefs of other people. I remain concerned about this issue. Is the conclusion offensive? Is it clear? Is it funny?

3

The Satiric Voice

SATIRE

The comic voices you have been hearing all share at least one purpose: the desire to amuse a reader. The satiric voices you are about to hear also share in that same objective. However, satire differs in that, at its core, it is a persuasive type of writing, and it has a different purpose from the sort of comic writing you have read earlier: it wishes to change things through its use of humor. Satire is essentially constructive, seeking not so much to destroy as to rebuild. Take a look at the comic section of your local newspaper and then look at the editorial cartoon on the editorial page in the same paper. These cartoons and comic strips, aside from the soap opera strips, have in common the desire to make the readers of the newspapers smile or laugh. However, the comic strips generally wish to accomplish nothing beyond provoking laughter (although many of the more contemporary strips in the *Doonesbury* mold are closer in spirit to editorial cartoons). On the other hand, because editorial cartoonists begin with the desire to change their readers' outlook on an important issue and merely use humor as the vehicle to effect that change, they are in many ways much closer to editorial writers than to comic strip artists.

IRONY

But perhaps it will be clearer to distinguish between the comic and satiric voices by discussing *irony*. *Irony* is a device used by writers, in which the literal meaning of a statement is actually the opposite of the writer's intended meaning. Thus when I clumsily knock over my son's glass of juice at the breakfast table, I say, "How graceful of me!" And he giggles, knowing full well that I have been just the opposite of graceful. While my example is rather simple, it does illustrate irony of the same sort used by satiric writers.

Certainly, irony is used by all sorts of writers, as in the comic essays you have already read. However, irony is a staple of the satiric voice to such a degree that it is difficult to imagine any satire that could still sound satiric without employing irony. Earlier I tried to distinguish between the comic, satiric, and sarcastic voices by commenting on the degree of hostility in each; now let me refine that statement a bit and suggest that the tone of the irony being used in the prose is perhaps a better way to distinguish between the three related voices.

GENTLE SATIRE

Satire has always come in two forms: gentle and harsh. Let's focus on the gentler form of satire at this point. Gentle as it may be, it still has a quality in its sound that differentiates it from the comic voice to which we have been listening, and that quality is a product, as I have said, of its intended purpose of changing the world in some way as a result of making fun of the way things are. Thus the satiric voice is based in part on the writer's conviction that the world could be a better place if only people would change their actions or beliefs, and thus subjects fit for satire would be any human behavior that does not measure up to the writer's preconceived ideal. The behavior of sports fans at our stadiums, the behavior of judges (or lawyers or doctors or teachers or plumbers or farmers or movie stars), our tax system, our foreign allies, the local ice cream parlor: these are all suitable topics for the satiric voice, provided the writer believes that they could stand a little improvement and provided that she writes about them humorously *and* ironically. Some portions of comic essays may manifest a satiric voice, and some portions of satiric essays may evidence a comic voice, for such distinctions really exist only in books like this one. In actuality, the voice created by the writer depends on the writer's intentions—upon the rhetorical situation behind that piece of writing.

TECHNIQUES

But if a writer intends to promote change through the use of satire, how does he do so? What are the techniques used by the satiric writer? They are really quite similar to those already described in the section on comic writing; exaggeration, oversimplification, and surprise still play a significant role in the writer's creation of his voice. Let me mention a few other techniques here too, however. One theory argues that all the devices used by satirists are based on a single concept: *distortion.* Satire operates by shocking the reader, by making us look at the world in a fun-house mirror: it's recognizably our world, yet it is also a distorted vision of our recognizable world being presented. The use of distortion is therefore a quite indispensable tool for the writer wishing to lampoon human fallibility.

One specific form of distortion worth mentioning is the use of *caricature,* a method of characterization that distorts one or two characteristics of a person to humorous effect. Charles Dickens' characters were frequently caricatures, like the loud gentleman in *Oliver Twist* whose every other sentence ended with his saying, "Or I'll eat my head." The editorial cartoonists I mentioned earlier draw caricatures of political figures, sketches that distort the person's nose or hairstyle or ears. So in a satiric essay that is complaining about the manner in which some English teachers bleed red ink all over their students' pages, the writer might construct a distorted description of the English teacher, making it sound as if she uses a pen hooked into an IV needle hooked in turn into the student's arm, thus permitting the teacher to suck the student's own blood out for use in marking the paper. The point? The satirist is distorting reality in an effort to get English teachers to reconsider their grading techniques (as many of us are doing these days).

Another technique used by the satirist to create a satiric voice is to distort a well-known work of art. And if we understand "work of art" to include films, TV scripts, popular music, advertisements, as well as paintings, operas, and poems, it becomes easy to realize that we have all probably read such satires, which are more precisely termed *parodies. Parody* is the mocking of a work of art by imitating its form and style in a humorous manner. The intention of *parody* is usually to effect a change in the way readers view the original work of art which, to the satirist's way of looking at things, has probably not been appreciated properly by the public. So the satirist writes a film script entitled *Rocky XVIII* and shows us a sixty-five-year-old Rocky Balboa defending his heavyweight title against some preposterous opponent. Rocky is still plagued by a greedy, annoying brother-in-law and a wife who fears for his health, even though he has been winning these boxing matches for forty years. And, parenthetically, you can count on the satirist to use caricature in his depiction of the characters so that Rocky will begin every sentence with "Aaaay" and will do one-handed push-ups—everywhere, on the sidewalk, in the shower, at the supermarket.

STRUCTURE

The satiric voice can rely upon the same organizational approaches as are used to create the comic voice, approaches such as cause and effect, comparison/contrast, definition. But let me also mention one or two other patterns for structuring satire:

Real-life documents. Satirists often pattern their writing after familiar documents encountered by readers in their everyday lives. For example, a satirist might lampoon American eating habits with a mock menu for a restaurant, or a satirist might comment on divorce by patterning her essay after the Declaration of Independence. An enterprising student might ridicule college English courses by writing a mock term paper.

Instructions. A good vehicle for the satiric voice is to be instructive to your reader. Dave Barry once wrote a set of instructions designed to help readers win arguments at cocktail parties, but his suggested steps in his set of instructions were distorted (and included making up facts, using meaningless Latin phrases, and speaking in a loud voice). His purpose? To get readers to reconsider their own silly misbehavior at cocktail parties.

Process Analysis. The process analysis is related to the set of instructions, but instead of offering directions to a reader who wishes to carry out a specific action, the process analysis offers an explanation of how a particular process occurs. Thus the student satirizing his English teacher's grading practices could write a process analysis which explains the steps taken by the English teacher in order to grade a paper. Although the reader does not intend to duplicate the activity, she will learn how the English teacher first hooks up her IV lines, and goes on to carry out all the steps in her satirized "grading process."

In the following essays, listen to the satiric voices. Examine the writing to learn what sorts of change the writers are seeking. Note the ironic quality of the writing, which makes it different from comic writing and which will make it different from the sarcastic writing to follow. Observe the structure of each piece. Then try to write in this satiric voice yourself. Where can you find topics for satire? In the aspects of the world around you which disappoint you because they fail to live up to your expectations of them. It's possible—although hardly likely I'm sure—that one of you somewhere, sometime, might satirize my book for not being as helpful as you would like it to be. Possible, but not likely—right?

Ex-Husbands for Sale
Delia Ephron

Delia Ephron is a writer who lives in Los Angeles with her husband and two stepchildren. Her writing has been published in a number of magazines including The *New York Times Magazine, Vogue, Esquire,* and *New York.* She has published three books, *How to Eat Like a Child, Teenage Romance,* and *Funny Sauce.*

"Ex-Husbands for Sale" first appeared in *Funny Sauce* (1988), a book whose title comes from a comment made by a stepchild to a stepmother at the dinner table: "I don't like chicken in funny sauce." Ephron writes in a prologue to *Funny Sauce* that "It occurred to me while writing this book that the extended family is in our lives again... We owe the return of the extended family, albeit in a slightly altered form, to an innovation called joint custody, in which two formerly married people share in raising their children. Your basic extended family today includes your ex-husband or -wife, your ex's new mate, possibly your new mate's ex, and any new mate that your new mate's ex has acquired." "Ex-Husbands for Sale" examines one facet of that "slightly altered" new extended family.

QUESTIONS ABOUT IDEAS

1. How realistic is the attitude toward ex-husbands depicted in Ephron's essay? How accurately has she depicted this relationship?
2. What concrete suggestions do you have for the ex-mates in this essay to enable them to get along better?
3. What chances for success do second marriages have, particularly if the attitude toward ex-spouses described in this essay is typical?

Are you worried about running out of things to talk about? Are you 1 worried that one day you will sit down to dinner with your husband or boyfriend and not have a single thing to say? BUY AN EX-HUSBAND AND KISS THIS WORRY GOODBYE—for you will find that you are always talking about him. You will even say the same things about him over and over and never bore yourself, continuing to find your comments fascinating and insightful. Some possible topics: How much you hate him. How happy you would be if he disappeared off the face of the earth. How thrilled you would be if he got a job in Kuwait. Why all the children's sneakers disappeared at his house. Whether he will pay half the cost of your daughter's Sweet Sixteen party and what it will say about him if he won't.

Is your son developing bad habits? Too much television? Too much 2 sugar? Blame it on the ex—he spoils him on weekends. Do any of your son's personality traits displease you? Is he reluctant to discuss his emotions? Is he unwilling to share? Is he fussy? Will he only wear socks that have no seam at the toe? "That's not my genes," you can say, or "He didn't get that from me." With an ex-husband in the picture, the chip will never be off YOUR block unless YOU want it. AND FURTHERMORE...

You need never again feel responsible for your child's misbehavior at   3 school. When the teacher calls to complain, you will suspect that the child is only acting up because he has problems with his father, your handy ex. You can even say, "He's always difficult right after he comes back from his dad's." Or, alternatively, "He's always difficult when he hasn't seen his father enough." If the teacher insists on a parent conference, we guarantee that your ex-husband will either refuse to attend, confirming your worst opinion of him, or attend, ensuring that you will never get anxious about your child's problems EVEN WHILE THE TEACHER IS ENUMERATING THEM. Instead you will be distracted by your ex, thinking, Why does he bitch all the time about paying child support when he can afford a Burberry raincoat?

And to show you just how terrific this offer is, WE ALSO PROMISE...   4

- Lifetime interference in your love life. Anytime you have planned a romantic weekend alone with the new man in your life, your ex-husband will cancel his plans to take the children. He can also, in our more deluxe model, arrive late to pick them up EVERY SINGLE WEEKEND THAT HE DOES TAKE THEM, ensuring that even though you get to be alone with your sweetheart, your plans for the day will be ruined. ALSO...
- Lifetime rage at a man you are not married to. This value is not to be underestimated, for it means that any new husband you acquire need never be the focus of your generalized man-hating tendencies, which you wouldn't have anyway if you hadn't married your ex. Yes, we promise that if you supply the anger and resentment, your ex-husband will channel it. ALSO...
- Belief in your own sainthood. For putting up with him.
- If possible, a higher self-image. Believing your ex-husband to be irresponsible, irrational, and childish will undoubtedly lead you to conclude that you are responsible, rational, and mature. This is known as the EX-HUSBAND EFFECT.
- Someone to measure your life by. Who has more money? Better values? A better job? A bigger house? Whose new mate is more attractive? Who remarried first? Who was smart enough to wait a while? Whose life is more stable? Whose life is more boring? If you can come out ahead in comparison to your ex-husband, you win the honor of being THE ONE WHO BENEFITED MORE FROM THE DIVORCE.
- A perpetual source of private amusement. His tie is crooked; he's suddenly becoming religious; he went on a raft river trip; he's gaining weight. To you these things are hysterically funny. In fact, the more ridiculous

you can find your ex-husband the better, for it is proof of your great intelligence—you were right to have divorced him.

But wait, THERE'S MORE...   5

A ONE-MONTH, UNCONDITIONAL, MONEY-BACK TRIAL   6
SEPARATION during which your new ex-husband will telephone you every single morning before eight and every evening after ten. You will never know what he is going to say and it will always upset you. Such as (1) he's calling his lawyer tomorrow to put a clause in the settlement that you can never go out of town with the children without his permission; (2) he's finally figured out what went wrong with your marriage; (3) why didn't you consult him on the selection of baby gym class when you supposedly have joint custody?

AND, TO MAKE ABSOLUTELY SURE YOU GET ALL THE RE-   7
SULTS POSSIBLE FROM YOUR EX, we will include free A BONUS IN-
STRUCTION BOOKLET, which tells you, among other things, how to use
your ex-husband to control the behavior of your new husband.

Let's say one day your new husband walks into the kitchen and sees   8
the milk sitting on the counter, and no one around planning to drink it. He
will say, "Is this milk out for a reason?" He will say this even though he
knows the answer. It is his own private joke—the milk is out because you
forgot to put it back. Ha, ha. Do not waste any time. Lose your temper immediately and generalize. Inform him that your ex-husband was always saying things like that and give examples, like, "Is the oven on for a reason?" or
"Is the flame on under the coffeepot for a reason?" If possible, cry, saying
that your ex-husband was always putting you down. Any overreaction will
be understandable if an ex-husband is involved, and you can be sure from
now on your new husband will put the milk back himself and keep quiet
about it. No husband ever wants to resemble an ex-husband. This is one of
the best reasons to have an ex-husband around.

And if we still haven't convinced you that what you need is an ex-   9
husband, we would like to point out this unique advantage: YOU WILL
NEVER HAVE TO FEEL YOUR EX-HUSBAND IS A REAL PERSON
WITH REAL FEELINGS. This is known as THE DIVORCE EFFECT.
He is simply the sum of his less attractive parts, a sort of cartoon character:
THE EX. So you don't have to feel sympathy for him. He's having trouble
with his business? He's short of money? You won't believe it for a minute.
You know he's only saying this to get out of paying money to you. And this
brings us to the best part: Even though an ex-husband is not real, YOU
GET TO TAKE EVERYTHING HE SAYS OR DOES PERSONALLY.
He brings your child home late? He's doing it to bug you. He goes to Paris?
It's just to show off because you always wanted to go to Paris when you were
married to him. He breaks his leg so he can't take the kids while you vaca-
tion? It's a plot to prevent you from going. Then he has to spend months

immobilized in a toe-to-hip cast? How ridiculous. He's just trying to make your friends, who blamed him for the divorce, feel sympathy for him now.

SO CALL OUR TOLL-FREE NUMBER RIGHT NOW and take ad- 10 vantage of this great opportunity to get an ex of your own. Don't settle for listening to your best friend discuss hers. We offer one easy payment plan: Buy now and pay for the rest of your life.

QUESTIONS ABOUT THE RHETORICAL SITUATION

1. Ephron's entire essay is written in the second person. Describe the "you" to whom the essay speaks. Is that "you" identical with the audience for her essay? Explain.
2. Since I am calling the voice in this essay a "satirical" one, I would also suggest that Ephron wishes to implement change through her essay. What do you think she hopes to change through this essay?
3. How would you characterize Ephron's attitude toward her subject—is she angry? is she treating the topic too seriously? seriously enough?

QUESTIONS ABOUT THE ESSAY'S VOICE

1. What is Ephron parodying in this essay? Which features of her parody are familiar? What does her parody say about the audience for whom she is writing this essay? (See question number 1 above.)
2. In this satirical essay Ephron has adopted a persona. How would you describe that persona? How does Ephron use capitalization to help create that persona? What other features of the essay establish her satiric persona?
3. What is the purpose of the long list in ¶4?
4. How does Ephron use surprise to create humor in her satirical piece? Where is the first instance of surprise in the essay? How does it help establish the essay's voice?
5. Ephron coins such terms as "The Ex-husband Effect" and "The Divorce Effect." Why does she do so?
6. Virtually every paragraph in the essay relies upon distortion to create humor in an ironic way. Select one paragraph and examine how the distortion creates humor.
7. What is particularly ironic about the essay's final sentence?

TOPICS TO WRITE ABOUT

1. Write a parody of your own about some aspects of family life. You might

write a mock menu for a family restaurant, a mock college bulletin listing all of the courses at the college, a mock sales letter for a —— of-the-month club. For example, you could write a mock course guide for a college program called "Coping with Your Divorced Parents." It might offer courses of study such as "Financial Manipulation 101" (a course in how to get divorced parents to buy the child gifts) and "Creative Date-Baiting" (a course in how to scare off potential step-parents when they begin to date the child's parent seriously). POTENTIAL AUDIENCES: married readers who have children/younger, single readers. POTENTIAL PURPOSES: to get them to modify in some way their attitudes toward a common family problem/to get them to view married responsibilities more realistically.

2. Write a satirical essay entitled " —— ing with Parents" (e.g. camping, vacationing, dancing, arguing, etc.), giving rules for survival. POTENTIAL AUDIENCES: children much younger than yourself/college students. POTENTIAL PURPOSES: to make them realize that any problems they have with parents are probably caused in part by themselves/to make them a bit more tolerant about their parents.

3. Write a satirical essay about a venerated institution in our society showing how perhaps our attitude toward this institution might be in need of reassessment. For example, patriotism or education or capitalism each might be satirized. POTENTIAL AUDIENCES: those most involved in the institution (military personnel, principals, bankers, in the above examples)/foreigners just coming to our country and needing a briefing about our institutions. POTENTIAL PURPOSES: to get them to rethink their conduct/to offer them an opportunity to see America more realistically.

No Hope on a Rope
Bill Cosby

Bill Cosby has been one of America's top stand-up comics for more than twenty years. Early in his career, he recorded several best-selling comedy record albums of his stand-up routines, frequently focusing on his childhood. His childhood character, Fat Albert, in fact became popular enough to be the "star" of a Saturday morning cartoon series.

Cosby has also been a television pioneer. In the 1960s he costarred as a secret agent in *I Spy*, one of the earliest starring roles on a network series for a black performer. More recently, in the 1980s, he has starred in *The Cosby Show*, a tremendously successful situation comedy in which he plays Cliff Huxtable, a New York doctor, married to an attorney.

"No Hope on a Rope" appeared in Cosby's best-selling 1987 book *Father-hood*, a wry look at family life from the perspective of the 1980s' most famous, thanks to television, father.

QUESTIONS ABOUT IDEAS

1. Are Mother's Day and Father's Day significant holidays or are they "compulsory holidays...meaningless greeting-card things?" Should they be significant holidays?
2. Is Cosby right about the lack of creativity in much gift selection? If it "is the thought that counts," what do inappropriate gifts communicate to their recipients?
3. If the money for these gifts comes from the father in the first place, then in what sense are the children buying him gifts? Isn't he buying himself the gifts?

I am never as happy as I deserve to be on Father's Day. The problem 1 is my presents. I trust my family to get them instead of simply buying them for myself; and so, I get soap-on-a-rope.

In the entire history of civilization, no little boy or girl ever wished on 2 a star for soap-on-a-rope. It is not the dumbest present you can get, but it is certainly second to a thousand yards of dental floss. Have you ever tried to wash your feet with soap-on-a-rope? You could end up with a sudsy hanging.

Of course, soap-on-a-rope is not the *only* gift that can depress a father 3 on Father's Day: there are many others, like hedge cutters, weed trimmers, and plumbing snakes. It is time that the families of America realized that a father on Father's Day does not want to be pointed in the direction of manual labor.

We could also do without a ninety-seventh tie or another pair of socks, 4 and we do not want a sweater in June. We appreciate the sentiment behind the buying of the sweater; it was on sale; but we still would rather have a Corvette.

Mothers do not permit Mother's Day to be run like this. Even General 5 Patton would have lacked the courage to give his mother soap-on-a-rope. Mothers, in fact, organize the day as precisely as Patton planned an attack. They make a list of things they want, summon their children, and say, "Go see your father, get some money from him, and surprise me with some of these."

The kids then go to the father and say, "Dad, we need eight thousand 6 dollars for some presents for Mom."

Mothers stress the lovely meaning of Mother's Day by gathering their 7 children and tenderly saying, "I carried every one of you in my body for nine months and then my hips started spreading because of you. I wasn't built like this until you were born and I didn't have this big blue vein on the back of my leg. *You* did this to me."

For Father's Day, however, this woman comes to you and says, "It's 8 one of those compulsory holidays again, one of those meaningless greeting-card things, so the kids are under pressure to buy some presents for you and the money is certainly not coming from *me*. Twenty bucks for each of them should do it—unless you'd rather have me put it on your charge."

You have five children, so you give her a hundred dollars. The kids 9 then go to the store and get two packages of underwear, each of which costs five dollars and contains three shorts. They tear them open and each kid wraps one pair of shorts for me. (The sixth pair is saved for a Salvation Army drive.) Therefore, on this Father's Day, I will be walking around in new underwear and my kids will be walking around with ninety dollars change.

Not every year, of course, do I get Old Spice or underwear. Many 10 times a few of my kids are away from home on this special day, but they always remember to call me collect, thus allowing the operator to join in the Father's Day wishes too. I have, in fact, received so many of these calls that I'm thinking of getting an 800 number.

On Father's Day, which is almost as exciting as Ground Hog Day, I 11 sometimes think of a famous writer named Dorothy Parker, who said that men were always giving her one perfect rose but never one perfect limousine. Well, I understand just how she felt. For just *one* Father's Day, I would like the kids to forget about the underpants, the tie, and the tin trophy saying WORLD'S GREATEST FATHER and instead surprise me with a Mercedes. Just put two hundred dollars down on it and I'll gladly finish the payments.

It will never happen, of course, because fathers are good actors who lie 12 well. A father can sound convincing when he says that he is delighted to have another bottle of Old Spice because he is down to his last six. A mother, however, will refuse to accept such a bottle or a little tin trophy and will send the children back to the store to get it right. After all, it's the thought that counts. And did you kids think she was crazy?

On every day of the year, both mothers and fathers *should* be given 13 more recognition than a jock or a trophy. I am still waiting for some performer to win an award and then step to the microphone and say, "I would like to thank my mother and father, first of all, for letting me live."

QUESTIONS ABOUT THE RHETORICAL SITUATION

1. In several of the essays in Cosby's *Fatherhood* book he is clearly addressing fathers in his reading audience. To what degree is that the case here?

Would mothers appreciate his humor? Would nonparents? How would Delia Ephron respond to this essay? (See the preceding essay in this chapter.) Would readers from foreign countries that do not celebrate Father's Day appreciate this essay?
2. Cosby, on his TV show, appears to be the model father. What is his attitude here toward children? Toward wives/mothers? Toward fatherhood itself? In what ways are his attitudes in this essay those of a model father?
3. What is Cosby hoping to see changed as a result of his satire? To what extent does your answer depend on your perception of his intended audience (see question number 1)?

QUESTIONS ABOUT THE ESSAY'S VOICE

1. If you are familiar with Cosby as a comedian or as Cliff Huxtable, would you describe the voice in this essay as similar to or different from the Cosby voice you have heard before on his albums or in his TV performances?
2. What is the effect of the dialogue Cosby uses (¶5–8)? How does it contribute to creating a satiric voice?
3. What other examples would be appropriate to Cosby's point besides the ones he has already included?
4. Where in this essay does Cosby distort the truth for the sake of his ironic humor? Where is his distortion particularly effective? Why?
5. How effectively does Cosby conclude his essay?
6. What might Cosby's reaction be to Delia Ephron's essay "Ex-Husbands for Sale?" What similarities/differences do you see in the two writers' perceptions and depictions of parenthood?

TOPICS TO WRITE ABOUT

1. Write a satire about a holiday which is either relatively meaningless or which once had meaning but has lost it. POTENTIAL AUDIENCES: the general reading public. POTENTIAL PURPOSES: to make it sound terribly significant as a means of satirizing our society's misguided ideas about holidays/to suggest that perhaps we need to celebrate these once important holidays in more meaningful ways.
2. Write a satire about the kinds of gifts parents give sons or daughters or the kinds of gifts boyfriends and girlfriends exchange. POTENTIAL AUDIENCES: Bill Cosby himself/members of the opposite gender. POTENTIAL PURPOSES: to get him to rethink his own gift giving as a parent/to suggest that more thought needs to be given to such gifts.

Glory, Those Shoes of Imelda Marcos
Nickie McWhirter

Nickie McWhirter is a newspaper columnist who was born in Peoria, Illinois. A graduate of the University of Michigan, McWhirter has worked as an editorial assistant for McGraw-Hill, a staff writer for the *Detroit Free-Press*, and as an advertising copywriter for a Detroit corporation. She has won awards for her writing from the Detroit Press Club Foundation, United Press International, and the Associated Press. She currently lives near Detroit.

"Glory, Those Shoes of Imelda Marcos" first appeared in the spring of 1986, shortly after news of Mrs. Marcos' extensive collection of shoes became public. The Marcoses were toppled from power in the Philippines after many years of virtual dictatorship, being replaced by a government led by Corazon Aquino.

QUESTIONS ABOUT IDEAS

1. To what extent is McWhirter describing a phenomenon with which you are familiar? Is this phenomenon a problem?
2. In ¶7, McWhirter makes an accusation of conspiracy, in jest. However, is there any truth to such accusations regarding the relationship between consumers and manufacturers?
3. What is an appropriate attitude for us, as private citizens, to take toward the leaders of foreign countries whose behavior does not conform to our notions of the way a national leader should behave?
4. The Marcoses' fall from power was a very significant news story at the time this satire was written. However, that was a couple of years ago. Is the satire still effective? What does this say about the importance of timing to a satire?

Imelda Marcos' shoes. The glory of them, the agony, the ecstasy—the 1 expense.

Imelda Marcos is said to have left an estimated 3,000 pairs of shoes 2 behind when she fled the Philippines. It must have broken her heart.

No woman collects 3,000 pairs of shoes overnight, you know. No 3 woman collects 3,000 pairs of shoes without suffering. I figure for every one of those 3,000 pairs of shoes, Imelda had to try on an average of four other pairs to find the shoes she wanted. That is 15,000 pairs of shoes—that we know about.

We can only guess the frustration, fatigue, and blistered heels Imelda 4 endured in order to assemble that glorious shoe collection. And then to just walk away from it. I don't think I could have done it. (I wonder what shoes she was wearing at the time.)

Imelda probably took some shoes with her, don't you think? Maybe   5
she packed her favorite 1,000 pairs. Those racks in her basement had a few empty shelves. Besides cash and looted treasures, we don't know what was in the crates the Marcoses carried out of the Philippines with them.

A woman without the proper footwear for every costume is a sad   6
woman, a deprived woman, a tragic figure moving in humiliation among her brothers and sisters on this earth. Many men don't seem to understand this, especially husbands and fathers who pay for their wives' and daughters' shoes. Even men who never pay for women's shoes, who have only been privileged on occasions to peek into women's closets, don't understand it. "Why all the shoes?" they frequently ask, in amazement. Why, indeed?

Because each pair of women's shoes is cruelly designed to complement   7
one dress, one suit, one gown only, that is why. I can't imagine the conniving that must go on between clothing and shoe designers, but don't tell me there isn't conniving. When it is over with, a shopper finds herself with no shoes to wear with the dress she has just purchased. The dress is perfect, just what she needs and was looking for. She got it on sale, too.

Despite a modest collection of 100 pairs of shoes in her closet, how-   8
ever, there will be none that looks right with this particular garment. Back at the store, however, perfectly positioned to catch her eye, will be a pair of shoes that fairly call out for mating with this very dress. They are exquisite, and only $192. Of course, she buys them. Otherwise, she couldn't wear the bargain dress.

I once figured out a shoe wardrobe that would free me from the need to   9
buy a pair of shoes almost every time I bought a dress or whatever. Stick to basics, I told myself. Men do it. Black or brown leather, tie or tassel, smooth or suede, for example. With just those Spartan choices, there are eight possibilities.

Add four or five heel heights, open or closed toe options, open or   10
closed heel options, all the colors of the rainbows, straps, buckles, baubles, bangles, and beads—there is no such thing as a basic shoe wardrobe for women. I gave up at 65 "absolute must haves."

I find nothing excessive in Imelda Marcos' shoe collection. There, but   11
for the pinch of wretched budgets and honesty, go I, and maybe you too. I wonder if Cory Aquino wears Imelda's size.

QUESTIONS ABOUT THE RHETORICAL SITUATION

1. Nickie McWhirter addresses her readers as "you" on several occasions. After reading her essay, try to describe the reader that McWhirter has in mind. Can you determine anything about that reader's gender, age, eco-

nomic class, awareness of public events, other attributes?

2. This essay originally appeared as a newspaper column with a picture of Imelda Marcos next to it. To what extent is McWhirter interested in satirizing Mrs. Marcos? At what other topics is she directing her satire? What does McWhirter seek to change through satire?

3. In another newspaper column published at the same time, Mrs. Marcos and her husband were accused of "wretched excess," "avarice," and "prodigality." McWhirter's attitude toward Mrs. Marcos seems much less hostile. Why? Does her attitude seem too nonchalant or unfeeling considering that Mrs. Marcos and her husband methodically accumulated billions of dollars while millions of Filipino people lived in abject poverty? Or is McWhirter's attitude justified by her purpose in writing this satire?

QUESTIONS ABOUT THE ESSAY'S VOICE

1. In ¶6, McWhirter describes in very distorted terms a woman without the proper footwear. Where else in the essay has she employed distortion to make satire? How much truth is there in her distortions?

2. Where else might she have distorted but chosen not to? What would have been the effect of such further distortion?

3. In ¶10, McWhirter is describing the options that would help a woman define the basic shoe wardrobe for all outfits. She mentions "buckles, baubles, bangles, and beads." Here she uses two literary devices for humorous purposes: *allusion* (to a Broadway show tune, "Baubles, Bangles, and Beads") and *alliteration* (in her repetition of the "b" sound). What are the effects on her voice of these techniques?

4. In discussing Mrs. Marcos in the opening four paragraphs, how does McWhirter poke fun at Mrs. Marcos without becoming excessively nasty or sarcastic? Why does she create this voice rather than a nasty or sarcastic one?

5. To what extent does McWhirter rely upon surprise to create humor in her essay? Find specific examples.

TOPICS TO WRITE ABOUT

1. Write a satirical essay about a hobby shared by many members of your gender: e.g., shopping at the mall, watching football on Sunday afternoons. POTENTIAL AUDIENCES: members of the opposite gender/people who might be interested in taking up that hobby. POTENTIAL PURPOSES: to get them to be a bit more understanding about the hobby/to offer a more realistic picture of the hobby.

2. Write a satirical essay about a public figure whose foibles are recognizably shared by many of your readers. For example: make your readers see themselves in a hypocritical politician or in a greedy game show contestant. POTENTIAL AUDIENCES: people just like yourself/the public figure herself. POTENTIAL PURPOSES: to force the readers to reexamine their own values/to nudge the public figure into appropriately modified behavior.

The P.G.A. Plays Through
Dan Jenkins

Dan Jenkins is a sportswriter who first became prominent when he wrote for *Sports Illustrated.* His greatest success, however, was the novel *Semi-Tough,* a comic look at professional football. Jenkins brought his hero, Billy Clyde Puckett, back in a sequel, *Life Its Own Self.* More recently, Jenkins has been writing a regular column entitled *Sports* for *Playboy* magazine.

In this essay, which first appeared in May 1986 in *Playboy,* Jenkins satirizes the Professional Golf Association (PGA), the organization that runs the men's professional golf tour.

QUESTIONS ABOUT IDEAS

1. Are organized sports in this country too commercialized, too businesslike? Is the money being charged, according to this essay, justifiable since it is for charity? Is the connection between big sport, big business, and big charity an appropriate one?
2. What is the appeal of professional golf tournaments? In fact, why is our society so intensely interested in pro sports?
3. Note the PGA players' response to the foreign golfer in this essay. Is their response an appropriate one to this foreign competition? Is their response different in any significant way from that of those domestic industries which seek to have the federal government restrict foreign competition through tariffs or trade barriers?

As one who has been unable to decide between the investment firms of 1 Arnold Palmer and Tom Watson on television, I was understandably excited when a big professional golf tournament came to my country club. I dashed right out to the club, of course, not only to pick up some portfolio advice but to see the famous golfers in their own flesh and checkered cottons.

The first shock came when I was forced to park on a playground five 2

miles away, ride a shuttle bus and then buy a badge just to get into my own
country club. The badge cost $5500, but the money was for charity, somebody
said.

The club certainly looked different. A lot of huge trucks and mobile 3
homes were sitting around, circus tents had been put up and a good many
wives of members I know were wearing the same bonnets, vests and polka-
dot skirts and were jumping in and out of white Pontiacs.

"Hi, Mildred," I said to one of the wives. "Where's Fred?" 4

"I can't talk now," she said, panting. "I have to take Mark Wiebe to 5
the dentist, and Don Pooley wants to stop by a discount store."

She sped away in the courtesy car. 6

My next shock came when I entered the clubhouse and a security 7
guard refused to admit me to my own locker room.

"I wish you wouldn't push me in the chest," I said, trying to smile. 8

"Players and officials only," he said. 9

"I'm a member." 10

"Move along, please. Can't you see this hallway's getting crowded?" 11

"I want to use the bathroom," I said. 12

The guard spoke into a walkie-talkie. 13

"Ralph, I've got a code three in the locker area. Want to send some 14
help to get the asshole outa here? Over."

I got the point and went downstairs to the Men's Grill to grab a bite to 15
eat. There was another guard at the door.

"Wrong badge," he said, stopping me. 16

"This is supposed to be good for the clubhouse," I explained, fondling 17
the badge pinned to my shirt.

"You're not a Patron," he said. 18

"I just want to go in the Men's Grill." 19

"Patrons only. Sorry." 20

"How do you get to be a Patron?" I asked. 21

"You buy a badge for ten thousand dollars." 22

I thought I might find a snack in the Mixed Foursome Room, but, 23
alas, there was another security guard on the door. He shoved me backward.

"My wife and I play bridge in this room," I argued. 24

"You're not a Saint." 25

"A what?" 26

"This room is for Saints only," said the guard. 27

"What does it cost to be a Saint?" 28

"Twenty thousand dollars." 29

The next place I looked for food was the teenage recreation parlor, 30
which our club calls the Peppermint Lounge.

It was reserved for the media. Yet another security guard was standing 31
watch.

I peeked inside the room and noticed several men and women with 32 cocktails in their hands. Others were loading up their plates at a sumptuous buffet spread.

"I gather those people are covering the tournament," I said cynically.   33

"Press only," the guard said. "You can't stand there."   34

"The tournament's outside," I said.   35

"They bring the leaders in here. Clarence Rose is on the way. Clear the   36
doorway, please."

It turned out that the only place for a clubhouse-badge holder to eat   37
was in the lobby, with 4000 other people. I stood in a line for two hours and
finally got a fat-roast-beef sandwich and a warm Coke.

"I'll just sign for this," I said when I reached the cashier.   38

"You need scrip," the cashier said. "Members can't sign this week.   39
You have to buy scrip."

"Buy what?"   40

"A book of tickets. You can buy a twenty-dollar book for a hundred   41
dollars or a forty-dollar book for five hundred."

Only 3000 people were in the scrip line.   42

Giving up on food, I went outdoors to watch the tournament. I wan-   43
dered down to the ninth green and stood behind 10,000 people. Eventually,
I squeezed into the crowd and managed to catch a glimpse of the action.
Three golfers were on their hands and knees, evidently staring at insects.

"Which one's Nicklaus?" I asked a fellow spectator.   44

"Nicklaus doesn't play in this tournament," the man said.   45

Moments later, another group came to the green and mostly walked in   46
circles.

"Is this Watson?" I asked.   47

"Watson never plays here."   48

"He doesn't?"   49

"Neither does Trevino or Crenshaw. Palmer always plays here, though."   50

"When's Arnie coming up?"   51

"He's not here this year."   52

"Oh."   53

I asked which players *were* here.   54

"That's Wayne Grady in the bunker," the spectator said. "David   55
Ogrin's the guy in the water. Bob Lohr's waiting for a ruling about the tree
trunk."

The player I really wanted to watch was Severiano Ballesteros of Spain.   56
I'd heard he was the greatest player in the world. Some people told me they
thought Ballesteros ought to be on the back nine.

I walked out to the 14th hole, the farthest point from the clubhouse.   57
There were about a dozen fans watching three players who were identified to
me as Tim Simpson, Ronnie Black, and Larry Mize.

"I guess the Spaniard will be coming along soon," I said to a man who   58
had brought his lunch and sat under a tree.

"You may have quite a wait," he said. "Ballesteros is barred from the 59
tour."

"He's not here?" I whimpered.   60

"Our pros won't let him play this country anymore."   61

"That's outrageous," I said, exhausted, hungry, thirsty. "Why am I at 62
a golf tournament if there's nobody here I've ever heard of?"

"Beats me," the man said. "I'm just sitting here till the thing's over. 63
The goddamn committee closed the street in front of my house, and I don't
have the right badge to get back home."

QUESTIONS ABOUT THE RHETORICAL SITUATION

1. Jenkins has been a sportswriter for many years. Does he come across as a
   sports fan in this essay? Is golf one of his favorite sports, based on what
   he writes here?
2. Jenkins seems remarkably patient throughout his story. Why? Do you
   think his story is faithful to the true facts of his experience? Why or why
   not? Why might he change the way he reacts in the essay from his actual
   real-life reactions?
3. Jenkins mentions quite a few golfers by name. How important is it for his
   readers to know who these players are? How well can someone who does
   not follow professional golf understand the essay? How familiar are Jenkins' references to his country club? How well can someone unfamiliar
   with country clubs follow this essay?
4. What changes do you think Jenkins would like to see in the way these
   tournaments are run?

QUESTIONS ABOUT THE ESSAY'S VOICE

1. How accurate is the picture of the security guards presented by the essay?
   Are these caricatures? How accurate a picture of these guards does the
   essay require?
2. Jenkins relies very heavily upon dialogue in this essay. How does his
   voice when he speaks in the story resemble the voice of the essay itself?
3. Jenkins uses language which some readers might find tasteless or offensive. How necessary is this language? How appropriate is it to his intended readers? Which characters in the essay use this language? What is
   significant about which characters speak this way?
4. How distorted are the dollar amounts mentioned in the essay? Are they
   exaggerated enough? Do they need to be exaggerated more?
5. What is the point of the essay's title? How does it help establish the essay's satiric voice?

6. How does ¶1 help establish the essay's voice?
7. The main target of Jenkins' satire is the pro golf tour. However, he satirizes other subjects as well to some extent. Which other subjects draw his ridicule? What is the effect on his essay's voice of this broad focus for his ridicule?
8. Why does Jenkins choose to let another character have the final say in this essay? How is this strategy in keeping with the voice he has adopted throughout the essay?

TOPICS TO WRITE ABOUT

1. Write a satirical essay about a sporting event: the local high school football championship game or wrestling tournament or Tee-ball game. POTENTIAL AUDIENCES: other fans at the sporting event/those who organize the event. POTENTIAL PURPOSES: to ridicule their behavior at these events, perhaps to get them to change that behavior/to criticize the arrangements that they have made.
2. Write a satirical essay about some exclusive organization such as a country club or fraternity/sorority. POTENTIAL AUDIENCES: members of the club/sociologists studying the behavior of club members. POTENTIAL PURPOSES: to mock the habits of the club members, perhaps to change their own view of themselves as being "special" because they belong to the club/to ridicule club members by suggesting that they are an endangered species who need to be studied while they still linger.

Is the Brown on My Nose Showing?
Tracy Eastman

Tracy Eastman, from Northbrook, Illinois, is a marketing major at Miami University. A college freshman when she wrote this essay, Tracy says, "I had, as usual, put off doing the paper until the night before it was due. I had no idea what to write about until finally I thought 'Hey, I'll persuade my professor to give me an A on the paper.'" This essay was the seventh and last essay written for a first-semester freshman writing course.

QUESTIONS ABOUT IDEAS

1. Is Eastman writing an essay in order to get a good grade, or is she writing it because she has something she wants to say? How large a role do grades

play in motivating students to write? How large a role *should* grades play in motivating students to write?

2. Is it important for student writers to have the "courage to be original"? Does it, in fact, take courage for any writer to be original? Is Tracy Eastman's essay a courageous one?

3. This is not a final draft. Tracy revised the paper one last time, making mostly minor adjustments. What do you think she needed to change? Why? How would you suggest she implement these changes? (*Note:* Following the essay and the questions and suggested topics, I have reprinted, "Is the Brown on My Nose Showing?" this time with the instructor's comments.)

    I think this paper deserves it. That should be reason enough, but after   1
the endless advice you've given us, you probably want to be more convinced. You've read them aloud, handed out guidelines for producing them and lectured about them. I'm talking about that elusive "A" paper, which I have yet to receive but think I richly deserve on this particular paper. Why this paper and not the others before it? I've got a few reasons I'd like to share with you now.

    Take it's appearance for instance. Neatly typed and double spaced, it   2
even looks like an "A" paper. I chose black type especially for you because I heard you mention something about it being your favorite color. It was between black and blue, the latter matching your eyes. Have I ever told you how much I love the color of your eyes? I've always wanted blue eyes. Also, please notice the quality of the paper. Not to brag, but I had it flown in from the finest paper mill in the country, just for this assignment. It wasn't cheap, mind you, and money is tight these days, but nothing but the best for English papers. Never mind the fact that I won't be able to afford to go uptown this weekend and hit Attractions. That's okay, I'd rather sleep easier knowing that my English paper is typed on only the very best paper available.

    Not only does it look good, but it sounds good, as well. I chose each   3
word as carefully as I choose what to order on my SDS pizza. My thesaurus has holes all over it and looks as if it's on it's last leg. Each punctuation mark is a carefully thought-out move. I even wrote to my senior English teacher to get advice on comma placement. I have been proofreading over and over and double-checking for misspellings. I am confident in saying that not one word is spelled incorrectly. Like you said, for an "A" paper we need to have a "reasonable grasp of grammar."

    I don't mean to quote you directly, but the way that you express your   4
thoughts is so effective that I can't seem to reword them. Especially when you say we have to have "the courage to be original." Courage is such a descriptive word, and I think it really fits this paper in particular. I could have written on abortion, capital punishment or suicide, but no, I had to be

unique and as you said—courageous. Also, you talk about how our papers should have a lot of voice. How much more voice could you ask for? It's like I'm sitting here talking to you. Which brings me to the audience of the paper. I don't think the paper could be intended for anyone but you and it is written appropriately.

Now I've illustrated how the paper fits the guidelines of an "A," I'd 5 like to discuss how it would benefit both you and me by giving it an "A." My father is a lawyer. I didn't want to bring him into this, but if I feel I've been graded unfairly, it could mean trouble. I'd hate to have to see you dragged into a messy court battle which could threaten your teaching career. I also didn't want to mention Grandpa Pearson, but since he is president of the university, he tends to get ornery when one of his employees is unfair to "his favorite little Redskin." See, he has this idea stuck in his head that I'm going to graduate and be a big success. Sometimes I'd just like to dropout and marry an oil tycoon, but that's such a copout. What does getting an "A" on this particular paper have to do with all that? I feel an "A" would give me the proper incentive to do well here. I would always remember this grade, believe me. Next year when I'm struggling through Econ. 201, I'll remember doing well on this paper and know that if I just keep at it, I will do well. So you'd be helping me shape my future and wouldn't that be self-satisfying? When I become a successful stockbroker, I'll remember you, maybe I'll even give you some tips.

So as you see, not only would it be beneficial for me to receive an "A," 6 it would benefit you as well. I would be ever grateful to you. I would worship the ground upon which you walk. I'd do your laundry. Got any bills you need paid? Hey, did I ever tell you I really like your taste in music? Can I borrow some tapes sometime? I also noticed your shoes needed to be polished. I do windows. Or....

QUESTIONS ABOUT THE RHETORICAL SITUATION

1. Eastman has a very specific audience in mind here: her English instructor. What can you tell about the instructor from the essay? What is she like? What has she been teaching her class? How do you think she responded to Tracy's essay?
2. A very real problem in freshman writing courses is that many times students have no audience to write for. They write essays simply because the teacher assigns them, often addressing them to no one in particular or at best to the teacher. Such writing is often designed with only a single purpose in mind: to obtain a high grade. Is Eastman's paper different from that kind of essay? If so, how?
3. The essay has a satiric voice; what is Tracy Eastman interested in changing through her satire? How many different topics does she satirize in the

piece? What other audience might she have addressed in a paper on this topic? How would her essay have needed to be changed?

4. Can you tell from the essay how Tracy Eastman probably really felt about her teacher and about her English class? What are the clues to her attitude?

QUESTIONS ABOUT THE ESSAY'S VOICE

1. How appropriate is Eastman's title? How effective is it as a title? What other titles might she have chosen instead?
2. Eastman organizes her essay into an implied process analysis. What, according to the essay, are the steps which can lead to an "A" paper?
3. In ¶4, Eastman addresses the entire question of voice. How effective is this paragraph in terms of the essay's purpose? To what extent do you agree with what Tracy says about her voice here?
4. Where in the essay does Eastman distort reality for ironic effect? How effectively does she use distortion in the essay?

TOPICS TO WRITE ABOUT

1. Write a letter to an authority figure in your own life, satirizing the advice and directions given you by that person even as you attempt to follow that advice. For example, write to your parents about your efforts to manage your own finances, or write to your high school athletic coach about your current training regimen.
2. Write an essay in a satiric voice about your college experiences. What could use improvement at your campus? The cafeteria? The library? The bookstore? The student body itself? POTENTIAL AUDIENCES: your dorm friends/the president of the university/your friends back in high school preparing to select a college. POTENTIAL PURPOSES: to suggest that they find alternative methods of feeding themselves or studying or buying supplies or interacting with other students/to suggest that changes need to be made/to get them to see college life more realistically.

THE WRITING PROCESS: A WRITING TEACHER'S COMMENTS

Below follows Tracy Eastman's draft with her instructor's comments inserted. [My gratitude to Dixie Neyer for her permission to use her comments on this paper.]

Is the Brown on My Nose Showing? [**Intriguing title!**]

I think this paper deserves it. [**what???**] That should be reason enough, but after the endless advice you've given us, you probably want to be more convinced. You've read them aloud, handed out guidelines for producing them and lectured about them. I'm talking about that elusive "A" paper, which I have yet to receive but think I richly deserve on this particular paper. Why this paper and not the others before it? I've got a few reasons I'd like to share with you now. [**Very clever intro—saving yr "subject" or thesis till later—a very effective "timing" break from convention.**]

Take it's appearance for instance. Neatly typed and double spaced, it even looks like an "A" paper. I chose black type especially for you because I heard you mention something about it being your favorite color. It [**what? yr choice of ribbons?**] was between black and blue, the latter matching your eyes. Have I ever told you how much I love the color of your eyes? [**I've always wanted *green* eyes!**] I've always wanted blue eyes. Also, please notice the quality of the paper. Not to brag, but I had it flown in from the finest paper mill in the country, just for this assignment. It wasn't cheap, mind you, and money is tight these days, but nothing but the best for English papers. Never mind the fact that I won't be able to afford to go uptown this weekend and hit Attractions. That's okay, I'd rather sleep easier knowing that my English paper is typed on only the very best paper available.

Not only does it look good, but it sounds good, as well. I chose each word as carefully as I choose what to order on my SDS pizza. [**funny!**] My thesaurus has holes all over it and looks as if it's on it's last leg. [**leg??? Better rethink this line.**] Each punctuation mark is a carefully thought-out move. I even wrote to my senior English teacher to get advice on comma placement. I have been proofreading over and over and double-checking for misspellings. I am confident in saying that not one word is spelled incorrectly. Like you said, for an "A" paper we need to have a "reasonable grasp of grammar."

I don't mean to quote you directly, [**Why not???**] but the way that you express your thoughts is so effective that I can't seem to reword them. Especially when you say we have to have "the courage to be original." Courage is such a descriptive word, and I think it really fits this paper in particular. [**I agree!**] I could have written on abortion, capital punishment or suicide, but no, I had to be unique and as you said—courageous. Also, you talk about how our papers should have a lot of voice. How much more voice could you ask for? It's like I'm sitting here talking to you. [**yr coming thru loud and clear, Tracy**] Which brings me to the audience of the paper. I don't think the paper could be intended for anyone but you and it is written appropriately.

Now I've illustrated how the paper fits the guidelines of an "A," I'd like to discuss how it would benefit both you and me by giving it an "A." My father is a lawyer. I didn't want to bring him into this, but if I feel I've been graded unfairly, it could mean trouble. I'd hate to have to see you dragged into a messy court battle which could threaten your teaching career. [**Beautiful! I'm quaking in my boots.**] I also didn't want to mention Grandpa Pearson, but since he is president of the university, he tends to get

ornery when one of his employees is unfair to "his favorite little Redskin."
See, he has this idea stuck in his head that I'm going to graduate and be a
big success. Sometimes I'd just like to dropout and marry an oil tycoon, but
that's such a copout. What does getting an "A" on this particular paper have
to do with all that? I feel an "A" would give me the proper incentive to do
well here. I would always remember this grade, believe me. Next year when
I'm struggling through Econ. 201, I'll remember doing well on this paper and
know that if I just keep at it, I will do well. So you'd be helping me shape my
future and wouldn't that be self-satisfying? **[very.]** When I become a
successful stockbroker, I'll remember you, maybe I'll even give you some tips.
[Here's hoping I have a few $ to invest.]

So as you see, not only would it be beneficial for me to receive an "A," it
would benefit you as well. I would be ever grateful to you. I would worship the
ground upon which you walk. I'd do your laundry. **[You're on!]** Got any bills
you need paid? **[gobs]** Hey, did I ever tell you I really like your taste in
music? Can I borrow some tapes sometime? **[They've been eaten.]** I also
noticed your shoes needed to be polished. **[Nobody's perfect]** I do windows.
Or....

[Tracy,

This was an utter pleasure to read—I grinned all the way thru (even laughed
out loud at times) and now my face is stiff. You've earned yr A in every way, and
if you'll retype w/minor corrections I'll give you an A + and submit it [to the
English Department's writing contest]—it's a definite winner! A/95DN]

QUESTIONS TO CONSIDER

1. How are Dixie Neyer's comments different in the latter part of the essay than
   in the beginning part of the essay? Why have they changed as they have?
2. How would you describe the voice you hear in Dixie's comments? Describe the rhetorical situation underlying her comments: who is her audience, what is her purpose, what is her attitude toward her material?
   (Compare this answer to your answer to question number 1, Questions
   about the Rhetorical Situation, p. 77).
3. Would you have given Tracy an A on this draft? Why or why not?

Final note: Tracy revised her draft; Dixie submitted it to the English
Department's writing contest, and it won a prize as one of the best essays of
the year.

4

The Sarcastic Voice

SATIRIC AND SARCASTIC VOICES

Much of what I wrote about the satiric voice in Chapter 3 is just as applicable here in Chapter 4 as we begin discussing the sarcastic voice: both voices use irony, distortion, caricature, parody. Both may use familiar patterns such as real-life documents, phony instructions, fabricated process analyses. However, there remains a significant difference between the satiric and sarcastic voices.

That difference is one of degree, not of kind. The sarcastic voice is satiric, but it is angrier, more hostile, nastier. Earlier I mentioned that there were two kinds of satire, a gentle form and a harsher form. The harsher form of satire is what I am calling the sarcastic voice; it is a hard-hitting, almost destructive, ridiculing of a subject. So while Bill Cosby may have made some gentle fun of the differences between mothers and fathers, in this chapter Mary Kay Blakely is not as gentle in discussing the differences between men's and women's incomes.

Later in this book, in Section Two, you will hear angry writers criticizing a variety of subjects, urging readers to change things in the world around them. But the sarcastic voice, like the satiric voice, is more subtle in its mode of criticizing, preferring the subtlety of art to the directness of propaganda or sermon. The criticism will lie below the surface, waiting for the reader to grasp the ironies and dig beneath them. The sarcastic voice is motivated by moral fervor, by a strong belief that life could be better. There is a constructive motive lurking beneath the denunciation and hostile laughter. The reader has to seek it out, however.

A SAMPLE

Read this paragraph from an essay by a first-year student named Cindy Wilson about her experiences at the local fast food drive-through window.

81

I am now in a semi-comatose state because of lack of food and drink. Finally the drive thru window is open. No cars are in front of me. It's my turn! There, in this window, is what looks to be a reject from Hee Haw. She says in an incredibly high voice, "Like...Hi! Your order comes to four dollars and sixty-seven cents." Her voice makes my stomach start to have spasms, and I begin to feel my eyes rolling into the back of my head. Dangling my arm out the window, I hand her my money. Then I happen to notice her nametag: this petite flower's name is Norma Faye Jean. Norma tells her co-workers to hurry with my order. She herself can't help because she doesn't want to risk breaking one of her priceless Lee Press On Nails. She manages to get my food to me, which at this point is like manna from heaven, and she says, "Thank you and have a nice day."

UNDERLYING HOSTILITY

What really distinguishes the sarcastic voice is the heaviness of the irony in the voice. Sarcastic writers are irate, outraged, infuriated, not merely amused or dismayed. Although irony is the tool, the sarcastic writer is much more *pointed* in attacking her subject, making little or no effort to be kind, compassionate, understanding of the target of her attack. Notice how hostile Cindy has been toward the fast food employee in the paragraph you have just read.

Sometimes the anger and pointed quality of the sarcastic voice can result in *name-calling*, but sarcastic writing is usually a bit more subtle than that. The name-calling is not likely to involve the use of epithets so much as the use of unpleasant labels. Notice that Cindy refers to Norma Faye Jean as a "petite flower" at one point in the essay, clearly a sarcastic label although not a nasty name.

Occasionally the writer writing sarcastically deliberately soft-pedals the criticism, employing the tactic of *understatement.* By minimizing the criticism, the writer hopes to emphasize it. You borrow your dad's car, scratch the door parking it, and then describe his reaction to your friends by saying, "He was just a *tad* angry." And you continue to note that you have been grounded until the turn of the century. Saying that he was a "tad angry" is sarcastic—and understated. It's an alternative to gross exaggeration ("My dad was so angry he popped three blood vessels in his forehead screaming at me"). In fact, understatement is a form of exaggeration in a sense, exaggerating in the opposite direction, making something seem smaller than it is instead of larger, sort of like looking through the wrong end of a telescope.

PERSONA

Sarcastic writers, it would seem, often pretend. This pretending—whether in the form of understatement or taking the opposite view of the issue—

causes the sarcastic writer to use what is known as a *persona*. A *persona* is a mask or personality adopted by the writer for purposes of the satire. This personality is not necessarily the writer's private personality. This speaker is an invented character, one who may be too dumb to understand the things he is saying or too insensitive to care, to name two possibilities. Dan Jenkins in "The P.G.A. Plays Through" adopted a persona, pretending to be a mild-mannered country club member who rather passively puts up with the changes wrought upon his familiar club by the P.G.A. golf tour. This mild-mannered persona provided Jenkins with an alternative to writing a furious-sounding attack on the golf tournament and its sponsors. The persona can say things that the writer would never say; Cindy's nasty remark about Norma's press-on nails is, for example, something that she would never say herself, being too polite a person. But her persona in the essay has no hesitation about making such a comment. Be careful when reading these sarcastic essays—as well as any satiric writing—to distinguish between the writer and her persona.

SARCASM AND HUMOR

But the more I talk about the sarcastic voice, the more I become concerned that one major point be clear: The sarcastic voice is still a variety of the humorous voice with which *Model Voices* started out. Despite its pointed qualities, its name-calling, its anger and hostility, sarcastic writing is intended to provoke laughter. The laughter may be of a bitter variety, but we are still supposed to laugh. When the anger overpowers the humor so totally that no laughter is possible, the writer has created a different voice (see Chapter 5, The Embittered Voice). As I pointed out above, like the satiric voice, the sarcastic voice desires reform or change; the writer is less patient, more upset about the changes needed, but she is still able to see the humor in the situation, however harsh and barbed the form of that humor may be.

One particularly barbed and harsh form of humor often present in sarcastic writing is known as *black comedy*. *Black comedy is cynical and rather negative in tone; it is humor of the absurd, perverted, morbid, sometimes called "sick" humor.* "Gallows humor" (jokes made about disasters and catastrophes) is a familiar form of black comedy. Joseph Heller's *Catch-22* is a good example of black comedy, as it finds laughter in the midst of war and death.

Black comedy produces the kind of laughter about which audiences may feel guilty ("Oh, that's awful," we say, attempting to stifle our laughter). In a modern world where instant global obliteration is possible, where new incurable diseases and cancers pop up almost daily, where technology seems to have gone haywire, one response, other than outright despair, is to laugh about these problems. The laughter is grim, but it is laughter nonetheless. The audience is frequently offended by lapses in taste, but they still laugh. Although we tend to think of black comedy as a modern genre of writing, examples of it can be found going back throughout literary history. Benjamin Franklin's "Sale of the Hessians" in this chapter is an excellent example.

WARNING: RISKS OF THE SARCASTIC VOICE

So read these essays and ask yourself what makes the voices, while still funny, so much less pleasant than the voices in the two preceding chapters and ask yourself what topics upset you enough to prompt you to write in this hostile voice. But also notice just at what point you, as a reader, have had enough hostility. When do these writers simply get too nasty for your taste? For that is one real risk of the sarcastic voice; it is possible to "turn off" the reader by being too nasty, too hostile.

It is also dangerous to use sarcasm because some readers will not recognize it as such, taking literally what may be meant ironically. I frequently show my classes a sarcastic editorial opposed to the use of physical discipline in school. This essay—entitled "Why Not Capital Punishment?"—advocates using corporal punishment in ways which more appropriately fit the student's "crime." The writer advocates poking out a bad speller's eye ("An eye for an I" he writes) and suggests execution for the football player whose fumble loses the big game, since that will emphasize that winning is indeed the only thing that counts. Unfortunately, a substantial portion of the class each time is unsure of the essay's intent; a number of students think the writer is serious (and pretty crazy!). Sarcasm is risky. The payoffs are big ones, however, for when effectively used, the writer's sense of outrage has a powerful impact on his readers.

So read these sarcastic voices and try writing in that voice. But remember that both reading and writing sarcastically can be tricky. As the circus ringmaster said to the tightrope walker about to begin her performance, "Be careful out there!"

The Sale of the Hessians

Benjamin Franklin

Benjamin Franklin was one of the founders of the United States. A diplomat, politician, scientist, printer, and writer, Franklin was one of the most versatile figures in American history. Franklin is best known as a writer for his *Autobiography* and for *Poor Richard's Almanac*, in which he published many sayings and epigrams that have become a part of the American cultural heritage.

In "The Sale of the Hessians," Franklin is concerned with King George III's hired mercenary troops, the Hessians, used by the king to fight against the colonists during the American Revolution (1776–1781). Franklin wrote this fictional letter during his stay in France as he sought French aid for the Colonies.

QUESTIONS ABOUT IDEAS

1. What is the significant difference between hiring foreign soldiers to fight in a war and training one's own citizens to be soldiers? Is there an important difference?
2. Is the need for a job a suitable motivation for soldiering? for fighting in a war? Why or why not?
3. The letter focuses on the differences between those who "run" a war and those who do the fighting. What responsibilities to their soldiers ought those in charge of the war to live up to?

Rome, February 18, 1777

Monsieur Le Baron:—On my return from Naples, I received at Rome   1
your letter of the 27th December of last year. I have learned with unspeakable pleasure the courage our troops exhibited at Trenton, and you cannot imagine my joy on being told that of the 1,950 Hessians engaged in the fight, but 345 escaped. There were just 1,605 men killed, and I cannot sufficiently commend your prudence in sending an exact list of the dead to my minister in London. This precaution was the more necessary, as the report sent to the English ministry does not give but 1,455 dead. This would make 483,450 florins instead of 643,500 which I am entitled to demand under our convention. You will comprehend the prejudice which such an error would work in my finances, and I do not doubt you will take the necessary pains to prove that Lord North's list is false and yours correct.

The court of London objects that there were a hundred wounded who   2
ought not to be included in the list, nor paid for as dead; but I trust you will not overlook my instructions to you on quitting Cassel, and that you will not

have tried by human succor to recall the life of the unfortunates whose days could not be lengthened but by the loss of a leg or an arm. That would be making them a pernicious present, and I am sure they would rather die than live in a condition no longer fit for my service. I do not mean by this that you should assassinate them; we should be humane, my dear Baron, but you may insinuate to the surgeons with entire propriety that a crippled man is a reproach to their profession, and that there is no wiser course than to let every one of them die when he ceases to be fit to fight.

I am about to send to you some new recruits. Don't economize them.   3
Remember glory before all things. Glory is true wealth. There is nothing degrades the soldier like the love of money. He must care only for honour and reputation, but this reputation must be acquired in the midst of dangers. A battle gained without costing the conqueror any blood is an inglorious success, while the conquered cover themselves with glory by perishing with their arms in their hands. Do you remember that of the 300 Lacedaemonians who defended the defile of Thermopylae, not one returned? How happy should I be could I say the same of my brave Hessians!

It is true that their king, Leonidas, perished with them: but things   4
have changed, and it is no longer the custom for princes of the empire to go and fight in America for a cause with which they have no concern. And besides, to whom should they pay the thirty guineas per man if I did not stay in Europe to receive them? Then, it is necessary also that I be ready to send recruits to replace the men you lose. For this purpose I must return to Hesse. It is true, grown men are becoming scarce there, but I will send you boys. Besides, the scarcer the commodity the higher the price. I am assured that the women and the little girls have begun to till our lands, and they get on not badly. You did right to send back to Europe that Dr. Crumerus who was so successful in curing dysentery. Don't bother with a man who is subject to looseness of the bowels. That disease makes bad soldiers. One coward will do more mischief in an engagement than ten brave men will do good. Better that they burst in their barracks than fly in a battle, and tarnish the glory of our arms. Besides, you know that they pay me as killed for all who die from disease, and I don't get a farthing for runaways. My trip to Italy, which has cost me enormously, makes it desirable that there should be a great mortality among them. You will therefore promise promotion to all who expose themselves; you will exhort them to seek glory in the midst of dangers; you will say to Major Maundorff: that I am not at all content with his saving the 345 men who escaped the massacre of Trenton.

Through the whole campaign he has not had ten men killed in conse-   5
quence of his orders. Finally, let it be your principal object to prolong the war and avoid a decisive engagement on either side, for I have made arrangements for a grand Italian opera, and I do not wish to be obliged to give it up. Meantime I pray God, my dear Baron de Hohendorf, to have you in his holy and gracious keeping.

QUESTIONS ABOUT THE RHETORICAL SITUATION

1. The letter is addressed to Baron de Hohendorf. What does the letter reveal about the Baron? What is he like?
2. Who are Franklin's intended readers? How are they different from Baron de Hohendorf?
3. What is Franklin's attitude toward the use of mercenary soldiers? What is his attitude toward the war? What can you tell about his attitude toward the nonmercenary soldiers in the war? Is he at all guilty of any of the same accusations his letter implies King George III is guilty of?
4. What is your response to this letter? How do you feel about King George's use of mercenaries? What do you think Franklin hoped to accomplish with such a letter?

QUESTIONS ABOUT THE ESSAY'S VOICE

1. In what ways does Franklin try to make his letter sound like an actual letter? Are there any parts of the piece which do not sound authentically "letterlike"?
2. How would you describe the personality of Franklin's persona in this letter?
3. What part or parts of the letter exemplify black comedy? Why does Franklin choose to write such passages? How necessary are they?
4. In ¶2, the letter writer argues that "we should be humane." How sincere is he at this point? How do you respond to his suggestion?
5. What is the portrait of the mercenary soldier that the letter writer paints? How does this portrait serve his purposes?
6. In ¶3, the letter writer argues that "glory is true wealth." What is ironic about this statement on his part? What is ironic about the rest of that paragraph?
7. In ¶4, the letter writer explains why it would be inappropriate for him to accompany the troops to the colonies: "it is no longer the custom for princes of the empire to go and fight in America for a cause with which they have no concern." What larger issue does this comment raise? How concerned with this larger issue is the letter writer?
8. What is ironic about the letter writer's complaints about Major Maundorff?

TOPICS TO WRITE ABOUT

1. Write a letter of your own similar to Franklin's, designed to criticize some aspect of public policy with which you disagree. Adopt the persona

of someone who supports this policy. (For example, if you are dissatisfied with the food in the school cafeteria, pretend you are one of the food suppliers and write a letter to the cafeteria's chef complimenting her on her varied and tasty uses for dehydrated, canned meat substitute and offer to sell her another truckload at a bargain rate, or if the local police are too aggressive in ticketing speeders, pretend you are the printer of the tickets and write to the local police chief praising his department for using up the tickets and ordering more.) POTENTIAL AUDIENCE: the part of the public most directly affected by the policy. POTENTIAL PURPOSE: to make them aware that something needs to be changed.

2. Write a sarcastic letter to an advice columnist, a letter which ridicules the kinds of letters usually published in this part of the newspaper. POTENTIAL AUDIENCE: readers of your local newspaper. POTENTIAL PURPOSE: to make the readers think twice before accepting the columnist's advice.

Just Like a Woman

Margaret Atwood

Margaret Atwood is one of Canada's most prominent writers. Born in Ottawa, she grew up in Ontario and subsequently in Toronto. Author of more than twenty books, including poetry, fiction, and nonfiction, Atwood is perhaps best known for her six novels, *The Edible Woman, Surfacing, Lady Oracle, Life Before Man, Bodily Harm,* and *The Handmaid's Tale. The Handmaid's Tale* is a novel in the tradition of Orwell's *1984* and Huxley's *Brave New World,* offering a grim view of a totalitarian state in the near future, a view from a distinctively female point of view. Atwood currently resides in Toronto.

"Just Like a Woman" appeared in *Harper's* magazine in 1985. It had earlier appeared under the title "Women's Novels" in the Spring 1985 issue of *Open Places,* a special issue on humor in America. *Open Places* is published twice yearly by Stephens College, in Columbia, Missouri.

QUESTIONS ABOUT IDEAS

1. How accurately has Atwood described men's and women's novels? Can you think of examples of both kinds of novels?
2. How can you explain why women, according to the essay, can only write one kind of novel while men can, it seems, write both kinds?
3. What, in your view, is wrong with the kinds of novels Atwood is so critical of? Or is she being unfair?

4. Might a similar essay be written about movies? How would it describe a "women's movie" and a "men's movie"? Can you think of examples of each kind?

1

Men's novels are about men. Women's novels are about men too but from a different point of view. You can have a men's novel with no women in it except possibly the landlady or the horse, but you can't have a women's novel with no men in it. Sometimes men put women in men's novels but leave out some of the parts: the heads, for instance, or the hands. Women's novels leave out parts of men as well. Sometimes it's the stretch between the belly button and the knees, sometimes it's the sense of humor. It's hard to have a sense of humor in a cloak, in a high wind, on a moor.

Women do not usually write novels of the type favored by men but men are known to write novels of the type favored by women. Some people find this odd.

2

I like to read novels in which the heroine has a costume rustling discreetly over her breasts, or discreet breasts rustling under her costume; in any case, there must be a costume, some breasts, some rustling, and, over all, discretion. Discretion over all, like a fog, a miasma through which the outlines of things appear only vaguely. A glimpse of pink through the gloom, the sound of breathing, satin slithering to the floor, revealing what? Never mind, I say. Never mind.

3

Men favor heroes who are tough and hard: tough with men, hard with women. Sometimes the hero goes soft on a woman, but this is always a mistake. Women do not favor heroines who are tough and hard. This leads to linguistic difficulties. Last time we looked, monosyllables were male, still dominant but sinking fast, wrapped in the octopoid arms of labial polysyllables, whispering to them with arachnoid grace: *darling, darling.*

4

Men's novels are about how to get power. Killing and so on, or winning and so on. So are women's novels, though the method is different. In men's novels, getting the woman or women goes along with getting the power. It's a perk, not a means. In women's novels you get the power by getting the man. The man is the power. But sex won't do; he has to love you. What do you think all that kneeling's about, down among the crinolines, on the Persian carpet? At least say it. When all else is lacking, verbalization can be enough. *Love.* There, you can stand up now, it didn't kill you? Did it?

5

I no longer want to read about anything sad. Anything violent, any thing disturbing, anything like that. No funerals at the end, though there can be some in the middle. If there must be deaths, let there be resurrections, or at least a heaven so we know where we are. Depression and squalor are for those under twenty-five; they can take it, they even like it, they still have enough time left. But real life is bad for you; hold it in your hand long enough and you'll get pimples and become feebleminded. You'll go blind.

I want happiness, guaranteed, joy all around, covers with nurses on them or brides, intelligent girls but not too intelligent, with regular teeth and pluck and both breasts the same size and no excess facial hair, someone you can depend on to know where the bandages are and to turn the hero, that potential rake and killer, into a well-groomed country gentleman with clean fingernails and the right vocabulary. *Always,* he has to say. *Forever.* I no longer want to read books that don't end with the word *forever.* I want to be stroked between the eyes, one way only.

6

Some people think a woman's novel is anything without politics in it. Some think it's anything about relationships. Some think it's anything with a lot of operations in it, medical ones I mean. Some think it's anything that doesn't give you a broad, panoramic view of our exciting times. Me, well, I just want something you can leave on the coffee table and not be too worried if the kids get into it. You think that's not a real consideration? You're wrong.

7

She had the startled eyes of a wild bird. This is the kind of sentence I go mad for. I would like to be able to write such sentences, without embarrassment. I would like to be able to read them without embarrassment. If only I could do these two simple things, I feel, I would be able to pass my allotted time on this earth like a pearl wrapped in velvet.

She had the startled eyes of a wild bird. Ah, but which one? A screech owl, perhaps, or a cuckoo? It does make a difference. We do not need more literalists of the imagination. They cannot read *a body like a gazelle's* without thinking of intestinal parasites, zoos, and smells.

She had a feral gaze like that of an untamed animal, I read. Reluctantly I put down the book, thumb still inserted at the exciting moment. He's about to crush her in his arms, pressing his hot, devouring, hard, demanding mouth to her as her breasts squish out the top of her dress, but I can't concentrate. Metaphor leads me by the nose, into the maze, and suddenly all Eden lies before me. Porcupines, weasels, warthogs, and skunks, their feral gazes malicious or bland or stolid or piggy and sly. Agony, to see the romantic *frisson* quivering just out of reach, a dark-winged butterfly stuck to an overripe peach, and not to be able to swallow, or wallow. *Which one?* I murmur to the unresponding air. *Which one?*

QUESTIONS ABOUT THE RHETORICAL SITUATION

1. Which kind of novels does Atwood seem to prefer—men's novels or women's novels? Or some third kind? Why?
2. Atwood's voice in this essay is rather sarcastic, a sign that she is angry. Why do you think Atwood feels so strongly about this subject?
3. Do you think that Atwood hopes to change her readers' reading habits? If so, why? And how? If not, then what is her purpose in this essay?
4. How does Atwood's essay seem directed toward a specific group of readers? Is she, for example, writing primarily for women or for men or doesn't it matter? Is she writing to other writers or novel readers or only certain kinds of novel readers?

QUESTIONS ABOUT THE ESSAY'S VOICE

1. Atwood's essay is very noticeably organized in an unorthodox fashion using short, numbered sections rather than transitions. How effective is this method? How does it affect the voice you hear in this essay?
2. What kind of novel does Atwood have in mind in her sarcastic remark in the last sentence of Section 1?
3. Why does Atwood talk about breasts so often in this essay? Is she always sarcastic when she does so? Why? How are the puns in section 3 of the essay related to this seeming preoccupation with breasts?
4. In sections 5 and 7, Atwood quotes from women's novels, using italics. Why does she select the specific examples she has selected? How do these examples help her to be sarcastic?
5. In section 6 of the essay, Atwood begins the first four sentences with virtually the same words. What is the effect of this strategy on the essay's voice? What is the point she is making in that particular section of the essay?
6. Describe the persona Atwood has adopted in this essay. (Notice section 5 in particular.)
7. How sincere is Atwood in section 7? What is the point of her concluding paragraph?

TOPICS TO WRITE ABOUT

1. Write a similarly sarcastic essay about movies or TV shows, discussing men's and women's films or shows. POTENTIAL AUDIENCES: readers of the Sunday newspaper's TV supplement/studio executives responsible for pro-

ducing these movies and shows. POTENTIAL PURPOSES: to make them think more carefully before wasting time watching such films or shows/to make them think about making films and shows with more substance to them.

2. Write an essay structured in a series of impressions about some topic you would like to criticize by falsely praising it. (For example, you might praise fast food over home-cooked meals with a section on the taste, one on nutrition, one on service, one on atmosphere; or you might praise some fashion that you actually find quite tasteless.) POTENTIAL AUDIENCES: those who actually like the thing you are criticizing/your one friend who has gone overboard in liking this particular thing. POTENTIAL PURPOSES: to make them feel uncomfortable about their own tastes/to make your friend reconsider his or her attitudes.

A Simpler Life for Consumers

Jeff Greenfield

Born in 1943, Jeff Greenfield has a law degree from Yale University. He worked as a speechwriter for Robert F. Kennedy and for John V. Lindsay, former mayor of New York City. Greenfield has been a sportswriter and television news commentator. He has published books such as *Where Have You Gone Joe DiMaggio?*, *Television: The First Fifty Years*, *The Real Campaign*, and *A Populist Manifesto*. He is perhaps best known for his widely anthologized 1975 essay "The Black and White Truth about Basketball," an insightful analysis of two different styles of play in the National Basketball Association. He is now a political and social commentator whose writing appears on editorial pages all over the country. Greenfield's "A Simpler Life for Consumers" was first published in the spring of 1987.

QUESTIONS ABOUT IDEAS

1. How important is having a wide choice for consumers? Would fewer choices result in a simpler life? A better life?
2. Greenfield really offers no solutions to the problem he is discussing. What possible solutions might there be? What would be the advantages and disadvantages of these solutions?
3. Does the ownership of an airline or a TV network really have any effect on the lives of most of us as consumers? How much does it matter that the ownership of a large corporation has changed hands?

Let's see, Chrysler Corporation is going to buy American Motors, 1
which Renault bought half of eight years ago. USAir is going to merge with
Piedmont, in order to block a takeover bid by TWA; USAir already owns
PSA.

Allegheny International, which makes Sunbeam and Oster appliances, 2
is being bought by an affiliate of the First Boston Corporation, which makes
deals. The Haft family of Washington D.C., blocked from taking over Safe-
way supermarkets, now wants to buy the Pathmark stores.

Donald Trump, who makes billions, has taken over Resorts Interna- 3
tional, which operates casinos. Walt Disney wants to buy Los Angeles television station KHJ.

Maybe you heard all about this news on NBC, which was taken over 4
last year by General Electric, or on ABC, which was taken over by Capital
Cities, or on CBS, which was effectively taken over by Lawrence Tisch, or
on one of the Fox TV stations, which were bought by Rupert Murdoch. Or
maybe you read about it in the *Detroit News,* which was taken over by the
Gannett Company, or in *Newsday,* owned by the Times-Mirror Corporation.

Maybe you read this news while flying the Eastern Shuttle, which is 5
now owned by Texas Air, which also owns Continental and People Express;
or maybe on a Western Airlines flight, now owned by Delta, or on Republic,
now owned by Northwest.

Did you ever think you would live in a world where the only increase 6
in competition has come from the telephone company? Yes, now you can
choose among dozens of long-distance services from which to call a friend
and talk about the fact that we are soon going to be living in a much simpler,
easier world.

No longer will you be staying up late at night, wondering what kind of 7
jobs your children are going to have. I can assure you that, whatever their
skills, your children are going to be working for The Company.

They will get up in the morning, read The Newspaper, jump into The 8
Car, get on The Plane and stay at The Hotel—each one a division of The
Company. Oh, they may call it something else for awhile, like Allegis, which
fuses United Airlines, Avis Rent-a-Car and Westin hotels, but not to worry:
By the time Junior and Sis are gulping down their first spoonfuls of Maalox,
Allegis and Esmark, and TRW, and USX and Nynex, and GE, GTE, GM,
MCI, ICM, and all the other letters of the alphabet will all be gathered to-
gether under the beneficent roof of The Company.

And won't the lives of our children be easier! Right now, for example, 9
I have to think about how I want to go to California: American, United,
TWA, Continental, what have you. If an airline suddenly cancels a flight
five minutes after telling the passengers the flight will leave on time—that
happened to me twice last month—I have to rush frantically to another airline, and worry that I made the wrong consumer choice among competitors.
No such anxiety for my kids.

They won't have to choose among hotels based on the quality of ser- 10
vice. They won't have to worry about which auto company builds the safest
cars, which supermarket provides the best prices, which news organization
is the fairest and most accurate.

Of course, there may be a few wrinkles in this brave new world of cor- 11
porate consolidation. For instance, when The Company decides to stream-
line its operations by laying off a few thousand workers, it may be a little
tricky to figure out where all these superfluous men and women will find
jobs. And it's going to be even harder to find rewarding labor for all those
bright young Wall Street investment bankers. Who, after all, is going to
merge with The Company, or take it over, once the last steel mill and newspaper have been gobbled up?

These technical details, however, are clouds no bigger than a man's 12
hand. The tide of history is clear; the future inexorably compelling. Welcome to America: where choice is not just a slogan—it's history.

QUESTIONS ABOUT THE RHETORICAL SITUATION

1. Greenfield's essay appeared on the editorial page of my city's newspaper.
   Would he have to change his essay in any way if he knew that it would be
   appearing on the financial page rather than on the editorial page? Why or
   why not? If changes were necessary, what would he need to change?
2. Why does Greenfield choose a sarcastic voice? What does that tell you
   about his feelings about this subject? Might he have written an editorial
   (of the sort found in Chapter 7 of *Model Voices*)?
3. What does Greenfield hope for in the way of a response from his readers?
   Does he want us to take action? If so, what sort of action does he want us
   to take? What does he want to see changed?
4. It is possible for readers to view the subject of this essay as too distant to
   be of great personal concern. Greenfield, however, does not view the issue that way. What has he done in this essay to try to make the readers as
   concerned with the issue of corporate mergers as he is?

QUESTIONS ABOUT THE ESSAY'S VOICE

1. Notice the mixed metaphors in the essay's final paragraph, where clouds
   turn into tides in two consecutive sentences. How might you rewrite this
   passage to be more consistent? What does this confusion suggest about
   Greenfield's attitude toward his topic?
2. The sentence that concludes ¶8 is a particularly difficult one to read.
   How might it be repunctuated or rewritten in order to make it more readable for the essay's audience?

3. How would you describe Greenfield's persona in this essay? In which paragraph is that persona first established clearly?
4. Most of the essay's first five paragraphs are devoted to giving the reader examples. Has Greenfield given the reader enough such examples? Too many? The right amount? Can you think of other appropriate examples that he might have used?
5. In ¶9, Greenfield sketches out the improvements he foresees in air travel. He is being sarcastic of course. Does his example sound worse than the current situation? If it doesn't sound worse to you, what problems does that present for his essay?
6. At the end of ¶11, Greenfield uses the phrase "gobbled up" to describe corporate takeovers. How effective is this phrase in keeping the voice of the essay consistent? Is this Greenfield or his persona speaking?
7. Which is the central paragraph of the essay, the one upon which the entire essay is built? Why does this paragraph appear where it does? Ought it to appear somewhere else in the essay? Could it?

TOPICS TO WRITE ABOUT

1. Write a sarcastic essay that criticizes some other current tendency in business, government, or education by praising it. POTENTIAL AUDIENCES: the readers of your local newspaper/the readers of a national magazine. POTENTIAL PURPOSES: to awaken them to the threat posed by the tendency you are writing about.
2. Write a sarcastic essay about the service you received from one of the companies mentioned in Greenfield's essay. POTENTIAL AUDIENCES: the complaint department of the company/potential customers of the same company. POTENTIAL PURPOSES: to have your problem corrected or an apology sent (after writing this essay, ask yourself whether the sarcastic voice is an effective one for such an objective)/to warn them not to use this company's services.

Fenimore Cooper's Literary Offences
Mark Twain

Mark Twain was the pseudonym used by Samuel Langhorne Clemens, a name adopted by Clemens from his days as a riverboat pilot on the Mississippi River. Twain, perhaps America's best-known humorist, wrote extensively in the latter half of the nineteenth century into the twentieth century about humanity's follies and foibles, his satire growing darker and angrier as the years passed. Author of *Tom Sawyer*, *A Connecticut Yankee in King Arthur's Court*, and *Life on the Mississippi*, Twain's greatest literary achievement was *The Adventures of Huckleberry Finn*, a much praised novel still read and reread 100 years after its publication.

James Fenimore Cooper (1789–1851), whose writing is the subject of Twain's sarcastic attack in the following essay, wrote novels about frontier New York state, novels which included adventures among the Indians. Cooper's best-known books include *The Pathfinder*, *Last of the Mohicans*, and *The Deerslayer*.

QUESTIONS ABOUT IDEAS

1. Have you ever read a very negative review of a book or movie or record album that you had enjoyed very much? What right have such critics to criticize the artistic efforts of others? Why is Twain so concerned with the literary efforts of a fellow writer? Is his concern legitimate?
2. What are the most significant of Cooper's literary offenses in Twain's view? Why do you think these are most significant to him?
3. If you have read any of Cooper's novels, how accurate an appraisal is Twain's essay? If you have not read any of the novels, do you think you would after reading this essay? Why did you answer as you did?
4. Twain's essay is longer than the other selections in this chapter. Could it have been shortened without damaging its effectiveness? Explain your answer.
5. What value have adventure novels of the sort written by Cooper, even when written well?

The *Pathfinder* and *The Deerslayer* stand at the head of Cooper's novels as artistic creations. There are others of his works which contain parts as perfect as are to be found in these, and scenes even more thrilling. Not one can be compared with either of them as a finished whole.

The defects in both of these tales are comparatively slight. They were pure works of art.—*Prof. Lounsbury.*

The five tales reveal an extraordinary fulness of invention....One of the very greatest characters in fiction, "Natty Bumppo."...

The craft of the woodsman, the tricks of the trapper, all the delicate art of the forest, were familiar to Cooper from his youth up.—*Prof. Brander Matthews.*

Cooper is the greatest artist in the domain of romantic fiction yet produced by America.—*Wilkie Collins.*

It seems to me that it was far from right for the Professor of English   1
Literature in Yale, the Professor of English in Columbia, and Wilkie Collins, to deliver opinions on Cooper's literature without having read some of it. It would have been much more decorous to keep silent and let persons talk who have read Cooper.

Cooper's art has some defects. In one place in *Deerslayer,* and in the   2
restricted space of two-thirds of a page, Cooper has scored 114 offences against literary art out of a possible 115. It breaks the record.

There are nineteen rules governing literary art in the domain of roman-   3
tic fiction—some say twenty-two. In *Deerslayer* Cooper violated eighteen of them. These eighteen require:

1. That a tale shall accomplish something and arrive somewhere. But the *Deerslayer* tale accomplishes nothing and arrives in the air.
2. They require that the episodes of a tale shall be necessary parts of the tale, and shall help to develop it. But as the *Deerslayer* tale is not a tale, and accomplishes nothing and arrives nowhere, the episodes have no rightful place in the work, since there was nothing for them to develop.
3. They require that the personages in a tale shall be alive, except in the case of corpses, and that always the reader shall be able to tell the corpses from the others. But this detail has often been overlooked in the *Deerslayer* tale.
4. They require that the personages in a tale, both dead and alive, shall exhibit a sufficient excuse for being there. But this detail also has been overlooked in the *Deerslayer* tale.
5. They require that when the personages of a tale deal in conversation, the talk shall sound like human talk, and be talk such as human beings would be likely to talk in the given circumstances, and have a discoverable meaning, also a discoverable purpose, and a show of relevancy, and remain in the neighborhood of the subject in hand, and be interesting to the reader, and help out the tale, and stop when the people cannot think of anything more to say. But this requirement has been ignored from the beginning of the *Deerslayer* tale to the end of it.
6. They require that when the author describes the character of a personage in his tale, the conduct and conversation of that personage shall justify said description. But this law gets little or no attention in the *Deerslayer* tale, as "Natty Bumppo's" case will amply prove.
7. They require that when a personage talks like an illustrated, gilt-edged, tree-calf, hand-tooled, seven-dollar Friendship's Offering in the beginning of a paragraph, he shall not talk like a negro minstrel in the end of

it. But this rule is flung down and danced upon in the *Deerslayer* tale.

8. They require that crass stupidities shall not be played upon the reader as "the craft of the woodsman, the delicate art of the forest," by either the author or the people in the tale. But this rule is persistently violated in the *Deerslayer* tale.

9. They require that the personages of a tale shall confine themselves to possibilities and let miracles alone; or, if they venture a miracle, the author must so plausibly set it forth as to make it look possible and reasonable. But these rules are not respected in the *Deerslayer* tale.

10. They require that the author shall make the reader feel a deep interest in the personages of his tale and in their fate; and that he shall make the reader love the good people in the tale and hate the bad ones. But the reader of the *Deerslayer* tale dislikes the good people in it, is indifferent to the others, and wishes they would all get drowned together.

11. They require that the characters in a tale shall be so clearly defined that the reader can tell beforehand what each will do in a given emergency. But in the *Deerslayer* tale this rule is vacated.

In addition to these large rules there are some little ones. These require that the author shall

12. *Say* what he is proposing to say, not merely come near it.
13. Use the right word, not its second cousin.
14. Eschew surplusage.
15. Not omit necessary details.
16. Avoid slovenliness of form.
17. Use good grammar.
18. Employ a simple and straightforward style.

Even these seven are coldly and persistently violated in the *Deerslayer* tale. 4

Cooper's gift in the way of invention was not a rich endowment; but 5 such as it was he liked to work it, he was pleased with the effects, and indeed he did some quite sweet things with it. In his little box of stage properties he kept six or eight cunning devices, tricks, artifices for his savages and woodsmen to deceive and circumvent each other with, and he was never so happy as when he was working these innocent things and seeing them go. A favorite one was to make a moccasined person tread in the tracks of the moccasined enemy, and thus hide his own trail. Cooper wore out barrels and barrels of moccasins in working that trick. Another stage-property that he pulled out of his box pretty frequently was his broken twig. He prized his broken twig above all the rest of his effects, and worked it the hardest. It is a restful chapter in any book of his when somebody doesn't step on a dry twig and alarm all the reds and whites for two hundred yards around. Every time a Cooper person is in peril, and absolute silence is worth four dollars a minute, he is sure to step on a dry twig. There may be a hundred handier things to step on, but that wouldn't satisfy Cooper. Cooper requires him to

turn out and find a dry twig; and if he can't do it, go and borrow one. In fact
the Leather Stocking Series ought to have been called the Broken Twig Series.

I am sorry there is not room to put in a few dozen instances of the   6
delicate art of the forest, as practiced by Natty Bumppo and some of the
other Cooperian experts. Perhaps we may venture two or three samples.
Cooper was a sailor—a naval officer; yet he gravely tells us how a vessel,
driving toward a lee shore in a gale, is steered for a particular spot by her
skipper because he knows of an *undertow* there which will hold her back
against the gale and save her. For just pure woodcraft, or sailor-craft, or
whatever it is, isn't that neat? For several years Cooper was daily in the society of artillery, and he ought to have noticed that when a cannon ball
strikes the ground it either buries itself or skips a hundred feet or so; skips
again a hundred feet or so—and so on, till it finally gets tired and rolls. Now
in one place he loses some "females"—as he always calls women—in the
edge of a wood near a plain at night in a fog, on purpose to give Bumppo a
chance to show off the delicate art of the forest before the reader. These mis-
laid people are hunting for a fort. They hear a cannon-blast, and a cannon-
ball presently comes rolling into the wood and stops at their feet. To the
females this suggests nothing. The case is very different with the admirable
Bumppo. I wish I may never know peace again if he doesn't strike out
promptly and *follow the track* of that cannon-ball across the plain through the
dense fog and find the fort. Isn't it a daisy? If Cooper had any real knowledge of Nature's ways of doing things, he had a most delicate art in conceal-
ing the fact. For instance: one of his acute Indian experts, Chingachgook
(pronounced Chicago, I think), has lost the trail of a person he is tracking
through the forest. Apparently that trail is hopelessly lost. Neither you nor I
could ever have guessed out the way to find it. It was very different with
Chicago. Chicago was not stumped for long. He turned a running stream out
of its course, and there, in the slush in its old bed, were that person's
moccasin-tracks. The current did not wash them away, as it would have
done in all other like cases—no, even the eternal laws of Nature have to va-
cate when Cooper wants to put up a delicate job of woodcraft on the reader.

We must be a little wary when Brander Matthews tells us that Cooper's   7
books "reveal an extraordinary fulness of invention." As a rule, I am quite
willing to accept Brander Matthews's literary judgments and applaud his lu-
cid and graceful phrasing of them; but that particular statement needs to be
taken with a few tons of salt. Bless your heart, Cooper hadn't any more invention than a horse, and I don't mean a high-class horse, either; I mean a
clothes-horse. It would be very difficult to find a really clever "situation" in
Cooper's books; and still more difficult to find one of any kind which he has
failed to render absurd by his handling of it. Look at the episodes of "the
caves;" and at the celebrated scuffle between Magua and those others on the
table-land a few days later; and at Hurry Harry's queer water-transit from

the castle to the ark; and at Deerslayer's half hour with his first corpse; and at the quarrel between Hurry Harry and Deerslayer later; and at—but choose for yourself, you can't go amiss.

If Cooper had been an observer, his inventive faculty would have **8** worked better, not more interestingly, but more rationally, more plausibly. Cooper's proudest creations in the way of "situations" suffer noticeably from the absence of the observer's protecting gift. Cooper's eye was splendidly inaccurate. Cooper seldom saw anything correctly. He saw nearly all things as through a glass eye, darkly. Of course a man who cannot see the commonest little everyday matters accurately is working at a disadvantage when he is constructing a "situation." In the *Deerslayer* tale Cooper has a stream which is fifty feet wide, where it flows out of a lake; it presently narrows to twenty as it meanders along for no given reason, and yet, when a stream acts like that it ought to be required to explain itself. Fourteen pages later the width of the brook's outlet from the lake has suddenly shrunk thirty feet, and become "the narrowest part of the stream." This shrinkage is not accounted for. The stream has bends in it, a sure indication that it has alluvial banks, and cuts them; yet these bends are only thirty and fifty feet long. If Cooper had been a nice and punctilious observer he would have noticed that the bends were oftener nine hundred feet long than short of it.

Cooper made the exit of that stream fifty feet wide in the first place, for **9** no particular reason; in the second place, he narrowed to less than twenty to accommodate some Indians. He bends a "sapling" to the form of an arch over this narrow passage, and conceals six Indians in its foliage. They are "laying" for a settler's scow or ark which is coming up the stream on its way to the lake; it is being hauled against the stiff current by a rope whose stationary end is anchored in the lake; its rate of progress cannot be more than a mile an hour. Cooper describes the ark, but pretty obscurely. In the matter of dimensions "it was little more than a modern canal boat." Let us guess, then, that it was about 140 feet long. It was of "greater breadth than common." Let us guess, then, that it was about sixteen feet wide. This leviathan had been prowling down bends which were but a third as long as itself, and scraping between banks where it had only two feet of space to spare on each side. We cannot too much admire this miracle. A low-roofed log dwelling occupies "two-third's of the ark's length"—a dwelling ninety feet long and sixteen feet wide, let us say—a kind of vestibule train. The dwelling has two rooms—each forty-five feet long and sixteen feet wide, let us guess. One of them is the bed-room of the Hutter girls, Judith and Hetty; the other is the parlor, in the day time, at night it is papa's bed chamber. The ark is arriving at the stream's exit, now, whose width has been reduced to less than twenty feet to accommodate the Indians—say to eighteen. There is a foot to spare on each side of the boat. Did the Indians notice that there was going to be a tight squeeze there? Did they notice that they could make money by climbing down out of that arched sapling and just stepping aboard when the ark scraped by? No; other Indians would have noticed these things, but Cooper's Indians never notice anything. Cooper thinks they are marvellous creatures for noticing, but he was almost always in error about his Indians. There was seldom a sane one among them.

The ark is 140 feet long; the dwelling is 90 feet long. The idea of the   10 Indians is to drop softly and secretly from the arched sapling to the dwelling as the ark creeps along under it at the rate of a mile an hour, and butcher the family. It will take the ark a minute and a half to pass under. It will take the 90-foot dwelling a minute to pass under. Now, then, what did the six Indians do? It would take you thirty years to guess, and even then you would have to give it up, I believe. Therefore, I will tell you what the Indians did. Their chief, a person of quite extraordinary intellect for a Cooper Indian, warily watched the canal boat as it squeezed along under him, and when he had got his calculations fined down to exactly the right shade, as he judged, he let go and dropped. And *missed the house!* That is actually what he did. He missed the house, and landed in the stern of the scow. It was not much of a fall, yet it knocked him silly. He lay there unconscious. If the house had been 97 feet long, he would have made the trip. The fault was Cooper's, not his. The error lay in the construction of the house. Cooper was no architect.

There still remained in the roost five Indians. The boat has passed un-   11 der and is now out of their reach. Let me explain what the five did—you would not be able to reason it out for yourself. No. 1 jumped for the boat, but fell in the water astern of it. Then No. 2 jumped for the boat, but fell in the water still further astern of it. Then No. 3 jumped for the boat, and fell a good way astern of it. Then No. 4 jumped for the boat, and fell in the water *away* astern. Then even No. 5 made a jump for the boat—for he was a Cooper Indian. In the matter of intellect, the difference between a Cooper Indian and the Indian that stands in front of the cigar shop is not spacious. The scow episode is really a sublime burst of invention; but it does not thrill, because the inaccuracy of the details throws a sort of air of fictitiousness and general improbability over it. This comes of Cooper's inadequacy as an observer.

The reader will find some examples of Cooper's high talent for inaccu-   12 rate observation in the account of the shooting match in *The Pathfinder*. "A common wrought nail was driven lightly into the target, its head having been first touched with paint." The color of the paint is not stated—an important omission, but Cooper deals freely in important omissions. No, after all, it was not an important omission; for this nail head is *a hundred yards* from the marksman and could not be seen by them at that distance no matter what its color might be. How far can the best eyes see a common house fly? A hundred yards? It is quite impossible. Very well, eyes that cannot see a house fly that is a hundred yards away cannot see an ordinary nail head at that distance, for the size of the two objects is the same. It takes a keen eye to see a fly or a nail head at fifty yards—one hundred and fifty feet. Can the reader do it?

The nail was lightly driven, its head painted, and game called. Then the 13 Cooper miracles began. The bullet of the first marksman chipped an edge of the nail head; the next man's bullet drove the nail a little way into the target—and removed all the paint. Haven't the miracles gone far enough now? Not to suit Cooper; for the purpose of this whole scheme is to show off his prodigy, Deerslayer-Hawkeye-Long-Rifle-Leather-Stocking-Pathfinder-Bumppo before the ladies.

> "Be all ready to clench it, boys!" cried out Pathfinder, stepping into his friend's tracks the instant they were vacant. "Never mind a new nail; I can see that, though the paint is gone, and what I can see, I can hit at a hundred yards, though it were only a mosquito's eye. Be ready to clench!"
>
> The rifle cracked, the bullet sped its way and the head of the nail was buried in the wood, covered by the piece of flattened lead.

There, you see, is a man who could hunt flies with a rifle, and command 14 a ducal salary in a Wild West show to-day, if we had him back with us.

The recorded feat is certainly surprising, just as it stands; but it is not 15 surprising enough for Cooper. Cooper adds a touch. He has made Pathfinder do this miracle with another man's rifle, and not only that, but Pathfinder did not have even the advantage of loading it himself. He had everything against him, and yet he made that impossible shot, and not only made it, but did it with absolute confidence, saying, "Be ready to clench." Now a person like that would have undertaken that same feat with a brickbat, and with Cooper to help he would have achieved it, too.

Pathfinder showed off handsomely that day before the ladies. His very 16 first feat was a thing which no Wild West show can touch. He was standing with the group of marksmen, observing—a hundred yards from the target, mind: one Jasper raised his rifle and drove the centre of the bull's-eye. Then the quartermaster fired. The target exhibited no result this time. There was a laugh. "It's a dead miss," said Major Lundie. Pathfinder waited an impressive moment or two, then said in that calm, indifferent, know-it-all way of his, "No, Major—he has covered Jasper's bullet, as will be seen if any one will take the trouble to examine the target."

Wasn't it remarkable! How *could* he see that little pellet fly through the 17 air and enter that distant bullet-hole? Yet that is what he did; for nothing is impossible to a Cooper person. Did any of those people have any deep-seated doubts about this thing? No; for that would imply sanity, and these were all Cooper people.

> The respect for Pathfinder's skill and for his *quickness and accuracy of sight* (the italics are mine) was so profound and general, that the

instant he made this declaration the spectators began to distrust their
own opinions, and a dozen rushed to the target in order to ascertain
the fact. There, sure enough, it was found that the quartermaster's
bullet had gone through the hole made by Jasper's, and that, too, so
accurately as to require a minute examination to be certain of the
circumstance, which, however, was soon clearly established by
discovering one bullet over the other in the stump against which the
target was placed.

They made a "minute" examination; but never mind, how could they 18
know that there were two bullets in that hole without digging the latest one
out? for neither probe nor eyesight could prove the presence of any more
than one bullet. Did they dig? No; as we shall see. It is the Pathfinder's turn
now; he steps out before the ladies, takes aim, and fires.

But alas! here is a disappointment; an incredible, an unimaginable dis- 19
appointment—for the target's aspect is unchanged; there is nothing there
but that same old bullet hole!

"If one dared to hint at such a thing," cried Major Duncan, "I should
say that the Pathfinder has also missed the target."

As nobody has missed it yet, the "also" was not necessary; but never 20
mind about that, for the Pathfinder is going to speak.

"No, no, Major," said he, confidently, "that *would* be a risky
declaration. I didn't load the piece, and can't say what was in it, but if
it was lead, you will find the bullet driving down those of the
Quartermaster and Jasper, else is not my name Pathfinder."

A shout from the target announced the truth of this assertion.

Is the miracle sufficient as it stands? Not for Cooper. The Pathfinder 21
speaks again, as he "now slowly advances towards the stage occupied by the
females:"

"That's not all, boys, that's not all; if you find the target touched at
all, I'll own to a miss. The Quartermaster cut the wood, but you'll
find no wood cut by that last messenger."

The miracle is at last complete. He knew—doubtless *saw*—at the dis- 22
tance of a hundred yards—that his bullet had passed into the hole *without
fraying the edges*. There were now three bullets in that one hole—three bullets imbedded processionally in the body of the stump back of the target.
Everybody knew this—somehow or other—and yet nobody had dug any of
them out to make sure. Cooper is not a close observer, but he is interesting.
He is certainly always that, no matter what happens. And he is more interesting when he is not noticing what he is about than when he is. This is a
considerable merit.

The conversations in the Cooper books have a curious sound in our 23 modern ears. To believe that such talk really ever came out of people's mouths would be to believe that there was a time when time was of no value to a person who thought he had something to say; when it was the custom to spread a two-minute remark out to ten; when a man's mouth was a rolling-mill, and busied itself all day long in turning four-foot pigs of thought into thirty-foot bars of conversational railroad iron by attenuation; when subjects were seldom faithfully stuck to, but the talk wandered all around and arrived nowhere; when conversations consisted mainly of irrelevances, with here and there a relevancy, a relevancy with an embarrassed look, as not being able to explain how it got there.

Cooper was certainly not a master in the construction of dialogue. Inaccurate observation defeated him here as it defeated him in so many other enterprises of his. He even failed to notice that the man who talks corrupt English six days in the week must and will talk it on the seventh, and can't help himself. In the *Deerslayer* story he lets Deerslayer talk the showiest kind of book talk sometimes, and at other times the basest of base dialects. For instance, when some one asks him if he has a sweetheart, and if so, where she abides, this is his majestic answer: **24**

> "She's in the forest—hanging from the boughs of the trees, in a soft rain—in the dew on the open grass—the clouds that float about in the blue heavens—the birds that sing in the woods—the sweet springs where I slake my thirst—and in all the other glorious gifts that come from God's Providence!"

And he preceded that, a little before, with this: **25**

> "It consarns me as all things that touches a fri'nd consarns a fri'nd."

And this is another of his remarks: **26**

> "If I was Injun born, now, I might tell of this, or carry in the scalp and boast of the expl'ite afore the whole tribe; or if my inimy had only been a bear"—and so on.

We cannot imagine such a thing as a veteran Scotch Commander-in- **27** Chief comporting himself in the field like a windy melodramatic actor, but Cooper could. On one occasion Alice and Cora were being chased by the French through a fog in the neighborhood of their father's fort:

> "*Point de quartier aux coquins!*" cried an eager pursuer, who seemed to direct the operations of the enemy.

> "Stand firm and be ready, my gallant 60ths!" suddenly exclaimed a voice above them; "wait to see the enemy; fire low, and sweep the glacis."

> "Father! father!" exclaimed a piercing cry from out the mist; "it is I! Alice! thy own Elsie! spare, O! save your daughters!"

> "Hold!" shouted the former speaker, in the awful tones of parental

agony, the sound reaching even to the woods, and rolling back in
solemn echo. " 'Tis she! God has restored me my children! Throw
open the sally-port; to the field, 60ths, to the field; pull not a trigger,
lest ye kill my lambs! Drive off these dogs of France with your steel."

Cooper's word-sense was singularly dull. When a person has a poor ear   28
for music he will flat and sharp right along without knowing it. He keeps
~·ar the tune, but it is *not* the tune. When a person has a poor ear for words,
the result is a literary flatting and sharping; you perceive what he is intend-
ing to say, but you also perceive that he doesn't *say* it. This is Cooper. He
was not a word-musician. His ear was satisfied with the *approximate* word. I
will furnish some circumstantial evidence in support of this charge. My instances are gathered from a half dozen pages of the tale called *Deerslayer*. He
uses "verbal," for "oral"; "precision," for "facility"; "phenomena," for
"marvels"; "necessary," for "predetermined"; "unsophisticated," for
"primitive"; "preparation," for "expectancy"; "rebuked," for "subdued";
"dependent on," for "resulting from"; "fact," for "condition"; "fact," for
"conjecture"; "precaution," for "caution"; "explain," for "determine";
"mortified," for "disappointed"; "meretricious," for "factitious"; "materi-
ally," for "considerably"; "decreasing," for "deepening"; "increasing," for
"disappearing"; "embedded," for "enclosed"; "treacherous," for "hostile";
"stood," for "stooped"; "softened," for "replaced"; "rejoined," for
"remarked"; "situation," for "condition"; "different," for "differing"; "in-
sensible," for "unsentient"; "brevity," for "celerity"; "distrusted," for
"suspicious"; "mental imbecility," for "imbecility"; "eyes," for "sight";
"counteracting," for "opposing"; "funeral obsequies," for "obsequies."

There have been daring people in the world who claimed that Cooper   29
could write English, but they are all dead now—all dead but Lounsbury. I
don't remember that Lounsbury makes the claim in so many words, still he
makes it, for he says that *Deerslayer* is a "pure work of art." Pure, in that
connection, means faultless—faultless in all details—and language is a detail.
If Mr. Lounsbury had only compared Cooper's English with the English
which he writes himself—but it is plain that he didn't; and so it is likely that
he imagines until this day that Cooper's is as clean and compact as his own.
Now I feel sure, deep down in my heart, that Cooper wrote about the poor-
est English that exists in our language, and that the English of *Deerslayer* is
the very worst than even Cooper ever wrote.

I may be mistaken, but it does seem to me that *Deerslayer* is not a work   30
of art in any sense; it does seem to me that it is destitute of every detail that
goes to the making of a work of art; in truth, it seems to me that *Deerslayer*
is just simply a literary *delirium tremens*.

A work of art? It has no invention; it has no order, system, sequence,   31
or result; it has no lifelikeness, no thrill, no stir, no seeming of reality; its
characters are confusedly drawn, and by their acts and words they prove that
they are not the sort of people the author claims that they are; its humor is

pathetic; its pathos is funny; its conversations are—oh! indescribable; its love-scenes odious; its English a crime against the language.

Counting these out, what is left is Art. I think we must all admit that.   32

QUESTIONS ABOUT THE RHETORICAL SITUATION

1. What purpose do you think Twain had in writing this essay? How do you think he wanted his readers to respond? What would he like to see changed as a result of his essay? How successful do you think he was in achieving this response?
2. How amusing was this essay? Can you find parts of the essay which were genuinely funny? What made them so funny? What makes this essay different from the earlier essays in Chapters 2 and 3?
3. To whom do you think Twain was addressing his essay? How important is it that his readers be familiar with Cooper's novels? How do you think his essay would need to be changed if it were written as a letter directly to Fenimore Cooper? What purpose might Twain have if he had written directly to Cooper?
4. During the course of his criticism of Cooper's writing, Twain mentions several other literary critics. What is his attitude toward these critics? Were you surprised at how he treats these other critics? Why or why not? Why do you think he adopts this attitude toward the other critics?

QUESTIONS ABOUT THE ESSAY'S VOICE

1. How does Twain use the opening series of quotations from other critics to help establish the sarcastic voice of his essay?
2. Given the high level of Twain's hostility toward Cooper, it would probably be understandable if he had called Cooper names, yet he does not. Examine closely how polite Twain is whenever he refers to Cooper directly. (For example, in ¶22, he writes, "Cooper is not a close observer, but he is interesting. He is certainly always that, no matter what happens.") Why does Twain take this approach when he refers to Cooper? How do you recognize that he is being sarcastic anyway?
3. Twain relies heavily upon understatement in this essay. For example, in ¶2, he writes that "Cooper's art has some defects." Then he observes that Cooper has "scored 114 offences against literary art out of a possible 115" and that Cooper has broken eighteen of the nineteen rules "governing literary art in the domain of romantic fiction." What does Twain gain by using such understatement in sentence number 1? In fact, is he really understating his point throughout the rest of the paragraph?

4. What is the effect on the essay's voice of the numbered list used by Twain? How would the essay be changed if he had chosen some other method for itemizing his objections to Cooper's work?

5. Twain goes into great detail about the ark and later about the shooting contest. What do you notice about the voice in the essay in those discussions, particularly when Twain is articulating his criticism?

6. If we are convinced by Twain's arguments, then Cooper clearly has some deficiencies as a writer. Couldn't Twain, however, have leveled the very same criticisms at Cooper with similar convincingness in a voice not so strongly sarcastic? In other words, what, if anything, does Twain gain by being sarcastic here? What does he lose by being so sarcastic?

7. Examine Twain's paragraphs, noting their varied lengths. Some are extremely long; some are but a sentence or two long. Can you reach some conclusions about why the paragraphs assume the length they do?

8. How would you describe the persona whose voice we hear in this essay? How tempted are you to see this persona as Twain himself? Why?

TOPICS TO WRITE ABOUT

1. Write a sarcastic essay about a movie or TV show or record album which, in your view, has been greatly overrated by the public. Be sure to be hostile and even nasty in your comments, but remain amusing at the same time. POTENTIAL AUDIENCES: others who might consider buying the record or watching the film/other critics who have already praised the artistic work in question. POTENTIAL PURPOSES: to warn them against wasting their time and money/to point out the deficiencies in their opinions.

2. Write a similar essay about Twain's essay on Cooper. Be polite, but be sure to be sarcastic about Twain. POTENTIAL AUDIENCE: your classmates who have read Twain's essay on Fenimore Cooper. POTENTIAL PURPOSE: to make clear that such a sarcastic examination of a writer is possible with any writer, even Twain himself.

3. Write a similar essay about your own writing entitled "[Your name]'s Literary Offenses." POTENTIAL AUDIENCE: your teacher. POTENTIAL PURPOSE: to suggest how well you understand where your writing needs improvement.

Psychic Income

Mary Kay Blakely

Mary Kay Blakely is a contributing editor for *Ms.* magazine. This essay, which was titled for *Model Voices,* was first published in March 1981, in the *New York Times* as part of its *Hers* column.

In 1976, the *Times* was about to start a new section of the paper entitled The Home Section. The editors of the *Times* decided to create a forum for women in that section, a column that would be written for men as well as for women, a column written not so much for women as by women. Since 1977 the weekly *Hers* column has been written by over fifty different women writers; in 1986 a collection of columns from the first nine years of *Hers* was published under the title *Hers: Through Women's Eyes.*

QUESTIONS ABOUT IDEAS

1. Women have been vigorously protesting inequality of pay for some time now. In your experience, have these protests produced results? Have pay inequities been reduced or eliminated?
2. Blakely's examples include nurses and clerical workers. Is she guilty of stereotyping? Should she have chosen other examples? Such as?
3. What would be a suitable recourse for women who feel they are being unfairly paid?
4. What valid points does the administrator in the essay have to make about this issue?

I used to be an unbeliever. I questioned the integrity of an economic system that valued women's work only half as much as men's. I was—and this seems almost preposterous to admit now—dissatisfied with the lot of women. 1

Before I reached enlightenment, I suffered from a common form of math anxiety caused by statistics from the Department of Labor. I was easily susceptible to depression whenever the words "supply and demand" came up in conversation. I kept getting lost in the void of the earnings gap. Years of investigation about women revealed many things to me, but didn't make sense of those numbers: Women earn 59 percent of what men earn. Until last week, I was like a haunted woman—devils of injustice chasing me, demons of inequity plaguing me. 2

My conversion happened unexpectedly, during a business meeting with a highly placed administrator. I had noticed—because skeptics habitually pay attention to damning facts—that the women employed by his pres- 3

tigious institution were being paid much less than the men. Like most unbelievers I was there to complain about the inequity. That's the major problem
with those who don't have the gift of faith in our economic system. They
have their visions trained on the temporal facts of their lives.

The discussion began predictably enough. With benign paternal toler-   4
ance, he reviewed the intricate principles of economics, the baffling nuances
of budgets, the confounding factors behind the salary schedules. With the
monosyllabic vocabulary educators use to address slow learners, he explained the familiar platitudes.

He invoked the dogma of salary surveys—the objective instruments   5
used to determine what "the market will bear." They prove, beyond a
shadow of doubt, that women workers are "a dime a dozen." That's reality,
he reported almost regretfully, that's how life is outside of Eden. Practitioners of sound business—the members of the faith, so to speak—can in good
conscience pay them no more. If he didn't adhere to the precepts of salary
surveys, it would cause economic chaos. Other women, in other institutions,
would begin to think they were worth more, too. The brethren in other ad-
ministrations would expel him from the faith.

"You have to think about what the job is worth, not the person in it,"   6
he cautioned me. It always gets you into trouble, thinking about what a person is worth. He warned me against engaging in the fallacy of "comparing
apples and oranges," a comparison odious to the members of the faith. It is
only the unbelievers, the kumquats, who try to argue for the fruits of their
labors. Mixing the categories would produce uncontrollable hybrids on the
salary scale. Men are men and women are women and their paychecks are
just further evidence of their vast biological differences, the powerful influence of the X and Y chromosomes.

I confess, I had heard these tenets of the faith many times before. It   7
was the kind of conversation that might inspire the vision of a lawsuit. So it
wasn't with an open heart that I asked the question one more time. How
could he accept women's invaluable contributions to the success of his institution, witness their obvious dedication, and withhold their just rewards?

He paused, regarding me carefully, deliberating, apparently, on   8
whether I was prepared to hear the truth, to embrace the amazing mystery of
women's wages. Then slowly, respectfully, he revealed the fantastic reason.

Women came seeking positions with an intense longing for work, but   9
with a paucity of credentials and experience. They were filled with gratitude
when they were offered a job. They worked in a pleasant environment, doing meaningful work, and had the privilege of writing the name of the prestigious institution on their résumés. They received such an extraordinary
sense of well-being, it would be almost a violation of female sensibilities to
compensate them with cold, hard cash. Instead, they received something
much more valuable; they earned a "psychic income."

I heard my voice becoming hysterical. Hysteria is not at all uncommon 10
during conversions. I was loud—perhaps I was even shouting—when I asked
him how much of his income was "psychic." Like many doubters, I didn't
immediately see the light. I thought one of us was mad.

But not an hour later, enlightenment came. I was in a car dealership, 11
chatting with the amiable mechanic who had repaired my transmission. He
seemed to enjoy his job, especially when he handed me the bill. I gasped,
knowing that the balance in my checkbook wouldn't cover the charge. Then
I remembered my "psychic income" and that people who love their work,
who are dedicated to it, are better paid with congratulations and a pat on the
back. I told him what a wonderful job he did, how much I appreciated it.
And then I wrote a "psychic check."

Suddenly, I was filled with the spirit. A happiness, a release flooded 12
over me. I realized that every act of spending my "psychic income" was an
act of faith. I had so much catching up to do. I worked steadily to increase
my state of grace. Immediately, I applied for a loan at the employee credit
union at the prestigious institution, authorizing payments through "psychic
payroll deductions." I used my "psychic credit cards" to charge two pairs of
spiritual Adidas for my kids, whose real toes were poking through their real
tennis shoes.

I was filled with a fervor to spread the Word. At a rally of working 13
women, I brought them the message of "psychic incomes," and many converts came into the fold.

Nurses, who had an extraordinary love for their work, felt "psychic 14
bonuses" coming to them. Their sense of self-esteem expanded miraculously, and they no longer bowed down to the false gods in the hospitals.

Clerical workers grasped the theory of "psychic work for psychic pay" 15
and began typing only intangible letters, filing transcendental folders, and
making celestial phone calls.

Prior to their conversions, working mothers thought they had to do all 16
the housework, because their earnings were only half of their husbands' salaries. But when they learned how to bank on their "psychic incomes," they
never cooked dinner again. They served their families supernatural pot
roasts.

Of course, everyone will not accept the gift of the Word. There are 17
those who will try to persecute us for practicing our faith. We must learn to
smile serenely at the unfortunate creditors who lack the vision. We must
have a charitable attitude toward the bill collectors whose interests are
rooted in temporal assets. Beware of the pharisees who pay spiritual salaries
but still demand physical work.

And judge not the angry women who file the interminable lawsuits, 18
who still rail against the status quo. Their daily struggle to exist prevents

them from accepting the good news. Remember that there, but for the gift of "psychic economics," go we.

QUESTIONS ABOUT THE RHETORICAL SITUATION

1. Blakely's essay originally appeared as one of the weekly *Hers* columns in the *New York Times.* What does this suggest about her intended audience? Is this the only audience she might address in this manner? How would her approach work if she had published this essay in the *Wall Street Journal?*
2. What suggestions are there that Blakely finds this topic anything but amusing despite the humor in her sarcastic voice? What evidence is there that she is angry about the situation she describes?
3. What is Blakely's objective in this essay? Does she hope to encourage women to file fewer lawsuits? More lawsuits? Or is she relatively unconcerned with legal action here? What other responses might she be hoping to arouse?
4. What response do you suppose the businessman with whom she spoke would have to this essay? Why didn't she write this essay in the form of a letter directly to him? How well would it have worked that way?

QUESTIONS ABOUT THE ESSAY'S VOICE

1. Describe the persona that Blakely has adopted in her essay. At what point in the essay does she adopt that persona?
2. Trace the religious diction used by Blakely throughout the essay. How consistently does she use it? How effective is it in sustaining the sarcasm of her voice? Which specific religious terms are particularly effective in the essay? Why? Are there any which are less effective?
3. How does Blakely depict the character of the "highly placed administrator"? How fair a depiction is this? Should it be fairer?
4. Twice in the essay Blakely leaves extra white space, separating the piece into three sections. Why does she divide the essay as she does? How would the essay be affected were the divisions absent?
5. To what extent does Blakely engage in name-calling in this essay? (See ¶6.) How does this approach help to establish her sarcastic voice?
6. Blakely is particularly good at taking an analogy and pushing it to ridiculous extremes. Examine what she has done with the administrator's reference to "apples and oranges" (¶6). What makes that exaggeration so effective? How does she use the same strategy with the concept of "psychic income?" Does she overdo this exaggeration (see ¶11–18)?

7. Why does Blakely seem apologetic about her behavior during her "conversion" (¶10)?
8. How does the final paragraph make its point through sarcasm? How could this paragraph—in fact the entire essay—have made the same point in a serious voice? Would it have been more or less effective?

TOPICS TO WRITE ABOUT

1. Write a sarcastic essay examining discriminatory work practices directed at teenagers. POTENTIAL AUDIENCES: teenagers/potential employers. POTENTIAL PURPOSES: to encourage them to stand up for their rights/to raise their awareness level and possibly instigate some change for the better.
2. Write a sarcastic essay about some unfair policy at your school in which you offer an unsatisfactory justification for the policy as if it were satisfactory. POTENTIAL AUDIENCES: other students at the school/the school's administration. POTENTIAL PURPOSES: to start some organized activity toward implementing change/to make clear to them that students are not accepting their explanations as valid.

The Voice of Concern

As I read the morning paper over coffee and a doughnut today, I flipped to the editorial page. There I found the following things to read:

- Two members of the League of Women Voters urging voters to pass an amendment on the upcoming ballot
- A columnist writing about Central American politics, urging readers to examine the issues carefully before deciding which policy to support
- An editorial about a superpower summit, suggesting great caution on the part of the President
- An editorial and a letter to the editor about upcoming tax levies for public schools, urging voters to support the increases
- An editorial about U.S. defense spending, suggesting that wasted tax dollars could be saved through careful and close examination of contractors' bids
- Two letters to the editor about women's roles in the Catholic church, one urging support for the traditional church view, one criticizing the Pope
- A letter to the editor from the president of a neighborhood association complaining that the city's urban renewal policy has been unfair to her neighborhood and needs to be overhauled
- A letter to the editor about the local baseball team's recent firing of its general manager, criticizing the team for doing so and suggesting that fans show their disapproval
- A letter mocking the President for some of his recent actions

Just a typical day on the editorial page.

What all these pieces of writing share is that they are motivated by the writer's strong concern. I myself have written several letters to the editor over the years: once about a teachers' strike, once about my favorite baseball team, once about a movie review to which I objected, to name a few examples. Each time I wrote because I was concerned about the subject to such an extent that I wanted to—had to—share my ideas and feelings with others, and, in fact, because I wanted to influence others

113

with my ideas. The focus in such writing is outward, as the writer tries to reach her readers forcefully. Of course, the voice of concern is not restricted to editorials and letters to the editor, but these forms of writing should be quite familiar to you. Certainly, they are easy to find every day in the newspapers and magazines that you read.

CONCERN

Of course, many, perhaps even most, of the essays you have already read in *Model Voices* were written because writers were concerned with their subjects and because they wished to reach their readers. But I mean "concern" here in a specific way, as in "worried about," or "troubled about." And I mean "reach readers" in a particular way—as in "bring them to change their beliefs" or "move them to take action" or "increase their awareness."

The concern you will hear in the voices in this section of *Model Voices* is frequently motivated by anger. In fact, the major distinction I want to make in this section among the three voices—the embittered voice, the angry voice, and the persuasive voice—is based on the degree to which the writers control that motivating anger. Take a look at these cartoons on page 115.

If the rushing waters in these cartoons represent anger, then the three cartoons illustrate the differences I think you will see in the three voices in this section of the book.

The embittered voice. This voice is the angriest of the voices you will hear. The writer's concern with her subject is so strong that her anger has become a raging torrent, carrying her away on a tide of bitterness. The writing hurtles along, like the flood, going where it will, destroying whatever is in its path. In my morning paper, the letter mocking the President was an embittered one. The writer made fun of the President's show-business background but offered no suggestions about how he should change and did not really try to convince his readers to cease supporting any particular policy of the President's. He was concerned with what he had observed recently and was so angered that he wrote a rather nasty letter about it.

The angry voice. This voice of concern shows a writer who is still quite angry, but who is making an attempt to control her anger, like the little Dutch boy in the cartoon, in order to communicate an important point to her reader. One of the letters in my morning paper about women's roles in the Catholic church demonstrated the angry voice. The writer, a middle-aged man with a small daughter, was concerned that she be able to participate in the church in whatever way she wished

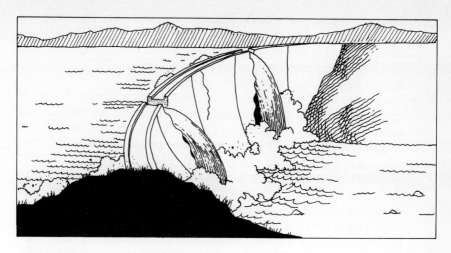

when she reached adulthood. That concern, however, was channeled into anger at recent pronouncements made by the Pope. The letter itself was not destructive, or even disrespectful to the Pope; the man was, however, clearly angry about the issue as he tried to communicate why he felt the church needed to change its views.

The persuasive voice. This voice demonstrates the most control. While the writer may have as much concern or even more for her subject than those writing in the embittered or angry voices, she has decided that changing readers' minds and actions is of greater significance. Thus this writer harnesses the energy of her anger, much as the dam and hydroturbine in the cartoon harness the water's energy, in order to be able to increase her readers' own concern with the subject. The other letter to the editor about women and the Catholic church in the paper today demonstrated the persuasive voice. This writer, a woman who has been a lifelong Catholic, was concerned that the traditions of the church were being attacked by those without enough reverence for those traditions. I gathered that she felt quite angry about the subject, but I could not hear that anger. Instead, what I heard was an attempt to be persuasive as she tried to get her readers to rethink their own positions on this issue. She acknowledged that times had changed since the early days of the church, and she agreed that women might well feel frustrated. But her final point was that tradition offers stability, and that in a world so frequently unstable, religion was very necessary for her and many like her.

THREE FAMILIAR CONCERNS

But what is the point of reading such writing, of listening to the varied voices of concern? What can you learn from these voices? I think this section of *Model Voices* will reinforce important lessons about the rhetorical situation and its relationship to voice. Remember the equation you have seen before:

$$\text{Awareness of audience} +$$
$$\text{understanding of purpose} +$$
$$\text{attitude toward subject} = \text{voice}$$

This section of the book will stress three familiar concepts:

The importance of your audience. The entire idea of expressing your concern about a subject is to communicate that concern to other people. You are no longer interested in making the readers smile or laugh. Your interest when you use the embittered voice, the angry voice, or the persuasive voice is to *involve* your reader, to make that reader feel the same concern that you do. As you write in the voice of concern, you will need always to be aware of the effect of your writing upon your reader.

The importance of your purpose. While the persuasive voice harnesses the anger or concern of a writer in an effort to influence readers, the embittered voice, to take the other extreme, is more concerned with communicating the strong sense of disapproval, the anger itself felt by the writer. But in all three voices, the writing itself matters intensely to the writer because she wants to have an effect on her readers. Whether that purpose is to raise the readers' sense of moral outrage to the same level as the writer's or to provoke the readers into signing a petition or writing to their legislators, it is this purpose that produces the writing in the first place.

The importance of your attitude toward your subject. The attitude you take toward the material about which you are writing has a tremendous impact not only on the voice of the writing, but also on your readers. If you wish to be persuasive, if that is your purpose, you must consider the effects of an embittered-sounding voice, for example. In order to achieve your purpose with the audience you have in mind, you will need to create an appropriate tone. The fellow who was so infuriated at the President did not really care if he changed the minds of his readers; he wanted to voice his outrage, let others know how angry he had become. He sounded embittered; I got the message. Although he didn't influence my own opinion one way or the other, I don't think he was interested in doing so. He made the right choice here, based on his own attitude toward the subject.

So as you read the writing in Section Two and try writing in these voices yourself, you should be gaining an ever increasing sense of just how important it is to a piece of writing for writers to know their audience and their purpose. While you may begin with nothing but that strong sense of concern, you need to become increasingly aware of whom you wish to write for and how you want them to respond. The concern you feel may emerge as bitterness or as anger, or you may control it enough to be persuasive—but unless you consider your audience and your purpose at some point in the writing, you will have a difficult time making it an effective piece of writing. We all have strong concerns about a variety of topics. In this section of the book, you can use those strong concerns as the subject of your writing. And then one day soon perhaps people in your town will sit down to a cup of coffee, a doughnut, and *your* ideas on the editorial page of the morning paper.

5

The Embittered Voice

WHEN ANGER ISN'T FUNNY

I remember as a teenager I would watch a popular late-night talk show and occasionally see as a guest a very unusual performer who called himself Brother Theodore. Brother Theodore's "performance" was unique. While he stood on stage with the microphone in front of him, the camera would zoom in for a close-up of his face, a middle-aged face with expressive, almost rubbery, features. Then for five or ten or fifteen minutes Theodore would harangue the audience. He would work himself into a rage as he spoke bitterly, free associating about politics, life, society, his own personal problems, the world around him. The audience's reactions were very interesting, for it seemed clear to me that they were having the same problem that I was having as a viewer at home: Should we laugh? Should we applaud? What do we do? Some audience members giggled but most were silent. Finally, Theodore would finish his "act," the audience would applaud, and that segment of the show would end.

There was something mesmerizing about Theodore, and I was not the only one entranced by his strange performance. Years later when I was working at a small magazine in New York, one of my colleagues, a writer with a quirky sense of humor, discovered Theodore performing at a small coffee house, approached him, and offered to become Theodore's manager! He had been so impressed as a young viewer with Theodore's uniqueness that he could not resist trying to help the performer resurrect his career. I asked the writer just what Theodore was—a comedian, a would-be prophet, or what? He couldn't really answer me. "Theodore is Theodore," he told me.

In Chapters 3 and 4 we read essays by angry writers, writers who converted their anger into satire and sarcasm, writers whose anger was funny. Those writers frequently adopted roles—personas—in order to make their points in their essays. I think Theodore too had adopted a persona. But his

118

anger was so vehement, so bitter, that as viewers we were unable to see much humor in his performance. The anger overpowered the humor.

I remember Theodore at times when I read an essay that has a satirical thrust to it but seems significantly devoid of humor, an essay in which the dominant voice is an embittered one. The motivation of the writers of these embittered essays is often the same motivation that serves as a catalyst for writers using the satiric voice or the sarcastic voice: they wish to change and improve things. But the degree of their concern with their topics prevents their voices from being truly humorous either because they, like the dam, cannot harness that concern or because they have no desire to do so.

While literary critics may not place much emphasis on the humorous content of a piece of satire, I think we as readers probably do. Just as the studio audience did not laugh at Brother Theodore's anger, so as readers we too may find ourselves interested in, troubled by, concerned with what we are reading in a piece of writing without feeling any impulse to smile or laugh. That's why I have separated the embittered voice from the earlier sarcastic and satirical voices, even though the essays in this section of the book may, in the classical sense, be satires and may even employ sarcasm.

AGGRESSION AND HOSTILITY

The important difference I want to note, then, is the degree of concern one can hear in essays that display an embittered voice. The writers care very deeply about their subjects, so much so that their disappointment and frustration about those subjects lead them to sound, well, "nasty" is about the best word I can come up with. The embittered voice is filled with *aggression* and *hostility*. That aggression is generally directed at a specific target: the government in power, a political party, a single individual, a group of people with a shared set of beliefs, society's attitudes toward a particular issue. Recently in class a student commented about one of her classmate's comic essays that she felt it might offend his audience. We talked for awhile about the aggressive nature of humorous writing, about how so many jokes are at the expense of some individual or some group of people, and about how those people might take offense. The conclusion we reached, however, was that the writer himself finally must make a judgment about whether the humor is worth the potential offense. If it is not, then the jokes are "toned down," the essay becomes less aggressive, less hostile.

However, in the essays you are about to read, the writers have made a different decision; they have not "toned down" their essays. In fact, the aggressive and hostile qualities of the writing dominate, often to the point where there is virtually no humor left in the voice at all.

Let me illustrate my point another way. We have all probably experienced at some point in life a bit of good-natured ribbing by our friends. One

way in which people show affection for one another is to poke fun, even sarcastic fun, at one another as if to say "Hey, you and I are secure enough in
our feelings for each other that we can make—and take—a joke at each other's expense." But the same sarcastic joking comment made by someone
who is not really a friend is no longer funny; it hurts instead. That latter
situation is what you will see in the essays in this chapter. There is nothing
good-natured about essays in the embittered voice; the sarcasm is so pointed
that it "draws blood," and few people are so good-humored that they laugh
at the sight of blood.

A LETTER TO THE EDITOR

Let's suppose that someone you knew had an unpleasant experience at the
local Motor Vehicle Bureau office while renewing his driver's license. He
might write a letter to the editor:

> Dear Editor,
>
> I recently experienced my annual ordeal at the Motor Vehicle Bureau
> in an attempt to renew my driver's license. I've seen slow-moving clerks
> before—usually at other offices of the MVB I should add—but this motley
> crew took the honors. Too embroiled in their own fascinating personal
> conversations with one another—about Dorrie's new designer hairdo and
> Waldo's new imported reptile skin boots—they couldn't be bothered talking
> with someone like me, a balding, tax-paying worker (wearing ordinary U.S.-
> made work shoes no less) who was trying to run an errand on his short
> lunch break.
>
> I asked if I could return after work to have my photo taken, a question
> greeted by a blank stare so profound that I suspect this clerk will soon be
> promoted to supervisor. Finally, the clerk deigned to say to her supervisor,
> "This one wants to know if he can come back for the picture later." "This
> one" certainly did not wish to return later for the enjoyment of the witty
> company....

The sarcasm in this letter is not really very funny; the writer is so frustrated that he has become bitter. And his voice sounds like it. He is not in
any laughing mood.

STEREOTYPING

One thing to be concerned about as you read the essays in this chapter is the
degree of fairness you sense in each piece. Motivated by sincere anger so

strong that it overpowers any hint of humor, these writers may not always be careful to be fair to their victims. Quite the opposite may be true in fact as some embittered-sounding essays seem intentionally unfair. *Stereotyping* may result, with certain people or groups of people being unfairly described as if they were all identical to one another. You may wish to ask whether the essay's point, the idea it wishes to communicate, is important enough to justify such stereotyping. Are, for example, all Motor Vehicle Bureau clerks as insensitive as the ones described in the letter above? Of course not. But some are. Has the writer created an unfair stereotype? That's a worthwhile question to consider.

THE STRAW MAN APPROACH

Suppose that while writing this letter to the editor, the writer had made an effort to appear fair by quoting from a brochure for new drivers written by the Motor Vehicle Bureau. What if this brochure began with a message from the Bureau chief emphasizing the importance to road safety of being courteous on the road? The letter writer might well take these well-intentioned words and use them to mock the lack of courtesy he experienced at the Bureau's hands. This strategy is known as *the straw man approach,* an effective, if rather hostile, way to structure a piece of writing.

You have probably seen *The Wizard of Oz.* Remember the straw man? He was quite floppy, always buckling at the knees, easily bowled over, a ready victim for a strong wind or a hard push. In a piece of writing, a weak opposing point of view may easily be set up as a straw man as the writer presents the opponent's views and then easily and firmly knocks the feet out from under that point of view, much as one could knock over the straw man in the movie. This is an appealing strategy to a writer using an embittered voice because it allows her to focus her hostility very specifically on an opponent, and it makes the reasons for that hostility quite clear. And at the same time it makes the essay seem more fair, at least initially.

A POWERFUL VOICE

I'm afraid that what I've written here sounds negative and critical, but that is not my intention at all. There is a time and place for writing in an embittered voice. It has always been a perfectly legitimate way of writing about a topic, as my inclusion in this chapter of one classic essay written more than two centuries ago demonstrates. I suspect that writing a letter as bitter as the one you've read above would not be terribly effective in bringing about changes; it would be a case of using a sledgehammer to kill an ant, and I doubt whether the clerks' behavior would change as a result of the letter.

But the letter did a fine job of expressing strong displeasure over the situation at the MVB.

Some situations do not permit their writers to write humorously or meditatively or even persuasively. Some writers feel their anger so strongly that they cannot help but sound embittered, and the strength of their feelings is not necessarily a flaw in their writing. Satiric voices are neither better nor worse than embittered voices, simply different. As *Model Voices* has been arguing all along, the combination of subject matter, attitude, audience, and purpose creates the rhetorical situation for a given piece of writing. In this chapter, writers with strong and deep concerns, with a sense of growing frustration at the wrongs they perceive around them, have found themselves in rhetorical situations that lead to an embittered voice. These are harsh voices, but powerful ones, voices worth listening to.

A Modest Proposal
Jonathan Swift

Jonathan Swift (1667–1745) is best known for his satire *Gulliver's Travels*
(1726). Although Gulliver and his travels to the lands of the Lilliputians and
other fantastic creatures have frequently been treated as children's stories in
recent times, Swift's book is actually a rather pointed—and at times harsh—
satire of the follies of humanity, particularly in the last of Gulliver's voyages
when he visits the land of the rational horses, the Houyhnhnms.

"A Modest Proposal," published in 1729, and subtitled "For preventing
the children of poor people in Ireland from being a burden to their parents or
country, and for making them beneficial to the public," focuses on the severe
plight of the Irish peasantry in the early part of the eighteenth century, when
overpopulation and poverty were pressing social concerns.

QUESTIONS ABOUT IDEAS

1. How does our society handle the problems of poverty and hunger? Are
   our solutions adequate? How appropriate would a satirical essay be in today's world if it proposed the same solution Swift offers in "A Modest
   Proposal"?
2. Why has Swift chosen such a horrifying proposal to protest the plight of
   the Irish? How effective is his strategy?
3. "A Modest Proposal" has been called by one critic "perhaps the most
   famous satiric essay in the English language." How do you account for its
   fame? Why is an essay written more than 250 years ago still being reprinted in college textbooks every year?

It is a melancholy object to those who walk through this great town or   1
travel in the country, when they see the streets, the roads, and cabin doors,
crowded with beggars of the female-sex, followed by three, four, or six children, all in rags and importuning every passenger for an alms. These mothers, instead of being able to work for their honest livelihood, are forced to
employ all their time in strolling to beg sustenance for their helpless infants,
who, as they grow up, either turn thieves for want of work, or leave their
dear native country to fight for the Pretender in Spain, or sell themselves to
the Barbadoes.

I think it is agreed by all parties that this prodigious number of chil-   2
dren in the arms, or on the backs, or at the heels of their mothers, and frequently of their fathers, is in the present deplorable state of the kingdom a
very great additional grievance; and therefore whoever could find out a fair,
cheap, and easy method of making these children sound, useful members of

the commonwealth would deserve so well of the public as to have his statue set up for a preserver of the nation.

But my intention is very far from being confined to provide only for   3 the children of professed beggars; it is of a much greater extent, and shall take in the whole number of infants at a certain age who are born of parents in effect as little able to support them as those who demand our charity in the streets.

As to my own part, having turned my thoughts for many years upon   4 this important subject, and maturely weighed the several schemes of other projectors, I have always found them grossly mistaken in their computation. It is true, a child just dropped from its dam may be supported by her milk for a solar year, with little other nourishment; at most not above the value of two shillings, which the mother may certainly get, or the value in scraps, by her lawful occupation of begging; and it is exactly at one year old that I propose to provide for them in such a manner as instead of being a charge upon their parents or the parish, or wanting food and raiment for the rest of their lives, they shall on the contrary contribute to the feeding, and partly to the clothing, of many thousands.

There is likewise another great advantage in my scheme, that it will   5 prevent those voluntary abortions, and that horrid practice of women murdering their bastard children, alas, too frequent among us, sacrificing the poor innocent babes, I doubt, more to avoid the expense than the shame, which would move tears and pity in the most savage and inhuman breast.

The number of souls in this kingdom being usually reckoned one million and a half, of these I calculate there may be about two hundred thousand couple whose wives are breeders; from which number I subtract thirty thousand couples who are able to maintain their own children, although I apprehend there cannot be so many under the present distresses of the kingdom; but this being granted, there will remain an hundred and seventy thousand breeders. I again subtract fifty thousand for those women who miscarry, or whose children die by accident or disease within the year. There only remain an hundred and twenty thousand children of poor parents annually born. The question therefore is, how this number shall be reared and provided for, which, as I have already said, under the present situation of affairs, is utterly impossible by all the methods hitherto proposed. For we can neither employ them in handicraft or agriculture; we neither build houses (I mean in the country) nor cultivate land. They can very seldom pick up a livelihood by stealing till they arrive at six years old, except where they are of towardly parts; although I confess they learn the rudiments much earlier, during which time they can however be looked upon only as probationers, as I have been informed by a principal gentleman in the country of Cavan, who protested to me that he never knew above one or two instances under the age of six, even in a part of the kingdom so renowned for the quickest proficiency in that art.

I am assured by our merchants that a boy or girl before twelve years   7
old is no salable commodity; and even when they come to this age they will
not yield above three pounds, or three pounds and a half a crown at most on
the Exchange; which cannot turn to account either to the parents or the
kingdom, the charge of nutriment and rags having been at least four times
that value.

I shall now therefore humbly propose my own thoughts, which I hope   8
will not be liable to the least objection.

I have been assured by a very knowing American of my acquaintance   9
in London, that a young healthy child well nursed is at a year old a most
delicious, nourishing, and wholesome food, whether stewed, roasted, baked
or boiled; and I make no doubt that it will equally serve in a fricassee or a
ragout.

I do therefore humbly offer it to public consideration that of the hun- 10
dred and twenty thousand children, already computed, twenty thousand
may be reserved for breed, whereof only one fourth part to be males, which
is more than we allow to sheep, black cattle, or swine; and my reason is that
these children are seldom the fruits of marriage, a circumstance not much
regarded by our savages, therefore one male will be sufficient to serve four
females. That the remaining hundred thousand may at a year old be offered
in sale to the persons of quality and fortune through the kingdom, always
advising the mother to let them suck plentifully in the last month, so as to
render them plump and fat for a good table. A child will make two dishes at
an entertainment for friends; and when the family dines alone, the fore or
hind quarter will make a reasonable dish, and seasoned with a little pepper
or salt will be very good boiled on the fourth day, especially in winter.

I have reckoned upon a medium that a child just born will weigh 11
twelve pounds, and in a solar year if tolerably nursed increaseth to twenty-
eight pounds.

I grant this food will be somewhat dear, and therefore very proper for 12
landlords, who, as they have already devoured most of the parents, seem to
have the best title to the children.

Infant's flesh will be in season throughout the year, but more plentiful 13
in March, and a little before and after. For we are told by a grave author, an
eminent French physician, that fish being a prolific diet, there are more children born in Roman Catholic countries about nine months after Lent than at
any other season: therefore, reckoning a year after Lent, the markets will be
more glutted than usual, because the number of popish infants is at least
three to one in this kingdom; and therefore it will have one other collateral
advantage, by lessening the number of Papists among us.

I have already computed the charge of nursing a beggar's child (in 14
which list I reckon all cottagers, laborers, and four fifths of the farmers) to
be about two shillings per annum, rags included: and I believe no gentleman
would repine to give ten shillings for the carcass of a good fat child, which,

as I have said, will make four dishes of excellent nutritive meat, when he hath only some particular friend or his own family to dine with him. Thus the squire will learn to be a good landlord, and grow popular among the tenants; the mother will have eight shillings net profit, and be fit for work till she produces another child.

Those who are more than thrifty (as I must confess the times require) 15 may flay the carcass; the skin of which artificially dressed will make admirable gloves for ladies, and summer boots for fine gentlemen.

As to our city of Dublin, shambles may be appointed for this purpose 16 in the most convenient parts of it, and butchers we may be assured will not be wanting; although I rather recommend buying the children alive, and dressing them hot from the knife as we do roasting pigs.

A very worthy person, a true lover of his country, and whose virtues I 17 highly esteem, was lately pleased in discoursing on this matter to offer a refinement upon my scheme. He said that many gentlemen of this kingdom, having of late destroyed their deer, he conceived that the want of venison might be well supplied by the bodies of young lads and maidens, not exceeding fourteen years of age nor under twelve, so great a number of both sexes in every county being now ready to starve for want of work and service; and these to be disposed of by their parents, if alive, or otherwise by their nearest relations. But with due reference to so excellent a friend and so deserving a patriot, I cannot be altogether in his sentiments; for as to the males, my American acquaintance assured me from frequent experience that their flesh was generally tough and lean, like that of our schoolboys, by continual exercise, and their taste disagreeable; and to fatten them would not answer the charge. Then as to the females, it would, I think with humble submission, be a loss to the public, because they soon would become breeders themselves: and besides, it is not improbable that some scrupulous people might be apt to censure such a practice (although indeed very unjustly) as a little bordering upon cruelty; which, I confess, hath always been with me the strongest objection against any project, how well soever intended.

But in order to justify my friend, he confessed that this expedient was 18 put into his head by the famous Psalmanazar, a native of the island Formosa, who came from thence to London above twenty years ago, and in conversation told my friend that in his country when any young person happened to be put to death, the executioner sold the carcass to persons of quality as a prime dainty; and that in his time the body of a plump girl of fifteen, who was crucified for an attempt to poison the emperor, was sold to his Imperial Majesty's prime minister of state, and other great mandarins of the court, in joints from the gibbet, at four hundred crowns. Neither indeed can I deny that if the same use were made of several plump young girls in this town, who without one single groat to their fortunes cannot stir abroad without a chair, and appear at the playhouse and assemblies in foreign fineries which they never will pay for, the kingdom would not be the worse.

Some persons of a desponding spirit are in great concern about that 19
vast number of poor people who are aged, diseased, or maimed, and I
have been desired to employ my thoughts what course may be taken to
ease the nation of so grievous an encumbrance. But I am not in the least
pain upon that matter, because it is very well known that they are every
day dying and rotting by cold and famine, and filth and vermin, as fast as
can be reasonably expected. And as to the younger laborers, they are now
in almost as hopeful a condition. They cannot get work, and consequently pine away for want of nourishment to a degree that if at any time
they are accidentally hired to common labor, they have no strength to
perform it; and thus the country and themselves are happily delivered
from the evils to come.

I have too long digressed, and therefore shall return to my subject. I 20
think the advantages by the proposal which I have made are obvious and
many, as well as of the highest importance.

For first, as I have already observed, it would greatly lessen the num- 21
ber of Papists, with whom we are yearly overrun, being the principal breeders of the nation as well as our most dangerous enemies; and who stay at
home on purpose to deliver the kingdom to the Pretender, hoping to take
their advantage by the absence of so many good Protestants, who have chosen rather to leave their country than to stay at home and pay tithes against
their conscience to an Episcopal curate.

Secondly, the poorer tenants will have something valuable of their 22
own, which by the law may be made liable to distress, and help to pay their
landlord's rent, their corn and cattle being already seized and money a thing
unknown.

Thirdly, whereas the maintenance of an hundred thousand children, 23
from two years old and upwards, cannot be computed at less than ten shillings a piece per annum, the nation's stock will be thereby increased fifty
thousand pounds per annum, besides the profit of a new dish introduced to
the tables of all gentlemen of fortune in the kingdom who have any refinement in taste. And the money will circulate among ourselves, the goods being entirely of our own growth and manufacture.

Fourthly, the constant breeders, besides the gain of eight shillings ster- 24
ling per annum by the sale of their children, will be rid of the charge of
maintaining them after the first year.

Fifthly, this food would likewise bring great custom to taverns, where 25
the vintners will certainly be so prudent as to procure the best receipts for
dressing it to perfection, and consequently have their houses frequented by
all the fine gentlemen, who justly value themselves upon their knowledge in
good eating; and a skillful cook, who understands how to oblige his guests,
will contrive to make it as expensive as they please.

Sixthly, this would be a great inducement to marriage, which all wise 26
nations have either encouraged by rewards or enforced by laws and penal-

ties. It would increase the care and tenderness of mothers toward their children, when they were sure of a settlement for life to the poor babes, provided in some sort by the public, to their annual profit instead of expense. We should see an honest emulation among the married women, which of them could bring the fattest child to the market. Men would become as fond of their wives during the time of their pregnancy as they are now of their mares in foal, their cows in calf, or sows when they are ready to farrow; nor offer to beat or kick them (as is too frequent a practice) for fear of a miscarriage.

Many other advantages might be enumerated. For instance, the addi- 27 tion of some thousand carcasses in our exportation of barreled beef, the propagation of swine's flesh, and improvement in the art of making good bacon, so much wanted among us by the great destruction of pigs, too frequent at our tables, which are no way comparable in taste or magnificence to a well-grown, fat yearling child, which roasted whole will make a considerable figure at a lord mayors's feast or any other public entertainment. But this and many others I omit, being studious of brevity.

Supposing that one thousand families in this city would be constant 28 customers for infants' flesh, besides others who might have it at merry meetings, particularly weddings and christenings, I compute that Dublin would take off annually about twenty thousand carcasses, and the rest of the kingdom (where probably they will be sold somewhat cheaper) the remaining eighty thousand.

I can think of no one objection that will possibly be raised against this 29 proposal, unless it should be urged that the number of people will be thereby much lessened in the kingdom. This I freely own, and it was indeed one principal design in offering it to the world. I desire the reader will observe, that I calculate my remedy for this one individual kingdom of Ireland and for no other that ever was, is, or I think ever can be upon earth. Therefore let no man talk to me of other expedients: of taxing our absentees at five shillings a pound: of using neither clothes nor household furniture except what is of our own growth and manufacture: of utterly rejecting the materials and instruments that promote foreign luxury: of curing the expensiveness of pride, vanity, idleness, and gaming in our women: of introducing a vein of parsimony, prudence, and temperance: of learning to love our country, in the want of which we differ even from Laplanders and the inhabitants of Topinamboo: of quitting our animosities and factions, nor acting any longer like the Jews, who were murdering one another at the very moment their city was taken: of being a little cautious not to sell our country and conscience for nothing: of teaching landlords to have at least one degree of mercy toward their tenants: lastly, of putting a spirit of honesty, industry, and skill into our shopkeepers; who, if a resolution could be now taken to buy only our native goods, would immediately unite to cheat and exact upon us in the price, the measure and the goodness, nor could ever yet be brought to make one fair proposal of just dealing, though often and earnestly invited to it.

Therefore I repeat, let no man talk to me of these and the like expedients, till he hath at least some glimpse of hope that there will ever be some hearty and sincere attempt to put them in practice. 30

But as to myself, having been wearied out for many years with offering vain, idle, visionary thoughts, and at length utterly despairing of success, I fortunately fell upon this proposal, which, as it is wholly new, so it hath something solid and real, of no expense and little trouble, full in our own power, and whereby we can incur no danger in disobliging England. For this kind of commodity will not bear exportation, the flesh being of too tender a consistence to admit a long continuance in salt, although perhaps I could name a country which would be glad to eat up our whole nation without it. 31

After all, I am not so violently bent upon my own opinions as to reject any offer proposed by wise men, which shall be found equally innocent, cheap, easy, and effectual. But before something of that kind shall be advanced in contradiction to my scheme, and offering a better, I desire the author or authors will be pleased maturely to consider two points. First, as things now stand, how they will be able to find food and raiment for an hundred thousand useless mouths and backs. And secondly, there being a round million of creatures in human figure throughout this kingdom, whose sole subsistence put into a common stock would leave them in debt two millions of pounds sterling, adding those who are beggars by profession to the bulk of farmers, cottagers, and laborers, with their wives and children who are beggars in effect; I desire those politicians who dislike my overture, and may perhaps be so bold to attempt an answer, that they will first ask the parents of these mortals whether they would not at this day think it a great happiness to have been sold for food at a year old in the manner I prescribe, and thereby have avoided such a perpetual scene of misfortunes as they have since gone through by the oppression of landlords, the impossibility of paying rent without money or trade, the want of common sustenance, with neither house nor clothes to cover them from the inclemencies of the weather, and the most inevitable prospect of entailing the like or greater miseries upon their breed forever. 32

I profess, in the sincerity of my heart, that I have not the least personal interest in endeavoring to promote this necessary work, having no other motive than the public good of my country, by advancing our trade, providing for infants, relieving the poor, and giving some pleasure to the rich. I have no children by which I can propose to get a single penny; the youngest being nine years old, and my wife past childbearing. 33

QUESTIONS ABOUT THE RHETORICAL SITUATION

1. Whom do you think Swift wants to read his essay? What clues to his intended audience are there in the essay?
2. Certainly Swift has no intention of convincing readers to start practicing cannibalism. What then does he hope to accomplish by writing "A Modest Proposal"? What would be the appropriate response for his readers to have? What was your response to the essay?
3. How can you tell that this subject is a very important one to Swift? Is he taking the situation too seriously?
4. Toward whom is Swift's hostility directed in this essay? Find specific passages to support your answer.

QUESTIONS ABOUT THE ESSAY'S VOICE

1. What is the effect on the essay's voice of the first seven paragraphs, which serve as an introduction to the actual proposal itself in ¶9?
2. What is the purpose of ¶17, in which Swift rejects serving young teenagers for dinner? Notice his final sentence. What is its purpose in the essay?
3. In ¶19, Swift says that the aged, diseased, and maimed poor people are dying "as fast as can be reasonably expected." What attitude does the essay's speaker display here? Why does Swift create such a persona for the essay?
4. Swift presents the advantages of his proposal in a very organized and clear manner (¶21–26). Why does he take this approach to making his argument? How does this section of the essay help establish the essay's persona?
5. Does Swift's voice change in ¶29? Explain your answer. What is the purpose of this paragraph in the essay?
6. In ¶32, Swift suggests that the impoverished and starving beggars he describes would probably "think it a great happiness to have been sold for food at a year old." What is ironic about that statement? Can you find other equally bitter passages in the essay? Where?
7. "A Modest Proposal" is generally classified as a satire, yet I have included it in this chapter on the embittered voice. What argument can you make that it really belongs in either Chapter 3 or 4? What argument can you make that it belongs in this chapter? Be sure to address the question of how funny Swift's essay is.

TOPICS TO WRITE ABOUT

1. Write an embittered essay in which you offer a "modest proposal" for the solution of some social problem that needs to be addressed and has not

been. (For example, you could propose that the national debt be reduced by the federal government's sale of national landmarks such as the Statue of Liberty, Mount Rushmore, and the Washington Monument to Japan or West Germany.) POTENTIAL AUDIENCES: government officials/other citizens. POTENTIAL PURPOSES: to offer them "help" in beginning to solve the problem/to make them feel guilty about their own lack of concern about the problem.

2. Write a "modest proposal" offering a solution to a problem on your campus. POTENTIAL AUDIENCES: campus administrators/the student body. POTENTIAL PURPOSES: to make them aware of how strongly you feel about the need to address the problem/to stimulate them to become more active in seeking a solution to the problem.

Real Democrats Don't Eat Quiche
Ishmael Reed

Ishmael Reed is a novelist whose books include *The Free-Lance Pallbearers, Yellow Back Radio Broke Down, Mumbo Jumbo,* and *The Terrible Twos.* Born in Chattanooga, Tennessee, Reed has also published several books of poems. He has been a Guggenheim fellow, a National Endowment for the Arts writing fellow, and a recipient of awards for his writing from the National Institute of Arts and Letters and the American Civil Liberties Union.

"Real Democrats Don't Eat Quiche" first appeared in *The Nation* in April of 1985 and comments on the Presidential election of 1984, which pitted Republican incumbent Ronald Reagan against the Democratic nominee, former Vice President Walter Mondale.

QUESTIONS ABOUT IDEAS

1. The political campaign described by Reed in his essay is decided by advertising and television appearances. To what extent is he exaggerating the importance in politics of the media? How appropriate a role do the media play in Presidential elections?

2. Bernhard Goetz became known as a symbol of vigilante justice as a result of his actions in a New York City subway station. To many people, Goetz was a hero. Why do you think that is the case? Should Goetz be viewed as a hero? Why or why not?

3. What basic problems does Reed feel the Democrats are facing as they prepare for the next Presidential election? To what extent are the prob-

lems discussed in this essay common to all political parties rather than just to the Democrats?

Despite his gallant and civilized attempt to win the Presidency, Walter 1
Mondale has been criticized by a number of columnists for his inability to control what they call special-interest groups. For the Democrats to regain the support of white males, more than 60 percent of whom voted for the Republican ticket, they argue, the Democrats must cease to be the party of wimps, a reputation they acquired during the campaign of 1984.

The Democrats can accomplish this in 1988 by nominating two men 2
who've proved that they will have no truck with minorities and "San Francisco Democrats," a ticket that will woo the white Chrysler-convertible-driving fraternity brothers and the he-men who boil beans in the kitchens of their Winnebagos and shoot bears from helicopters.

By nominating Bernhard Hugo Goetz for President and former San 3
Francisco Supervisor Dan White for Vice President, the Democrats will send a clear signal to millions of virile Americans that the party is abreast of the times, no longer a dispenser of milky, outdated New Deal mush.

Goetz became a hero to millions of potential voters by shooting four 4
young blacks—two of them in the back—when they "accosted" him by asking for $5. According to early news reports, three were carrying sharpened screwdrivers, though New York *Daily News* columnist Jimmy Breslin said on the CNN show *Crossfire* that the screwdrivers weren't sharpened. As for those who felt that Goetz's reaction was way out of proportion to the crime—assuming it can be established that a crime was committed—well, what do you expect from those epicene supporters of secular humanism and other wimpy philosophies?

Dan White showed his opposition to the weak-sister political ideas of 5
the Democratic left by assassinating Harvey Milk, a gay Supervisor, and Mayor George Moscone, a charismatic Democrat who brought the locked-out into San Francisco City Hall. Some say that had he lived, Moscone would have become Governor of California or a candidate for national office.

White's lawyer said that the defendant, who finished off Moscone 6
while he lay wounded from earlier gunshot wounds, killed the two men because he had eaten too many Twinkies. The Democrats can expect large contributions to the Goetz-White ticket from the manufacturers of junk food.

The 1988 Republican ticket, composed of Vice President George Bush 7
and Representative Jack Kemp, won't have a chance against Goetz-White. During his debate with Goetz, a poised Bush will display an impressive knowledge of both foreign and domestic affairs. But he will lose the debate in one dramatic moment when Goetz will turn to him and say, "You only tried to kick a little ass; I went out and burned some." Bush will have no rejoinder, and in his network commentary following the debate, George Will

will award the debate to Goetz and will describe his dramatic flourish as truly Hobbesian.

Although the Republicans will run on a complicated platform, Goetz 8 and White will be vague about theirs, or limit themselves to a couple of promises. Maybe the Army of God will be appointed to screen all potential Supreme Court nominees, that is if we need a Supreme Court. Hell, what's wrong with the law of the jungle?

As for foreign policy, Grenada already having been occupied, maybe 9 the pair will promise to send the marines into Berkeley, California, to take care of those City Council members who are reluctant to salute the flag.

If support for the Goetz-White ticket falls off as Election Day ap- 10 proaches, the team can always galvanize the voters by staging some sort of electrifying event. Perhaps Goetz can shoot some young black patrons of a video-game arcade, saying he was once accosted there, or, if he wants to take the high road and leave the hatchet job—or shall we say trigger job—to his Vice-Presidential nominee, White can always get loaded on candy, sneak into the basement window of some City Hall and correct a left-leaning mayor the way he corrected George Moscone, who didn't even have a screwdriver to protect himself.

The Republicans will spend millions on their campaign; the Goetz- 11 White ticket will cost very little. A full-page advertisement in the *National Enquirer* with the slogan "You Know Where We Stand," or "Why Not the Worst?" or, a week before the election, "Vote Tuesday: Make Their Day," will do.

President Goetz's first appointment will be George Will as press secre- 12 tary. During his first news conference Will will admit that he was the person who suggested that Goetz challenge Bush on who was the better "ass-kicker"—the challenge that some will say gave the debate, and thus the election, to Goetz. Will will then comment on the morality of the new "state of nature" Administration, quoting seventeenth-century British philosopher Thomas Hobbes, who was also a bootlicker for royalty. In a wink at traditional values, Washington will be renamed Dodge City, but the biggest surprise will come after pollsters analyze the voting trends. The black backlash that was expected against Goetz and White will have failed to materialize. Millions of blacks like Clint Eastwood, too.

QUESTIONS ABOUT THE RHETORICAL SITUATION

1. Is Reed writing to Democrats, Republicans, conservatives, moderates, liberals, or readers of all political persuasions? Is he writing only to readers with a strong interest in politics and current events? Explain your answers.

2. Is Reed writing this essay simply to get something off his chest, to release

his anger, or does he have some other purpose in mind also? What might that other purpose be?

3. Why do you suppose Reed is so angered by this subject? In fact, about what subjects is he angry in this essay besides recent criticism of Walter Mondale's campaign?

QUESTIONS ABOUT THE ESSAY'S VOICE

1. Is the essay at all funny? Where? If not, which parts of Reed's essay come closest to being humorous? If the essay is funny, does it really belong in Chapters 2, 3, or 4?
2. Which parts of this essay are quite the opposite of funny? To what extent is Reed's essay tasteless or offensive? Why would he risk being either tasteless or offensive in the essay? How effective is this strategy?
3. In ¶2, Reed characterizes white male voters in rather derogatory terms. What other groups does Reed disparage? Are his exaggerations fair? Is he stereotyping?
4. George Will is a conservative newspaper columnist. Thomas Hobbes (1588–1679) was a British philosopher whose view of government included a defense of the rights of an absolute monarch. Why does Reed bring these two references into his essay?
5. What is the straw man in Reed's essay? How does he use the straw man approach to set up his entire essay?
6. In ¶8, Reed asks a rhetorical question. How would his persona in this essay answer that question? How do you think Reed himself would answer the question?
7. Reed's title is an allusion to a best-selling humor book entitled *Real Men Don't Eat Quiche,* which made fun of men whose behavior had changed as a result of the women's movement. How is this title an appropriate one for Reed's essay?
8. Why does Reed's essay end as it does? What effect on your answer does it have to learn that Reed himself is black?

TOPICS TO WRITE ABOUT

1. Write an embittered letter to the editor about some local political issue that upsets you. POTENTIAL AUDIENCES: readers of your hometown newspaper/readers of your campus newspaper. POTENTIAL PURPOSE: to express your anger and stir up opposition.
2. Write an embittered essay focusing on someone held up by the public for praise whom you feel does not deserve that praise. POTENTIAL AUDIENCES: the public figure himself or herself/the general reading public. POTENTIAL

PURPOSES: to let him or her know that not all members of the public approve of his or her behavior/to force them to reconsider their adulation.

Why I Want a Wife
Judy Syfers

Judy Syfers was born in 1937 in San Francisco and earned a Bachelor of Fine Arts degree in painting at the University of Iowa in 1962. Hopeful of pursuing graduate degrees in painting as preparation for a university teaching career, Syfers was discouraged by male instructors who advised her that, as a woman, she needed to seek work as a high school teacher. Syfers dropped out of school, married, and had two children. Subsequently divorced, she returned to live in San Francisco.

Syfers has published articles on topics such as union organizing and abortion but remains best known for this essay. "Why I Want a Wife" was originally published in 1971 in the very first issue of *Ms.* magazine.

QUESTIONS ABOUT IDEAS

1. How accurate a depiction of a "wife" is Syfers' essay in the late 1980s, close to two decades after it was first written? Has this essay become dated?
2. Syfers' essay is frequently described as a piece of feminist writing. Why? Can you make an argument that Syfers' central concern need not be considered a feminist one? How would you do so?
3. What would be a more appropriate set of duties for a wife than the ones to which Syfers objects? Why?
4. Would you, as Syfers suggests in her final paragraph, want a "wife" like the one she has described? Why or why not?

I belong to that classification of people known as wives. I am A Wife. 1
And, not altogether incidentally, I am a mother.

Not too long ago a male friend of mine appeared on the scene from the 2
Midwest fresh from a recent divorce. He had one child, who is, of course, with his ex-wife. He is obviously looking for another wife. As I thought about him while I was ironing one evening, it suddenly occurred to me that I, too, would like to have a wife. Why do I want a wife?

I would like to go back to school so that I can become economically 3
independent, support myself, and, if need be, support those dependent

upon me. I want a wife who will work and send me to school. And while I am going to school I want a wife to take care of my children. I want a wife to keep track of the children's doctor and dentist appointments. And to keep track of mine, too. I want a wife to make sure my children eat properly and are kept clean. I want a wife who will wash the children's clothes and keep them mended. I want a wife who is a good nurturant attendant to my children, arranges for their schooling, makes sure that they have an adequate social life with their peers, takes them to the park, the zoo, etc. I want a wife who takes care of the children when they are sick, a wife who arranges to be around when the children need special care, because, of course, I cannot miss classes at school. My wife must arrange to lose time at work and not lose the job. It may mean a small cut in my wife's income from time to time, but I guess I can tolerate that. Needless to say, my wife will arrange and pay for the care of the children while my wife is working.

I want a wife who will take care of *my* physical needs. I want a wife 4 who will keep my house clean. A wife who will pick up after my children, a wife who will pick up after me. I want a wife who will keep my clothes clean, ironed, mended, replaced when need be, and who will see to it that my personal things are kept in their proper place so that I can find what I need the minute I need it. I want a wife who cooks the meals, a wife who is a *good* cook. I want a wife who will plan the menus, do the necessary grocery shopping, prepare the meals, serve them pleasantly, and then do the cleaning up while I do my studying. I want a wife who will care for me when I am sick and sympathize with my pain and loss of time from school. I want a wife to go along when our family takes a vacation so that someone can continue to care for me and my children when I need a rest and a change of scene.

I want a wife who will not bother me with rambling complaints about 5 a wife's duties. But I want a wife who will listen to me when I feel the need to explain a rather difficult point I have come across in my course of studies. And I want a wife who will type my papers for me when I have written them.

I want a wife who will take care of the details of my social life. When 6 my wife and I are invited out by my friends, I want a wife who will take care of the babysitting arrangements. When I meet people at school that I like and want to entertain, I want a wife who will have the house clean, will prepare a special meal, serve it to me and my friends, and not interrupt when I talk about the things that interest me and my friends. I want a wife who will have arranged that the children are fed and ready for bed before my guests arrive so that the children do not bother us. I want a wife who takes care of the needs of my guests so that they feel comfortable, who makes sure that they have an ashtray, that they are passed the hors d'oeuvres, that they are offered a second helping of the food, that their wine glasses are replenished when necessary, that their coffee is served to them as they like it. And I want a wife who knows that sometimes I need a night out by myself.

I want a wife who is sensitive to my sexual needs, a wife who makes 7
love passionately and eagerly when I feel like it, a wife who makes sure that
I am satisfied. And, of course, I want a wife who will not demand sexual
attention when I am not in the mood for it. I want a wife who assumes the
complete responsibility for birth control, because I do not want more children. I want a wife who will remain sexually faithful to me so that I do not
have to clutter up my intellectual life with jealousies. And I want a wife who
understands that *my* sexual needs may entail more than strict adherence to
monogamy. I must, after all, be able to relate to people as fully as possible.

If, by chance, I find another person more suitable as a wife than the 8
wife I already have, I want the liberty to replace my present wife with another one. Naturally, I will expect a fresh, new life; my wife will take the
children and be solely responsible for them so that I am left free.

When I am through with school and have acquired a job, I want my 9
wife to quit working and remain at home so that my wife can more fully and
completely take care of a wife's duties.

My God, who *wouldn't* want a wife?   10

QUESTIONS ABOUT THE RHETORICAL SITUATION

1. Syfers' essay first appeared in *Ms.* magazine. However, it is reprinted frequently in books like this one. How appropriate was Syfers' essay for its
   original audience? Why? How appropriate is Syfers' essay for the more
   general readership of a college class? Why?
2. What reaction do you think Syfers sought from her original readers?
   Could her essay have been written by a man? Could her essay have been
   published in a men's magazine as is, or would it need to be changed
   somewhat? If so, what would she have to change?
3. What evidence can you find in the essay that Syfers is angry about the
   status of wives in American society?

QUESTIONS ABOUT THE ESSAY'S VOICE

1. In the first two paragraphs, Syfers sounds rather calm. What is the point
   of this beginning? Why does she capitalize the words "A Wife" in ¶1?
   Why does she add "of course" to the second sentence in ¶2? At which
   point in the essay does Syfers' voice begin to sound embittered?
2. Syfers writes "I want a wife" many times throughout the essay. What
   effort has she made to avoid becoming repetitious? You might examine
   her sentences carefully.
3. In ¶3, Syfers notes that child-raising duties might cut into the wife's income, "but I guess I can tolerate that." How does this comment help to

characterize the essay's persona? What does this attitude say about that persona?

4. What is Syfers' purpose in using italics in ¶4?

5. Which of the persona's attitudes seems most repugnant to you? Why?

6. What reasons does Syfers have for placing the essay's ideas in this sequence?

7. How would you describe the voice you hear in the essay's final paragraph? Why is this an effective way for Syfers to conclude her essay?

8. "Why I Want a Wife" is often referred to as a piece of satirical writing. What case can you make for its inclusion in Chapter 3 or 4 of *Model Voices*? What argument can you make that it is properly included in this chapter on the embittered voice? How does its voice compare with Delia Ephron's voice in Chapter 4 "Ex-Husbands for Sale"?

TOPICS TO WRITE ABOUT

1. Write an embittered essay entitled "Why I Want a Husband" or "Why I Want a Mother" or "Why I Want a Father," in which you address the stereotyped roles of husbands, mothers, fathers. POTENTIAL AUDIENCES: readers of *Playboy* magazine/readers of *Parents* magazine. POTENTIAL PURPOSE: to explain to a sympathetic audience how people who fill these roles are exploited in our society.

2. Write an embittered essay about magazines, books, television programs, films, that are directed at one small or specific special interest group (examples might include men's magazines, women's magazines, self-improvement books, hunting or fishing television shows, pornographic films). POTENTIAL AUDIENCE: readers who may not have paid much attention to such magazines, books, films. POTENTIAL PURPOSE: to point up the dangerous narrow-mindedness of such media productions.

Common Women
Philip Wylie

"Common Women" is an excerpt from Chapter 11 of *Generation of Vipers* (1942), a book described by one critic as "an abusive satire on American types, attitudes, and institutions." In the Introduction to the twentieth printing written in 1955, Wylie explained that he had chosen not to rewrite the book, even though the passage of time had led many readers to call it "dated." He explained, "It is not 'dated' but it does exhibit the lapse of time: much that is mere prediction in the text as it stands has become history." He goes on to say that rewriting a "book of opinion," as he views *Generation of Vipers*, is a "kind of cheating." Judge for yourself, thirty years after that twentieth printing, whether "Common Women" seems dated to you.

QUESTIONS ABOUT IDEAS

1. Can Wylie's essay be dismissed as a crude piece of sexist writing? Is he criticizing all women? Most women? Are there women at all like the ones he criticizes here? Are there men like these "moms"?
2. What is Wylie's basic complaint about the "moms" he attacks in his essay?
3. Has the passage of thirty years made this essay a dated one?
4. What do you think Judy Syfers would have to say about Wylie's essay?

Mom, however, is a great little guy. Pulling pants onto her by these 1 words, let us look at mom.

She is a middle-aged puffin with an eye like a hawk that has just seen 2 a rabbit twitch far below. She is about twenty-five pounds overweight, with no sprint, but sharp heels and a hard backhand which she does not regard as a foul but a womanly defense. In a thousand of her there is not sex appeal enough to budge a hermit ten paces off a rock ledge. She none the less spends several hundred dollars a year on permanents and transformations, pomades, cleansers, rouges, lipsticks, and the like—and fools nobody except herself. If a man kisses her with any earnestness, it is time for mom to feel for her pocketbook, and this occasionally does happen.

She smokes thirty cigarettes a day, chews gum, and consumes tons of 3 bonbons and petits fours. The shortening in the latter, stripped from pigs, sheep and cattle, shortens mom. She plays bridge with the stupid voracity of a hammerhead shark, which cannot see what it is trying to gobble but never stops snapping its jaws and roiling the waves with its tail. She drinks moderately, which is to say, two or three cocktails before dinner every night and a brandy and a couple of highballs afterwards. She doesn't count the two cocktails she takes before lunch when she lunches out, which is every day she can. On Saturday nights, at the club or in the juke joint, she loses count of her drinks and is liable to get a little tiddly, which is to say, shot or blind. But it is her man who worries about where to acquire the money while she worries only about how to spend it, so he has the ulcers and colitis and she has the guts of a bear; she can get pretty stiff before she topples.

Her sports are all spectator sports. 4

She was graduated from high school or a "finishing" school or even a 5 college in her distant past and made up for the unhappiness of compulsory education by sloughing all that she learned so completely that she could not

pass the final examination of a fifth grader. She reads the fiction in the three
women's magazines each month and occasionally skims through an article,
which usually angers her so that she gets other moms to skim through it, and
then they have a session on the subject over a canister of spiked coffee in
order to damn the magazine, the editors, the author, and the silly girls who
run about these days. She reads two or three motion-picture fan magazines
also, and goes to the movies about two nights a week. If a picture does not
coincide precisely with her attitude of the moment, she converses through all
of it and so whiles away the time. She does not appear to be lecherous toward the moving photographs as men do, but that is because she is a realist
and a little shy on imagination. However, if she gets to Hollywood and encounters the flesh-and-blood article known as a male star, she and her sister
moms will run forward in a mob, wearing a joint expression that must make
God rue his invention of bisexuality and tear the man's clothes from his
body, yea, verily, down to his B.V.D.'s.

Mom is organization-minded. Organizations, she has happily discov-   6
ered, are intimidating to all men, not just to mere men. They frighten politicians to sniveling servility and they terrify pastors; they bother bank pres-
idents and they pulverize school boards. Mom has many such organizations,
the real purpose of which is to compel an abject compliance of her environs
to her personal desires. With these associations and committees she has double parking ignored, for example. With them she drives out of the town and
the state, if possible, all young harlots and all proprietors of places where
"questionable" young women (though why they are called that—being of all
women the least in question) could possibly foregather, not because she
competes with such creatures but because she contrasts so unfavorably with
them. With her clubs (a solid term!) she causes bus lines to run where they
are convenient for her rather than for workers, plants flowers in sordid spots
that would do better with sanitation, snaps independent men out of office
and replaces them with clammy castrates, throws prodigious fairs and parties
for charity and gives the proceeds, usually about eight dollars, to the janitor
to buy the committee some beer for its headache on the morning after, and
builds clubhouses for the entertainment of soldiers where she succeeds in
persuading thousands of them that they are momsick and would rather talk
to her than take Betty into the shrubs. All this, of course, is considered social service, charity, care of the poor, civic reform, patriotism, and self-
sacrifice.

As an interesting sidelight, clubs afford mom an infinite opportunity   7
for nosing into other people's business. Nosing is not a mere psychological
ornament of her; it is a basic necessity. Only by nosing can she uncover all
incipient revolutions against her dominion and so warn and assemble her co-
cannibals.

Knowing nothing about medicine, art, science, religion, law, sanita-   8
tion, civics, hygiene, psychology, morals, history, geography, poetry, liter-

ature, or any other topic except the all-consuming one of momism, she seldom has any especial interest in *what*, exactly, she is doing as a member of any of these endless organizations, so long as it is *something*.

I, who grew up as a "motherless" minister's son and hence was smoth- 9 ered in multimomism for a decade and a half, had an unusual opportunity to observe the phenomenon at zero range. Also, as a man stirring about in the cesspool of my society, I have been foolhardy enough to try, on occasion, to steer moms into useful work. For example, owing to the fact that there was no pasteurization law in Miami and hundreds of people were flecking the pavement with tubercular sputum, while scores, including my own wife, lay sick and miserable with undulant fever, I got a gaggle of these creatures behind a move toward a pasteurization law, only to find, within a few weeks, that there was a large, alarmed, and earnest committee at work in my wake to *prevent* the passage of any such law. This falange, fanned by the milk dealers, who would not even deliver the stuff if they could get their money without, had undone even that one small crusade because it had uncovered a quack doctor, unknown and unheard-of, who had printed the incandescent notion that cancer, the big boogie of the moms, was caused by the pasteurization of milk!

In the paragraph above I have given, I know, the golden tip for which 10 any moms able to read this volume have been searching all the long way. I had no mother: therefore, all my bitterness and—especially—this cruel and wanton attack of moms for which, they will doubtless think, I should be shot or locked up. Well, let them make the most of that. All mothers are not such a ravening purulence as they, and mine was not. Mine, I can show, felt much as I do about the thundering third sex, as do all good women, of whom there are still a few. But I have researched the moms, to the beady brains behind their beady eyes and to the stones in the center of their fat hearts. I am immune to their devotion because I have already had enough. Learning the hard way, I have found out that it is that same devotion which, at the altar, splits the lamb from his nave to his chaps. And none of the moms, at least, will believe that I am a lamb. Let them mark time on that.

In churches, the true purpose of organized momhood is to unseat bish- 11 ops, snatch the frocks off prelates, change rectors just for variety, cross-jet community gossip, take the customary organizational kudos out of the pot each for each, bestow and receive titles, and short-circuit one another.

Mom also has patriotism. If a war comes, this may even turn into a 12 genuine feeling and the departure of her son may be her means to grace in old age. Often, however, the going of her son is only an occasion for more show. She has, in that case, no deep respect for him. What he has permitted her to do to him has rendered him unworthy of consideration—and she has shown him none since puberty. She does not miss him—only his varletry— but over that she can weep interminably. I have seen the unmistakable evidence in a blue star mom of envy of a gold star mom: and I have a firsthand account by a woman of unimpeachable integrity, of the doings of a shipload of these super-moms-of-the-gold-star, en route at government expense to France to visit the graves of their sons, which I forbear to set down here, because it is a document of such naked awfulness that, by publishing it, I would be inciting to riot, and the printed thing might even rouse the dead soldiers and set them tramping like Dunsany's idol all the way from Flanders to hunt and haunt their archenemy progenitrices—who loved them—to death.

But, peace or war, the moms have another kind of patriotism that, in the department of the human spirit, is identical to commercialized vice because it captures a good thing and doles it out for the coin of unctuous pride—at the expense of deceased ancestors rather than young female offspring. By becoming a Daughter of this historic war or that, a woman makes herself into a sort of madam who fills the coffers of her ego with the prestige that has accrued to the doings of others. A frantic emptiness of those coffers provides the impulse for the act. There are, of course, other means of filling them, but they are difficult, and mom never does anything that is difficult—either the moving of a piano or the breaking of a nasty habit.   13

Some legionnaires accept, in a similar way, accolade due their associates only. But legionnaires learned a little wisdom, since they still can function in ways that have some resemblance to normality. Furthermore, competition with the legions from the new war will probably make veritable sages out of thousands.   14

But mom never meets competition. Like Hitler, she betrays the people who would give her a battle before she brings up her troops. Her whole personal life, so far as outward expression is concerned, is in consequence, a mopping-up action. Traitors are shot, yellow stars are slapped on those beneath notice, the good-looking men and boys are rounded up and beaten or sucked into pliability, a new slave population continually goes to work at making more munitions for momism, and mom herself sticks up her head, or maybe the periscope of the woman next door, to find some new region that needs taking over. This technique pervades all she does.   15

In the matter of her affiliation of herself with the Daughters of some war the Hitler analogue especially holds, because these sororities of the sword often constitute her Party—her shirtism. Ancestor worship, like all other forms of religion, contained an instinctual reason and developed rituals thought to be germane to the reason. People sedulously followed those rituals, which were basically intended to remind them that they, too, were going to be ancestors someday and would have to labor for personal merit in order to be worthy of veneration. But mom's reverence for her bold forebears lacks even a ritualistic significance, and so instructs her in nothing. She is peremptory about historical truth, mandates, custom, fact, and point. She brushes aside the ideals and concepts for which her forebears perished fighting as if they were the crumbs of melba toast. Instead, she attributes to the noble   16 dead her own immediate and selfish attitudes. She "knows full well what they would have thought and done," and in that whole-clod trumpery she goes busting on her way.

Thus the long-vanished warriors who liberated this land from one 17 George in order to make another its first president guide mom divinely as she barges along the badgering boulevard of her life, relaying fiats from the grave on birth control, rayon, vitamins, the power trust, and a hundred other items of which the dead had no knowledge. To some degree most people, these days, are guilty of this absurd procedure. There has been more nonsense printed lately detailing what Jefferson would say about matters he never dreamed of than a sensible man can endure. (I do not have any idea, for instance, and I am sure nobody has any idea, what Jefferson would think about the giddy bungle of interstate truck commerce; but people, columnists especially, will tell you.)

Mom, however, does not merely quote Thomas Jefferson on modern 18 topics: she *is* Thomas Jefferson. This removes her twice from sanity. Mom wraps herself in the mantle of every canny man and coward who has drilled with a musket on this continent and reproduced a line that zigzagged down to mom. In that cloak, together with the other miters, rings, scepters, and power symbols which she has swiped, she has become the American pope.

People are feebly aware of this situation and it has been pointed out at 19 one time or another that the phrase "Mother knows best" has practically worn out the staircase to private hell. Most decriers of matriarchy, however, are men of middle age, like me.

Young men whose natures are attuned to a female image with more 20 feelings than mom possesses and different purposes from those of our synthetic archetype of Cinderella-the-go-getter bounce anxiously away from their first few brutal contacts with modern young women, frightened to find their shining hair is vulcanized, their agate eyes are embedded in cement, and their ruby lips casehardened into pliers for the bending males like wire. These young men, fresh-startled by learning that She is a chrome-plated afreet, but not able to discern that the condition is mom's unconscious preparation of somebody's sister for a place in the gynecocracy—are, again, presented with a soft and shimmering resting place, the bosom of mom.

QUESTIONS ABOUT THE RHETORICAL SITUATION

1. Is Wylie writing primarily to a male readership? A female readership? A mixed readership? How can you tell?
2. At what point in the essay do you first sense Wylie's anger? Which are his harshest criticisms of the "moms" he attacks in "Common Women"?
3. Is Wylie interested in more than just stirring up his readers' anger? What purpose do you think Wylie has in his essay?

QUESTIONS ABOUT THE ESSAY'S VOICE

1. What effect does Wylie create in his very first sentence?
2. Wylie compares "moms" to animals on several occasions in the essay. Examine those metaphors. What kinds of animals does he choose? What is the effect of these descriptions?
3. In ¶5, Wylie uses Biblical-sounding phrasing at one point. Why?
4. Later in the piece, Wylie compares "moms" to Hitler. What is the effect of such a comparison on the essay's voice? How do you respond to such a comparison?
5. Wylie criticizes the women he is writing about for their attitudes, their beliefs, and even their appearance. Where in the essay has he been unfair? How might he justify his stereotyping in this essay?
6. Why does Wylie call the women he is criticizing "moms"? What does he mean by the term "momism" (¶8)?
7. Where does Wylie hint that there are other women whom he prefers to the "moms" he so strongly criticizes in the essay?
8. What is the point of the final paragraph?
9. Wylie's book *Generation of Vipers* is widely considered to be a piece of satirical writing. To what extent is "Common Women" satirical in voice? How strong is the humor in the piece? What portions of the essay did you find amusing? Is there enough humor in the essay to qualify it for inclusion in Chapter 3 or 4?

TOPICS TO WRITE ABOUT

1. The "moms" in this essay are not the only people who misuse patriotism for their own ends. Write an embittered essay about some other group of people who also do so. POTENTIAL AUDIENCES: members of that group of people/high school students. POTENTIAL PURPOSES: to make clear that you are aware of their spurious sense of patriotism/to warn them to be careful about what they accept when they hear the ideas of such people.
2. Write an embittered essay about the way men and women treat one another in romantic relationships or about the way parents and children treat one another within family relationships. POTENTIAL AUDIENCES: a men's or women's magazine/a magazine for parents. POTENTIAL PURPOSES: to rally support or confront the "enemy" depending on the audience you have chosen/to make clear your generation's strong feelings.

6

The Angry Voice

ANGER AS A PHYSICAL BURDEN

"I just had to get it off my chest."

"I'm fed up to here."

"Let it all out."

These are all familiar phrases, and they all describe situations in which someone is feeling angry. You might have made the first of these comments after shouting at a friend, or you may have uttered the second as a complaint. Perhaps you have advised a friend who was struggling to control her anger to "let it all out."

One form of psychological treatment makes use of something known as the "primal scream" and advocates that the person in therapy scream as a means of releasing tensions, anger, stress. An assumption underlying all of the three expressions I have quoted as well as the primal scream therapy is that anger is a heavy burden to carry. Releasing it therefore becomes a relief; it can be therapeutic. And of course it is quite possible to emit a "primal scream," "to let it all out," "to get it off your chest" in writing. When a writer does so, obviously the voice she creates is likely to be an angry one.

There are several important features to note in the angry voices you will be hearing in this chapter. First is the writers' strong sense of principle. The targets of their anger are those who have not lived up to the standards deemed appropriate by the writer. Sometimes these criteria are moral in nature, but they might easily be a code of conduct based on common sense, personal etiquette, or professional standards, for example.

In other words, a writer who feels that marriage is a sacred contract not to be treated lightly might write an angry essay about the number of couples who now live together without getting married or about the number of people who remarry after a divorce, condemning all these individuals for their immoral, in his view, behavior. But a writer who feels that the local department store no longer offers merchandise of as high a quality as it once did might also write in an angry voice because her set of standards has been violated.

THE URGE TO JUDGE

There is, therefore, a *judgmental* quality to angry writing. The writer assumes some standards against which she judges the behavior of certain individuals or institutions. Were the behavior of those individuals satisfactory, the writer would not be angry and would not sound angry when writing about that subject. But when the behavior the writer has observed does not measure up to the standards she has set, she judges those individuals, often rather harshly.

How is all this different from the embittered voice in the last chapter? Like the writers in Chapter 5, the writers in Chapter 6 are also motivated by deep concern about their subjects. Because the embittered writers' judgment is so harsh and so destructive, little that is constructive can develop out of the writing, while the angry writers, although judging harshly, have hopes that something constructive can be done to improve the situation that they have judged so harshly.

ANOTHER LETTER TO THE EDITOR

For example, the workingman in Chapter 5 who was so incensed about his poor treatment at the hands of the clerks at the Motor Vehicle Bureau wrote a very bitter letter to the editor. What if, instead, he felt that since modern society tends to depersonalize human beings, public employees, such as clerks at the Motor Vehicle Bureau, must make an effort to acknowledge the basic humanity of their clients by being courteous. Writing about the situation in a letter to the editor, for example, he might well sound angry, but he may be interested in more than merely getting things off his chest, as he seemed to be in the earlier version of this letter.

Dear Editor,

I recently went to the local Motor Vehicle Bureau to renew my driver's license and was quite displeased with the treatment I received. While the slow-moving line may not have been entirely the fault of the clerks, they certainly made little effort to work more quickly. Additionally, they were singularly unhelpful in answering questions posed by confused clients.

When I asked if I could return at a later time to get my photo taken, I received at first a blank stare, as if to say, "What a stupid question." Finally, after at least thirty seconds of silence, the clerk turned to her supervisor and said, "This one wants to know if he can come back for the picture later." I resent being referred to in this manner.

Motor Vehicle Bureau clerks are public employees and ought to be polite to the public they serve. They have no right to be so rude and inconsiderate. Furthermore....

Because this writer is making judgments, it is not surprising that he felt offended, even hurt. He takes it personally when those clerks violate his standards of appropriate behavior.

CONTROLLING ANGER

But let's return for a moment to the image of someone screaming in order to get something off his chest. Yes, it's therapeutic, but it isn't always communicative. The sounds I make when I, in my clumsy fashion, stub yet another toe or bang my leg into the corner of yet another coffee table, are angry but communicate little to any listeners other than that I am angry. In order to communicate a message about my anger—"I wish my parents had not let me quit ballet lessons when I was five. I might be more graceful now instead of always bumping into furniture."—I would need to make some effort to control my feelings. In Chapter 5, anger was channeled by the writers into rather bitter sarcasm; in Chapter 6, the anger appears in the writing. However, that anger is generally under control to some extent, as most writers wish to convey more to their readers than the mere fact that they are angry.

So, as you read these essays, notice how the writers set up standards by which they can make judgments, notice how at times they seem offended or hurt by the failures of others to measure up to those standards. But also notice what efforts the writers have made to control their anger and communicate. For these essays are not primal screams on paper. The writers are not involved in a personal therapy session, at least not entirely; they are involved in a rhetorical situation. These writers are struggling to make sure that their attitude toward their subjects does not overpower the other important factors of that rhetorical situation: their purpose and their audience.

What Is Poverty?

Jo Goodwin Parker

Jo Goodwin Parker is a writer about whom virtually nothing is known. As George Henderson, a professor at the University of Oklahoma, was preparing his book, *America's Other Children: Public Schools Outside Suburbia,* he received the following essay in the mail, postmarked West Virginia. The essay appeared in Henderson's book in 1971. Nothing else is known about either the essay or its author.

QUESTIONS ABOUT IDEAS

1. What did Parker's essay teach you about poverty in America that you had not already known? Were you surprised at all by what you read?
2. Some readers have questioned the authenticity of this essay, expressing doubts about whether Parker actually lived the experiences she describes. Why would readers question the essay in that manner? Do you have any doubts about its authenticity? If Parker has not actually lived through poverty as she describes, how has she come to be so knowledgeable about it?
3. What evidence is there that the grim situation described by Parker in this essay written almost two decades ago has changed for the better? The worse? Not changed at all?
4. What role should government play in dealing with poverty? What role should individual citizens—both the poor and the affluent—play in dealing with poverty?

You ask me what is poverty? Listen to me. Here I am, dirty, smelly, 1 and with no "proper" underwear on and with the stench of my rotting teeth near you. I will tell you. Listen to me. Listen without pity. I cannot use your pity. Listen with understanding. Put yourself in my dirty, worn out, ill-fitting shoes, and hear me.

Poverty is getting up every morning from a dirt- and illness-stained 2 mattress. The sheets have long since been used for diapers. Poverty is living in a smell that never leaves. This is a smell of urine, sour milk, and spoiling food sometimes joined with the strong smell of long-cooked onions. Onions are cheap. If you have smelled this smell, you did not know how it came. It is the smell of the outdoor privy. It is the smell of young children who cannot walk the long dark way in the night. It is the smell of the mattresses where years of "accidents" have happened. It is the smell of the milk which has gone sour because the refrigerator long has not worked, and it costs money to get it fixed. It is the smell of rotting garbage. I could bury it, but where is the shovel? Shovels cost money.

Poverty is being tired. I have always been tired. They told me at the hospital when the last baby came that I had chronic anemia caused from poor diet, a bad case of worms, and that I needed a corrective operation. I listened politely—the poor are always polite. The poor always listen. They don't say that there is no money for iron pills, or better food, or worm medicine. The idea of an operation is frightening and costs so much that, if I had dared, I would have laughed. Who takes care of my children? Recovery from an operation takes a long time. I have three children. When I left them with "Granny" the last time I had a job, I came home to find the baby covered with fly specks, and a diaper that had not been changed since I left. When the dried diaper came off, bits of my baby's flesh came with it. My other child was playing with a sharp bit of broken glass, and my oldest was playing alone at the edge of a lake. I made twenty-two dollars a week, and a good nursery school costs twenty dollars a week for my three children. I quit my job.

Poverty is dirt. You say in your clean clothes coming from your clean house, "Anybody can be clean." Let me explain about housekeeping with no money. For breakfast I give my children grits with no oleo or cornbread without eggs and oleo. This does not use up many dishes. What dishes there are, I wash in cold water and with no soap. Even the cheapest soap has to be saved for the baby's diapers. Look at my hands, so cracked and red. Once I saved for two months to buy a jar of Vaseline for my hands and the baby's diaper rash. When I had saved enough, I went to buy it and the price had gone up two cents. The baby and I suffered on. I have to decide every day if I can bear to put my cracked, sore hands into the cold water and strong soap. But you ask, why not hot water? Fuel costs money. If you have a wood fire it costs money. If you burn electricity, it costs money. Hot water is a luxury. I do not have luxuries. I know you will be surprised when I tell you how young I am. I look so much older. My back has been bent over the wash tubs for so long, I cannot remember when I ever did anything else. Every night I wash every stitch my school-age child has on and just hope her clothes will be dry by morning.

Poverty is staying up all night on cold nights to watch the fire, knowing one spark on the newspaper covering the walls means your sleeping children die in flames. In summer poverty is watching gnats and flies devour your baby's tears when he cries. The screens are torn and you pay so little rent you know they will never be fixed. Poverty means insects in your food, in your nose, in your eyes, and crawling over you when you sleep. Poverty is hoping it never rains because diapers won't dry when it rains and soon you are using newspapers. Poverty is seeing your children forever with runny noses. Paper handkerchiefs cost money and all your rags you need for other things. Even more costly are antihistamines. Poverty is cooking without food and cleaning without soap.

Poverty is asking for help. Have you ever had to ask for help, know- 6
ing your children will suffer unless you get it? Think about asking for a
loan from a relative, if this is the only way you can imagine asking for
help. I will tell you how it feels. You find out where the office is that you
are supposed to visit. You circle that block four or five times. Thinking
of your children, you go in. Everybody is very busy. Finally, someone
comes out and you tell her that you need help. That never is the person
you need to see. You go see another person, and after spilling the whole
shame of your poverty all over the desk between you, you find that this
isn't the right office after all—you must repeat the whole process, and it
never is any easier at the next place.

You have asked for help, and after all it has a cost. You are again told 7
to wait. You are told why, but you don't really hear because of the red cloud
of shame and the rising black cloud of despair.

Poverty is remembering. It is remembering quitting school in junior 8
high because "nice" children had been so cruel about my clothes and my
smell. The attendance officer came. My mother told him I was pregnant. I
wasn't, but she thought that I could get a job and help out. I had jobs off
and on, but never long enough to learn anything. Mostly I remember being
married. I was so young then. I am still young. For a time, we had all the
things you have. There was a little house in another town, with hot water
and everything. Then my husband lost his job. There was unemployment
insurance for a while and what few jobs I could get. Soon, all our nice things
were repossessed and we moved back here. I was pregnant then. This house
didn't look so bad when we first moved in. Every week it gets worse. Nothing is ever fixed. We now had no money. There were a few odd jobs for my
husband, but everything went for food then, as it does now. I don't know
how we lived through three years and three babies, but we did. I'll tell you
something, after the last baby I destroyed my marriage. It had been a good
one, but could you keep on bringing children in this dirt? Did you ever
think how much it costs for any kind of birth control? I knew my husband
was leaving the day he left, but there were no good-byes between us. I hope
he has been able to climb out of this mess somewhere. He never could hope
with us to drag him down.

That's when I asked for help. When I got it, you know how much it 9
was? It was, and is, seventy-eight dollars a month for the four of us; that is
all I ever can get. Now you know why there is no soap, no needles and
thread, no hot water, no aspirin, no worm medicine, no hand cream, no
shampoo. None of these things forever and ever and ever. So that you can
see clearly, I pay twenty dollars a month rent, and most of the rest goes for
food. For grits and cornmeal, and rice and milk and beans. I try my best to
use only the minimum electricity. If I use more, there is that much less for
food.

Poverty is looking into a black future. Your children won't play with 10
my boys. They will turn to other boys who steal to get what they want. I can

already see them behind the bars of their prison instead of behind the bars of my poverty. Or they will turn to the freedom of alcohol or drugs, and find themselves enslaved. And my daughter? At best, there is for her a life like mine.

But you say to me, there are schools. Yes, there are schools. My chil- 11 dren have no extra books, no magazines, no extra pencils, or crayons, or paper and the most important of all, they do not have health. They have worms, they have infections, they have pink-eye all summer. They do not sleep well on the floor, or with me in my one bed. They do not suffer from hunger, my seventy-eight dollars keeps us alive, but they do suffer from malnutrition. Oh yes, I do remember what I was taught about health in school. It doesn't do much good. In some places there is a surplus commodities program. Not here. The county said it cost too much. There is a school lunch program. But I have two children who will already be damaged by the time they get to school.

But, you say to me, there are health clinics. Yes, there are health clin- 12 ics and they are in the towns. I live out here eight miles from town. I can walk that far (even if it is sixteen miles both ways), but can my little children? My neighbor will take me when he goes; but he expects to get paid, *one way or another*. I bet you know my neighbor. He is that large man who spends his time at the gas station, the barbershop, and the corner store complaining about the government spending money on the immoral mothers of illegitimate children.

Poverty is an acid that drips on pride until all pride is worn away. 13 Poverty is a chisel that chips on honor until honor is worn away. Some of you say that you would do *something* in my situation, and maybe you would, for the first week or the first month, but for year after year after year?

Even the poor can dream. A dream of a time when there is money. 14 Money for the right kinds of food, for worm medicine, for iron pills, for toothbrushes, for hand cream, for a hammer and nails and a bit of screening, for a shovel, for a bit of paint, for some sheeting, for needles and thread. Money to pay *in money* for a trip to town. And, oh, money for hot water and money for soap. A dream of when asking for help does not eat away the last bit of pride. When the office you visit is as nice as the offices of other governmental agencies, when there are enough workers to help you quickly, when workers do not quit in defeat and despair. When you have to tell your story to only one person, and that person can send you for other help and you don't have to prove your poverty over and over and over again.

I have come out of my despair to tell you this. Remember I did not 15 come from another place or another time. Others like me are all around you. Look at us with an angry heart, anger that will help you help me. Anger that will let you tell of me. The poor are always silent. Can you be silent too?

QUESTIONS ABOUT THE RHETORICAL SITUATION

1. In both her opening and concluding paragraphs, Jo Parker addresses her readers directly. Is she speaking to Professor Henderson alone? Is she speaking to other impoverished readers? To whom is she speaking?
2. Clearly, Parker is angry about the situation in which she and many others find themselves. Which aspects of poverty seem to anger her most? Why?
3. In her opening paragraph, Parker says she does not want pity. Why is she so definite about not wanting pity? In her closing paragraph, she suggests that her readers become angry. Does she have any other objective beyond arousing her readers' anger?

QUESTIONS ABOUT THE ESSAY'S VOICE

1. Parker's essay is not always "grammatically correct." For example, her opening sentence would, if employing standard usage, read "You ask me, 'What is poverty?'" How do her occasional stylistic or grammatical lapses affect the essay's voice? Are such lapses mistakes that ought to be corrected?
2. Paragraph 2 discusses a number of rather distasteful subjects. Why has Parker begun answering the question "What is poverty?" with this particular paragraph?
3. In ¶3, the essay focuses on some disturbing examples about Parker's children. Although she comes close to sounding bitter ("The poor are always polite. The poor always listen."), she basically sounds rather neutral in this paragraph. Why?
4. Over half of the essay's paragraphs begin with the word "poverty." In fact, many sentences begin either with "Poverty is" or "I." Is this repetition effective? Why or why not?
5. Parker often asks her readers questions and often uses command verbs (see ¶6 for example). What is the effect on the essay's voice of her doing so?
6. In ¶12, Parker uses italics in describing her neighbor. Why? What is she angry about here? What is the connection between this paragraph and the use of italics later on in ¶14?
7. Parker vividly describes poverty as an "acid" in ¶13. How has she illustrated the corrosive effects of poverty throughout her essay? Which examples in particular illustrate the truth of this metaphor?
8. Parker's essay consists of a series of examples of what poverty is like. What is Parker's reason for placing her examples in the sequence in which they appear?
9. Does Parker sound too angry in this essay? Does her anger put off her readers? Does she sound angry enough? Does she seem genuinely concerned with her subject? Explain your answer.

TOPICS TO WRITE ABOUT

1. Write an essay about a social issue that angers you: for example, health care, public education, the prison system, the criminal justice system. Be sure that you know enough about the issue to write intelligently about it. You might consider drawing upon personal experiences in writing this essay. POTENTIAL AUDIENCES: readers who have ignored the problem/a university professor doing research into the problem. POTENTIAL PURPOSES: to wake them up to what they have been ignoring/to bring the human dimension of the problem into focus.

2. Write an angry essay that concretely defines an abstract term such as *terminal illness* or *divorce* or *unemployment* or *insanity*. POTENTIAL AUDIENCE: readers who have not paid much attention to the term you are defining. POTENTIAL PURPOSES: to make the abstraction seem real to the readers/to stimulate the readers to want to know more.

In Our Own Image
De'Lois Jacobs

De'Lois Jacobs lives in New York City and is a free-lance writer. "In Our Own Image" was published in the "Speak!" column of *Essence* magazine, a magazine targeted for a readership of black women. The editors describe "Speak!" to their readers as "your chance to express yourself about the issues that concern you and other *Essence* readers." This column appeared in the June 1986 issue of *Essence*.

QUESTIONS ABOUT IDEAS

1. Why should Jacobs be so concerned about this issue? Since America is reputed to be a "melting pot," why would she find it desirable for young black people to look different from the majority of Americans?

2. To what extent is the preoccupation with appearance common throughout all of our society, not just the black population? How healthy is this concern with what Jacobs calls "face value"?

3. Another issue touched on in this essay but not really developed is the question of which people are chosen as role models by our younger generation. Notice that Jacobs focuses on entertainers. How accurate is she

in portraying the influence of musicians and other performers on teenagers? Do such celebrities exert too much influence on the young? Why?

Recently one of my greatest concerns and fears was realized when my   1
younger sister told me about a story she had read in a popular Black publication: A teenager committed suicide because his mother would not allow
him to have cosmetic surgery on his nose in imitation of his idol, Michael
Jackson. This story is more than just sad; it is an outrage. What is it about
this society that gets us so completely involved in the material and physical
world? Why is it that our Black public figures, particularly in entertainment,
tend to be turning more and more to this way of presenting themselves?
What are these false images they worship and aspire to look like?

When I look in a mirror, I can clearly see where I come from—the   2
influences of my father's genes and my mother and grandmother in me. It
gives me a feeling of warmth, pride and reassurance to be able to see my
roots every single day of my life. There is nothing there that needs "fixing."

Yet I've had at least one lover (now "ex") tell me that my nose "spoils"   3
my looks. This was a man who was constantly talking about Black unity,
solidarity, beauty and pride. Well, I asked him whether it would please him
to see me with a straight or aquiline nose, or maybe one like a popular white
model's. This response not only surprised him, but it also shut him up on
the subject forever when he realized the absurdity of his remark.

Here in America we are increasingly buying and selling goods and ser   4
vices based on "face value." We are inundated with images that beckon us
through advertising, shape attitudes through film and television, and influence thinking through the printed, recorded and spoken word. Before we lay
down our hard-earned cash and our principles, let's take a close look at who
is selling us this bill of goods and why. As the ads have changed from extolling the wonders of Afro-hairstyle products to those of "curl" activators, so
has our idea of ourselves and what we look like.

Now, I have heard many defensive arguments in justification of the   5
things we do to our hair and skin color. Why are some of us so embarrassed
by our natural physical traits? I like to look into other Black faces and see
the tribes from which we have descended. Lineage is something to be aware
of, and pride in it is something to pass on to our young, from generation to
generation. I will not renounce that, ever. And here is my question: When
we try to change our looks so drastically, what messages are we conveying to
our young? Think about it—think long and strong. Think about that young
teenager, and then let your conscience be your guide.

This innate insecurity that drives us to change our images must come   6
to an end. Surely we must realize that such changes will not make our most
popular and revered singers sing any better, our musicians perform any
more brilliantly, or when you take a really close look, appear any more at-

tractive. For instance, although I like Michael Jackson's music, as I always have, I must admit I now feel a remoteness when I look at him, since there is not much there that I can relate to and admire anymore. I do not wish to chastise any particular entertainers, but I am curious about the reasons behind their decisions regarding their looks. Do they even know?

It is sad that our children's heroes seem to want to look like images 7 from which we Black people are the farthest removed. Straighten your nose, then your lips are too full; fix that, then your hips are too wide; tuck those, then your hair is too kinky; relax that, then your hair is too short, wonder-weave that, then your skin is too dark; and on and on it goes.

Although the 20-inch Afro is a thing of the past, the feeling of Black 8 pride that accompanied it was fortifying. Let us not lose that feeling. The once often-heard phrases from the sixties—"I'm Black and I'm proud" and "Black is beautiful"—are sorely missed. I thought we didn't need to proclaim them so loudly in the eighties because, finally, we truly believed them. Do we? Look at the conflicting signals our young people get every day about their self-images. We who are parents and grandparents, aunts and uncles, godparents and older siblings have a responsibility to our young. Let us take the time to examine and explain to them those things that have real value and those that do not, so that they can make sounder judgments and better choices in conducting their own lives. Let us help them develop strong self-esteem by setting examples they can follow that are in our own images.

QUESTIONS ABOUT THE RHETORICAL SITUATION

1. This essay appeared in a magazine read primarily by black women. What clues are there in the essay that this is the case? What changes, if any, does Jacobs need to make in order to make her essay equally effective for male readers? For nonblack readers?
2. How angry is Jacobs? How well has she controlled her anger in this essay? Does she still seem concerned enough with her subject, or has she put her readers off by sounding too angry?
3. Is Jacobs' goal to get something off her chest, or does she have another purpose in writing this essay? Does she want her readers to become angry? What other reactions might she be seeking from her readers?

QUESTIONS ABOUT THE ESSAY'S VOICE

1. In ¶1, Jacobs objects to black public figures who turn to "this way" of presenting themselves. What does she mean when she says "this way"? How could she have expressed her idea more clearly in this sentence?

2. Why does Jacobs make it a point to add in parentheses that the lover she quotes is now her ex-lover (¶3)? How does this parenthetical comment help create her voice in this essay?

3. In ¶4, Jacobs makes a joke out of a familiar expression about laying down hard cash. Is the joke funny? What is the purpose of the joke? She continues the metaphor of a financial exchange in the next sentence, using the familiar expression "bill of goods." How is this paragraph helping to establish her angry voice?

4. In ¶5, Jacobs writes about her lineage that "I will not renounce that, ever." What effect does the final word have on the sentence? On the essay's voice?

5. Also in ¶5, Jacobs advises her readers to "Think about it—long and strong." Here she has played with another familiar expression, substituting "strong" for "hard," thus creating a rhyme. Why? How effective is this strategy? What purpose does the dash serve in the sentence? What is her reason for writing this sentence using an imperative, or command, verb form? Where else in the essay does she speak directly to the reader this way?

6. Michael Jackson figures prominently in this essay. Why is Jacobs so careful in what she says about him in ¶6? Is she angry with him? How can you tell if she is or isn't?

7. Does Jacobs seem offended or hurt at any point in this essay? Explain your answer.

8. Does Jacobs sound sarcastic or bitter at any point in the essay? How could she have written this essay in the embittered voice we heard in the previous chapter? Why has she not done so?

TOPICS TO WRITE ABOUT

1. Using an angry voice, write an essay about the changing self-image of some group of which you are a member. For example, you might write about the vanishing ethnic traditions in your family or the lessening importance of regional and civic pride in your local community. POTENTIAL AUDIENCES: other members of the group/nonmembers of the group. POTENTIAL PURPOSES: to make them pay more attention to what is happening within the group/to inform outsiders of the problems faced by the group.

2. Write an angry-sounding essay about the undue emphasis placed on physical appearance in our society. POTENTIAL AUDIENCES: other college students/parents/members of the opposite gender. POTENTIAL PURPOSES: to make them examine their own attitudes about other people and themselves/to help them understand the pressures placed upon their children to create a certain appearance or image before their peers/to criticize their gender's emphasis on appearance.

America's Grandmother Fixation
Sally Wendkos Olds

Sally Wendkos Olds is a professional writer with numerous magazine articles and books to her credit. A summa cum laude graduate of the University of Pennsylvania where she majored in English literature and minored in psychology, Olds is the author of *The Eternal Garden: Seasons of Our Sexuality* and *The Complete Book of Breastfeeding*, a classic guide for nursing mothers. She is the co-author of several successful textbooks including *A Child's World* and *Human Development*. Among the topics of her other books are the concerns of working parents, sexual development throughout life, and development of values by children. As her essay indicates, she is a wife, mother, grandmother, and runner.

"America's Grandmother Fixation," subtitled "A Venerable Status I Could Sometimes Do Without," first appeared in the January 1987 issue of *Ms.* magazine.

QUESTIONS ABOUT IDEAS

1. Is Olds concerned with sexism in her essay or with ageism? Or both?
2. Olds titles her essay *"America's"* fixation. Is the fixation singularly American?
3. What is the mental image that comes to your mind when you hear the word "grandmother"? How does that image support or refute Olds' central point?
4. Both De'Lois Jacobs and Sally Wendkos Olds are concerned with the image created by a specific group of people. What similarities do you see in their concerns? What differences between them?

I read recently of a community that's cracking down on speeding by 1 giving tickets to people going two or three miles per hour faster than the speed limit. To illustrate how unfair the police were being, one local merchant said, "They're nailing grandmothers."

In still another report a woman who wanted to become grand marshal 2 of New York's St. Patrick's Day Parade was identified not as a leader of Irish-American organizations or the host of an Irish music radio show, which she was, but as "a soft-spoken Irish grandmother from Queens."

And on the radio the other day, I heard about a woman convicted of 3 killing her fiancé with arsenic. The murderer was identified not by her occupation as a nurse, which was pertinent to the story, but by her indirect procreative status as a "51-year-old grandmother," which was not.

I've been saving little nuggets like these since that happy day four 4 years ago when my daughter gave birth to a darling little boy, thereby conferring upon me the status of grandmother. While I love the idea of being a grandmother, I'm both amused and bemused by the notion of using this new status to describe me exclusive of my other activities in life.

For example, I wrote a book about sexuality throughout life, and a re-   5
porter who interviewed me about the book identified me in one sentence as "a grandmother who lives in New York with her husband of 29 years, grew up in Philadelphia, and attended the University of Pennsylvania." The only element of this description that was really irrelevant was my status as a grandmother.

I can see how being married to the same man for 29 years might have   6
some bearing on my point of view about sexuality. I can see why readers of a Philadelphia newspaper might be interested in my local origins and why my residence in that hotbed of liberalism, New York, might also be pertinent. But I really don't think that my daughter's fecundity, resulting in the birth of a child a continent's breadth away whom I (regrettably) see only twice a year, has had an appreciable influence on my outlook about sex or my ability to write about it. It would have been more appropriate to describe me as the mother of three grown children, since the experience of parenthood has had a profound impact upon my adult development.

If this reporter had wanted to indicate my stage in life and didn't want   7
to ask me my age or describe the salt in my once all-pepper hair, his phrase "her husband of 29 years" would have done the trick. It would have been obvious that I was at least in my mid- to late-forties and that therefore my opinions had undergone some of the seasoning of maturity.

Following another scenario, should I enter a five- or six-mile race (as   8
I've been doing from time to time over the past few years) and should I win in the 50-to-59-year category (as I've done in a few small and unheralded events), would my little triumph be hailed as "Grandmother earns trophy in 10-kilometer run"? Does this imply that my daughter's delivery of a baby affected my endurance, stamina, or speed on the road?

For me, as for other grandparents I know, this role, while emotionally   9
gratifying, is usually secondary to most of the other roles in our lives. Even for my friends who live near their children's children, grandmothering has not become the major focus in their lives. (I'm focusing on grand*mothers* here, since men are almost never described by their relationship to another generation, unless that's what the story is about.)

Most grandmothers continue to pursue the same career and leisure in-   10
terests that they had before their daughters or sons added a third generation to the family. According to research, few see their grandchildren more than once a week, and in the peripatetic society we live in these days many see them far less often than that. For practically none of them is their day-to-day life changed to any appreciable degree. Why, then, is "grandmother" such a ubiquitous designation for any woman who fits it?

Reporters who identify a woman as a grandmother don't mean, I'm 11
sure, to imply that she spends her days cooing at babies or shopping for extravagant children's clothes and toys in "grandmother boutiques." They just
want to peg her at a certain stage in life. We hear the word "grandmother"
and picture a kindly, white-haired, prim little old lady, content to sit in a
rocking chair. But for most American women, grandmotherhood arrives
when they're in their forties or fifties, and in some segments of our society
women become grandmothers in their early thirties.

For whatever reason the current popularity of "grandmother" as an 12
identity tag, when women are achieving more than ever before in history,
has a sinister result. Defining women—and not men—this way becomes a
means of keeping us in our place, of tying us to our anatomy, of saying to us
that our prime purpose on earth is to bear babies who will then grow up to
beget or bear babies. Using the word "grandmother" to define a woman is
just as sexist as the old joke in which a middle-aged man tells a friend, "I
don't mind being a grandfather—I just don't like the idea of going to bed
with a grandmother."

Don't get me wrong—I *like* being a grandmother. I just don't like the 13
idea of being identified as one unless you're prepared to say something about
my adorable little grandson. Wait, let me show you some pictures...

QUESTIONS ABOUT THE RHETORICAL SITUATION

1. The majority of readers of *Ms.* magazine are women. How can you tell
   that Olds is writing directly to a predominantly female audience? To
   what extent can male readers appreciate this essay? To what extent do
   you think the age of the readers influences their response to the essay?
2. Olds does not ask for any specific change of behavior on society's part. Is
   her purpose simply to get her anger off her chest, to let it all out? What
   is the purpose behind Olds' essay?
3. What in particular has angered Olds? Does she dislike her new role in life
   as a grandmother? Explain your answers.

QUESTIONS ABOUT THE ESSAY'S VOICE

1. When you first read Olds' opening three paragraphs, each of which relates an anecdote, did you understand the point she was making?
2. Why does she call these three anecdotes "little nuggets" in ¶4? How does
   this paragraph help to establish her angry voice? She writes in ¶4 that she
   is amused at the situation. How amused does she seem to be throughout
   the remainder of the essay?

3. Olds devotes three paragraphs (¶5–7) to the story of her interview with the reporter. Why does she spend so much time on this short episode? How angry does she sound in this part of the essay?
4. What is the effect on the essay's voice of the question that ends ¶8? Is the voice the same in the question that concludes ¶10?
5. In ¶11, Olds discusses reporters again. This time she makes an effort to understand why reporters behave as they do. Why is she being so understanding here when earlier she seemed rather displeased with the reporter's behavior in writing about her?
6. Why does Olds use the word "sinister" in ¶12? What is its effect on the essay's voice? How concerned with this issue does Olds seem to be at this point?
7. Is the humor that concludes the essay in ¶13 a mistake on Olds' part? Why is she making grandmother jokes in her own essay?

TOPICS TO WRITE ABOUT

1. Write an angry essay about college students' mistaken ideas about some group of which you are a member: For instance, cheerleading squad, athletic team, chess club, honor society, a specific fraternity or sorority, a specific academic major. POTENTIAL AUDIENCES: your campus newspaper/ your classmates. POTENTIAL PURPOSES: to force them to rethink their stereotyped views/to share with them your feelings about being misunderstood by others on campus.
2. Sally Wendkos Olds is angry about how labeling women as grandmothers creates a wrong impression of an entire group of people, an impression that diminishes their worth as individuals. Write an angry essay about the power of labels when attached to individuals. You might write about labels such as "boy," "girl," "kid," "teen," "nontraditional student." POTENTIAL AUDIENCES: readers who use such terminology without realizing it/other victims of the same label. POTENTIAL PURPOSES: to force them to realize the implications of the language they use/to arouse their concern about an issue directly related to themselves.

To Kill a Wolf

Farley Mowat

Farley Mowat (1921–) was born in Ontario and grew up in a number of Canadian cities including Saskatoon and Toronto. After serving in World War II,

Mowat pursued his lifelong interest in the Canadian Arctic by living in or visiting almost every part of Canada. He describes himself as "a Northern Man...a reincarnation of the Norse saga men...." Like the Norse storytellers he admires, Mowat's chief concern has been to tell stories about people and animals living under conditions of, as he phrases it, "natural adversity." His books include *People of the Deer, The Desperate People, A Whale for the Killing,* and *Never Cry Wolf.*

"To Kill a Wolf" comes from *Never Cry Wolf,* first published in 1963. The book is based on a summer that Mowat spent living among the arctic wolves in that subarctic part of Canada known as the Barren Lands. This section of the book focuses on the hunting of wolves by human beings, who are, in Mowat's view, misinformed about their prey.

QUESTIONS ABOUT IDEAS

1. Mowat is not alone in his concern over the dwindling numbers of wolves. After reading this excerpt, how well do you understand his concern? Why should people who do not depend on the caribou of the Barren Lands for subsistence be concerned about this issue?

2. Mowat, throughout his book, discusses evidence he has accumulated about the true behavior of the arctic wolves, yet he has great difficulty finding anyone to accept what he says. This is not an uncommon experience for naturalists, scientists, and social scientists. Why are people so frequently resistant to the findings of scientific studies?

3. Can you understand why Mowat would be willing to study the wolves when they were believed to be so fierce? What explanations can you offer for why people undertake such potentially dangerous activities?

For the Barren Land wolves winter is the time of death.   1

Once they have entered timber they are exposed to a concentrated,   2
highly skilled, and furious assault from men. Trappers cannot bear them,
for wolves not only compete for caribou but can wreak havoc with a trapline,
springing the light traps used for foxes without getting caught themselves.
Furthermore, most white trappers are afraid of wolves—some of them
deathly afraid—and there is nothing like the whip of fear to lash men into a
fury of destruction.

The war against wolves is kept at white heat by Provincial and Federal   3
Governments, almost all of which offer wolf bounties ranging from ten dollars to thirty dollars per wolf; and in times when the value of foxes and other
furs is depressed, this bounty becomes in effect a subsidy paid to trappers
and traders alike.

Much is said and written about the number of deer reputedly slaugh-   4
tered by wolves. Very little is said about the actual numbers of wolves

slaughtered by men. In one case a general falsehood is widely and officially disseminated; in the other the truth seems to be suppressed. Yet one trapper operating along the boundary between Manitoba and Keewatin, in the winter of the first year of my study, collected bounty on a hundred and eighteen wolves of which one hundred and seven were young ones born the previous spring. According to law he should have killed those wolves by trapping or shooting them. In fact he did what everyone else was doing—and still does in the Far North, with the covert permission of Governments: he spread strychnine so indiscriminately over an immense area that almost the entire population of foxes, wolverines and many lesser flesh-eaters was wiped out. That did not matter since foxes fetched no price that year. Wolves were worth twenty dollars each for bounty.

Traps and poison are the commonest wolf-killers; but there are other 5 methods in wide use as well. One is the airplane, a favorite of those civic-minded sportsmen who serve society by sacrificing their time and money to the destruction of vermin. The crew of a high-flying aircraft keeps watch for wolves in the open, preferably on the ice of a lake. When one is found the aircraft is flown low over him and the beast is pursued so long and hard that he frequently collapses and sometimes dies even before a blast of buckshot strikes him.

However, I know of one occasion when this method failed of its pur- 6 pose. Two men in their own light aircraft had flown out from a large city to help rid the world of wolves. During previous hunts they had killed many, and the pilot had become adept at chasing the beasts so closely that his skis would almost strike them. One day he came too close. The harassed wolf turned, leaped high into the air, and snapped at one of the skis. He died in the ensuing crash; but so did the two men. The incident was described in an article in a widely distributed sportsman's magazine as an example of the cunning and dangerous nature of the wolf, and of the boundless courage of the men who match themselves against him. This is, of course, a classic gambit. Whenever and wherever men have engaged in the mindless slaughter of animals (including other men), they have often attempted to justify their acts by attributing the most vicious or revolting qualities to those they would destroy; and the less reason there is for the slaughter, the greater the campaign of vilification.

Antiwolf feelings at Brochet (the northern Manitoba base for my win- 7 ter studies) when I arrived there from Wolf House Bay were strong and bitter. As the local game warden aggrievedly described the situation to me: the local people had been able to kill 50,000 caribou each winter as recently as two decades past, whereas now they were lucky if they could kill a couple of thousand. Caribou were becoming scarce to the point of rarity, and wolves were unanimously held to be to blame. My rather meek remonstrance to the effect that wolves had been preying on caribou, without decimating the herds, for some tens of thousand of years before the white men came to Brochet, either fell on deaf ears or roused my listeners to fury at my partisanship.

One day early in the winter a trader burst into my cabin in a state of great excitement.   8

"Listen," he said challengingly, "you've been screaming for proof   9
wolves butcher the herds. Well, hitch up your team and get out to Fishduck Lake. You'll get your proof! One of my trappers come in an hour ago and he seen fifty deer down on the ice, all of 'em killed by wolves—and hardly a mouthful of the meat been touched!"

Accompanied by a Cree Indian companion I did as I was bid, and late   10
that afternoon we reached Fishduck Lake. We found a sickening scene of slaughter. Scattered on the ice were the carcasses of twenty-three caribou, and there was enough blood about to turn great patches of snow into crimson slush.

The trapper had been correct in stating that no use had been made of   11
the carcasses. Apart from some minor scavenging by foxes, jays and ravens, all but three of the animals were untouched. Two of those three were bucks—minus their heads; while the third, a young and pregnant doe, was minus both hindquarters.

Unfortunately for the "proof," none of these deer could have been at-   12
tacked by wolves. There were no wolf tracks anywhere on the lake. But there were other tracks: the unmistakable triple trail left by the skis and tailskid of a plane which had taxied all over the place, leaving the snow surface scarred with a crisscross mesh of serpentine lines.

These deer had not been pulled down by wolves, they had been shot—   13
some of them several times. One had run a hundred yards with its intestines dragging on the ice as a result of a gut wound. Several of the others had two or more bullet-broken limbs.

The explanation of what had actually happened was not far to seek.   14

Two years earlier, the tourist bureau of the Provincial Government   15
concerned had decided that Barren Land caribou would make an irresistible bait with which to lure rich trophy hunters up from the United States.* Accordingly a scheme was developed for the provision of fully organized "safaris" in which parties of sportsmen would be flown into the subarctic, sometimes in Government-owned planes, and, for a thousand dollars each, would be guaranteed a first-rate set of caribou antlers.

During the winter sojourn of the caribou inside the timberline they   16
feed in the woods at dawn and dusk and spend the daylight hours yarded on the ice of the open lakes. The pilot of the safari aircraft, therefore, had only to choose a lake with a large band of caribou on it and, by circling for a while at low altitude, bunch all the deer into one tight and milling mob. Then the aircraft landed; but kept under way, taxiing around and around the panic-

---

*In 1963 the Newfoundland Government is using the same gambit.

stricken herd to prevent it from breaking up. Through open doors and windows of the aircraft the hunters could maintain a steady fire until they had killed enough deer to ensure a number of good trophies from which the finest might be selected. They presumably felt that, since the jaunt was costing a great deal of money, they were entitled to make quite certain of results; and it is to be assumed that the Government officials concerned agreed with them.

When the shooting was over the carcasses were examined and the best   17
available head taken by each hunter, whose permit entitled him to "the possession of" only a single caribou. If the hunters were also fond of venison a few quarters would be cut off and thrown aboard the plane, which would then depart southward. Two days later the sports would be home again, victorious.

The Cree who accompanied me had observed this sequence of events   18
for himself the previous winter while acting as a guide. He did not like it; but he knew enough of the status of the Indian in the white man's world to realize he might just as well keep his indignation to himself.

I was more naïve. The next day I radioed a full report of the incident   19
to the proper authorities. I received no reply—unless the fact that the Provincial Government raised the bounty on wolves to twenty dollars some weeks afterwards could be considered a reply.

QUESTIONS ABOUT THE RHETORICAL SITUATION

1. What assumptions does Mowat seem to make about his readers' opinion of killing wolves? Does he assume that readers will be sympathetic or unsympathetic to his point of view? How can you tell?
2. Near the end of this excerpt, Mowat refers to his Indian companion's "indignation." He implies that he too felt indignant. What clues are there in the essay itself that Mowat feels indignant, that he is extremely angry, even outraged?
3. Does this excerpt make you angry? Is it supposed to? What other purposes might Mowat have in writing this portion of his book?

QUESTIONS ABOUT THE ESSAY'S VOICE

1. What clue is there in ¶2 that Mowat is angry at the hunters?
2. What can you tell about Mowat's attitude toward the government from his choice of words in ¶3?
3. In ¶5, Mowat is quite bitter about the use of airplanes to hunt wolves. Throughout most of the excerpt, however, he keeps his bitterness from

being heard by the reader. Why has he chosen to do otherwise in this paragraph? Is the bitter anger effective here? Explain your answer.

4. At the end of ¶6, Mowat offers an explanation of what he calls a "classic gambit." What is the effect of his parenthetical aside? What is his point in using the word "slaughter" to describe the hunters' activities?

5. In ¶12, Mowat places the word "proof" inside quotation marks. What is his purpose in doing so? How is the reader supposed to read that sentence with the word "proof" in quotation marks? Would the sentence read differently if there were no quotation marks?

6. Why has Mowat provided such a graphic description in ¶10–12? At the same time, he does not sound terribly angry in those paragraphs. Why not? Should he have sounded more angry? Does he sound concerned enough in this part of his essay?

7. Similarly, in ¶16, Mowat does not sound very angry. Why not? In general, are you surprised that he does not sound angrier throughout the essay?

8. How would you describe the voice you hear in the final paragraph of "To Kill a Wolf"? Is this voice the same one you have been hearing throughout or has it changed at all? Explain your answer.

TOPICS TO WRITE ABOUT

1. Write an angry-sounding editorial about some environmental concern of yours, perhaps a local park that is beset by litterers and vandals or a ballfield used by dog owners as a rest stop for their pets or a campground filled with the noise pollution of TV sets and boom boxes. POTENTIAL AUDIENCES: a magazine devoted to recreational activities/a neighborhood newspaper. POTENTIAL PURPOSES: to demonstrate to readers that something is quite wrong with the situation you describe/to stir the readers into caring about their neighborhood parks and playgrounds.

2. Over the years my students have complained about dogs being abandoned by their owners, abused by cruel dogcatchers, and locked up in closed automobiles in the hot summer. Pick a similar concern having to do with the treatment of animals by human beings and write a letter to the editor about it. POTENTIAL AUDIENCE: the local newspaper. POTENTIAL PURPOSE: to make clear that there are concerned citizens in the area.

7

The Persuasive Voice

A FINAL LETTER TO THE EDITOR

Our letter-writing workingman has written a third letter to the editor about his unfortunate trip to the Motor Vehicle Bureau.

Dear Editor,

Yesterday I experienced another frustrating visit to the Motor Vehicle Bureau. Unfortunately, this is not the first time I have been mistreated by the employees at the MVB; it's time things changed for the better.

Slow-moving lines are, it seems, an inevitable feature of the MVB. I understand that budgetary concerns prevent the MVB from hiring more clerks to service the public; however, it seems unwise to allow so many of the clerks to take their lunch breaks at the same time, leaving the counter understaffed. Additionally, many working people use their own lunch hours to renew their driver's licenses, as I did, thus guaranteeing that the lunch hour will be among the busier times of the day at the MVB. Clearly, it is time for the supervisory staff to reevaluate its policy regarding lunch break schedules for their clerks.

While I do understand the staffing problems faced by the MVB, I do not understand why the clerks need to treat the public so rudely and inconsiderately. Yes, the clerks are human beings subject to stress, and yes, they may well be entitled to an occasional off-day while on the job. But the rudeness still seems counterproductive to me. When I asked if I might return later in the day, after work, to have the photo for my license taken, I received a blank stare from the clerk. Then she said to her supervisor, "This one wants to come back later for his picture." I had been polite in my request, despite my frustration at waiting almost an hour to reach the counter. Why could the clerk not have been polite in return? I realize now that she was probably frustrated at my failure to read the notice on the wall that clearly states the photo policies. But wouldn't a polite answer referring me to that notice have helped me to avoid asking such inappropriate questions again in the future?

166

The clerks may say that their job is to process applications and that they do an efficient job of doing so. I agree that, by and large, they are efficient. But I would argue that they do more than process applications; they serve people. Each application belongs to an applicant—a person. And the clerks are public servants who must remember to serve the public, not merely process applications. The man in line behind me finally pointed out the notice to me. Shouldn't that have been the clerk's job?

My point is a simple one. The Motor Vehicle Bureau performs necessary functions and does so fairly efficiently. But does the Bureau need to conduct itself in such an adversarial manner toward the public it serves? With a little planning and a small effort to be cooperative, the employees of the Bureau would find that their jobs might go more smoothly and that the public might have fewer complaints to register about the MVB.

His earlier letters sounded angrier, more embittered. This time, however, he has a different sound and a different purpose: he sounds persuasive because he wants to see the situation changed.

THE NEED FOR CHANGE

Can you still hear the strong sense of concern on his part as he writes about one of life's minor annoyances? While the nasty sarcasm of his first letter may have felt good to him, it really did not address the situation with any hope of improving it. In his angry-sounding version of the letter, the writer communicated that he felt things needed to improve, but he really was not trying to initiate the changes through his letter. In his third version, however, he has harnessed the energy provided by his anger because he now would like very much to convince the workers at the MVB to make some specific changes.

Perhaps the most important feature of the persuasive voice is the writer's *desire to implement change*. Sometimes the changes desired require the reader to take action: write a letter to her congressman, sign a petition, vote against a specific proposition on the election ballot, mail a donation to a political candidate, or change the lunch break schedules of the MVB clerks. Sometimes, however, the change desired requires not action but a change of belief or attitude. Perhaps the writer wants readers to reconsider one of their political beliefs or to decide that a social issue needs to be addressed or to treat the public with more courtesy on the job. But when you hear the persuasive voice in a piece of writing, you should realize that the writer's central purpose is to influence the reader to change in some way. The pouring out of anger for the sake of release, as in the primal scream I mentioned earlier has changed; the writers now channel their anger into an effort to persuade.

DIFFERENT KINDS OF APPEALS

How does a writer writing in the persuasive voice attempt to change the reader? By appealing to that reader in several different ways:

Appealing to Reason

One effective method of trying to persuade readers to change is to appeal to their reason by offering logical explanations of your point of view. These logical explanations may better be called *arguments,* not in the sense of quarreling but in the same sense in which attorneys are said to argue a case in court. The writer appealing to his readers' reason offers evidence and logic in an effort to make an effective argument.

Notice the arguments presented in the letter to the editor that appeared at the start of this introduction. The speaker suggested that lunch break scheduling needed to be changed because there were not enough clerks on duty; he also pointed out that lunch hour required a larger clerical staff because of greater numbers of drivers needing assistance. The logic is simple but clear:

- There are not enough clerks as it is.
- The budget will not allow for more to be hired.
- There is a greater need for clerks at certain times of the day.
- More of the available clerks need to be on duty during those certain times.

As part of appealing to the readers' reason, the persuasive writer needs to remember that there is always another side to the issue, an opposing point of view, and that intelligent people of good will may believe in that opposing point of view. The smart writer doesn't ignore the opposing point of view by trying to pretend that it doesn't exist; instead he addresses that point of view and offers *counterarguments* against it. In the letter to the editor we have been examining notice how, in ¶4, the writer presents an argument that the clerks might make and then refutes it.

Arguments, evidence, counterarguments, refutation: these are all aspects of the appeal to reason that you will frequently find when you hear the persuasive voice, particularly if the writer is addressing readers who do not hold the opinion advanced in the writing itself, as in the letter above, which is designed to prod the Motor Vehicle Bureau into changing.

Appealing to Emotions

What if the letter writer really did not think he could change the minds of the people who work at the MVB? What if he had addressed his letter to the editor to those members of the public who felt pretty much as he did about the MVB?

He might still try to appeal to their reason, but he might also try appealing more strongly to their emotions. He might have focused on the rudeness addressed to an old woman with a cane who had to wait the same hour that he did. He could have described her as she visibly tired, and then he might have reported on the rude treatment she received from a clerk forty years younger than she. His hope would be to arouse his readers' sympathy for the old woman and their anger at the clerks as a means of persuading them to write to their state legislators about the situation.

Of course, the same appeal to the emotions could have been included in the version of the letter that you have seen, the one designed to be read by both the public and the MVB workers. In that case, the idea would be not to make the workers angry but to make them feel guilty enough to want to change their policies and behavior. The writer decided that in this case he wished to deal with the situation on the basis of reason alone, but at other times he might want to include an appeal to the readers' emotions. In any event, using an appeal to emotions requires great care lest the essay get carried away on a wave of strong feeling that might actually offend some readers. A little bit goes a long way when it comes to using the appeal to the reader's emotions.

Appealing to Ethics

Neither of the letter writer's first two efforts at discussing the MVB situation were particularly persuasive. And one reason was that he sounded so bitter in the first letter and so angry in the second.

Here, however, as a part of sounding persuasive, he is trying to create a picture of himself as a fair person, a reasonable guy trying to implement a necessary change. He is appealing to his readers' sense of fair play, their sense of right and wrong, their sense of ethics.

In his embittered letter, he blamed the clerks; in fact, he blamed *all* MVB clerks. Here, however, not only does he avoid blaming all the clerks, he even makes an effort to understand and excuse the poor behavior of the few clerks he has most recently encountered. He is not interested in vengeance here but in change. One method by which he creates this impression of being fair is called *concession*. The writer concedes at times that the situation is not entirely the fault of the workers (¶2 when he mentions budget problems), and he even concedes that he himself has been wrong (¶3 about the notice on the wall).

So while the writer no longer sounds very bitter or even very angry, he does sound deeply concerned, yet in a reasonable way. He doesn't call the workers names, and he doesn't call for them to be fired. He's calm, rational, likable—persuasive.

TOPICS FOR PERSUASION

I've deliberately used the example of the clerks at the MVB because it is not of earthshattering significance. If the letter to the editor I have been using was about nuclear disarmament or the safe disposal of toxic waste, it would have needed to be longer and would have undoubtedly included more evidence: statistics, expert opinions, fuller counterarguments. But I chose the simpler topic to illustrate that the persuasive voice is a product of the writer's concern, not of the writer's topic. After all, writing about nuclear disarmament without any deep sense of concern would not produce a very persuasive piece of writing. So as you read the essays in this chapter, note closely how deeply concerned the writers are to make you see things as they do, and notice how they appeal to your reason, your emotions, and your sense of fair play in order to do so.

The Rent-a-Womb Dilemma
Cleo Kocol

Cleo Kocol was born in Cleveland, Ohio, and has also lived in California, Nevada, Virginia, and New Jersey, before making Seattle, Washington, her home. As a playwright and actor she spent five years presenting her plays, Heroines Past and Present, Bus to the White House, and A Celebration of Women's Work, throughout the United States. She has described her plays as "an entertaining way to educate about women's history and touch on issues with which we as a nation and culture have struggled." Kocol's writing career began late in her life, but she now writes a column, "Feminist Update," for The Humanist magazine and teaches creative writing part-time at a Seattle high school. Winner of several writing awards in the Pacific northwest area, Kocol has recently completed a novel. "The Rent-a-Womb Dilemma" first appeared in The Humanist.

QUESTIONS ABOUT IDEAS

1. Has Kocol taken a feminist stance on the issue of surrogate mothering? What would a feminist stance be? Would the behavior of either of the two women in the Baby M case, Mrs. Whitehead and Mrs. Stern, be appropriate from a feminist point of view?
2. Why would parents go through the expense and difficulty of surrogate pregnancies rather than adopting a child?
3. As Kocol describes it, the judge in the Baby M case awarded custody to the Sterns not based on the legality or illegality of their contract with Mrs. Whitehead, but based on the "best interests of the child." In most cases, when one party to a contract does not fulfill the contract, that person is said to be in "breach of contract." What is there about the Baby M case that makes it different from a typical breach of contract lawsuit? Or shouldn't it be treated differently?

     Elizabeth and William Stern engaged Mary Beth Whitehead to bear a 1
child for them for ten thousand dollars. When the baby was born, Mrs.
Whitehead reneged on her contract. For a year she managed to keep a shaky
hold on the child she had named Sara.
     The Sterns did not want to give the baby up either. After all, the infant 2
had Mr. Stern's genes. Of course, it had Mrs. Whitehead's genes also. The
only one who had no genetic stake was Mrs. Stern. But, then, she had
agreed to the contract. In fact, the matter of legality was the overriding issue

in many minds. The press had a field day with the story that came to be known as that of "Baby M."

Litigation followed. The judge rendering the decision needed the wisdom of Solomon. But wisdom and the law are not necessarily synonymous. Judge Sokrow ruled in favor of the Sterns, citing the best interests of the child. 3

The decision has to be questioned. Not that the child's best interests lie with the birth mother either, but it can be argued that Melissa Elizabeth (as she was subsequently named by the Sterns) was denied an option relatively free of the circus atmosphere of competing parents. Already the Sterns and Whitehead have issued pronouncements. In the April 13, 1987, issue of *Newsweek*, Mr. Stern said, "I'm going to tell her [Melissa Elizabeth] about the kind woman who did something nice for us and then changed her mind and how it wasn't a lot of fun." The words undoubtedly will make an impression on Baby M, as will Mrs. Whitehead's continued battle for custody. She declared, "We will not accept the decision of one judge...that we should be permanently separated." 4

For the good of the child, why wasn't removing her from both the Sterns and the Whiteheads considered? A qualified couple, unable to bear their own child, would have been ideal. It is debatable, however, given the voracious appetite of the public for sensation and the propensity of journalism for drama, that Baby M could remain anonymous forever, but her chances for a normal childhood would have been increased. 5

Today we view surrogate motherhood as a modern event. But surrogacy had biblical origins. In Genesis 21:1–2, we read, "The Lord visited Sarah...and did as He had planned. And Sarah conceived and bore Abraham a son...." Throughout the Old Testament, women were impregnated by the Lord, his angels, and the Holy Ghost. All this was a precursor to the virgin birth, foretold in Matthew 1:20: "...that which is conceived in her is of the Holy Spirit." 6

That is not to say that William Stern's sperm was in any way hallowed, except perhaps in his mind. Genetically, Whitehead's hold on Baby M was equal to his. It was also argued very well by columnist Ellen Goodman that the input of each was as unequal as "ejaculation and gestation." 7

The tug-of-war will undoubtedly continue. As a society, we are only now coming to grips with the problems of ordinary adoptions. Should we burden society with the added difficulties of a procedure that isn't needed? Children are available for adoption, not only in the United States but also worldwide. Couples with money can have a child in their arms in approximately the same time it takes to arrange for artificial insemination, gestation, and birth in a surrogacy program. And regular adoptions are far less expensive. 8

Yet, money is a consideration in surrogacy. The overriding reason to carry a child that one is legally bound to give up is money. Rich women don't become surrogate mothers. 9

The opportunities for abusing the system are immense. Without blink- 10 ing an eye, the judge in the Baby M case called surrogacy "an alternative reproductive vehicle." His words brought visions of a future in which lower-class women became baby factories. In these days of fundamentalist religious fervor, it's not difficult to imagine a scenario with surrogacy carried to extremes, as portrayed by Margaret Atwood, the 1987 Humanist of the Year, in her bestselling novel, *The Handmaid's Tale.*

Still, surrogacy is relatively rare—750 cases reported in the United 11 States to date. Let's quit before we're caught in a quagmire from which we cannot extricate ourselves.

QUESTIONS ABOUT THE RHETORICAL SITUATION

1. Kocol's statement in opposition to surrogacy appeared in a magazine for humanists. What is there about her essay that makes it appropriate for that audience? How appropriate is her essay for other readers who do not think of themselves as humanists?
2. Why is Kocol so concerned about this issue? Why is she not angry or embittered about the issue? What does her title convey about her attitude toward surrogacy?
3. What action or change does Kocol seek to implement through her persuasive essay? How did you respond to her essay? If her view is representative of the humanist point of view on the issue, what purpose has she in addressing an audience of humanists?

QUESTIONS ABOUT THE ESSAY'S VOICE

1. Kocol describes the facts of the Baby M case in rather neutral terms in the opening two paragraphs of her editorial. In ¶3, she expresses her opinion that the judge's decision may have been wrong. At this point in the essay she appears to be on Mrs. Whitehead's side. Yet in the next paragraph we learn that she is not. Why has she presented her opinion in this manner instead of saying straight out what she thinks about the issue?
2. Kocol offers another alternative solution to the problem in ¶5, doing so in the form of a question. Later, in ¶8, she again uses a question to suggest her own opinion. What is the effect on the essay's voice of using questions to advance her own point of view?
3. Humanists are often criticized as being atheists (an oversimplified and overgeneralized criticism). Many readers will be quite surprised to find Kocol, an avowed humanist, quoting scripture in ¶6. Why does she do so? How effective is her strategy here?

4. Although Kocol advocates placing Baby M with a childless couple rather than with either the Sterns or Mrs. Whitehead, she is not truly neutral toward both sets of litigants in the case. What evidence can you find of Kocol's attempts to appeal emotionally to the women in her reading audience?

5. Part of Kocol's argument against surrogate pregnancies is to refer to Margaret Atwood's *The Handmaid's Tale*. In that novel, set in the middle of the twenty-first century, few women remain fertile, and those who do—called handmaids—are assigned to the more prominent men in the community with the sole purpose of being impregnated by them since their wives cannot have children. Why doesn't Kocol explain more about the Atwood novel? How effective a strategy is it for her to use this novel as evidence to support her point of view?

6. In her concluding paragraph, Kocol writes in the first-person plural. Why hasn't she done so earlier in the essay? She also describes the situation as a "quagmire." Has she provided enough details of the situation in the earlier paragraphs of the essay to support her use of the word "quagmire," or of the word "dilemma" used in the title?

TOPICS TO WRITE ABOUT

1. Write an essay in which you present an opposing point of view to Kocol's either by arguing that the Sterns deserved to keep Baby M, that Mrs. Whitehead deserved to keep the baby, that surrogate pregnancies serve an important and justifiable purpose, or that solutions to the dilemma described by the essay are possible. Be sure you have enough evidence to support your own point of view. POTENTIAL AUDIENCES: the same readers who have read Kocol's essay/married couples considering surrogate pregnancy. POTENTIAL PURPOSES: to persuade them to accept a different outlook on this issue/to persuade them to plan carefully for all the possible consequences of such an arrangement.

2. Write an essay about other recent developments in human procreation: in vitro pregnancies, artificial insemination, fertility drugs. Take a position in favor of one or more of these methods of reproduction or against one or more of them. POTENTIAL AUDIENCES: the general public/married couples considering the use of one of these methods. POTENTIAL PURPOSES: to persuade them of the positive and/or negative social implications of some of these methods/to persuade them that some of these methods should be viewed as acceptable and others as not acceptable.

They Could Do No Other

Robert McAfee Brown

Robert McAfee Brown, born in Carthage, Illinois, received a Masters in Divinity from Union Theological Seminary in 1945. He was ordained to the Presbyterian ministry in 1944 and served as a chaplain in the U.S. Naval Reserve in 1945–1946. After receiving a Ph.D. from Columbia University in 1951, Brown commenced a career as an educator, holding a number of academic posts, including a fifteen-year tenure as a professor of religion at Stanford University. Also an author, Brown has written many articles and books, including *Is Faith Obsolete?* (1974), and *Elie Wiesel: Messenger to All Humanity* (1983). Brown more recently served as a member of the U.S. Holocaust Memorial Council.

"They Could Do No Other" first appeared in 1986 in a book entitled *The Courage to Care: Rescuers of Jews During the Holocaust,* edited by Carol Rittner and Sondra Myers. The book, based on an award-winning film, examines why, during the period of the Nazi persecutions, deportations, and murders, some Europeans chose to aid the Jews of Europe despite the danger and despite the fact that the majority of their fellow citizens did not have the "courage to care." Brown's essay appears in a section of the book entitled "Reflections."

QUESTIONS ABOUT IDEAS

1. Brown suggests that in the same situation as the Danes, most of us would have great difficulty deciding what to do. Is he right in making this comment?
2. Why should the United States be erecting a memorial to Holocaust victims when the war itself took place in Europe?
3. Would you term the Danes and others who helped rescue persecuted Jews during the war heroes and heroines?
4. Which of the five considerations offered by Brown are most convincing to you? Why?

As a member of the United States Holocaust Memorial council, I was   1
privileged to visit Europe in 1979 with other members of the Council, to get ideas for an appropriate Holocaust memorial in the United States. We visited Warsaw and Treblinka, Auschwitz and Birkenau, Kiev and Babi-Yar, and Moscow. Our final destination was Israel.

During the early part of the trip, in both Poland and Russia, we saw   2
monuments, but they were all monuments of dead stone, reminding us of human degradation. In Denmark, however, we encountered monuments of living flesh that testified to power of human goodness. These were the Danes themselves, those members of the Resistance who, by extraordinary and selfless heroism, reversed the normal experience of Jews in countries occupied

by the Nazis. Thanks to these living monuments, 95 percent of Denmark's Jews survived the war.

Why did the Danes side with and shelter Jews, at great risk to themselves, when most of Europe did not? We met with some of them, heroes and heroines now in their seventies and eighties, and asked them why they behaved so nobly. And every time, the reaction was the same: not only did they refuse to be labeled heroes and heroines, they discounted the notion that they had done anything exceptional. Their answer to our question was always to ask another question: "Wouldn't you have helped your neighbors if they had been in trouble?"

And the deeply disturbing thing is that most of us do not know. Would we have tried to save another's life if it had meant risking ours? Most of us, if we are honest, must acknowledge that we become cautious in the face of such a question. When the price can be very high, we search for, and usually find, reasons to excuse ourselves from involvement. The Danes did not.

About three weeks after my return, I received a copy of a then forthcoming book, Philip Hallie's *Lest Innocent Blood Be Shed* (Harper and Row, 1979). So enthralling was it that I read it in a single sitting in a day. I remain grateful for that book, which not only reminded me of the horror of those years, but also highlighted that tiny moment of human splendor that was revealed when the people of the village of Le Chambon-sur-Lignon united at their own risk to save the Jews who needed their help. What struck me in my reading, so soon after the time I had spent in Denmark, was that the people in Le Chambon had reacted in the same way as the Danes: they refused to see anything unusual in what they had done.

The people of Denmark and Le Chambon are not alone in reflecting such an attitude. It seems to have been almost universal among rescuers of Jews during this period. But they are "alone," in the sense that they were atypical of most people confronting similar choices almost all of whom capitulated to the Nazi mentality toward Jews when forced to choose. Why, then, did a few Europeans see it as a matter of course to risk their lives for Jews, while most, if they ever had such impulses, efficiently curbed them so as not to run afoul of the Nazis?

There are surely times when religion is the dominant motive. Le Chambon's André Trocmé was, after all, a French Reformed pastor, and many who worked fearlessly with him were members of his congregation, people who had learned in their Protestant upbringing that "God alone is Lord of the conscience." In addition, at least some of the Danes must have retained vestiges of the Lutheranism that had informed their national history, and knew well that a time might come when Lutherans, like Luther, might have to say, "Here we stand, we can do no other." Many rescuers in other parts of Europe came from families, or even countries, in which religion was a central feature. During a visit to Poland, for example, I had the privilege of going with Eli Zborowski, a survivor, to visit the Catholic family that had sheltered his family 35 years earlier, and

thereby saved their lives. I asked the mother in that home why, in a town
and a culture that had little use for Jews, she and her family had taken in
the Zborowskis? A simple, unlettered woman, she gave a clear and un-
complicated response: "I do not understand," she said, "why the rest did
not hide Jews. We are all Catholics here. How could anyone refuse to
hide Jews when our Lord told us that we should help those in need?"

It is a shared resource, then, in the Reformed, Lutheran, and Catholic   8
faiths, and in the Jewish faith as well, that all people, without exception, are
made in God's image and therefore must be treated as infinitely precious;
they must be afforded whatever protection can be provided by a fellow human being. No other conclusion is possible for those with a true commitment either to God or God's creatures.

It would be comforting if we could stop there and announce the ver-   9
dict, "case proven." We know, however, that we cannot stop there. The
case is not proven, and for two reasons at least. First, there are too many
people whose actions on behalf of those in danger spring from other motivations for us to claim that their actions are the result of religious commitment. Second, the overall track record of religious people is abysmally weak;
despite the fact that their articles of faith assert that to believe in a just God
means to challenge human injustice. More often than not they fail to honor
this conviction.

The sad truth is that when we cite instances in which religious faith has   10
led people to protect the weak, we are describing a few brilliant exceptions
to the general rule of cowardice or apathy in the face of human need. Those
of us who are Christians must remember that we cannot let the few who took
risks—the occasional Father Delp, Bishop Lichtenberg, Dietrich Bonhoef-
fer, or Martin Niemoeller—absolve the rest of us of our failure. St. Paul was
not enunciating some complicated doctrine of sin, but merely making a descriptive comment, when he said of himself, in words that describe the rest
of us, "The good that I would I do not; the evil that I would not, that I do."
(Romans 7:19)

The value, then, of the appeal to religion, in dealing with our ques-   11
tion, is that it provides both a way of challenging members of the religious community with the moral yardstick against which they must be
measured, and of reminding them (in Johannine terms) that if any persons say they love God but hate their brothers and sisters, they are liars.
(1 John 4:20)

So I do not think that religiously inclined people can convincingly offer   12
religion as the full explanation for righteous behavior of those who are not so
inclined. "By their fruits you shall know them" (Matthew 7:16) is an awesome and yet justifiable criterion for testing the authenticity of any religious
claim. We are to be judged by the quality of our actions rather than by the
quantity of our affirmations, by the immediacy of what we do rather than by
the intensity of what we say. "Love must not be a matter of words or talk; it
must be genuine and show itself in action." (1 John 3:18)

So we need to reflect further on considerations that may lead to righ- 13
teous behavior. Let me suggest five:

1. It is important to take the disclaiming of heroic deeds seriously. Such
   statements may be less an instance of false humility than true indications about those who make them. For some people, it may be that the
   ingrained habits of a lifetime do make it "easy" for them to do what
   others will not. We need to reflect on the biographies of those who, for
   whatever reasons, did rise to heights of selflessness to a degree that
   most did not.
2. Does not involvement in the life of a community of like-minded people
   render exceptional actions more likely? It is hard as an individual to initiate and maintain actions that go against the accepted mores of one's society. If there are others involved, taking similar stands, it may sometimes be easier for individuals or minority groups to defy the prevailing
   wisdom of the majority. This communal support surely helped both the
   Danes and those in Le Chambon.
3. Those who took risks were, by and large, ordinary people. The comment
   is not made demeaningly, but as a source of encouragement. The evidence is that the instinct for love ran deep in unexpected places, and was
   present not only among leaders or highly gifted people. We need to reflect on the fact that there may be more potential for disinterested action
   on behalf of others than we usually assume.
4. In addition, however, we may find a further clue to selfless action in
   the presence of role models for the initially timid. The people of Le
   Chambon had André Trocmé, providing an example they could not
   ignore. Trocmé himself had Kindler, the German soldier he met during World War I who was a conscientious objector, as well as Jesus of
   Nazareth. Martin Luther King had Gandhi. And who knows how
   many black children, whose names we will never know, had the courage to suffer in the civil rights struggles of the sixties because King
   himself was their model?
5. These questions deserve fuller treatment than is possible here, but
   even in this brief presentation it is clear that they pose another question for all of us: Is it not a part of our own obligation today to anticipate crises, to try to determine ahead of time how we wish to act in an
   emergency?

We should at least be clear that certain attitudes and actions are to be 14
ruled out, come what may—informing on innocent people or being craven
before the perpetrators of injustice in the hope of salvaging something for
ourselves.

We can at least anticipate a spectrum of possible responses and begin 15
to train ourselves in the discipline necessary to carry them out. One of our
main resources will surely be to continue listening to stories from the Nazi

era in which ordinary people like ourselves did rise to heroic actions, stories that confront us as well as their participants with the necessity of moral choice and empower us to deal with our own dilemmas by letting us live through the decisions that others had to make for themselves. In this way we can prepare ourselves for the challenges, whether routine or extraordinary, that lie ahead, so that we may act against injustice and inhumanity, and for justice and humanity in whatever situations we find ourselves.

QUESTIONS ABOUT THE RHETORICAL SITUATION

1. How much prior knowledge of World War II does Brown's essay require on the part of his readers? Most members of your class were born after the war. How difficult is the essay to follow because it concerns events that happened almost fifty years ago? Does Brown explain historical references fully enough?
2. The final paragraph of the essay suggests that Brown is concerned with more than merely explaining the behavior of "those who could do no other." What is the purpose of this essay?
3. Is Brown's attitude toward the Holocaust a familiar one to you? Is it in any way surprising? Explain your answers.

QUESTIONS ABOUT THE ESSAY'S VOICE

1. What is the effect on the essay's voice of Brown's decision to write in the first person, making himself a character in the anecdotes he tells? How effective a strategy is this?
2. In ¶7, Brown wishes to make a point about the role of religious faith in the behavior of the rescuers. Why does he choose to make his point by telling the story of Eli Zborowski's rescuer? How effective a strategy is the use of the anecdote here?
3. Brown quotes scripture throughout his essay. Is his purpose in doing so the same or different as Cleo Kocol's purpose in doing so in "The Rent-a-Womb Dilemma"? What is the effect on his essay's voice of the scriptural references?
4. Why does Brown use language appropriate to a courtroom in ¶9?
5. Also in ¶9, Brown makes two significant assertions about human behavior without offering evidence to support them. This suggests that he feels his readers will accept the assertions as valid ones. Has he made a mistake here, or will most readers agree with his points?
6. Can you sense the logic behind Brown's sequence of five considerations? Might he reorganize them for any reason or is this the best order in which to make his presentation? Explain your answer.

7. Since Brown is not writing about a controversial issue, one likely to provoke serious disagreement, does this essay really demonstrate the persuasive voice? In what other chapters of *Model Voices* might this essay fit?

TOPICS TO WRITE ABOUT

1. Some groups and individuals have claimed that the Holocaust never occurred, that it is a hoax. Write a persuasive essay in which you argue that
   the Holocaust did in fact occur. POTENTIAL AUDIENCE: younger students
   who may not have studied the Holocaust in school yet. POTENTIAL PUR-
   POSE: to persuade them not to believe any false claims they may hear
   about the Holocaust.
2. Write an essay in which you attempt to prove that some individual or
   group of individuals were heroes. For example, you might write about
   those veterans who served in Vietnam and make the case that they were
   heroes. Or you might write about those individuals who protested the
   war in Vietnam and argue that they were heroes. POTENTIAL AUDIENCES:
   the general reading public/those who disagree with you. POTENTIAL PUR-
   POSES: to convince them that your view is accurate/to try to get them to
   examine their own beliefs a bit more carefully.

The Star Who Went Astray

David Bradley

David Bradley was born in 1951. Son of a minister, he grew up in the small
town of Bedford, Pennsylvania, and later attended the University of Pennsylvania. He has since become a novelist and a teacher at Temple University in
Philadelphia. Among his novels is the award-winning *The Chaneysville Incident.*

"The Star Who Got Away" was originally published in *Esquire* magazine in
1983 under the title "My Hero, Malcolm X."

QUESTIONS ABOUT IDEAS

1. How does Bradley's portrait of Martin Luther King differ from the image
   of King generally painted in the media?
2. How might the approaches and messages of Malcolm and Martin Luther
   King be received by the American people in the 1980s?

3. How are we to interpret the word "hero" in the *Esquire* title? Is this definition of "hero" different than the one used in Robert McAfee Brown's "They Could Do No Other?"

Martin Luther King Jr. should have been my hero. I was a middle-class black kid, the son of a preacher, carefully trained in the Ways I Should Go: Christianity, the Protestant Ethic, the social responsibility and respectability prescribed by W.E.B. Du Bois for the Talented Tenth—that cadre of "colored, college-bred men" whose mission, Du Bois wrote, would be to keep the black masses from "brooding over the wrongs of the past and the difficulties of the present, so that all their energies may be bent toward a cheerful striving and cooperation with their white neighbors." I should have been inspired by another middle-class black kid—also the son of a preacher, a product of Atlanta and Atlanta University, the very city and institution that inspired Du Bois's thoughts—who became a white-shirted revolutionary, the most brightly shining example of Christian idealism this nation has ever produced.

But Martin Luther King Jr. left me cold. For me there was something missing in both him and his philosophy. I did not know what. I could only say (as I once did to my father in a moment of ill-advised and quickly withdrawn candor) that King knew more of Christ and Gandhi than he did of white people—at least the ones of my acquaintance.

That insight came to me after I read King's "Letter from Birmingham Jail," in which he expressed a disappointment with the lack of activity of the white moderates. Then, dimly and intuitively, I saw that King's ideas were based on the belief that there existed in American society a moral white majority that would be disgusted by the actions of an immoral white minority against a passive black minority and that would take swift and correct action. Clearly a fallacy.

I could not so quickly analyze King's philosophy when I first read "Letter from Birmingham Jail." But then I came across a wholly irreverent but deadly accurate evaluation of King's adoption of Gandhi's philosophy: "Gandhi was a big dark elephant sitting on a little white mouse. King was a little black mouse sitting on top of a big white elephant." When I read that, I knew not only what I had been trying to say but that, in the expression of the thought, there was a mighty intelligence at work. I had found my hero. He was Malcolm Little, aka Detroit Red, Satan, El-Hajj Malik El-Shabazz—Malcolm X.

For someone like me to identify with someone like Malcolm was not as far-fetched as it might sound. In fact, the similarities between Malcolm and King are almost bizarre, given the popular perception that their natures were totally different—that King was a master of cool intellectual protest, while Malcolm was a thoughtless firebrand. Both were born in the latter part of the 1920s, Malcolm in 1925, King four years later. Both of their fathers were Georgia Baptist preachers, and both had the early and intense exposure to Christian teaching that such parentage implies. Both had below-standard secondary educations, which forced them to play educational catch-up: Malcolm leaving school in the eighth grade; King, on entering college, having only an eighth-grade reading level. Despite that, both were voracious readers and scholars, primarily of religion and philosophy—both were especially familiar with the writings of Thoreau. Both became ministers as well as scholars, in faiths that emphasized discipline, hard work, abstention from vice, and public service; both were married, with children; both were pilgrims abroad, King having journeyed to Gandhi's India, Malcolm having become, like all good Muslims, a pilgrim to Mecca; both were assassinated when they were just about forty.

Their dissimilarities, however, were crucial. King was a child of relative privilege, his family affluent, fixed, secure, traditionally nuclear. Malcolm grew up in poverty, in a family that moved frequently and was finally broken up after his father's death and his mother's dissolution into insanity. King was a product of the urban South, Malcolm of the North, with experience in rural, suburban, and hard-core urban settings. King's educational handicaps did not interfere with a traditional pattern of study; Malcolm was a dropout. King was a product of black schools until after he received his B.A.; Malcolm knew the dubious benefits of school integration firsthand. In addition to his Baptist training, Malcolm had experience with other religions. His mother, before her breakdown, became a Seventh-Day Adventist, a sect whose practices preadapted him to the laws of Islam. But, perhaps most significantly, unlike King, Malcolm had experience not just with poverty but with the entire underside of American society. A street hustler who graduated from shoeshine boy to dope seller, numbers runner, burglar, drug addict, zoot-suiter, chaser of morally depraved white women, jiver, hipster, and convict, Malcolm knew the welfare system, the criminal justice system, the practical workings of American society that contradicted idealistic theory.   6

He was also the living embodiment of every negative stereotype popularly associated with the American black. As Carl Rowan, then the head of the United States Information Agency, said in response to foreign eulogizing of Malcolm, "All this about an ex-convict, ex-dope peddler who became a racial fanatic."   7

What Rowan, and almost all of America, failed to understand was that Malcolm's life was truer than King's, his experience more broad and typical. King was the prototype of the New Negro, Malcolm the stereotype Nigger. King was a saint (a woman tried to stab him through the heart; the surgeon who closed the wound set his sutures in the pattern of a cross), Malcolm a sinner (inspired by his atheism, remarkable even in a prison, his fellow inmates named him "Satan"). King said the good things that middle-class   8 black and white America wanted to hear said; Malcolm said what no one in any establishment wanted said. On subject after subject, Malcolm kicked ass.

On the idea that blacks should develop as immigrant groups had: "Everything that comes out of Europe, every blue-eyed thing, is already an American. And as long as you and I have never been over there, we aren't Americans yet. They don't have to pass civil rights legislation to make a Polack an American." On the hypocrisy surrounding the position of blacks in America: "I'm not going to sit at your table and watch you eat, with nothing on my plate, and call myself a diner." On blacks and the American heritage: "We didn't land on Plymouth Rock. It landed on us." On white influence in the civil rights movement: "The white man pays Reverend Martin Luther King, subsidizes Reverend Martin Luther King...." On nonviolence as a way of life: "If they make the Klan nonviolent, I'll be nonviolent." On nonviolence as a universal tactic: "...if he only understands the language of a rifle, get a rifle. If he only understands the language of a rope, get a rope. But don't waste time talking the wrong language to a man if you really want to communicate with him." On King's reliance on the promise of protection by federal officials from white southern officials: "...asking the fox to protect you from the wolf." In speaking this way, with ideas that sprang from the same works of philosophy and religion as King's ideas, but in an idiom that came from earthier experience, Malcolm spoke in a pungent voice for many blacks, especially those least likely to themselves be articulate, least likely to have access to public attention.

Malcolm certainly was articulate and he certainly got attention, probably contributing to acceptance of King. Malcolm was the horrible alternative. King was aware of this effect and used it, referring to Malcolm repeatedly by warning that a failure to redress black grievances might force blacks into more-violent actions, while acknowledging, at the same time, that business leaders had become "prepared to tolerate change in order to avoid costly chaos."

Malcolm was the spokesman of that chaos. For although the Nation of Islam had been around since the Thirties, it was not until 1959 that it was represented by a regular publication, *Muhammad Speaks,* a creation of Malcolm's. And it was also not until 1959 that the Nation received nationwide media attention. That year CBS aired the documentary *The Hate That Hate Produced.* An inflammatorily edited piece of yellow journalism (even Malcolm described it as being "edited to increase the shock mood" and likened public reaction to "what happened back in the 1930s when Orson Welles frightened America with...an invasion by 'men from Mars'"), the CBS program featured Malcolm and thrust him into the public spotlight. In part because Elijah Muhammad had declared him a Muslim spokesman, in part because it was Malcolm who had pushed the Muslim faith into media-conscious urban centers of the East—Boston, Philadelphia, then New

York—but mainly because his style of expression brought the kind of pro-
vocative drama into a live talk-show studio that King could offer only on
taped news broadcasts, by 1963, when King spoke of the positive effect of
the violent alternative, Malcolm had become the symbol of that alternative.
Although the Nation of Islam, which had come to be called the Black Muslims, was not and never had been violent, and in fact strictly eschewed violence save in self-defense, Malcolm chose to go along with the media repre-
sentation.

Why he went along was never entirely clear. In his *Autobiography* he 12
claims to have been motivated by a desire to defend the Nation of Islam and
Elijah Muhammad from the false image presented in *Life, Look, Time,
Newsweek,* and nearly every major media outlet in America. However, it is
true that he spoke repeatedly to the white media and was, by design, un-
tempered in speech. And he was as aware of some of his effect on the nonviolent struggle as King was, for he told King's wife while King was jailed in
Selma: "If the white people realize what the alternative is, perhaps they will
be more willing to hear Dr. King."

Which is not to say that Malcolm's strident pronouncements had no 13
effect on the civil rights movements. For it was at the time of his greatest
prominence (greater television presence in 1963 than King) that elements of
the movement began to espouse Malcolm-like rhetoric and ideas. The planning of the Mississippi Freedom Summer of 1964 was complicated by the
notion that it should be a black struggle carried on without white assistance.
Nonviolence was seen as a tactical option rather than a moral imperative; in
the wake of the triple killing of civil rights workers near Philadelphia, Mississippi, the field workers of both the Student Nonviolent Coordinating
Committee and the Congress of Racial Equality asserted their right to wear
guns for self-protection. Later, SNCC also adopted Malcolm's position opposing military service for blacks, coining the slogan "Hell no, we won't
go," which became the rallying cry of the antidraft movement, and pushing
King to consider and oppose the Vietnam War, as Malcolm had done years
before.

Within the Nation of Islam, Malcolm's influence waned, due to jeal- 14
ousy, specifically that of Elijah Muhammad. Yet Malcolm's prominence
made the Muslims prominent, bringing in a wave of converts and making
the Muslim dreams of economic independence more a reality and the Muslim programs of rehabilitation more effective than ever before. These dreams
and programs were models for those of other groups, such as the Republic of
New Africa and the Black Panthers, whose leaders found that there was a
new acceptance in publishing for words written from prison because of the
success of Malcolm's *Autobiography.*

Indeed, Malcolm established the rhetorical style that became the hall- 15
mark of the various movements of the late Sixties and Seventies. While the
antidraft and antiwar movements drew their strategic and tactical models

from the nonviolent civil rights movement, their rhetoric, like that of later black groups, was poured hot from the mold of Malcolm rather than beaten in the shape of King's learned, lofty dissertations. From Malcolm came the sharp turns of phrase, the euphony and rhythm that gave Eldridge Cleaver "If you're not part of the solution, you're part of the problem" and H. Rap Brown "Violence is as American as cherry pie."

At the time of his death, Malcolm's influence was only beginning to be 16 felt. Then he was still popularly seen as a madman, a racist, a man of violence. King, with ironic self-righteousness, considering the circumstances of his own demise, on the occasion of Malcolm's assassination said Malcolm was a victim of the violence that had spawned him.

Precisely what Malcolm was the victim of is hard to say. He himself 17 spoke of the danger from other Muslims. "Any number of former brothers felt they would make heroes of themselves in the Nation of Islam if they killed me....No one would kill you quicker than a Muslim if he felt that's what Allah wanted him to do." But assassinations are not always done quickly. Although the likelihood of international involvement has been widely denied, Malcolm was establishing ties with black leaders in Africa and with Muslim leaders in the Middle East. These connections, especially the Middle Eastern ones, which transcended racial lines and which involved a region in which American foreign policy and economic interests were greatly concerned, surely would have made Malcolm's death a source of some relief to many. We do not know who killed Malcolm. We do know that of the four great political assassinations of the Sixties, Malcolm's was most clearly a conspiracy.

And it was a successful conspiracy. For not only did it result in Mal- 18 colm's death but that death obscured what is perhaps the greatest importance of Malcolm as a man, a leader, and an example: that by the time he died, Malcolm had changed.

That change was totally unexpected, in fact virtually impossible, given 19 the racial and social theories of the day. Those theories held that once blacks allowed themselves to leave the high road of moral purity, exemplified by Christian forbearance and *agape* love, once they began to hate their oppressors, they would be lost to hopeless, mindless rage. But Malcolm negated that. "In the past," he said after his pilgrimage to Mecca, "yes, I have made sweeping indictments of *all* white people. I never will be guilty of that again—as I know now that some white people *are* truly sincere, that some truly are capable of being brotherly toward a black man."

Impossible as it supposedly was, such a change might have been ac- 20 ceptable had it been simply extreme (America would have loved to have Malcolm recant). But Malcolm insisted on *developing*. He did not give up his hating or his accusation of racism. He simply learned to hate institutions: "Here in America, the seeds of racism are so deeply rooted in the white people collectively, their belief that they are 'superior' in some way is so deeply rooted, that these things are in the national white subconsciousness.... The white man's racism toward the black man here in America is what has got him in such trouble all over this world, with other non-white peoples.... That's why you've got all of this trouble in places like Viet Nam."

Malcolm's new ideas were, like many of his ideas, ahead of his time. 21 Fortunately, by means of texts of speeches, interviews, and the tapes from which Alex Haley would create his *Autobiography*, Malcolm spoke beyond his time into an era and to ears, like mine, that were able to understand him and needed to.

For while many of his pronouncements seem silly, overly rhetorical, 22 and extreme, he not only made them and admitted to them but he meant them and moved beyond them. His experience encompassed that of so many of us. His example applies to so many of us. He experienced, as every black does, the alienation, isolation, deprivation, elimination, exploitation, and subjugation that is dished out by American society. He saw, as every thinking person must see, the terror of racism, the awesome depth of its roots, the awful subtlety of its poisoned fruit. He felt, as every human person must feel, rage and despair and hatred so powerful as to warp the mind. He acknowledged the damage he had suffered. But he survived. Not just physically. Emotionally. Spiritually. He survived.

To any of us who have at times allowed the pain to defeat us and have 23 wondered, while in the throes of it, if this were the anguish of death, to any of us who have succumbed to the feelings and feared that this was a madness from which we could not recover, to any of us who know we could never, because of our lacking or its lacking, follow a philosophy of saintly forbearance, to any of us who have hated so thoroughly that we have wondered if we could ever love again, Malcolm's example did make and continues to make more than a difference. It gives us hope

QUESTIONS ABOUT THE RHETORICAL SITUATION

1. *Esquire* magazine is intended for a male audience. Is there any indication that Bradley is writing primarily with male readers in mind? Can female readers understand and appreciate this essay just as much as male readers might? How might Bradley's essay be different if it were written for a predominantly black audience instead of the racially mixed audience of *Esquire?*

2. Bradley is writing about a subject that has been on his mind since he was a boy, that is clearly very important to him. Which portions of the essay most forcefully demonstrate his deep concern with his subject? How?

3. What is Bradley trying to persuade us to believe in this essay?

QUESTIONS ABOUT THE ESSAY'S VOICE

1. Bradley's essay was, in *Esquire*, subtitled "Some Boys Weren't Made to Be Credits to Their Race." In what ways is that an appropriate title for this essay?

2. Since Bradley's essay is to focus on Malcolm X, why does he spend his opening three paragraphs discussing Martin Luther King, Jr., instead? How does the final sentence of ¶3 begin to establish Bradley's voice as persuasive?

3. In ¶5 and ¶6, Bradley discusses the similarities and differences between King and Malcolm. What is the point of this discussion? How does it relate to the argument that Malcolm X was a hero? Why does he term the similarities between the two men "bizarre" (¶3)?

4. What does Bradley mean in ¶8 when he describes Malcolm's life as "truer" than King's? What is the importance of this paragraph to Bradley's point? Why does he use such a colloquial term to describe Malcolm at the conclusion of this paragraph ("Malcolm kicked ass")? How does such language advance his argument?

5. In ¶13–15, Bradley sketches out the influence that Malcolm had upon the civil rights movement and the antiwar/antidraft movements of the 1960s. Why does he spend so much time tracing these influences? What purpose have these paragraphs?

6. Note the interesting variety of sentences in the essay's concluding two paragraphs. Among the noteworthy features, ¶22 includes a series of sentence fragments at the end, and ¶23 begins with a sentence more than 100 words long. The rhythms of the sentences are also noteworthy. What is the effect on the essay's voice of these two paragraphs? What is the effect on you as a reader of these paragraphs?

7. In ¶22, Bradley concedes that many of Malcolm's pronouncements seem "silly, overly rhetorical, and extreme." Is this an example of *concession* in the essay? Does Bradley use concession anywhere else in the essay in an effort to sound reasonable? Should he have done so more often? Explain your answers.

8. Is Bradley's essay written in the persuasive voice, or would it be better described as having some other voice? Explain your answer. How is this essay's voice similar to or different from the voice you have heard in the other essays you have read in this chapter?

TOPICS TO WRITE ABOUT

1. Write an essay in which you attempt to persuade your readers that one specific person influenced not only you but an entire generation. For ex-

ample, depending upon your age, you might argue that John Lennon of the Beatles, Gloria Steinem of *Ms.* magazine, or Bob Geldof of Live Aid has been a tremendous influence upon you and your generation. POTENTIAL AUDIENCES: readers who are members of your own generation/readers who are younger than yourself. POTENTIAL PURPOSES: to persuade them that they too have been influenced by this person/to persuade them to seek out similar role models for their own generation.

2. Write a persuasive essay about the current state of the civil rights movement. You might focus on the civil rights of blacks, Hispanics, women, or gays or any other minority that has at some time in the past been subject to prejudice. POTENTIAL AUDIENCE: the general reading public. POTENTIAL PURPOSES: to persuade them either that the battle for full civil rights is not yet over or that there is no battle to fight any longer.

A Letter to the House of Representatives
Barbara W. Tuchman

Barbara W. Tuchman is an historian who has published a number of books including *The Zimmermann Telegram* (1956), *The Guns of August* (1962), *The Proud Tower* (1966), and *A Distant Mirror: The Calamitous 14th Century* (1978).

"A Letter to the House of Representatives" was originally published in the *Washington Post* on October 28, 1973; it was written during the difficult days when the nation was growing more and more concerned with the extent of President Nixon's involvement in the Watergate break-in and cover-up. This version comes from Tuchman's 1981 collection of her writings, entitled *Practicing History*.

QUESTIONS ABOUT IDEAS

1. How has Tuchman's training as an historian helped her to make her argument in this letter to the newspaper?
2. How has the entire Watergate episode proved to be significant in recent American history?
3. What do you recall about Watergate either through personal experience or through history classes in school? How have the media and the educational system handled the Watergate episode in the years since President Nixon's resignation?

"Those who expect to reap the blessings of freedom," wrote Tom 1
Paine, "must undergo like men the fatigue of supporting it."

In the affairs of a nation founded on the premise that its citizens pos- 2
sess certain "inalienable" rights, there comes a time when those rights must
be defended against creeping authoritarianism. Liberty and authority exist
in eternal stress, like the seashore and the sea. Executive authority is forever
hungry; it is its nature to expand and usurp.

To protect against that tendency, which is as old as history, the farm- 3
ers of our Constitution established three co-equal branches of government.
In October 1973 we have come to the hour when that arrangement must be
called upon to perform its function. Unless the Executive is brought into
balance, the other two branches will dwindle into useless appendages. The
judiciary has done its part; by defying it the President brought on the crisis.
The fact that he reversed himself does not alter the fact that he tried, just as
the fact that he reneged on the domestic-surveillance plan of 1970—a fundamental invasion of the Bill of Rights—does not cancel the fact that he earlier authorized it, nor does withdrawing from Cambodia cancel the fact of
lying to the public about American intervention.

The cause for impeachment remains, because President Nixon cannot 4
change—and the American people cannot afford—the habit of illegality and
abuse of executive power which has been normal to him. Responsibility for
the outcome now rests upon the House of Representatives, which the fram-
ers entrusted with the duty of initiating the corrective process. If it does not
bring the abuse of executive power to account, it will have laid a precedent
of acquiescence—what the lawyers call constructive condonement—that will
end by destroying the political system whose two-hundredth birthday we are
about to celebrate.

No group ever faced a more difficult task at a more delicate moment. 5
We are in the midst of international crisis; we have no Vice-President; his
nominated successor is suddenly seen, in the shadow of an empty Presidency, as hardly qualified to move up; the administration is beleaguered by
scandal and criminal charges; public confidence is at low tide; partisan politics for 1976 are in everyone's mind; and the impeachment process is feared
as likely to be long and divisive and possibly paralyzing. Under the circumstances, hesitancy and ambivalence are natural.

Yet the House must not evade the issue, for now as never before it is the 6
hinge of our political fate. The combined forces of Congress and the judiciary
are needed to curb the Executive because the Executive has the advantage of
controlling all the agencies of government—including the military. The last
should not be an unthinkable thought. The habit of authoritarianism, which the
President has found so suitable, will slowly but surely draw a ruler, if cornered,
to final dependence on the Army. That instinct already moved Mr. Nixon to
call out the FBI to impound the evidence.

I do not believe the dangers and difficulties of the situation should 7
keep Congress from the test. Certainly the situation in the Middle East is full
of perils, including some probably unforeseen. But I doubt if the Russians
would seize the opportunity to jump us, should we become embroiled in impeachment. Not that I have much faith in nations learning from history;
what they do learn is the lesson of the last war. To a would-be aggressor, the
lesson of both world wars is not to count on the theory held by the Germans
and Japanese that the United States, as a great lumbering mush-minded degenerate democracy, would be unable to mobilize itself in time to prevent
their victory. I am sure this lesson is studiously taught in Russian General
Staff courses.

Nor should we be paralyzed by fear of exacerbating divisions within 8
this country. We are divided anyway and always have been, as any indepen-
dently minded people should be. Talk of unity is a pious fraud and a politician's cliché. No people worth its salt is politically united. A nation in con-
sensus is a nation ready for the grave.

Moreover, I think we can forgo a long and malignant trial by the Sen- 9
ate. Once the House votes to impeach, that will be enough. Mr. Nixon, I
believe, will resign rather than face an investigation and trial that he cannot
stop. If the House can accomplish this, it will have vindicated the trust of
the founders and made plain to every potential President that there are limits
he may not exceed.

QUESTIONS ABOUT THE RHETORICAL SITUATION

1. Tuchman's letter was about current events at the time that it was published. She has chosen to include it in her collection of essays published a
   decade later. How well can readers who did not live through the events
   alluded to in the letter follow Tuchman's argument? Has her letter become irrelevant to most readers?
2. Many people were very angry throughout the Watergate investigations
   and hearings, some at the President and his staff, others at those inves-
   tigating the President. Do you get any impression that Tuchman herself
   is angry? What suggestions are there in this essay that she is writing
   about a subject that concerns her deeply?
3. Although her letter is addressed to the House of Representatives, Tuchman did not send it to her representative, but instead published it in the
   newspaper, where it would be read by many other people as well. The
   general reading public does not have the power to impeach the President,
   only the House of Representatives does. What then is her purpose in
   publishing this letter in the newspaper?

QUESTIONS ABOUT THE ESSAY'S VOICE

1. Why does Tuchman quote Thomas Paine at the opening of her letter? What is the relevance of the quotation to her argument? Why does she quote Paine rather than some other American patriot of that era?
2. In ¶2 and 3, Tuchman makes the point that the expanding power of the executive branch of government is not a new development. Why would she want to place the Watergate scandal into an historical context?
3. In ¶4, Tuchman moves from discussing the situation historically and abstractly to discussing the personality of Richard Nixon. What proof does she offer to support her assertion about Nixon in the first sentence of that paragraph? How convincing is she in this paragraph?
4. In ¶5, she asserts that some doubt exists about the qualifications of Gerald Ford to assume the presidency should Nixon be removed from office. Why does she choose not to mention Ford by name? Why does she use the passive voice in making this point ("his nominated successor *is seen*...as hardly qualified to move up")? What is the point of this entire paragraph? (Note the final sentence of the paragraph.)
5. In ¶6, Tuchman offers what she sees as a compelling reason for immediate action by the House. How compelling a reason do you find this? Is her evidence convincing here?
6. In ¶7, she discusses the Russian military threat, and in ¶8, she focuses on the possibly divisive consequences of impeachment. What is her purpose in these paragraphs? How do they help her make her major argument more persuasively? How appropriate is her voice in these paragraphs to her purpose?
7. What is Tuchman trying to accomplish in her final paragraph? How successful is she in achieving that purpose?

TOPICS TO WRITE ABOUT

1. Write your own letter to the editor urging Congress to take some specific action. POTENTIAL AUDIENCES: the readers of your local newspaper/the readers of a national news magazine. POTENTIAL PURPOSES: to persuade them to contact your local congressperson supporting the action you have written about/to persuade them to write their own representatives supporting your position.
2. In Chapter 5, one of the Topics to Write About (topic number 1 following Ishmael Reed's "Real Democrats Don't Eat Quiche") suggested writing an embittered letter to the editor about some local political issue that upset you. Now try rewriting that letter, using a persuasive voice. POTENTIAL AUDIENCES: readers of your hometown newspaper/readers of your

campus newspaper. POTENTIAL PURPOSE: Instead of expressing your anger and stirring up opposition, try to persuade your readers to, for example, sign a petition, join a protest movement, write a protest letter. In other words, persuade them to take constructive action to correct the situation.

Goose Music
Aldo Leopold

Aldo Leopold was a naturalist and conservationist. "Goose Music" appeared in his book *A Sand County Almanac* (1949). Leopold died before the book could be published; his son edited a draft of the manuscript.

In the foreword to *A Sand County Almanac,* Leopold describes himself. "There are some who can live without wild things, and some who cannot. These essays are the delights and dilemmas of one who cannot." He continues by observing that for some, including himself, "the opportunity to see geese is more important than television, and the chance to find a pasque-flower is a right as inalienable as free speech." His writing objected to the modern view of land as a commodity. "When we see land as a community to which we belong, we may begin to use it with love and respect," he wrote, concluding his foreword with the hope that such a shift of values might be possible, offering his own thoughts and reflections in *A Sand County Almanac* as a step toward that shift of values.

QUESTIONS ABOUT IDEAS

1. Who are the "villains" in this essay about hunting? Are you at all surprised at Leopold's attitude toward hunting and fishing? How does his attitude compare to your own?
2. Delight in wildlife, Leopold asserts, is instinctive for human beings. To what extent does your own experience confirm this assertion?
3. What do you value as highly as Leopold values goose music? Why?
4. "Goose Music" was written more than forty years ago. How have attitudes toward wildlife, hunting, and conservation changed since Leopold wrote his essay?

Some years ago the game of golf was commonly regarded in this country as a kind of social ornament, a pretty diversion for the idle rich, but hardly worthy of the curiosity, much less of the serious interest, of men of affairs. Today scores of cities are building municipal golf courses to make golf available to the rank and file of their citizens.

The same change in point of view has occurred toward most other out-   2
door sports—the frivolities of fifty years ago have become the social necessities of today. But strangely enough, this change is only just beginning to
permeate our attitude toward the oldest and most universal of all sports,
hunting and fishing.

We have realized dimly, of course, that a day afield was good for the   3
tired businessman. We have also realized that the destruction of wildlife removed the incentive for days afield. But we have not yet learned to express
the value of wildlife in terms of social welfare. Some have attempted to justify wildlife conservation in terms of meat, others in terms of personal pleasure, others in terms of cash, still others in the interest of science, education,
agriculture, art, public health, and even military preparedness. But few have
so far clearly realized and expressed the whole truth, namely, that all these
things are but factors in a broad social value, and that wildlife, like golf, is a
social asset.

But to those whose hearts are stirred by the sound of whistling wings   4
and quacking mallards, wildlife is something even more than this. It is not
merely an acquired taste; the instinct that finds delight in the sight and pursuit of game is bred into the very fiber of the race. Golf is sophisticated exercise, but the love of hunting is almost a physiological characteristic. A man
may not care for golf and still be human, but the man who does not like to
see, hunt, photograph, or otherwise outwit birds or animals is hardly normal. He is supercivilized, and I for one do not know how to deal with him.
Babes do not tremble when they are shown a golf ball, but I should not like
to own the boy whose hair does not lift his hat when he sees his first deer.
We are dealing, therefore, with something that lies very deep. Some can live
without opportunity for the exercise and control of the hunting instinct, just
as I suppose some can live without work, play, love, business, or other vital
adventure. But in these days we regard such deprivations as unsocial. Opportunity for exercise of all the normal instincts has come to be regarded
more and more as an inalienable right. The men who are destroying our
wildlife are alienating one of these rights, and doing a thorough job of it.
More than that, they are doing a permanent job of it. When the last corner
lot is covered with tenements we can still make a playground by tearing
them down, but when the last antelope goes by the board, not all the playground associations in Christendom can do aught to replace the loss.

If wild birds and animals are a social asset, how much of an asset are   5
they? It is easy to say that some of us, afflicted with hereditary hunting fever, cannot live satisfactory lives without them. But this does not establish
any comparative value, and in these days it is sometimes necessary to choose
between necessities. In short, what is a wild goose worth? I have a ticket to
the symphony. It was not cheap. The dollars were well spent, but I would
forgo the experience for the sight of the big gander that sailed honking into
my decoys at daybreak this morning. It was bitter cold and I was all thumbs,

so I blithely missed him. But miss or no miss, I saw him, I heard the wind whistle through his set wings as he came honking out of the gray west, and I felt him so that even now I tingle at the recollection. I doubt not that this very gander has given ten other men a symphony ticket's worth of thrills.

My notes tell me I have seen a thousand geese this fall. Everyone of these in the course of their epic journey from the arctic to the gulf has on one occasion or another probably served man in some equivalent of paid entertainment. One flock perhaps has thrilled a score of schoolboys, and sent them scurrying home with tales of high adventure. Another, passing overhead of a dark night, has serenaded a whole city with goose music, and awakened who knows what questionings and memories and hopes. A third perhaps has given pause to some farmer at his plow, and brought new thoughts of far lands and journeyings and peoples, where before was only drudgery, barren of any thought at all. I am sure those thousand geese are paying human dividends on a dollar value. Worth in dollars is only an exchange value, like the sale value of a painting or the copyright of a poem. What about the replacement value? Supposing there were no longer any painting, or poetry, or goose music? It is a black thought to dwell upon, but it must be answered. In dire necessity somebody might write another *Iliad*, or paint an 'Angelus,' but fashion a goose? 'I, the Lord, will answer them. The hand of the Lord hath done this, and the Holy One of Israel created it.'

Is it impious to weigh goose music and art in the same scales? I think not, because the true hunter is merely a noncreative artist. Who painted the first picture on a bone in the caves of France? A hunter. Who alone in our modern life so thrills to the sight of living beauty that he will endure hunger and thirst and cold to feed his eye upon it? The hunter. Who wrote the great hunter's poem about the sheer wonder of the wind, the hail, and the snow, the stars, the lightnings, and the clouds, the lion, the deer, and the wild goat, the raven, the hawk, and the eagle, and above all the eulogy of the horse? Job, one of the great dramatic artists of all time. Poets sing and hunters scale the mountains primarily for one and the same reason—the thrill to beauty. Critics write and hunters outwit their game primarily for one and the same reason—to reduce that beauty to possession. The differences are largely matters of degree, consciousness, and that sly arbiter of the classification of human activities, language. If, then, we can live without goose music, we may as well do away with stars, or sunsets, or Iliads. But the point is that we would be fools to do away with any of them.

What value has wildlife from the standpoint of morals and religion? I heard of a boy once who was brought up an atheist. He changed his mind when he saw that there were a hundred-odd species of warblers, each bedecked like to the rainbow, and each performing yearly sundry thousands of miles of migration about which scientists wrote wisely but did not understand. No 'fortuitous concourse of elements' working blindly through any number of millions of years could quite account for why warblers are so beautiful. No mechanistic theory, even bolstered by mutations, has ever quite answered for the colors of the cerulean warbler, or the vespers of the woodthrush, or the swansong, or—goose music. I dare say this boy's convictions would be harder to shake than those of many inductive theologians. There are yet many boys to be born who, like Isaiah, 'may see, and know, and consider, and understand together, that the hand of the Lord hath done this.' But where shall they see, and know, and consider? In museums?

What is the effect of hunting and fishing on character as compared 9 with other outdoor sports? I have already pointed out that the desire lies deeper, that its source is a matter of instinct as well as of competition. A son of a Robinson Crusoe, having never seen a tennis racket, might get along nicely without one, but he would be pretty sure to hunt or fish whether or not he were taught to do so. But this does not establish any superiority as to subjective benefits. Which helps the more to build a man? This question (like the one we used to debate in school about whether boys or girls are the best scholars) might be argued till dooms-day. I shall not attempt it. But there are two points about hunting that deserve special emphasis. One is that the ethics of sportsmanship is not a fixed code, but must be formulated and practiced by the individual, with no referee but the Almighty. The other is that hunting generally in-volves the handling of dogs and horses, and the lack of this experience is one of the most serious defects of our gasoline-driven civilization. There was much truth in the old idea that any man ignorant of dogs and horses was not a gentleman. In the West the abuse of horses is still a universal blackball. This rule of thumb was adopted in the cow country long be-fore 'character analysis' was invented and, for all we know, may yet out-live it.

But after all, it is poor business to prove that one good thing is better 10 than another. The point is that some six or eight millions of Americans like to hunt and fish, that the hunting fever is endemic in the race, that the race is benefited by any incentive to get out into the open, and is being injured by the destruction of the incentive in this case. To combat this destruction is therefore a social issue.

To conclude: I have congenital hunting fever and three sons. As little 11 tots, they spent their time playing with my decoys and scouring vacant lots with wooden guns. I hope to leave them good health, an education, and pos-sibly even a competence. But what are they going to do with these things if there be no more deer in the hills, and no more quail in the coverts? No more snipe whistling in the meadow, no more piping of widgeons and chat-tering of teal as darkness covers the marshes; no more whistling of swift wings when the morning star pales in the east? And when the dawn-wind stirs through the ancient cottonwoods, and the gray light steals down from the hills over the old river sliding softly past its wide brown sandbars—what if there be no more goose music?

QUESTIONS ABOUT THE RHETORICAL SITUATION

1. To whom is Leopold addressing this essay? Is he writing to hunters? Conservationists? Men? Women? Refer to the text to support your answer.
2. Leopold writes of his great love for wildlife. To what extent does the way the essay is written make clear the importance of the subject to Leopold?
3. How would most conservation-minded readers respond to Leopold's essay? How would most hunters respond to the essay? How did you respond to the essay? Explain your answer.

QUESTIONS ABOUT THE ESSAY'S VOICE

1. What purpose does Leopold's opening comparison between golf and hunting serve? Why has he chosen this strategy?
2. In ¶4, Leopold calls the person who does not wish to outwit animals "abnormal." Does he offer enough evidence to support this assertion? How is this argument a part of his larger overall argument?
3. Leopold often asks questions and offers his own answers (see ¶5 and ¶6 for example) as a means of furthering his arguments. How effective a strategy is this?
4. In ¶7, Leopold appears to be answering anticipated objections from those who favor art. To what extent will this paragraph satisfy such objectors?
5. In ¶8, Leopold offers a religious argument in favor of conserving wildlife. How effective is this argument?
6. In ¶9, Leopold argues that hunting builds character. How convincing is this paragraph? Does Leopold mean "human being" when he writes "man" in this paragraph, or does he mean the male of the human species only?
7. Look at Leopold's first sentence in ¶10. Why does he write this sentence? What is his purpose in this paragraph?
8. How would you describe the tone of Leopold's final paragraph? Why does he choose to end his essay this way? How effective a conclusion is this paragraph?

TOPICS TO WRITE ABOUT

1. Check your answer to question number 3 in the Questions about Ideas. Write a persuasive essay about that response. POTENTIAL AUDIENCES: Aldo Leopold/readers without the same appreciation you have. POTENTIAL PURPOSES: to persuade him that there are other things in life to value as im-

portant as wildlife/to convince them that they are missing something important in life.

2. Write a persuasive essay on the subject of hunting. POTENTIAL AUDIENCES: hunters/the general public. POTENTIAL PURPOSES: to persuade them that indiscriminate hunting destroys irreplaceable wildlife/to persuade them that hunting is not a destructive activity.

When Thou Prayest, Enter into Thy Closet
James Pokas

James Pokas, from Martins Ferry, Ohio, was a first-year student at Miami University when he wrote this essay in fulfillment of an assignment for English 111, the first part of Miami's yearlong first-year composition course. Pokas, a history major, describes his thought process in writing this essay: "Only after clear consideration of both sides did I arrive at a conclusion." "When Thou Prayest, Enter into Thy Closet" was named a first-prize winner for 1985–1986 in the English Department's annual writing competition and was subsequently published in the following year's *Freshman English Manual*, a publication read by all first-year students enrolled in composition courses at Miami.

QUESTIONS ABOUT IDEAS

1. Are there any arguments either for or against prayer in the public schools that Pokas has omitted from his essay? Ought he to have included them? Explain your answer.
2. As Pokas presents his case, it appears that there is an either/or situation here: either prayer is allowed in school or it isn't. Is there an in-between position, a compromise that might satisfy proponents and opponents alike?
3. What should the role of public education be in your view? What should teachers try to teach and what should they not try to teach? (See ¶8 for Pokas' answer to this question.)

In the early 1960's, the Supreme Court of the United States declared unconstitutional an order by the New York Board of Regents for an obligatory prayer to be recited in the classrooms of the public schools of that state. Reading the majority opinion, Justice Hugo Black—who had long been a Baptist Sunday school teacher—maintained that "the constitutional prohibition against laws respecting an establishment of religion must mean at least that, in this country, it is no part of the business of government to compose official prayers for any group of the American People to recite as part of a religious program carried on by the government" (Katcher, 422). This historic Warren Court decision helped to fuel a holy war over the role of religion in the public schools. Many feel that this ruling is an affront to the religious freedom of this country. However, I feel that the justices made a wise and prudent decision which—instead of decreasing religious liberty—has made this country more religiously pluralistic.

Those who wish to return prayer to the public schools contend that the 2 Founding Fathers certainly intended for children to engage in organized prayer in the public schools. Some have noted that when our Founding Fathers passed the First Amendment, they sought to protect churches from government interference. They didn't mean to construct a wall of hostility between government and the concept of religious belief.

However, these assertions rely, to a good extent, on wishful history. 3 The father of the Declaration of Independence, Thomas Jefferson, was a member of the Deist movement which asserted the belief in a watchmaker God who created the world and left it on its own. While it is true that the Founding Fathers did not create a "wall of hostility," they nonetheless did create a wall—one of neutrality. Jefferson also spoke of "a wall of separation between church and state" that needed to be defended (Katcher, 422). In addition, James Madison, the author of the First Amendment, said that "religion flourishes in greater purity without than with the aid of government" ("Pro and Con," 40).

Moreover, the Founding Fathers lived in a society much different from 4 ours. In the 18th century, the United States was essentially a religiously homogeneous country. Throughout the years, however, this scenario has changed. Many different religions have emerged in this nation whose members total in the millions. There presently is a need to accommodate and protect the various religious groups as well as those without religious beliefs. The Warren Court decision was a logical adaptation of the system to changing circumstances, much like the decisions to allow women to vote and blacks to become citizens, implemented at times in which our society became more enlightened. If one scrupulously adhered to what the Founding Fathers believed, then one would think it morally acceptable to own slaves or to deny women the franchise.

Pro-prayer advocates maintain that the majority of Americans favor the 5 reinstitutionalization of vocal school prayer. Their proof: a recent Gallup poll showed that 81 percent of the American people favor the reinstitutionalization of prayer in the public schools, ("The American Way," 18), suggesting that the decision should be overturned to benefit the overwhelming majority.

The statistic, though, is not sufficient to have the decision overturned. 6 The very reason that the Bill of Rights was formulated was to prevent a tyranny of the majority. If a law violates what Jefferson called the "inalienable rights" of an individual, it should be struck down even if the majority of people approve of it. A case in point: the majority of Americans are "pro-choice" in their feelings toward abortion. However, if the Supreme Court decides that a fetus is a person, it does not matter how many people feel that abortion is a woman's choice; the fetus would be protected by the 14th amendment.

Advocates of prayer in the public schools contend that there has never 7 been a true wall of separation between government and religion. This assertion is true. Church property is tax-exempt if used for church purposes. There are chaplains in both houses of Congress, as well as in the military and in prisons. Also, "In God We Trust" is the U.S. national motto and the phrase "under God" is used in the Pledge of Allegiance (Trueblood, 12, 18). Prayer advocates assert that vocal school prayer is no more of a violation of the Constitution than any of the previously stated instances of church/state intermingling.

However, the current areas in which church and state overlap are not 8 analogous to having a non-sectarian prayer read aloud in a classroom of a public school. Church property of all religions is given tax-exempt status: no single sect is given preferential treatment. The use of the word "God" in our Pledge of Allegiance and motto refers to an abstract and non-sectarian Creator. Because our nation, in general, is composed of religious people, there are certain cases in which religion in the abstract and government intermix. Prayer in public schools is not one of them.

It is also important to note the function of the public schools. Many 9 who wish to restore prayer to the schools maintain that the recital of prayer is an integral part of a pupil's education. This may be true in some cases, but leading a classroom in prayer is not what the states hire teachers to do. The role of a public schoolteacher is to develop minds, not to save souls. A good teacher should give his or her students the pertinent facts and let them draw their own conclusions—not impose dogma on students. Still a good teacher should instill positive values in students. The best way to do that is not by reciting a committee-written prayer, but by serving as a positive role model for students to emulate.

Jesus discussed his thoughts on prayer only once: 10

> When thou prayest, thou shalt not be as the hypocrites are for they
> love to pray standing in the synagogues and in the corners of the
> streets, that they be seen of men. Verily I say to you, they have their
> reward. When thou prayest, enter into thy closet, and when thou has
> shut thy door, pray to thy Father which is in secret; and thy Father
> which seeth in secret shall reward thee openly   (Matthew 6:5, 6).

Jesus' statements show the difference between true, heartfelt prayer 11 and ritual. The Supreme Court can no more ban true prayer than it can ban thought. What has been disallowed is rote and sectarian ritual—something that Jesus found to be pharisaical.

Works Cited

"The American Way," Editorial, *National Review*, 6 April 1984: 17, 18.

The Holy Bible

Katcher, Leo. *Earl Warren: A Political Biography*. New York: McGraw-Hill Book Company, 1978.

"Pro and Con: Permit Prayer by Students in Public Schools?" (Interview with Senator Lowell Weicker) *U.S. News and World Report*, 12 March 1984: 40.

Trueblood, D. Elton. "Church and State: The Myth and Separation." *Saturday Evening Post*, July/August 1983: 12.

QUESTIONS ABOUT THE RHETORICAL SITUATION

1. To whom is Pokas writing his essay? Is he addressing his classmates? The general public? Readers of a particular religious outlook? Some other audience? Explain your answer.

2. Pokas clearly wants his readers to oppose organized prayer in public schools. Has he convinced you to agree with him? Has he changed your original opinion? How successful an essay has he written?

3. Does this essay convey a deep sense of concern on its author's part, or does it come across as an academic exercise? Explain your answer.

4. Unlike the rest of the essays in this chapter, this one makes use of formal research, making sure to include a bibliography and specific references to sources. What does Pokas' use of research suggest about his perception of the rhetorical situation surrounding the essay? How effective are the materials he has consulted? Explain your answer.

QUESTIONS ABOUT THE ESSAY'S VOICE

1. Why does Pokas make a point of observing that Justice Black was a Sunday school teacher (¶1)?

2. Later in ¶1, Pokas refers to the entire controversy as a "holy war." How does this reference affect the essay's voice?

3. Where in the essay does Pokas make clear for the first time what his point of view will be? How effective a strategy is it for him to make his point when he does?

4. Pokas discusses the intentions of the Founding Fathers for several paragraphs (¶2–4). Why does he do so? How effective is this section of his essay?

5. In several parts of his essay, Pokas offers his opponents' point of view only to follow up by refuting their arguments. Which of these sections of the essay is most effective? Why? Which is least effective? Why? How would you describe Pokas' voice in these sections of his essay? Is the voice appropriate?

6. In ¶6, Pokas uses the abortion issue as an analogy to the school prayer issue. Of course, feelings run as high if not higher on the Supreme Court's decision legalizing abortion, so Pokas is taking a risk in introducing such potentially controversial material into his own discussion. How wise a strategy is this one? How effectively has it worked?

7. Why does Pokas concede a point to his opponents in ¶7? Could any readers who otherwise support Pokas object to his concession? How effectively does he handle this section of his essay?

8. Why does Pokas decide to conclude his essay by quoting scripture? What is the effect here on his essay's voice? How effective a strategy is this closing one?

TOPICS TO WRITE ABOUT

1. Write a persuasive essay in which you disagree with Pokas. POTENTIAL AUDIENCES: your classmates who have read Pokas' essay/Pokas himself. POTENTIAL PURPOSES: to persuade them that Pokas is wrong, and you are right in your view of this issue/to convince him that he has made several serious mistakes in arguing his point of view.

2. Write a persuasive essay in which you argue your opinion regarding some educational issue at your university. For example, you might argue either in favor of or against a required core curriculum, or in favor of or against the current intercollegiate athletic policy in practice at your school. POTENTIAL AUDIENCES: your class, including your teacher/college students in general. POTENTIAL PURPOSES: to convince them to support or oppose the current policy on campus/to offer your university's policy as an example of one that should either be followed or avoided.

SECTION THREE

The Personal Voice

A PERSONAL TOUCH

The weekend is over, and you've just returned to class. Outside the classroom, you bump into one of your best friends, whom you have not seen since Friday.

"How was your weekend?" your friend says to you.

You smile and move closer. Leaning forward toward your friend a bit, you say quietly, "Let me tell you about the wild time I had Saturday night."

And the conversation continues in soft tones as the other students file past you into class.

I am sure that this situation is a familiar one to you. "So what?" you think. My point is that when we wish to conduct a personal conversation, we often move closer and speak more softly to our listener. Personal congratulations must be expressed from close enough by that the two parties can shake hands; fatherly or motherly advice may well be administered with a parental arm thrown around the child's shoulder. Distance is reduced and a voice is used which says to the listener: "I'm talking directly to you about something important to us both which I'd like you to pay close attention to."

A FAMILIAR KIND OF LETTER

The same situation exists in writing also. That note pinned on my refrigerator door—the one I spoke of in the first section of this book—is a personal communication from me directly to my family. Of course, any personal letter you have ever written or received is also an example of a personal communication. Listen to the voice in this familiar type of letter:

203

Dear Mr. Somers:

You have been chosen, Mr. Somers, to receive this letter which explains an extraordinary offer only being made to selected homeowners in Cincinnati, Mr. Somers. And you are one of them!

We know, Mr. Somers, how important your new home in Cincinnati is to you. That's why....

Have you ever received letters like this? Such letters always spell my name incorrectly—it seems like it, anyway—but even if the spelling were correct, I don't think I would be likely to confuse this letter with one from a friend. Contrast the false heartiness of this form sales letter with a genuine letter written to you by a friend or relative; you can hear the falseness, the artificiality, of the one and the genuineness of the other.

Yet personal writing need not be limited to the single form of letters from one person to another. Perhaps you remember listening to notable citizens delivering commencement addresses at high school graduations you have attended. Some, perhaps most, of these speakers sound as if they were up on a stage delivering a formal address to a large group of strangers—which of course they are. But some of the most effective commencement addresses I have heard were delivered by speakers who made an effort to use a more personal form of address, speakers who sounded as if they were talking *with* their listeners rather than *at* them. Often valedictorians are more successful at capturing that personal voice because they have an advantage over the commencement speaker: they are not only speaking *to* their audience, but in a sense they are *part* of that same audience, sharing mutual interests, concerns, memories.

It is quite possible for writers, just as it is for speakers at commencements, to create a voice which is best described as a personal one. Indeed, writing instructors for more than 100 years have been urging students to write personally, often assigning topics for papers or themes that are designed to produce personal writing. "How I Spent My Summer Vacation" is one such assignment, although not a very interesting one.

DEFINING THE PERSONAL VOICE

While it was easy to define the humorous voice (in Section One of this book) as a voice which sounds humorous, defining the personal voice is a bit more difficult because virtually all the voices in this textbook have a personal quality to them. Yet in this section of *Model Voices,* the voices

are somehow different from those in the other chapters and do have a
distinctive and unique personal sound to them.

The personal voice is most easily understood by examining its purpose.
Section Two focused on writing that desired to change readers' beliefs,
attitudes, behavior. *But what do writers seek to achieve when they employ a
personal voice? They wish to reach out to their readers in a direct way in order
to appeal either to the reader's heart or to the reader's mind.* In other words,
the writers in this section of *Model Voices* will not be attempting to
influence what you believe or how you act. They will be trying to make
you feel an emotion or ponder an idea.

The writer need not be writing about personal subjects; in other words,
the topic of the piece of writing does not have to be the writer herself,
although it frequently is. But the vantage point of the writing is clearly the
writer's own; the writer is not writing dispassionately about abstract ideas
but rather is speaking with a high level of commitment about a subject of
some personal importance to her. A survivor of the Nazi concentration
camps may record his thoughts about recent war crimes trials, as Elie
Wiesel will do in Chapter 9, or a middle-aged writer may reminisce about
his childhood days at his family's lakeside cabin, as E. B. White will do in
Chapter 8. What these essays have in common is that high degree of
personal commitment to the topic—and the personal voice that comes
through to the reader.

I mentioned that writers using the personal voice may appeal to the
readers' hearts on some occasions and to their minds at others. In this section
of *Model Voices* you will read one chapter, *The Evocative Voice, that focuses
on essays that appeal powerfully to readers' emotions, essays that will make you
experience strong feelings yourself, essays in which you will be able to hear the
emotion in the writers' voices as they write about the subjects that aroused those
emotions.* Then you will read another chapter, *The Meditative Voice,* that
focuses on essays that appeal to readers' minds. In the *Meditative Voice*
selections, *you will hear a different, yet still very personal voice, a voice that
has the quality of musing aloud as the writers seek not so much to move you or
even inform you as to make you think, to provoke your thoughts.* What all the
essays in these two chapters have in common, however, is that they
demonstrate *a type of writing in which the distance between writer and reader
is deliberately kept to a minimum.* In fact, many of these essays will sound
very much like that conversation in the hallway outside your classroom:
like one person speaking directly to another rather than like the phoniness
of a computer-generated sales letter "speaking" to you.

BENEFITS OF USING THE PERSONAL VOICE

Using the personal voice can help you write effectively in several ways:

By Providing Fresh Ways to Deal with Familiar Subjects

As I mentioned in the introductory section to the Humorous Voice, students too often feel as if they have nothing much to write about. Even though their instructors—and textbooks like this one—offer the advice that writers "should write about what they know," many students, especially when confronted with the need to write an assigned paper, are inclined to despair, convinced that they know very little. Using the personal voice is a way to find something to say, something about which the student *does* know a great deal. Although an old expression says that there is nothing new under the sun, suggesting that there are no new things to write about, when a writer draws upon her own experiences, her own recollections, her own feelings and thoughts, she is more likely to produce a piece of writing that *seems* new, fresh, novel.

I have read many essays over the years about students' unfortunate experiences with automobiles: car crashes, driver's license exams. And yet every so often I read one that makes an old, familiar subject seem brand new—such as the essay that one woman wrote about her boyfriend's rather severe car accident.

She focused the entire essay on herself rather than on him. So instead of the more typical description of squealing tires and breaking glass, I read about her being awakened in the middle of the night by a phone call, her hurried and anxious trip to the emergency room, her fearful emotions as she saw her injured boyfriend for the first time. The following day she journeyed out to the scene of the crash; she wrote movingly of her feelings as she gazed at the tire marks on the road and the scattered bits of metal and glass. While the subject may not have been new, the treatment of it was. The voice was personal; I heard her speaking directly to me (and the rest of her readers).

Similarly, I have read quite a few essays about students' humorous experiences while taking their driving tests. One paper that stands out, however, took the form of a letter from the student to her younger brother. Out of sad personal experience—she had received a drunk driving citation and had had her newly acquired license suspended—she told him of the added responsibilities that come with the added freedoms a driver's license gives. Her ambition was not to lecture him or to tell him what to do; she wanted to get him to think about the meaning of the new driver's license he was hoping to get. Although the letter was not really addressed to me, I could still hear the concern in her voice, and I suspect her letter would indeed have made her brother think in a more responsible way about driving. She achieved her objective by using a personal voice, taking a humdrum subject and making it fresh and original.

By Providing a Wealth of Material to Write About

If you write about subjects you care about—an approach that I would encourage you to accept as an essential one for effective writing—then another advantage of writing in the personal voice is the wealth of material available to you. By selecting topics to write about which are of some personal significance to you, you can begin to draw upon your personal treasury of experiences, opinions, recollections, feelings, thoughts, ideas, sensations, and you will find that you have ample sources of evidence to help make your ideas specific and clear.

An Exercise

Try this exercise: In the next minute or so make a list of subjects that are of great personal interest to you without worrying about how interesting the list may be. Here's my list, compiled in about thirty seconds:

N.Y. Yankees baseball players, especially Mickey Mantle
the movie *Sophie's Choice*
terrible things I've said to people I care about
the New Jersey ocean shore at dawn
my great failure as a Little League ballplayer
spending time with my two sons
cooking special meals for family celebrations

This list includes a variety of different topics, but they are all of genuine personal interest to me. Could I write about them in the personal voice I have been discussing? I am pretty sure I could.

My next step would be to dig into that treasury of personal experiences, recollections, feelings, of which I wrote above. Once I actually wrote an essay about my failures as a Little League player, using a personal voice. I wanted to share my own feelings about playing sports with my older son, who had just begun his first experience in organized sports by joining a recreational soccer team.

BRAINSTORMING

I began working on my essay by *brainstorming*. In other words, I tried to make a list as quickly as I could of the details I could remember about my Little League experience. Here is that list:

I was 10
Quit the team—frustrated and *afraid*
The change-up strikeout. Crying. HUMILIATED!

{The Dodgers. 3 levels of ball—this was top
{sketch in background of "career"
Characters: me, Dad, coach (Larsen—the tugboat captain—big man, rough
       huge hands and skin, kind, concerned, gentle), other kids (Larsen's
       kid—the catcher—good, confident player not interested in my prob-
       lems); Grammarosa—the "speedball king"—grinning.
1st sentence: "Get in there, Sommers..."
Sun shining. Strikeout—running away. Remember fear of ball at other
       times? (grounders, etc.)
Next practice—called Larsen and quit. Leave message; he's out.
He comes to visit, to talk. No go: "They're all laughing at me." "So what?
       You have to do it for yourself not for them."
Next game day friends go play and I'm left alone—feeling miserable.

Now you need to select one of the subjects you listed a few moments ago.
Try brainstorming for a couple of minutes on that selected topic. You
should find that you do have a wealth of material to use in an essay, just
as I did.

     Remember that one of the lessons to be learned from the humorous
voice you listened to in the first section of this book was that an audience
of readers needs *specific details*. Writing in the personal voice continues to
emphasize *specific details* at the same time that the choice of "personal"
subject matter provides a source for them. As a writing instructor, my
favorite two words in student essays are *for example*. When I see those
words in a student's essay, I know that the writer is going to get more
specific. After awhile, the students realize that it is the examples that
matter, not the words "for example," and although that two-word phrase
disappears, the examples themselves continue to appear. I think you will
find it easy to discover those relevant and useful examples when you write
in the personal voice.

By Engaging the Readers'—and the Writer's—Interest

The effective commencement speaker makes an effort to speak *with* her
listeners rather than *to* them, making eye contact as she speaks, trying to
sound enthusiastic about or committed to the ideas she is talking about.
The effective writer must also sound enthusiastic or committed, must
seem interested in what he is writing about because if *he* doesn't, then
why would his readers be at all interested in what he has to say? The
personal voice, as I have said, encourages writers to write about subjects
which do interest them and to create a voice that displays that interest.
The odds increase that the reader will also be more interested.

TOPICS

A worried girlfriend writing about her injured boyfriend; a man who suffered through Nazi persecution during World War II contemplating one of those men responsible for causing such suffering; a middle-aged professor recalling the time he quit playing baseball rather than suffer continued humiliation; a sister lovingly offering her own mistakes in life as an example to her brother of how not to behave; a father taking his son to the site of some of his own favorite childhood memories—these are people writing about subjects they themselves genuinely care about. Reading these essays—some of which are included in the upcoming two chapters— you will hear in these personal voices concern and a strong interest in evoking feelings or provoking thought. Because these writers care, we as readers will also care about their subjects.

So it may not be the topic itself that matters so much as the relationship between the writer and the topic. An important advantage of the personal voice is that as a writer you get to share with your readers something of great importance; that's good for you and it's good for your readers also.

In the next two chapters, then, be prepared to hear a number of personal voices; be prepared to be touched, to be moved, to be provoked to think and feel. Pay close attention because these "commencement speakers" won't be putting you to sleep—they will be waking you up to feel and think.

8

The Evocative Voice

FEELING WHILE READING

When I teach literature courses, I find that my students generally approach the literature, especially the poetry, as if it were a code to decipher, a sort of mental puzzle. They like to intellectualize about and interpret the poems, seeking the "hidden" meanings in the symbols.

And of course I try to encourage that sort of inquisitive reading. But I worry sometimes, that in the desire to interpret, these readers will lose sight of something equally important: the emotional response generated by the poem or story or play. Aren't we to feel grief for Oedipus when he learns the awful secret of his life? Aren't we to be uplifted when Shakespeare describes his beloved in his sonnets? Aren't we to hate Bill Sykes when he kidnaps Oliver Twist from his benevolent foster father?

Certainly we are. And the interesting thing is that as children we do respond emotionally to stories and poems. Somehow we lose some of that freshness of response as we grow up. Yet often writers want, more than anything else perhaps, to make us *feel* things, to make us feel what *they* are feeling or have felt. It's an aspect of that very human need to be a part of humanity, not to be isolated and left on one's own, a need that produces personal writing.

THE EVOCATIVE VOICE

One variety of personal writing that attempts to share emotions with readers is writing in what I call the *evocative* voice, *a voice designed to evoke emotions.* Love letters use the evocative voice, but so do funeral orations or eulogies as well as many testimonials. I'm not speaking about sentimentality—such as the trite phrasing that appears on most greeting cards—but genuine heartfelt emotion. Sentimentality is like a computer program: show a picture of a

210

small child playing with a cuddly puppy, and the audience feels all warm inside and goes "Ahhhhhhh." Show a picture of a weeping, emaciated child, and the audience goes "Awwwwwww." Now, I am not a hardhearted ogre who has no interest in small children and puppies. My point is that these stock pictures elicit stock responses. Like a computer program, the picture is shown and the reaction occurs. The photographer doesn't have to *earn* the response; it's programmed in.

When you write in the evocative voice, you have *to earn the response* of the reader. You have experienced strong emotions, and you wish to share them. You don't necessarily want to explain them or analyze them or generalize about them; you simply want to share them. This is a worthwhile and legitimate goal for you to try to achieve. But how might you go about achieving such a goal, creating such a voice?

A Sample

Read this selection from an essay that appeared in the *New York Times* in September 1980. The author is Jane Adams, a novelist.

> Her son is leaving to live with his father. He is funny, and kind, and creative, and smart, this boy; underneath the anger and apart from the surging hormones that have changed him from a laughing, loving child to a silent, surly teenager is a son a father would be proud to call his own. And inside him, too, is the man he will become. She has taught him what she could, but this she cannot show him. This he will have to learn from someone else, someone she does not know anymore, someone whose ways are strange to her, whose life has taken turns and taught him lessons unfathomable to her. It's time I paid my dues, her ex-husband told her when they talked about their son; it's my turn to worry. She believes him, for she has no other choice. And the shrunken knot of that old pain, ten years dead now, expands and fills the void.
>
> He is leaving to live with his father, and she does not know if he will return.

FEATURES OF THE EVOCATIVE VOICE

There are several features to notice in this selection, features that help to create the evocative voice.

Creating a Sense of Time

Evocative essays often are tied very effectively into the reader's sense of time. That is not to say that such writing always begins, "It was 3:21 P.M.

Eastern Standard Time, on a sultry Wednesday afternoon in late July, 1987"
or even "Once upon a time..." However, the evocative essay frequently
takes the reader back into the past, often the writer's own past. The ability
to reflect upon earlier events in one's own life is a power that is enjoyed from
a vantage point only the passage of time can provide—and it seems quite
natural for writers to take a journey back to their childhood or early adulthood in an effort to recapture a strong and memorable feeling. One reason
that Adams' essay rings true emotionally is its wistfulness as she looks back
on a ten-year period of change in her life at the very moment when another
great change is about to occur.

When you think about the essays you read in the first section of *Model
Voices,* you may recall individual jokes or comments or funny descriptions.
But I doubt that you are very aware of when Lewis Grizzard had his cardiac
catheterization or even that James Thurber's university days occurred years
earlier. The location of these humorous essays in time isn't that vital. With
the evocative voice it seems to be.

Not all essays in the evocative voice journey into the past, however.
Some immerse themselves in the present; in fact, Adams is as interested in
the emotions of the present as she is in the remembered heartache of the
past. The evocative voice can also look to the future. And in the very moving
final paragraph in Adams' piece, we see her looking ahead to an uncertain
future.

The point then is that it is important for the evocative voice to be sit-
uated firmly in a particular time in the writer's life, whether the past, the
present, the future, or a combination of the three.

Showing, Not Telling

As young children we all looked forward to that portion of the school day
devoted to "show and tell," when we had a chance to show our classmates
the really neat seashell we had brought back from a vacation to the ocean or
the oddly shaped rock we had dug up in the back yard or the photo of our
new baby brother. All eyes were on us along with all ears as we told about
what we were showing.

But if we forgot to bring the rock or the seashell or the photo to class
there seemed to be no point in trying to explain to the class. Kids use their
hands to "see" new things by touching them, making them concrete and
real. The showing, therefore, was a vital part of the telling. While you
couldn't bring your baby brother to the class to be "seen," you could bring
his photo to pass around.

Adult readers are not really very different. They too need to be shown,
not merely told. As the evocative voice essays demonstrate, in order to evoke
emotion, the writer must provide concrete details, must *show* the reader the
emotions. We have to see the beautiful lake, hear the beloved grandmother,
feel the strength of the horse being described if we are to accept what the

writers have to tell us about these topics. "Grandma was a loving soul" may have meaning, but it will not create an emotional response until the reader has a chance to see Grandma's loving soul as she places her hands on her granddaughter's head and prays over her, as Diane Rawlings describes her grandmother doing in her essay in this chapter entitled "Reflections."

Emotions are abstractions: love, pity, pride. And merely reciting these abstractions or *telling* the reader about them will rarely evoke any strong responses. *Showing* the reader, however, can arouse emotions. Think of the movie scenes you have watched that have no dialogue: Rocky thrusting his arms to the sky atop the staircase at the Philadelphia Art Museum, E.T. boarding his spaceship to return home, Humphrey Bogart watching Ingrid Bergman's plane take off from the airstrip. It's the showing that matters, not the telling. The essays in this chapter *show*, just as Jane Adams shows us the "shrunken knot of pain" that "expands and fills the void" of her narrator's life.

Using a Personal Point of View

"Point of view" as I am using it is not a synonym for "opinion." "What's your point of view on that issue?" is an appropriate way to use the phrase; however, that's not how I intend to use it here.

In a piece of writing, *point of view refers to the angle of vision from which the writing views the material.* Jane Adams is writing an essay about a mother saying good-bye to her teenage son who is about to go live with her ex-husband. Will her story be told in the first person ("I") by Adams herself? Or by the son, who is leaving one parent for another? Or will the writer tell the story in the third person, using words like "she," "he," "father," "son"? The facts of the story may remain the same in all these instances. But the point of view has changed.

With the evocative voice, the point of view tends to be first-person, as the author frequently plays the part of a character in her own story or description. But not all essays written in the evocative voice are narratives or descriptions, and not all of them are written in the first person. Even when the essays are not explicitly first person, even when the pronoun "I" doesn't actually appear in the essay, the point of view remains a personal one in essays written in the evocative voice. Notice that Adams' essay is in the third person. However, it is not a newspaper account of the event. The reader learns what the woman is thinking, remembering, feeling, because Adams is seeking to evoke emotion. If Adams wrote a journalistic account of the scene, it would indicate that she had decided that she was not interested in evoking emotion so much as in informing her readers.

The evocative voice is a personal voice, and the point of view of the writing is inevitably a personal one, whether the writer chooses the first or third person.

Writing with Sincerity

Writers, I believe, have certain ethical obligations to their readers. Being honest about facts and sources is essential (except, perhaps, for those humorous essays that clearly exaggerate for comic effect).

In these evocative voice essays, however, there is another kind of honesty, a sincerity that underlies the entire essay. As you read these essays I think you will sense that the writers are being forthright and very earnest about their experiences and feelings.

This is perhaps at the heart of what makes an essay evoke emotions: readers can sense a genuineness of emotion as they read. Adams is writing about an extraordinarily painful moment in the life of this mother. As readers, we suspect that she is writing about herself; perhaps the pain has led her to adopt a more distant third-person point of view rather than using the first person. But the essay still sounds sincere as we listen to the mother's mixture of emotions: she knows she cannot be the role model for her son that he needs; at the same time she also knows that she does not want him to leave even if, in some ways, it is right that he do so. There are no good guys and bad guys in this essay; it's too honest and true to life for that.

I have read essays over the years written by my students that have evoked many emotions in me as a result of their honesty about themselves and their own experiences, at times a painful sort of honesty. What is most important, however, is not so much that you unburden your soul on your reader as that you write sincerely, for readers seem to have finely tuned antennae that pick up artificiality and pretense.

PERSONAL VS. PRIVATE

All this encouragement to write more personally, to write out of your own experiences and feelings, to be sincere, makes some students uncomfortable. "Why should I tell my readers—a bunch of strangers—all about myself? I'd be embarrassed."

This is a very important and valid point. I am not encouraging you to write things about yourself that might make you uncomfortable or that might embarrass you. I never would write such things about myself, so why should you?

I mentioned earlier that I had written an essay about my failure as a Little League ballplayer. I don't mind writing about that experience because it happened long ago when I was a completely different person. I have, of course, failed at other things since those long ago days on the baseball diamond. Some of these later failures I would be quite willing to write about for you to read, but others I would only write about for those people very close to me, while I can think of one or two personal failures that I think I would write about only in my personal journal and would let no one read. What I am saying is that I draw a line that divides the personal—which I am willing to share in my teaching and in my writing—from the private—which I am not willing to share.

Look at these two diagrams:

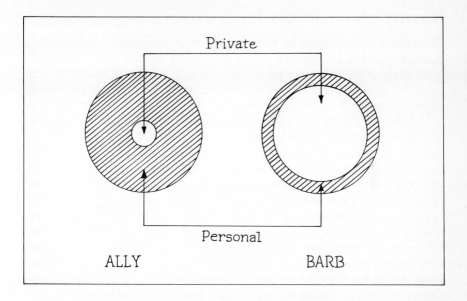

Ally is a very open student. She may not mind writing about her drug rehabilitation or her feelings when she learned that her father was being unfaithful to her mother or her miscarried pregnancy or her attempted suicide. I have had students like Ally; all of these topics have actually been written about by different students in my classes who felt comfortable dealing with such personal topics. Barb, on the other hand, is much more private. She will write about her high school prom, her trip to Acapulco, her reaction to the film *Platoon*. She will not mention that her date embarrassed her at the prom by flirting with all the cheerleaders; she will not discuss her passionate evening with the Mexican bullfighter; she will not refer to her older brother's death in Vietnam.

It would be wrong, I think, for either Ally or Barb to cross that boundary between personal and private. But, aside from scientific manuals, legal contracts, and other forms of technical and business writing, it would be difficult to write effectively if one were not willing to be personal at all. Maybe we should redefine "personal": I mean writing about experiences, memories, ideas, feelings which the writer herself has experienced directly *or through friends, relatives, neighbors.* So put yourself into your writing—but only to the degree that feels comfortable and right to you.

STRUCTURES

The evocative voice may appear in any number of different sorts of essays, but two structures in particular seem conducive to writing an evocative essay: (1) descriptions and (2) narratives, or stories.

Descriptions

For a descriptive essay to be effective it must be concrete; it must show a place or a person or an event vividly from some definite point of view. It quite likely is anchored in a particular time and usually embodies a strong emotional quality. No wonder description is an effective pattern for writing an evocative essay!

Effective description, as I've said, must show rather than tell. Sunset at Key West is breathtakingly beautiful. However, if I want you to feel its wonder, experience its beauty, I'm going to have to show it to you rather than merely asserting that it is astonishing. In order to do that, I will rely upon the five senses. Certainly, most descriptive writing emphasizes the visual, but there are four other senses also, and as a writer you need to rely upon them all. What can you hear as the sun sets at Key West—gulls, waves breaking on the beach, the breathing of other sunset watchers? What aromas are there—the ocean, suntan oil, cocktails in the hands of the sunset watchers? Can you taste anything—the salt air, the margarita in your glass? What about the sense of touch—are you barefoot on wet sand, is the approaching night air giving you goose bumps, is there a mist from the waves?

Thoughts/Feelings But in an effort to focus on sensory impressions, don't forget that you are also a thinking and feeling human being out there observing the sunset. What thoughts are running through your mind as you watch the beautiful end of day? Are you seeing patterns in the clouds, making associations between the varied shades of the sky and other colorful sights you've seen? Is your awe at the beauty so strong that you cannot swallow that margarita because of a lump developing in your throat? Do you find yourself inclined to speak in whispers or to grow altogether silent? These are the sort of responses that can show your reader just what it feels like to experience sunset at Key West.

Selecting Details Frequently, descriptions make an attempt to convey a single dominant impression of the scene, event, or person being described. In the example I've been using, the dominant impression is one of experiencing awe-inspiring beauty. In an effort to convey that feeling, to evoke it in the reader, as a writer I would pick the details for my description very carefully, only using the ones that best create the picture I want to convey. So I choose to ignore the squalling baby whose crying marred the sunset on

Tuesday night, and I overlook the pain of my sunburned shoulders, caused by my own carelessness during a day of swimming in the ocean, because these details, while genuine, work against my goal. Am I being dishonest in omitting these details? I don't think so. I'm trying to communicate the emotions I felt as I watched a number of such sunsets, so I focus on typical details, leaving out the singular ones that really don't fit the mood I am evoking.

I have described a place, but it is just as likely that you can evoke emotion by describing a person important to you such as a grandparent or teacher (!!), or by describing an event such as the Indianapolis 500 or your high school commencement.

Narration

Another effective way to evoke emotion is by telling a story. Actually, "telling" a story is an unfortunate way to describe narration because here, as with the descriptive writing I've just described, you really don't want to "tell" the reader so much as you want to "show" the reader.

Dramatizing   So you don't merely tell us that the mother was hurting as she watched her son get ready to move out of her home and into her ex-husband's. You let us see what the son is like so that we know why she will miss him. You let us hear the conversation between the parents that has brought about this change. You tell us what the mother's insides feel like and what her fears are as the son leaves. If it sounds as if I am suggesting that you describe the event, you're right. (And, of course, Jane Adams has done all these things in her essay.) There is a certain overlap between narration and description. Sometimes your description includes action on the part of the people involved; sometimes your narration of actions includes description of people or places. In narrative writing, however, the emphasis is on what happens more than on appearances.

And if the narration is to be effective in evoking emotions, it must create a sense of vicarious participation on the part of the reader. In other words, the readers need to feel as if they *were* there, experiencing the same things that the characters in the narrative are experiencing. Done effectively, narrative is thus quite powerful in evoking emotions. In other words, the writer *shows* the readers things happening—dramatizing events—rather than merely telling us what occurred in summarizing fashion.

Points to Remember   To create this sense of vicarious participation in the experience, I'd suggest that you remember several factors as you write your story:

Pace   Too many stories move too slowly. They begin somewhere way before the beginning ("One Tuesday night, I was out celebrating my new driver's license. Little did I know that by that Sunday I would have had that license suspended"), forcing the reader to wait and wait and wait for something significant to happen. Often the stories bog down in unnecessary details.

What you need to remember is that as the writer of the story you have the power to control time. Notice that Jane Adams gives us a view of the ten years of the mother's single parenthood in just a few sentences. She does not want to slow the story down with a long account of what happened during those years. She wants to keep her reader focused on the important actions, not the trivial ones.

Dialogue Too many stories forget to share the sound of the human voice with the reader. While indirect dialogue has its place in keeping the pace of the story moving, direct dialogue can make the reader feel a part of the scene. So instead of writing, "Her husband had said that it was time he paid his dues; it was his turn to worry about the boy," Adams writes, "It's time I paid my dues, her ex-husband told her when they talked about their son; it's my turn to worry." And we get to hear the actual conversation.

When writing dialogue, just remember that the conversations we have every day are often unexciting and, to be honest, relatively trivial. The dialogue in your narrative essays, however, needs to be purposeful; it has to be dialogue that will reveal something about the character's emotions.

Conclusions There is a tendency in narrative writing to "reach a conclusion," to add a lesson or make a point such as Aesop always did with his fables. And of course there are times when such conclusions make sense.

There are other times, however, when the story suggests its point, shows its conclusion, and a tacked-on lesson becomes unnecessary. In fact, if you are writing in the evocative voice, evoking strong emotions in your audience, I suspect that there will be little need for you to conclude your story with a lesson or moral. If you've told the story well, your reader will be feeling the emotions you wish him to feel; that's conclusion enough. (See Chapter 10 for narratives that tend to make a point or teach a lesson.)

So in this chapter you will be hearing honest, sincere voices, emotional voices, describing, narrating, simply speaking to you about heartfelt emotions that these writers wish to share with you. Read these essays looking for the qualities they share, and then try writing in the evocative voice yourself. It's a powerful experience to know that your own writing has moved other people to feel something you have felt yourself, a powerful experience worth trying.

Once More to the Lake
E. B. White

Elwyn Brooks White (1899–1985) is one of the most widely anthologized American writers of this century. Familiar to college students as coauthor (with William Strunk, Jr.) of *The Elements of Style,* a writer's handbook, White's most enduring fame may be as the author of the beloved children's classics *Charlotte's Web* and *Stuart Little.* White, recipient of The Presidential Medal for Freedom as well as a citation from the Pulitzer Prize Committee, was a regular contributor to magazines such as *The New Yorker* and *Harper's.* "Once More to the Lake," arguably his best-known essay, appeared most recently in *The Essays of E. B. White,* published in 1967.

QUESTIONS ABOUT IDEAS

1. White expects the lake to have changed for the worse over the years but is pleased to find that the changes have not been major. Why is he initially so pessimistic? Do you tend to view change as negative or positive? Why?
2. What is the appeal of nature trips to urban Americans? Why do so many city dwellers spend their vacations in the woods or the mountains? What does this phenomenon say about our society?
3. Evidently, White has chosen to vacation without his wife, whom he never mentions in the essay. In fact, he never mentions his mother either, although she undoubtedly was there during his family's vacations at the lake. Are there trips and vacations where it is important for men to get away without their spouses, daughters, mothers? Would the same be true for women?

AUGUST 1941

One summer, along about 1904, my father rented a camp on a lake in   1
Maine and took us all there for the month of August. We all got ringworm from some kittens and had to rub Pond's Extract on our arms and legs night and morning, and my father rolled over in a canoe with all his clothes on; but outside of that the vacation was a success and from then on none of us ever thought there was any place in the world like that lake in Maine. We returned summer after summer—always on August 1 for one month. I have since become a salt-water man, but sometimes in summer there are days when the restlessness of the tides and the fearful cold of the sea water and

the incessant wind that blows across the afternoon and into the evening make me wish for the placidity of a lake in the woods. A few weeks ago this feeling got so strong I bought myself a couple of bass hooks and a spinner and returned to the lake where we used to go, for a week's fishing and to revisit old haunts.

I took along my son, who had never had any fresh water up his nose   2 and who had seen lily pads only from train windows. On the journey over to the lake I began to wonder what it would be like. I wondered how time would have marred this unique, this holy spot—the coves and streams, the hills that the sun set behind, the camps and the paths behind the camps. I was sure that the tarred road would have found it out, and I wondered in what other ways it would be desolated. It is strange how much you can remember about places like that once you allow your mind to return into the grooves that lead back. You remember one thing, and that suddenly reminds you of another thing. I guess I remembered clearest of all the early mornings, when the lake was cool and motionless, remembered how the bedroom smelled of the lumber it was made of and of the wet woods whose scent entered through the screen. The partitions in the camp were thin and did not extend clear to the top of the rooms, and as I was always the first up I would dress softly so as not to wake the others, and sneak out into the sweet outdoors and start out in the canoe, keeping close along the shore in the long shadows of the pines. I remembered being very careful never to rub my paddle against the gunwale for fear of disturbing the stillness of the cathedral.

The lake had never been what you would call a wild lake. There were   3 cottages sprinkled around the shores, and it was in farming country although the shores of the lake were quite heavily wooded. Some of the cottages were owned by nearby farmers, and you would live at the shore and eat your meals at the farmhouse. That's what our family did. But although it wasn't wild, it was a fairly large and undisturbed lake and there were places in it that, to a child at least, seemed infinitely remote and primeval.

I was right about the tar: it led to within half a mile of the shore. But   4 when I got back there, with my boy, and we settled into a camp near a farmhouse and into the kind of summertime I had known, I could tell that it was going to be pretty much the same as it had been before—I knew it, lying in bed the first morning smelling the bedroom and hearing the boy sneak quietly out and go off along the shore in a boat. I began to sustain the illusion that he was I, and therefore, by simple transposition, that I was my father. This sensation persisted, kept cropping up all the time we were there. It was not an entirely new feeling, but in this setting it grew much stronger. I seemed to be living a dual existence. I would be in the middle of some simple act, I would be picking up a bait box or laying down a table fork, or I would be saying something and suddenly it would be not I but my father who was saying the words or making the gesture. It gave me a creepy sensation.

We went fishing the first morning. I felt the same damp moss covering   5
the worms in the bait can, and saw the dragonfly alight on the tip of my rod
as it hovered a few inches from the surface of the water. It was the arrival of
this fly that convinced me beyond any doubt that everything was as it always
had been, that the years were a mirage and that there had been no years. The
small waves were the same, chucking the rowboat under the chin as we
fished at anchor, and the boat was the same boat, the same color green and
the ribs broken in the same places, and under the floorboards the same fresh
water leavings and debris—the dead hellgrammite, the wisps of moss, the
rusty discarded fishhook, the dried blood from yesterday's catch. We stared
silently at the tips of our rods, at the dragonflies that came and went. I lowered the tip of mine into the water, tentatively, pensively dislodging the fly,
which darted two feet away, poised, darted two feet back, and came to rest
again a little farther up the rod. There had been no years between the ducking of this dragonfly and the other one—the one that was part of memory. I
looked at the boy, who was silently watching his fly, and it was my hands
that held his rod, my eyes watching. I felt dizzy and didn't know which rod
I was at the end of.

We caught two bass, hauling them in briskly as though they were   6
mackerel, pulling them over the side of the boat in a businesslike manner
without any landing net, and stunning them with a blow on the back of the
head. When we got back for a swim before lunch, the lake was exactly where
we had left it, the same number of inches from the dock, and there was only
the merest suggestion of a breeze. This seemed an utterly enchanted sea, this
lake you could leave to its own devices for a few hours and come back to,
and find that it had not stirred, this constant and trustworthy body of water.
In the shallows, the dark, water-soaked sticks and twigs, smooth and old,
were undulating in clusters on the bottom against the clean ribbed sand, and
the track of the mussel was plain. A school of minnows swam by, each min-
now with its small individual shadow, doubling the attendance, so clear and
sharp in the sunlight. Some of the other campers were in swimming, along
the shore, one of them with a cake of soap, and the water felt thin and clear
and unsubstantial. Over the years there had been this person with the cake
of soap, this cultist, and here he was. There had been no years.

Up to the farmhouse to dinner through the teeming dusty field, the   7
road under our sneakers was only a two-track road. The middle track was
missing, the one with the marks of the hooves and the splotches of dried,
flaky manure. There had always been three tracks to choose from in choosing which track to walk in; now the choice was narrowed down to two. For
a moment I missed terribly the middle alternative. But the way led past the
tennis court, and something about the way it lay there in the sun reassured
me; the tape had loosened along the backline, the alleys were green with
plantains and other weeds, and the net (installed in June and removed in
September) sagged in the dry noon, and the whole place steamed with mid-

day heat and hunger and emptiness. There was a choice of pie for dessert, and one was blueberry and one was apple, and the waitresses were the same country girls, there having been no passage of time, only the illusion of it as in a dropped curtain—the waitresses were still fifteen; their hair had been washed, that was the only difference—they had been to the movies and seen the pretty girls with the clean hair.

Summertime, oh, summertime, pattern of life indelible with fadeproof **8** lake, the wood unshatterable, the pasture with the sweetfern and the juniper forever and ever, summer without end; this was the background, and the life along the shore was the design, the cottages with their innocent and tranquil design, their tiny docks with the flagpole and the American flag floating against the white clouds in the blue sky, the little paths over the roots of the trees leading from camp to camp and the paths leading back to the outhouses and the can of lime for sprinkling, and at the souvenir counters at the store the miniature birch-bark canoes and the postcards that showed things looking a little better than they looked. This was the American family at play, escaping the city heat, wondering whether the newcomers in the camp at the head of the cove were "common" or "nice," wondering whether it was true that the people who drove up for Sunday dinner at the farmhouse were turned away because there wasn't enough chicken.

It seemed to me, as I kept remembering all this, that those times and **9** those summers had been infinitely precious and worth saving. There had been jollity and peace and goodness. The arriving (at the beginning of August) had been so big a business in itself, at the railway station the farm wagon drawn up, the first smell of the pine-laden air, the first glimpse of the smiling farmer, and the great importance of the trunks and your father's enormous authority in such matters, and the feel of the wagon under you for the long ten-mile haul, and at the top of the last long hill catching the first view of the lake after eleven months of not seeing this cherished body of water. The shouts and cries of the other campers when they saw you, and the trunks to be unpacked, to give up their rich burden. (Arriving was less exciting nowadays, when you sneaked up in your car and parked it under a tree near the camp and took out the bags and in five minutes it was all over, no fuss, no loud wonderful fuss about trunks.)

Peace and goodness and jollity. The only thing that was wrong now, **10** really, was the sound of the place, an unfamiliar nervous sound of the outboard motors. This was the note that jarred, the one thing that would sometimes break the illusion and set the years moving. In those other summertimes all motors were inboard; and when they were at a little distance, the noise they made was a sedative, an ingredient of summer sleep. They were one-cylinder and two-cylinder engines, and some were make-and-break and some were jump-spark, but they all made a sleepy sound across the lake. The one-lungers throbbed and fluttered, and the twin-cylinder ones purred and purred, and that was a quiet sound, too. But now the campers all had

outboards. In the daytime, in the hot mornings, these motors made a petu-
lant, irritable sound; at night in the still evening when the afterglow lit the
water, they whined about one's ears like mosquitoes. My boy loved our
rented outboard, and his great desire was to achieve single-handed mastery
over it, and authority, and he soon learned the trick of choking it a little (but
not too much), and the adjustment of the needle valve. Watching him I
would remember the things you could do with the old one-cylinder engine
with the heavy flywheel, how you could have it eating out of your hand if
you got really close to it spiritually. Motorboats in those days didn't have
clutches, and you would make a landing by shutting off the motor at the
proper time and coasting in with a dead rudder. But there was a way of reversing them, if you learned the trick, by cutting the switch and putting it
on again exactly on the final dying revolution of the flywheel, so that it
would kick back against compression and begin reversing. Approaching a
dock in a strong following breeze, it was difficult to slow up sufficiently by
the ordinary coasting method, and if a boy felt he had complete mastery over
his motor, he was tempted to keep it running beyond its time and then re-
verse it a few feet from the dock. It took a cool nerve, because if you threw
the switch a twentieth of a second too soon you would catch the flywheel
when it still had speed enough to go up past center, and the boat would leap
ahead, charging bull-fashion at the dock.

We had a good week at the camp. The bass were biting well and the 11
sun shone endlessly, day after day. We would be tired at night and lie down
in the accumulated heat of the little bedrooms after the long hot day and the
breeze would stir almost imperceptibly outside and the smell of the swamp
drift in through the rusty screens. Sleep would come easily and in the morning the red squirrel would be on the roof, tapping out his gay routine. I kept
remembering everything, lying in bed in the mornings—the small steamboat
that had a long rounded stern like the lip of a Ubangi, and how quietly she
ran on the moonlight sails, when the older boys played their mandolins and
the girls sang and we ate doughnuts dipped in sugar, and how sweet the music was on the water in the shining night, and what it had felt like to think
about girls then. After breakfast we would go up to the store and the things
were in the same place—the minnows in a bottle, the plugs and spinners dis-
arranged and pawed over by the youngsters from the boys' camp, the Fig
Newtons and the Beeman's gum. Outside, the road was tarred and cars
stood in front of the store. Inside, all was just as it had always been, except
there was more Coca-Cola and not so much Moxie and root beer and birch
beer and sarsaparilla. We would walk out with the bottle of pop apiece and
sometimes the pop would backfire up our noses and hurt. We explored the
streams, quietly, where the turtles slid off the sunny logs and dug their way
into the soft bottom; and we lay on the town wharf and fed worms to the
tame bass. Everywhere we went I had trouble making out which was I, the
one walking at my side, the one walking in my pants.

One afternoon while we were at that lake a thunderstorm came up. It 12 was like the revival of an old melodrama that I had seen long ago with childish awe. The second-act climax of the drama of the electrical disturbance over a lake in America had not changed in any important respect. This was the big scene, still the big scene. The whole thing was so familiar, the first feeling of oppression and heat and a general air around camp of not wanting to go very far away. In midafternoon (it was all the same) a curious darkening of the sky, and a lull in everything that had made life tick; and then the way the boats suddenly swung the other way at their moorings with the coming of a breeze out of the new quarter, and the premonitory rumble. Then the kettle drum, then the snare, then the bass drum and cymbals, then crackling light against the dark, and the gods grinning and licking their chops in the hills. Afterward the calm, the rain steadily rustling in the calm lake, the return of light and hope and spirits, and the campers running out in joy and relief to go swimming in the rain, their bright cries perpetuating the deathless joke about how they were getting simply drenched, and the children screaming with delight at the new sensation of bathing in the rain, and the joke about getting drenched linking the generations in a strong indestructible chain. And the comedian who waded in carrying an umbrella.

When the others went swimming my son said he was going in, too. He 13 pulled his dripping trunks from the line where they had hung all through the shower and wrung them out. Languidly, and with no thought of going in, I watched him, his hard little body, skinny and bare, saw him wince slightly as he pulled up around his vitals the small, soggy, icy garment. As he buckled the swollen belt, suddenly my groin felt the chill of death.

QUESTIONS ABOUT THE RHETORICAL SITUATION

1. To what age groups is White's essay most likely to appeal? Why?
2. White's feelings about the lake are very strong ones. Where in the essay does he show us these feelings through the use of concrete details? Where in the essay does he tell us about these feelings through direct commentary? How would you describe the feelings he has toward his subject?
3. How did you react to White's description of his vacations at the lake? How did you react to his final sentence? What is the purpose of that final sentence?

QUESTIONS ABOUT THE ESSAY'S VOICE

1. How would you describe the voice you hear in the essay's opening paragraph? How does that voice change as the essay progresses? Why does it change?

2. In ¶10 White describes the sound of the outboard motors at some length. What other sounds does he describe in the essay? In fact, which of the five senses does he rely on in painting his picture of the lake? What is the effect of all his sensory description?

3. White is an adult, a father, as he writes the essay. How clearly does he recall what it was like to be a child at the lake? Where in the essay does he re-view the lake through his own child's eyes? Through his own remembered eyes as a boy? How does the voice sound at these moments in the essay?

4. Starting at about ¶4, White begins to feel that the lake has really not changed. What examples does he provide to make this point? Why has he chosen these specific examples instead of others? Notice how his certainty about the unchanging qualities of the lake gets stronger and stronger. Why is it important to the essay that he convey this growing certainty?

5. In ¶9, White uses the second person ("you" and "your"). What is his reason for doing so? What effect does this strategy have on the essay's voice? On the reader's response to the essay?

6. Part of the essay's interest is created by White's perceptions of himself as both child and adult. (See the end of ¶5 for instance.) How do these perceptions contribute to creating the evocative voice of this essay?

7. As mentioned earlier, this essay is widely anthologized. Why do you suppose the compilers of so many textbooks like *Model Voices* choose to include "Once More to the Lake"? Does the voice have anything to do with the essay's popularity?

TOPICS TO WRITE ABOUT

1. Write an essay about the changes you have observed in a favorite place which you have just recently revisited. POTENTIAL AUDIENCES: people who have lived through the changes as they occurred/ the general reading public. POTENTIAL PURPOSES: to make them feel the effect of the passage of time in a way they probably have not felt before/to make them feel the same emotions you did—good or bad, uplifting or disturbing.

2. Write an essay in which you describe a significant change in one of the roles you play (White deals with being a son and later a father; you might write about being a novice swimmer and later a pool lifeguard teaching new swimmers or about being a baby sister and now having a new baby sister of your own). POTENTIAL AUDIENCES: others who play the role you currently play/readers who play the role you played formerly. POTENTIAL PURPOSES: to remind them of what things were like before they adopted this current role/to make them identify with the feelings aroused in you by your recollections of what it was like to play that role.

The Odors of Homecoming

Pablo Neruda

Pablo Neruda was a Chilean poet who published a number of volumes of poetry. Born the son of a railway worker in 1904, Neruda published five volumes
of poems by the age of 22. Neruda was also an active politician, serving as a
member of the Chilean senate and as a diplomat representing Chile abroad. A
Communist, Neruda spent several years after World War II in exile, but after
his return in 1952, he remained active as a politician in his native land for the
final twenty-one years of his life. He died in 1973. The following essay, from
Passions and Impressions (1983), is a vivid description of a familiar and important scene. The essay has been translated by Margaret Sayers Peden and was
first published in 1952.

QUESTIONS ABOUT IDEAS

1. How long do you think the writer has been away from his home? Is the
   length of his absence a factor in his response to his homecoming?
2. It is often said that "you can't go home again." In what sense is this idea
   right? Wrong? Based on your reading of this essay, how do you think
   Neruda might answer these questions?
3. This essay is set in a different hemisphere in a quite distant and, for us,
   exotic locale. How familiar is the scene Neruda describes? How difficult
   is it to identify with the emotions he presents?

   My house nestles among many trees. After a long absence, I like to lose   1
myself in hidden nooks to savor my homecoming. Mysterious, fragrant
thickets have appeared that are new to me. The poplar I planted in the back
of the garden, so slim it could barely be seen, is now an adult tree. Its bark
is patterned with wrinkles of wisdom that rise toward the sky to express
themselves in a constant tremor of new leaves in the treetop.
   The chestnut trees were the last to recognize me. When I arrived, their   2
naked, dry branches, towering and unseeing, seemed imperious and hostile,
though the pervading spring of Chile was germinating amid their trunks.
Every day I went to call on them, for I understood that they demanded my
homage, and in the cold of morning stood motionless beneath the leafless
branches, until one day a timid green bud, high overhead, came out to look
at me, and others followed. So my reappearance was communicated to the
wary, hidden leaves of the tallest chestnut tree, which now greets me with
condescension, tolerating my return.
   In the trees the birds renew their age-old trills, as if nothing ever hap-   3
pened beneath the leaves.

A pervasive odor of winter and years lingers in the library. Of all 4 places, this was the most suffused with absence.

There is something of mortality about the smell of musty books; it as- 5 saults the nostrils and strikes the rugged terrain of the soul, because it is the odor of oblivion, of buried memory.

Standing beside the weathered window, staring at the blue and white 6 Andean sky, I sense that behind my back the aroma of spring is pitting its strength against the books. They resist being rooted out of their long ne-glect, and still exude signs of oblivion. Spring enters every room, clad in a new dress and the odor of honeysuckle.

The books have been unruly in my absence. None is missing, but none 7 is in its place. Beside an austere volume of Bacon, a rare seventeenth-century edition, I find Salgari's *The Captain of Yucatan,* and in spite of everything, they've got along rather well together. On the other hand, as I pick up a solitary Byron, its cover drops off like the dark wing of an albatross. Labo-riously, I stitch spine and cover, but not before a puff of cold Romanticism clouds my eyes.

The shells are the most silent occupants of my house. They endured 8 the years of the ocean, solidifying their silence. Now, to those years have been added time and dust. Their cold, glinting mother-of-pearl, their con-centric Gothic ellipses, their open valves, remind me of distant coasts, long-ago events. This incomparable lance of rosy light is the *Rostellaria,* which the Cuban malacologist Carlos de la Torre, a magus of the deep, once con-ferred upon me like an underseas decoration. And here, slightly more faded and dusty, is the black "olive" of the California seas, and, of the same prov-enance, the oyster of red spines and the oyster of black pearls. We almost drowned in that treasure-laden sea.

There are new occupants, books and objects liberated from boxes long 9 sealed. The pine boxes come from France. The boards smell of sunny noon in the Midi, and as I pry them open, they creak and sing, and the golden light falls on the red bindings of Victor Hugo. *Les Misérables,* in an early edition, arrives to crowd the walls of my house with its multitude of heartrending lives.

Then, from a large box resembling a coffin, comes the sweet face of a 10 woman, firm wooden breasts that once cleaved the wind, hands saturated with music and brine. It is the figure of a woman, a figurehead. I baptize her María Celeste, because she has all the mystery of a lost ship. I discovered her radiant beauty in a Paris *bric-à-brac,* buried beneath used hardware, disfig-ured by neglect, hidden beneath the sepulchral rags and tatters of the slums. Now, aloft, she sails again, alive and new. Every morning her cheeks will be covered by mysterious dew or saltwater tears.

All at once the roses are in bloom. Once I was an enemy of the rose, of 11 its interminable literary associations, of its arrogance. But as I watched them grow, having endured the winter with nothing to wear and nothing to cover their heads, and then as snowy breasts or glowing fires peered from among hard and thorny stems, little by little I was filled with tenderness, with admiration for their ox-like health, for the daring, secret wave of perfume and light they implacably extract from the black earth at just the right moment, as if duty were a miracle, as if they thrived on precise maneuvers in harsh weather. And now roses grow everywhere, with a moving solemnity I share—remote, both they and I, from pomp and frivolity, each absorbed in creating its individual flash of lightning.

Now every wave of air bears a soft, trembling movement, a flowery 12 palpitation that pierces the heart. Forgotten names, forgotten springs, hands that touched briefly, haughty eyes of yellow stone, tresses lost in time: youth, insistently throbbing with memories and ecstatic aromas.

It is the perfume of the honeysuckle, the first kisses of spring.   13

QUESTIONS ABOUT THE RHETORICAL SITUATION

1. Neruda wrote this essay in Spanish. Is there any evidence that he has targeted his writing to a Spanish-speaking audience? Would a Chilean reader get more out of this essay than an English-speaking reader?
2. How would you describe Neruda's attitude toward his home? What makes his home a home? How would you describe his attitude toward the various objects in his home? Does he feel the same way about all these belongings? Which seem most important? Why?
3. What emotions does Neruda evoke in you as you read his essay? Do these emotions change over the course of the essay? If so, how?

QUESTIONS ABOUT THE ESSAY'S VOICE

1. What is appropriate about Neruda's description of the honeysuckle in the essay's final paragraph? What emotion(s) does this paragraph evoke?
2. The essay's title refers to the sense of smell. What odors does the essay actually describe? What impression do these descriptions create? Which of the other five senses does Neruda include in his description? What impression do these other sensory details create?
3. In ¶11, Neruda's third sentence is more than eighty words long. What effect does this long sentence create? What do you notice about the sentences before and after this one?
4. What impact does the essay's verb tense have on you as you read this essay? How would the essay's voice be affected if the tense were different?

5. Examine Neruda's movements in the essay as he describes his homecoming. Why is he so careful to tell us where he is as he examines his familiar belongings?

6. How effective is Neruda in showing us his homecoming and emotions rather than merely telling us about them? Which concrete details stand out most vividly for you? Why?

7. Neruda's essay is about his return to a favorite place. So is E. B. White's "Once More to the Lake." What significant differences do you see between these two "homecomings"? How do these differences account for the difference in the voice in the two essays?

TOPICS TO WRITE ABOUT

1. Write a description of your own home when you have returned to it after being away for awhile. POTENTIAL AUDIENCES: the other people you live with/someone who has just moved into your part of the country. POTENTIAL PURPOSES: to make them recall the feelings which are a part of your home/to make them feel what it is like to live in your part of the country.

2. Write a description of someplace important to you, emphasizing one of the senses other than sight (for example, your favorite campsite or your favorite bakery). POTENTIAL AUDIENCES: someone you love who has never been able to visit this special place/someone with whom you have shared special times in this special place. POTENTIAL PURPOSES: to make the place come alive and to make your readers feel as if they were there/to remind your readers of what it was like when you shared those special times in this special place.

Grandma's Veranda
Jackie Pfeifer

At the time this essay was written, Jackie Pfeifer was a nontraditional student taking a degree in nursing. In addition to her coursework, she worked as a student assistant to a zoology professor. Pfeifer is married, and mother of a young son. Her essay was in response to an assignment that asked the students to write something that would be enjoyed by an audience of senior citizens. About "Grandma's Veranda," Jackie says, "It was one of those rare occasions when everything seemed to 'gel'—I couldn't get my thoughts onto the paper

fast enough. In writing the essay, I wanted to convey the warm, secure feeling
I had growing up and the special relationship I had with my grandmother, and
possibly evoke similar memories in my audience."

QUESTIONS ABOUT IDEAS

1. What is it that makes the grandma's veranda special? Is there anything
   truly special about the veranda that a casual visitor would notice?
2. Everything Pfeifer remembers about the veranda is pleasant and positive,
   yet undoubtedly life was not wonderful 100 percent of the time on the
   veranda. How typical is Pfeifer's "selective memory" here? Why do we
   tend to "misremember" in this way?
3. No specific time or place is given in the essay. Approximately when and
   where is the story taking place? What impression did you form? How important is it to know the when and where?

When my two brothers and I were young, we spent our summers at   1
Grandma's house. More specifically, we spent our summers on Grandma's
"veranda." She never called it a porch. "Porches are ordinary," she would
say. "Lots of people have porches, but a veranda is special—an extension of
home."

Her veranda was a large, two-sided structure that wrapped around the   2
house, halfway down one side and along the back. It looked not as if it had
been built as part of the original house, but as an afterthought, added long
after the house had been built. Every floorboard creaked when we stepped
on it, and the steps sagged a bit in the middle from the years of use. There
were large bamboo shades hanging from the ceiling that Grandma would roll
down in the late afternoon to ward off the hot summer sun and give us a cool
nook in which to shade ourselves. Furniture was sparse: a potpourri of mis-
matched tables and tattered wicker chairs, and a squeaky glider with heavy
vinyl cushions that stuck to our legs when we sat on them.

The veranda was quite literally an extension of home, for we lived   3
there all summer. Early in the morning, Grandma would sit in her petticoat
on the glider, fanning herself, and watch as my brothers and I would play
tag or hide-n-seek, using the veranda as "home base." Or she would watch
as we climbed up an old mulberry tree in her backyard. We'd pick the
purplish-red berries and take them back to the veranda to be washed and
sorted. After that, we'd take our assigned seats on the steps and eat the berries, staining our mouths with berry juice that took days to wear off.

In the afternoon when the summer sun was unmercifully hot or on   4
days when it rained, Grandma would roll down the shades and the veranda
would then be transformed into a cool oasis where we could shut out the rest
of the world. We would draw and color, read our Nancy Drew and Hardy

Boy mysteries, or best of all, imagine we were on a spaceship, in an enchanted castle, or on a pirate ship crossing the ocean. We'd let our imaginations soar and play out our fantasies while Grandma, still fanning herself, looked on and marveled at us. All our energies being spent, we would settle down into the chairs or glider, listen to the sparrows call to each other, and watch our shadows, cast by the sun glowing through the bamboo slats, as they danced on the floor. One by one we would fall asleep, Grandma being first, lulling the rest of us with her gentle snoring.

Of all the times to be on the veranda, evening was the best. The air was   5
cooler, and everything seemed more settled and calm. Friends and neighbors would walk by and stop to visit, always remarking on what a lovely evening it was and how grown up my brothers and I were getting. When it grew darker, Grandma would light the citronella candles she had on the tables to keep the mosquitoes away and watch as we ran through the backyard catching lightning bugs. Holding them prisoner in old mayonnaise jars with holes punched in the lids, we'd take them back to the veranda, place them on the tables, and watch the bugs light up while we ate our before-bedtime snack. Before long, it would be time for bed. We'd reluctantly leave the veranda, with its cool breezes, and go inside the house where it was hot and sticky. There we would anxiously wait until the next morning, when we could break free from the house and get back to the veranda.

I never thought about the veranda that much until several years ago   6
when my grandmother died. Her house had been sold, and my brothers and I were there for the last time, packing up the rest of her belongings, deciding who should take what. Taking a long-needed break on the veranda, we were transported back in time as we took turns asking each other, "Remember when...?" Amid tears and laughter, memories came flooding back to all of us. Although each of us had slightly different versions of those memories, we all agreed on one thing. Grandma was right—verandas are special.

QUESTIONS ABOUT THE RHETORICAL SITUATION

1. As mentioned above, the essay was written to be read by senior citizens living in the local retirement village. How appropriate for those readers is this essay? Why? Are changes necessary to make it more appropriate? Why? Where? The odds are that your class is much younger than Pfeifer's target audience. Can this essay work for a younger audience? Why or why not?
2. Pfeifer's objective in this essay was to "make my readers remember fondly their own childhood special places." What was your reaction to the essay? What do you think the senior citizens' reaction would be? How successful is Pfeifer in achieving her objective?
3. Compare Pfeifer's recollections about her grandmother to Diane Rawl-

ings' (which follow). Both essays were written subsequent to the death of the author's grandmother. How are Pfeifer's attitudes toward her grandmother similar to and different from Rawlings'?

QUESTIONS ABOUT THE ESSAY'S VOICE

1. Pfeifer was concerned that her title and opening paragraph were "too bland," that her readers would lose interest in the essay very early. How accurate an assessment of her own work has she made? Can you compose a better title? A better introduction?
2. What is the effect on the opening paragraph's final sentence of Pfeifer's inserting "she would say" in the middle of the quotation? How would the sentence's impact be changed, how would its voice be affected, if those words were either omitted or placed at the beginning or end of the quotation instead of in the middle?
3. In ¶2, Pfeifer describes how Grandma lowers the bamboo shades to "ward off the hot summer sun and give us a cool nook in which to shade ourselves." Pfeifer is careful to provide sensory details relating to more than just the sense of sight. Which other such details help to create a full picture of Grandma's veranda?
4. Although she does not tell us how long ago these childhood days of playing on the veranda took place, Pfeifer is very clear in the final paragraph about when she came to value the veranda. Why is it important to her essay for her to be more specific about dates in that final paragraph?
5. What effect does her final sentence have on the reader? What does Pfeifer gain by having the essay's final thought focus on her grandmother rather than on her own happy memories?
6. Like Neruda and White, Pfeifer is writing about a place very important to her. In what ways are the three essays similar? different? While all three essays evoke emotion, how would you describe the emotions evoked in each?
7. Unlike Neruda, Pfeifer writes her essay using the conditional form of her verbs ("Grandma *would roll down* the shades"). Why doesn't she simply use past tense ("rolled down") or present tense ("rolls down"), as Neruda does? What is the effect of her using the contraction "d" instead of the word "would" at times (see ¶3)?

TOPICS TO WRITE ABOUT

1. Write an essay in which you remember fondly some old-fashioned way of doing things. POTENTIAL AUDIENCES: others who would recall the same old-

fashioned ways/people younger than yourself or from another part of the country who will be unfamiliar with your topic. POTENTIAL PURPOSES: to remind them of a fondly recalled past which in at least one way may have been better than the present/to make them feel that they might have missed out on something special.

2. Write about how you learned that some piece of advice or observation made by someone older than yourself was an accurate way of looking at life. POTENTIAL AUDIENCES: that person himself or herself/other readers who have probably heard the same observation or advice. POTENTIAL PURPOSES: to make him or her feel your gratitude for the advice/to share your feelings about learning this lesson with readers who may have learned the same lesson at some point.

Royal Exile
Beryl Markham

Beryl Markham was born in England in 1902 and moved to East Africa with her father at the age of four. She spent her childhood playing with the native children and living on her father's farm. An experienced horse trainer and breeder, Markham became a pilot in the early 1930s and carried passengers, mail, and supplies throughout East and Central Africa. In September 1936 she became the first person to fly solo across the Atlantic Ocean from east to west. Her book *West with the Night* (1942) is a memoir of her life, a book about which Ernest Hemingway wrote, "...she has written so well, and marvelously well, that I was completely ashamed of myself as a writer.... [Markham] can write rings around all of us who consider ourselves as writers." In this selection from Markham's book, she reminisces about the horse that was her very favorite when she was a girl.

QUESTIONS ABOUT IDEAS

1. What makes human relationships with dogs and horses different from human relationships with other animals? How do humans interact differently with dogs than with horses?
2. Is the relationship between the girl and her horse a fair one? In other words, does the horse have rights? If so, what are they? Does the girl acknowledge these rights?
3. What is your impression of the girl's reaction to Camciscan's disobedience? How effective a horse trainer does she seem to be?

4. Does this essay bring back memories of a childhood pet? or of a childhood challenge which you met and conquered?

To an eagle or to an owl or to a rabbit, man must seem a masterful and   1
yet a forlorn animal; he has but two friends. In his almost universal unpop-
ularity he points out, with pride, that these two are the dog and the horse.
He believes, with an innocence peculiar to himself, that they are equally
proud of this alleged confraternity. He says, 'Look at my two noble
friends—they are dumb, but they are loyal.' I have for years suspected that
they are only tolerant.

Suspecting it, I have nevertheless depended on this tolerance all my   2
life, and if I were, even now, without either a dog or a horse in my keeping,
I should feel I had lost contact with the earth. I should be as concerned as a
Buddhist monk having lost contact with Nirvana.

Horses in particular have been as much a part of my life as past birth-   3
days. I remember them more clearly. There is no phase of my childhood I
cannot recall by remembering a horse I owned then, or one my father
owned, or one I knew. They were not all gentle and kind. They were not all
alike. With some my father won races and with some he lost. His black-and-
yellow colours have swept past the post from Nairobi to Peru, to Durban.
Some horses he brought thousands of miles from England just for breeding.

Camciscan was one of these.   4

When he came to Njoro, I was a straw-haired girl with lanky legs and   5
he was a stallion bred out of a stud book thick as a tome—and partly out of
fire. The impression of his coming and of the first weeks that followed are
clear in my mind.

But sometimes I wonder how it seemed to him.   6

He arrived in the early morning, descending the ramp from the noisy   7
little train with the slow step of a royal exile. He held his head above the
heads of those who led him, and smelled the alien earth and the thin air of
the Highlands. It was not a smell that he knew.

There was a star of white on his forehead; his nostrils were wide and   8
showed crimson like the lacquered nostrils of a Chinese dragon. He was tall,
deep in girth, slender-chested, on strong legs clean as marble.

He was not chestnut; he was neither brown nor sorrel. He stood un-   9
certainly against the foreign background—a rangy bay stallion swathed in
sunlight and in a sheen of reddish gold.

He knew that this was freedom again. He knew that the darkness and   10
the terrifying movement of the ship that strained his legs and bruised his
body against walls too close together were gone now.

The net of leather rested on his head in those same places, and the long   11
lines that he had learned to follow hung from the thing in his mouth that
could not be bitten. But these he was used to. He could breathe, and he

could feel the spring of the earth under his hooves. He could shake his body, and he could see that there was distance here, and a breadth of land into which he fitted. He opened his nostrils and smelled the heat and the emptiness of Africa and filled his lungs and let the rush of air go out of them again in a low, undulant murmur.

He knew men. In the three quick years of his life he had seen more of 12 them than of his own kind. He understood that men were to serve him and that, in exchange, he was to concede them the indulgence of minor whims. They got upon his back and most often he let them stay. They rubbed his body and did things to his hooves, none of which was really unpleasant. He judged them by their smells and by the way they touched him. He did not like a hand with a tremor, or a hand that was hard, or one that moved too quickly. He did not trust the smell of a man that had nothing of the earth in it nor any sweat in it. Men's voices were bad, but there were some not too loud that came to his ears slowly, without insistence, and these he could bear.

A white man came up to him now and walked around him. Other men, 13 all of them very black—as black as his own mane—stood in a circle and watched the first man. The stallion was used to this. It was always the same, and it made him impatient. It made him bend the sleek bow of his neck and jab at the earth with his hooves.

The white man put a hand on the stallion's shoulder and said a word 14 that he knew because it was an old word and almost all men said it when they touched him or when they saw him.

The white man said, "So you are Camciscan," and the black men re- 15 peated, more slowly, "Camciscan," one after another. And a girl, who was white too, with straw-coloured hair and legs like a colt's, said "Camciscan" several times.

The girl seemed foolishly happy saying it. She came close to him and 16 said it again and he thought her smell was good enough, but he saw that she was familiar in her manner and he blew a little snort into her straw-coloured hair to warn her but she only laughed. She was attended by a dog, ugly with scars, who never left her heels.

After a little while the girl tugged gently on the lines Camciscan had 17 learned to follow, and so he followed.

The black men, the white girl, the scarred dog, and the bay stallion 18 walked along a dirt road while the white man rode far ahead in a buggy.

Camciscan looked neither to one side nor another. He saw nothing but the 19 road before him. He walked as if he were completely alone, like an abdicated king. He felt alone. The country smelled unused and clean, and the smells of the black men and the white girl were not outside of his understanding. But still he was alone and he felt some pride in that, as he always had.

He found the farm large and to his liking. It harboured many other 20 horses in long rows of stables, but his box was separate from theirs.

He remembered the old routine of food and saddle and workout and 21 rest, but he did not remember ever being attended before by a girl with straw-coloured hair and legs that were too long, like a colt's. He did not mind, but the girl was too familiar. She walked into his stall as if they had been old friends, and he had no need of friends.

He depended upon her for certain things, but, in turn, she got on his 22 back in the morning and they went to a valley bigger than any he had ever seen, or sometimes up the side of a certain hill that was very high, and then they came back again.

In time he found himself getting used to the girl, but he would not let 23 it be more than that. He could feel that she was trying to break through the loneliness that he lived by, and he remembered the reasons there were to mistrust men. He could not see that she was any different, but he felt that she was, and that disturbed him.

In the early morning she would come to his stable, slip his head-collar 24 on and remove his heavy rug. She would smooth him down with a cloth and brush his black mane and his tail. She would clean the urine from his floor, and separate the good bedding from that spoiled with manure. She did these things with care. She did them with a kind of intimate knowledge of his needs and with a scarcely hidden sense of possession which he felt—and resented.

He was by Spearmint out of Camlarge, and the blood flowed arro- 25 gantly in arrogant veins.

Mornings came when Camciscan waited for the girl with his ears and 26 with his eyes, because he had learned the sound of her bare feet on the ground that was still unsoftened by any sun, and he could distinguish the tangle of straw-coloured hair among other things. But when she was in his stable, he retreated to a far corner and stood watching her work.

He sometimes felt the urge to move closer to her, but the loneliness of 27 which he was so proud never permitted this. Instead, the urge turned often to anger which was, to himself, as unreasonable as the unprovoked anger of another might have been. He did not understand this anger; when it had passed, he would tremble as if he had caught the scent of something evil.

The girl vaulted to his back one morning, as she always did when they 28 went to the hill or the valley, and the anger surged suddenly through his body like a quick pain. He threw her from him so that she fell against the root of a tree and lay there with blood running through the straw-coloured hair. Her legs that were too long, like a colt's, did not move even when the white man and the black men carried her away.

Afterward, Camciscan trembled and sweated in his box and let his mis- 29 trust of the men who tried to feed him boil into hate. For seven mornings the girl did not return.

When she did return, he moved again to the farthest corner and 30 watched her work, or stood still as death while she lifted his feet, one by one, and cleaned them with a hard tool that never hurt. He was a Thoroughbred stallion and he knew nothing of remorse. He knew that there were things that made him tremble and things that filled him with anger. He did not know, always, what these things were.

He did not know what the thing was that made him tremble on the 31 morning he saw the chestnut filly, or how it happened that there was suddenly a voice in his throat that came to his own ears unfamiliar and distant, startling him. He saw his dignity slip away like a blanket fallen from his back, and pride that had never before deserted him was in an instant shamefully vanished.

He saw the filly, smooth, young, and with a saunter in her pose, stand- 32 ing in an open field, under the care of four black men. Unaccountably, he had been led to this field, and unaccountably he strained against restraint toward this filly.

Camciscan called to her in a tone as unfamiliar to him as it was to her, 33 but there must have been danger in it. It was a new sound that he did not know himself. He went toward her, holding his head high, lifting his clean legs, and the filly broke from the kicking-straps that held her and fled, screaming, in a voice as urgent as his own.

For the first time in his life he would have exchanged the loneliness he 34 lived by for something else, but his willingness had gained him only the humility of rejection and disdain. He could understand this, but not more than this. He returned to his stable, not trembling. He returned walking with careful steps, each as even as another.

When the girl came as she always did and kneaded the new dead hairs 35 from his bright coat with supple fingers and ran the soft body-brush over him, he turned his head and watched her, accepting the soothing stroke of her hand, but he knew that the old anger was in him again. It had welled up in his heart until now it burst and made him whirl round and catch her slender back with his teeth, biting until the brush dropped from her hand, flinging her bodily against the far wall of the box. She lay there huddled in the trampled bedding for a long time, and he stood over her, trembling, not touching her with any of his feet. He would not touch her. He would have killed any living creature that touched her then, but he did not know why this was so.

After a while the girl moved and then crawled out of the box and he 36 pawed through the bedding to the earthen floor, tossing his head up and down, letting the anger run out of him.

But the girl was there again, in the stable, the next day. She cleaned it 37 as she had cleaned it each other day and her touch on his body was the same, except there was a new firmness in it, and Camciscan knew, without knowing, that his strength, his anger, and his loneliness at last were challenged.

Nothing about the morning ride was different. The black men worked 38 with the other horses and about the stables in their usual positions, with their usual movements. The large tree against which he had thrown the girl was still there making the same little pond of shade, bees criss-crossed the unresisting air like golden bullets, birds sang or just dipped in and out of the sky. Camciscan knew that the morning was slow with peacefulness. But he also knew that this thing would happen; he knew that his anger would come and would be met by the girl's anger.

By then he understood, in his own way, that the girl loved him. Also **39** he understood now why it was that when she had lain hurt in his box, he could not trample her with his hooves, nor allow any other living thing to touch her—and the reason for this frightened him.

They came to a level spot on the green hill and he stopped suddenly **40** with sweat stinging his blood-bay neck and his blood-bay flanks. He stopped because this was the place.

The girl on his back spoke to him, but he did not move. He felt the **41** anger again, and he did not move. For the first time her heels struck against his ribs, sharply, and he was motionless. He felt her hand relax the lines that held his head so that he was almost free. But she did not speak; she rapped him again with her heels, roughly, so that it hurt, and he whirled, baring his teeth, and tried to sink them into her leg.

The girl struck his muzzle with a whip, hard and without mercy, but **42** he was startled by the act more than by the pain. The alchemy of his pride transformed the pain to anger that blinded him. He bit at her again and she struck again making the whip burn against his flesh. He whirled until their world was a cone of yellow dust, but she clung to his back, weightless, and lashed at him in tireless rhythm.

He reared upward, cutting the dust cloud with his hooves. Plunging, **43** he kicked at her legs and felt the thin whip bite at his quarters, time after time, until they glowed with pain.

He knew that his bulk could crush her. He knew that if he reared **44** high enough, he would fall backward, and this terrified him. But he was neither mastered by the girl nor by his terror. He reared until the ground fell away before him, and he saw only the sky, through bulging eyes, and inch by inch he went over, feeling the whip on his head, between his ears, against his neck. He began to fall, and the terror returned, and he fell.

When he knew that the girl was not caught under his weight, his anger **45** left him as quickly as the wind had whisked the dust away. This was not reason, but it was so.

He got up, churning the air awkwardly, and the girl stood, watching **46** him, still holding the lines and the whip, her straw-coloured hair matted with dust.

She came to him and touched the hurt places on his body and stroked **47** his neck and his throat and the place between his eyes.

In a little time she vaulted again to his back and they went on along the **48** familiar road, slowly, with no sound but the sound of his hooves.

Camciscan remained Camciscan. In relation to himself, nothing 49
changed, nothing was different. If there were horses on the farm that whin-
nied at the approach of certain men or forsook their peculiar nobility for the
common gifts of common creatures, he was not one.

He held a heritage of arrogance, and he cherished it. If he had yielded 50
once to a will as stubborn as his own, even this had left no bruise upon his
spirit. The girl had triumphed—but in so small a thing.

He still stood in the far corner of his stable each morning while she 51
worked. Sometimes he still trembled, and once in the late evening when
there was a storm outside and a nervous wind, she came and lay down in the
clean bedding under his manger. He watched her while there was light, but
when that failed, and she must surely have been asleep, he stepped closer,
lowering his head a little, breathing warmly through widened nostrils, and
sniffed at her.

She did not move, and he did not. For a moment he ruffled her hair 52
with his soft muzzle. And then he lifted his head as high as he had ever held
it and stood, with the girl at his feet, all through the storm. It did not seem
a strong storm.

When morning came, she got up and looked at him and spoke to him. 53
But he was in the farthest corner, where he always was, staring, not at her,
but at the dawn, and at the warm clouds of his breath against the cold.

QUESTIONS ABOUT THE RHETORICAL SITUATION

1. How important is it for the reader to be knowledgeable about horses
   when reading "Royal Exile"? About Africa? Why do you think Markham
   has directed her essay at this group of readers?
2. What emotion or emotions does this essay evoke in you? Compare your
   reactions with your classmates' reactions. How consistent is the response
   to this essay? Why do you suppose Markham wishes to evoke these emotions with this essay instead of, for example, writing an essay that explains how horsetrainers teach horses to obey?
3. How would you describe Markham's attitude toward Camciscan? Her attitude toward herself as a girl? How do these attitudes on her part contribute to the essay's effectiveness?
4. Is there any point, or lesson, to this story? If so, what is it? If not, how
   great a deficiency in the essay is this lack?

QUESTIONS ABOUT THE ESSAY'S VOICE

1. Which of the five senses does Markham rely upon in order to show the
   readers what happened rather than just tell them? Find particularly ef-

fective examples. (My favorite? "... bees criss-crossed the unresisting air like golden bullets, birds sang or just dipped in and out of the sky."—¶37)

2. This story is a recollection of events that occurred long before they are being narrated. What technique does Markham use on p. 236 to introduce the flashback to the past? How effective is this technique? Why doesn't she simply start her story on p. 236, ¶7? What does she gain with her first six paragraphs?

3. The body of Markham's story is written from a most unusual point of view: Camciscan's. In fact, Markham refers to herself consistently in the third person. What does she gain in the essay by using this unorthodox approach? How might the voice be affected were the story narrated in the first person all the way through?

4. How convincingly does Markham adopt the point of view of Camciscan? Which passages seem most like the way in which a thoroughbred horse might think about events? How does your understanding of the events differ from the horse's?

5. How would the essay's voice be affected if Markham had entitled it "My Horse" or "Camciscan" rather than "Royal Exile"? Where in the essay does she focus on the royal qualities of the horse?

6. Eventually, Markham broke the wild stallion. Describe the emotions she seems to have experienced at her triumph. Is she triumphant? How do these emotions help to define the sound of her voice in the essay?

7. What effect did the essay's conclusion have on you as a reader? Should the essay have returned to the first-person approach used in the introductory paragraphs? Should a lesson of some sort, a point, be included at the end? (See question number 4, Questions about the Rhetorical Situation).

TOPICS TO WRITE ABOUT

1. Write an essay about a childhood pet or toy or friend whose memory is still quite important to you. POTENTIAL AUDIENCES: the friend or pet or toy/other people your own age. POTENTIAL PURPOSES: to make the reader feel how you felt about him or her or it/to evoke similar memories on the part of your readers.

2. Write an essay about some major obstacle you had to overcome as a child or a challenge you had to meet. POTENTIAL AUDIENCES: Write to your parents/write to a child you know well. POTENTIAL PURPOSES: to recreate for them the feelings you experienced as a child/to help them understand that adults have felt the same anxieties and fears they feel.

Reflections

Diane Rawlings

Diane Rawlings, formerly a high school English teacher at Ansonia High School in Ansonia, Ohio, has been teaching writing and literature courses for the past eight years. She has attended the Ohio Writing Project Summer Institute and Advanced Summer Institute and has been an Ohio Writing Project Teacher-Scholar, working on her Masters in Composition and Rhetoric at Miami University. An accomplished teacher, Rawlings has conducted numerous workshops for writing teachers all over the state of Ohio in the past three years.

In the summer of 1987, Rawlings was enrolled in a graduate seminar on the teaching of writing. One of the course assignments asked the students to create a writing assignment to be used with their own composition students and then to write their own essay in response to that assignment. "Reflections" is Diane Rawlings' essay in response to her own assignment. Following the final draft of the essay, you will find Rawlings' assignment sheet for her students, from which she created her own essay. You will also find two earlier drafts, her initial journal free writing on the subject, and her own comments to the graduate course instructor about her essay.

QUESTIONS ABOUT IDEAS

1. Rawlings' grandmother is unique because of her accomplishments. Is that what makes her unique to Rawlings herself? To what extent are the people of great significance in our own lives significant because of what they do? because of who they are?
2. Who was the most important person in your life when you were a child? Why? How has your understanding of that person changed as you have matured?

The young girl sat stiffly in the wooden pew next to the only stained   1
glass window in the plain, white-walled country church. She wished she had the courage to look at the window more closely, but, at the moment, it was too painful. Instead, she chose to stare at the front of the church. The brown attendance record on the wall had resigned itself to its usual numbers concerning last Sunday's service: attendance—49, visitors—2, offering—$79.63. The mahogany organ seemed asleep in the corner, the pews before her barren, cold, lonely. And there was the pulpit—empty. The white hanky that usually rested on the edge next to the hymnbook was noticeably gone.

At sixteen she had thought everything was permanent, eternal, that life   2
would never change. But life had become different. The one person who understood her was gone although somehow she couldn't say the word "dead."

That seemed too final. She hadn't even cried at the funeral. Her grandma wouldn't have wanted that.

Her grandma had told her many times, "Just bury me by the cemetery   3 road 'cause I want to be the first to leave this old world with a shout when Judgment Day comes!" Today she was living her life without Grandma. Now the only place that brought her comfort was this church where her grandma had preached during most of her thirty years in the ministry. And, of course, there was the window.

She couldn't stop herself from looking at it. She didn't want to remem-   4 ber. The bright light shining through the glass nearly blinded her as she studied the simple patterns carved in the window. It was so much like her grandma. Grandma in the garden. On those days when the asthma didn't make her "poorly," she'd be bent over in the midst of her sunflowers, red peonies, and hearty vegetables. Diligently pulling the stubborn weeds, she would whistle hymns and munch on the sunflower seeds. Her tanned complexion made her look healthy, but she used a metal scrubber on her skin to get rid of the darkness because it "didn't look clean." Faded from many days of wear, her "everyday" thin, light blue cotton dress covered her stout, short frame. Occasionally, she would wipe her hands, weathered by age and hard work from raising five children on the farm, onto her full white apron. The girl had watched her iron the soft fleece-white material on Tuesdays. Monday was wash day; Tuesday the day to iron. Not that there were ever many clothes to iron. Grandma took little stock in worldly possessions. She was saving the "egg" money to buy a nice Sunday dress: a plain, conservatively-styled one of good quality. Grandma had instructed the young girl many times, "Dresses shouldn't draw attention to yourself. People should see God in you and not get caught up in your outward appearance."

And when the corn grew a bit taller, the girl would still find her   5 grandma in the garden, her blue sunbonnet hardly visible, bobbing up and down in a playful hide-and-go-seek game with the outdoors she loved so much. When the girl would arrive to spend the afternoon, as she did often, her grandma would step quickly down the garden path to greet her. Grandma's face would be flushed a beet red from the heat. Her welcome was always the same: biting down on her tongue, she would squeeze the girl's hands together tightly. It was the expression of affection she reserved for those she loved deeply.

"How beautiful the stained glass becomes when the light shines   6 through it!" the young girl observed thoughtfully. It seemed as though God himself were shining through the window. Her grandma would like that.

Basking in the warm streams of sunlight, the girl noticed how the   7 quaint, reverent building seemed to be filled with a kind of aura. This, too, was like her grandma, whose presence seemed to fill the room when she entered it. To the young girl, she was "grandma," but, to others, her grandma was set apart and revered. It was her grandma's grey-framed eyes that were unforgettable: her eyes that seemed to look straight into people's hearts. Her words were always comforting, spoken with an authority that brought strength and relief to those who were hurting. People talked of "Lina's prayers" and called her when they were in trouble.

The young girl wished for the opportunity to hear her grandma pray 8 again. If the girl walked into the living room of the clean white farmhouse in the morning, she would find her grandma kneeling beside the couch with the Bible open before her. The granddaughter would kneel beside her. The prayers would last at least an hour, as each family member would be named, and every friend and parishioner's need prayed for. Then her grandma would place her hands firmly on the young girl's head and begin to pray. The voice would start out in a quivery tone. The words would become louder, building in intensity into a cadence that flowed. It was a soothing rhythm. The girl was afraid to breathe, as though the slightest movement would interrupt this holy moment when they seemed to be transported before the throne of God just on Grandma's mere words.

"God has his hand on your life for a special purpose," her grandma 9 would say. But the girl was too afraid to ask what that meant. Now she wished she had.

The girl began to study the picture of Christ that nearly encompassed 10 the entire glass. The Good Shepherd with the staff in his hand, carrying the little lamb, cradling the lamb to comfort it after it had been lost. Grandma cradling the girl in her arms. The two sitting on the creaky, front porch swing. Grandma listening to the girl's confusion and guiding her with scripture verses from her black Scofield Bible, tattered and wrinkled around the edges from the hours of reading. Grandma and the girl enjoying the afternoon together while Grandma played "Skip to My Lou" on the French Harp, and the girl sang the words. Grandma's hearty cackling when she and her granddaughter were "tickled" by something that happened. And then...Grandpa cradling her grandma in his arms after the stroke that left her confused, frightened, no longer able to recognize the people or the world around her.

The gold plate at the bottom of the window read, "In Memory of Lina 11 Rawlings." The young girl read the words and felt much older. It wasn't just the window that carried her grandma's name. And she cried.

QUESTIONS ABOUT THE RHETORICAL SITUATION

1. Why, in an essay about a topic of such personal significance, has Rawlings chosen to write in the third person? How would her attitude toward her subject seem different if the essay were written in the first person?
2. Rawlings' earlier versions (p. 248 and p. 249) were written either for her

high school students to read or for her graduate student classmates to read. Which of these audiences would the version you have just read be most appropriate for? Why? What other audiences would this essay be suitable for?

3. Rawlings herself clearly loved and admired her grandmother. How are we as readers supposed to respond to her reminiscence about Grandma Rawlings?

QUESTIONS ABOUT THE ESSAY'S VOICE

1. How does the essay rely upon a sense of time to help create the evocative voice? Notice, for example, how old the girl in the essay is. How old is the narrator of the story?
2. How does Rawlings' use of dialogue help to bring her grandmother to life in this essay? Notice the kinds of things Rawlings quotes.
3. Which details about the grandmother make her easier to picture? How do Rawlings' strategies in describing a favorite person resemble Markham's strategies in describing a favorite pet?
4. Notice the transition that begins ¶5. Rawlings is concerned here with maintaining the pace of her story. Why is this a suitable transition at this point in the essay?
5. In ¶10, Rawlings relies heavily upon sentence fragments. How effective is this strategy in creating the voice she wants in her essay?
6. What is your reaction to the essay's final paragraph? How has Rawlings prepared the reader for this final paragraph?

TOPICS TO WRITE ABOUT

1. Write an essay in which you pay tribute to a person in your life who played a very significant role. Be sure that your feelings about that person are shown vividly. POTENTIAL AUDIENCES: the special person himself or herself/your classmates. POTENTIAL PURPOSES: to say thanks in a vivid way/ to make them remember the important people in their own lives.
2. Write an essay in which you describe how your feelings about an important person in your life (a parent, early role model, childhood friend) have changed over the years, or about how mixed those feelings remain. POTENTIAL AUDIENCES: a close friend or a sibling who knew this person/ people of the generation right before yours. POTENTIAL PURPOSES: to strike a sympathetic chord in people who might have felt the same way you did/ to help them understand your responses.

THE WRITING PROCESS

Diane Rawlings wrote this essay in response to an assignment she had made for her own students. She was interested in learning whether or not her assignment was a good one.

Here is the assignment sheet she gave her own class.

Assignment: Descriptive Essay

For this assignment, I want you to consider the following question:
Who was the most important person in your life when you were a child?

Consider how you would describe this person to an audience who has never met him/her. How did this person influence your life? What traits, physical description, experience do you recall about him/her?

Rawlings often uses samples of her own writing in class to illustrate one possible approach to the assignments she makes for her students. In order to test out her own assignment, therefore, she decided to write the kind of description she had asked them to write. In searching for a topic, she returned to a free-writing entry she had made in her own journal a year or two previously. Here is that entry.

Free Writing

What do I remember about Grandma? Sturdiness and strength. A woman who could preach the Word of God, waving her hanky and pacing quickly around the pulpit. A woman who could be found several times during the day on her knees in the living room, praying for her family, for the church people, for me. A grandma who took the time to sit with me on the porch swing and talk about my boyfriends and manage to apply my problems to what the Bible had to say. A mother who could make the best noodles in the world and sugar cookies that melted in my mouth.

Grandma died when I was sixteen. How I've wished over and over again for the chance to sit on that porch swing again and ask her advice about things. How I've longed to see her run over to hug me when I've walked through the door of her house. When Grandma died, it seemed as though our family was never the same. There was no one who had that kind of love to draw the family home again.

One of my favorite memories as a child was visiting Grandma's house in the summertimes. She only lived four miles from my house, so trips to her house were often. I'd wear her nightgown and jump into the huge feather tick on the upstairs bed. I'm not sure what adventures I imagined, but I do remember how much fun I had doing that.

I remember that ominous black Scofield Bible she carried. I suppose because I was a small child that made her Bible seem even bigger. It just carried such authority when it was in her hands. Inside the pages were worn by her underlining passages and constant use.

Everyone else remembered Grandma for the way she'd ride next to Grandpa whenever they'd go somewhere. She was so loving and affectionate. And Grandpa enjoyed that. One of the reasons why I admire her so much is that she was able to have the romance in her marriage even after 56 years.

I remember that she usually wore a dustcap on her head when working in the house. She preferred the outdoors though, loving to grow sunflowers and vegetables in her garden. That is, as long as her asthma didn't make her "poorly." Her grey-framed glasses still didn't hide her alert, darting eyes. Before her illness, she was quick to react and full of enthusiasm for life. She knew how to make small things into special moments. She always had time for me.

A lot of people who knew my grandma say that I remind them of her. That's a tremendous compliment to me. "You have my gift for gab" she'd say. "Choose a job where you'll work with people." I think she has influenced me to care about people and to be devoted to the cause of helping others. That's more important to me than anything else I do.

I think I'm getting off topic here. It's interesting to me that someone who died when I was sixteen could still have so much of an impact on my life. Being loved and accepted unconditionally by someone is an experience that no one ever forgets. And the memory of my grandma and how I felt when I was near her will never leave me as long as I live.

Rawlings then turned this free-writing entry into a draft that she shared with her students. Here is her draft.

Rough Draft

Grandma Rawlings once told me that I have her "gift for gab" and that she saw many of her own traits in me. I was a nine-year-old child at the time—more interested in warm cookies lying on the cabinet top and in sitting in the old willow tree in the front yard than in her insight into my life. My memories are as a child would remember—small, insignificant happenings, bits and pieces of memories. Grandma died when I was 16. How I wish now, as an adult, I could talk to her, because to understand her would be to understand myself.

Grandpa and Grandma Rawlings lived nearby on a farm. I thought at the time it was a mansion, but when I drive by now, I am almost embarrassed that they lived in such a run-down, dilapidated house. There was so much love inside that I guess the outside of the buildings never mattered.

My favorite activity at Grandma's house (besides eating her homemade cookies) was jumping in the old feather tick upstairs. I would put on Grandma's flannel nightgown and with an acrobatic dive, land in the middle of the soft, "billowy" tick! I don't remember what I actually pretended I was doing, but there were several adventures in that upstairs room.

Grandma loved people and people loved her. A unique trait of my Grandma is that she was a minister, which in her day was considered radical. She didn't become a minister to prove that women are as capable as men. She felt strongly that she had been called of God to minister to others and, because of that, she was a minister, even if some of her family didn't accept it.

Grandma had a big, black Bible. I viewed it with awe and respect. In the afternoons we'd sit on the front porch swing and talk. Grandma wanted to share scripture verses, many times from memory. Then she'd hold me and pray for me. I remember that I felt loved and that even as a child, I understood that giving of myself to others was the highest calling in life because my Grandma had enriched my life in so many ways.

A strong woman, a lover of the simple things in life, who appreciated everyone and everything around her, my grandma influenced all of us who knew her. In my teaching and in my youth work at church, I see myself giving a part of myself to others as Grandma gave a part of herself to me.

When the graduate seminar in which she was enrolled required Rawlings to write an assignment sheet and an accompanying essay, she went back to this piece about her grandma. She says, "I wasn't entirely satisfied with what I had shown my own students. They too really weren't all that impressed. I knew that this piece of writing needed more work." She worked on the essay further. Here is her later draft.

Second Draft: A Reflection of My Grandma

The Antioch Congregational Christian Church rests at the corner of a quiet street in Losantville, Indiana. It is a small, intimate building with a majestic stained glass window dedicated to the memory of Lina Rawlings—my grandmother. It is an appropriate symbol of my grandmother's life—fragile glass in a sturdy frame, simple patterns in a maze of rainbow colors, all radiating warm streams of sunlight on those who enter there for worship. Knowing her was a life changing experience for those she had the opportunity to love.

Grandpa and Grandma Rawlings lived on a small farm about three miles from our house. Their horse and buggy courtship resulted in a happy marriage of 56 years. Even in their latter years together, Grandma still rode in the middle of the seat next to Grandpa whenever they would ride somewhere. After Grandma had raised her five children, she accepted what she believed to be a call into the ministry. Without the approval of her family, this 42-year-old woman with only an eighth grade education enrolled in a correspondence course and later at Merom College in Indianapolis, Indiana, to attain a degree in pastoral ministries. She endured the week long stay in Indianapolis, coming home on weekends to face the disapproval of her family. No one wanted to believe that she was doing the right thing. In spite of this she became a minister and served as pastor to various churches in the Losantville area for over thirty years.

But Grandma did not spend all of her time in the pulpit. She loved the outdoors as long as her asthma did not make her "poorly" as she called it. When I'd step through the back door at her house, she would be standing at the kitchen sink, dustcap on her head, whistling to herself as she baked cookies or pies. She would run over and squeeze me tightly. Grandma never seemed too busy to love me.

I don't remember that Grandma had toys and material things for me to play with; nevertheless, I had fun with whatever I could find. My most memorable times with Grandma were on the front porch swing in the afternoons. This was a special time when Grandma would talk to me and listen to my problems. At her side, she always had her well worn black Scofield Bible with its notes and underlinings. Grandma would share scripture verses with me, many times from memory. She would give me advice about boys: "Marry someone two years older; you're more mature than most boys your age." She also talked to me about my future: "You have my 'gift for gab,' you know, so choose a job where you'll work with people." I was only a child at the time. I don't remember all that she said to me, but I do remember that I felt loved and accepted when I was with her. She taught me that the highest calling in life is in giving myself to others.

Grandma loved people and people loved her. A simple woman who loved unconditionally, Grandma influenced all of us who knew her. She died when I was sixteen—our friendship fragmented and shattered by eternal distance. I have always felt cheated because of all the things I have never been able to share with her: high school and college graduations, my wedding, and, of course, lazy afternoons spent together on the front porch swing. In my teaching and in my youth work at church, I see myself giving a part of myself to others as Grandma gave a part of herself to me. Her life reflected in mine—as sunlight reflects rainbow colors through a fragile stained glass window in a quaint old country church.

Still unhappy with this new draft, she showed it to a classmate, Steve Barrett (who is represented in *Model Voices* in Chapter 9). She explains her own reactions to the second draft she had shown Barrett, the one you have just read:

> I wasn't happy with it....I was at a loss. [Steve] read it and began to question me about the window, which I had briefly mentioned in the other paper. "What picture was on the window? What does the window say? Is there any writing?" He said he would try this from a different point of view like third person and would focus on the relationships my grandma had with others, especially me....The next night I started completely over in third person, choosing the church scene and the flashback technique.

Her conversation with her classmate led to the version of this essay,

"Reflections," that you have read on pages 243–245. About this final version, Diane Rawlings said,

> ...I was very pleased. This is much better than the other one. The ending (last two paragraphs) was so powerful to write and read that I started crying when I wrote the words. It was kind of like when I write poetry and the words are flowing so fast that I can hardly get them written down. The last paragraph was not written until I sat down at the typewriter. It sort of popped onto the page.

Looking back at her original assignment sheet for her students, Rawlings then added to what she had originally written, having learned from her own work on her essay that something more was needed. The revised assignment sheet now reads as follows (notice how Rawlings has expanded her instructions to the students).

Assignment: Descriptive Essay (Revised Assignment Sheet)

For this assignment, I want you to consider the following question:
Who was the most important person in your life when you were a child?
Consider how you would describe this person to an audience who has never met him/her. How did this person influence your life? What traits, physical description, experience do you recall about him/her?
Now...the jolt:
To avoid the too familiar (and too safe) structure of the five-paragraph essay, I want you to try this essay from a different angle to see where it takes you. Take a risk. Think of an out of the ordinary way to present this person to your readers.
The following are some suggestions:

You are given a chance to return to your childhood to relive
    your favorite memory that you shared with this person.
    Focus on this incident, retelling it to your audience in a
    way that shows us what this person was like.
Use the flashback technique: begin in the present and
    "flash back," or retell one or more incidents from the
    past that you shared with this person. Connect those
    experiences to the present, if you can.
Call up the voice of the child within you and describe a day
    spent with this person through a child's eyes.
Tell about this person in a fictional short story, letting one of
    your main characters take on his/her personality.
Your option.

Rawlings explains her objectives for this assignment by noting that

"the goal of this assignment is twofold: to provide students with an opportunity to describe a person who has been important in their lives and to provide an assignment that makes them look at that relationship in a different or more analytical way rather than just 'telling' details about a person. The assignment will achieve this goal by either switching point of view, using a change in time, or using the fictional genre to describe the person."

She attributed her own dissatisfaction with her earliest efforts at writing about her grandmother to the assignment itself. "I found that I wrote a more traditional form of essay that needed to be more focused rather than telling about the entire life of my grandma." Her conversation with a classmate jolted her into reconceiving her entire essay and resulted not only in a better essay but a better assignment for her students.

QUESTIONS ABOUT THE PROCESS

1. Can you hear the evocative voice in any of the writing that precedes Rawlings' final draft (the journal entry, first draft, second draft)?
2. Have you ever experienced the same kind of "jolt" that Rawlings did through discussing a piece of writing with another reader? When? Why did it occur?
3. The final paragraph, Rawlings says, "was not written until I sat down at the typewriter. It sort of popped onto the page." She compares this to her experiences in writing poetry when the words just flow onto the page. Have you ever had such an experience while writing? When? Why? Rawlings' final comment about her final paragraph was "I know. The process at work!" She is referring to the writing process. Why does she make this comment? What does she mean?

9

The Meditative Voice

A QUESTION TO PONDER

One day several years ago, as I was driving around town running errands in my car, I pulled up to a stoplight, and my son, who must have been about six years old at the time, asked me a question. "Dad, how many birds would it take to lift this car?"

I was—and remain—unable to answer that question. Being an alert parent, however, I simply said to him, "Good question. How many birds do *you* think it would take?" I did not hear a peep out of him the rest of the trip as he computed the possibilities in his mind.

I remember this little exchange because my son's curiosity, his willingness to work out a possible answer to his own question, seems to me a good example of the impulse that leads to another variety of the personal voice—the meditative voice, a form of writing that provokes thought rather than evokes emotion, that stimulates the mind rather than the heart.

WHY "MEDITATIVE"?

Actually I have had some difficulties in titling this chapter, having considered calling the voice presented here "the thought-provoking voice," "the thoughtful voice," "the pensive voice," "the meditative voice." All seem appropriate. The quality that makes this voice distinctive is the writer's willingness to ponder difficult questions without necessarily coming to a definite conclusion or a final answer. My son, for instance, decided that about 50,000 birds might be able to do it ("Unless they were real big then it wouldn't take so many"). However, even though we were unable to test this scientific hypothesis, he seemed quite pleased to have considered the question in some detailed manner. And that is usually what writers who write in the meditative voice are content with also—considering the question.

251

Pensive suggests not only thoughtful but sad or wistful, and the essays you are about to read, while thoughtful, are not always sad or wistful. *Thought-provoking* is an appropriate adjective, but it suggests that the writer is totally focused on the reader's response. *Thoughtful* is an accurate description of the voices you will hear, but *meditative* is even better because a meditation is intended to express its author's reflections, perhaps even offer guidance to a reader in contemplating the very same ideas. And that is what these essays have in common: not only do they display the writer's interest in making the reader stop to think about the subject, but they manifest the writer's desire to share his thoughts as well. In other words, with the meditative voice, the writer himself seems to be part of the intended audience along with the other readers.

A Sample

Read this excerpt from William Least Heat Moon's *Blue Highways* (you will be reading a longer selection from *Blue Highways* in Chapter 10):

> I was sitting in the northeast corner of the great Sonoran Desert, while at my feet a pair of water bugs swam in slow tandem as if shadows of each other. Evergreens resinated in the air, and bleached clouds moved high over three rhylite monoliths cut from the spewings of ancient volcano to which the Chiricahuas are a tombstone. Before any men, wind had come and inscribed the rock, and water had incised it, but who now could read these writs?
>
> I was in one of the strangest pieces of topography I'd ever seen, a place, until now, completely beyond my imaginings. What is it in man that for a long while lies unknown and unseen only one day to emerge and push him into a new land of the eye, a new region of the mind, a place he has never dreamed of? Maybe it's like the force in spores lying quietly under asphalt until the day they push a soft, bulbous mushroom head right through the pavement. There's nothing you can do to stop it.

FEATURES OF THE MEDITATIVE VOICE

There are a number of features to notice in Least Heat Moon's writing that help to create its meditative voice:

Developing a Sense of Wonder/Curiosity

One feature of the meditative voice is the author's sense of wonder about the topic, his curiosity. Just as my little boy's sense of curiosity led to his asking about the vehicle-lifting birds, so is curiosity often the impulse that brings about the meditative voice. Notice that Least Heat Moon sounds curious; he wants to know why humans act as they do. He displays a sense of awe or wonder at the natural surroundings in which he finds himself and the speculations those surroundings engender in him.

So one notable feature of the meditative voice is to be found in the subject selected. The writer usually chooses to write about a topic of great personal interest, but the topic is generally one the writer does not quite understand completely, not so much in the sense of being confused about it but more in the sense of not knowing or understanding as much as he would like to about it. These topics, it is important to remember, do not always have to raise "major" questions about human behavior.

Smaller Possibilities For example, I wonder about

- Most people's fascination with mail: almost everyone I know eagerly checks the mailbox at work and at home each day even though so much mail is unwanted in one sense or another (bills and junk mail, for example).
- UFOs, not so much about whether they exist as about why people want so much for them to exist, about why a horror novelist's recent book about his encounter with alien beings was recently on the *nonfiction* best-seller list.
- Why the sight of a carefully manicured, well-tended, lush, green lawn makes me happy and content. In fact, I'd say that I have a sense of wonder about my reaction because that same lawn is anything but inspiring to me in late March right after the snow melts, when it's patchy and browning, awaiting the warmer days of spring.
- Why every book I want to find in the library's card catalog or in the stacks is always on the bottom shelf. Do shorter people always find the books they want on the top shelves? This last question really isn't about behavior; it's about the universe in which we live, in a sense.

These are not "deep" subjects, and they may not really interest you. But my point is that we all have such subjects we might write about, subjects that fascinate us, that make us curious to know more, that seem perhaps beyond full explanation, subjects that make us wonder. But how can the writer convey this sense of curiosity or wonder in a piece of writing? Two ways include *asking questions* and *thinking aloud.*

Asking Questions

One way that the writer's sense of wonder, her curiosity, becomes apparent to the reader is through the use of questions. Let me distinguish between two different forms of questions, rhetorical and interrogative. Rhetorical questions are the kind of questions that do not really require an answer because the question itself provides its own answer. For example, one of my students wrote a letter to the editor in which she argued that proliferating restrictions placed on smokers in public places were unfair to those who wanted to smoke. Her letter concluded with the question, "After all, smokers have rights too, don't they?" The context, or situation, of that letter made an answer to the question unnecessary; whether the reader agrees with the author's point or not, it's clear that she expects her reader to answer "yes" to this question.

Another Kind of Question But rhetorical questions are asked by writers who *know* the answers, or who feel they know the answers. In fact, so strongly do they know the answers that they ask questions of their readers that will compel the readers to supply the very same answers. *Interrogative questions*, on the other hand, are the kind of question to which the answer is not self-evident or self-contained, to which context does not matter because the answer itself is open to disagreement, to opinion. Look at the questions raised by Least Heat Moon in the passage quoted above. The question that concludes the first paragraph may well be a rhetorical question with the answer being, "No one." But the question in the final paragraph is not one easily answered.

The meditative voice is a voice that asks interrogative questions, often tentatively suggesting answers, but only as possibilities because the writer is still not sure. Certainly, some forms of writing make use of questions to which the writer then supplies what he feels are definitive answers, but those forms of writing create a very different voice (see Section Four—The Voice of Authority). With the meditative voice, the questions are raised, but the answers provided are tentative at best because finding the answer is not the goal; finding a number of answers is. The meditative voice produces an open-ended essay.

And it is important to note that the questions are not always explicit, but are sometimes implied. As you read the selections in this chapter, look not only for the questions that actually appear in the text of an essay, but for the unasked questions that underlie the entire piece of writing.

Thinking Aloud/Expressing Uncertainty

Another noteworthy feature of essays written in the meditative voice is that reading them at times will make you feel like an eavesdropper, as if you were intruding into a private conversation. Sometimes the writer may be a character in his own essay, although the essay may just as well avoid a narrative structure. Always, however, the writer's personal point of view—that open-minded seeking, wondering about an issue—is central, even if the writing is not in the first person.

"Talking" to Yourself I think this quality of the self speaking to the self is what makes the voice meditative rather than thought-provoking. Certainly, the writers wish to provoke you to think; that's the main goal of the writing. But the sense of wonder and curiosity that prompted the essay in the first place is also apparent in the voice, as if the writer needs to say aloud what she has been thinking silently in order to try out the ideas.

Think about how often you talk to yourself when you are puzzled or trying to figure out which decision to make. I don't necessarily mean speaking aloud to yourself—although I suspect many of you do that just as I do—so much as I mean talking to yourself in your own voice in your mind. This speaking to yourself, or musing about a subject, when written out, can create the meditative voice.

When my son pondered the answer to his own unanswerable question about the birds and the car, he did so silently. He was speaking to himself. Eventually he spoke to his audience, me, but I think he was still speaking to himself as he tried to explain his answer, testing out his ideas aloud.

Notice how Least Heat Moon is only able to offer a very tentative answer to his own question. "Maybe" he says, indicating that he is unsure, "it's like the force in spores...." Notice the "like." Not only is Least Heat Moon's answer only a possibility, but it is not really an answer at all but only a comparison to something else. He is still puzzling this one out, and he is inviting us to puzzle it out along with him.

The structure of meditative writing seems to be based on observing details and trying to reach some larger conclusion about these details. What meditative writers are often doing can be called *effect-to-cause writing*.

One form out of which the meditative voice may grow is the *causal analysis, a type of writing in which the writer observes a phenomenon and attempts to ascertain its causes*. Looking once again at Least Heat Moon's piece, we can see him discussing an effect that he has observed: he finds himself visiting an unimaginably foreboding desert. He seeks to learn the cause of such behavior: why do people feel the urge to explore such desolate areas? The answers are not clear; the causes are not evident. But his essay may well take the form of a causal analysis as he describes the effect and then investigates its causes even though he may be unable to point at any one cause and say, "This is the one."

Another way to explain this movement from details to larger conclusions is to speak of *moving from the specific to the general*. Suppose I receive a speeding ticket every time I pass a police cruiser with a radar gun. After several days, I start automatically slowing down whenever I see a police cruiser. I take my specific observations and eventually reach a conclusion about them. In other words, I form a generalization: "Generally, whenever I see a police cruiser, it is a radar unit monitoring speed, so I'd better slow down."

So Least Heat Moon notices that he is drawn to unusual topography: deserts, volcanic mountain ranges. By observing such specifics and seeking larger explanations for them, Least Heat Moon can produce a piece of writing with a meditative voice. The difference is that Least Heat Moon's explanation is a more tentative one than was mine.

The actual meditative essay may present to the reader the writer's speculative responses to her own observations. What are the causes of the observed effects? What generalizations can the writer reach based on the specifics he has noticed? What are the answers to the writer's questions? Least Heat Moon begins trying to answer his own question immediately after asking it; writing in the meditative voice frequently does this.

Being an Explorer, Not an Expert

The essence then of the meditative voice is that the writer is an explorer, not an expert. She stands before us not as a professor in an introductory course in sociology or American history would stand before you, as an authority prepared to explain her subject to you, but stands rather as an equal, as an individual who has been thinking hard about a puzzling, confusing, perplexing, awe-inspiring subject. Her goal is to make you think along with her. The old cruise ship ads used to claim that "getting there is half the fun." With the meditative voice, getting there is *most* of the fun, because neither the writer nor the reader is really sure that the essay will actually arrive *there* at all! Writers who write in the meditative voice may not know all the answers, but they do know the important questions.

The Tree People: A Man, A Storm, A Magnolia

David Quammen

David Quammen writes the column "Natural Acts" for *Outside* magazine. A published novelist, Quammen was a 1984 National Magazine Award finalist for his essays and columns. His work has appeared in the *New York Times Book Review, Audubon, Esquire,* and *Rolling Stone,* among other publications. He was educated at Yale and Oxford and has worked as a fishing guide in Montana.

Quammen is not a scientist. "What I am," he has written, "is a dilettante and a haunter of libraries and a snoop, the sort of person who has his nose in the way constantly during other people's field trips, asking too many foolish questions and occasionally scribbling notes." He argues that "lively writing about science and nature depends less on the offering of good answers, I think, than on the offering of good questions." "The Tree People" first appeared in *Outside* magazine in 1984.

QUESTIONS ABOUT IDEAS

1. Why are people drawn to trees and flowers and plants? What is the appeal of plant life to us?
2. Has Quammen's father gone overboard in his planting and caring for the trees, especially the magnolia? What is the reason for your answer?
3. The wilderness behind the Quammens' house is eventually replaced by homes and other buildings. This is a common situation in the twentieth century as human beings continue to domesticate the wild areas of the earth. Many naturalists, ecologists, conservationists, and nature lovers are quite disturbed about the loss of natural habitat. What is your view on this issue?
4. In ¶12, Quammen talks about how this essay turned out to be very different from the one he originally intended to write. Has this happened to you as a writer? How do you deal with such a situation?

Some humans have a special relationship with trees.   1

I'm thinking here not of the professional foresters, nor the academic   2
dendrologists, certainly not the barrel-chested flannel-shirted fallers. No, it's gentler folk I have in mind. Persons neither scientific nor pragmatic, whose encounters with trees tend to be more intimate, more spontaneous, marked by an altogether different degree of sensitivity and—it might not be going too far to insert the word *mutual*—appreciation. People who can actually quiet themselves sufficiently to gaze at one individual tree and perceive there

a real living creature conducting its own mortal business. This isn't so easy as it sounds. "The tree which moves some to tears of joy is in the eyes of others only a green thing which stands in the way," wrote William Blake. These genuine tree people are rare.

John Muir was one—read his account of riding out the thrills of a ³ mountaintop storm while perched in the upper branches of a hundred-foot spruce. Another was that curious historical figure Jonathan Chapman, dead in 1845, later sentimentalized and Disneyfied under the name Johnny Appleseed. Still another is the British novelist John Fowles, who has written an interesting and little-known nonfiction book titled *The Tree*, in which he avows: "If I cherish trees beyond all personal (and perhaps rather peculiar) need and liking of them, it is because of this, their natural correspondence with the greener, more mysterious processes of mind—and because they also seem to me the best, most revealing messengers to us from all nature, the nearest its heart." Among this group of tree-loving people, too, is my own father.

Unlike Muir, he has never rambled solitarily among the California se- ⁴ quoias, my father. Unlike Fowles, he offers no elaborate philosophical theories for his special attachment. Like Chapman, he is simply a planter. Ever since I can remember—let's say at least thirty years—this man has been planting and tending and doting upon trees. He has never sold a board-foot of timber. He has never carried a bushel of fruit to a fair. He barely consents to own a saw. And behind him his life stretches out like a burgeoning, flourishing wood lot.

For a long time it made no particular sense to me.   ⁵

At the beginning there was a half acre of nearly bare real estate, for- ⁶ merly farmland, at the suburban fringe of a city in the southern Midwest, not far from the Mason-Dixon line. Upon the half acre sat a new house and a stately old black walnut tree, not much else; beyond a fence marking the west edge was a wild stand of high grass and thistle, through which a foot trail led to unspoiled hardwood forest that went on for several miles. Across that fence was a miniature wilderness area for the delectation of young boys. Then, gradually, bits of the forest came to the half-acre lot.

A soft maple was planted up front near the road. A hard maple, just ⁷ out the kitchen window. A sweet gum beside the driveway. A pin oak near the old well. An apple tree, off at the northwest corner, keeping company with the compost heap. A little dogwood. A Scotch pine, which often seemed to be struggling against heat prostration. More maples along that west fence. Eventually, getting fancy, a ginkgo. And a magnolia tree, a hapless and delicate magnolia, to the right of the front door. The earliest of these were poached as saplings from the adjacent woods, carefully trotted home on the foot path and replanted; later it became necessary to patronize a nursery. From my point of view (roughly waist-high then), the place had

become a nursery itself. Finally the man in question bought me a rake, and
I was not amused.

It had become necessary to patronize a nursery because, by the time I 8
was old enough to operate that new rake, the wilderness area over the back
fence had disappeared. Bulldozers had scraped it away. In its place there was
now a tract suburb of medium-sized boxes. Paved driveways and sidewalks.
Tulips. Myrtle in neat patches. Precious few trees.

I sat high in the crow's nest of that old black walnut tree, years pass- 9
ing, and watched this transformation. A valuable early lesson, with the res-
onance of a parable. Still grudging my time at the rake, I could see after a
while that the man, the planter, my father, was not insane after all. Not even
perverse. As the forest was massacred, as the neighborhood turned into concrete and crabgrass, on our small island there was a continual spreading of
new branches. Local trees and exotics thrown together in strange juxtaposi-
tions, most of them thriving, fighting each other genially for sunlight and
water and the attentions of the chief arborist. He was running his own gene
bank. I would not want to be so high-flown as to call this half acre a *sym-
phonic* orchestration of trees; but it represented, at least, a pretty good Dixieland band. The planter enjoyed his son's complete approbation for a couple more years, until an ice storm hit the magnolia, at which point it seemed
that things were perhaps being taken too far.

This would have been about 1963. In that peculiar borderland climate, 10
ice storms were a familiar enough (though not common) feature of what
passed for winter. Cold sleet would begin falling at night, as the temperature
dropped, and by morning the entire city would be glazed with a very beautiful and extremely treacherous eighth-of-an-inch layer of clear ice. Power
lines down. Fender smashing against fender. Hips being fractured. The ice
storm in 1963 was especially bad, and instead of an eighth-inch thickness
there was a quarter-inch. Over any large surface area, like the crown of a
tree, that amounted to considerable weight. The conifers, adapted to serious
snows, could take it. The hardwoods were bare and streamlined. But the
magnolia tree, a southern-bred creature, too trusting to drop its big trowel-
shaped leaves from its brittle limbs after the autumn frosts, was caught in a
wretched position.

Every leaf was lacquered thickly with ice, hundreds of pounds in all, 11
the whole tree about to collapse like so much Steuben glass under a garbage
compactor. And so, on that Saturday morning, there was the droll spectacle
of a man and his fifteen-year-old son (the latter an unwilling draftee, with
places to go and other enormously pressing things, now forgotten, to do)
taking turns on a stepladder to break the ice—gingerly, one leaf at a time,
with raw cold hands—off that desperate magnolia.

I remembered the magnolia's trauma, and its rescue, just yesterday 12
while reading some scientific papers on an extraordinary species of tree

called the bristlecone pine. The bristlecone was originally to be the main subject of this essay, since largely preempted, but never mind about that. The bristlecone will get its full starring role some other time. It can wait. It knows how. It is a tree accustomed to taking the long view. Unrecognized by biologists until about thirty years ago, bristlecone pines in the mountains of the American southwest are today known to be the oldest living creatures on Earth.

We're not talking about the age of a *species*, understand, but about ven- 13 erable *individuals*. One noble specimen of bristlecone, found alive in 1964 on the shoulder of a high peak in eastern Nevada, was calculated to be 4,900 years old. That single tree sprouted from its seed and began putting out needles, in other words, around the same time the Egyptians established their first kingdom. No pyramids yet. The book of Genesis was still in galleys. This was a very old tree.

A number of curious facts emerged from those journal papers on the 14 bristlecone—it is a species of paradoxical superlatives—most of which have no pertinence here, no bearing upon that image of the man, the ice, the stepladder, the magnolia. But two of them do.

First: Dendrologists have discovered that longevity, among individuals 15 of this most long-lived of earthly creatures, is inversely related to the hospitableness of its living conditions. Age-wise, the tree thrives on adversity. The more harsh and ungiving its particular locale, the longer a bristlecone tends to live. At lower elevations within the mountains of its native range, places where soil is decent, wind and erosion are not extreme, water is available in good supply, the bristlecone grows large and robust—but does not seem to survive much beyond 1,500 years. (These ages can be gauged rather precisely, from a core sample or a full cross-section, by counting the annual rings laid down through the trunk.) At higher elevations, right up at the edge of the timberline, on steep south-facing slopes of stony soil that is poor in organic material and chemical nutrients, where little water is available, winds are relentless, growing conditions are generally lousy—here the bristlecone lives as a gnarled dwarf. But long. Often enough in this harshest environment a bristlecone survives its 4,000th birthday. Obvious moral: When the growing is tough, the tough keep growing.

The second odd fact is corollary to that one. Certain dendrologists who 16 count bristlecone tree-rings have taken to writing of two separate characters of tree within the species. These are the "sensitive" bristlecones and the "complacent" bristlecones. The sensitive bristlecones are those that respond to climatic fluctuations, such as a year of exceptional drought, by laying down a drastically narrower growth ring that year, or possibly no ring at all. A complacent tree records no such response. Maybe it shouldn't be surprising that the complacent trees (as reported in *Science*, 1968) tend to be those that are younger and more comfortable. Meanwhile the ancient trees, struggling through 4,000 years of thirst and starvation, solitary on exposed ridges, grotesquely shaped, hunkered down, clinging to life with only one or two green branches—these are the ones that leave a record of sensitivity.

Now it seems to me that this discernment of "sensitivity" and "com- 17 placency" among various individual pine trees, silently living to millennial ages on their high mountain slopes, must constitute some sort of breakthrough percipience for the botanical sciences. And it compels me to wonder about that beleaguered magnolia on the half-acre wood lot at the edge of the Midwestern city.

Was the magnolia, by disposition, a complacent creature? Or was it, as 18 I hope, sensitive? Did it *appreciate,* during the year of growth following that 1963 ice storm, what the man with the stepladder and the raw hands had done for it?

The house and the half acre have long since been sold to strangers. The 19 magnolia, last time I drove past, looked neglected: a broken crown, whole branches on which the leaves were a sickly brown. Too bad. It may not survive another big ice storm. Certainly it will not live to see 4,000.

But does there perhaps remain, in its heartwood, some record—just a 20 slight thickening to one annual ring, like a grateful sigh—of that mildly eccentric act of love? Can a magnolia remember a man?

QUESTIONS ABOUT THE RHETORICAL SITUATION

1. What would you expect readers of a magazine entitled *Outside* to be like? How has Quammen taken his readers into account? What can you tell about those readers from Quammen's essay?
2. What does Quammen's subtitle tell you about his attitude toward his essay? Why has he placed the three nouns in that order instead of another one?
3. Quammen as a boy did not understand much of his father's behavior. How would you describe his attitude toward his father in the past versus in the present? Why does Quammen take the time to show us his earlier attitudes?
4. How does Quammen want the reader to answer the questions that conclude his essay? How does he want you to respond to tree people? Did you?

QUESTIONS ABOUT THE ESSAY'S VOICE

1. Quammen writes an extraordinary number of sentence fragments in the essay. Can you locate several successfully used fragments? What makes them successful? What purpose do Quammen's one-sentence paragraphs

serve (¶1, ¶5)? How effective are these paragraphs? Why is he using this style?

2. What is the purpose of mentioning William Blake, John Muir, Jonathan Chapman, and John Fowles in ¶3? How does the essay's voice change when Quammen writes about his father?

3. As mentioned in the Questions about Ideas, many people are very concerned and even angry about the destruction of the earth's wilderness. In ¶8 and ¶9, Quammen discusses this phenomenon. How would you describe his voice in that paragraph? Does he seem at all upset? Why or why not?

4. Quammen occasionally uses metaphors in an attempt to explain his ideas (see the Dixieland band metaphor in ¶9 and the Steuben glass metaphor in ¶11). How do such metaphors help to establish Quammen's voice? How would the voice be different if he had not used these metaphors? How would the essay's voice be changed if he had described the tree-filled yard as "not a Louvre of a forest but a pretty good local art gallery of a woods"?

5. Is Quammen right about trees and tree people? How does he write about the trees in this essay? Has he become a tree person? (Note the description of the magnolia in ¶10 and the bristlecones in ¶16.)

6. Since the essay is about "a man, a storm, a magnolia," what is the purpose of the five paragraphs on the bristlecone?

7. What is the effect on the essay's voice of the final three paragraphs?

TOPICS TO WRITE ABOUT

1. Write an essay about some nature topic which has always fascinated you even though you may not fully understand it. (For example, I discussed earlier the sense of contentment a well-tended, lush, verdant lawn gives me. I am not alone in this response. You might write a serious consideration of the joys of bird watching as opposed to Dave Barry's humorous account of that pastime.) POTENTIAL AUDIENCES: readers who do not spend much time outdoors in nature/the same readers addressed by Quammen. POTENTIAL PURPOSES: to make them think about some of the natural wonders they have overlooked/to share your sense of wonder with a sympathetic audience.

2. Write an essay in which you attempt to understand how your parents' behavior made them a part of a special group of people and what made those people special. (Quammen's dad was one of the "tree people" he has noticed. Perhaps your mother or father felt that same affinity for automobile engines or roses, or loved Chinese wok cooking.) POTENTIAL AUDIENCES: your parent/the general reading public. POTENTIAL PURPOSES: to show your parent that you appreciated his or her specialness although

you may still not fully understand it/to make some readers recognize themselves as members of that same special group and to make them ask themselves why they are so drawn to cars or roses or....

Was He Normal? Human? Poor Humanity
Elie Wiesel

Elie Wiesel, winner of the 1986 Nobel Peace Prize, was 15 years old when the Nazis entered his hometown of Sighet, Hungary, in 1944. Miraculously, he managed to survive the death camps of Auschwitz and Buchenwald, and at war's end he became a journalist in Paris. He would not speak out about the unspeakable for ten years. When that self-imposed vow of silence ended, he devoted his life to writing and talking, with rare eloquence and power, about the despair of the past and the concerns of the present. His autobiographical account of his sojourn in Auschwitz, *Night*, remains one of the most powerful testaments to the horrors of the Holocaust. Now a U.S. citizen, Wiesel, 56, has written some thirty books and is widely acknowledged, in the words of the Nobel committee chairman, as a "messenger to mankind."

Klaus Barbie, the infamous Butcher of Lyons, was deported by the Bolivian government after close to forty years of being a fugitive. This piece by Wiesel appeared in *Time* magazine shortly before Barbie's trial as a war criminal commenced in France in 1987. Barbie was convicted and sentenced to life imprisonment. Wiesel begins by recalling the war crimes trial of Adolf Eichmann, the Nazi official who presided over the Final Solution, the systematic execution of six million Jews during World War II.

QUESTIONS ABOUT IDEAS

1. There is some debate over the appropriateness of putting Nazi officials and soldiers on trial in the 1980s for their actions in the 1940s since so many years have passed. What rationale does the essay offer for such trials? Is it a convincing one?
2. Wiesel is concerned with the fact that Barbie was assisted in fleeing postwar Europe by the American intelligence community. What is your reaction to this information?
3. The essay is also critical of the behavior of the French people during the World War II occupation of their country by Nazi Germany. What is your reaction to the essay's description of French conduct during the war? How understandable is that conduct? How excusable is it?

4. In other, similar trials, defendants have generally argued that they were
   merely soldiers or officials who were following orders. How convincing a
   defense is that? What should such defendants have done?
5. What would be a suitable punishment for Barbie given the crimes he has
   been accused of by the French government?

I remember the nearsighted, balding man in his glass cage in Jerusa- 1
lem. During the April-to-December trial in 1961, I listened to witnesses
whose words and silences contained the tormented memory of an entire people. Yet I was not watching them. Most of the time I was watching the defendant. It was to see him that I had come to Israel, anxious to find out for
myself if he was human, if there was any humanity in him. I had hoped to
find myself in the presence of a disfigured creature, a monster whose unspeakable crimes would be clearly legible in his three-eyed face. I was disappointed: Adolf Eichmann seemed quite normal, a man like other men—he
slept well, ate with good appetite, deliberated coolly, expressed himself
clearly and was able to smile when he had to. The architect of the Final Solution was banal, just as Hannah Arendt had said.

Will the same now be said of Klaus Barbie, who was less important but 2
whose work was no less cruel? Barbie's trial is bound to attract worldwide
attention. People are already saying this will be the last great courtroom
drama to result from the Holocaust. They may be right.

For even behind bars, Barbie throws a long shadow. From the day of 3
his capture, there were whispers that retribution could bring political catastrophe: the prisoner knows too much about too many. His lawyer is Jacques
Vergès, most recently the defender of the Arab terrorist Georges Ibrahim
Abdallah, sentenced last February to life imprisonment by a French tribunal
for complicity in the killings of two diplomats, one of them an American,
and in the attempted murder of a third. With Vergès' help, Barbie is quite
capable of turning the tables, of forcing a trial of France under the Occupation.

But despite these fears, there will be a Judgment Day. The official ex- 4
amination of Klaus Barbie begins on May 11 in Lyons, France. No one
knows how the story will end. But we know now how it all began.

Barbie, who grew up in Trier, a small town in Germany, and dreamed 5
of becoming a minister, first arrived in Lyons at the age of 28. He was assigned the task of fighting the Resistance and getting rid of the Jews. The
young, dedicated Nazi excelled at this job. He is accused of having executed
4,000 people and deported 7,500 Jews. His career grew so bloodstained that
he was dubbed the "Butcher of Lyons." Yet only a fragment of this past will
be weighed in the deliberations: the accusation is primarily concerned with
the forty-four Jewish children who, along with their guardians, were ar-

rested on his orders in the village of Izieu and then sent to the gas chambers of Auschwitz.

How can Barbie justify what was done to the children of Izieu? Here, 6 the proofs of his crimes are beyond dispute: the Nazi hunters Beate and Serge Klarsfeld, the best known of his pursuers, have turned up a striking document: "This morning, the Jewish children's home, 'Children's Colony,' at Izieu has been removed. Forty-one children in all, aged three to thirteen, have been captured. Beyond that, the arrest of all the Jewish personnel has taken place, namely ten individuals, among them five women. It was not possible to secure any money or other valuables. Transportation to Drancy will take place on 4.7.44." The arrest is signed in the name of Klaus Barbie.

This trial represents an extraordinary victory for Beate Klarsfeld, who, 7 as it happens, was born and raised in Germany. A victory over the forgetfulness, the willingness to compromise, the indifference that an overly politicized world has shown for too long toward escaped SS killers. A victory too over the governments that helped Barbie. It was the Klarsfelds who picked up his trail—he had disappeared for almost forty years into the identity of a prosperous and peaceful businessman named Klaus Altmann living in Bolivia. They were the ones who managed to persuade François Mitterrand's Socialist government to act, to induce the Bolivian government to expel "Altmann" so that he could be returned to the country of his crimes.

The former head of the Gestapo at Lyons re-entered France on Feb- 8 ruary 5, 1983. On orders from Minister of Justice Robert Badinter, he was locked in the same Montluc prison where his own victims had been subjected to maltreatment and torture. It is said he spent his first night in the very cell Badinter's father occupied before he was deported to Auschwitz, never to return.

How had Barbie eluded prosecution, not to say detection, for so long? 9 For one thing, he had collaborated with the American Counter Intelligence Corps in postwar Europe, supplying information about Communist activities in Germany and Austria. The services of the CIC made it possible for him to flee to South America. (Most ironically, it was a young Jewish officer, 23-year-old Leo Hecht, who was ordered to provide him with his false travel documents.) For another, he had powerful friends throughout Europe. It is known that an international network existed after World War II to aid war criminals. No such escape system was ever created for their victims.

Will Barbie tell us how the network operated? Will he reveal the iden- 10 tity of his highly placed friends? If he does, other questions are certain to arise. The upper echelons of the CIC knew what Barbie had done; how could they reward him for it? Even in the first frosts of the cold war, was it really necessary to call upon individuals like the Butcher of Lyons? Where was honor in all this? And memory?

The French have even more to fear from the revelations or digressions 11 of their special prisoner. Ever since Marcel Ophuls's documentary *The Sorrow and the Pity* unreeled in Europe and America, people have stopped believing in the myth that France united to resist the occupying forces. On the contrary, France under Pétain fully collaborated with Hitler's Germany. It handed its Jews over to the Nazi executioners—76,000 were deported, few came back. French militia competed with the Gestapo for efficiency. French police organized the roundups. Will the nation be forced to remember its sins? Or will its citizens allow themselves to be manipulated by Barbie and Vergès, who will certainly try to show that even the Resistance was not blameless? That Jean Moulin, a leader of the Resistance who died under the hands of Barbie, was betrayed by his own comrades? In a different domain and on another level, there is some concern that the trial will conveniently and simplistically group the various victims together—dump them all into the same file: Jews and Resistance fighters, Jews and anti-Nazis, Jews and political prisoners. In other words, that the specific, the unique, even ontological aspect of the Jewish tragedy will be lost.

Vergès and Barbie will probably try to blur the distinctions. They may 12 go further and remind France that the nation was itself guilty of torture and murder during the Algerian conflict. War is war, they may say. In war everything is allowed. As Barbie remarked to one journalist, "The point is to win. It doesn't matter how."

In fact, *The State of France v. Klaus Barbie* is not a matter of war. It is 13 a matter of truth. In Lyons, Barbie will have to answer not for his war crimes but for his crimes against humanity. For these there is no statute of limitations.

He will have to explain, for example, why he condemned the Jewish 14 children of Izieu. Listen to the words of one of those children, eleven-year-old Liliane Gerenstein, in a letter scrawled to God before she was taken on the road that led to the gas chambers: "It is thanks to You that I enjoyed a wonderful life before, that I was spoiled, that I had lovely things, things that others do not have. God? Bring back my parents, my poor parents, protect them (even more than myself) so that I may see them again as soon as possible. Have them come back one more time. Oh! I can say that I have had such a good mother, and such a good father! I have such faith in You that I thank You in advance." Of what was this child guilty?

No, Lyons will not provide a restaging of the Eichmann trial. Barbie 15 did not make policy. He was only a regional executioner, a local hangman— he merely participated, did what he was told. His operations only extended to Lyons and its surroundings. Yet if Klaus Barbie was not "important," his trial is. It can serve a vital purpose, for future generations and for our own. Certain witnesses have to be heard; certain truths have to be uttered, repeated. Will they clarify the mystery of what happened? It does not seem possible. The determination of the killer to kill, the passivity of the bystander are likely to remain incomprehensible. There is something about this

Event that eludes rational thought. Only those who were there know what it meant to be there. The others can, at best, come close to the gate. There they must stop. They will never see the fire. They will never witness the sight of children thrown into flames alive. They will never experience the fear of selections for the execution chambers. Knowledge can be shared; experience cannot. Surely not in matters related to Auschwitz.

Still, we must hear the testimonies, from the victims, and from Klaus   16
Barbie himself. For in the end they may help us to understand the deeper motivations of a Nazi killer who chose to make himself the enemy of those children and who even now thinks of himself as innocent. Was he normal, like Eichmann? Human, perhaps?

Poor humanity.   17

QUESTIONS ABOUT THE RHETORICAL SITUATION

1. Wiesel's article appeared in *Time* magazine. Describe the typical readers of that weekly news magazine. Which of your assumptions does Wiesel also seem to have made as he addressed his essay to those readers?
2. What subject or subjects does Wiesel's essay encourage us to ponder? To what extent does he suggest *how* he wants us to view Barbie and the trial? To what extent does he *assume* certain responses on our part?
3. Wiesel lived through the horrors of Auschwitz. Which part or parts of his essay display an understandably strong point of view about this topic? Which details demonstrate clearly Wiesel's continued strong feelings about his own experiences?
4. How might this essay have been changed if Wiesel had focused more on his own feelings? If, for example, the essay had been more personal than it is, would the voice have been changed? How? Would this have been an improvement or not? Why?
5. How is Wiesel's attitude toward the Holocaust similar to or different from Robert McAfee Brown's attitude in his essay (in Chapter 7) "They Could Do No Other"?

QUESTIONS ABOUT THE ESSAY'S VOICE

1. What point of view does Wiesel use in this essay? How is this point of view effective in creating the meditative voice? How does Wiesel's essay about human behavior sound different from Quammen's essay, also about human behavior?
2. Wiesel makes extensive use of questions throughout his essay. Which questions are rhetorical (see p. 255)? Which are interrogative (see p. 256)? Which interrogative questions does Wiesel leave open? Why?

3. In ¶15, Wiesel capitalizes the word "Event." Why?

4. Why does Wiesel include the excerpted letter by Liliane Gerenstein in ¶14? What effect does this letter have on the reader? On the essay's voice?

5. Why does Wiesel begin this essay by discussing a different trial and a different war criminal? How does this strategy help to create the meditative voice in this essay?

6. Wiesel's voice is not consistently pensive or meditative. What other voice(s) can you hear? Where in the essay? How effective is it for Wiesel to change voices in this essay?

7. At the end of ¶15, Wiesel writes: "Knowledge can be shared; experience cannot." What does he mean? Do you agree? How can this comment help to explain the differences between a meditative writing voice and an authoritative writing voice (see Chapter 10)?

TOPICS TO WRITE ABOUT

1. Write an essay about an historical event that puzzles or confuses you (be sure you know enough about the historical event to write convincingly of your wonderment). POTENTIAL AUDIENCES: the readers of *Time* magazine/ the members of your history class. POTENTIAL PURPOSES: to make them think carefully about the same event/to make them look critically at the event as a history scholar might.

2. Read Wiesel's book *Night* and write an essay which seeks to understand how the adult writer of "Was He Normal?" grew out of the teenager who lived in Auschwitz. POTENTIAL AUDIENCE: the members of your composition class who have also read this essay. POTENTIAL PURPOSE: to make the class ponder how a great and sympathetic writer grew out of a boy who underwent such suffering.

A Small Moral Quandary
Otto Friedrich

Otto Friedrich was born in Boston, Massachusetts. After graduating *magna cum laude* from Harvard University in 1948, Friedrich began a career as a journalist. He has worked as an editor and writer for United Press International, the *New York Daily News, Newsweek, The Saturday Evening Post,* and *Time* magazine. Friedrich has published over a dozen books, ranging from fiction to nonfiction to children's books, in addition to publishing a large number of magazine articles and short stories. He also serves as an essayist for *Time* magazine, in which publication "A Small Moral Quandary" first appeared in the spring of 1987.

QUESTIONS ABOUT IDEAS

1. Friedrich is dealing with a thorny constitutional problem: what happens when an individual's right to the pursuit of happiness conflicts with another individual's right to the pursuit of happiness. In fact, his friend talks about this very issue (¶16). What are your views on this issue?
2. What other situations in our society exemplify the same sort of quandary explored by Friedrich in his essay? Which of these situations seem more significant? Less significant? Why do you think Friedrich chooses a "small moral quandary" to examine when larger ones exist?
3. Various opinions are expressed in this essay and varied advice is given, either explicitly or implicitly, to the author. Which advice seems most sensible to you? Did Friedrich do the right thing?

"Let's meet for lunch at 1 o'clock at the Millennium Club," the distinguished person said.   1

"O.K.," the essayist said.   2

The essayist doesn't much like the Millennium Club and has not been   3
there for quite a while. The club's food is generally overcooked and its atmosphere musty—all leather armchairs and dark green table lamps and bound sets of people like Bulwer-Lytton. But there are compensations of a sort. It is always faintly possible that one might meet some celebrated old walrus.

But the essayist faced a small dilemma: Is it really socially acceptable to   4
go to lunch at places like the Millennium Club, which practices the weird ritual of barring women from its cobwebbed sanctuary? The club has a token black or two—nothing racist about the dear old Millennium—but a spirited faction among its members insists that the admission of women would "alter the character" of the institution. The essayist, who rather prefers the company of women to that of men, agrees. The character of the club would indeed be changed, by being improved. The essayist might even want to join.

Actually, the essayist doesn't see why any self-respecting woman   5
would want to enter a club filled with moss-backed Millenarians, but there is a popular theory that social clubs of this sort represent a kind of secret power center, where the old-boy network twines from armchair to armchair and the old boys negotiate million-dollar contracts between the clam chowder and eggs Benedict. The essayist doubts that there is much truth in this. It seems like one of those fantasies that the excluded often concoct about the places and people that exclude them. The essayist has been to a reasonable number

of clubs, and although he has had pleasant conversations there, he cannot recall ever having heard anyone say a very useful word about anything. The clubs, of course, deny that they are places of business; in fact, some even have rules against any piece of paper lying on a table. On the other hand, the mere fact that the clubs deny the women's charges suggests that they may be true after all. In any case, a number of local governments have ordered the clubs to stop discriminating against blacks or women or anybody else. In theory, a private club that gets tax benefits or serves as a place of business has no right to exclude people.

New York City's human rights commission, for example, has filed 6
charges against the University Club, the Union League and the Century Club to force them to admit women. The University Club is fighting in court, and lost its latest appeal in February. The Los Angeles city council is considering a new ordinance that would prohibit any club from barring people on grounds of race, religion, or gender.

Around the country, a number of such clubs have politely surren- 7
dered—the Houston Club, for example, and the Detroit Athletic Club—but others keep maneuvering with all the grace of frightened schoolboys. (Speaking of which, the Princeton University council last month asked New Jersey authorities whether Princeton's last two all-male eating clubs could escape going coed by severing all connections with the university, as several all-male clubs at Harvard have done.) Washington's splendiferous Cosmos Club, which boasts Woodrow Wilson and Oliver Wendell Holmes among its past members, has even tried (unsuccessfully) to require new members to sign a pledge that they will not try to change the club's by-laws, which limit membership to "men of accomplishment." Critics of the Cosmos' policies have formally asked the D.C. alcoholic beverage-control board to cancel the club's liquor license.

It was getting on toward 1 o'clock, and still the essayist, who is given 8
to idly wondering, idly wondered: Is it really acceptable to go to lunch at the Millennium Club? He casually asked a colleague whether he was a member, and the colleague said he had been but had resigned. That seemed very high-toned and impressive, but the essayist is not a member, and it would seem excessive to join an organization solely to resign from it in protest. The colleague then explained that his wife had given him no peace on the subject, and he valued peace. So now would he go to lunch there if another member invited him? Sure. Would he go to lunch at a club that barred blacks? No. "What's the difference?" the essayist inquired. The colleague paused. "I don't know," he said.

These are small things, to be sure, and not a single sick or hungry child 9
will feel better because the Millennium Club opens its doors to women. On the other hand, is life not made up of small things? Lots and lots of small things? And isn't there considerable truth in that old banality of Edmund Burke's about the only thing necessary for the triumph of evil being for

good men to do nothing (he presumably meant good people or good individuals, but never mind—the creation of aphorisms was simpler in Burke's day)?

So down with the Millennium Club and all its partners in crime! Far 10 from having lunch there, let us march against it and wave our banners before its marble portals. Down with all discrimination! Equality for all! We *demand* justice!

"Wait a minute," said a woman who works down the hall. "I hope 11 you're not going to be one of those people who try to argue that women have to let men into the Colony Club."

"Sure I am," said the essayist, all filled with revolutionary enthusiasm. 12

"But that's one of the most important discoveries of the women's 13 movement," she said, "that women need to have some place where they can talk about their experiences."

"They can do that with men on the premises too," the essayist said. 14 "I'm for desegregation in all things."

"No, they *can't*," said the woman who works down the hall. 15

"As a matter of fact," said the colleague who had resigned from the 16 Millennium Club, "I'm enough of a libertarian to think that as long as a club is *really* private, it ought to be free to exclude anybody it wants, women or blacks or Greeks or people with red hair or whatever. Let them all start their own clubs."

"Ah, well, I think it is now just about time for lunch," said the essay- 17 ist, whose revolutionary impulses rarely last very long.

Just a little bit guiltily, he went to lunch at the Millennium Club. The 18 conversation with the distinguished person was very pleasant. He didn't meet anyone else, and no business of any kind was transacted. The bound sets of people like Bulwer-Lytton looked much the same as ever, and the shish kebab was overdone.

QUESTIONS ABOUT THE RHETORICAL SITUATION

1. Friedrich is sarcastic throughout the essay (see ¶3, ¶4, and ¶17, for example). At what subjects is his sarcasm directed? Why is he sarcastic? What does this sarcasm say about his attitude toward the small moral quandary he faces? How effective a strategy is this use of sarcasm?
2. How would you describe Friedrich's opinion of private clubs? Men? Women? Feminism? How do these attitudes affect his purpose in the essay? How do these attitudes affect your response to Friedrich?
3. How did you respond to Friedrich's essay? Would you experience this situation as a moral quandary? A small one? A large one? Would you respond to the situation differently now as a result of having read this essay? Why or why not? Would you respond as Friedrich would want you

to? In fact, how does Friedrich want you to respond to his essay? How would he wish you to act in the same situation?

4. As Wiesel was in his essay, Friedrich is addressing the readers of *Time* magazine. What assumptions has he made about his readers? How are his assumptions about his audience similar to or different from Wiesel's? How might his essay have taken a different form if it had been written for a different magazine, e.g., *Seventeen, Cosmopolitan, Ms.,* or *Playboy?* (Notice the geographical locations from which he draws his examples.)

QUESTIONS ABOUT THE ESSAY'S VOICE

1. As part of his meditating on the subject, Friedrich is careful to present more than one point of view on the issue (see ¶5 and ¶9). Does he have no opinion of his own? How would the voice of the essay have been affected had he only expressed one point of view in each of these paragraphs? How would the voice have been affected by the choices he might have made in each case?

2. Why does Friedrich call himself "the essayist"? Clearly, the essay is being written out of first-hand experience. Why isn't the essay written in the first person? How would the voice of the essay be affected if the essay were written in the first person? What would be the gains or losses for the essay of such a change?

3. In ¶5, Friedrich writes: "In theory, a private club that gets tax benefits or serves as a place of business has no right to exclude people." Why does he begin the sentence by saying "in theory?" Why does he make a distinction about the kind of private club he means ("that gets tax benefits or serves as a place of business")?

4. In ¶8, Friedrich uses both indirect quotation, telling us in his words what a colleague said, and direct quotation, telling us in the colleague's exact words what he said. Why does he switch from indirect to direct quotation? What is the effect on the essay's voice of the use of dialogue throughout the essay?

5. Describe the other two major characters in Friedrich's essay. Do they have anything in common? Why does the man seem to say one thing but be willing to do another? Is the woman down the hall different in this regard or the same?

6. Where in the essay does a sense of wonder or of questioning surface most explicitly? How has Friedrich used questions in a manner similar to or different from the other writers in this section of *Model Voices?*

7. What is the point of the essay's concluding paragraph? Can you think of a more appropriate final paragraph? How does the final paragraph contribute to creating the meditative voice in this essay?

TOPICS TO WRITE ABOUT

1. Write an essay in which you meditate about why people frequently claim to hold a specific set of beliefs but often behave counter to those beliefs. (For example, the Little League coach who tells the parents that the goal of the team is for the kids to have fun, but who then benches the player who makes an error or strikes out; or the parent who tells a child not to say anything rather than say something critical about a classmate, but who then engages in negative gossip about the neighbors; or the television clergyman who preaches spirituality but accepts a million dollar salary.) PO-TENTIAL AUDIENCE: Select an appropriate popular magazine, such as *Time*, and write to that audience of readers. POTENTIAL PURPOSE: to make your readers stop to ponder the inherent contradiction in such behavior.

2. Write an essay about a moral quandary in which you have found yourself. (For example, should you tell a friend a small truth which will hurt her feelings or should you tell a small lie and save her feelings?) POTENTIAL AUDIENCES: readers who are likely to have been in the very same quandary/readers who are unlikely to have been in the same quandary. POTENTIAL PURPOSES: to make them think about what they have done or ought to have done in similar situations/to make them think about what they might or should do in similar situations.

Strangers to Darkness
Annie Dillard

Annie Dillard was born in Pittsburgh, Pennsylvania, in 1945. She earned undergraduate and graduate degrees from Hollins College in the 1960s. In 1973, she began a long association with *Harper's* magazine as a contributing editor. She has published poetry (*Tickets for a Prayer Wheel*), literary analysis (*Living by Fiction*), and collections of essays (*Teaching a Stone to Talk, Holy the Firm, Encounters with Chinese Writers*). Dillard has also published in magazines such as the *Atlantic Monthly, Sports Illustrated, Prose, Cosmopolitan, Living Wilderness,* and *American Scholar,* among others.

Perhaps her best-known work is *Pilgrim at Tinker Creek* (1974), an account of a year spent observing nature on a tract of land in Virginia, for which she won the Pulitzer Prize for nonfiction. "Strangers to Darkness" first appeared in *Pilgrim at Tinker Creek.*

QUESTIONS ABOUT IDEAS

1. Nothing dramatic actually occurs in this essay, yet Dillard's responses are

quite dramatic. What is there about this natural scene that is causing such
a strong response in Dillard?
2. How would a scientist perhaps respond differently to the same scene?
3. What is the connection between light and dark made by the essay? Why
is it important?
4. What is it that most concerns Dillard, that allows her to use things as
small as an amoeba and as large as the galaxy as her examples?

Where Tinker Creek flows under the sycamore log bridge to the tear 1
shaped island, it is slow and shallow, fringed thinly in cattail marsh. At this
spot an astonishing bloom of life supports vast breeding populations of insects, fish, reptiles, birds, and mammals. On windless summer evenings I
stalk along the creek bank or straddle the sycamore log in absolute stillness,
watching for muskrats. The night I stayed too late I was hunched on the log
staring spellbound at spreading, reflected stains of lilac on the water. A
cloud in the sky suddenly lighted as if turned on by a switch; its reflection
just as suddenly materialized on the water upstream, flat and floating, so
that I couldn't see the creek bottom, or life in the water under the cloud.
Downstream, away from the cloud on the water, water turtles smooth as
beans were gliding down with the current in a series of easy, weightless
push-offs, as men bound on the moon. I didn't know whether to trace the
progress of one turtle I was sure of, risking sticking my face in one of the
bridge's spider webs made invisible by the gathering dark, or take a chance
on seeing the carp, or scan the mudbank in hope of seeing a muskrat or follow the last of the swallows who caught at my heart and trailed it after them
like streamers as they appeared from directly below, under the log, flying
upstream with their tails forked, so fast.

But shadows spread and deepened and stayed. After thousands of years 2
we're still strangers to darkness, fearful aliens in an enemy camp with our
arms crossed over our chests. I stirred. A land turtle on the bank, startled,
hissed the air from its lungs and withdrew to its shell. An uneasy pink here,
an unfathomable blue there, gave great suggestion of lurking beings. Things
were going on. I couldn't see whether that rustle I heard was a distant rattlesnake, slit-eyed, or a nearby sparrow kicking in the dry flood debris slung
at the foot of a willow. Tremendous action roiled the water everywhere I
looked, big action, inexplicable. A tremor welled up beside a gaping muskrat burrow in the bank and I caught my breath, but no muskrat appeared.
The ripples continued to fan upstream with a steady, powerful thrust. Night
was knitting an eyeless mask over my face, and I still sat transfixed. A distant airplane, a delta wing out of nightmare, made a gliding shadow on the
creek's bottom that looked like a stingray cruising upstream. At once a black
fin split the pink cloud on the water, shearing it in two. The two halves
merged together and seemed to dissolve before my eyes. Darkness pooled in

the cleft of the creek and rose, as water collects in a well. Untamed, dreaming lights flickered over the sky. I saw hints of hulking underwater shadows, two pale splashes out of the water, and round ripples rolling close together from a blackened center.

At last I stared upstream where only the deepest violet remained of the   3
cloud, a cloud so high its underbelly still glowed, its feeble color reflected from a hidden sky lighted in turn by a sun halfway to China. And out of that violet, a sudden enormous black body arched over the water. Head and tail, if there was a head and tail, were both submerged in cloud. I saw only one ebony fling, a headlong dive to darkness; then the waters closed, and the lights went out.

I walked home in a shivering daze, up hill and down. Later I lay open-   4
mouthed in bed, my arms flung wide at my sides to steady the whirling darkness. At this latitude I'm spinning 836 miles an hour round the earth's axis; I feel my sweeping fall as a breakneck arch like the dive of dolphins, and the hollow rushing of wind raises the hairs on my neck and the side of my face. In orbit around the sun I'm moving 64,800 miles an hour. The solar system as a whole, like a merry-go-round unhinged, spins, bobs, and blinks at the speed of 43,200 miles an hour along a course set east of Hercules. Someone has piped, and we are dancing a tarantella until the sweat pours. I open my eyes and I see dark, muscled forms curl out of water, with flapping gills and flattened eyes. I close my eyes and I see stars, deep stars giving way to deeper stars, deeper stars bowing to deepest stars at the crown of an infinite cone.

"Still," wrote Van Gogh in a letter, "a great deal of lights falls on ev-   5
erything." If we are blinded by darkness, we are also blinded by light. Sometimes here in Virginia at sunset low clouds on the southern or northern horizon are completely invisible in the lighted sky. I only know one is there because I can see its reflection in still water. The first time I discovered this mystery I looked from cloud to no-cloud in bewilderment, checking my bearings over and over, thinking maybe the ark of the covenant was just passing by south of Dead Man Mountain. Only much later did I learn the explanation: polarized light from the sky is very much weakened by reflection, but the light in clouds isn't polarized. So invisible clouds pass among visible clouds, till all slide over the mountains; so a greater light extinguishes a lesser as though it didn't exist.

In the great meteor shower of August, the Perseid, I wait all day for   6
the shooting stars I miss. They're out there showering down, committing hara-kiri in a flame of fatal attraction, and hissing perhaps at last into the ocean. But at dawn what looks like a blue dome clamps down over me like a lid on a pot. The stars and planets could smash and I'd never know. Only a piece of ashen moon occasionally climbs up or down the inside of the dome, and our local star without surcease explodes on our heads. We have really only that one light, one source for all power, and yet we must turn away

from it by universal decree. Nobody here on the planet seems aware of this strange, powerful taboo, that we all walk about carefully averting our faces, this way and that, lest our eyes be blasted forever.

Darkness appalls and light dazzles; the scrap of visible light that   7
doesn't hurt my eyes hurts my brain. What I see sets me swaying. Size and distance and the sudden swelling of meanings confuse me, bowl me over. I straddle the sycamore log bridge over Tinker Creek in the summer. I look at the lighted creek bottom: snail tracks tunnel the mud in quavering curves. A crayfish jerks, but by the time I absorb what has happened, he's gone in a billowing smoke screen of silt. I look at the water: minnows and shiners. If I'm thinking minnows, a carp will fill my brain till I scream. I look at the water's surface: skaters, bubbles, and leaves sliding down. Suddenly, my own face, reflected, startles me witless. Those snails have been tracking my face! Finally, with a shuddering wrench of the will, I see clouds, cirrus clouds. I'm dizzy, I fall in.

This looking business is risky. Once I stood on a humped rock on   8
nearby Purgatory Mountain, watching through binoculars the great autumn hawk migration below, until I discovered that I was in danger of joining the hawks on a vertical migration of my own. I was used to binoculars, but not, apparently, to balancing on humped rocks while looking through them. I reeled. Everything advanced and receded by turns; the world was full of unexplained foreshortenings and depths. A distant huge object, a hawk the size of an elephant, turned out to be the browned bough of a nearby loblolly pine. I followed a sharp-shinned hawk against a featureless sky, rotating my head unawares as it flew, and when I lowered the glass a glimpse of my own looming shoulder sent me staggering. What prevents the men on Palomar from falling, voiceless and blinded, from their tiny, vaulted chairs?

I reel in confusion; I don't understand what I see. With the naked eye   9
I can see two million light-years to the Andromeda galaxy. Often I slop some creek water in a jar, and when I get home I dump it in a white china bowl. After the silt settles I return and see tracings of minute snails on the bottom, a planarian or two winding round the rim of water, roundworms shimmying frantically, and finally, when my eyes have adjusted to these dimensions, amoebae. At first the amoebae look like *muscae Volitantes*, those curled moving spots you seem to see in your eyes when you stare at a distant wall. Then I see the amoebae as drops of water congealed, bluish, translucent, like chips of sky in the bowl. At length I choose one individual and give myself over to its idea of an evening. I see it dribble a grainy foot before it on its wet, unfathomable way. Do its unedited sense impressions include the fierce focus of my eyes? Shall I take it outside and show it Andromeda, and blow its little endoplasm? I stir the water with a finger, in case it's running out of oxygen. Maybe I should get a tropical aquarium with motorized bubblers and lights, and keep this one for a pet. Yes, it would tell its fissioned descendants, the

universe is two feet by five, and if you listen closely you can hear the buzzing
music of the spheres.

Oh, it's mysterious, lamplit evenings here in the galaxy, one after the 10
other. It's one of those nights when I wander from window to window, looking for a sign. But I can't see. Terror and a beauty insoluble are a riband of
blue woven into the fringes of garments of things both great and small. No
culture explains, no bivouac offers real haven or rest. But it could be that we
are not seeing something. Galileo thought comets were an optical illusion.
This is fertile ground: since we are certain that they're not, we can look at
what our scientists have been saying with fresh hope. What if there are *really*
gleaming, castellated cities hung upside-down over the desert sand? What
limpid lakes and cool date palms have our caravans always passed untried?
Until, one by one, by the blindest of leaps, we light on the road to these
places, we must stumble in darkness and hunger. I turn from the window.
I'm blind as a bat, sensing only from every direction the echo of my own
thin cries.

QUESTIONS ABOUT THE RHETORICAL SITUATION

1. What assumptions has Dillard made about her audience? Could her essay
   be read by anyone in the general reading public? Who does she mean
   when she uses the pronoun *we* in ¶2? What does the final sentence of ¶6
   suggest about Dillard's perception of herself and her audience?
2. David Quammen also wrote about nature and the outdoors ("The Tree
   People"). Is there any difference between his intended readers and Dillard's? Is Dillard's attitude toward nature any different from Quammen's?
3. See Dillard's description of herself sitting on the log (in ¶1). Which adjective in particular is significant in describing her attitude? How accurately does this adjective describe her attitude throughout the remainder
   of the essay?
4. How did Dillard's essay affect your attitude toward nature? The stars?
   Darkness? How did she produce that response in you?

QUESTIONS ABOUT THE ESSAY'S VOICE

1. Virtually every paragraph includes concrete details describing the scene.
   Which concrete details are used by Dillard to speculate and to make
   larger generalizations about nature? How does she expand the scope of
   her ideas from these details to the possible generalizations?

2. Words like *inexplicable* (¶2) and *mystery* (¶5) tell us that Dillard is uncertain. How does she manage also to *show* her uncertainty? (See ¶4, 7, 8, 9, for example.)

3. What are possible answers to the questions posed by Dillard in ¶8 and ¶10? What possible answers does she suggest? How concerned is she with finding the answers?

4. What is Dillard describing in ¶3? Is the description clear enough to serve her purposes? How does this description help to create the meditative voice in this essay?

5. How does ¶4 help to establish the essay's meditative voice?

6. Look at Dillard's use of similes in the essay. In ¶1, she says the water turtles move "as men bound on the moon." In ¶9, she says the bluish-tinted amoebae in her bowl are "like chips of sky in the bowl." Why does she choose such similes? How are they appropriate to her essay's voice?

7. Is Dillard's voice closer in sound to David Quammen's, which also deals with nature, or to those of Elie Wiesel and Otto Friedrich, which focus exclusively on human behavior?

8. Dillard begins her final paragraph with the word *oh*. What is the effect of this sentence on her voice?

TOPICS TO WRITE ABOUT

1. Visit a special place at night and then again during the day (a nearby pond, the downtown business district, a local park, for example). Write an essay in which you speculate about the meaning of the differences you have observed in this setting during your two visits. POTENTIAL AUDIENCE: readers who will likely have visited the place either only during the day or only during the night. POTENTIAL PURPOSE: to make them ponder the very different place this familiar environment seems to be at an unfamiliar time of day.

2. Write an essay in which you meditate about the meaning and impact on your own life of the tremendous technological advances of the past twenty years (men on the moon, organ transplants, low-cost pocket calculators and personal computers, lasers). POTENTIAL AUDIENCES: the members of your class/scientists, inventors, physicians, researchers. POTENTIAL PURPOSES: to make them also consider the impact of these often-taken-for-granted technologies/to make them consider what the future impact of their technological breakthroughs might be.

Private and Public Writer
Steve Barrett

Steve Barrett is a 1987 graduate of Miami University in Ohio. Barrett returned
to college after spending five years immediately after his high school graduation working as a plumber. Following graduation from Miami University, he
entered Florida State University's graduate program in English, working toward a goal of becoming a creative writing instructor on the college level.

An inveterate journal keeper who had about seven cartons of journals
tucked away in his closets, Barrett had been meditating for some time about
his own writing at the time when he wrote this essay, and struggling to determine where the boundary line between private and public lies for writers.

QUESTIONS ABOUT IDEAS

1. Have you ever been unsure about how much of yourself to reveal in a
   piece of writing? How have you solved the problem?
2. What is the value of using personal experiences, ideas, feelings, thoughts
   in a piece of writing designed to be read by strangers?
3. In what ways are you also both a private and public person? In what ways
   have you experienced a conflict between these two people that you are?

Just yesterday afternoon, I 1
unthreaded the plug in my oil pan,
drained the oil in my engine,
changed the filter, and added three
new quarts of Kendall Superb 100
and a can of STP oil treatment.
Now what does any of this have to
do with me as a writer? I think it is
symbolic of where I stand as a human being (and therefore as a
writer) at this point in my life, for I
have owned my car nine years now,
have travelled each of its 158,000
miles with it, and yet yesterday afternoon was the first time I
changed its oil *myself*. It is no big
deal, I know, but it is symbolic, I
think.

Do I dare admit that my fa- 2
ther asked me earlier in the week if
I had changed the oil in my car
lately? Do I dare try to capture in
words the grimace that wracked his
face when I confessed that I had
not? Does this confession detract
from my evolving independence
and self-reliance?

Just the night before, Shelley's parents had sat down with Shelley and me, talking with us about the possibility/impossibility, the practicality/impracticality, of Shelley and me getting married next summer at the end of only our first year of graduate school. This, too, I think, is symbolic of the point I have come to in my life.   3

At points there were tears in the eyes of each of them as they remembered and shared with us the financial and emotional burdens they had borne as students and newlyweds twenty-four years ago. Do I share that here? Do I admit that I could not help taking it all rather personally? Do I admit that in the days since, the discussion has stirred up my own fears that deep down Tom and Marilyn would prefer to see Shelley have an easier, more comfortable life than the one I would help her to make for herself next year, or five years, or even ten years from now?   4

And in eight days, I will be standing in front of a classroom filled with twenty-five lean and hungry students, and I will be beginning my own first year of graduate studies, and that, too, I think, is symbolic.   5

And do I admit here how frightened I have been of the prospect for six or eight months now? And do I complicate this piece by trying to describe and make sense of the opposing desire to stand in front of these students, share something of myself with them, make some positive impact upon their lives, and in the process overcome the obstacles to my own growth? How much do I share? And what determines how much I share? Reason? Fear?   6

These seemingly unrelated events suggest that I stand on the brink of something significant—something that, for lack of a better term, I will call adulthood, something that my parents might call "the real world" or "the cold, hard facts of life." I think that is where I stand as a writer, too. I have been an adult for some time now, at least a young one, and in many ways a   7

These seemingly unrelated events were among the most difficult I have ever tried to write for a paper. And I must admit I find that both a little surprising and a little troubling. I am after all a journal writer and take great delight in delving as deeply as time and emotional energy will permit into just such scenes as these. So what is the difficulty? It is not that   8 very immature one; and I have been a writer for some time, too. Though still very much a young and immature writer, I have been writing consistently for almost seven years and have in my possession a piece of paper that proclaims to all who care that I have studied creative writing for four years now.

I think they are terribly private. But they are events from my own life, recent events, events from which I cannot distance myself yet to gain perspective. And with the writing of each one, real fears emerge, fears which at heart all ask: What will readers think of me? What perspective would a thirty, a forty, or a fifty year old individual have on the events I have described? In addition to the significance I obviously see, I also wonder what each scene reveals about me—my youth? my naiveté?

My life it seems is something of a paradox or a dichotomy or something. On the one hand, I am a very private, usually quiet, always introspective person. My friends tend to be few and close. Friendships with women are often the most rewarding. And I am a journal writer. I have been one for some time. At this point in my journal writing I get the most satisfaction out of those entries where I feel I have truly exerted myself, have truly searched myself and stretched the boundaries of my own self-awareness. And consequently my writing grows more private all the time. 9

On the other hand, I am striving to become a creative writer—a writer of prose. My writing is therefore also becoming more public all the time. Yet I find myself turning to my own experiences, to my journals, more and more often, and each time I am faced with just the kinds of questions I have raised in this piece. The questions are ones I might easily raise in my journals, but when I am writing more public pieces I raise them and answer them almost unconsciously, and when answered I dismiss them. It is then as if I had never raised them at all. 10

How private do I want my public writing to be? Perhaps that as much as anything else is the significant brink I feel I now stand upon. An interesting question was raised yesterday: Have I chosen fiction because it is something I can safely hide behind while truly dealing with my own thoughts and feelings and life experiences? Am I hiding behind my fiction? I do not think so. The greatest excitement and release for me as a writer of either fiction or journals is when I feel I have worked successfully with difficult material, which usually translates "private material." 11

I do believe that the two modes of writing I love and practice most often are distinct and disparate forms, but I do not believe that they are nec- 12 essarily irreconcilable, for I believe that as I turn my focus inward and delve more deeply into myself, I am at the same time and *by the very same gesture* turning my focus outward and travelling among the people around me. Though certainly unique and individual and irreplaceable, each of us, I think shares much more with the people around us than we may often realize. And I truly believe that by taking the time to sit down with my journal and concentrate all my attention and emotional energies upon myself, and upon discovering myself, I am also coming to a growing understanding of and empathy for the people who share my life. Turning inward can be turning outward. We most often think in terms of dichotomies—of introversion and extroversion, in this case. But I feel strongly that introversion can be extroversion.

So what about those questions that arise each time I go to the closet, 13 pull down the shoe boxes that contain the thousands of daily entries I have made in the last seven years, and huddle over what will be a "public" paper? Those questions, I believe are some of the tools of my trade. Writing, and particularly creative writing, is of growing significance in my life, and as I continue writing increasingly significant work I must constantly reconsider and redefine the narrow line between private and public writing, and come to terms with myself as a private and public person.

QUESTIONS ABOUT THE RHETORICAL SITUATION

1. Is Barrett writing for an audience of other writers? Can his essay be of interest to nonwriters? He submitted his essay to the editors of a journal read by high school English teachers. How appropriate would his essay be to those readers? How appropriate is his essay to students in a composition course?
2. How is the essay itself an indication of the importance of the subject to Barrett? How does it illustrate the quandary in which he finds himself whenever he writes?
3. What does he want his reader to meditate about? How did you respond to his essay? Do his private passages make you uncomfortable? If so, why? Does he want them to?

QUESTIONS ABOUT THE ESSAY'S VOICE

1. What is the effect of the essay's unusual format through its first several pages? How else might Barrett have written this part of his essay? Is this an effective strategy?
2. Barrett uses people's names in his essay without identifying them. Does this strategy work? Explain your answer.

3. In ¶11 of his essay, Barrett raises several questions. Which of these questions lead to further meditations? Which do not? Why not?
4. In ¶12 Barrett uses italics for emphasis. Does he need to? Would the passage work as effectively without the italics? Explain your answer.
5. In his conclusion, Barrett says he must come to terms with himself as a private and public person. Has he done so in this essay? Why is the meditative voice an appropriate voice for such an activity?
6. In ¶12, Barrett writes "I feel strongly that introversion can be extroversion." This is an apparent paradox. How does this paradox help to create the meditative voice in his essay? Are there any other paradoxes in this essay?

TOPICS TO WRITE ABOUT

1. Write a meditative essay about some activity that you feel quite ambivalent about: you do it, but you don't know why. For example, you continue to perform in amateur theatrical productions even though you suffer greatly from stage fright. POTENTIAL AUDIENCES: others who participate in the same activity/your friends and others who know you well. POTENTIAL PURPOSES: to make them think about why they participate in this activity/to make them think about whether or not they understand your behavior.
2. Write a meditative essay about why some people are more private than others and about how different people define *private* so differently. POTENTIAL AUDIENCES: the general reading public/people from another country. POTENTIAL PURPOSES: to make them think about their own definitions of *private*/to make them think about whether their own culture defines *private* differently.

SECTION FOUR

The Voice of Authority

BOOKS I REMEMBER

My love for baseball began when I was a small boy. In addition to playing
the game (with varied degrees of success!), I also loved reading about it. I
read all sorts of baseball novels for boys, later graduating to reading
biographies of ballplayers. But as I got older still, I read three baseball
books that really changed my view of the sport.

First I read a biography of Ty Cobb, perhaps the greatest ballplayer of
all time, certainly the meanest and most vicious. All the biographies I had
been reading were like children's books compared to this one. All the
others made the ballplayers sound like knights in shining armor; the one
about Cobb made him sound like a very real, if not very nice, human
being. At about the same time, I read *Eight Men Out* by Eliot Asinof, a
meticulously researched book that told the sad story of how a few New
York gamblers were able to bribe members of the 1919 Chicago White Sox
to throw the World Series. I had heard about the infamous Black Sox
Scandal, as it was called, but reading about the gamblers and the players
and how the World Series itself was played, game by game, really made
me feel as if I had been there.

The final of the three books was Jim Bouton's *Ball Four,* a sort of diary
of a baseball season written by an active player. This book was reviled by
the baseball world because it told the truth about ballplayers: some liked
to drink, some weren't particularly faithful to their wives while on road
trips, some were bigoted, some were plain ornery or dumb. Again, I felt
as if my eyes had been opened! This guy Bouton knew his stuff!

I still love baseball, but I no longer need the players to be King Arthur
or Superman. I can accept that they are human beings with their own
problems, humans who just happen to be skilled athletes. I'm sure I
would have eventually learned this lesson on my own, but reading these

three knowledgeable books opened my eyes for me. What all three books shared was a similar voice, the voice of authority. Each of the writers knew his subject inside and out and, quite simply, sounded expert to me.

THE ROLE OF EXPERT

In *Model Voices* you have already read personal voices that encouraged you to write meaningfully about yourself. You have read writing that included larger concerns (such as persuasion). Now this book offers you an opportunity to combine both the "smaller," more personal, and "larger," more public, focus in the voice of authority. Here the writer starts out with the assumption that she knows more than the reader does about the topic. The objective is not so much to amuse, entertain, even persuade, as it is to explain, inform, enlighten. Your readers will learn something, either by being directly and explicitly taught or by being shown in such a vivid way that they will understand something they have not understood before.

This voice of the expert, the voice of authority, may be the most familiar of the voices you hear in this book because it is the voice you hear in school in your other textbooks, in your lecture classes. This is the writing voice that is called upon most frequently in an academic setting: reports, essay exams, term papers, literary criticism all employ the voice of authority.

But this voice is in a sense a voice you have been using all along—because how could you have written anything sensible without knowing a great deal about the subject? Weren't you an expert when you wrote humorously and satirically? Weren't you an expert when you wrote angrily and persuasively?

WRITING WITH POWER AND CONFIDENCE

In this section, the writers write with the power and confidence that comes of *knowing* that they are experts. But the actual voices may at times make use of humor or sarcasm or may evoke emotion or persuade a reader as part of instructing. They may use already familiar structures: narration, description, exposition. Here, more than in the other sections of the book, you will hear a variety of voices because the voice of authority varies from one expert to another just as the voices of your professors, who are authorities in their fields, vary from one lecture class to another. One professor is a comic virtuoso explaining the significance of the five senses in her introduction to psych course; another is earnest, sincere, passionate in explaining the workings of Marxist economic theory; another is reflective and calm as he explains Aristotle's view of tragedy; and yet another is bitter, sarcastic, nasty as she explains the initially shortsighted reaction of many geologists to the theory of plate tectonics in a course on the history of science.

But they are all experts, voices of authority, and they speak with the power and confidence that is born of knowing that they know what they are talking about. That's the point you have reached in this book and in your course—you should be able to write with that same sense of power and confidence.

DRAWING CONCLUSIONS

The voices in this chapter are voices of experts speaking knowledgeably and forcefully about the things they know best. *These writers make extensive use of details, but they also tend to move beyond merely reporting facts. They frequently draw general conclusions from specific data, an important trait of the voice of authority, a trait that distinguishes it from the personal voice.* The writing in Section Four usually moves outward from the self, sometimes using the self as a starting point but generally expanding the scope of the discussion to include other people, ideas, and issues.

You will find four chapters in Section Four, exemplifying three different voices of authority:

The voice of firsthand experience. With this voice, we hear the writer writing out of personal experience. The writer has become an authority simply by living and by being observant. A description of an exotic location has been acquired by visiting that location. An explanation of how spiders and wasps interact has been acquired by observing them over a period of years. An explanation of the significance of the Vietnam War to those who fought in that war is the product of having been a soldier in Southeast Asia. An explanation of the quality of a new movie is the result of the writer's having seen many, many movies over the years and having evolved a set of standards against which any new movie can be judged. The writing in this voice is divided into two chapters, one with narrative and descriptive essays and one with expository or explanatory essays.

The interview voice. With this voice, we hear a writer who has become an expert by virtue of consulting a primary source. In other words, although the writer has not enough expertise on her own to write her essay, she does not scurry off to the library in order to see what others have written about the subject. Instead, the writer speaks to someone who is already an expert on the subject and uses that information to become an "instant" expert. Regardless of whom the writer interviews, the voice is still one of authority, although a secondhand kind of authority. That is not meant to be a criticism. In fact, the voices you will hear in Chapters 10 and 11 (The Voice of Firsthand Experience) could very easily turn up in Chapter 12 demonstrating the interview voice if some enterprising writer had interviewed the Vietnam veteran or the entomologist about the war or about the spiders and wasps. The voice would have been somewhat different; the sense of immediacy in the voice of firsthand experience would be somewhat diminished.

The research voice. The most formal-sounding voice of authority may well be the research voice, a voice created as the end product of an active process of acquiring information. In a sense, the interview voice is the product of research, but writing that is the culmination of a more traditional researching of a subject through other written sources (secondary sources) has its own sound. While the voice of firsthand experience can give the reader the impression that the writer simply *knows* his subject, the research voice, by carefully suggesting in one way or another the sources of the writer's information, makes clear that the writer has worked diligently to reach the state of being an expert. Yet even the research voice sounds different from one rhetorical situation to another, depending on the targeted audience, the amount and complexity of the information acquired, and the writer's objectives.

SOME BENEFITS OF USING THE VOICE OF AUTHORITY

Section Four of *Model Voices* should prove useful to you in a number of ways.

It will reconfirm the lessons you learned earlier about the need to be specific and to consider your audience. When you started out in this textbook, you were concerned with whether or not your audience would smile or laugh at your humorous voice. Now you will be focusing on whether or not they will understand your explanations of unfamiliar materials. They will—if you remember to provide them with the details they need in a language they can understand.

It will illustrate the variety of ways to acquire information. Using your college library to find information is a very valuable method for acquiring materials necessary to writing. However, there are other equally valuable methods for obtaining information—for example, interviewing experts, and making use of your own firsthand experiences. Section Four will illustrate the value of all three of these methods for obtaining materials for writing.

It will prepare you to write essay exams and research papers and to do other academic writing. By reading the essays in this section and trying some of your own, you should be able to strengthen your skills in presenting information in a clear, informative manner—the skill needed to write effectively on exams as well as in research papers.

RISKS

As with all the different voices you have been hearing in this textbook, the voice of authority presents many advantages—but it also presents some risks. Remember how excited you were when you got home with your first stereo system (or video recorder or bicycle or food processor)? You tore open the box or boxes and looked at all the beautiful components. Then, unless you just happened to already know about such things, you quickly found the owner's manual and began to read through it, learning about how to set up the equipment, how to maintain it, how to use it.

That manual, or instruction sheet, spoke to you as a teacher would speak to a student, as the voice of an expert instructing a novice. The voice you heard was the voice of authority. Of course, some of us ignore these manuals, either because we already know how to set up a stereo system or because (this is my usual mistake), we *think* we know how to set up a stereo system. At other times, we eagerly read the instructions only to be disappointed that we are not learning enough.

Several years ago I purchased an automatic garage door opener, convinced that I could save money by buying it on sale and installing it myself, even though I usually am lucky to hammer two consecutive nails into a wall without mashing my thumb. I lugged the box into the garage, opened it, sought out the instructions for installation, and finally found them—thirty-five pages' worth! I started reading, growing glummer by the minute. The instructions sounded bright and cheery but soon began talking about tools and tasks that I had never heard of. It took only fifteen minutes for me to learn that I was not going to be able to install this garage door opener, so I called the store and paid for them to install it for me.

The instructions were simply too technical for me, although probably not for a more practiced do-it-yourselfer. (And of course the installer from the store never once looked at the instructions.)

PROBLEMS TO SOLVE

There is a point to this story. When you write with the voice of authority you face two likely problems:

Your audience may already know what you have to tell them. Your job then is to try to be so knowledgeable that this won't happen. However, there will always be some readers who already know what you are writing about; the idea is to keep that number to a minimum.

Your audience may not be able to understand the information you provide. Because you are so much more knowledgeable than your readers are, it is more than likely that you could write about your subject in such a fashion that few readers could follow what you were saying (my problem with the instructions for the garage door opener). The solution is to remember what your readers need to know and what they already know so that you can write to them at the proper level of technicality. My proposal to McGraw-Hill suggesting that they offer me a contract to write *Model Voices* included references to concepts and research studies that would serve no purpose if I included them in the text that you have been reading. However, such references were important to my explanation of the proposed textbook's objectives when they were being judged by a trained editor.

WE ARE ALL EXPERTS

By paying close attention to the essays in this section of the book, you will learn how to avoid both these pitfalls. Remember—all of us are experts on a myriad of topics because we have all lived on this planet for a number of years and have been accumulating experiences every minute of every day. It is not the subjects you choose that will make you sound like an expert— it is how much you know about those subjects. More than ever before in this book, this section asks you to write about what you know, what you are interested in. And that's often the most rewarding type of writing to do. See if that isn't the case for you as you try out the voice of authority in your own work.

10

The Voice of Firsthand Experience: Narration and Description

An Exercise

Try this exercise: in the next minute or minute and a half, compile a list of subjects about which you are an expert, an authority. When I suggest this to my students—I usually have them try this activity in class—they generally groan and roll their eyes. "Me, an expert?" is the thought running through their minds. That's because they have misinterpreted the word *expert*. They are thinking of Einstein and Newton—you know, *real experts*. Let me illustrate, however, the kind of expert I mean. Here's my list, compiled in about a minute and a half.

Charles Dickens
Jack Nicholson movies
vegetables I absolutely will not eat
fights I had with my brothers when we were kids
strategies for playing Trivial Pursuit
things in my closet
teaching Freshman Composition
supermarket shopping

As you can see, some of these topics are "serious topics," but some of them are trivial or frivolous. Could I develop each of them into a complete essay? I suspect so; however, I am skeptical right now that I could interest either myself or you in a discussion of the things in my closet. My goal in compiling this list, however, was merely to take inventory of the things I know about.

PURPOSE

I actually did write an essay on teaching Freshman Composition several years ago. In it I wrote about many of the mistakes I had made when I first began teaching, mistakes such as only offering criticism to students and never praising their work. I went on to discuss how I had made an effort to change my approaches to teaching Freshman Composition. The purpose of my essay was to try to explain to my readers, other teachers of Freshman Composition, that there was a better way to teach the course than many of us had been using. That essay was published in *Freshman English News,* a journal read by college English instructors.

I wrote out of personal experience in the classroom, and I sounded like an expert because I felt very confident that I knew what I was talking about. I'm sure that some of my readers disagreed with my ideas and that many others had already reached similar conclusions, but I wrote with the intention of informing my readers of my experiences and ideas because I felt that those ideas and experiences had general relevance to all teachers of freshman composition.

And I think that the impulse to speak to readers about personal ideas and experiences that are as relevant to *their* lives as to the writer's own life is the most distinctive feature of the voice of firsthand experience. In the last two chapters, you read a number of essays that employed personal voices, voices that compelled us to feel what the writer had felt at a significant personal moment, voices that provoked us to ponder some of the small and large mysteries of our lives as human beings. In this chapter, however, the voice is different; the objective is different.

Here the voices are not tentative, uncertain, meditative; they are certain, confident, powerful, strong. The writers *know* the answers to any questions they may be raising; the search for an answer is over. These essays report on those answers rather than on the search itself. So Kieu Ly's essay about her flight from Vietnam belongs in this chapter because she is less interested in making us feel the emotions she felt than she is in explaining to us what it feels like to escape to freedom through great adversity. And Philip Caputo, in his essay in the next chapter, is not nearly as interested in making us meditate about the significance of the U.S. involvement in Vietnam as he is interested in explaining what he thinks that significance was.

TOPICS

Now look at your list of topics. Which ones could you use to instruct, inform, educate your readers? Remember that it is not the topic which matters here so much as your degree of expertise about that topic. I have read powerfully informative essays by my students about subjects as diverse as living with a parent who has mental problems, vacationing in Tahiti, collecting beer cans (or baseball cards or ceramic dolls), working in a fast food restaurant, growing up as an abused child, driving a race car for the first time, being a singer in a rock band, repairing a roller coaster, and laying a concrete driveway. All of those essays were effective; I learned something from every one of them.

And most of them were written by students whose first response to my assignment was, "ME? An expert? No way."

FEATURES TO NOTE

The voice of firsthand experience has several features worth noting:

Abundant Evidence

A colleague of mine, a linguist, once wrote an essay for the Sunday newspaper's magazine section about what it was like being a linguist. In his essay, he told stories about famous linguists, he made jokes about linguists, he illustrated linguistic research by offering the reader examples of ordinary speech variations of interest to the linguist. In fact, his examples were so interesting that they virtually forced his readers into participating in the essay by sounding out different words in their heads. Why go to all this effort? Because he felt that the typical reader of the Sunday magazine probably had no intrinsic interest in linguistics or linguists. He pulled out all the stops.

What is worth noting is that although he pulled out all the stops, using a ton of interesting details, he hardly used up all the possible material he might have included. He was a professional linguist, spending his entire adult working life studying language. He could have told anecdotes about linguists for days. In fact, he could have told anecdotes just about himself for days.

Expertise and Evidence Experts are experts because they understand their subjects, but that understanding is a product of their close study and observation of "evidence." I placed the word *evidence* in quotation marks because it sounds too formal for what I mean. I said earlier that I was an authority on the things in my closet; I can tell you in great detail (excruciating detail, in fact) what's in there. These details are what I mean by "evidence." All the details of which you would be aware if you went backpacking in the Canadian Rockies—the details of terrain, equipment, wildlife, climate, food and supplies, adventures, dangers, speculations, feelings—would make you an expert on your backpacking trip to the Canadian Rockies. When you write your essay on that trip, you will draw upon all of those details, just as the linguist drew on his experiences as a linguist and just as I would draw upon my nightmarish adventures in my closet.

To put it in a nutshell: Experts know so much about their subjects that they usually have to leave things out when they write because there is simply too much to include.

The Tendency to Generalize

The expert feels confident enough to use his material as a means by which he can form general conclusions about a larger topic. For instance, Philip Caputo writes about Vietnam, but he reaches conclusions about the behavior of all men in all wars. In this chapter you will also read Nell Irvin Painter's description of her two-year visit to an African nation: a concrete description that becomes the foundation for her more abstract observations about life in two different countries. In Chapter 11, Alexander Petrunkevitch, a famous zoologist, will describe a fascinating life-or-death struggle between two insects, but he will also carefully point out the greater scientific significance of this miniature war.

Understanding Evidence As a result of studying the world around her, the expert writer comes to a deeper understanding of that world, or at least of some facet of that world. Writers who deliberately choose to focus on the mysteries of the world end up writing in the meditative voice; the writers you are about to read deliberately choose to write about subjects that they feel they understand. They share their understanding with us, enlightening us by making us see the greater implications of their smaller observations.

So you write about your trip to the Canadian Rockies, and you generalize about it by observing that a trip to the mountains refreshes the spirit of most urban office workers or that these mountains are unlike any other mountains to be found anywhere else or that each mountain has its own personality that sets it apart from all other mountains or that dawn in the mountains is more special than sundown. If your goal is to make us feel the exhilaration of a trip to the Rockies, your voice will most likely be an evocative one. If your goal is to ruminate about what the significance of this natural beauty might be in a world beset by social problems, you will probably write in a meditative voice. But if your goal is to inform us about this trip and to make us understand one of the generalizations mentioned above, you will undoubtedly adopt the voice of authority, the voice of firsthand experience.

Connectedness

In a creative writing class several years ago, the students and I tried to make a list of the characteristics of effective writers. One student suggested that good writers are writers who can make connections, who can see the connectedness of events, people, phenomena, ideas in the world around them.

That is a sharp insight. Think about how often an effective teacher has illuminated an idea for you in a lecture by making a comparison to something else, perhaps something less complex or more familiar. In his piece on

Vietnam, Philip Caputo makes connections to Shakespeare, Rudyard Kipling, the American Civil War, and World War II. He compares different aspects of his experiences to being in prison, to leaving the womb, to getting married. Since his goal is to explain, he is willing to use any tool he can find to get his meaning across. And this leads him to forge connections.

Forging Links   In your hypothetical Canadian Rockies essay, you might compare the feeling of being in the mountains to the feeling a scuba diver gets on his first dive or to the feeling a child experiences the first time she rides a bicycle on her own. Or you might refer to John Denver's song "Rocky Mountain High" or, less obviously, to Keats' line about standing "silent upon a peak in Darien." Or you might talk about the mountain that Richard Dreyfuss sculpted out of mashed potatoes in the movie *Close Encounters of the Third Kind.* It all depends on what you're trying to explain.

Allusions and Analogies   Some of these connections take the form of *allusions (references made to things outside the essay),* and some take the form of *analogies (comparisons to unlike things which share one startling similarity, such as the mountain of mashed potatoes and the snow-covered Rocky Mountains).* Certainly these connections are observable in most of the essays you have read so far in this book, but with essays that manifest the voice of authority, it is particularly appropriate for these techniques of explaining to be used.

STRUCTURE

The voice of firsthand experience, perhaps the most common voice of authority, can be divided into two forms, according to structure: (1) narration/description and (2) exposition. Chapter 10 will focus on narrative and descriptive writing; Chapter 11 will focus on expository writing.

Narration/Description

Back in Chapter 8 (The Evocative Voice), I discussed writing descriptions and narratives, and what I said then still applies. But I would like to add just a little more here.

A Sample   When the writer's objective in writing a story or a description is to make the reader feel the same emotions he felt when he underwent a particular experience, he will likely create the evocative voice. But when the writer tries to create a scene that the reader can almost see or to relate a series of events so that the reader can almost feel as if she were there, so that the reader can understand the events, the voice is likely to be the voice of authority. For example, here is an excerpt from an essay by a first-year student, Laurie Lehrter, in which she recalls her fears of being the last one in the house to go to bed on a Saturday night. The essay is titled "Who's Afraid?"

> The breathing seems to fill my head now. It's the only thing I can hear. Some mysterious trick of the night seems to have amplified it a million times blocking out any other sounds that might exist. Slowly, slowly, the cover pulls back to reveal…my sister's blond head resting serenely on her pillow. I quickly check to make sure the rest of her body is attached and then sit back on my heels listening to my own self breathing rather heavily.
>
> I make my way back to the doorway, shaking my head and giggling at my foolishness. "I'm not really afraid of the dark," I whisper aloud. "Not really."

Laurie's essay always reminds me of similar experiences of my own in my younger days. The loudness of one's own breathing, the need to double check that the familiar head is attached to its usual body, the self-conscious giggling and talking to oneself—these are the kinds of details that allow a reader to experience the scene along with Laurie. These are the details that convince us that she is indeed an expert, that she knows what she is talking about.

Laurie's interest was in recreating the scene so that her readers could experience it along with her; she's not trying to make us feel fear. Jane Adams, quoted in the introduction to Chapter 8, wanted to make her readers feel her character's pain. So here the voice is authoritative and earlier it was evocative. Remember that no writer sets out to create a particular voice so much as she sets out to achieve a particular objective with her readers. So if you have a story to tell or a description you wish to convey, go to it. If you really know your material—as you will need to—the voice will grow out of it.

In this chapter, therefore, I think you'll hear a different voice in the narratives and descriptions from the one you heard several chapters ago—because these writers are really most interested in informing their readers through narration and description, rather than in evoking emotion.

ON TRUTHFULNESS

A final word about this type of writing. I was returning student essays once and got to the last one, a rather well-written story by a freshman about how lonesome he had felt at the beginning of the new school year. Having grown in Louisville, Kentucky, he knew no one at all in Cincinnati, where he was attending college. The essay described his feelings quite vividly. Since I had relatives in Louisville, I started up a conversation with the student.

"My brother lives in Louisville," I said. "What part of the city are you from?"

The student chuckled. "Oh, I'm from Cincinnati. I grew up right down the street from the university. I made all of that up," he laughed.

Well, he certainly fooled me, because he really sounded as if he knew his subject. Actually, I suspect he was writing out of experience anyway. Perhaps he was recalling his loneliness as a high school freshman or as a new sleepaway camper. At some point in his life, he must have experienced loneliness to write so convincingly about it, or else he had an extraordinary imagination.

My students have frequently asked me if their narratives must be "true." My answer is to tell them the anecdote I have just related and to make the point that what matters when telling a story is not whether the story is true or not, but whether it sounds true, whether it is true to the emotions of the event. Remember the equation I used in Chapter 1:

$$\text{Awareness of audience } +$$
$$\text{understanding of purpose } +$$
$$\text{attitude toward subject } = \text{voice}$$

When your purpose is to provoke laughter, truthfulness is not terribly important. When your purpose, on the other hand, is to explain something or to persuade a reader, truthfulness is vital if you are to write in an ethical way. It is dishonest to make up stories to suit a persuasive purpose, just as surely as it is dishonest to fabricate statistics. However, if your purpose is to relate a story in so vivid a fashion that your readers will feel as if they were experiencing the events themselves, it is probably permissible to "make up" the story.

On another occasion I read a narrative by a woman student about her psychic experiences in foretelling the future. She insisted that her experiences were not imagined, that they were true. Unfortunately, her essay was written in a manner which seemed more like fiction; it simply wasn't as convincing as it could have been.

When you write description or narration, I would recommend sticking to the truth. It's much easier to remember accurately than it is to think up an entire scene imaginatively with all the details necessary to create that feeling of reality. Remember that you yourself will not be there to tell a skeptical reader, "But that's the way it really happened." The words on the page have to stand on their own and be convincing on their own. Your story or description must have the ring of authenticity to have the impact you want upon your reader; it must have the voice of firsthand experience.

Blizzard

William Least Heat Moon

William Least Heat Moon is a writer who lives in Columbia, Missouri. Born William Trogdon, he adopted his father's Sioux Indian name. As he explains, "My father calls himself Heat Moon, my elder brother Little Heat Moon. I, coming last, am therefore Least."

After a divorce, Least Heat Moon left his job and traveled the United States, recording his adventures in his first published book, entitled *Blue Highways* (1982). He explains that on old highway maps of America, the main routes appeared in red and the back roads appeared in blue. In his truck, Ghost Dancing, Least Heat Moon chose to travel those blue highways. In the following selection (titled by the editor), the traveler spends a memorable night in the mountains.

QUESTIONS ABOUT IDEAS

1. During his night in the storm, Least Heat Moon experiences some irrational fears. Why do you think he focuses on an unlikely threat when such very real threats surround him?
2. One of the author's interesting reactions is his surprise that he should be in such a difficult situation in the latter part of the twentieth century. Have you ever found yourself in similar trouble, where our modern conveniences and technology have been of no help? Was your reaction similar to Least Heat Moon's?
3. What was your reaction to the author's attempts at surviving the storm? Would you have done what he did? Why or why not?

Somewhere out there was the Colorado River perfectly hidden in the   1
openness. The river wasn't more than a mile away, but I couldn't make out the slightest indication of it in the desert stretching level and unbroken for twenty or thirty miles west, although I was only fifty miles above where it enters Grand Canyon. This side of the Colorado gorge was once an important Hopi trail south, and, some say, the route Hopi guides took when they first led white men to the canyon. While the arid path followed the river cleft, water was an inaccessible four hundred feet down. Typically, the flexible Hopi solved the desert: women buried gourds of water at strategic points on the outward journey for use on the return.

The highway made an unexpected jog toward Navajo Bridge, a meld-   2
ing of silvery girders and rock cliffs. Suddenly, there it was, far below in the deep and scary canyon of sides so sheer they might have been cut with a stone saw, the naturally silted water turned an unnatural green (*colorado*

means "reddish") by the big settling basin a few miles upriver called Glen Canyon Dam. Navajo Bridge, built in 1929 when paved roads began opening the area, is the only crossing over the Colorado between Glen Canyon and Hoover Dam several hundred river miles downstream.

West of the gorge lay verdant rangeland, much of it given to a buffalo 3 herd maintained by the Arizona Game Commission; the great beasts lifted their heads to watch me pass, their dark, wet eyes catching the late sun. To the north rose the thousand-foot butt end of the Vermillion Cliffs; the cliffs weren't truly vermillion, but contrasting with the green valley in the orange afternoon light, they seemed so.

In 1776, a few months after white-stockinged men in Philadelphia had 4 declared independence, a Spanish expedition led by missionaries Francisco Silvestre Velez de Escalante and Francisco Atanasio Dominguez, returning from an unsuccessful search for a good northern route to the California missions, wandered dispiritedly along the Vermillion Cliffs as they tried to find in the maze of the Colorado a point to cross the river chasm. They looked for ten days and were forced to eat boiled cactus and two of their horses before finding a place to ford; even then, they had to chop out steps to get down and back up the four-hundred-foot perpendicular walls. My crossing, accomplished sitting down, took twenty seconds. What I saw as a remarkable sight, the Spaniards saw as a terror that nearly did them in.

Escalante's struggles gave perspective to the easy passage I'd enjoyed 5 across six thousand miles of America. Other than weather, some bad road, and a few zealous police, my difficulties had been only those of mind. In light of what was about to happen, my guilt over easy transit proved ironic.

I went up an enormous geologic upheaval called the Kaibab Plateau; 6 with startling swiftness, the small desert bushes changed to immense conifers as the Kaibab forest deepened: ponderosa, fir, spruce. At six thousand feet, the temperature was sixty: a drop of thirty degrees in ten miles. On the north edge of the forest, the highway made a long gliding descent off the plateau into Utah. Here lay Kane and Garfield counties, a place of multicolored rock and baroque stone columns and, under it all, the largest unexploited coalfield in the country. A land certain one day to be fought over.

At dusk I considered going into the Coral Sand Dunes for the night, 7 but I'd had enough warmth and desert for a while, so I pushed north toward Cedar Breaks in the severe and beautiful Markagunt Plateau. The cool would refresh me. Sporadic splats of rain, not enough to pay attention to, hit the windshield. I turned onto Utah 14, the cross-mountain road to Cedar City. In the dim light of a mountainous sky, I could just make out a large sign:

ELEVATION 10,000 FEET
ROAD MAY BE IMPASSIBLE
DURING WINTER MONTHS.

So? It was nearly May. The rain popped, then stopped, popped and stopped. The incline became steeper and light rain fell steadily, rolling red desert dust off the roof; I hadn't hit showers since east Texas. It was good. The pleasant cool turned to cold, and I switched on the heater. The headlights glared off snowbanks edging closer to the highway as it climbed, and the rain became sleet. That's when I began thinking I might have made a little miscalculation. I looked for a place to turn around, but there was only narrow, twisted road. The sleet got heavier, and the headlights were cutting only thirty feet into it. Maybe I could drive above and out of the storm. At eight thousand feet, the wind came up—a rough, nasty wind that bullied me about the slick road. Lear, daring the storm to "strike flat the thick rotundity of the world," cries, "Blow, winds, and crack your cheeks! Rage! Blow!" And that's just what they did.

A loud, sulphurous blast of thunder rattled the little truck, then an-   8
other, and one more. Never had I seen lightning or heard thunder in a snowstorm. Although there were no signs, the map showed a campground near the summit. It would be suicide to stop, and maybe the same to go on. The wind pushed on Ghost Dancing so, I was afraid of getting blown over the invisible edge. Had not the falling snow taken away my vision, I might have needed a blindfold like the ones medieval travelers wore to blunt their terror of crossing the Alps. A rule of the blue road: Be careful going in search of adventure—it's ridiculously easy to find.

Then I was on the top, ten thousand feet up. UP. The wind was hor-   9
rendous. Utah 14 now cut through snowbanks higher than the truck. At the junction with route 143, a sign pointed north toward Cedar Breaks campground. I relaxed. I was going to live. I puffed up at having beaten the mountain.

Two hundred yards up 143, I couldn't believe what I saw. I got out   10
and walked to it as the raving wind whipped my pantlegs and pulled my hair on end. I couldn't believe it. There it was, the striped centerline, glowing through the sleet, disappearing under a seven-foot snowbank. Blocked.

Back to the truck. My heart dropped like a stone through new snow.   11
There had to be a mistake. I mean, this wasn't 1776. The days of Escalante were gone. But the only mistake was my judgment. I was stopped on state 143, and 143 lay under winter ice.

I turned up the heater to blast level, went to the back, and wrapped a   12
blanket around the sleeping bag. I undressed fast and got into a sweatsuit, two pairs of socks, my old Navy-issue watch cap, a pair of gloves. When I cut the engine, snow already had covered the windshield. Only a quarter tank of gas. While the warmth lasted, I hurried into the bag and pulled back the curtain to watch the fulminous clouds blast the mountain. That sky was bent on having a storm, and I was in for a drubbing.

At any particular moment in a man's life, he can say that everything he   13
has done and not done, that has been done and not been done to him, has

brought him to that moment. If he's being installed as Chieftain or receiving a Nobel Prize, that's a fulfilling notion. But if he's in a sleeping bag at ten thousand feet in a snowstorm, parked in the middle of a highway and waiting to freeze to death, the idea can make him feel calamitously stupid.

A loud racketing of hail fell on the steel box, and the wind seemed 14 to have hands, it shook the Ghost so relentlessly. Lightning tried to outdo thunder in scaring me. So did those things scare me? No. Not *those* things. It was something else. I was certain of a bear attack. That's what scared me.

Lightning strikes the earth about eight million times each day and kills 15 a hundred and fifty Americans every year. I don't know how many die from exposure and hypothermia, but it must be at least a comparable number. As for bears eating people who sleep inside steel trucks, I haven't been able to find that figure. It made no sense to fear a bear coming out of hibernation in such weather to attack a truck. Yet I lay a long time, waiting for the beast, shaggy and immense, to claw through the metal, its hot breath on my head, to devour me like a gumdrop and roll the van over the edge.

Perhaps fatigue or strain prevented me from worrying about the real 16 fear; perhaps some mechanism of mind hid the true and inescapable threat. Whatever it was, it finally came to me that I was crazy. Maybe I was already freezing to death. Maybe this was the way it happened. Black Elk prays for the Grandfather Spirit to help him face the winds and walk the good road to the day of quiet. Whitman too:

O to be self-balanced for contingencies,
To confront night, storms, hunger, ridicule, accidents,
rebuffs, as the trees and animals do.

I wondered how long I might have to stay in the Breaks before I could drive down. The cold didn't worry me much: I had insulated the rig myself and slept in it once when the windchill was thirty-six below. I figured to survive if I didn't have to stay on top too long. Why hadn't I listened to friends who advised carrying a CB? The headline showed darkly: FROZEN MAN FOUND IN AVALANCHE. The whole night I slept and woke, slept and woke, while the hail fell like iron shot, and thunder slammed around, and lightning seared the ice.

QUESTIONS ABOUT THE RHETORICAL SITUATION

1. Is the intended audience for this essay a general reading audience? Would the essay work for any reader at all? Or has Least Heat Moon narrowed his audience somewhat? If so, how?
2. How does the author now seem to view his experience? How has his viewpoint changed since the night of the storm?

3. Is Least Heat Moon trying to get us to feel the same fear that he felt or is he trying to teach us something? What is his purpose in this selection?

QUESTIONS ABOUT THE ESSAY'S VOICE

1. What purpose do ¶1–3 serve in this essay? How do they help to establish Least Heat Moon as an expert?
2. What is the point of including ¶4 and ¶5? Least Heat Moon describes Escalante and his men as wandering "dispiritedly." This is not the usual objective historical recounting of facts. Why has he chosen this adjective? How does this description figure significantly later in the essay?
3. In ¶7, Least Heat Moon focuses on what he was thinking about during the journey. How does this paragraph help to create the voice of firsthand experience in the essay?
4. At one point Least Heat Moon observes a "rule of the blue road: Be careful going in search of adventure—it's ridiculously easy to find" (¶8). How does this generalization strengthen his credentials as an expert? At what point in his travels is he when the storm hits? Do you think this is his first "adventure"? What other generalizations does he make in this essay? Does he seem qualified to make these generalizations?
5. In ¶10, the author makes an effort to create suspense. At what point in this paragraph does he reveal the major piece of information? How has he structured his sentences in order to create suspense?
6. Throughout the essay there is evidence that Least Heat Moon has done research. Where do you find such evidence? Does this researched material make his voice sound different? Or does he continue to sound like a firsthand authority?
7. Notice how the author describes the weather conditions. What do you find particularly effective in these descriptions?
8. This section was written as a single complete chapter in *Blue Highways* rather than as an essay. Does Least Heat Moon's conclusion work as the conclusion of an essay? Does it work as the conclusion of a chapter in a book? Is there a difference? What do you think the next chapter is about?

TOPICS TO WRITE ABOUT

1. Write an essay about an experience you had that was caused by bad judgment on your part. POTENTIAL AUDIENCES: the same readers Least Heat Moon is addressing in his essay/a potential employer. POTENTIAL PURPOSES: to make them understand how your bad judgment was at fault/to demonstrate your resourcefulness in handling a difficult situation.

2. Write an essay about some experience you have had with nature. For example, you might write about a sailing trip or a scuba diving experience; you might write about a parachute jump you made or your first night camping out in your backyard treehouse. POTENTIAL AUDIENCES: your friends/an appropriate magazine of your choice. POTENTIAL PURPOSES: to make them understand what your experience was like/to entertain the readers with your vivid telling of the story.

Waking Up
Beverly Slater and Frances Spatz Leighton

Beverly Slater was a typical middle-class American homemaker on a vacation with her husband when she was struck by an automobile. The accident caused her to suffer a severe case of amnesia. Through years of therapy, she has managed to recover much of her memory and has returned home to lead a relatively normal life.

She told her story in a book entitled *Stranger in My Bed*, written with the assistance of Frances Spatz Leighton, a professional writer. A physician who treated her says of her condition: "Mrs. Slater described her amnesia as though she were a newborn babe who knew nothing about anything and had to be taught about the smallest details of everyday living."

In this selection, "Waking Up," Slater awakens in a hospital room after her traumatic accident.

QUESTIONS ABOUT IDEAS

1. Remember a time when you suffered from a small lapse of memory (forgetting someone's name, forgetting that you went a certain place). How did you feel when someone else reminded you of what you had forgotten? Did your feelings resemble Slater's feelings when she cannot remember?
2. Most of us remember very little of our first several years of life, reconstructing those years from family stories, photographs, and home movies. What is the earliest memory you have? Have people in your family told you things about yourself as a small child that you find hard to believe of yourself? How does Slater's amnesia resemble these "lost" early years?
3. One of the difficulties of treating patients with serious problems such as Slater's is balancing the needs of the patient and the needs of the patient's family and loved ones. How fairly does the medical staff seem to be treating Slater? Her family?

4. Slater eventually made a nearly full recovery. What adjustments do you
   expect her family had to make as a result of her injuries? Can a family
   recover fully from such a catastrophic experience?

I woke up to a world of hazy white. Strangers stood around my bed, 1
their mouths opening and closing, making sounds that had no meaning.

I closed my eyes.   2

"Beverly, are you awake? Oh, nurse, I think she's awake." The voices. 3
Every time I opened my eyes there were the voices. "Nurse, I think she's
coming to."

I felt the pain in my head, my throat. I tried to pull the tubes out but 4
something was restraining my hand. I wanted to touch the pain, wipe it away.

Questions. Always questions. "Beverly Slater, do you know where you 5
are? Beverly, do you know who you are? Nod your head if you do." I closed my
eyes. I didn't know what everyone wanted. Why wouldn't they leave me alone?

If I slept, I could hide from them. But I kept opening my eyes. "Bev- 6
erly, are you awake?" "Beverly, do you know who you are?" "No, you
mustn't try to pull the tubes out. No, no."

"Do you know who this is?" "Do you recognize what I'm holding? 7
Nod your head if you do."

I did not nod.   8

I wished they would shut up.   9

Slowly the blurry faces came into focus, but I still didn't understand 10
the noises they were making. I would look at these mouths taking different
shapes as they opened and closed—overlapping faces moved forward and
backward, fading in and out. Disjointed conversations around me. *Strangers*
peering at me. Everyone was a stranger.

But there was one voice I was getting used to. "Hi, hon, how are you? 11
You're looking better. Do you know who I am? I'm your husband. I'm
Harold, and I'm with you. You're going to be all right."

What was "all right"?   12

"You know who is here to see you? Your mother and your dad. Ev- 13
erybody's here."

I had no idea what he meant.   14

Time seemed endless, the questions seemed endless... "What is your 15
name?" "Do you recognize me?" "Nod your head if you understand me—
do you understand me?"

I refused to nod for these silly fools. I couldn't talk with all the tubes 16
in my nose and throat anyway. I didn't know who they were and I didn't
care. For that matter, I didn't know who *I* was and I didn't care. Why did
they keep bothering me?

One day a doctor took a tube out of my throat. "I think we'll see if she 17
can get along without the respirator." I was so glad to have it out and I tried

to talk, but all that came out were guttural sounds. Soon I was gasping for breath and the doctor was forcing the respirator back down my throat. I tried to stop him. I didn't want that pain again. The doctor won.

In a few days the respirator was removed again and this time it stayed out. 18

Now I could talk. At first it was only gibberish, but then suddenly I 19 could say a few words that people did understand. I liked seeing their amazement. "She's coming around," said the doctors. "She understands. That's great. Do you know where you are?"

"No," I croaked. "Am I supposed to?" 20

"You're in the hospital. You're going to be all right." 21

There were those words *all right* again. I still didn't know what they 22 meant.

"Do you know where you live?" 23

"No. Am I supposed to?" 24

A nurse was leaning over me. "Hello, what's your name?" 25

"I don't know, what's *your* name?" 26

"I'm Nurse Louise. Now tell me your name." 27

"Go to hell." 28

One person had the right idea. He always came in booming, "Hi, Bev- 29 erly Slater. *You* are Beverly Slater and I am Dr. O'Connor. How is Beverly Slater today?"

I liked him. He didn't make me try to remember who I was—he *told* 30 me. And if he thought I was Beverly Slater, well, that was good enough for me—especially since it seemed to make him happy.

Beverlyslater, Beverlyslater. At first I thought it was all one word. I 31 would say it in a rush, "Beverlyslater."

But the man called Harold confused me—he kept calling me Beverly. 32 If I was Beverlyslater, why was he calling me Beverly?

And he was calling me other things that made no sense at all— 33 "honey," "darling," "sweetheart." Who were *they?* Who was he? Not that I cared particularly. I kept wishing he wouldn't hang around so much. Whenever I opened my eyes he'd be there, looking at me, talking at me, telling me he loved me.

Everyone was saying that. "We love you." "I love you." "We *all* love 34 you." Who cared? What was love? I hadn't the foggiest.

At first it was fun showing off that I could speak, even if none of it 35 made much sense. But eventually the game palled. I became tired of the same old questions.

"What's your name?" 36

"Do you know who I am?" 37

"Where do you live?" 38

Did I know what this or that was? And if I did give the right name, 39 they would ask what it was for. They showed me a clock, I could point out the numbers on it—"That's a two and that's a four and that's twelve."

"What do you call it?"   40

"I don't know."   41

"Do you know what time it is?"   42

"What's time?"   43

"Can you tell time with a clock?"   44

"What? What do you mean?"   45

They explained it to me, and I relearned it very quickly.   46

What did I know? What could I do? That's what the doctors wanted to   47
know.

I could speak. I could read words—but I still had to keep asking what   48
so many things meant. At least I knew how to ask a question and sometimes
I even understood their explanation. But why did they have to speak so fast?

I started to remember faces but I still couldn't remember names—   49
sometimes not even my own.

"Hi, babe, I'm here again. I'm Harold, your husband. Do you remem-   50
ber me now?"

I just looked at him. "I'm Harold," he repeated. "What's your name?"   51

"I'm Harold," I rasped.   52

"No," he said. "*You're* Beverly. I'm Harold. You're my wife. Beverly.   53
Say it. Beverly. Say it—Beverly."

I didn't want to say it. "I don't know you," I lashed out. "Shit, shit,   54
shit. Bitch, get out."

I could see that he was shocked. It pleased me. He left. But he came   55
back the next day. Sometimes I was happy and eager to listen to him and
other times I was irritable and shouted curses.

When I was happy and did not curse, Harold called me a good girl and   56
when I went into a tantrum and cursed, he said I was a bad girl. When I was
a good girl, he sat and stroked my hair and kissed my cheek before he left.
When I was a bad girl, he just got up and left.

So now I thought I knew how to get rid of all those people standing   57
around my bed, looking at me sadly or with forced smiles. I would just
throw tantrums.

I swore at all those smiling faces—the doctors, the nurses, the rela-   58
tives—everyone who kept assuring me of his or her love.

"Goddamn son of a bitch," I said. "Fuck you. Shut up."   59

Harold apologized to a nurse for my language and she laughed, saying   60
that cursing was not at all uncommon for head injury patients, often such
patients behave in a manner exactly opposite to their normal selves. A nun
had awakened from a concussion screaming obscenities.

"Your wife will get over it, Mr. Slater."   61

Harold said he had *never* heard me swear like this and was tremen-   62
dously relieved that it wouldn't last forever.

Sometimes the doctors laughed. Sometimes they said, "There, there.   63
That's not nice, is it?"

"Damn bastard."   64

Relatives did not react so mildly. They looked hurt, stricken. I was 65
glad. Maybe now they would stay away and quit tormenting me with all
those questions. "Do you remember this? Do you remember that?"

"Get out, get out, get out, son of a bitch." 66

"Better let her cool down," a nurse would say. "Perhaps she shouldn't 67
have this much company."

But no matter what I did, the man they called Harold kept coming 68
back. Why?

With the I.V. out of my arm, I was now feeding myself. I picked up 69
food with my fingers, stuffed it into my mouth. The nurses urged me to take
more. I didn't know why I should bother pleasing them but sometimes I'd
oblige anyway.

One day a nurse brought in the tray with something particularly ugly 70
on it—long, long strands of things intertwined. "What is this shit?" I demanded, lifting up a handful.

"It's called spaghetti," the nurse said, wiping my hand and handing 71
me a fork. I threw the spaghetti on the floor.

"Who the hell are you?" I roared at the stranger who had just come in. 72

"Mother, I'm your child. I'm Joanie. Don't you recognize me?" 73

Hateful creature. She was fiddling in her purse, pulling something out. 74
She showed me a picture. "Pretty girl," I said. "Who is that?"

"Mother, that's me." 75

She burst into tears and ran out of the room. 76

"Go to hell, bitch," I yelled after her. 77

Now the other one was coming in. "Get the hell out, miss," I hissed. 78

"Now, now, Beverly. I'm your husband. I'm Harold, remember?" 79

"Who the shit cares. Get out, get out, get out." 80

He just stood there looking at me. "I'll get the nurse." He came in 81
with a nurse and doctor. "I think she's getting overexcited. My daughter is
very upset—"

"Shut up, shut up, shut up." I wanted to drown out his voice. 82

"—and I think maybe we'd better not let any more visitors come for a 83
few days. It just makes her like this."

I wanted to hit him. "Shut up, shut up, shut up." 84

"There, there," said Dr. O'Connor, patting my hand, smiling at me. I 85
calmed down and smiled back. "That's a good idea," he said. "For a time it
might be better if she sees just you and gets used to you."

In a way, I understood. They were going to do something about those 86
people and if Dr. O'Connor said so, it was all right.

"Shit, shit, shit," I rasped. I didn't want Dr. O'Connor to stop paying 87
attention to me.

"Now, Beverly Slater," he said, "now, now. Quiet down." 88

Somehow the one they called my son, Stuart, didn't annoy me as much 89
as Joanie did.

The face that became most familiar to me was Harold's. He came all 90 the time. Every day. Some times several times a day. Sometimes I called him "sir," sometimes "miss." I didn't know him. I didn't like him.

He kept trying to explain things to me. "I'm your husband and I love 91 you, so I come to see how you are."

"I'm okay, how are you?"   92

"A lot better now that you're talking. I brought you something—a 93 lovely nightgown. You have more in your house."

That was truly where everything nice was. "I want to go house."   94

"No, dear, say, 'I want to go *home.*' Your *home* is your *house.*" 95

"I don't understand."   96

"Well, it's not easy to explain. Your home could be just a trailer or an 97 apartment in a big building, but it's still *home. You* live in a *house.* That's home to you."

I had no idea what he was talking about. I tuned him out.   98

When he'd finished I tried again. "Are you taking me house?"   99

"Not today, dear. Not for a while."   100

"Okay." I was distracted—Dr. O'Connor was coming in, beaming at 101 me. "How's Beverly Slater today?"

I didn't curse. I gave him my best smile as he touched my wrist, 102 looked into my eyes, examined the back of my head. He was so gentle and cheerful I wished I could follow him out of the room. I watched him as he walked over to the nurses' station.

Then Harold left the room to talk to him. I felt as though I'd been a 103 good little girl.

Once I had cut down on my cursing and cleaned up my act a bit, 104 Harold let the children visit me again. He did his best to make Joanie's re-entry into my life a little smoother.

The idea was to make me curious to see this newcomer. Stepping out 105 into the hall, he said, "Oh, look who is here to see Beverly. I'm so glad to see you. Beverly will be, too." In the few days since I'd last seen anyone in my family aside from Harold, he had mentioned many times that I had a daughter named Joanie whom I was going to like very much. Now, when he brought her in, she seemed so friendly, putting her arms around me. I decided I liked her. Especially since she brought me a present. So, we were over the first hurdle.

Harold had warned Joanie not to ask me questions I couldn't answer— 106 he'd learned from experience that nothing infuriated me more—and she was nervously bringing up safe subjects. She mentioned that she had to get a dress fixed because she was going to a party. "There's a dressmaker upstairs in Haddonfield," I said.

Harold looked stunned. "Where in Haddonfield?"   107

"Kings Highway and Haddon Avenue."   108

Harold rushed out to get a nurse and told me to tell her what I had just 109 said.

"I don't know," I said. I really didn't. I couldn't remember, and when 110 they told me the address it still didn't jog my memory. "I don't know," I said. They dropped it, but I could tell that this had made them excited and hopeful.

In the second week, with the tubes out, I had become ambulatory and 111 soon I was here, there and everywhere, exploring this wonderful, magical new world. Bells rang, walls opened. People appeared and disappeared.

One day a wall opened and I walked in. A door closed and I was caged 112 in a box. Suddenly it moved. I was shocked. The door opened. I ran out, bumping into people. Finally I was found and returned to my floor. A nurse showed me the elevator door and said, "No, no. Beverly, don't get on the elevator. It's a no-no unless we are with you. Do you understand?"

"Go to hell," I croaked. "Shit, shit, shit."   113

Her solution was to put a sign on the back of my hospital gown: 114 "RETURN TO INTENSIVE CARE, NEUROSURGERY, 3RD FLOOR."

One day I wandered into the cafeteria, drawn by the sight of so many 115 people. For a time I stood in the line with them, just staring at their faces, listening to them talk, and then I wandered off to a brightly lighted place where rows and rows of pretty foods were sitting in a long shiny box. I walked up and down, putting my fingers into the various dishes. I found a pretty red cherry in one of them and popped it into my mouth.

I was having so much fun I didn't even notice that a crowd of people 116 had gathered around me, all talking excitedly. "Where does she belong?" "Who is she?" Someone read the sign on my back, "RETURN TO INTEN- SIVE CARE, NEUROSURGERY, 3RD FLOOR." Gently, a doctor intro- duced himself and led me back to my ward.

I prattled happily all the way back. Finally we were standing by my 117 bed. "Good-bye, Beverly," he said.

"Are you taking me home today?"   118

I had an obsession about going home.   119

"No, Beverly."   120

"Go to hell, you bastard."   121

I was angry—he had betrayed me. I had walked with him like a good 122 girl and he wouldn't take me where I wanted to go—wherever that was.

QUESTIONS ABOUT THE RHETORICAL SITUATION

1. Is "Waking Up" appropriate for all readers? Is there any indication that Slater has aimed at a specific audience?
2. What do you think is the purpose of this opening chapter of Slater's book? Is there anything to learn from this selection, or is it just entertaining?

3. How does Slater view these first experiences? Is she still frustrated by them? Is she amused by them? What other reactions might she have even now to these memories?

QUESTIONS ABOUT THE ESSAY'S VOICE

1. Slater is likely to offend some readers by including harsh language. How necessary to the essay is the harsh language? Would its absence affect the essay's voice? How?
2. What details surprise you in this essay? How do such details make Slater's voice convincing?
3. Notice the opening of the essay. What is the effect of beginning this way? Compare Slater's opening to the opening of the chapter of *Blue Highways* that you have just read. What do these two different introductions suggest about the two authors' intentions?
4. "Waking Up" is narrated from a first-person point of view. How consistent is this point of view? How would the voice be different if someone else—Harold Slater, Dr. O'Connor, Nurse Louise—had narrated the essay?
5. Slater described herself as a "newborn babe." How does her behavior in the essay support this generalization?
6. When she describes meeting her daughter for the first time, Slater says she "roared" at her. How effective is this choice of verb? Notice the other verbs used instead of "said." How effective are these other verbs? Frequently, Slater uses no verb at all, but merely quotes the dialogue. How effectively has she decided when to use or not use a verb indicating speech?
7. Slater writes of "exploring this wonderful, magical new world" during the second week of her "waking up." How effective are the examples she supplies to support her generalization about her world?
8. Like the selection from *Blue Highways*, "Waking Up" really does not bring the story to an end. Is the conclusion disappointing or is it appropriate? Why?

TOPICS TO WRITE ABOUT

1. Write an essay about a serious illness suffered either by you or by someone you care about. (For example, you might tell a story about your emergency appendectomy or about your grandfather's heart attack or about your friend's battle with multiple sclerosis or, as one student did, about a small child's courageous fight against spina bifida.) POTENTIAL AUDIENCES: others who suffer from the illness/the general public. POTENTIAL PURPOSES: to explain how you coped with the illness in an effort to show

them how they might also cope/to make them see the problems associated with the ailment more clearly.

2. There are times in our lives when we recognize that we need help in order to accomplish some goal, yet we are reluctant to accept such assistance because of pride or stubbornness. Write an essay about one time in your life when you either refused assistance or were rebuffed when you tried to offer help. POTENTIAL AUDIENCES: the other person in your story/your classmates. POTENTIAL PURPOSES: to let him or her know how your feelings have changed since that earlier time/to make them understand how this story explains in part why you are the person they know you to be.

Darkness at Noon
Harold Krents

Harold Krents practices law in Washington, D.C. after attending Harvard University and Oxford. Krents, who was born blind as his essay indicates, has long been interested in the plight of the handicapped. He is the author of *To Race the Wind* (1972).

"Darkness at Noon" originally appeared in May 1976 in the *New York Times*. While the *Times* publishes its own editorial opinions along with those of syndicated columnists, it also offers its readers an opportunity to express their opinions. "Darkness at Noon" appeared on what the *Times* calls its "Op-Ed page," a page reserved for readers who wish to express their opinion in an editorial form.

QUESTIONS ABOUT IDEAS

1. In what ways are Krents' experiences as a blind person typical of the experiences of other people with disabilities? Why do they receive such treatment?
2. What is your own reaction to Krents as a person whom you get to know through his essay?
3. In the decade that has elapsed since "Darkness at Noon" was written, what changes have you seen in society's attitudes toward people with disabilities? Has the situation hoped for by Krents in his essay's conclusion come into being? Are his hopes realistic?

Blind from birth, I have never had the opportunity to see myself and   1 have been completely dependent on the image I create in the eye of the observer. To date it has not been narcissistic.

There are those who assume that since I can't see, I obviously also cannot hear. Very often people will converse with me at the top of their lungs, enunciating each word very carefully. Conversely, people will also often whisper, assuming that since my eyes don't work, my ears don't either. 2

For example, when I go to the airport and ask the ticket agent for assistance to the plane, he or she will invariably pick up the phone, call a ground hostess and whisper, "Hi, Jane. We've got a 76 here." I have concluded that the word "blind" is not used for one of two reasons: either they fear that if the dread word is spoken, the ticket agent's retina will immediately detach or they are reluctant to inform me of my condition of which I may not have been previously aware. 3

On the other hand, others know that of course I can hear, but believe that I can't talk. Often, therefore, when my wife and I go out to dinner, a waiter or waitress will ask Kit if "*he* would like a drink" to which I respond that "indeed *he* would." 4

This point was graphically driven home to me while we were in England. I had been given a year's leave of absence from my Washington law firm to study for a diploma in law degree at Oxford University. During the year I became ill and was hospitalized. Immediately after admission, I was wheeled down to the X-ray room. Just at the door sat an elderly woman—elderly I would judge from the sound of her voice. "What is his name?" the woman asked the orderly who had been wheeling me. 5

"What's your name?" the orderly repeated to me. 6

"Harold Krents," I replied. 7

"When was he born?" 8

"November 5, 1944," I responded. 9

"November 5, 1944," the orderly intoned. 10

This procedure continued for approximately five minutes at which point even my saint-like disposition deserted me. "Look," I finally blurted out, "this is absolutely ridiculous. Okay, granted I can't see, but it's got to have become pretty clear to both of you that I don't need an interpreter." 11

"He says he doesn't need an interpreter," the orderly reported to the woman. 12

The toughest misconception of all is the view that because I can't see, I can't work. I was turned down by over forty law firms because of my blindness, even though my qualifications included a cum laude degree from Harvard College and a good ranking in my Harvard Law School class. 13

The attempt to find employment, the continuous frustration of being told that it was impossible for a blind person to practice law, the rejection letters, not based on my lack of ability but rather on my disability, will always remain one of the most disillusioning experiences of my life. 14

Fortunately, this view of limitation and exclusion is beginning to 15 change. On April 16 [1976], the Department of Labor issued regulations that mandate equal-employment opportunities for the handicapped. By and large, the business community's response to offering employment to the disabled has been enthusiastic.

I therefore look forward to the day, with the expectation that it is cer- 16 tain to come, when employers will view their handicapped workers as a little child did me years ago when my family still lived in Scarsdale.

I was playing basketball with my father in our backyard according to 17 procedures we had developed. My father would stand beneath the hoop, shout, and I would shoot over his head at the basket, attached to our garage. Our next-door neighbor, aged five, wandered over into our yard with a playmate. "He's blind," our neighbor whispered to her friend in a voice that could be heard distinctly by Dad and me. Dad shot and missed; I did the same. Dad hit the rim; I missed entirely: Dad shot and missed the garage entirely. "Which one is blind?" whispered back the little friend.

I would hope that in the near future when a plant manager is touring 18 the factory with the foreman and comes upon a handicapped and non-handicapped person working together, his comment after watching them work will be, "Which one is disabled?"

QUESTIONS ABOUT THE RHETORICAL SITUATION

1. How would a reader who is blind or deaf or in need of a wheelchair to move about respond differently to this essay than a reader without any such disability? Is Krents writing only to the reader with no disability or is his essay addressed to all readers? Explain your answer.
2. At times Krents sounds sarcastic, amused, angry, resigned, even optimistic. What do these varied responses communicate to the reader about Krents' attitude toward his subject?
3. How does Krents seem to feel about the people with whom he has contact in the anecdotes he relates in this essay?
4. As Krents notes, legislative support for disabled workers has been enacted. Since he does not need to rally support for legislative change, why is he writing this essay? What does he hope to accomplish by writing "Darkness at Noon"?

QUESTIONS ABOUT THE ESSAY'S VOICE

1. What is the tone of Krents' voice in the final sentence of ¶1? What is the tone of Krents' voice in ¶3 when he tells his airport story?
2. Krents, like Beverly Slater, has a physical condition with which he must cope. How is his voice similar to and different from hers? Which of these

      similarities/differences are a product of their quite different physical problems?

3. While Krents has not written a narrative like Least Heat Moon's in which he goes into great detail about a single episode in his life, he has written an essay that frequently uses the narrative form. Why does he dramatize some of the stories he includes (his hospital experience in ¶5–12, the basketball story in ¶17), while he summarizes others (¶2, ¶3, ¶4, ¶14, ¶15)?

4. Krents does not tell his anecdotes in a chronological order. Why does he save the story about his childhood ballplaying for last? What connection does he wish to make by doing so?

5. Clearly, the Department of Labor's 1976 mandate regarding equal employment opportunity for the handicapped is of great significance to Krents. Why does he wait until so late in his essay to discuss this ruling?

6. Krents, based on a lifetime of experience, attempts on several occasions in the essay to interpret the behavior of the sighted toward the blind. How accurate are his interpretations, do you think? Why are all of these interpretations not offered with the same degree of seriousness?

7. What has Krents' essay taught you about his subject? How convincing an expert is he?

TOPICS TO WRITE ABOUT

1. Write an essay about a personal encounter of your own with a disabled person and what you learned about disabled people as a result. POTENTIAL AUDIENCES: the members of your class/disabled people. POTENTIAL PURPOSES: to let them learn something important about disabled people through your experience/to make clear how you have grown as a person through this experience.

2. People frequently make wrong assumptions about other people based on their appearance or their gender or their names or their occupations. Write an essay about typical misunderstandings you have encountered on the part of people unfamiliar with who you are as an individual. POTENTIAL AUDIENCES: the members of your class/your teacher. POTENTIAL PURPOSES: to make sure your classmates do not make the same mistake in their interactions with you/to introduce who you *really* are to your reader.

3. Write a narrative about a childhood experience that helps explain your current outlook on an important issue in your life, similar to Krents' basketball story. POTENTIAL AUDIENCES: your parents/your future children. POTENTIAL PURPOSES: to help them understand why you are who you are now as an adult/to help them understand what you were like when you were young.

Sympathy for the Devil
Gerri Hirshey

Gerri Hirshey is a freelance writer whose articles have appeared in *Esquire*, *New York* magazine, *Family Circle*, the *New York Daily News*, the *New York Times*, and primarily in *Rolling Stone* magazine. She lives in New York City.

Hirshey, who is white, remembers watching soul singer James Brown on the Ed Sullivan show when she was a girl. "Watching him dance inflicted a momentary, ecstatic paralysis; the three-cape, collapse-and-resurrection exit left me white-knuckling the vinyl hassock." The next day she threw away her Beatles magazines and began a lifelong fascination with soul music, a fascination that eventually led her to write *Nowhere to Run: The Story of Soul Music* (1984). In "Sympathy for the Devil," Hirshey vividly describes not only the performance of Screamin' Jay Hawkins, a rock 'n roll pioneer, but also the reaction of an audience that is not familiar with Hawkins.

QUESTIONS ABOUT IDEAS

1. Hirshey claims that "at its most dangerous, rock *is* a scream. The fads and styles of the marketplace control the volume and the pitch." Do you agree or disagree with this comment?
2. How important an element in our modern culture is rock 'n roll music? Is today's popular music going to stand the test of time as Mozart's, Beethoven's, Wagner's have?
3. How recognizable a picture of a rock concert does Hirshey paint in "Sympathy for the Devil"? Is the scene familiar? Is it important that the scene seem familiar and recognizable?
4. How well does Hirshey manage to convince you that Jay Hawkins is a significant figure in the history of rock music?

Twenty-two thousand fans move between the molded plastic seats in   1
New York City's Madison Square Garden. Most of them entered a vast mail lottery to win the privilege of buying tickets; some have paid scalpers as much as $200 to be here. We are at a Rock Event at the outset of the eighties. Check all bottles at the door; have your tickets ready to show the officers....

"Get yer ya-yas out," bawls a T-shirt vendor at the gate. The escalator   2
is a twitching artery of fifteen- to twenty-year-old haunches vacuum-packed into denim and spandex, all come to shake it with the Rolling Stones, who were singing as a group before many of these kids were born.

Besides solid, reliable, kick-ass rock and roll, some rock theater is an-   3
ticipated. Enormous plastic bladders hang from the ceiling, bulging with

thousands of colored balloons. A squadron of sneakered young men washes the custom-crafted kidney-shaped stage with swirling pastel lights. Stage left, a cherry picker reaches up from below the loge seats like a monster-movie crab claw. Mick Jagger will confer his pouty benedictions from aloft. The question is on many lips: "You think Mick's gonna throw rose petals like he did in Philly?"

There is so much going on no one seems to have noticed the tall black   4
man who has wandered out onstage in a long red cape and gold lamé turban. He checks the miking on a huge concert grand and smiles at a pretty black woman who sits sipping a soft drink just left of the drum set. A four-piece band has begun to fiddle with the clutch of breadbox-size monitors and amps. Before half the crowd even notices that the recorded Top Forty music has stopped blaring from the Stones' mammoth speakers, the band has jumped into a springy blues.

"Ladies and gentlemen," the PA system booms, "will you please wel-   5
come blues and rock *legend*, Mr. Screamin' Jay Hawkins."

"Whoooo?" Bewilderment whistles through scores of high-glossed   6
lips.

Screamin' Jay Hawkins, children. Piano sideman turned blues shouter   7
turned rock and roll pioneer. In the mid-fifties he was one of rock's arche-typal wild men, a fiendish dandy in polka-dot shoes and zebra coattails, leaping out of coffins and clouds of smoke with the same manic drive that let Jerry Lee Lewis mule-kick a piano stool halfway to the second balcony. Owing to his screaming delivery, his spiritualism (albeit demonic), and his stage antics, Screamin' Jay Hawkins stood, as music critic. Arnold Shaw put it, "on the surrealistic borderline between rhythm and blues and soul." After thirty years on the road, he still screams hard but travels light (no coffin). He is selective with his bookings and still proud of his name.

Born Jalacy Hawkins in 1929 in Cleveland, he was renamed Screamin'   8
Jay one whiskey-mist West Virginia night when a lusty club patron shook her size no-end bootie and sent a galaxy of sticky shot glasses into orbit, yelling all the while, "Scream, baby, scream! Go on, Jay, scream it!"

It sounds like a hoarse gargle at first, this scream, snapping heads in   9
the direction of the Garden stage.

"Auwwwwrargaieeeeeee. Ow. Ohhhhhhh. Mmm."   10

Jay tamps it to a low moan and bears down on the keyboard with a   11
greasy tangle of river-deep blues chords. Screamin' Jay does not so much sing a song as assault it. He will beat, stretch, and hammerlock a lyric and all but suffocate a melody. Though his style and training are rooted in postwar urban blues, his is not the noble detachment of the great mid-western blues-men. Those guys knew the devil, but they never went so far as to lend him their voices.

Jay's voice, that terrible, changeling voice, is suffused with moans,   12
growls, gurgles, and snuffles, a churning swamp of unchecked emotion that

would, in the years following Jay's flaming fifties, be refined, politened, in many cases churchified and pumped out as soul by the next wave of black popular artists.

Singers like Ray Charles would replace the hoodoo spiritualism with a 13 gospel sensibility and, like Hawkins, ignite it with sex. James Brown would raise the soul scream to sacramental heights. The voice of Aretha Franklin would take a holiness shout and wrap it around an audience until it, too, screamed for the sheer wonder of it. By the late sixties, along with other singers like the Soul Screamer himself, Wilson Pickett, they would take the human howl to unprecedented commercial success.

Of course, the soulful scream is as old as the blues, as old as desolation 14 itself, and, in that sense, just as fundamental to gospel. Gospel sufferers can ask, "Why, O Lord?" and seek relief in the balm of faith. The bluesman must listen for his answer in a piney woods wind, a train whistle, a dog howl.

Either way, it's no surprise that America, a nation that began with Pil- 15 grim martyrs and enslaved tribes, that a people so bound up with persecution would come up with a music so ripe with rebellion and a headlong run at deliverance: rock. At its most dangerous, rock *is* a scream. The fads and styles of the marketplace control the volume and the pitch.

What Jay Hawkins and other rock pioneers did was to let the scream 16 loose in a way that both scared and delighted the kids. Crooners were too tame for the postwar baby-boom kids. And classic bluesmen were simply too strong. To white kids, horror was a zit, not a lynch mob. Black kids were familiar with the blues but distanced in their own way.

"As a kid in the fifties I was taught to be *ashamed* of the blues," Isaac 17 Hayes told me. "We thought of it as plantation darkie stuff. And that was miles from where *we* wanted to be."

As a teenager in Detroit Smokey Robinson ignored his mother's blues 18 records. "The blues is torment or some degrading type of thing," he says. "Kids weren't ready for that. I liked Frankie Lymon, Sam Cooke, or Jackie Wilson—the plush, pop kind of singers whose music wasn't hardcore blues."

All in all, fifties kids' tastes were just 3.2 beer compared to Muddy 19 Water's 90-proof barrel of blues. Screamin' Jay kept the chords and rhythms and learned to burlesque some of the pain. He could conjure fright but make it fun. In doing so, Jay Hawkins became one of the original bards of rock theater, a funky Iago whose favorite prop is still a human skull on a stick.

He is at it now, rushing from behind the piano to center stage, toting 20 the skull and a rubber rattlesnake, big hips rumbling like a haywire Maytag.

"Is he for real?" asks a blow-dried subteen. 21

"Fuckin' weird," says a boy in a Black Sabbath T-shirt. "Like he's 22 rippin' off the Sabbath."

Black Sabbath's former lead singer Ozzy Osbourne does real neat stuff 23

like bite the heads off live doves. Oz has performed some of his most outrageous stunts at record company conventions to demonstrate his commercial appeal. Such genteel corporate arenas were not available to rock's pre-
historic wild men.

Most of the artists Oz went to school on are dead or convalescing now. 24
Elvis, the King, is dead. The Killer, Jerry Lee Lewis, was recently resur-
rected from yet another near-fatal bout with bleeding ulcers, pills, and
booze. Chuck Berry has been quieted by a jail sentence and financial woes.
Once again Little Richard has gone back to screaming for the Lord. Jackie
Wilson, after collapsing on stage with a heart attack in 1975 and remaining
semi-comatose in a nursing home, died in January of 1984. For a while punk
tried to butt its matted head into the pantheon of True Lunacy, but with
little lasting impact. Sex Pistol Sid Vicious was just perfecting his projectile
vomiting when heroin spaded him under.

"Nah, you got it wrong," says Sabbath T-shirt's friend. "This guy 25
Hawkins is rippin' off *Kiss.*"

Playing to squealing teen angels, Kiss spit fake blood and wore horror- 26
flick makeup. Kiss sing dem surburban Clearasil blues. Kiss was in diapers
when Screamin' Jay Hawkins pumped the full clip of a military automatic
rifle into a wild boar on the rim of a Hawaiian volcano to extract the tusk
that now thumps against his chest on a big gold chain.

Sweat has begun to bead up above the penciled mustache Hawkins has 27
drawn on his upper lip; rivulets seep from beneath the turban, which is listing to the right with all the exertion. He has roared and shaken through half
a dozen songs, gutbucket stuff like "She Put the Wammee on Me," "Lawdy
Miss Clawdy," and "Alligator Wine." Now he has retreated back behind the
piano, fishing for a wandering mike with his right hand, reaching down past
Hades for some sulfurous chords with his left. Remarkably, a good portion
of the audience seems to have passed beyond curiosity and into listening.

"I hear," says Sabbath T-shirt, "this guy's an old favorite of Keith and 28
Mick or somethin'."

It is a long-standing habit of the Rolling Stones to pay tribute to the 29
font of their music by touring and jamming with black musicians. The
alumni include Howlin' Wolf, Tina Turner, Billy Preston, and Stevie Wonder, among others. Were it not for a last-minute contractual snag, James
Brown would have opened this very show at the Garden. One of the first
things Mick Jagger did on the Stones' first U.S. tours in the sixties was to
make a beeline for Brown's dressing room at the Apollo. It was an infatua-
tion that began in *his* youth.

In the late fifties and early sixties, aspiring rockers like Jagger, Keith 30
Richards, Eric Clapton, and John Lennon would queue up outside the doors
of London "palais" like the Flamingo and the Marquis, stubbing out cigarette butts with pointy black boots while they waited in the skanky urban
rain to dig the American madmen.

"To English and French kids," Eric Burdon of the Animals has said, 31 "names like Chuck Berry, Etta James, and Screamin' Jay Hawkins and countless others are *gods.*"

The Stones' audience is hardly worshipful tonight, but after thirty min- 32 utes they are still with Screamin' Jay. He is gearing up for his finale now, marking the beat with his skull like some satanic drum major, leaning into the mike to howl out the title line of his 1956 hit, "I Put a Spell on You."

Sabbath T-shirt is impressed. "That's a Creedence song," he tells his 33 friends, who nod sagely. He is referring to a 1968 version of the song by a white rock group, Creedence Clearwater Revival.

Screamin' Jay vamps and shakes through the number, waving the skull 34 at bewildered teenies in the front row. About to wrap it up, he signals to the woman who has been sitting beside the drums. She puts down her soda and ambles toward center stage, where she sets a small black box in front of the singer. He has ground the song down to spasmodic growls and yelps.

"*Yo' miiiiiiine, mine, mi-i-i-i-ine...*"   35

Unrolling an attached wire, the woman walks back to the drums, and 36 at the agreed-upon cue, she throws a switch. The black box releases a flash and a wheezy puff of smoke.

"*Aaaeeeeeeyowwwwwww.*"   37

The last of the scream whangs off the Garden scoreboard as the artist 38 and his rubber totems exit through the smoke, stage right.

"Far out," says Sabbath T-shirt, rolling his eyes. "We got time till the 39 Stones," he says to his girl friend. "You wanna buy a T-shirt or somethin'?"

Afterward the opening act passes on the backstage banquet, the wine and 40 Perrier, the celebrity corner. As Mick Jagger bounds onstage in yellow football pants and kneepads, Screamin' Jay tucks his skull under his arm, collects his snake and his woman, and heads uptown to his West Side apartment.

QUESTIONS ABOUT THE RHETORICAL SITUATION

1. For which magazines would "Sympathy for the Devil" be appropriate? How much must a reader already know about rock music in order to appreciate this essay?
2. What age group is Hirshey addressing in her essay? What clues are there that she is not really writing for readers of all ages?
3. How important is the topic of this essay? How important does the topic appear to be to Hirshey? What passages in particular can you point to in support of your answer?
4. What does Hirshey wish to teach her listener? (Remember your answer to question number 2 above. If she is writing to a young audience, what is her goal? If she is writing to a somewhat older audience, doesn't her goal need to be different?)

QUESTIONS ABOUT THE ESSAY'S VOICE

1. Hirshey's essay describes a specific place. How is her voice different from the voices of Pablo Neruda, E. B. White, and Jackie Pfeifer (Chapter 8), who also describe specific places?
2. Hirshey works very hard to describe sounds, a particularly challenging task. How effective is it when she quotes Hawkins as he sings? How effective is her description of his voice in ¶12?
3. Not only is Hirshey a close observer of the Rolling Stones concert she is describing, but she is obviously a close observer of the rock scene. What does the essay's voice sound like as she discusses rock history (¶13–19)?
4. Some of the connections Hirshey forges in her essay are understandable—references to other singers and rock critics. Other references are more of a surprise—Pilgrims and Indian tribes (¶15), Shakespeare's Iago (¶19). What is the point of these connections? How effective are they?
5. What is the point of the break in the essay between ¶19 and ¶20?
6. What do Hirshey's descriptions of the concertgoers tell us about her attitude toward them? (Note her descriptions in ¶2, ¶6, and ¶39.) In ¶20–26 two of the concertgoers comment on Hawkins. Notice how Hirshey comments on their comments. How has her voice changed in this section? How effective is this change?
7. How effective is the essay's conclusion? Why does Hirshey make a point of describing Mick Jagger's costume and Jay Hawkins' stage props?
8. Hirshey quotes a number of rock and R&B performers in her essay. Later in her book she quotes Jay Hawkins extensively. Why does she choose not to quote him in this essay? How would the voice of the essay have been affected if she had quoted him?

TOPICS TO WRITE ABOUT

1. Write an essay in which you describe a large-scale spectacle. Your description should be personal observation. (For example, describe the running of the bulls in Pamplona, Spain, or the Indy 500 or the Kentucky Derby or spring break at Daytona or the opening game of the baseball season or high school commencement ceremonies or a neighborhood block party.) POTENTIAL AUDIENCES: readers who have never even heard of the event/readers with an intense interest in and familiarity with the event. POTENTIAL PURPOSES: to make them understand what they have been missing/to show them an underlying significance they probably have not thought of before.

2. Write an essay about some recent development in popular culture, explaining how it has developed from a past development. (For example, you might explain how outer space movies, Saturday morning cartoons, current stand-up comics, comic book heroes, television situation comedies have developed from *Star Wars,* Bugs Bunny, Steve Martin, Superman/Spiderman, Archie Bunker and *All in the Family.*) POTENTIAL AUDIENCES: current fans of your subject/readers old enough to remember the earlier versions of your subject. POTENTIAL PURPOSES: to provide an historical understanding of how these popular shows and performers developed/to explain the superiority of either the originals or the newer versions of the subject.

English and Inglés
Richard Rodriguez

Richard Rodriguez was born in 1944 and was raised in Sacramento, California. Rodriguez, the son of working-class Mexican immigrant parents, attended Catholic schools as a child. He later attended Stanford University, Columbia University, Warburg Institute in London, and the University of California at Berkeley, where he obtained a doctorate in English. A writer and journalist, he lives in Mexico City.

Rodriguez is best known for his autobiography, *The Hunger of Memory: The Education of Richard Rodriguez* (1982), which he wrote with the assistance of a National Endowment for the Humanities fellowship. Portions of *The Hunger of Memory* have also appeared in more than half a dozen periodicals.

"English and *Inglés*" (editor's title) comes from Chapter 1, "Aria," of *The Hunger of Memory* and was published as an essay in 1981 in *The American Scholar.*

QUESTIONS ABOUT IDEAS

1. To what extent have you experienced personally the difference between public and private individuality discussed by Rodriguez in his essay? Does this part of the essay speak only to those raised in a bilingual household?
2. What advantages are there to being bilingual?

3. Should foreign-language-speaking students be compelled to learn English
   in American schools? Why? Why not?

Supporters of bilingual education today imply that students like me 1
miss a great deal by not being taught in their family's language. What they
seem not to recognize is that, as a socially disadvantaged child, I considered
Spanish to be a private language. What I needed to learn in school was that
I had the right—and the obligation—to speak the public language of *los gringos*. The odd truth is that my first-grade classmates could have become bilingual, in the conventional sense of that word, more easily than I. Had they
been taught (as upper-middle-class children are often taught early) a second
language like Spanish or French, they could have regarded it simply as that:
another public language. In my case such bilingualism could not have been
so quickly achieved. What I did not believe was that I could speak a single
public language.

Without question, it would have pleased me to hear my teachers ad- 2
dress me in Spanish when I entered the classroom. I would have felt much
less afraid. I would have trusted them and responded with ease. But I would
have delayed—for how long postponed?—having to learn the language of
public society. I would have evaded—and for how long could I have afforded
to delay?—learning the great lesson of school, that I had a public identity.

Fortunately, my teachers were unsentimental about their responsibil- 3
ity. What they understood was that I needed to speak a public language. So
their voices would search me out, asking me questions. Each time I'd hear
them, I'd look up in surprise to see a nun's face frowning at me. I'd mumble, not really meaning to answer. The nun would persist, "Richard, stand
up. Don't look at the floor. Speak up. Speak to the entire class, not just to
me!" But I couldn't believe that the English language was mine to use. (In
part, I did not want to believe it.) I continued to mumble. I resisted the
teacher's demands. (Did I somehow suspect that once I learned public language my pleasing family life would be changed?) Silent, waiting for the bell
to sound, I remained dazed, diffident, afraid.

Because I wrongly imagined that English was intrinsically a public lan- 4
guage and Spanish an intrinsically private one, I easily noted the difference
between classroom language and the language of home. At school, words
were directed to a general audience of listeners. ("Boys and girls.") Words
were meaningfully ordered. And the point was not self-expression alone but
to make oneself understood by many others. The teacher quizzed: "Boys
and girls, why do we use that word in this sentence? Could we think of a
better word to use there? Would the sentence change its meaning if the
words were differently arranged? And wasn't there a better way of saying
much the same thing?" (I couldn't say. I wouldn't try to say.)

Three months. Five. Half a year passed. Unsmiling, ever watchful, my 5 teachers noted my silence. They began to connect my behavior with the difficult progress my older sister and brother were making. Until one Saturday morning three nuns arrived at the house to talk to our parents. Stiffly, they sat on the blue living room sofa. From the doorway of another room, spying the visitors, I noted the incongruity—the clash of two worlds, the faces and voices of school intruding upon the familiar setting of home. I overheard one voice gently wondering, "Do your children speak only Spanish at home, Mrs. Rodriguez?" While another voice added, "That Richard especially seems so timid and shy."

That Rich-heard!   6

With great tact the visitors continued, "Is it possible for you and your   7
husband to encourage your children to practice their English when they are home?" Of course, my parents complied. What would they not do for their children's well-being? And how could they have questioned the Church's authority which those women represented? In an instant, they agreed to give up the language (the sounds) that had revealed and accentuated our family's closeness. The moment after the visitors left, the change was observed. "*Ahora,* speak to us *en inglés,*" my father and mother united to tell us.

At first, it seemed a kind of game. After dinner each night, the family   8
gathered to practice "our" English. (It was still then *inglés,* a language foreign to us, so we felt drawn as strangers to it.) Laughing, we would try to define words we could not pronounce. We played with strange English sounds, often overanglicizing our pronunciations. And we filled the smiling gaps of our sentences with familiar Spanish sounds. But that was cheating, somebody shouted. Everyone laughed. In school, meanwhile, like my brother and sister, I was required to attend a daily tutoring session. I needed a full year of special attention. I also needed my teachers to keep my attention from straying in class by calling out, *Rich-heard*—their English voices slowly prying loose my ties to my other name, its three notes, *Ri-car-do.* Most of all I needed to hear my mother and father speak to me in a moment of seriousness in broken—suddenly heartbreaking—English. The scene was inevitable: One Saturday morning I entered the kitchen where my parents were talking in Spanish. I did not realize that they were talking in Spanish however until, at the moment they saw me, I heard their voices change to speak English. Those *gringo* sounds they uttered startled me. Pushed me away. In that moment of trivial misunderstanding and profound insight, I felt my throat twisted by unsounded grief. I turned quickly and left the room. But I had no place to escape to with Spanish. (The spell was broken.) My brother and sisters were speaking English in another part of the house.

Again and again in the days following, increasingly angry, I was   9
obliged to hear my mother and father: "Speak to us *en inglés.*" (*Speak.*) Only then did I determine to learn classroom English. Weeks after, it happened: One day in school I raised my hand to volunteer an answer. I spoke out in a loud voice. And I did not think it remarkable when the entire class under-

stood. That day, I moved very far from the disadvantaged child I had been
only days earlier. The belief, the calming assurance that I belonged in public, had at last taken hold.

Shortly after, I stopped hearing the high and loud sounds of *los gringos*. 10
A more and more confident speaker of English, I didn't trouble to listen to
how strangers sounded, speaking to me. And there simply were too many
English-speaking people in my day for me to hear American accents anymore. Conversations quickened. Listening to persons who sounded eccen-
trically pitched voices, I usually noted their sounds for an initial few seconds
before I concentrated on *what* they were saying. Conversations became
content-full. Transparent. Hearing someone's *tone* of voice—angry or questioning or sarcastic or happy or sad—I didn't distinguish it from the words it
expressed. Sound and word were thus tightly wedded. At the end of a day,
I was often bemused, always relieved, to realize how "silent," though
crowded with words, my day in public had been. (This public silence measured and quickened the change in my life.)

At last, seven years old, I came to believe what had been technically 11
true since my birth: I was an American citizen.

But the special feeling of closeness at home was diminished by then. 12
Gone was the desperate, urgent, intense feeling of being at home; rare was
the experience of feeling myself individualized by family intimates. We remained a loving family, but one greatly changed. No longer so close; no
longer bound tight by the pleasing and troubling knowledge of our public
separateness. Neither my older brother nor sister rushed home after school
anymore. Nor did I. When I arrived home there would often be neighborhood kids in the house. Or the house would be empty of sounds.

Following the dramatic Americanization of their children, even my 13
parents grew more publicly confident. Especially my mother. She learned
the names of all the people on our block. And she decided we needed to have
a telephone installed in the house. My father continued to use the word
gringo. But it was no longer charged with the old bitterness or distrust.
(Stripped of any emotional content, the word simply became a name for
those Americans not of Hispanic descent.) Hearing him, sometimes, I wasn't
sure if he was pronouncing the Spanish word *gringo* or saying gringo in English.

Matching the silence I started hearing in public was a new quiet at 14
home. The family's quiet was partly due to the fact that, as we children
learned more and more English, we shared fewer and fewer words with our
parents. Sentences needed to be spoken slowly when a child addressed his
mother or father. (Often the parent wouldn't understand.) The child would
need to repeat himself. (Still the parent misunderstood.) The young voice,
frustrated, would end up saying, "Never mind"—the subject was closed.
Dinners would be noisy with the clinking of knives and forks against dishes.
My mother would smile softly between her remarks; my father at the other

end of the table would chew and chew at his food, while he stared over the heads of his children.

My *mother!* My *father!* After English became my primary language, I 15 no longer knew what words to use in addressing my parents. The old Spanish words (those tender accents of sound) I had used earlier—*mamá* and *papá*—I couldn't use anymore. They would have been too painful reminders of how much had changed in my life. On the other hand, the words I heard neighborhood kids call *their* parents seemed equally unsatisfactory. *Mother* and *Father; Ma, Papa, Pa, Dad, Pop* (how I hated the all-American sound of that last word especially)—all these terms I felt were unsuitable, not really terms of address for *my* parents. As a result, I never used them at home. Whenever I'd speak to my parents, I would try to get their attention with eye contact alone. In public conversations, I'd refer to "my parents" or "my mother and father."

My mother and father, for their part, responded differently, as their 16 children spoke to them less. She grew restless, seemed troubled and anxious at the scarcity of words exchanged in the house. It was she who would question me about my day when I came home from school. She smiled at small talk. She pried at the edges of my sentences to get me to say something more. (What?) She'd join conversations she overheard, but her intrusions often stopped her children's talking. By contrast, my father seemed reconciled to the new quiet. Though his English improved somewhat, he retired into silence. At dinner he spoke very little. One night his children and even his wife helplessly giggled at his garbled English pronunciation of the Catholic Grace before Meals. Thereafter he made his wife recite the prayer at the start of each meal, even on formal occasions, when there were guests in the house. Hers became the public voice of the family. On official business, it was she, not my father, one would usually hear on the phone or in stores, talking to strangers. His children grew so accustomed to his silence that, years later, they would speak routinely of his shyness. (My mother would often try to explain: Both his parents died when he was eight. He was raised by an uncle who treated him like little more than a menial servant. He was never encouraged to speak. He grew up alone. A man of few words.) But my father was not shy, I realized, when I'd watch him speaking Spanish with relatives. Using Spanish, he was quickly effusive. Especially when talking with other men, his voice would spark, flicker, flare alive with sounds. In Spanish, he expressed ideas and feelings he rarely revealed in English. With firm Spanish sounds, he conveyed confidence and authority English would never allow him.

The silence at home, however, was finally more than a literal silence. 17 Fewer words passed between parent and child, but more profound was the silence that resulted from my inattention to sounds. At about the time I no longer bothered to listen with care to the sounds of English in public, I grew careless about listening to the sounds family members made when they spoke. Most of the time I heard someone speaking at home and didn't distinguish his sounds from the words people uttered in public. I didn't even pay much attention to my parents' accented and ungrammatical speech. At least not at home. Only when I was with them in public would I grow alert to their accents. Though, even then, their sounds caused me less and less concern. For I was increasingly confident of my own public identity.

I would have been happier about my public success had I not some- 18 times recalled what it had been like earlier, when my family had conveyed its intimacy through a set of conveniently private sounds. Sometimes in public, hearing a stranger, I'd hark back to my past. A Mexican farmworker approached me downtown to ask directions to somewhere. "*Hijito*...?" he said. And his voice summoned deep longing. Another time, standing beside my mother in the visiting room of a Carmelite convent, before the dense screen which rendered the nuns shadowy figures, I heard several Spanish-speaking nuns—their busy, singsong overlapping voices—assure us that yes, yes, we were remembered, all our family was remembered in their prayers. (Their voices echoed faraway family sounds.) Another day, a dark-faced old woman—her hand light on my shoulder—steadied herself against me as she boarded a bus. She murmured something I couldn't quite comprehend. Her Spanish voice came near, like the face of a never-before-seen relative in the instant before I was kissed. Her voice, like so many of the Spanish voices I'd hear in public, recalled the golden age of my youth. Hearing Spanish then, I continued to be a careful, if sad, listener to sounds. Hearing a Spanish-speaking family walking behind me, I turned to look. I smiled for an instant, before my glance found the Hispanic-looking faces of strangers in the crowd going by.

Today I hear bilingual educators say that children lose a degree of "in- 19 dividuality" by becoming assimilated into public society. (Bilingual schooling was popularized in the seventies, that decade when middle-class ethnics began to resist the process of assimilation—the American melting pot.) But the bilingualists simplistically scorn the value and necessity of assimilation. They do not seem to realize that there are *two* ways a person is individualized. So they do not realize that while one suffers a diminished sense of *private* individuality by becoming assimilated into public society, such assimilation makes possible the achievement of *public* individuality.

The bilingualists insist that a student should be reminded of his dif- 20 ference from others in mass society, his heritage. But they equate mere separateness with individuality. The fact is that only in private—with intimates—is separateness from the crowd a prerequisite for individuality. (An intimate draws me apart, tells me that I am unique, unlike all others.) In public, by contrast, full individuality is achieved, paradoxically, by those who are able to consider themselves members of the crowd. Thus it happened for me: Only when I was able to think of myself as an American, no longer an alien in *gringo* society, could I seek the rights and opportunities necessary for full public individuality. The social and political advantages I enjoy as a man result from the day that I came to believe that my name, indeed, is *Rich-heard Road-ree-guess*. It is true that my public society today is often impersonal. (My public society is usually mass society.) Yet despite the anonymity of the crowd and despite the fact that the individuality I achieve in public is often tenuous—because it depends on my being one in a crowd—I celebrate the day I acquired my new name. Those middle-class ethnics who scorn assimilation seem to me filled with decadent self-pity, obsessed by the burden of public life. Dangerously, they romanticize public separateness and they trivialize the dilemma of the socially disadvantaged.

My awkward childhood does not prove the necessity of bilingual edu-   21 cation. My story discloses instead an essential myth of childhood—inevitable pain. If I rehearse here the changes in my private life after my Americanization, it is finally to emphasize the public gain. The loss implies the gain: The house I returned to each afternoon was quiet. Intimate sounds no longer rushed to the door to greet me. There were other noises inside. The telephone rang. Neighborhood kids ran past the door of the bedroom where I was reading my schoolbooks—covered with shopping-bag paper. Once I learned public language, it would never again be easy for me to hear intimate family voices. More and more of my day was spent hearing words. But that may only be a way of saying that the day I raised my hand in class and spoke loudly to an entire roomful of faces, my childhood started to end.

QUESTIONS ABOUT THE RHETORICAL SITUATION

1. This piece of writing appeared in two different places: Rodriguez's book and *The American Scholar*. What changes do you think Rodriguez might have made in this version, the magazine version, because of his different audience? What changes might he make now to accommodate his essay's new audience: first-year composition classes? Explain your answers.
2. Can you read Rodriguez's essay as an attempt to argue for a particular approach to educating foreign-language-speaking students in American schools? Is Rodriguez trying to write persuasively here? What other purpose might he have in this essay?
3. How would you describe Rodriguez's attitude toward his own story—amused, saddened, angered, troubled, moved? Or would you find another word to describe that attitude? Explain your answer.

QUESTIONS ABOUT THE ESSAY'S VOICE

1. Which of the earlier narratives in this chapter does this piece resemble more: the chapter from *Blue Highways* or "Darkness at Noon"? Why? Is

    this essay predominantly narrative or descriptive?

2. What details does Rodriguez offer that make the story seem authentic, that make it clear that he did indeed go through these experiences?

3. Time passes very rapidly in this essay. In ¶5, for example, three quick sentences account for six months. Examine the portions of his autobiography that Rodriguez dramatizes. What is the principle behind his choices to summarize some events and dramatize others?

4. Rodriguez uses parentheses to comment on his own story in a number of places (see ¶3, ¶4, ¶8, ¶10, ¶13, to cite a few such instances). Why does he do so? Is the voice the same in the parenthetical comments as in the rest of the text? Explain your answer.

5. One significant omission from Rodriguez's narrative is any attempt on his part to reproduce his early attempts at speaking English. He writes about them, but he never employs dialogue. Why do you suppose he has chosen this strategy? How effective a strategy is it?

6. In the essay's last three paragraphs, Rodriguez draws a conclusion from his experiences. Do the events he has recounted seem to lead to this conclusion? How would his essay be changed if it did not end with Rodriguez generalizing about the significance of his story?

TOPICS TO WRITE ABOUT

1. Write an essay in which you examine a crucial episode in your life when you realized that your relationship with your parents had changed forever. POTENTIAL AUDIENCES: your parents/your class. POTENTIAL PURPOSES: to give them a new insight into an event they may remember well/to make them reexperience the moment as they read, perhaps identifying it with similar experiences of their own.

2. Write an essay in which you tell a story about an important moment in your life as a student. For example, you might tell about an important competition that you entered and lost and what you learned about yourself as a result. POTENTIAL AUDIENCES: your younger brother or sister/your former teacher. POTENTIAL PURPOSES: to illustrate to him or her that you understand some of their recent experiences in growing up/to show her that you remember an important learning experience of which he or she was a part.

A Taste of Reality

Kieu K. Ly

Born in Cho-Lon, Vietnam, Kieu K. Ly was a first-year student at Miami University in Ohio when she wrote "A Taste of Reality," an essay for which she won first prize in the annual English Department Writing Awards for Excellence in Writing.

Ly went on to become a systems analysis major with career plans that include working in an international company. Since she wrote "A Taste of Reality," she notes that she has written several other essays continuing where she left off in her narrative. About this essay, Ly says, "It was quite an emotional period for me trying to remember as much detail as I could about the 'trip,' but I am glad I did because I sure have learned a lot from those memories."

QUESTIONS ABOUT IDEAS

1. In recent years the U.S. government has been grappling with its policy toward immigrants. Does the United States have a moral or ethical responsibility to accept refugees from oppressed countries? Should the United States have any sort of immigration quotas? If so, what sort?
2. Who is to blame for the plight in which Ly and her fellow refugees find themselves? Does Ly blame anyone in particular for her troubles?
3. Have these refugees been courageous in leaving behind their troubled homeland? Would it have been more courageous to stay? Why or why not?

May 4, 1979, was just another day of school or work for many people. However, for the five hundred refugees escaping from their country, it became a memorable day that would affect the rest of their lives. We found it very difficult to leave our friends and relatives and especially the place of birth for many of us. Our little house will become a place we can only have in our memories.

We had decided to escape from Vietnam, hoping to find freedom in another country. This decision was a dangerous one because we could all be put in jail if the Communist officials learned of our plan. Also, we didn't really know what our chances were as far as survival was concerned. As the tension mounted while we were waiting to get in the boat, an older gentleman, stout and dark, said, "I don't care where we will end up as long as I get out of here." His words clearly expressed what we were all feeling at that moment.

As a young man held out his hands to help us climb onto the boat, the captain carefully checked our names off his list. He had to keep track of the number of people to prevent those who didn't pay the required amount from getting on board. Some of this money was his profit, and the rest was used to blackmail some local officials.

When all the procedures were finished and all the people were checked 4 in, I realized how tiny this boat was, compared to the number of people present. This craft should carry only about two hundred passengers, not five hundred. Tears drowned everyone's faces as our hands waved endlessly at the people on shore, the ones who were left behind.

With confidence, the captain announced that we were heading straight 5 for Australia. We were informed that the trip would take only three days. Sighing with relief, everyone felt more relaxed and was able to enjoy the beauty of the sea.

As the days went by, our optimism, however, grew weaker. By the 6 fourth day, we were still at sea, and there was no land in sight. We were just slowly drifting across the wide ocean. Everyone was very tired by now. For the past three days, we had been crammed together in this tiny boat. The young and strong passengers, mostly men, were directed to sit in the cargo hold, where the air was damp and was heavy with the smell of sweat. They took turns climbing up to the main level to breathe in and feel the coolness of the fresh ocean air. The rest of the passengers, my family and myself included, had been sitting in the same position for the last few days, only moving our arms and legs once in a while to keep our circulation flowing. Due to the size of the boat, we had to sit with our legs locked together. Our knees were below our chins, a position which caused them to touch occasionally when the brown boat was tossed about by the crashing waves.

The food and water had been gradually running low. Since our third 7 day at sea, only the older people and small children were given some soup and water. The rest of us had to control our hunger as well as the thirst that was welling in our parched throats. I found myself staring enviously at my three-year-old sister drinking the water. I swallowed hard and licked my lips with the dry, tasteless saliva. Late that afternoon, the captain finally admitted that he had lost his way and had no idea where we were, except that we were aimlessly floating in the Pacific Ocean. Moreover, the condition of our decrepit boat was becoming worse because it had accidentally hit a rock the night before and a small leak had resulted.

Everyone was panicking. People began to move around, wanting to see 8 where they were, causing the boat to become unstable and tilt from one side to another. At that moment, an anguished cry pierced the air. Everything became still, and everyone turned toward the center of the noise. A passenger had just died. She had been quite ill since she boarded the ship. This woman had been lying awkwardly across her children's laps. No longer able to carry on, she died in her husband's arms.

The silence was interrupted when someone screamed in tears, "We 9 ought to get help!" The reality of the situation finally hit all of us. Some people cried out uncontrollably, while others frightfully turned away, not wanting to witness this madness. We were all terribly disturbed, and no one was in a state of mind to think logically. Meanwhile, quite a distance away, a small boat was approaching. A young man yelled, "Wave, everybody! That must be one of those American boats that have rescued other boats before." We all waved, and our faces instantly lit up. Our terrified white faces were beginning to gain back their healthy pink color.

Nobody had stopped to think how a tiny "American" fishing boat 10 could have survived in the heart of the Pacific Ocean or could have even travelled across the world. I believe that we were all too tired then to think of other consequences or even to maintain our senses.

The other boat, very small and painted with an ugly green, was coming 11 up beside our boat. A few of our people began conversing with the fishermen, but none understood their responses. It turned out that they were from Thailand. The other boat was right next to us now. One Thai fisherman quickly tied a rope connecting the two vessels. Not wasting a minute, nine men, dark and dirty, climbed on our boat, each holding one or two weapons. "Xyzlmonqup...," they screamed, but none of us understood their language. Frustrated, the men pointed at our jewelry and other personal belongings and motioned for us to surrender them.

Terror and confusion overcame the passengers. Some people ran 12 down into the cargo hold to hide, while others, held motionless by shock, began handing over whatever the pirates wanted. As they moved toward us in the boat, the first thing they did was to throw the dead body of the woman into the ocean because she was in their way. I felt the pain her family was suffering. Then, a young man came up to me with a devilish grin and pointed at my gold ring. He was only about my height and looked my age, fourteen. He was holding a sharp knife in one hand and a huge hammer in the other. I was petrified and my legs threatened to crumble under me at any minute. I backed away from him, a move which made him angrier. Violently, he held the knife to my neck and grabbed the jade charm which was connected to my gold necklace and pulled hard. A sharp pain went through my neck, and the touch from his hand sent goose bumps through my body. He mumbled something, "...," and returned his greedy eyes to my ring again. I quickly slipped the ring off my finger and handed it to him as my face turned whiter, and tears streamed down my cheeks. At last, he moved away to pick on the next victim.

With a sigh of relief, I closed my eyes and tried to slow my breathing. 13 However, my misfortune did not stop there. A very large man was shouting at me when I opened my eyes. He moved his hands all over my body, supposedly searching for more valuables. I could feel my face turning red and hotter as I stood there in shame. When he was convinced that I had no more valuable items, he headed toward my younger sister.

At age twelve, my sister was very stubborn. She refused to open her 14 mouth when the man ordered her to do so. Angrily, he was about to smack her when I screamed, "Vi, open your mouth!" Bitterly, she did, and nothing was in there. He then "searched" her in the same fashion and left. Vi moved toward me and said, "I did it...." "What?..." she opened her mouth carefully without being seen by the pirates and showed me a gold ring placed secretly beneath her tongue.

After a complete search of everyone, the fishermen signaled each other 15 and moved toward their boat. Passing where my family was, one man grabbed my older sister and pulled her along. Filled with anger, my mother ran after him as my sister sobbed and screamed for help. He then pushed her back against my mother and jumped into his boat. "Ha! Ha! Ha!..." They had hit the jackpot with all the valuable items they had forcibly taken from all of us.

Ironically, as if they felt sorry that we had no food, the men sailed off, 16 leaving behind a bucket of raw fish. The smell of the dead fish made me want to throw up. I felt sicker when the people, too hungry to care, took the fish and ravenously ate them. I climbed over a few people to get to the other side of the boat and to get away from the crazed crowd.

Looking down at the clear water made me thirstier than ever. This 17 thirst had finally reached its peak now after my two days without water. I reached for the silver can, tied my blue hair ribbon to it and dipped it into the ocean. Happily, I took several gulps without stopping.

"Yuck...," I felt sick to my stomach. My throat suddenly seemed to 18 have caught on fire. My thirst was becoming worse because of my stupidity in drinking the salted water. On another occasion, this incident would probably have made me laugh, but at that particular moment, it was a nightmare. Looking around, I felt hatred toward everything. I hated the pirates, the sun, the boat, the sea...

The sun was bright as ever as I stood there just staring, and the ocean 19 was more beautiful than words could describe. Our boat rocked as the billowing foam pushed against its sides. Beneath the vast ocean, green seaweed surrounded the multicolored corals. Deeper down, the baby fish were enjoying their tour of this exotic kingdom. In a distance ahead, the flying fish seemed to be having a race as the stingrays swam flatly across the water. This scene was delightful, but no one seemed to care anymore. Ironically, for the other refugees and myself, it seemed that dark clouds covered the blue sky, and that the water appeared to be very murky.

We were all very tired, hungry, thirsty, and afraid. The beauty of 20 nature no longer mattered. The dream of freedom was being weighed against the price we had to pay. For the first time in my sheltered childhood, I understood the real meaning of life. It was not just the wonderful things my parents had been giving me. These good things were just one phase of reality. Pirates, sinking ships, fear, hunger, thirst, and inhuman behavior weren't just acts on television screen and movies. They existed and were actually presenting another phase of reality. I had learned so much yet knew so little.

Silently, I cried and wondered, "Is there any hope left for us, the four 21 hundred ninety-nine refugees, who only long for one simple thing: 'FREEDOM!'"

QUESTIONS ABOUT THE RHETORICAL SITUATION

1. This essay was written in a freshman composition class. Is there any suggestion that Ly's audience is restricted to her teacher? Her classmates? (You might compare this essay to Tracy Eastman's "Is the Brown on My Nose Showing?" in Chapter 3). Are there any other audiences that would be able to appreciate this essay?
2. Is Ly interested in generating sympathy from her readers in this essay? In arousing their admiration? What is her objective in the essay? How well has she achieved that objective?
3. What, if anything, is surprising about the attitude taken by Ly toward the local officials, the boat's captain, her fellow passengers, the pirates? How might you expect her to react to these people?

QUESTIONS ABOUT THE ESSAY'S VOICE

1. Why doesn't Ly simply start her story with ¶3? What is the purpose of the opening two paragraphs? How effective are these paragraphs? Do they establish her voice as an authoritative one?
2. How appropriate is Ly's title? Can you suggest any alternative titles that might be more appropriate?
3. Ly uses very little dialogue in her essay. Examine the dialogue that she does use. How does she make it effective? What is the point of the quotation marks with no words in between them in ¶12? Is this strategy more or less effective than her earlier quoting of the pirate in ¶11? Why?
4. At times in this essay, Ly refrains from telling us what she was thinking or from interpreting behavior (¶12–13) while at other times she does so (final sentence of ¶15, first sentence of ¶16). Why does she interpret sometimes but not at other times? Does she still sound expert when she does not interpret? How effective is her description of the pirate raid in *showing* us what the pirates were thinking and what she and the other passengers must have been thinking?

5. Why does her sentence concluding ¶18 fade away by using ellipses? How does this sentence affect the voice of the essay?

6. In ¶19, Ly describes the scene quite vividly, even interpreting the behavior of the fish. She then contrasts the scene with the refugees' feelings. Could Ly have made the same point without making this interpretation? Can you see any alternative way for her to make the same point? Would there be any advantages to making the point more subtly or is it valuable to be blunt at this point in the essay?

7. Ly's story does not end with a fairy tale rescue. Are you disappointed by its ending? Why do you think Ly ends the story where she does? Does her final sentence sound like what she must have thought at the time or does it sound more like what she thinks now about that moment in her life? Is this an important question?

TOPICS TO WRITE ABOUT

1. Write an essay telling the story of the hardships your family underwent in coming to your current home or to this country in the first place. You may want to speak with older relatives. POTENTIAL AUDIENCES: your future children/your classmates. POTENTIAL PURPOSES: to pass along family history in an effort to give them an appreciation of their ancestors' courage and pluck/to provide them with a vividly told experience against which they can contrast their own family history.

2. Write an essay about a memorable journey—one where you overcame many hardships or fulfilled a longtime dream. (For example, tell about your family camping trip during a hurricane or your five-mile hike through the desert to get gas for your empty gas tank or your ten-mile hike with full rucksack during basic training or your successful completion of your first minimarathon or your trip to your ancestral home in Europe or your backpacking tour of the Middle East.) POTENTIAL AUDIENCES: the readers of a travel magazine/a general reading audience. POTENTIAL PURPOSES: to make clear the advantages of such a trip/to make clear the joys of achieving a long-sought goal.

11

The Voice of Firsthand Experience: Exposition

EXPERTS EXPLAIN

Another common mode of writing that uses the voice of firsthand experience is exposition, or explanation. Writing designed to explain ideas is writing composed by experts, for who else could explain the ideas in the first place if not those who already understand them? Exposition takes many forms, all of which rely fairly heavily on the use of *examples: specific details offered to substantiate general ideas.* Actually, all writing relies upon the use of specific details or examples to clarify and support the writer's ideas, as you have been seeing since the earliest chapters in this book. Many textbooks of this kind will have an entire chapter devoted to essays that explain through exemplification; however, almost every essay in those books could be included in that single chapter. Explaining through examples is not a structural technique; it's simply good writing practice.

A Sample

Here is an example. This excerpt comes from an essay entitled "'Aack!' (Or an Analysis of 'Bloom County')" by Susan Glueck, Kathryn O'Connor, and Stephanie Turner, three high school students who wrote this collaborative essay for a local writing contest.

"Bloom County" breaks free from the stereotypical comic syndrome. For years, most comic strips have been presenting humor on an intellectual par with advertisements for sugar-coated cereals. The domestic themes of features like "Hi and Lois" and "Dennis the Menace" have gone stale, as have Dagwood sandwiches of "Blondie" fame. Their values and sit-com humor are outdated. Shouldn't the intelligent teen have some comic strip which not only is funny and enjoyable but also serves as a funhouse mirror, reflecting and distorting the world around them? Fortunately, "Bloom County" introduces a new era of comic strip humor.

In "'Aack!'" the authors sound like experts because they know what they are talking about. They make a generalization based on specific first-hand observation: comic strip humor is in a rut except for "Bloom County." They use many examples of the old-fashioned comic strips to illustrate their point about domestic humor, mentioning Dagwood's once-amusing sandwiches in particular. They make connections to help illustrate their point, comparing these older strips to cereal commercials. In their next paragraph, they go on to offer illustrations of "Bloom County's" humor, mentioning characters such as Opus the penguin, the little boy Milo, and Bill the Cat, whose cry of "Aack!" gives the essay its title.

STRUCTURES

There are a number of common patterns for using examples that will help you explain your ideas. One of these patterns is the *process analysis, which explains how a particular process, procedure, or activity takes place.* Dave Barry's little play, his conversation between a bird-watcher and a non-bird-watcher in "For the Birds" (Chapter 2), used the technique of process analysis for humorous purposes, showing how a non-bird-watcher might cope in a conversation with an avid ornithologist.

When your objective is a bit more serious, however, you may find yourself explaining how a process occurs as a means of illuminating your subject. Some essays are "pure" process analyses: their main objective is to explain the process. But it is also very likely that only a smaller portion of an essay in the voice of firsthand experience might be a process analysis. My linguist colleague, to whom I referred in Chapter 10, spent a brief part of his essay explaining how linguists collect data for their research; your hypothetical essay on a backpacking trip to the Canadian Rockies may devote three paragraphs to explaining how a climber uses ropes to rappel down the side of a steep decline. Process analysis is a technique available to the expert writing about her field of expertise; use it when appropriate. Just be sure you are complete and chronological, offering your less-than-expert reader the full process in a logical sequence.

At other times writers who are experts make an effort *to distinguish between related ideas. When they are dealing with two such ideas, they may organize their ideas in a comparison/contrast pattern.* The three high school students writing about "Bloom County" used a comparison/contrast approach to analyze the appeal of "Bloom County," contrasting it frequently with older comic strips. In *Model Voices,* you have read E. B. White's "Once More to the Lake," which makes use of the contrast between two visits to the same-lake, and David Quammen's "The Tree People," which contrasted two different kinds of bristlecone firs and then contrasted the bristlecone with a magnolia tree. David Bradley contrasted Martin Luther King and Malcolm X in Chapter 7. You will see Derek Rowntree using this pattern for a portion of his essay "What Is Statistics?" in this chapter. The idea of comparing two subjects to one another is that it becomes easier to explain each by pointing out how it differs from and resembles the other. Notice how often in this section of *Model Voices* I have compared the voice of authority to the other voices we have heard throughout the book's first nine chapters.

When the writer focuses on contrasting more than two different subjects, she may use a pattern known as classification, placing the several subjects into categories. You have also read essays using classification in the humorous voice section of the book (Dave Barry created nonsense categories of birds in "For the Birds," and Nickie McWhirter tried to narrow down the essential shoes for a fashionable wardrobe into categories in "Glory, Those Shoes of Imelda Marcos.") Some essays are organized completely as classification essays: three types of tennis players, four types of student loans, and so forth. Equally likely is that a small part of a whole essay designed to explain and inform might take the form of a classification. You might need to explain that there are three categories of backpackers: the novice who is just starting, the expert who takes the sport seriously, and the weekender who is just sort of visiting. Then you can proceed to focus on any one of the three in the remainder of your essay.

Another possible organizational pattern is *definition, a pattern of exposition in which a writer attempts to describe the subject clearly enough to convey to the reader the subject's essential qualities, the qualities that differentiate it from other related subjects.* Think about how often your teachers define terms during lectures. Definitions are an important feature of the voice we are discussing because experts frequently must prepare their readers to understand complex concepts by first explaining less complex concepts or by establishing a common vocabulary. In Chapter 2, Lewis Grizzard spent considerable time in his essay "This Might Sting a Little" offering definitions. You will probably find examples of short definitions in almost every one of the upcoming essays. Sometimes, however, the entire intention of an essay is to offer a definition, and thus every part of the essay offers more information intended to define the central term. Derek Rowntree's "What Is Statistics?" is an essay designed to define; Rowntree's goal is to describe the science of statistics so clearly that his readers will be able to differentiate between it and even a closely related discipline such as mathematics. As you read Rowntree's essay, notice the various strategies he employs in an effort to answer the question posed by his title.

Sometimes the voice of firsthand experience is heard in *analysis, in which a writer attempts to explain what makes his subject "tick"; analysis takes a subject apart in order to explain its inner workings.* By answering the question "Why?" a writer is assuming the pose of an authority. Philip Caputo examines the Vietnam War in an effort to explain why American soldiers in Vietnam behaved as they did during that war. Nell Irvin Painter explains why feeling ordinary is a positive feeling. When you attempt to answer the question "Why?" and are unsure of your answer, you will sound meditative, but when you *are* sure, you will sound authoritative. Offering reasons and explaining causes are at the heart of the voice of authority.

One last pattern worth mentioning is *evaluation, in which a writer offers her judgment of the worth of her subject.* Experts know enough about their subjects to be able to form opinions and justify those opinions. Thus Alexander Petrunkevitch will conclude his discussion of spiders and wasps by offering his considered opinion about the likeliest explanation for their behavior. Caputo will evaluate the reasons he himself has offered in explaining American conduct in Vietnam. You might explain why certain manufacturers make better equipment for backpacking than certain others. Or you may just organize your entire essay into an evaluation by reviewing a new film, book, play, record album, concert, restaurant. If you take this approach, remember that you have two major objectives to fulfill when you write a review:

You must clearly articulate your opinion of the value of what you are reviewing by explaining your standards for judgment and applying them. Notice that many newspaper reviews use a system of stars to rate films, with four or five being a great movie and one being a bomb.

You must give your readers a clear picture of what the film, book, concert, or restaurant is like so that they can decide for themselves if they have any interest in it. Notice that reviews will tell you if the restaurant serves French, Mexican, or Japanese cuisine, or that the movie is full of foul language and nudity, or that the novel is an historical romance.

Your goal in writing a full-length review is most likely to help your readers make a consumer decision: should they invest their time and money in that particular film or book or restaurant? That's why those television shows in which two movie critics—one thin and one chubby, or one nice and one nasty, or one with glasses and a mustache and one with glasses but no mustache—discuss new movies always show film clips before anyone holds a thumb up or down on the film. The clip and the discussion allow the audience to grasp what kind of movie is being reviewed. Your job, as the sort of expert known as a reviewer, is to provide enough information and opinion to allow readers to make their own decisions.

PATTERNS OF EXPOSITION AND RHETORICAL SITUATIONS

While all of these patterns—*definition, analysis, evaluation, comparison/ contrast, process analysis, classification*—are used in essays based on firsthand experience, few writers if any begin with the pattern in mind. Rather they begin with the subject and a need to communicate about it. Remember the familiar equation:

$$\text{Awareness of audience} +$$
$$\text{understanding of purpose} +$$
$$\text{attitude toward subject} = \text{voice}$$

As writers attempt to deal with the different aspects of the rhetorical situation in an effort to inform their readers, they may use one or more of the patterns I have been discussing. Why not? They are helpful tools, but all they are is tools. If you decide to build yourself a bookcase, you start out with wood and plans (the equivalent of the subject to be written about and our equation). Then you buy the necessary hammers, saws, planes, and other tools (the possible patterns of exposition). It would be rather unusual to buy the tools and then decide you ought to build something that might use just those tools.

So pick your subject, one about which you know a great deal from firsthand experience, decide for whom you are writing, and then select the appropriate tools to do the job. The finished product should be a new book-case: the tools you used to build it only matter if they have worked effectively.

The Spider and the Wasp

Alexander Petrunkevitch

Alexander Petrunkevitch (1875–1964) was born in Russia and studied in his homeland and Great Britain before emigrating to the United States while in his mid-twenties. A leading expert on spiders, Petrunkevitch published a standard reference text, *Index Catalogue of Spiders of North, Central, and South America*. He taught zoology at a number of American universities including Harvard and Yale.

"The Spider and the Wasp" first appeared in *Scientific American* in 1952. This essay has been widely read in freshman composition courses over the past three decades.

QUESTIONS ABOUT IDEAS

1. What parallels to human behavior can you make with Petrunkevitch's spider and wasp? Could Aesop have made a fable out of this confrontation, à la the famous tortoise and the hare?
2. The relationship between the spider and the wasp is, of course, a common enough one in nature between a hunter and its victim. Would a similar story about a lion and a gazelle have a different impact? Why or why not?
3. Why do you think this essay has been so popular in courses like the one you are taking?

To hold its own in the struggle for existence, every species of animal   1
must have a regular source of food, and if it happens to live on other animals, its survival may be very delicately balanced. The hunter cannot exist without the hunted; if the latter should perish from the earth, the former would, too. When the hunted also prey on some of the hunters, the matter may become complicated.

This is nowhere better illustrated than in the insect world. Think of   2
the complexity of a situation such as the following: There is a certain wasp, *Pimpla inquisitor*, whose larvae feed on several years in succession. In a Paris museum is a tropical specimen which is said to have been living in captivity for 25 years.

A fertilized female tarantula lays from 200 to 400 eggs at a time; thus it   3
is possible for a single tarantula to produce several thousand young. She takes no care of them beyond weaving a cocoon of silk to enclose the eggs. After they hatch, the young walk away, find convenient places in which to dig their burrows and spend the rest of their lives in solitude. Tarantulas feed mostly on insects and millipedes. Once their appetite is appeased, they

digest the food for several days before eating again. Their sight is poor, being limited to sensing a change in the intensity of light and to the perception of moving objects. They apparently have little or no sense of hearing, for a hungry tarantula will pay no attention to a loudly chirping cricket placed in its cage unless the insect happens to touch one of its legs.

But all spiders, and especially hairy ones, have an extremely delicate 4 sense of touch. Laboratory experiments prove that tarantulas can distinguish three types of touch: pressure against the body wall, stroking of the body hair, and riffling of certain very fine hairs on the legs called trichobothria. Pressure against the body, by a finger or the end of a pencil, causes the tarantula to move off slowly for a short distance. The touch excites no defensive response unless the approach is from above, where the spider can see the motion, in which case it rises on its hind legs, lifts its front legs, opens its fangs and holds this threatening posture as long as the object continues to move. When the motion stops, the spider drops back to the ground, remains quiet for a few seconds, and then moves slowly away.

The entire body of a tarantula, especially its legs, is thickly clothed 5 with hair. Some of it is short and woolly, some long and stiff. Touching this body hair produces one of two distinct reactions. When the spider is hungry, it responds with an immediate and swift attack. At the touch of a cricket's antennae the tarantula seizes the insect so swiftly that a motion picture taken at the rate of 64 frames per second shows only the result not the process of capture. But when the spider is not hungry, the stimulation of its hair merely causes it to shake the touched limb. An insect can walk under its hairy belly unharmed.

The trichobothria, very fine hairs growing from disklike membranes of 6 the legs, were once thought to be the spider's hearing organs, but we now know that they have nothing to do with sound. They are sensitive only to air movement. A light breeze makes them vibrate slowly without disturbing the common hair. When one blows gently on the trichobothria, the tarantula reacts with a quick jerk of its four front legs. If the front and hind legs are stimulated at the same time, the spider makes a sudden jump. This reaction is quite independent of the state of its appetite.

These three tactile responses—to pressure on the body wall, to moving 7 of the common hair, and to flexing of the trichobothria—are so different from one another that there is no possibility of confusing them. They serve the tarantula adequately for most of its needs and enable it to avoid most annoyances and dangers. But they fail the spider completely when it meets its deadly enemy, the digger wasp *Pepsis*.

These solitary wasps are beautiful and formidable creatures. Most spe- 8 cies are either a deep shiny blue all over, or deep blue with rusty wings. The largest have a wing span of about four inches. They live on nectar. When excited, they give off a pungent odor—a warning that they are ready to attack. The sting is much worse than that of a bee or common wasp, and the pain and swelling last longer. In the adult stage the wasp lives only a few months. The female produces but a few eggs, one at a time at intervals of two or three days. For each egg the mother must provide one adult tarantula, alive but paralyzed. The tarantula must be of the correct species to nourish the larva. The mother wasp attaches the egg to the paralyzed spider's abdomen. Upon hatching from the egg, the larva is many hundreds of times smaller than its living but helpless victim. It eats no other food and drinks no water. By the time it has finished its single gargantuan meal and becomes ready for wasphood, nothing remains of the tarantula but its indigestible chitinous skeleton.

The mother wasp goes tarantula-hunting when the egg in her ovary is 9 almost ready to be laid. Flying low over the ground late on a sunny afternoon, the wasp looks for its victim or for the mouth of a tarantula burrow, a round hole edged by a bit of silk. The sex of the spider makes no difference, but the mother is highly discriminating as to species. Each species of *Pepsis* requires a certain species of tarantula, and the wasp will not attack the wrong species. In a cage with a tarantula which is not its normal prey the wasp avoids the spider, and is usually killed by it in the night.

Yet when a wasp finds the correct species, it is the other way about. To 10 identify the species the wasp apparently must explore the spider with her antennae. The tarantula shows an amazing tolerance to this exploration. The wasp crawls under it and walks over it without evoking any hostile response. The molestation is so great and so persistent that the tarantula often rises on all eight legs, as if it were on stilts. It may stand this way for several minutes. Meanwhile the wasp, having satisfied itself that the victim is of the right species, moves off a few inches to dig the spider's grave. Working vigorously with legs and jaws, it excavates a hole 8 to 10 inches deep with a diameter slightly larger than the spider's girth. Now and again the wasp pops out of the hole to make sure that the spider is still there.

When the grave is finished, the wasp returns to the tarantula to com- 11 plete her ghastly enterprise. First she feels it all over once more with her antennae. Then her behavior becomes more aggressive. She bends her abdomen, protruding her sting, and searches for the soft membrane at the point where the spider's leg joins its body—the only spot where she can penetrate the horny skeleton. From time to time, as the exasperated spider slowly shifts ground, the wasp turns on her back and slides along with the aid of her wings, trying to get under the tarantula for a shot at the vital spot. During all this maneuvering, which can last for several minutes, the tarantula makes no move to save itself. Finally the wasp corners it against some obstruction and grasps one of its legs in her powerful jaws. Now at last the harassed spider tries a desperate but vain defense. The two contestants roll over and over on the ground. It is a terrifying sight and the outcome is always the same. The wasp finally manages to thrust her sting into the soft spot and holds it there for a few seconds while she pumps in the poison.

Almost immediately the tarantula falls paralyzed on its back. Its legs stop twitching; its heart stops beating. Yet it is not dead, as is shown by the fact that if taken from the wasp it can be restored to some sensitivity by being kept in a moist chamber for several months.

After paralyzing the tarantula, the wasp cleans herself by dragging her 12 body along the ground and rubbing her feet, sucks the drop of blood oozing from the wound in the spider's abdomen, then grabs a leg of the flabby, helpless animal in her jaws and drags it down to the bottom of the grave. She stays there for many minutes, sometimes for several hours, and what she does all that time in the dark we do not know. Eventually she lays her egg and attaches it to the side of the spider's abdomen with a sticky secretion. Then she emerges, fills the grave with soil carried bit by bit in her jaws, and finally tramples the ground all around to hide any trace of the grave from prowlers. Then she flies away, leaving her descendant safely started in life.

In all this the behavior of the wasp evidently is qualitatively different 13 from that of the spider. The wasp acts like an intelligent animal. This is not to say that instinct plays no part or that she reasons as man does. But her actions are to the point; they are not automatic and can be modified to fit the situation. We do not know for certain how she identifies the tarantula—probably it is by some olfactory or chemotactile sense—but she does it purposefully and does not blindly tackle a wrong species.

On the other hand, the tarantula's behavior shows only confusion. Ev- 14 idently the wasp's pawing gives it no pleasure, for it tries to move away. That the wasp is not simulating sexual stimulation is certain, because male and female tarantulas react in the same way to its advances. That the spider is not anesthetized by some odorless secretion is easily shown by blowing lightly at the tarantula and making it jump suddenly. What, then, makes the tarantula behave as stupidly as it does?

No clear, simple answer is available. Possibly the stimulation by the 15 wasp's antennae is masked by a heavier pressure on the spider's body, so that it reacts as when prodded by a pencil. But the explanation may be much more complex. Initiative in attack is not in the nature of tarantulas; most species fight only when cornered so that escape is impossible. Their inherited patterns of behavior apparently prompt them to avoid problems rather than attack them. For example, spiders always weave their webs in three dimensions, and when a spider finds that there is insufficient space to attach certain threads in the third dimension, it leaves the place and seeks another, instead of finishing the web in a single plane. This urge to escape seems to arise under all circumstances, in all phases of life, and to take the place of reasoning. For a spider to change the pattern of its web is as impossible as for an inexperienced man to build a bridge across a chasm obstructing his way.

In a way the instinctive urge to escape is not only easier but more ef- 16 ficient than reasoning. The tarantula does exactly what is most efficient in all cases except in an encounter with a ruthless and determined attacker dependent for the existence of her own species on killing as many tarantulas as she can lay eggs. Perhaps in this case the spider follows its usual pattern of trying to escape, instead of seizing and killing the wasp, because it is not aware of its danger. In any case, the survival of the tarantula species as a whole is protected by the fact that the spider is much more fertile than the wasp.

QUESTIONS ABOUT THE RHETORICAL SITUATION

1. Petrunkevitch's essay first appeared in *Scientific American*. What assumptions can you make about his intended readers? How has he made an effort to reach those intended readers? How would his essay need to be changed if it were written for a journal called *Entomology Quarterly?* How would the essay need to be changed for *Readers' Digest?*
2. What do you suppose the essay's audience learned from this essay? What did *you* learn from reading this essay? How much did you enjoy reading this essay?
3. What is Petrunkevitch's attitude toward his subject? What are his attitudes toward the spider and the wasp? How does his use of adjectives help to convey his attitudes? (See ¶10 and ¶11, for example.)

QUESTIONS ABOUT THE ESSAY'S VOICE

1. What is the purpose of the essay's opening paragraph?
2. In ¶11, Petrunkevitch writes, "...the outcome is always the same." What does this sentence tell you about Petrunkevitch's source of information? What other clues are there in the essay that also suggest this same source of information?
3. In ¶13, Petrunkevitch discusses the wasp's behavior, offering his own interpretation of that behavior. How does offering an interpretation help to create the essay's authoritative voice?
4. In ¶15, Petrunkevitch compares spinning a spider's web to building a bridge. What is he trying to explain by using this analogy? How effective an analogy is this?
5. In discussing the behavior of the spider, Petrunkevitch confesses to being unsure of its motivation. Why doesn't the essay's final section (¶14–16) create a meditative voice (see Annie Dillard's essay "Strangers to Darkness" in Chapter 9) instead of an authoritative voice?
6. How effective is the essay's concluding paragraph? Could it be improved? How?
7. Petrunkevitch explains the process by which the *Pepsis* wasp lays its eggs. How many distinct steps, or stages, are there in the process? What is the point of the parts of the essay that do not directly describe the stages in the process?

TOPICS TO WRITE ABOUT

1. Write a process analysis in which you explain how people perform some specific task (for example, performing a dismount from the parallel bars, shearing sheep, starting a rock collection, applying a tourniquet, decorating a gym for a prom, publicizing a school drama club production, decorating a wedding cake). POTENTIAL AUDIENCES: readers who are already involved in similar activities/readers who are unlikely to be very interested in the subject. POTENTIAL PURPOSES: to provide additional insight into a fairly familiar activity/to show how interesting the subject really can be.
2. Write a process analysis in which you explain a natural or mechanical process (how blood clots, how perspiration cools the body, how leaves fall in the autumn, how an automobile engine works, how a microchip works, how a metronome keeps time). POTENTIAL AUDIENCE: non-scientifically or non-mechanically inclined readers. POTENTIAL PURPOSE: to explain an unfamiliar and perhaps even mysterious process in everyday terms.

The Joys of Being Ordinary
Nell Irvin Painter

Nell Irvin Painter was born in Oakland, California. After earning a Ph.D. in American history at Harvard University in 1974, she has taught history at the University of Pennsylvania, the University of North Carolina, and at Princeton University. Author of numerous scholarly articles and reviews, Painter has also published three books on American history, two of which focus on the black experience after the Civil War.

In addition to her scholarly writing, Painter has also published in newspapers and magazines such as the *New York Times*, the *Boston Globe*, and *The Nation*. "The Joys of Being Ordinary" originally appeared without a title in the "Hers" column of the *New York Times* in December 1981.

QUESTIONS ABOUT IDEAS

1. What insights into racism does this essay offer?
2. Many people who are proud of their ethnic heritage feel a divided allegiance at times between being an American and being a member of that ethnic group. How can one resolve any conflicts that may arise? (For ex-

ample, in addition to the situation described by Nell Painter, American
Jews are often torn by their allegiance both to the United States and to
Israel as are many Irish Americans torn by their allegiance to both the
United States and Northern Ireland.)
3. What are the major adjustments that Painter has to make in order to live
   in a foreign country? To what degree are these adjustments common to
   all expatriates? To what degree is she experiencing a unique situation?

Ghana is one of the best things that ever happened to me, even though   1
it was a long time ago. My family and I lived there for two years in the mid-
1960's. Ghanaians impressed me from the moment I stepped off the plane.
For aside from a few travelers, everyone was black, an even, opaque, velvety
black that I had never seen in the United States. The customs officials, families greeting passengers, taxi drivers, policemen, they were all intensely and
beautifully black.

The people in the airport not only looked different from American Ne-   2
groes, they also carried themselves differently. They stood with self-
assurance and spoke without implied apology. Their dress seemed to announce that they were sure of themselves. They wore the bright colors and
large prints that respectable American Negroes eschewed for fear of being
conspicuous or seeming to reinforce unfortunate stereotypes. Ghanaian
women wore long, two-piece dresses of a batiklike print that I learned was
called wax print. The dresses were designed to flatter African figures and to
take advantage of the prints, whether they were flowers or portraits of public
figures.

Most of the men wore Western dress, white shirts with plain, dark ties   3
and trousers. The contrast between dark skins and white shirts dramatically
reinforced the blackness of skin and the whiteness of cloth. A few men wore
traditional dress, a toga-wrapped cloth of either printed cotton or Kente
cloth, made of several narrow hand-woven strips of blue, yellow, red, and
white silk sewn together. Kente cloth, which is both beautiful and expensive, announced the wearer's national pride and his importance. Men wearing traditional dress showed off their calves and their sumptuously decorated
sandals. In comparison, the American men travelers in their boxy suits
seemed dowdy.

The city of Accra and the university at Legon presented me with a new   4
spectrum of color. I squinted into an enormous, brilliant sky. All the buildings and walls presented complex patterns of textures and colors, for something grew on every surface—bushes, flowers or mold. The California Bay
Area that I had left was a gray-blue place with mostly light-colored people.
But now I moved in a world of bright contrasts. The dirt was red, the trees

and grass blue-green, the buildings white with red-tiled roofs. Cerise bou-
gainvillea climbed whitewashed walls and cascaded over fences. This colorful landscape and the very black people in white or brilliant clothes together
altered my visual sense of everyday life.

Many Ghanaians invited us into their homes, chemistry professors, a   5
carpenter, an herb doctor, and our landlord, among others. We ate in man-
sions more luxurious than anything we could ever afford and in bungalows
so crowded that we winced. At every point on the scale of wealth, the people
were Ghanaian, each one as black as the others.

As black Americans unaffiliated with the United States Embassy, we   6
enjoyed several advantages. Nearly everyone regarded us as kindred, and
they called us Afro-Americans, not American Negroes. Ghanaians disassoci-
ated us from their main grievances against the United States: imperialism
and racial discrimination. Those who had studied in the United States or
visited for any length of time included us in their nostalgia, if their memories
were fond.

With our unstraightened hair and in wax-print dresses, Mother and I   7
looked enough like locals to pass, provided we kept our mouths shut. This
silent assimilation made me something new. I felt inconspicuous and free.
This is not to say that I felt like a Ghanaian. The better I came to know the
various sorts of Ghanaian lives and customs, the more I realized how thoroughly American I was. Yet I never felt terribly foreign in Ghana. Knowing
full well that I could never take part in Ghanaian national life, I felt far less
an outsider than I had sometimes felt in California. As a black person in a
black country, I was very much at home.

At first I found being a member of the racial majority disorienting. I   8
had grown up in Northern California as a member of one of several racial
minorities. In the 1940's and 1950's my family had encountered outright discrimination in housing and occasional difficulties in getting decent service in
restaurants. But by and large, racism didn't present us with serious problems on a day-to-day basis. My parents taught me about racial discrimination, however, and for as long as I could remember, I felt connected to people of African descent in the South, the West Indies and Africa. Any failure
of mine, I was convinced, reflected badly on 400 million black people
throughout the world. My successes, of course, made them all proud. I bore
my responsibilities without complaint, certain that my actions counted in the
world.

Growing up as I did with a strong Pan-African orientation, I took my   9
social and political bearings by race. How to decide which team to root for?

Favor the one with the black players, then later, the one with the most black players. (This system doesn't work so well anymore.) Which side of a political issue to support? See how it will affect black people as a whole. Which movie to see? The one with a black character. Without my realizing it, my response to racism was a keen sense of race.

In Ghana, however, racial solidarity and the American way made little 10 sense. I realized this first in politics, mostly at the Star Hotel. Ghanaian and Afro-American students and my friends and I spent many tropical nights at the tables around the Star's outdoor dance floor, drinking Ghanaian beer, smoking Ghanaian cigarettes and talking politics. That is, my friends talked politics. All I could sort out was colonialism, which was related to racism.

In the independent republic of Ghana, however, the issues were not 11 racial, but economic. Should the inefficient collective state farms expand, although they were losing money hand-over-fist? Should the prosperous, private cocoa farms, which brought in most of the nation's hard currency, be nationalized? Should the government emphasize the development of agriculture or industry? When those who profited and those who suffered were all equally black, I couldn't figure the racial angle. But as economic questions superseded racial ones in my mind, I slowly discovered the politics of class.

Similar processes occurred in other areas of my life, as the racial think- 12 ing I had brought from the United States gave way. At the university, where geniuses, dumbbells and average students were black, I discovered the quality of ordinariness, which American race relations denied to blacks. In my studies of African history, I began to separate the politics of power from color. The outlines of human nature emerged.

Ordinary humanness affected me deeply as a woman. In the United 13 States I was a woman, but always—outside the tight circle of family and close friends—a Negro woman. A Negro woman in the United States was not the same thing as just a woman, without a racial qualifier.

In Ghana, I became just a woman. I let down my burden of responsi- 14 bility to the 400 million people of African descent, for I was surrounded by friends who were thinking seriously about the future and also having a good time. I had love affairs. I had my heart broken and broke hearts in my turn. I was free to enjoy myself and be something I have often missed intensely in the years since I came home—ordinary.

QUESTIONS ABOUT THE RHETORICAL SITUATION

1. Painter's essay appeared in a newspaper read by people of all racial backgrounds. How might she have changed her essay if it were written for a Ghanaian newspaper? For an American magazine primarily read by black Americans?

2. What is a "wax print"? What is "Kente cloth"? How do you know the answers to these questions?
3. How does Painter want her readers to respond to her essay? How would the response be different if she had written for the Ghanaian newspaper or the magazine for black Americans?
4. As a victim of prejudice, Painter most likely has felt anger and bitterness at times. Why does her essay present a different attitude toward her experiences with racism? How would you describe her attitude toward her stay in Ghana?

QUESTIONS ABOUT THE ESSAY'S VOICE

1. Painter's essay seems to have a "thesis statement." Where is it? Is it effective in this position in the essay? How is this a surprising location for this thesis statement?
2. Painter is an expert in this essay not only on life in Ghana but also on life as a black woman in California. What evidence is there in the essay of this dual expertise?
3. Unlike writers who are meditating about the significance of their own experiences, Painter is quite certain about the significance of hers. How might she change ¶7 to make her voice more meditative?
4. In ¶9, Painter adds parenthetically that it has become difficult to root for sports teams based on the percentage of black players on the team. What voice do you hear in that parenthetical statement? Has she made a mistake in changing her voice here? Why or why not?
5. How would you describe Painter's voice in ¶9 when she writes "my response to racism was a keen sense of race"? What other voices can you imagine her using at this point in the essay?
6. Why does Painter initially have problems participating in political discussions in Ghana? How does she resolve these problems?
7. What is the purpose of the dash in the essay's final sentence? How would the sentence sound if it were rewritten so that it did not use that dash?
8. How appropriate is the title I have assigned to this essay? What else might I have called it?

TOPICS TO WRITE ABOUT

1. Write an essay that explains the unexpected value you received from a personal experience. Begin the essay with the sentence: "———was one of the best things that ever happened to me." (For example, you might write about moving from one state to another while you were a child; or you might write about the death of a pet or being falsely accused by a

teacher of some sort of misbehavior.) POTENTIAL AUDIENCES: readers who have been through the same experience/readers who may never have thought about such an experience being positive. POTENTIAL PURPOSES: to explain to them what there is that makes such a potentially negative experience worthwhile to so many people/to enable them to see the experience in a different light.

2. Write an essay which explains the *significant* differences and similarities between two different places, reaching some general conclusion about the two places (For example, you might describe the startling similarities between life in Manhattan and life where you live now or you might discuss the essential differences between the United States and some other English-speaking country.) POTENTIAL AUDIENCES: readers who live in one of the two places/readers of a travel magazine. POTENTIAL PURPOSES: to make them understand that some differences are merely superficial while some similarities can be quite significant/to prepare them for a stay in an unfamiliar place.

Black Men, Public Spaces
Brent Staples

Brent Staples was born in Chester, Pennsylvania, in 1951 and received a bachelor's degree from Widener University in 1973. He holds a Ph.D. in psychology from The University of Chicago. While in Chicago, he worked at a number of newspapers and magazines, including The *Chicago Reader* and The *Chicago Sun-Times*, where he was a staff reporter.

He moved to the *New York Times* as an editor of The *New York Times Book Review* in 1985 and was later promoted to assistant metropolitan editor. He has published in a variety of publications, including the *New York Times Magazine, Harper's*, and *Ms.* He is currently writing a book about his childhood and hometown with the working title "Parallel Time." He has received grants and awards for his writing and his studies from the Illinois Arts Council, the Ford Foundation, and the Danforth Foundation.

"Black Men, Public Spaces" first appeared in *Ms.* magazine in 1986 under the title "Just Walk on By."

QUESTIONS ABOUT IDEAS

1. How would you relate Staples' experiences to those of Nell Irvin Painter in Ghana? Are they discussing similar ideas?

2. How understandable are the reactions of the other pedestrians in this essay? How understandable are Staples' reactions? Have you observed the behavior he describes in this essay?
3. The events Staples uses as examples take place in San Francisco, New York, Chicago. Does the same situation occur in smaller cities and towns? Does this situation occur on campus?
4. Staples offers his own personal solution but does not offer any larger solution to the problem. What solutions are there?

My first victim was a woman—white, well dressed, probably in her 1
early twenties. I came upon her late one evening on a deserted street in Hyde Park, a relatively affluent neighborhood in an otherwise mean, impoverished section of Chicago. As I swung onto the avenue behind her, there seemed to be a discreet, uninflammatory distance between us. Not so. She cast back a worried glance. To her, the youngish black man—a broad six feet two inches with a beard and billowing hair, both hands shoved into the pockets of a bulky military jacket—seemed menacingly close. After a few more quick glimpses, she picked up her pace and was soon running in earnest. Within seconds she disappeared into a cross street.

That was more than a decade ago. I was 22 years old, a graduate stu- 2
dent newly arrived at the University of Chicago. It was in the echo of that terrified woman's footfalls that I first began to know the unwieldy inheritance I'd come into—the ability to alter public space in ugly ways. It was clear that she thought herself the quarry of a mugger, a rapist, or worse. Suffering a bout of insomnia, however, I was stalking sleep, not defenseless wayfarers. As a softy who is scarcely able to take a knife to a raw chicken— let alone hold it to a person's throat—I was surprised, embarrassed, and dismayed all at once. Her flight made me feel like an accomplice in tyranny. It also made it clear that I was indistinguishable from the muggers who occasionally seeped into the area from the surrounding ghetto. That first encounter, and those that followed, signified that a vast, unnerving gulf lay between nighttime pedestrians—particularly women—and me. And I soon gathered that being perceived as dangerous is a hazard in itself. I only needed to turn a corner into a dicey situation, or crowd some frightened, armed person in a foyer somewhere, or make an errant move after being pulled over by a policeman. Where fear and weapons meet—and they often do in urban America—there is always the possibility of death.

In that first year, my first away from my hometown, I was to become 3
thoroughly familiar with the language of fear. At dark, shadowy intersections in Chicago, I could cross in front of a car stopped at a traffic light and elicit the *thunk, thunk, thunk, thunk* of the driver—black, white, male, or female—hammering down the door locks. On less traveled streets after dark, I grew accustomed to but never comfortable with people who crossed to the

other side of the street rather than pass me. Then there were the standard unpleasantries with police, doormen, bouncers, cab drivers, and others whose business it is to screen out troublesome individuals *before* there is any nastiness.

I moved to New York nearly two years ago and I have remained an   4 avid night walker. In central Manhattan, the near-constant crowd cover minimizes tense one-on-one street encounters. Elsewhere—visiting friends in SoHo, where sidewalks are narrow and tightly spaced buildings shut out the sky—things can get very taut indeed.

Black men have a firm place in New York mugging literature. Norman   5 Podhoretz in his famed (or infamous) 1963 essay, "My Negro Problem— And Ours," recalls growing up in terror of black males; they "were tougher than we were, more ruthless," he writes—and as an adult on the Upper West Side of Manhattan, he continues, he cannot constrain his nervousness when he meets black men on certain streets. Similarly, a decade later, the essayist and novelist Edward Hoagland extols a New York where once "Negro bitterness bore down mainly on other Negroes." Where some see mere panhandlers, Hoagland sees "a mugger who is clearly screwing up his nerve to do more than just *ask* for money." But Hoagland has "the New Yorker's quick-hunch posture for broken-field maneuvering," and the bad guy swerves away.

I often witness that "hunch posture," from women after dark on the   6 warrenlike streets of Brooklyn where I live. They seem to set their faces on neutral and, with their purse straps strung across their chests bandolier style, they forge ahead as though bracing themselves against being tackled. I understand, of course, that the danger they perceive is not a hallucination. Women are particularly vulnerable to street violence, and young black males are drastically overrepresented among the perpetrators of that violence. Yet these truths are no solace against the kind of alienation that comes of being ever the suspect, against being set apart, a fearsome entity with whom pedestrians avoid making eye contact.

It is not altogether clear to me how I reached the ripe old age of 22   7 without being conscious of the lethality nighttime pedestrians attributed to me. Perhaps it was because in Chester, Pennsylvania, the small, angry industrial town where I came of age in the 1960s, I was scarcely noticeable against a backdrop of gang warfare, street knifings, and murders. I grew up one of the good boys, had perhaps a half-dozen fist fights. In retrospect, my shyness of combat has clear sources.

Many things go into the making of a young thug. One of those things   8 is the consummation of the male romance with the power to intimidate. An infant discovers that random flailings send the baby bottle flying out of the crib and crashing to the floor. Delighted, the joyful babe repeats those motions again and again, seeking to duplicate the feat. Just so, I recall the points at which some of my boyhood friends were finally seduced by the perception of themselves as tough guys. When a mark cowered and surrendered his money without resistance, myth and reality merged—and paid off. It is, after all, only manly to embrace the power to frighten and intimidate. We, as men, are not supposed to give an inch of our lane on the highway; we are to seize the fighter's edge in work and in play and even in love; we are to be valiant in the face of hostile forces.

Unfortunately, poor and powerless young men seem to take all this 9 nonsense literally. As a boy, I saw countless tough guys locked away; I have since buried several, too. They were babies, really—a teenage cousin, a brother of 22, a childhood friend in his mid-twenties—all gone down in episodes of bravado played out in the streets. I came to doubt the virtues of intimidation early on. I chose, perhaps even unconsciously, to remain a shadow—timid, but a survivor.

The fearsomeness mistakenly attributed to me in public places often 10 has a perilous flavor. The most frightening of these confusions occurred in the late 1970s and early 1980s when I worked as a journalist in Chicago. One day, rushing into the office of a magazine I was writing for with a deadline story in hand, I was mistaken for a burglar. The office manager called security and, with an ad hoc posse, pursued me through the labyrinthine halls, nearly to my editor's door. I had no way of proving who I was. I could only move briskly toward the company of someone who knew me.

Another time I was on assignment for a local paper and killing time 11 before an interview. I entered a jewelry store on the city's affluent Near North Side. The proprietor excused herself and returned with an enormous red Doberman pinscher straining at the end of a leash. She stood, the dog extended toward me, silent to my questions, her eyes bulging nearly out of her head. I took a cursory look around, nodded, and bade her good night. Relatively speaking, however, I never fared as badly as another black male journalist. He went to nearby Waukegan, Illinois, a couple of summers ago to work on a story about a murderer who was born there. Mistaking the reporter for the killer, police hauled him from his car at gunpoint and but for his press credentials would probably have tried to book him. Such episodes are not uncommon. Black men trade tales like this all the time.

In "My Negro Problem—And Ours," Podhoretz writes that the hatred 12 he feels for blacks makes itself known to him through a variety of avenues— one being his discomfort with that "special brand of paranoid touchiness" to which he says blacks are prone. No doubt he is speaking here of black men. In time, I learned to smother the rage I felt at so often being taken for a criminal. Not to do so would surely have led to madness—via that special "paranoid touchiness" that so annoyed Podhoretz at the time he wrote the essay.

I began to take precautions to make myself less threatening. I move 13 about with care, particularly late in the evening. I give a wide berth to nervous people on subway platforms during the wee hours, particularly when I

have exchanged business clothes for jeans. If I happen to be entering a building behind some people who appear skittish, I may walk by, letting them
clear the lobby before I return, so as not to seem to be following them. I
have been calm and extremely congenial on those rare occasions when I've
been pulled over by the police.

And on late-evening constitutionals along streets less traveled by, I em- 14
ploy what has proved to be an excellent tension-reducing measure: I whistle
melodies from Beethoven and Vivaldi and the more popular classical composers. Even steely New Yorkers hunching toward nighttime destinations
seem to relax, and occasionally they even join in the tune. Virtually everybody seems to sense that a mugger wouldn't be warbling bright, sunny selections from Vivaldi's *Four Seasons*. It is my equivalent of the cowbell that
hikers wear when they know they are in bear country.

QUESTIONS ABOUT THE RHETORICAL SITUATION

1. Staples' essay first appeared in *Ms.* magazine, a magazine directed to
   women readers. Later it was reprinted in *Harper's* magazine, a magazine
   directed to an audience of both men and women. Is the essay more appropriate to one group of readers or another? Why? Why would a wom-
   en's magazine publish this essay?
2. How did you react to reading Staples' essay? What do you think he
   wanted his readers to get out of reading his essay?
3. Once again, we see a writer who probably has every right to feel angry
   about his experiences, yet Staples does not sound angry. What attitude
   has Staples adopted toward his subject? Is his anger a thing of the past?

QUESTIONS ABOUT THE ESSAY'S VOICE

1. How effective is Staples' opening paragraph? What did you think his essay would be about? What was your response to that opening paragraph?
   Does his voice change after that introductory paragraph?
2. After more than ten years of observations, Staples has formed a generalization about his experiences (¶2). How convincing do you find his generalization?
3. Staples' essay relies upon vivid details and examples to make its point.
   (Note the use of sound imagery in ¶3 to make the scene come alive.) Why
   then does he summarize so much material at the end of ¶3 instead of offering further details and examples? How effective is this strategy?
4. Throughout his essay, Staples makes a number of connections between
   his own firsthand experiences as a pedestrian and his childhood, the experiences of others, two essays written by white writers, the feelings of

frightened pedestrians. What is the effect on his voice of all of these connections?

5. Why does Staples spend so much time discussing "young thugs" (¶7–9)? How necessary to his essay is this section? What would be the result of his omitting these explanations?

6. Why does he focus so strongly on the essays by Norman Podhoretz and Edward Hoagland? What does this add to his essay?

7. In ¶6, Staples discusses his own feelings about being feared by other pedestrians. He then returns to those feelings in the final two paragraphs of the essay. What is the significance of his final sentence? What does it say about the depth of his emotions?

TOPICS TO WRITE ABOUT

1. Write an essay about your own experiences with prejudice and what you have learned about others and about yourself as a result. (Prejudice, unfortunately, is widespread and is not restricted to race. Harmful stereotypes also exist about various religions and ethnic groups, for example. But similar harmful stereotypes and prejudices also exist about students who study a great deal, athletic students, students interested in computers, people who are extraordinarily good-looking, librarians, teachers, construction workers, weightlifters, soldiers.) POTENTIAL AUDIENCES: readers who are likely to be prejudiced themselves/readers who may have been unaware of this particular form of prejudice. POTENTIAL PURPOSES: to explain to them how victims of their prejudice feel about being victimized/to make them aware that such prejudice exists.

2. Write an essay in which you analyze some form of public behavior, explaining its significance. (For instance, you might discuss how people behave on elevators or at shopping malls or in their cars as they try to merge onto the highway or at the university library.) POTENTIAL AUDIENCES: either a women's or men's magazine/your local Sunday newspaper. POTENTIAL PURPOSES: to explain your gender's viewpoint on either male or female behavior/to explain some recognizable local behavior to those who may not have paid close attention to it before.

Prologue to *A Rumor of War*
Philip Caputo

Philip Caputo, a novelist and journalist, served in Vietnam as an infantry officer and later as a news correspondent. His most recent book is a novel entitled *Horn of Africa*, a story of mercenary soldiers in Ethiopia. *A Rumor of War*
(1977) is his story of his time in the Vietnam war. A best-seller, the book takes
its title from the Book of Matthew (24:6–13):

> And ye shall hear of wars and rumors of wars. See that ye be not
> troubled, for all these things must come to pass, but the end is not
> yet....For nation shall rise against nation and kingdom against
> kingdom...Then shall they deliver you up to be afflicted and shall
> put you to death...but he that shall endure unto the end, he shall be
> saved.

In this excerpt from the book, the Prologue, Caputo offers some explanation of
what the war experience was like for those who fought in Vietnam.

QUESTIONS ABOUT IDEAS

1. Both those who supported the American involvement in Vietnam and
   those who opposed it considered themselves patriotic. In what sense
   could they both be right? Or is that contradictory?
2. Caputo's feelings about the war are complex. He fought in it; he fought
   against it. And he wanted to return to it afterward. Do his reactions to
   the war surprise you? Why or why not?
3. To what extent do you think Caputo's observations about the Vietnam
   War are probably true of most wars? to what extent are they true only of
   this particular war?

*In thy faint slumbers I by thee have watch'd And heard thee murmur tales of iron
wars....*

—Shakespeare
Henry IV, Part I

   This book does not pretend to be history. It has nothing to do with   1
politics, power, strategy, influence, national interests, or foreign policy; nor
is it an indictment of the great men who led us into Indochina and whose
mistakes were paid for with the blood of some quite ordinary men. In a general sense, it is simply a story about war, about the things men do in war and
the things war does to them. More strictly, it is a soldier's account of our

longest conflict, the only one we have ever lost, as well as the record of a long and sometimes painful personal experience.

On March 8, 1965, as a young infantry officer, I landed at Danang 2 with a battalion of the 9th Marine Expeditionary Brigade, the first U.S. combat unit sent to Indochina. I returned in April 1975 as a newspaper correspondent and covered the Communist offensive that ended with the fall of Saigon. Having been among the first Americans to fight in Vietnam, I was also among the last to be evacuated, only a few hours before the North Vietnamese Army entered the capital.

Although most of this book deals with the experiences of the marines I 3 served with in 1965 and 1966, I have included an epilogue briefly describing the American exodus. Only ten years separated the two events, yet the humiliation of our exit from Vietnam, compared to the high confidence with which we had entered, made it seem as if a century lay between them.

For Americans who did not come of age in the early sixties, it may be 4 hard to grasp what those years were like—the pride and overpowering self-assurance that prevailed. Most of the thirty-five hundred men in our brigade, born during or immediately after World War II, were shaped by that era, the age of Kennedy's Camelot. We went overseas full of illusions, for which the intoxicating atmosphere of those years was as much to blame as our youth.

War is always attractive to young men who know nothing about it, but 5 we had also been seduced into uniform by Kennedy's challenge to "ask what you can do for your country" and by the missionary idealism he had awakened in us. America seemed omnipotent then: the country could still claim it had never lost a war, and we believed we were ordained to play cop to the Communists' robber and spread our own political faith around the world. Like the French soldiers of the late eighteenth century, we saw ourselves as the champions of "a cause that was destined to triumph." So, when we marched into the rice paddies on that damp March afternoon, we carried, along with our packs and rifles, the implicit convictions that the Viet Cong would be quickly beaten and that we were doing something altogether noble and good. We kept the packs and rifles; the convictions, we lost.

The discovery that the men we had scorned as peasant guerrillas were, 6 in fact, a lethal, determined enemy and the casualty lists that lengthened each week with nothing to show for the blood being spilled broke our early confidence. By autumn, what had begun as an adventurous expedition had turned into an exhausting, indecisive war of attrition in which we fought for no cause other than our own survival.

Writing about this kind of warfare is not a simple task. Repeatedly, I 7 have found myself wishing that I had been the veteran of a conventional war, with dramatic campaigns and historic battles for subject matter instead of a monotonous succession of ambushes and fire-fights. But there were no Normandies or Gettysburgs for us, no epic clashes that decided the fates of armies or nations. The war was mostly a matter of enduring weeks of expectant waiting and, at random intervals, of conducting vicious manhunts through jungles and swamps where snipers harassed us constantly and booby traps cut us down one by one.

The tedium was occasionally relieved by a large-scale search- 8 and-destroy operation, but the exhilaration of riding the lead helicopter into a landing zone was usually followed by more of the same hot walking, with the mud sucking at our boots and the sun thudding against our helmets while an invisible enemy shot at us from distant tree lines. The rare instances when the VC chose to fight a set-piece battle provided the only excitement; not ordinary excitement, but the manic ecstasy of contact. Weeks of bottled-up tensions would be released in a few minutes of orgiastic violence, men screaming and shouting obscenities above the explosions of grenades and the rapid, rippling bursts of automatic rifles.

Beyond adding a few more corpses to the weekly body count, none of 9 these encounters achieved anything; none will ever appear in military histories or be studied by cadets at West Point. Still, they changed us and taught us, the men who fought in them; in those obscure skirmishes we learned the old lessons about fear, cowardice, courage, suffering, cruelty, and comradeship. Most of all, we learned about death at an age when it is common to think of oneself as immortal. Everyone loses that illusion eventually, but in civilian life it is lost in installments over the years. We lost it all at once and, in the span of months, passed from boyhood through manhood to a premature middle age. The knowledge of death, of the implacable limits placed on a man's existence, severed us from our youth as irrevocably as a surgeon's scissors had once severed us from the womb. And yet, few of us were past twenty-five. We left Vietnam peculiar creatures, with young shoulders that bore rather old heads.

My own departure took place in early July 1966. Ten months later, 10 following a tour as the CO of an infantry training company in North Carolina, an honorable discharge released me from the Marines. I felt as happy as a condemned man whose sentence has been commuted, but within a year I began growing nostalgic for the war.

Other veterans I knew confessed to the same emotion. In spite of ev- 11 erything, we felt a strange attachment to Vietnam and, even stranger, a longing to return. The war was still being fought, but this desire to go back did not spring from any patriotic ideas about duty, honor, and sacrifice, the myths with which old men send young men off to get killed or maimed. It arose, rather, from a recognition of how deeply we had been changed, how different we were from everyone who had not shared with us the miseries of the monsoon, the exhausting patrols, the fear of a combat assault on a hot landing zone. We had very little in common with them. Though we were civilians again, the civilian world seemed alien. We did not belong to it as much as we did to that other world, where we had fought and our friends had died.

I was involved in the antiwar movement at the time and struggled, un- 12 successfully, to reconcile my opposition to the war with this nostalgia. Later, I realized a reconciliation was impossible; I would never be able to hate the war with anything like the undiluted passion of my friends in the movement. Because I had fought in it, it was not an abstract issue, but a deeply emotional experience, the most significant thing that had happened to me. It held my thoughts, senses, and feelings in an unbreakable embrace. I would hear in thunder the roar of artillery. I could not listen to rain without recalling those drenched nights on the line, nor walk through woods without instinctively searching for a trip wire or an ambush. I could protest as loudly as the most convinced activist, but I could not deny the grip the war had on me, nor the fact that it had been an experience as fascinating as it was repulsive, as exhilarating as it was sad, as tender as it was cruel.

This book is partly an attempt to capture something of its ambivalent 13 realities. Anyone who fought in Vietnam, if he is honest about himself, will have to admit he enjoyed the compelling attractiveness of combat. It was a peculiar enjoyment because it was mixed with a commensurate pain. Under fire, a man's powers of life heightened in proportion to the proximity of death, so that he felt an elation as extreme as his dread. His senses quickened, he attained an acuity of consciousness at once pleasurable and excruciating. It was something like the elevated state of awareness induced by drugs. And it could be just as addictive, for it made whatever else life offered in the way of delights or torments seem pedestrian.

I have also attempted to describe the intimacy of life in infantry bat- 14 talions, where the communion between men is as profound as any between lovers. Actually, it is more so. It does not demand for its sustenance the reciprocity, the pledges of affection, the endless reassurances required by the love of men and women. It is, unlike marriage, a bond that cannot be broken by a word, by boredom or divorce, or by anything other than death. Sometimes even that is not strong enough. Two friends of mine died trying to save the corpses of their men from the battlefield. Such devotion, simple and selfless, the sentiment of belonging to each other, was the one decent thing we found in a conflict otherwise notable for its monstrosities.

And yet, it was a tenderness that would have been impossible if the 15 war had been significantly less brutal. The battlefields of Vietnam were a crucible in which a generation of American soldiers were fused together by a common confrontation with death and a sharing of hardships, dangers, and fears. The very ugliness of the war, the sordidness of our daily lives, the degradation of having to take part in body counts made us draw still closer to one another. It was as if in comradeship we found an affirmation of life and the means to preserve at least a vestige of our humanity.

There is also the aspect of the Vietnam War that distinguished it from 16
other American conflicts—its absolute savagery. I mean the savagery that
prompted so many American fighting men—the good, solid kids from Iowa
farms—to kill civilians and prisoners. The final chapter of this book concen-
trates on this subject. My purpose has not been to confess complicity in
what, for me, amounted to murder, but, using myself and a few other men
as examples, to show that war, by its nature, can arouse a psychopathic violence in men of seemingly normal impulses.

There has been a good deal of exaggeration about U.S. atrocities in 17
Vietnam, exaggeration not about their extent but about their causes. The
two most popularly held explanations for outrages like My Lai have been the
racist theory, which proposes that the American soldier found it easy to
slaughter Asians because he did not regard them as human beings, and the
frontier-heritage theory, which claims he was inherently violent and needed
only the excuse of war to vent his homicidal instincts.

Like all generalizations, each contains an element of truth; yet both 18
ignore the barbarous treatment the Viet Cong and ARVN often inflicted on
their own people, and neither confront the crimes committed by the Korean
division, probably the most bloody-minded in Vietnam, and by the French
during the first Indochina war.

The evil was inherent not in the men—except in the sense that a devil 19
dwells in us all—but in the circumstances under which they had to live and
fight. The conflict in Vietnam combined the two most bitter forms of warfare, civil war and revolution, to which was added the ferocity of jungle war.
Twenty years of terrorism and fratricide had obliterated most reference
points from the country's moral map long before we arrived. Communists
and government forces alike considered ruthlessness a necessity if not a virtue. Whether committed in the name of principles or out of vengeance,
atrocities were as common to the Vietnamese battlefields as shell craters and
barbed wire. The marines in our brigade were not innately cruel, but on
landing in Danang they learned rather quickly that Vietnam was not a place
where a man could expect much mercy if, say, he was taken prisoner. And
men who do not expect to receive mercy eventually lose their inclination to
grant it.

At times, the comradeship that was the war's only redeeming quality 20
caused some of its worst crimes—acts of retribution for friends who had
been killed. Some men could not withstand the stress of guerrilla-fighting:
the hair-trigger alertness constantly demanded of them, the feeling that the
enemy was everywhere, the inability to distinguish civilians from combat-
ants created emotional pressures which built to such a point that a trivial
provocation could make these men explode with the blind destructiveness of
a mortar shell.

Others were made pitiless by an overpowering greed for survival. Self- 21
preservation, that most basic and tyrannical of all instincts, can turn a man

into a coward or, as was more often the case in Vietnam, into a creature who destroys without hesitation or remorse whatever poses even a potential threat to his life. A sergeant in my platoon, ordinarily a pleasant young man, told me once, "Lieutenant, I've got a wife and two kids at home and I'm going to see 'em again and don't care who I've got to kill or how many of 'em to do it."

General Westmoreland's strategy of attrition also had an important ef- 22 fect on our behavior. Our mission was not to win terrain or seize positions, but simply to kill: to kill Communists and to kill as many of them as possible. Stack 'em like cordwood. Victory was high body-count, defeat a low kill-ratio, war a matter of arithmetic. The pressure on unit commanders to produce enemy corpses was intense, and they in turn communicated it to their troops. This led to such practices as counting civilians as Viet Cong. "If it's dead and Vietnamese, it's VC," was a rule of thumb in the bush. It is not surprising, therefore, that some men acquired a contempt for human life and a predilection for taking it.

Finally, there were the conditions imposed by the climate and country. 23 For weeks we had to live like primitive men on remote outposts rimmed by alien seas of rice paddies and rain forests. Malaria, blackwater fever, and dysentery, though not the killers they had been in past wars, took their toll. The sun scorched us in the dry season, and in the monsoon season we were pounded numb by ceaseless rain. Our days were spent hacking through mountainous jungles whose immensity reduced us to an antlike pettiness. At night we squatted in muddy holes, picked off the leeches that sucked on our veins, and waited for an attack to come rushing at us from the blackness beyond the perimeter wire.

The air-conditioned headquarters of Saigon and Danang seemed thou- 24 sands of miles away. As for the United States, we did not call it "the World" for nothing; it might as well have been on another planet. There was nothing familiar out where we were, no churches, no police, no laws, no newspapers, or any of the restraining influences without which the earth's population of virtuous people would be reduced by ninety-five percent. It was the dawn of creation in the Indochina bush, an ethical as well as a geographical wilderness. Out there, lacking restraints, sanctioned to kill, confronted by a hostile country and a relentless enemy, we sank into a brutish state. The descent could be checked only by the net of a man's inner moral values, the attribute that is called character. There were a few—and I suspect Lieutenant Calley was one—who had no net and plunged all the way down, discovering in their bottommost depths a capacity for malice they probably never suspected was there.

Most American soldiers in Vietnam—at least the ones I knew—could 25 not be divided into good men and bad. Each possessed roughly equal measures of both qualities. I saw men who behaved with great compassion toward the Vietnamese one day and then burned down a village the next. They were, as Kipling wrote of his Tommy Atkins, neither saints "nor black-guards too/But single men in barracks most remarkable like you." That may be why Americans reacted with such horror to the disclosures of U.S. atrocities while ignoring those of the other side: the American soldier was a reflection of themselves.

This book is not a work of the imagination. The events related are true, the characters real, though I have used fictitious names in some places. I have tried to describe accurately what the dominant event in the life of my generation, the Vietnam War, was like for the men who fought in it. Toward that end, I have made a great effort to resist the veteran's inclination to remember things the way he would like them to have been rather than the way they were.   26

Finally, this book ought not to be regarded as a protest. Protest arises from a belief that one can change things or influence events. I am not egotistical enough to believe I can. Besides, it no longer seems necessary to register an objection to the war, because the war is over. We lost it, and no amount of objecting will resurrect the men who died, without redeeming anything, on calvaries like Hamburger Hill and the Rockpile.   27

It might, perhaps, prevent the next generation from being crucified in the next war.   28

But I don't think so.   29

QUESTIONS ABOUT THE RHETORICAL SITUATION

1. In this essay, the opening chapter of his book about his Vietnam war experiences, Caputo is clearly addressing readers of his book. To whom is Caputo addressing himself in his book—other veterans? War protestors? Someone else? All of the foregoing? What are your reasons for your answer?
2. As Caputo himself insists, it does no good to object to a war that is long over. So why did he write this book? Why did he write this specific prologue to precede his book? What would you expect to read about in the remainder of *A Rumor of War?*
3. What might Benjamin Franklin's reaction be to Caputo's essay (based on your reading of "The Sale of the Hessians" in Chapter 4)?
4. What is surprising, if anything, to you about Caputo's attitude toward his subject? How do you think you would feel about the subject if you were he?

QUESTIONS ABOUT THE ESSAY'S VOICE

1. Caputo quotes Shakespeare and Kipling (¶25). Why does he do so instead of merely saying in his own words what he wanted to say? Why does

Caputo allude to Normandy and Gettysburg in ¶7? Why has he chosen those particular examples?

2. In ¶5, Caputo observes that "war is always attractive to young men who know nothing about it," one of a number of generalizations he makes about men and war. What other such observations can you locate in the essay? What is the effect on Caputo's voice of these generalizations?

3. Throughout the essay Caputo writes not in the first person singular (*I*), but in the first person plural (*we*). What is his purpose in choosing this strategy? How successful a tactic is this?

4. It would be understandable if Caputo were angry, yet his voice is quite calm. Does the anger ever surface? If so, where? Would the essay be more effective if it were calmer? Angrier?

5. Examine Caputo's use of analogies to explain himself (see the birth analogy in ¶9, the prison analogy in ¶10, the love analogy in ¶14). Which of these analogies is particularly effective in helping Caputo explain himself? Which most effectively establish his voice as that of an authority?

6. Which details used by Caputo most clearly convince you that he was indeed a foot soldier in Vietnam? Which, if any, of these details surprise you? Do these surprising details make Caputo a more or less convincing expert?

7. Paragraph 23 begins with the word *finally*. What train of thought does this paragraph conclude? How is this section of the essay clearly written in the voice of authority?

8. In ¶11, Caputo is writing about his life in two different worlds, much as Nell Painter did in "The Joys of Being Ordinary." Are Caputo's feelings about his two worlds essentially the same as Painter's feelings about her two worlds or are they essentially different? Why?

TOPICS TO WRITE ABOUT

1. Write an essay about an historical period of great stress in your life and the lives of other members of your generation (for example, living through the assassinations of John Kennedy, Martin Luther King, and Robert Kennedy, or living through the Watergate hearings and Richard Nixon's resignation, or living through the explosion of the *Challenger* space shuttle) and explain its significance to all of you. POTENTIAL AUDIENCES: readers of all generations/readers too young to remember the events. POTENTIAL PURPOSES: to offer your interpretation of the significance of the event/to educate the readers about this important period.

2. Write an essay in which you explain how you were changed by an experience you underwent, an experience typical for your age. POTENTIAL AUDIENCES: readers of your parents' generation/readers much younger than yourself. POTENTIAL PURPOSES: to help close the communications gap be-

tween the generations by offering some insight into your generation's behavior/to help them better understand some of the conflicts that they will encounter as they grow up.

What Is Statistics?

Derek Rowntree

Derek Rowntree has written a number of books on education. A teacher at the Open University in England, Rowntree has a degree in economics and a Certificate in Education and has taught in schools and colleges in England and Canada.

"What Is Statistics?" is an excerpt from Chapter 1 of Rowntree's 1981 book, *Statistics Without Tears: A Primer for Non-Mathematicians.* In the introduction to his book, Rowntree writes that from his chosen title readers may infer that his motivation is to save them "from the weeping (and/or wailing and/or gnashing of teeth) that is so often to be heard among students drawn willy-nilly into the study of statistics." In the following selection, Rowntree begins to explain the approach his book will take to this often daunting subject.

QUESTIONS ABOUT IDEAS

1. What role does statistics play in your chosen major? How important will it be for you to understand statistics in your field?
2. It has often been said that statistics can be used to prove anything. How does Rowntree's essay explain why that statement is meaningful?
3. *Model Voices,* along with other English textbooks, may be among the few textbooks you read that does not rely upon statistics to any great extent. How do you respond to the statistics in your other textbooks? How clearly and effectively do these textbooks present their statistics? How important is the rhetorical situation to the presentation of statistical information?

Before we go any further, we'd better take note, in passing, that the   1
word 'statistics' is used in at least four different senses. First of all, it can indicate, very broadly, a whole *subject* or *discipline,* and everything that gets studied or practiced in its name. Secondly, and more specifically, the term may refer to the *methods* used to collect or process or interpret quantitative

data. Thirdly, the term may be applied to *collections of data* gathered by those methods. And fourthly, it may refer to certain *specially calculated figures* (e.g. an average) that somehow characterize such a collection of data. Thus, to illustrate the four meanings in turn, a researcher in a firm's *statistics* department may use *statistics* (statistical methods) to gather and interpret *statistics* (data) about the revenue from sales of a new detergent, and may summarize his findings by quoting the *statistics* of 'average sales per thousand of population' in various towns and 'range of sales revenue from town to town.'

The meaning I shall emphasize in this book is the second of those mentioned above: statistics as a set of *methods of inquiry*. It is these methods that enable us to think statistically—a very powerful way to think—about a variety of situations that involve measurements or observations of quantities.   2

Statistical thinking (of one kind or another) has a long history. From earliest times, kings and governments have been collecting stat(e)istics about the population and resources of their states. The Domesday Book compiled for William the Conqueror is a comparatively recent example. Even the Old Testament mentions rulers, like the Pharaohs of ancient Egypt, who had a keen interest in data about how many people they had available to build pyramids or fight wars, and how much wealth they could conceivably squeeze out of them in taxation. Today, governments are the most prolific generators of statistics (in the sense of collections of data): on cost of living, unemployment, industrial production, birth-rates, imports and exports, etc. (See the *Statistical Abstracts of the United States,* several hundred pages of data produced by the government, or the equivalent publications in most other industrialized countries.)   3

Gamblers, too, have made an indispensable contribution to statistical thinking. To them, and their desire to 'figure out the odds' in games of chance, we owe the theory of probability. Such theory only began to develop in the seventeenth century, largely due to the interest aroused in the French mathematician, Blaise Pascal, by (so it is said) the problems posed by a dice-playing friend. The gambling table proved a good test-ground for a theory concerned with prediction, but probability theory soon began to reveal its explanatory and predictive powers in areas like astronomy, heredity and genetics, business, and even warfare.   4

Today, few professional activities are untouched by statistical thinking, and most academic disciplines use it to a greater or lesser degree. Its applications in science, especially the 'biological sciences' like genetics, medicine and psychology, are both numerous and well known. But the physical sciences (e.g. meteorology, engineering and physics) also need statistical methods. And even in the humanities, the dating of ancient fragments of textile or pottery has been revolutionized by the essentially statistical technique of radio-carbon dating; while statistical methods have also been used in literary studies to help decide such questions as whether a particular au-   5 thor wrote a certain work, or at what point in his lifetime it was written. Statistics has developed out of an aspect of our everyday thinking to become a ubiquitous tool of systematic research.

But it is time we got down to discussing what it is about statistical 6 thinking that can lend itself to such a variety of pursuits. Statistics arises out of caution in the face of uncertainty. Statistical thinking is a way of recognizing that our observations of the world can never be totally accurate; they are always somewhat uncertain. For instance, a child we record as being four feet in height will not be exactly that—somewhere between 3 feet 11½ inches and 4 feet ½ inch maybe, but not exactly four feet. And the chance of inaccuracy is even greater if we use our present observations to estimate what observations elsewhere might reveal. Thus, we might want to use our knowledge that four feet is the average height in this child's class to predict the average height in another class.

In such matters there can be no certainty. But statistics enables us to 7 estimate the extent of our errors. Thus, we may express near certainty that the child's height lies within a range of four feet plus or minus half an inch; or we may calculate that the chances are ninety-nine in a hundred that the average height in another class lies within two inches of four feet.

Statistics

You will find that statistics textbooks commonly make a distinction be- 8 tween (1) DESCRIPTIVE STATISTICS (methods used to summarize or describe our observations), and (2) INFERENTIAL STATISTICS (using those observations as a basis for making estimates or predictions, i.e. inferences about a situation that has not yet been observed).

Look again at those three 'everyday' statements I mentioned earlier. 9 Which of them appear(s) 'descriptive' and which 'inferential,' in the sense indicated above?

(i) 'On average, I cycle about 100 miles a week';

(ii) 'We can expect a lot of rain at this time of year';

(iii) 'The earlier you start reviewing, the better you are likely to do in the exam.'

Statement (i) is descriptive (an attempt to summarize experience), 10 while (ii) and (iii) go beyond what has been observed, in order to make inferences about what is likely to happen in the future.

The distinction between descriptive and inferential statistics depends 11 upon another: the distinction between *samples* and *populations*.

In statistical jargon, 'POPULATION' does not necessarily refer to a 12 body of people. It may refer to people, but it may equally well refer to white mice, to light-bulbs of a particular brand, to substandard dwellings in inner cities, to meteorites, to future examination results in secondary schools, and so on. The point is that population refers to *all* the cases or situations that the 'statistician' wants his inferences or guesses or estimates to apply to. Thus, different statisticians may be making inferences about the learning ability of (all) white mice; predicting how long (all) light-bulbs of a particular type are likely to burn; estimating the cost of renovating (all) substandard dwellings; predicting the composition of (all) meteorites; guessing the (total) numbers of candidates passing various examinations, and so on.

Perhaps it is also worth pointing out that the researcher will not be interested in every aspect of members of a population. Rather, he is interested in just some—maybe only one—of the many attributes or characteristics that members might have in common. Thus a psychologist may not be concerned to speculate about the tail-length or litter-size of white mice (though these characteristics might interest other researchers); he is interested simply in their learning ability. Neither might the astrophysicist be interested in predicting the geographical distribution or the size of falling meteorites as well as their composition. 13

However, even if he is interested in only one characteristic of his population, the researcher will be most unlikely to study all members of it. Usually he has to do the best he can with a SAMPLE—a relatively small selection—from within the population. Often he must do this to save time and expense. For the astrophysicist to tour the world inspecting every meteorite that has ever been known to fall would be prohibitively expensive. Again, an industrial researcher who is estimating the burning-life of a brand of light-bulb by 'testing to destruction' cannot test all the population or there will be none left to sell. 14

In some cases, it may be logically impossible to study all members of the population. The population may be infinite, or simply not yet available for study. Thus, the psychologist who is studying learning ability in white mice will hope his results, and therefore his inferences, will have some application to all white mice—not just the millions that exist at this moment but also the further millions not yet born. He may even hope his results can be generalized to explain *human* learning. Likewise, the astro-physicist may well use his statistics to generalize not just about the meteorites that have already fallen to earth, or even about those that will fall in the future; he may hope to speculate also about the composition of other objects flying around in space. 15

All such researchers go *beyond* the available information. They generalize from a sample to the population, from the seen to the unseen. (So do we all, though often in a rather careless, uncontrolled way, when using everyday 'common sense.') This idea of generalizing from a sample applies to research in the arts as well as in the sciences. For example, one would not need to have read everything ever written by, say, D. H. Lawrence and Joseph Conrad before one could begin generalizing about how they compared 16 and contrasted as novelists. One could work from a sample of two or three books by each author.

Anyway, *descriptive* statistics is concerned with summarizing or de- 17 scribing a sample. *Inferential* statistics is concerned with generalizing from a sample, to make estimates and inferences about a wider population. Consider a biologist experimenting with the feeding of chicks. He may report (using descriptive statistics) that a particular sample of 60 chicks, fed a particular compound, grow faster than a similar sample fed on some standard diet. So much (the weight gain) he reports as a fact. But he goes beyond the fact. He uses inferential statistics to suggest that *all* similar chicks (the wider population) would grow faster if given similar treatment.

How safe are such generalizations from a part to the whole? Well, that 18 is largely what statistics is about: quantifying the probability of error. We will be looking at the underlying ideas in subsequent chapters. One thing we can say at this stage, however: the reliability of the generalization will depend on how well the sample mirrors the population. Is the sample truly representative of the population?

QUESTIONS ABOUT THE RHETORICAL SITUATION

1. The subtitle of Rowntree's book refers to his audience as "non-mathematicians." What evidence is there in this essay of his awareness of his audience? If you are a nonmathematician, how clear was this essay? If you are a mathematician, to what degree did you find Rowntree explaining concepts that you already understood?
2. What would you assume the purpose of this chapter to be? Rowntree has already written a three-page introduction to his book. In what sense is this selection a second introduction? What would you expect to find next in his book? How is Rowntree's opening chapter similar to and different from Philip Caputo's Prologue to *A Rumor of War?*
3. Rowntree probably never wept or wailed or gnashed his teeth over a statistics course. How would you describe his attitude toward his subject? How does this attitude affect his voice? How effective is his attitude in making this selection achieve its purpose?
4. How suitable would Rowntree's book be in a statistics course, based on your reading of this opening chapter? Why?

QUESTIONS ABOUT THE ESSAY'S VOICE

1. Take a close look at the examples Rowntree uses. Why does he choose examples of this type? (See ¶6, ¶16 for example.)

2. Throughout his chapter, Rowntree makes use of italics to emphasize specific words and phrases. What pattern is there to the words and phrases he singles out?

3. What purpose has Rowntree in addressing a question directly to his reader (see ¶9)? How does this question help to establish Rowntree's voice as an authority?

4. In his chapter, Rowntree writes in the first-person singular, the first-person plural, and the second person (*I, we, you*). Is there any pattern to the use of these pronouns? What is the effect on the voice of this approach?

5. In ¶1, Rowntree defines *statistics* by offering four definitions. Why doesn't he simply offer the single definition he plans to use in his book (as he explains in ¶2)? Is he simply showing off his expertise at this point?

6. Since he has already defined statistics in ¶1, why does Rowntree continue, in ¶3–4, to discuss the history of statistics?

7. Notice how Rowntree defines descriptive and inferential statistics: he offers a short definition (¶8), uses examples to illustrate the distinctions between descriptive and inferential statistics (¶12–15), and concludes by defining the two concepts again in terms of how they are used (¶17). Why does he spend so much time and use so many strategies to define these two terms? How is his strategy here similar to his earlier approach to defining the entire science of statistics (¶1–4)?

TOPICS TO WRITE ABOUT

1. Write an essay in which you define something rather technical from your major field of study or from your own work experience (for example, you might define tensile strength if you are a mechanical engineer or amortization if you are an accounting major or the Petrarchan sonnet if you are an English major or framing a new house if you work on a construction site or Pascal if you are a systems analysis or computer major). POTENTIAL AUDIENCE: nonexperts from outside your field of interest. POTENTIAL PURPOSE: to explain an unfamiliar technical concept to them.

2. Write an essay in which you explain the distinctions between two or more related concepts. (For example, you might explain the differences between the hit-and-run play, the sacrifice bunt, and the straight steal as means of advancing runners in a baseball game. Or you might explain the differences among Cape Cods, split levels, and bilevel floor plans for new homes. Or you might explain the differences between a crèpe and a pancake or between a fracture and a broken bone. Or you might discuss the various meanings of the word *romance*.) POTENTIAL AUDIENCES: readers who know something already about the subject/the general reading pub-

lic. POTENTIAL PURPOSES: to show them some of the more subtle and complex differences/to explain the basic and significant distinctions between
the things you are describing.

Review of *The Color Purple*

Pauline Kael

Pauline Kael has been a film critic for many years. Her reviews have appeared
regularly in the *New Yorker* magazine since 1968. She has also published several collections of her reviews including *I Lost It at the Movies, When the Lights
Go Down,* and *5001 Nights at the Movies.* Kael won the National Book Award
for arts and letters for her 1974 collection *Deeper into Movies* and has received
more than half a dozen honorary degrees from American universities. Perhaps
the most highly regarded film critic in the United States, Kael has also won the
Newswomen's Club of New York Front Page Award for Distinguished Journalism (1983).

The *Color Purple* (1985) was a much-honored film directed by Steven Spiel-
berg, based on the highly regarded novel of the same name by Alice Walker.
Kael's review of *The Color Purple* appeared in December 1985 in the *New
Yorker.*

QUESTIONS ABOUT IDEAS

1. Critics frequently compare works of art to other works of art, sometimes
   in a different medium. Is this a helpful approach to discussing Spielberg's
   film in this review? How appropriate is this technique? Might it be argued that works of art are not meant to compete with one another?
2. What similarities do you see between Kael's role as a critic of Spielberg's
   film and your instructor's role in responding to your writing in this
   course? What differences do you see? What is the significance of these
   similarities and differences?
3. Film director Stanley Kubrick, who directed *A Clockwork Orange, The
   Shining,* and *Full Metal Jacket,* recently commented about film critics, "I
   wouldn't like to have to write an appreciation of a movie that I liked,
   because I think it's so elusive, and the things that critics are forced to
   do—make connections and conceptualizations of it—seem at best minor,
   and at worst fairly irrelevant to what seems almost inexpressibly beautiful
   about the movie." Kubrick was speaking of a positive review. How,
   based on his observation, do you think he would respond to this largely
   uncomplimentary review?

During the making of *The Color Purple*, Steven Spielberg's version of   1
the Alice Walker novel about black women's lives in the South in the first
half of the century, the advance publicity suggested that he was attempting
something "serious." But when you see the movie you realize that he was
probably attracted by Walker's childlike heroine, Celie, and the book's lyr-
ical presentation of the healing power of love. He may not have understood
this, because he approaches the material with undue timidity. It's no wonder
the novel was popular. On the first page, the fourteen-year-old black drudge
Celie is raped by the man she believes to be her father. She gives birth to two
children by this brute; he takes the babies away, and she has no idea what he
has done with them. Tired of her, he forces her to marry another brute—a
widowed farmer who needs her to take care of his children. This man uses
her sexually and beats her. When her younger sister, Nettie—the only person who cares for her and doesn't think she's ugly—runs away from the rap-
ing father and comes to stay with her, her husband makes advances to Nettie
and, when Nettie fights him, throws her off the property. Poor Celie toils
on, with never a kind word coming her way, until her husband brings home
Shug Avery, a honky-tonk singer—his true love and sometime mistress—
who is sick and needs care. Celie falls in love with the raucous, gutsy Shug
(short for "sugar"), and Shug, seeing Celie's true worth, makes love to her.
It's the turning point of Celie's life: after experiencing sexual pleasure, she
becomes confident of her self-worth, goes out into the world, and returns to
make a success of herself running a small business.

But *The Color Purple* isn't just the story of Celie; it's an extended-   2
family saga spanning generations and two continents. (The cast-out Nettie
has gone to Africa, with a missionary couple.) The novel is about the bond-
ing of the generous, artistically gifted, understanding black women (no matter how worn down they are, they never speak a harsh word to a child). It's
also about the insensitivity, cowardice, and meanness of the black men
(Nettie is able to brief us on how the men oppress the women in Africa, too).
The glue that holds it all together is a pop-folk religiosity that also serves to
keep the book's anti-male attitudes in check. Walker allows some of the
lazy, lecherous oppressors to redeem themselves by accepting their inferiority to their wives and developing their aptitudes for cooking and sewing. So the many characters all come together for a series of reconciliation
scenes.

Probably Alice Walker gets by with so much rampant female chauvin-   3
ism because it's put in the mouth of her battered fourteen-year-old heroine.
The book—or, rather, the best part of it, roughly the first third—is made up
of Celie's letters to God, which are written in a raw, cadenced dialect, an
artful version of a rural near-illiterate's black English. The book has a joyous
emotional swing to it, and this swing can carry a reader right through inspi-
rational passages such as the one where Shug teaches Celie that God is inside
her and inside everybody else, that everything wants to be loved and "it

pisses God off if you walk by the color purple in a field somewhere and don't notice it."

Spielberg has been quoted in the *Times* as being worried about "doing   4
a movie about *people* for the first time in my career," and fearing that he'll be "accused of not having the sensibility to do character studies." But the Walker material has about as much to do with character studies as Disney's *Song of the South* did. Spielberg's *The Color Purple* is probably the least authentic in feeling of any of his full-length films; the people on the screen are like characters operated by Frank Oz. But they're not much phonier than the people in the book: Spielberg's problem is that he can't give the material the emotional push of that earthy folk style of Walker's. He just doesn't have the conviction that she has.

Spielberg's version comes from a man who filters everything through   5
movies. He sees Georgia in 1909 the way a European director might; visually, the picture suggests *Song of the South* remade by Visconti. When Celie (played in the early scenes by Desreta Jackson and then by Whoopi Goldberg) and Nettie (Akosua Busia) do their jive talk—clapping their hands in fast, intricate rhythms as they chant—it seems to be going on in a faraway, magical kingdom, in a field of pink flowers from the florists who supplied the daffodils for David Lean's *Doctor Zhivago.* Spielberg has all this facile, pretty camera technique, but he can't find an appropriate tone, and so the incidents don't click into place. The movie is muffled, bombed out, and a gooey score by Quincy Jones calls attention to the emotional void—Jones seems to have been waiting all his life to metamorphose into Max Steiner.

Spielberg soft-pedals the lesbian side of the Celie and Shug romance,   6
and the men may be more buffoonish than they are in the book and so less threatening, but he has tried to be faithful to Walker. This doesn't do the movie a lot of good. Working from a script (by Menno Meyjes) that hasn't reshaped the novel into a dramatic structure, Spielberg has trouble getting about two dozen characters in and out of the action, which spans some thirty years. (Performances, such as Rae Dawn Chong's as Squeak—Celie's stepson's mistress, who wants to be a singer—have obviously been truncated.) A scene of several women standing on Celie's porch is the worst piece of staging this director ever dreamed up. It tops even the crowd scene where the people singing outside a church converge with the people singing inside—a jubilee that reminds you of fire drills in junior high. And this is the only film that Spielberg has ever made where the editing looks to be from desperation. The crosscutting between Nettie's experiences in Africa and Celie's life back home is staggeringly ineffective. In one sequence, we hop back and forth between Celie, who has just learned of her husband's full treachery to her and picks up a straight razor to shave him, and Shug, who is at a distance and starts running to the house because she intuits that Celie is about to cut his throat, and Nettie in Africa dashing to a ritual of initiation where children are to have their faces incised. The passage rivals the famous parody of

editing in *The Apprenticeship of Duddy Kravitz,* where Denholm Elliott played a drunken filmmaker who, having been hired by a father to record his son's bar mitzvah, got carried away with his art and intercut the gathering with bloody primitive rites. (Spielberg's African ritual may even be a first on film: a coed tribal initiation.)

Except for the dimpled Oprah Winfrey as the powerhouse Sofia, whose 7 mighty punch at a white man lands her in jail for twelve years, the performers don't make a very strong impression. Whoopi Goldberg's Celie may be little less "real" than the title character in *E.T.,* but, given the conception of Celie—who has to be meek and then discover her power—she does a respectable job. (If we feel a letdown when she takes over from Desreta Jackson's teen-age Celie, it's because Jackson is warmer and more open to the camera.) Willard Pugh is likable and peppy as Celie's stepson, who keeps falling through roofs, and Danny Glover, in the difficult role of the husband who slaps her around, probably does as well as anybody could with material such as the stupid comedy routine where he proves the ineptitude of men by trying to prepare a meal for the bedridden Shug and burning everything. (It's the kind of humiliation that Katharine Hepburn went through long ago in *Woman of the Year;* it's no less offensive when the sexual tables are turned.) As Shug, Margaret Avery is in a tough spot, because of all the press attention to Tina Turner's being offered the role and turning it down. (You can't help imagining how Turner might have played it.) Margaret Avery makes a terrific entrance, grinning, with a jagged front tooth sticking out, and she looks great singing in a glittering red dress in a juke joint. (She's dubbed by Tata Vega.) But then an awful thing happens, which has to be at least partly the director's fault: she plays the rest of her scenes in a refined, contemporary manner that dulls out all interest in Shug. If you're among the millions of people who have read the book, you probably expect the actors to be more important than they turn out to be. The movie is amorphous; it's a pastoral about the triumph of the human spirit, and it blurs on you.

QUESTIONS ABOUT THE RHETORICAL SITUATION

1. What assumptions about her readers does Kael make? To what extent is she writing for serious filmgoers? To what extent would her essay be understandable to readers who do not see many movies? To what extent is she counting on her readers' familiarity with the technical side of moviemaking?

2. What evidence is there that Kael is writing about a firsthand experience that she has had but that she assumes the reader has not (that is, she has already seen the film; her readers have not)? Is the review just as effective now that many readers have seen the film? Why did you answer as you did?

3. Read "Beyond *The Color Purple*" in Chapter 12. How do you think Margaret Avery would reply to Kael's review?
4. Reviewers often get personal in their reviews, sometimes reviewing a great film as if the director had deliberately given them a gift, or, more often, writing about a bad film as if it were a personal insult directed at them. To what extent is Kael's attitude toward the film a personal one? How fair has she been in her criticism and praise?
5. Reviewing is one type of authoritative writing that has a clearly understood purpose: it is designed to advise readers about whether or not to experience the work of art being reviewed. Does Kael want her readers to see the film or to stay away from it? How can you tell?

QUESTIONS ABOUT THE ESSAY'S VOICE

1. The essay's style is quite noticeable. What is the effect of the very long paragraphs on the essay's voice?
2. How is the voice affected by some of Kael's other stylistic tactics: her heavy use of parentheses, colons, and dashes?
3. Kael's vocabulary is varied: she uses words like "truncated," "intuits," and "incised," but she also says the film's incidents "don't click into place," "Nettie is able to brief us...." and "the movie is muffled, bombed out...." She also writes the review in the second person. How effective are all of these choices together? Does the essay's voice seem consistent enough?
4. Kael establishes herself as a firsthand authority largely by referring to related films as well as the novel; she has clearly seen many movies and read the book. How effectively does Kael establish herself as qualified to offer an intelligent opinion of the film? To what extent are all of these references necessary? Does the essay rely too heavily on them? Or do they successfully assist Kael in explaining her view of the film?
5. How well does Kael fulfill the primary objective of a reviewer—to inform the reader of her opinion along with a clear explanation of that opinion? Where in the review is she explaining her opinion of the film? Many film reviewers assign a rating to a film: for instance, five stars for excellent, going down to one star for terrible. How many stars do you think Kael's review is assigning to *The Color Purple?*
6. How well does Kael fulfill the secondary objective of a reviewer—to present the reader with a clear picture of what the work being reviewed is like, what it is about? Based on this review, do you know enough about *The Color Purple* to determine if it is the type of film you might wish to see?

TOPICS TO WRITE ABOUT

1. Write a review of a film or TV show or book. POTENTIAL AUDIENCES: the readers of a specific newspaper or popular magazine. POTENTIAL PURPOSE: to help the readers decide whether to see the film or TV show or read the book.
2. Write a review of a something other than a work of art, such as an automobile, a restaurant, a vacation resort, a stereo system. (The objectives of the review will remain the same: to express an opinion clearly and to give the reader a clear sense of what the subject being reviewed is like.) POTENTIAL AUDIENCES: the readers of a specific newspaper or popular magazine. POTENTIAL PURPOSE: to help the readers decide whether to try the product or location.

Mark Twain and Bret Harte: Social Critics
Karen Stubbs

Karen Stubbs wrote this essay for a survey course in American Literature. A student at Miami University's Middletown campus, Stubbs majored in English and Library Sciences with a minor in Anthropology and planned a teaching career. She now lives in Camden, Ohio, with her husband and two children.

Stubbs says writing is always "frustrating" to her, this essay proving to be "particularly troublesome."

"Despite spending a good bit of time formulating the essay in my mind before even attempting to corral it on paper," she says, "this essay still required extensive revision....I ended up with at least eight drafts of this paper before I was finished." She notes that when she reread the essay a year after writing it, she noticed further revisions that she would like to make. "But then I never seem to be entirely finished with any writing that I do," she says.

QUESTIONS ABOUT IDEAS

1. How recognizable are the social types and problems identified in this essay in our modern day society?
2. Assuming that you have read "The Outcasts of Poker Flat" (see Section Five of *Model Voices*) and *Huckleberry Finn*, to what extent does this essay add to your appreciation and understanding of those two literary works?

3. What does Stubbs gain by discussing both stories in the same essay instead of writing two separate essays, one on each literary work?

Both Mark Twain, in *Adventures of Huckleberry Finn*, and Bret Harte, 1
in "The Outcasts of Poker Flat" deal with the serious issue of moral and
social responsibility. Distinct similarities exist in the authors' respective efforts to expose elements of society as tragically cruel and unjust. In a general
sense, the same society which unrestrainedly condones slavery in the novel
also piously exiles the outcasts in the short story. Both authors incisively
criticize the cultural institutions which tend to classify human beings on a
cursory and inequitable basis. In addition, both authors place their characters in precarious positions in which decisions dealing with moral responsibility ultimately decide their fate.

Twain's character, Huck, and Harte's character, Mr. Oakhurst exhibit 2
many corresponding qualities. They both appear to be loners, alienated from
other members of a society in which they are forced to exist. Even as Huck
attempts to conform to the standards of Widow Douglas, he remains exiled
by his loneliness. "I [Huck] felt so lonesome I most wished I was dead"
(p.28). Oakhurst pauses to reflect on "...the loneliness begotten of his [Oak-
hurst's] pariah-trade, his habits of life, his very vices..." (p.271).

These two loners of seemingly unconscionable reputation are unlikely 3
heroes, yet heroes they are in responding to the stimulus of their respective
intuitions. They both possess a great capacity to sympathize with the suffering of others, even those with whom they are not intimately acquainted.
Huck cannot bear the sight of a slave auction and states—"I can't ever get it
out of my memory, the sight of them poor miserable girls and niggers hanging round each others necks and crying..." (p.171). Oakhurst's simple
kind-heartedness is evidenced in his seeking to alleviate the physical discomfort of the Duchess. As a gesture of concern, Oakhurst insists upon
"...exchanging his own riding-horse, 'Five Spot', for the sorry mule which
the Duchess rode" (p.270).

Huck, although suffering considerably from self-condemnation, sub- 4
mits to a moral decision not to turn Jim in as an escaped slave—"All right,
then, I'll *go* to hell..." (p.193), he says. The motivation stems from his
heart and he refuses to propitiate a conscience ruled by the accepted code of
the ante-bellum South. Rather than yielding to the guise of conventional societal expectations, Huck turns inward and discovers that Jim is "white
inside" (p.238). Huck's ultimate decision to abide by his ethically sound
emotions exemplifies his admirable moral responsibility.

On superficial examination, Huck and Oakhurst appear to be very dif- 5
ferent; one is an unsophisticated child, the other a worldly adult; Huck is
ruled primarily by his emotional response, Oakhurst relies on logical reasoning. On closer examination, however, it is apparent that Oakhurst shares

with Huck a common understanding of the feelings, thoughts, and motives of others. A gambler by trade, Oakhurst easily wins the entire fortune of an inexperienced young man, but Oakhurst's compassionate nature permits him to return the youth's money and offer considerate advice—"'Tommy, you're a good little man, but you can't gamble worth a cent. Don't try it over again'" (p.272).

Oakhurst's moral sensitivity is introduced early in the story—"The 6 thought of deserting his weaker and more pitiable companions never perhaps occurred to him" (p.271). He selflessly encourages Tom to take the improvised snow shoes as a last effort to avoid their certain deaths from starvation, yet in doing so Oakhurst ultimately relinquishes the only opportunity available to save his own life. Realizing also that the two women may be able to survive on the remaining provisions, Oakhurst provides enough fuel to sustain the women a few days longer and then calmly takes his own life. Thus Oakhurst heroically accepts his ultimate fate as dictated by his honorable degree of moral duty.

Both Twain and Harte also present characters whose principles are di- 7 ametrically opposed to those of Huck and Oakhurst. Twain's king and duke represent a conscienceless element of society. The two scoundrels' abominable behavior relegates them to the position of social outcasts whose exclusive goal in life is to dupe and cheat as many people as possible. They prey on the gullibility and ignorance of the river-town inhabitants they encounter. Their deceit in the plot to steal the Wilks family's inheritance leads Huck to exclaim—"It was enough to make a body ashamed of the human race" (p.156). The king's deliberate callousness is best evidenced in the episode in which he sells Jim for forty dollars. Twain's method of characterizing the king and the duke obviously expresses a grave conviction that unprincipled cruelty is an objectionably strong element of society.

Comparably self-serving and equally contemptuous of what is right 8 and honorable is Harte's character, Uncle Billy. Much like Twain's king and duke, Uncle Billy is deserving of censure by society because of his contemptible behavior. He is described as "...a suspected sluice-robber and confirmed drunkard" (p.270). The disdain with which he regards the innocence of the young lovers, Tom and Piney, is confirmation of his corrupt and sordid nature. Comparable to the king and the duke, Uncle Billy's own survival is his exclusive intention. Inspired by unqualified egoism, he stealthily steals the mules, heedless of the outcasts' probable resulting fate. Huck's statement—"Human beings can be awfully cruel to one another" (p.205) succinctly sums up the disturbing aspect of human failing represented by the king, the duke, and Uncle Billy.

While the moral attitudes of the king, the duke, and Uncle Billy are 9 not surprising, both Twain and Harte also present characters whose moral responsibility is not consistent with what one would immediately expect. Twain's model of local southern aristocracy, the Grangerfords, seems thor-

oughly admirable while Harte's prostitute character, Mother Shipton, seems
utterly reprehensible in nature. Under closer scrutiny, however, the Grangerfords' dignity, glory, and honor are exposed as based upon a false social
conscience, while Mother Shipton's socially offensive characteristics disguise
a sound heart.

For example, the Grangerfords are seemingly sentimentalists who lov- 10
ingly keep their deceased daughter's room exactly as she left it. The family
stands as a paragon of culture, refinement, and religious righteousness. Yet,
the Grangerfords carry guns to church in case any opportunity to continue
the senseless feud with the Shepherdsons arises. Huck is troubled by the
lack of moral integrity he intuitively perceives as he reflects on a church service he attends with the family—

> It was pretty ornery preaching—all about brotherly love, and such-like
> tiresomeness; but everybody said it was a good sermon, and they all
> talked it over going home, and had such a powerful lot to say about
> faith, and good works, and free grace, and preforeordestination, and I
> don't know what all, that it did seem to me to be one of the roughest
> Sundays I had run across yet (p.117).

The feud is almost immediately resumed and several members of both families are senselessly murdered; obviously Huck recognizes the hypocrisy the
sermon demonstrates while, sadly, the Shepherdsons and Grangerfords do
not. The families feel compelled to follow the traditional code as established
by the past without consideration of moral and social responsibility.

As compared to the Grangerfords, Harte's character, Mother Shipton, 11
represents the lowest class as regarded by society. Her reputed wrongs
against the town of Poker Flat lead to her banishment by a morally indignant
group of pseudo righteous citizens. Although Mother Shipton's crude swearing and her spoken "...desire to cut somebody's heart out..." (p.270) disguise her truly admirable moral strength, Harte effectively demonstrates the
genuine moral responsibility she possesses. She hoards her ration of food in
order to improve the chances of survival of the young girl.

> "Give 'em [rations] to the child," she [Mother Shipton] said, pointing
> to the sleeping Piney. "You've starved yourself," said the gambler.
> "That's what they call it," said the woman querulously, as she lay
> down again, and turning her face to the wall, passed quietly away
> (p.276).

Without doubt, Mother Shipton's magnanimous sacrifice of her own life
represents a commendable inner moral conscience in contrast to the outward
appearance she flaunts.

The cruelties committed by the Grangerfords for the sake of pride and 12
honor are morally reprehensible to a much greater extent than the considerably less offensive wrongs perpetrated by Mother Shipton. It is evident that

both authors intended to express the same concerns in much the same manner. Twain presents the seemingly ethical Grangerfords as an example of a society lacking moral and social responsibility while Harte offers the supposedly degenerate Mother Shipton as representative of a morally sound conscience.

In a broader sense, both Twain and Harte criticize society collectively 13 for its hypocritical moral attitude. Twain uses the Sherburn-Boggs incident to illustrate the mob cowardice aspect of a society dismally lacking moral responsibility. An agitated crowd rushes to lynch Sherburn for shooting the harmless old drunk, Boggs, who had "...never hurt nobody, drunk nor sober" (p.141). A scornful Sherburn scathingly denounces the crowd as "...beneath pitifulness" (p.144) as he refers to the group's despicable cowardice in the face of any resistance. The crowd's predictable, skulking retreat reiterates Twain's conviction that society's motivations in general rest on weak and self-centered principles.

In much the same manner, society's lack of moral rectitude is further 14 exemplified in the sanctimonious citizens of Poker Flat. Essentially, the same craven crowd which attempts to lynch Sherburn also banishes the outcasts to their uncertain end. The moral atmosphere of the town fulminates in "...a spasm of virtuous reaction, quite as lawless and ungovernable as any of the acts that had provoked it" (p.269). Society's hypocrisy is additionally evidenced in the manner in which judgment is passed on those to be exiled— "A secret committee had determined to rid the town of all improper persons" (p.269). The ignoble lack of courage plus the essential brutality of society is well represented by both groups of citizens.

Both Twain and Harte recognized the integral harshness of a society 15 that only pretends to be benevolent, lawful, and righteous. With similar technique, Twain and Harte chose character demonstration rather than didactic lecturing to teach the precept of moral and social responsibility. Certainly, the two literary works allow significant insight to be gained into the patterns and traps of traditionally accepted societal values. Both *Adventures of Huckleberry Finn* and "The Outcasts of Poker Flat" speak expressively of somber moral issues which society continues to confront.

QUESTIONS ABOUT THE RHETORICAL SITUATION

1. What evidence is there in the essay that Stubbs assumes that her readers have read "The Outcasts of Poker Flat" and *Huckleberry Finn?* How would her essay need to be changed if she were writing for readers who had not already read these two literary works?

2. Is Stubbs' primary purpose analytical or evaluative? In other words, is she interested in explaining or in judging? Or is she doing both? Explain your answer.

3. Stubbs herself expressed a concern that she was treating Bret Harte's story "too seriously," given that it is not all that profound a piece of literature. How appropriate is her essay's attitude toward Harte's story? How appropriate is her essay's attitude toward *Huckleberry Finn,* a story many of you may have read as children? Explain.

QUESTIONS ABOUT THE ESSAY'S VOICE

1. How does Stubbs use her first paragraph to establish a common ground for the two literary works? Why does she do so?
2. One of the notable features of her essay is Stubbs' use of quotations. At times she uses partial quotations (see ¶3 for instance), and at other times she uses long quotations (see ¶10). How effective is her use of quotations? Has she quoted too much? Too little? Why is she quoting at all in an essay to be read by readers who have already read both Twain's and Harte's works?
3. When writing about literary works, writers usually observe a number of conventions: they write in the present tense, they refer to the complete title of the literary work and the author's full name, they subsequently refer only to the author's last name, they identify the page numbers of quotations. How consistently has Stubbs observed these conventions? What sense do these conventions make?
4. Comparison/contrast essays move back and forth between topics, presenting the writer with a problem in keeping the essay from fragmenting into unrelated parts. How has Stubbs attempted to organize her essay in order to keep it unified? Examine some of her transitions (see ¶7 and ¶9 for instance). How effective are they in keeping the essay unified?
5. In ¶8, Stubbs uses a quotation from Twain's book to describe characters from both stories. What does she gain by doing so?
6. In ¶5, Stubbs talks about a "superficial examination" and a "closer examination" of Harte's character, Oakhurst. How does this paragraph help to create the voice of the expert in her essay?
7. Experts, I have been arguing, offer much specific data but also reach conclusions. In ¶13, Stubbs draws a conclusion about society's hypocrisy. Where else in the essay does she draw conclusions from her evidence? Does she do so enough to sound like an expert?
8. In what sense is "Mark Twain and Bret Harte: Social Critics" an essay based on firsthand experience?

TOPICS TO WRITE ABOUT

1. Write an essay that compares and contrasts the ways in which two writers handle related ideas in a pair of essays in *Model Voices* (for instance, Elie

Wiesel's (Chapter 9) and Robert McAfee Brown's (Chapter 7) essays on the Holocaust; Philip Caputo's (Chapter 11) and Wallace Terry's (Section Five) selections on Vietnam. POTENTIAL AUDIENCE: your classmates who have read both selections from the book. POTENTIAL PURPOSE: to interpret both essays in a way that will illuminate their significance for your readers.

2. Write your own essay about Bret Harte's "The Outcasts of Poker Flat," examining some feature of the story (such as the role of nature in the story) not discussed by Karen Stubbs. POTENTIAL AUDIENCES: readers who have read the story/readers who have not read the story. POTENTIAL PURPOSES: to explain the workings of the story and add to their understanding of it/to evaluate the story's effectiveness and let them know whether or not to spend the time it takes to read the story.

12

The Interview Voice

BECOMING AN INTERVIEWER

We've all seen scenes like these dozens of times: the attorney and her client come out of the courtroom and are mobbed by several reporters, all sticking microphones in their faces and shouting questions. Or the President stands in the front of a large auditorium and points to one of the dozens of reporters waving their arms in the air, shouting "Mr. President!!" Or the hard-nosed TV journalist asks tougher and tougher questions as the person he is asking starts to squirm and sweat, in a tight close-up.

Have you ever fantasized yourself in this role of interrogator? Some of us might have, but most of us, I would guess, have not. Then why is there a chapter in *Model Voices* devoted to the interview voice? The answer is that conducting the kind of interview suitable to writing an essay is not that difficult and requires neither the flash, the nerve, nor the hunger to be on TV that you might think it would. In fact, *interview* may even be too formal a word; perhaps *conversation* would work better. If you have ever told a friend an anecdote that you had been told by another friend, you have already had some practice in the skills you need to write in the interview voice.

A BRIDGE

The interview voice is a voice of authority. It is a bridge between the voice of firsthand experience and the more formal research voice. Somewhat different from the voice of firsthand experience, which draws upon a vast reservoir of accumulated information acquired by seeing and doing, *the interview voice nevertheless has the sound of firsthand experience, acquired in this case by interviewing an authority.* As with the research voice, you will find the writers make it a point *to identify the source of their information*—the interview subject—although perhaps in a much less formal manner. Here the writer serves at times almost as *a master of ceremonies,* introducing the voice of the true authority—the interview subject. Thus the interview voice is the voice that holds the essay together—the voice of the writer who brings the information to the reader, who has become an authority on the subject, who steps aside periodically to allow the firsthand authority to be heard.

This is one of the easier voices to find in the casual, everyday reading you do. Newspapers are full of the interview voice: stories about last night's football or baseball or basketball game or about yesterday's plane crash or court case will usually include comments made by those involved. Magazines regularly offer profiles of significant individuals, articles that include direct quotations from the people being profiled.

THE INTERVIEW ESSAY

Let me clarify for a moment the type of essay I am describing. While *Playboy* magazine runs an interview in every issue, usually with entertainment celebrities or famous athletes but sometimes with political figures (the interview with presidential candidate Jimmy Carter in 1976 even had a brief effect on the campaign), those interviews are not essays at all. Instead they are edited transcriptions of the interview. The interviewer asks a question and the subject responds, and both question and answer are printed verbatim, thus presenting the reader with a transcribed conversation in which two distinct and separate voices can be heard.

What you will be reading in this chapter, however, are *essays,* composed and shaped by the interviewers. In some of the essays you may not read a single one of the questions asked by the interviewer, and the interviewer may, as is frequently the case, not appear in the essay at all. But you will still hear that interviewer's voice as it reports on the information the writer has gleaned through interviewing the expert. At times the interviewer will let you hear the interviewee, but the entire piece of writing will be seamless as it flows back and forth between the interviewer and the person interviewed. In short the piece will *sound* like an essay, and the primary voice you hear will be the writer's.

A SAMPLE

Here is an excerpt from an article written by a sophomore, Pamela Schramm, who had interviewed one of her professors for the campus newspaper.

So with the encouragment of his wife, children, and friends in Oxford, Professor James Lehman went back to school at the age of 42 to earn his masters degree in history at Miami University. "You know," Lehman says slowly, "when I went back to school, people said I deserved a lot of credit. I could never understand that. I loved every minute of it. It was so exciting!"

Lehman stresses that it is his wife and children who deserved credit since he couldn't have done it without their support and encouragement. "I was a student on Monday, Wednesday, and Friday, and a businessman on Tuesday, Thursday, and Saturday. That's why I have a special sympathy for the non-traditional student...I know how frightened they are."

FEATURES OF THE INTERVIEW VOICE

There are several features to look for in the essays in this chapter, features that frequently appear in essays with the interview voice, features that you can see in the excerpt from Pamela's essay.

Use of Quotations

While you may have seen dialogue or quotations used in earlier essays in this book, there is a strong likelihood, almost a certainty, that you will see quotations used in the essays that create an interview voice. And for obvious reasons. Without those quotations, the essay would not really seem to be an interview. There are times when writers interview experts and use the information they have obtained without quoting the experts. These essays may create the voice of authority, probably sounding as if they have come from firsthand experience, or, if the writer identifies his interview subject, they may sound like the research voice, but without the quotations, they will not sound much like an interview. That second voice in the essay, the interview subject's voice, is the major distinguishing feature of the essays in this chapter.

Look at the illustration below. It shows the spectrum of possibilities when you are using material you have obtained by conducting an interview. If you write your essay without using any (or enough) quotations, it will sound very much like the essays in Chapters 10, 11, or 13; if you simply report what the interviewee said or rely almost entirely upon direct quotation, you will write something that sounds more like a *Playboy* interview than an essay.

No quotations————**Some quotations**————**Entirely quotations**
Voice of firsthand————The interview voice————Transcription
  experience
Research voice

Of course, one of the major problems encountered by the writer working with an interview is deciding when and how much to quote. There are no formulas, of course, but one good rule of thumb is that you ought to quote only when the quotation serves two purposes: it provides information, and it provides the reader with a better picture of what the interviewee is like as a person.

Notice that in reporting the historical facts of Professor Lehman's graduate education, the student used her own words (in the first sentence of the passage.) However, when she asked a question that received an answer that revealed a great deal about the professor's personality, she quoted him directly, as she does in sentence two of the passage.

She included this direct quotation in her essay because it told her readers something about both the history professor's life and about his personality at the same time. Having become an expert about the dry facts of his background through her interview, she reported that information in her own words as effectively as he had reported it to her. But when he expressed himself memorably, she quoted him.

Use of Characterizing Description

Because the interviewer has actually spoken to the expert, she simply knows much more about that person than does her reader. Quoting what the interviewee has said is one way to convey an impression of that person to the reader. Trying to show the reader *how* the interviewee spoke is another way to convey that impression.

Did the interviewee chuckle when she made a comment? Did she think quietly for a moment before answering a question? Did she sound angry? Enthusiastic? Sad? Did she smile, grimace, clap her hands? Including such details is an effective—and common—strategy used in essays that display the interview voice. Notice that Pamela characterizes Professor Lehman's comments in ¶1 by mentioning that he spoke "slowly," as if he were thinking carefully as he answered. An effectively chosen adverb can describe how the interviewee made a response. A short descriptive phrase or clause can illustrate the interviewee's facial expression, gestures, posture, attitude. It is neither necessary nor desirable to modify every comment made by the interviewee, but judicious use of such description is effective in painting a picture of the interview subject.

Attention to Pace

Perhaps one of the more difficult features to master in writing in the interview voice is creating an effective pace for the essay. *Playboy* does not have such a problem since the interviews are merely transcriptions. But for writers who wish to include some effectively selected quotations, the problem is not only *what* should be quoted, but also *how much* should be quoted and *where* in the essay the quotations should appear.

Ideally, the writer will quote enough to give the reader a sense of the interviewee's personality. The essay will flow back and forth between the quotations and the other exposition. The writer strives for a balance between direct quotation, indirect quotation, and completely rephrased (paraphrased) passages.

Let's suppose you have interviewed the local mortician, who turns out to be a surprisingly vivacious and bubbly sort of person. To the question "What keeps you in this profession?" he has responded by saying, "I love my job to death!" You might quote him directly:

He says, almost gleefully, "I love my job to death!"

Or you might quote him indirectly:

Almost gleefully, he talks about how much he loves his job.

Or you might use a mixture of direct and indirect quotation:

Almost gleefully, he talks about how he loves his job "to death!"

Or you might paraphrase his comments.

Smithers seems to love his work in an almost gleeful fashion.

None of these approaches is necessarily the best one; they all have their places, and the writer must decide when to use each approach. If the mortician has not been quoted for several paragraphs, then the direct quotation might be best. If this part of the essay follows immediately after several lengthy quotations from him, perhaps the mixed approach—which produces a much briefer quotation—would be effective for balance. If the intended readers are a squeamish bunch to whom the interviewee's glee will sound ghoulish, the indirect quotation might be best. If the information is important as background only, then paraphrasing might be the best approach.

Notice how the student who interviewed her professor has balanced the paragraphs; both paragraphs allow the professor to speak, but they also speak in the writer's own voice. As you read the interview essays that follow, be aware of the essay's pace, and try to see what principles were used by each writer to decide when to use each strategy.

INTERVIEWS AS EXPOSITION

The structure of essays written in the interview voice tends to be expository, explaining something. However, the interview voice can be heard in essays that use a great variety of organizational patterns. The danger in using an interview to tell a story is that it may be tempting to rely entirely upon the interviewee's voice to tell that story. And a story told almost entirely through quotations, direct and indirect, from a person other than the writer himself is going to sound much different than a story told by the person who had experienced the event herself. The power of the firsthand experience will be somewhat lost. Thus essays that demonstrate the interview voice tend not to be narratives—or at least tend to be only partly narrative. So it is quite likely that the interview subject will tell a story, but that the story will appear as but a part of a larger essay with explanatory goals. (See Lynn Sawyer's essay in this chapter for an example.)

STRUCTURE

Most of the time then, you will hear the interview voice in an essay designed to explain something, and the essay may take whatever form or structure the writer sees as appropriate: comparison/contrast, classification, definition, or some other form. In fact, it's most likely that the essay will not really stick to a single of these structures at all. What you will be able to notice, however, is that the essays in this chapter all tend to use the material culled from the interviews in similar ways. The writer/interviewer forms generalizations based on the interviewing; the quotations and paraphrases are used as examples to support these generalizations. At the conclusion of her interview essay, Pamela Schramm called Professor Lehman "courageous enough to change professions in mid-life." That generalization had been supported by the material she had included earlier in the essay, including his comment about his wife and children and his full-time job, quoted in the excerpt above.

To illustrate the many ways in which an interview essay might be organized, let's suppose that you have interviewed jolly Mr. Smithers, the local mortician. You might find that he has explained in detail how he arranges a funeral (*process analysis*), the differences between being a mortician and a coroner (*comparison/contrast*), and the different types of burial preparation used over the centuries (*classification*). He might tell a story about how he grew interested in his chosen profession, or he might describe the decor of his establishment. All this information could appear in an essay designed to demystify for your readers what goes on at a funeral home (much as Jessica Mitford actually did in her famous book *The American Way of Death*).

So it may be that you will mix comparison, classification, process analysis, narrative, description in an effort to explain Mr. Smithers' job. What you will undoubtedly have to do, however, is use his information to support your generalizations. You might write, "Morticians fulfill a very different function than do coroners." You would then quote Smithers, directly or indirectly, or paraphrase him to clarify and illustrate your point.

Using the information you have gained through the interview in this manner makes the interview voice a voice of authority. You will become an expert, an authority, by listening to an expert, interpreting that expert's ideas, and explaining those ideas to the reader. Of course, sometimes the expert will do the interpreting for you, and you will simply pass along these ideas; even so, you are still going to sound authoritative as you pass the ideas along. More often, you will have to reach conclusions on your own and use the collected information to illustrate your conclusions. The actual form you choose for your essay, however, will be dictated by the rhetorical situation. Remember that

$$\begin{aligned}
\text{Awareness of audience } + \\
\text{understanding of purpose } + \\
\text{attitude toward subject } = \text{ voice}
\end{aligned}$$

as you strive to achieve your purpose, whether it be to inform or entertain or both.

SOME TIPS ON INTERVIEWING

At the beginning of this chapter, I suggested that conducting the sort of interviews I had in mind would not be terribly difficult. Let me offer you a few suggestions for interviewing, based not only on my own experiences but on those of my students who have conducted interviews and subsequently written essays.

1. Interview someone who has done something interesting (work, travel, accomplishment, hobby, attitude). *Remember:* You must capture your readers' interest.

     Some jobs just automatically sound interesting; for instance, many readers will want to know what being an astronaut is like. However, less "exciting" sounding jobs may be interesting too. One of my students interviewed his friend whose job with the local power company was to cut down tree limbs that might damage high-voltage powerlines. The interviewee had a number of amusing and exciting stories to tell. Another student interviewed a piano tuner, whose clear and witty explanations of his job made the essay quite readable. Interviews with expert Dungeon and Dragon players or supermarket coupon collectors were also quite readable, as was a recent student interview with the local barber—whose job was not terribly interesting but whose outgoing personality was. Interviews with the professors on our campus were of intrinsic interest to readers of our campus newspaper.

     Be sure you keep your readers in mind; if you cannot interest them in your interview subject, you may find it very difficult to write a successful essay. My student interviewed her history professor because she knew that readers of the campus paper would be interested in learning more about one of their instructors.

2. Interview someone you feel comfortable speaking with.

     Unless you are extremely outgoing or a prospective reporter, you quite likely will not feel all that comfortable interviewing a total stranger. Most of my students have interviewed relatives, neighbors, friends, coworkers, employers, teachers—people with whom they have spoken before, or with whom they think they can speak comfortably. My student had had many conversations with her history professor and knew that she could talk comfortably with him.

3. Interview someone who likes to talk.

You shouldn't be doing all the talking during the interview. Be sure you interview someone who enjoys talking about the subject. That's not hard: choose someone who usually talks about the subject you have in mind and then tape record the conversation! This was another factor in my student's decision to interview her professor; she had been listening to him in class for weeks and knew that he enjoyed talking to students.

4. Interview someone who is readily available.

Since you may find that you will have to return to the interviewee to ask additional questions—a common experience—it becomes important that you interview someone who is available for a second interview. Interviewing your cousin at the airport as she departs for her attempt to climb Mt. Everest may prove unwise. What if you need to ask her several more questions? How would you get in touch with her? With the history professor, my student simply made appointments with him during his regularly scheduled office hours and conducted two interview sessions with him in his office.

5. Find an angle or focus for the interview.

When preparing for your interview, you probably need to start out with some angle or focus in mind as you think up questions to ask. You do not wish to find out everything there is to know about your interviewee; that will not only be exhausting for both of you but will also make writing your essay that much harder since you will have to sift through all of your notes looking for useful information. My student focused her questions to her professor on his education rather than on his entire life, just as she had planned. Sometimes, however, during the actual interview, you will discover that you have found a more interesting angle, in which case you should certainly switch to a new line of questioning, as I am sure the student would have done had the history professor begun reminiscing about his days as an international spy (at which point she might also have begun thinking about writing to a different audience for a different purpose).

6. Prepare questions ahead of time.

After deciding on a focus for the interview, it makes sense to think up a number of specific questions to ask. The prepared questions will serve as prewriting of a sort, as you continue to think about your topic; they will serve to give the interview some structure and guarantee that you stay focused on the topic you are interested in. Additionally, you will be less likely to be nervous as you begin the interview if you have prepared several questions ahead of time.

7. Follow up with more questions during the interview.

You need to be ready to ask questions in addition to the ones you have prepared in advance. When the interviewee has been unclear, ask for clarification. When she has said something really interesting, ask for more information; it's particularly useful to ask for examples because the interviewee may then relate an anecdote that you might be able to use in your essay. After listening to a number of answers, you might try to interpret or summarize what you have heard during the interview in the form of a question just to see if the interviewee agrees with your interpretation or summary.

8. Use a tape recorder.

Although both you and the interviewee may feel uncomfortable at first speaking in front of a tape recorder, you will both get used to it quickly. The advantage is that you can concentrate on the give and take of the conversation without having to worry about remembering everything you hear. The taped approach will also allow you to quote accurately when writing your essay.

9. Convert the tape into notes.

You will probably find it easier to write your essay if you can transfer your taped interview into written notes. That way you can refer to specific comments with ease. My student laboriously transcribed every word of her taped interviews; I think you can accomplish the same objective by taking abbreviated notes. Of course, when you are preparing to write the paper and need to quote the interviewee, you will need to transcribe the exact words spoken on the tape.

THE ADVANTAGES

So even if you are not a trained journalist and have no dreams of becoming one, you probably have the conversational skills needed to conduct an informal interview and turn it into a piece of writing. The advantage of writing in the interviewer's voice is that you can expand the range of your expertise by relying upon the expertise of others; you don't need to be an authority on funeral practices if you can find a talkative Mr. Smithers to interview.

Another advantage of writing in the interview voice is that it will give you excellent practice in using information acquired from sources other than you yourself, the same kind of skill required in writing research papers and essay exam questions. You acquire the information; you reach conclusions about it; you organize it into a readable form; you teach your reader something valuable. These are the skills needed for successful academic writing also. Listen to the interview voices in the essays that follow, observe how the writers have made use of their acquired information. Then try an interview essay yourself—tape recorder recommended, camera not necessary.

Foot Soldiers in the War on Imports
Randy McNutt

Randy McNutt joined the staff of the Cincinnati *Enquirer* in 1976 as the news-paper's Clermont County bureau chief. Since then he has worked as a general assignment reporter, columnist, and roving feature writer. In his present job, McNutt, 39, is a special projects reporter for the Metro section of the *Enquirer*, writing feature stories from around Ohio, Indiana, and Kentucky. In May 1987, he won a Gannett Well-Done Award for his story about the struggles and successes of the Amish in relocating from Indiana to Adams County, Ohio. McNutt has also written numerous freelance articles in the last ten years, and was named contributing editor to *Ohio* magazine in 1985. McNutt's book *We Wanna Boogie: An Illustrated History of the American Rockabilly Movement* was published in 1987. He and his wife reside in Hamilton, Ohio, a suburb of Cincinnati.

McNutt's article on Harry and Evelyn Dean appeared in the Cincinnati *Enquirer*'s Metro section, a section devoted to local news, on June 1, 1987.

QUESTIONS ABOUT IDEAS

1. This essay links the local economy it describes with the national econ-omy. What effects have you observed the national economy having on your local area?
2. Harry Dean calls companies that import foreign-made goods "traitors." What would your response to Dean's assertion be? Why?
3. According to the article, the Deans' business would have been eligible for government funding assistance had they applied at the right time. Should the government provide such funding for private enterprises? Why or why not?

Every weekday morning, Harry Dean walks into his small shoe factory 1 and hears the quiet. It is noticeable—no, *pervasive*—this malevolent quiet that is consuming his life and future.

By now, Harry expected to have at least ten employees busily stitching 2 shoes, but the only people available for work each day are he and his wife, Evelyn. They can produce enough shoes to fill orders for a few companies, but the Deans know their factory's capacity is limited.

Harry thinks the inconvenience is temporary. He has to think that 3 way. At 64, he has finally achieved his dream of owning a shoe factory. He is determined not to fail.

Every morning he and Evelyn drive about 35 miles from their Nor- 4

wood home to the factory in this Ohio River village in Clermont County.
Just to make shoes.

The former Adler Sock factory is an eerie place—fully equipped, ready 5
for work, but lacking people. For the past four years, the Deans have struggled alone to remodel the rectangular, two-story building. It is as sturdy as a
Civil War fort, with a weathered brick front, thick walls, a stone foundation,
and more than 11,000 feet of space. This factory was built when work was
work.

The Deans financed the entire project with their personal savings and 6
by selling a piece of real estate. They spread 185 gallons of white paint on
the walls, repaired the high ceilings and generally revived the turn-of-the-
century building. When they had finished, Harry and Evelyn stood proudly
in front and erected a sign: DEAN SHOE COMPANY.

Friends in the business traced hard-to-find manufacturing equipment, 7
much of it made from 1895 to 1960. Harry bought roughers, buffers, click-
ers, folders, cutters, cementers, molders, stitchers—all manner of machine.

He obtained rolls of foam rubber, stacks of leather, and boxes of metal 8
for buckles. He was so confident that he opened a repair shop and a main
workroom with about fifty old sewing machines.

As an act of ultimate faith, he set up an attractive lunchroom for em- 9
ployees.

That the trend in the domestic shoe industry leans lopsidedly toward 10
imported footwear does not faze Harry. He is, after all, an unemployed shoe
worker who spent forty years sweating his life away in the factories of America. He is not going to quit because of something called trade imbalance.

"I'm a *pattern* man," Harry says defiantly. "Show me a picture, any- 11
thing, and I'll make it into a shoe. I can make you any kind of shoe you
want. I'm going to make a good shoe or I ain't going to make it at all. If you
buy an imported shoe and it falls apart in six weeks, you don't have much,
do you?"

Harry says he knows that 100 million pairs are imported annually, and 12
that 700 shoe factories have closed in the past fifteen years. But here he sits
in the empty lunchroom, laughing at the odds and talking confidently of
business. He thinks his shoes will sell because they are well-crafted and sell
for only $6.50 to $18.50.

White shoe boxes line the shelves of the Deans' outlet store in the front 13
of the factory. Harry and Evelyn make the shoes, wait on customers, fit
them, make change, talk about life, and offer a cup of coffee.

On this sunny day, a silver coffee pot spews and wheezes in a corner. 14
Harry stands behind a table, chuckling in a deep, smoky laugh and pondering the rate of inflation and the size of women's feet.

"You've got no idea how *big* some of these women's feet are," he says 15
in amazement. "I mean to tell ya. We'll make shoes for 'em, though, sizes

four to 12½, whole and half sizes. I had to come up with a lot of money to buy the dies and everything, but somebody had to do it for these gals. I'll make the shoes, but I'll also wonder: Are my boxes big enough to hold 'em?"

Harry met Evelyn in the Monogram Footwork factory in Trenton, Il- 16 linois. He was a pattern man. She was a stitcher.

In thirty-seven years their marriage has produced two children, thou- 17 sands of shoes, and a factory filled with dreams.

The Deans toiled twenty-three years in a shoe factory in St. Louis be- 18 fore moving to Cincinnati fourteen years ago to work in the U.S. Shoe Company plant.

Everything went well until four years ago—Harry was laid off for the 19 first time in his life. He says that applying for unemployment benefits is an experience he will not soon forget.

He was outraged. He was angry. If the U.S. footwear industry had 20 dropped this low, he reasoned, then the only thing left to do was to start his *own* shoe company.

Evelyn knew he was serious. Was this not the same Harry Dean who 21 once told a shoe company president to resign if he wanted to save his company some unnecessary costs? "But we would miss you, fella," Harry laughed as he left the meeting.

He is that bold. And stubborn. He is a blue-collar philosopher with 22 enough spirit for three men. That's one reason why friends think he can succeed despite an industry seemingly obsessed with foreign goods.

"I'd always thought about owning my own shoe factory," he says, 23 "but I never did pursue it. Why should I? A few years ago you could quit your job one morning and get another by the end of the day. Nowadays, though, the shoe industry is hurting. You know what *kills* me? The state has all these training programs, but where are the trainees going to work? The state gives money to all these other companies, including Japanese ones, but not to me. If I had $35,000, well, man, I could roll."

As he talks, the wife of a retired automobile worker walks into the out- 24 let wearing a blue United Auto Worker windbreaker. She inspects the boxes of shoes and selects a pair of leather sandals.

"Jobs are getting hard to find," she says. "Don't know what we're go- 25 ing to do."

"It's a *crime*," Harry says, spitting out the word.   26

"Folks come in here and see 'Made in the U.S.A.' on our boxes, and 27 they like that," Evelyn says.

"I still say," Harry goes on, "that if you don't like this nation, get out. 28 There's the plane, man. Get on! These companies that import stuff are trai-

tors. If we import our clothes, shoes, equipment—everything—then what
are we going to do when a war breaks out?"

Harry is excited now. His thin, gray hair stands up wildly on the top of   29
his head. A cigarette dangles from his lips as he talks in rapid-fire fashion.

"If I owned four large shoe factories, I couldn't hire all the people who   30
have filed applications with me for jobs," he says. "Hey, they're riding bicycles here because they don't even have cars...."

Harry limps up the old walnut staircase carrying a load of leather.   31
Sewing-machine motors line the hall like black carcasses. He moves into a
room, slowly, carefully, a result of a severe leg wound suffered in the South
Pacific during World War II.

He smiles shyly as he looks over the rows of antique sewing machines,   32
for he knows he has put together a shoe industry anomaly.

He puffs on a cigarette and leans against a table near seven long,   33
arched windows that invite the sunshine in. The room is bright and neatly
kept. The black Singers look as if they belong in some 1890s photograph.
Harry is at home here.

"My machinery is old," he says, "but unlike today's equipment, it was   34
built to last ten lifetimes. You don't pick up this stuff on any corner. I've
had it shipped here from as far away as Puerto Rico and California. Equipment like this is flowing out of the country today."

Now all he needs are a few employees to operate the machines, but he   35
knows he can't afford to hire them. So he waits, and binds soles with Evelyn.

"We're trying desperately to get some money for you," Mayor Betty J.   36
Hinson tells him, "But so far we've been ignored. We have a lot of unskilled
workers in New Richmond who need jobs. About forty percent of our three-
thousand residents are low-income and welfare people."

The Deans aren't asking for a lot of money, as grants go. They could   37
put $10,000 to good use. The problem is that they asked too late.

Had they requested the village's help four years ago, when they were   38
ready to buy the building, they might have been eligible for federal community development funds. They could have spent their own money on expan-
sion.

"When I come down here to the factory and see how you people have   39
struggled and persevered," Hinson says, "I think you've kept alive a great
idea. If only you had come to the village first. It's a shame."

Harry Dean remains undaunted.   40

"Somebody's got to help turn this country around," he says, striking   41
his fist gently on a table. "We're going to put some people to work in this
town. I know it. I just *know* it."

QUESTIONS ABOUT THE RHETORICAL SITUATION

1. Since McNutt's interview appeared in a Cincinnati newspaper, he obviously wrote it to be read by people who live in the greater Cincinnati area. How understandable would the essay be for readers from outside that geographical area? How interesting would it be to readers from outside the Cincinnati area? What could be done to make the essay more understandable? More interesting?
2. How did you feel about the Deans after reading about their shoe factory and its problems? How has McNutt tried to elicit this response from you?
3. How would you describe McNutt's own response to the Deans? Why?
4. Does the essay have a larger concern than the Deans? Does McNutt make an effort to enlarge the focus of his essay? If you think so, what is your response to any larger issues you may have identified? If you think not, *should* he have expanded the scope of his essay?

QUESTIONS ABOUT THE ESSAY'S VOICE

1. How effectively has McNutt quoted Harry Dean? Which quotations in particular show the reader what Dean's personality is like? Were any of the quotations less effective than the others? Why?
2. Notice where McNutt uses indirect quotations attributed to Dean and where he simply rephrases the information into his own words. Why has he made these decisions? How effectively does the essay flow from direct quotation to indirect quotation to paraphrase?
3. Is there enough direct quoting of Harry Dean in this essay? Why? Why not? How effective do you find it when McNutt spells words in an unusual manner in order to suggest Dean's pronunciation ("ya," "'em," for example)?
4. Why does McNutt end his essay by quoting Harry Dean instead of writing his own conclusion? How effective is this strategy of ending with a quotation from the interviewee?
5. Notice when McNutt chooses to describe Harry Dean as he speaks. What methods of description has he used? Which in particular are effective in painting a picture of Harry Dean? Why?
6. What is the purpose of including the anecdote in ¶21? What would the essay lose if this anecdote were omitted?
7. McNutt establishes himself as an authority in this essay in more than one way. Where does he reach conclusions or form generalizations? Where does he offer evidence of firsthand experience? How effective are these strategies in creating a voice of authority?
8. The essay is divided into three sections. What is the logic behind these divisions?

9. McNutt himself never appears in the essay nor does he report any of the questions he asked Dean. Can you infer what some of these questions were? What focus do the questions seem to have had? To what extent does McNutt stray from the essay's central focus?

TOPICS TO WRITE ABOUT

1. Interview a worker nearing retirement about the changes in his or her job over the years. POTENTIAL AUDIENCES: your local newspaper's readers/ students whose majors might lead them to careers in the same field. PO-TENTIAL PURPOSES: to enlighten the readers about how an industry of some local importance has evolved over the years/to give them an historical perspective on their future careers.
2. Interview a resident of a small town about life in a small town in the late twentieth century. POTENTIAL AUDIENCES: a city magazine such as *New York* or *Cincinnati* magazine/your sociology class. POTENTIAL PURPOSES: to show the readers an important way of life unfamiliar to them/to draw some conclusions about social norms in a small town.

Beyond *The Color Purple*
Stephanie Stokes Oliver

Stephanie Stokes Oliver is originally from Seattle, Washington. Currently Editor of *Essence* magazine, she is responsible for editing all articles published in each issue of the magazine. Second in command at *Essence,* Oliver facilitates the development of editorial ideas into article assignments, manages the editorial staff, and works with contributing editors. Oliver joined *Essence* as the editor of the Contemporary Living department and was later promoted to senior editor. In 1984, she became West Coast Editor and subsequently became Editor in 1986. Formerly an editor with *Glamour* magazine, Oliver is a journalism graduate of Howard University. She is a member of the American Society of Magazine Editors and the National Association of Black Journalists. She currently lives with her husband and daughter in New Jersey.

"Beyond *The Color Purple*" originally appeared in the September 1986 issue of *Essence.*

QUESTIONS ABOUT IDEAS

1. In your opinion, how significant a problem is the underrepresentation of racial minorities in television shows and movies? Avery talks about this

situation from her perspective as a working actress having difficulty making a living. Does this problem have larger implications for society itself?
2. Avery talks about being bothered by some of the roles she has played. Did this surprise you? Should actors and actresses care about the type of characters they portray? For example, several notable actors (Alec Guinness and Anthony Hopkins to mention two) have played Adolf Hitler on screen. Should they have done so?
3. Avery talks about the black community exerting pressure on Hollywood to open up more roles for black performers. Other minority groups might want to do the same thing. How might these groups exert this pressure? Should they do so?

   The film version of Alice Walker's immensely popular *The Color Pur-*   1
ple showcased an explosion of Black talent and put more Black actresses on the screen than did the TV movie *Roots*. But moviegoers expecting to see more Black women in feature roles will just have to make do with reruns. Good lead parts for Black women come along every now and then—mostly then. It's still feast or famine, even for a proven talent.

   Margaret Avery is a case in point. She received a well-deserved Acad-   2
emy Award nomination and countless honors for her portrayal of *Purple*'s free-spirited, feisty and supersensual Shug. But so far the applause hasn't had many results. "I still don't work as an actor," she concedes. "The scripts I get don't have a deal with a studio. They [producers] want me to say yes so that they can have a name to sell it with. That's okay if they have a strong script, but I haven't read one yet."

   Avery's professional ups and downs are still the norm for Black ac-   3
tresses. Once upon a time, however, things seemed to be changing. In 1969, when she decided to give up her steady job teaching school in Oakland for the uncertainty of a Hollywood film career, it was a time of hope and optimism. "Martin Luther King, Jr., had inspired me to challenge myself and believe in equality," she recalls.

   Avery was among the horde of black actors and actresses at that time   4
who descended upon the movie industry and found work. Her first parts were in television commercials and as prostitutes in several so-called Blaxploitation films. "The parts bothered me," she admits. "But I didn't do anything I was ashamed of. I just wanted to work so that I could be seen. Those movies allowed me and other Blacks the experience we needed."

   At about the same time, Avery and her husband, director Robert Gor-   5
don Hunt, formed the Zodiac Theater. Together they put on the play *Does the Tiger Wear a Necktie?* It won her an L.A. Drama Critics Circle Award for Outstanding Performance in 1972 and the attention of Clint Eastwood, who

saw her in the play and cast her as a hooker in *Magnum Force.* "That," she recalls, "was my first crossover film."

Work then began to come more regularly, and this time in the form of 6 quality jobs. She played Billy Dee Williams' wife, Belle, in the TV movie *Scott Joplin.* Then, in 1977, Avery landed the part for which she is probably best remembered prior to *Purple,* that of Richard Pryor's country wife, Annie Mae, who in her heightened sexual awareness handcuffs Pryor to the bed in *Which Way Is Up?*

But after the sex- and violence-studded Black formula films became passé 7 in the late seventies, the demand for Black actresses came to a screeching halt. "Black men still got jobs in police stories," Avery recalls, "but all of a sudden no one thought any of these Black male characters needed a woman."

As recently as last year, Margaret Avery was still out of work. Things 8 got so bad for the now-divorced mother that she had to rent out her Hollywood Hills home to meet her mortgage payments. Living downstairs in the one-bedroom guest quarters with her daughter Aisha, now 12, Avery went back to school to become a court reporter.

But she could never let go of her dream of making it as a working actress. "I decided to put my energies back into my career," she recalls. But it 9 meant making some sacrifices. She went on a six-month singing tour of Japan and Indonesia while Aisha stayed behind in Los Angeles with her father and stepmother.

When Avery returned to the United States, she heard that *The Color* 10 *Purple* was being cast. Although the role of Shug seemed destined to be hers—after all, she shares her character's last name—it was her uncompromising determination that got her foot in the door. "I asked my agent if he had put me up for it. He said he had, but that the casting director thought I was wrong for the role. So I wrote a letter asking to be auditioned, saying I wouldn't take no for an answer. After I read for the role, I was one of four actresses asked to screen-test for it. Then Steven [Spielberg, the director] saw me on film, and I got it."

Avery got a plum role—the one that Tina Turner was offered but 11 turned down.

"It was a challenge," Avery says, "working in the heat of North Caro- 12 lina and trying to capture the spirit of that woman who was so free. But that's what attracted me to the Shug role—to do someone so different from me. I was excited and fearful, wondering, *Am I going to be able to pull this off?* The joy is that people think I did."

Avery says *The Color Purple* "made people think," and that it will be- 13 come a classic. "Its worth will be recognized in the years to come. The things we're criticizing it for now will be downplayed twenty years from now, when it will still be shown."

That criticism was—and still is—hot and heavy. Many Black men, and 14 women, cried foul, charging that the abusive Black male characters, played by Danny Glover and the late Adolph Caesar, cast a negative light on all brothers.

Did the controversy surprise Avery? "Not a whole lot," she replies. 15 "The book was controversial, and the film was picketed before it was released. When more Black films are made, we won't have to expect one to represent all our people."

In addition to that controversy, Avery found herself embroiled in one 16 of her own. This past January, in response to her nomination for Best Supporting Actress, she placed an ad in the *Hollywood Reporter,* in which Oscar nominees often do a little self-promoting in an attempt to steer Academy votes their way. This practice is sometimes unpopular, but what got Avery in trouble was the wording of her ad: "Dear God...I knows dat I been blessed by Alice Walker, Steven Spielberg, and Quincy Jones who gave me the part of 'Shug' Avery in *The Color Purple*...I guess the time has come fo' the Academy voters to decide whether I is one of the Best Supporting Actresses this year or not!" It was signed "Your little daughter, Margaret Avery" and featured a photograph of her as Shug.

Critics called the ad "exploitation," pointing out that Avery didn't play 17 Celie, the character who wrote the letters to God; Whoopi Goldberg did. Nor was Shug's way of speaking so exaggerated.

To this day, Avery is puzzled by the critics' reaction. "I didn't under- 18 stand the flak I got for the ad. All the votes were in, so the ad said thank you to God for the opportunity. It was written the way Celie wrote and Shug spoke, and it was signed by Margaret Avery. The people who didn't like it didn't like the movie, either. And they didn't care anything about Margaret Avery when Margaret Avery wasn't working. The Man upstairs did."

How did she feel when she didn't walk away with the Oscar? "When I 19 won the Academy nomination I said, 'Thank you, Jesus!'" she exclaims. "When I didn't win the award I still felt I had won. It couldn't diminish my self-worth because I know I'm a winner. The winning is inside. If I had to wait for the establishment to tell me, I'd never have anything."

After the awards ceremony, Avery was honored at a dinner for the 20 Black nominees. "I broke into tears," she says, "because it is so important to be recognized by your own. We are survivors. Did you know that 75 percent of the people working *behind* the scenes of *Purple* were Black? They did the sound, music, hair, wardrobe. It was incredible and beautiful."

Today Margaret Avery is looking forward to a career beyond *The Color* 21 *Purple.* On the surface, she appears to be a talented woman who enjoyed her moment in the sun and is now fading into obscurity. Scratch the surface and you might find some disturbing reasons why. Avery asserts that her life as an actress has always been unpredictable—she just doesn't expect the same breaks that white actesses get. "They automatically go into a television series," she says. "There have been Black exceptions. Isabel Sanford and Nell Carter are two. But percentage-wise, the numbers aren't the same.

There are a lot of good parts that Black actresses don't get to read for because 'They' have decided those parts won't be Black."

This explains the dearth of Black female superstars in the film industry. "And the male superstars were stars before they got into the movie business," she says, citing comedians Richard Pryor, Eddie Murphy and Bill Cosby. 22

Avery's other pet peeve is salaries. "If you compared the white salaries with the Black, the white would be higher," she insists. "I was recently offered a series, and the figure was real lowball. It was a slap in the face. If I can't get equality I'd rather not take the jobs; I'll go back to Japan. Getting low-paying parts is as bad as not getting high-quality jobs. It's a way of keeping us 'in our place.'" 23

That's not all that's fueling Avery's dissatisfaction. "I shouldn't be limited to Black projects," she adds. "The latest new Black project is *Uncle Tom's Cabin!* Can you believe that?" she asks with an incredulous laugh. "Is this the hand that's going to feed me?" 24

Always looking for a hopeful sign, Avery points out that Rae Dawn Chong recently broke through the "blackcasting" barrier with her role in *Commando.* But she believes that overall, in spite of the huge number of Black moviegoers, Black actors aren't being recognized. "Don't take for granted that when you haven't seen Black actors in a long time, it's by their choice." 25

Avery says it's up to the Black community to pressure the movie industry to change. "We as actors can't demand these things or we'll be blacklisted. It's an insecure business." She also encourages Blacks to take more control of the industry, to buy cable-TV stations, and to get into some of the power positions so that they won't always have to depend on others. "We need to support each other." 26

When the going gets really tough, Avery gets inspiration from those Black actresses who have made it despite the odds—Lena Horne, Cicely Tyson, Diahann Carroll, and, most recently, Oprah Winfrey. "If I had let all the problems get me down, I wouldn't have gotten to do *The Color Purple.* If Lena and the others can do it, I can too. You have to keep on steppin.'" 27

Avery says that if she could direct the steps of her own career, she would like to do a Broadway comedy. "Stage acting was my beginning," she explains. "I'm hoping that *The Color Purple* will open this door for me." 28

In the meantime, she is taking her life in stride, basking in the publicity from the recent release of *Purple* in Europe. She's also overseeing the renovation of her reclaimed home, traveling the college lecture circuit, reading scripts and accepting honors. The only thing she doesn't like about her life now, she says, is that all her time is planned to the minute, with little left for herself. 29

"It's a struggle to find time for myself, time for Aisha and time for my boyfriend," she says, referring to a man she'll identify only as someone 30 who's "in the business" too. "Fortunately, he's been very understanding," Avery continues. "And he has never made me choose between my career and him, or my child and him."

Avery says that she'd like to take a vacation, then consider the scripts 31 she's been offered. One is for a television movie that her manager, Dave Nelson, who is Black, says may lead to a series. Called *Stagecoach Mary,* it's based on the true story of ex-slave Mary West, who lived in Montana. "She was a gun-toting Black woman," according to Nelson, "who delivered the mail and punched men out."

In spite of it all, Avery for now is counting her blessings. "The most 32 important thing *The Color Purple* did for me was what it was supposed to do for Celie," she notes. "It was supposed to give that character self-worth. And it also gave Margaret Avery self-worth. It came at a time when I could appreciate it. I feel good because I earned it."

QUESTIONS ABOUT THE RHETORICAL SITUATION

1. At one point in the essay, Oliver refers to black men as "brothers." Is there any other evidence that this essay is directed primarily to black readers? To what degree is the essay difficult to follow for nonblack readers?

2. Avery, at one point, talks about her first "crossover" film, meaning that the part was her first one in a film intended for a racially mixed audience as opposed to her earlier work in films marketed for black audiences. To what extent does Oliver assume that her readers are conversant with the film industry? To what degree can a casual moviegoer or nonmoviegoer understand this essay?

3. Avery appears to have been involved in several controversies surrounding *The Color Purple,* her Academy Award nomination, and the professional lives of Black performers. What is Oliver's attitude toward Avery in this essay? Is she on Avery's side or is she a neutral reporter? What reasons do you have for your answer?

4. When readers have completed reading "Beyond *The Color Purple,*" what have they learned about? About what subject or subjects is Oliver trying to inform her readers? How appropriate is her essay's title in reflecting the subject(s) of her essay?

QUESTIONS ABOUT THE ESSAY'S VOICE

1. How does the first paragraph of the essay establish Oliver's voice as the voice of authority?

2. Only rarely does Oliver use descriptive phrases to portray Avery's manner of speaking, yet she still conveys a vivid picture of the way Avery speaks. How does she do so?

3. Oliver quotes Avery extensively throughout the essay. But she also paraphrases information frequently. By examining both the quotations and the paraphrases, can you discern a pattern behind Oliver's decisions about what information to offer in the form of direct quotation, indirect quotation, and paraphrase?

4. Unlike Randy McNutt in "Foot Soldiers in the War on Imports," Stephanie Oliver makes little or no effort to reflect Avery's pronunciation by use of unorthodox spelling. Should Oliver reconsider this decision? Why or why not?

5. On occasion Oliver includes one of the questions she asked Avery during their interview. What is the purpose of her doing so? How effective is this strategy? How would the essay's voice be changed if she did so more frequently? Less frequently?

6. How effective is Oliver's conclusion? What is her purpose in concluding with a quotation from Avery?

7. Many magazines use subheads, small headlines, to highlight different sections of a long article. Where in this essay might such subheads be used? How might the subheads read? What would such subheads reveal about the essay's organizational plan? How would you describe the organization of the essay?

TOPICS TO WRITE ABOUT

1. Interview a friend who is a member of a racial, ethnic, religious, social, or professional minority about her opinions and impressions of, her reactions to, her ideas about the depiction of the group of which she is a member on television shows and in the movies (for example, black, Indian, Hispanic, or Asian people; or Italian, Irish, or Arab people; or Jewish, Buddhist, or fundamentalist Christian people; or overweight, short, wheelchair-bound, or blind people; or nurses, garbage collectors, or teachers). POTENTIAL AUDIENCES: readers of *TV Guide*/the general reading public. POTENTIAL PURPOSES: to explain to readers interested in TV and film how one member of such a minority group feels/to inform them about the significant impact of stereotyping upon those being stereotyped.

2. Interview a performer—actor, singer, dancer, musician. POTENTIAL AUDIENCES: those who might have seen the performer perform/other performers of the same type. POTENTIAL PURPOSES: to provide readers with a better understanding of the performer through a behind-the-scenes look at what is involved in such performances/to give the readers a better understanding of the personality of one of their fellow performers.

James Harrington
Edward Feit

Edward Feit is professor emeritus of political science at the University of Massachusetts, where he taught for over twenty years. He has also taught at universities in Germany and France. Feit has published six books on political subjects including four about political problems in his native land of South Africa.

A longtime art enthusiast and collector, Feit is currently a freelance writer on art subjects. Feit's interview with James Harrington, a painter who works primarily with oil paint and whose work is displayed in art galleries in the midwest and New England, first appeared in *American Artist* magazine.

QUESTIONS ABOUT IDEAS

1. In Feit's essay, the painter's techniques are described in some detail. (See ¶16 for an example.) What parallels can you observe between Harrington's process of painting and your own process of writing? What is the significance of such parallels? What insights into writing does this essay on painting provide?
2. In one anecdote, Harrington suggests that his opinion about one of his paintings was right while the gallery director's was wrong because two people wanted to buy his painting. Does this suggest that the ultimate decision about the value of a piece of art rests with the collector? Would the price offered by the two women collectors be significant in establishing whether Harrington or the gallery director was "more" right than the other?
3. At the beginning of his career, Harrington had to support himself as a bricklayer, thus reducing the amount of time he could spend on his painting. A number of foundations and government agencies offer support to talented artists so that they do not have to worry about making ends meet. Should more such support be given? Less? Why?
4. Should teachers treat special children, such as Harrington, in such a special way, as his elementary school teachers evidently did? Why or why not?

If the true impressionist spirit is one of spontaneity and light, no one   1
could live up to it more than Jim Harrington. Harrington, who loves the
challenge of a blank canvas, often begins a painting with only a composition
in mind. By coming to his easel without a set subject, he is able to enjoy the
challenge of turning his ideas into paintings that evolve as he works. A painting that starts out as a pumpkin field may turn into a battlefield and perhaps
end up as a view of the Hudson River covered with moving ice floes. Yet it

would be misleading to see this method as a lack of direction; it is simply that Harrington is fully at ease in what he does and he does not have to struggle for a painting to emerge.

"The joy is in pushing the paint around," Harrington says, "and I of- 2 ten cannot get a brush in my hand fast enough. This morning, for instance, I went to my studio with a composition in mind, although I was unsure what the final painting would be. I knew it would have figures, but I did not know what they would be doing. I was certain only of their places on the canvas."

The ease with which Harrington can set human figures in a landscape 3 is the result of practice dating back to childhood when he traveled the subways of New York City armed with a sketch pad. He would draw the people across the aisles and note how they sat, stood, and behaved.

Fascinated with paints, Harrington loves to mix them, and he keeps a 4 collection of paints that laid side by side would fill a seven-foot shelf. Although he uses only a few colors in each painting, he experiments with a range of them and especially enjoys creating different shades of gray. "Gray, to me, is the queen of the colors," Harrington explains. "Properly used, it sets the stage for all the others."

Since Harrington was tough and rebellious in grammar school, his 5 teachers found that the only way to deal with him was to let him draw murals with colored chalk on the blackboard at the back of each classroom. His teachers would assign a theme, such as transport or agriculture, and then leave him alone to do the mural. Indeed, in his last year in grammar school, Harrington did not go to class at all. "I was a terrible, terrible kid," he recalls with a grin.

Next, Harrington tried the New York School of Industrial Art, which 6 he felt taught him nothing of painting and little of draftsmanship. He was disappointed with the school, so he left it and, in 1946, joined the Marines. After his discharge in 1948, he attended the Cartoonists and Illustrators Institute of New York City on the GI Bill, which again proved to him that he could not find what he wanted in the classroom. "I realized that I could not be taught how to paint at a school," Harrington explains. "I had to study on my own, and can truly say that I am entirely self-taught."

To earn a living, Harrington went into his father's craft—that of a 7 bricklayer. He found bricklaying both creative and satisfying. He would lay bricks for six to eight months and paint for the rest of the year. Since he could pick up work in any part of the country, he had the opportunity to paint in different places. Now that he devotes himself entirely to painting, he still travels and paints—from the mid-Atlantic states to the Maritime Provinces of Canada.

As a successful painter, Harrington has had his work exhibited at some 8 of this country's major galleries, among them the Mongerson Gallery in Chicago; the Albany Institute of History and Art in Albany, New York; and the

Mystic Maritime Gallery in Mystic, Connecticut. He is presently repre-
sented by the Seraphim Fine Art Gallery in Englewood, New Jersey; the
Hermine Merel Smith Fine Art Gallery on Martha's Vineyard; the South
Wharf Gallery on Nantucket; and by other prominent private galleries.

Independent of spirit, Harrington enjoys bending the rules of compo- 9
sition and at times will deliberately center the horizon or set a figure in the
middle of a painting. In one such painting, the figure was 11" high in a 24"-
× -36" painting and was set squarely in the middle. It was of a beach scene,
with his wife serving as the model for the figure. She was wearing a long
dress and a broad-brimmed hat, and was standing with her back to the
viewer. "When I took it to a gallery," Harrington recounts, "the director
would not exhibit it. In the end, I persuaded him to hang it, and later that
day, I overheard two women arguing over which of them was to have it."
Harrington contends it is not where a figure is placed that matters, but if its
placement serves an artistic purpose. The overall balance, space, mood,
color, and texture should give enough meaning to the composition for it to
seem natural to the viewer.

Harrington does most of his painting in the studio, for on beaches, his 10
favorite subject, canvases can become sand magnets. He makes many
sketches on the site, on either a French easel or a pochade box, and uses
these sketches for reference in his studio. "If, for instance, I want to paint a
scene with horses," he explains, "I begin by making many drawings of
horses and surrounding myself with them. In fact, if I had my way, I'd bring
a bale of hay into the studio. Once I begin painting, however, I do no more
drawings. I won't even have a pencil in my studio."

Harrington finds a pochade box especially valuable in sketching since 11
it combines a palette with an easel and can be held in one hand. In it he
usually carries a few tubes of paints and a 5"- × -7" canvas board. Where the
French easel or the pochade box proves impractical, he makes quick notes in
his sketch pad, using a pen for the facts and watercolor for indicating dis-
tances and local color. Harrington makes a point of drawing every day; he
regards this as practice—in the same sense that a musician plays scales on his
or her instrument.

Harrington's studio faces north, with its justly prized north light. 12
However, because he begins painting at five in the morning and finishes at
about eight at night, he has fitted his studio with four-foot-long, full-
spectrum, fluorescent lights, which, to avoid drastic changes in light quality,
he keeps burning day and night. Full-spectrum lights, unlike normal fluorescent or incandescent lamps, do not affect color and are long-lasting. Although he bought them in 1976, Harrington has not had to replace his
lights, making them a technically sound and cost-effective method of studio
illumination.

After mixing color with medium on a glass 20"- × -30" palette, the art- 13
ist begins by working the basic colors onto the canvas with swatches of

either linen or unbleached muslin. "I must work quickly at this point," Harrington explains, "and by touching the paint to canvas without a brush to separate me from it, my person and my materials become as one. If the painting is to have an horizon, once I know where it will be—what is to be land and what is to be sky—the painting starts to grow under my hand."

Dipping the muslin rags into the paint with quick hand motions, Harrington blocks in the painting. He may begin the composition with one basic color or with two or three—as the subject demands. Only when the painting is completely blocked in does he turn to the can holding his favorite brushes. A second can is used to hold worn brushes so that when he needs to replace them, he can simply pack them off to his suppliers for them to send him the same brands and sizes. 14

Before leaving his studio in the evening, Harrington scrapes down much of the painting done that day—an important element of his technique. He may begin by painting a face blue and the background in flesh tones, scrape it all down, and then the next day put positive on negative, completely reversing the colors. The scraping is done with twelve palette knives of different sizes and shapes. Harrington believes that letting the underpainting peep through in this way gives a painting a patina that cannot be gained in any other way. 15

Scraping a painting down can be painful. Harrington recalls that John Singer Sargent could not bring himself to do it and had a student or an apprentice do it for him. Although he shares some of these feelings, he forces himself to scrape down the painting and bring it up again and again until he is satisfied. 16

An artist, Harrington holds, should not skimp on materials but should use the best. With this in mind, he uses only natural bristle and pure sable brushes, and although they are among the most expensive, Blockx oil paints. "If I use the best brushes, the best paints, and put the best canvas on the best easel," Harrington explains, "I have no room for excuses. This way I cannot later argue that I could have done better with finer materials." 17

Although Harrington will often visit museums and galleries to refresh his eye, he emulates no one artist and follows no one school. Much as he admires Frans Hals, considering him perhaps the greatest Master and possibly the first true impressionist, he does not borrow Hals's style or technique. Nor, much as he loves them, does he imitate any of the French or American Impressionists. It is the inspiration behind their paintings that moves him, which is why he has given copies of Robert Henri's *The Art Spirit* to both friends and fellow artists—some fifty or sixty. 18

To younger artists, Harrington's advice is that in art there is no fixed level of achievement. "If a young artist believes there is a plateau on which the artist can rest on his or her laurels," he says, "then he or she will be sadly disappointed. Success is only the foundation for further progress, for there is no resting place." 19

QUESTIONS ABOUT THE RHETORICAL SITUATION

1. A number of Feit's terms and references may be unfamiliar to you unless you are a regular reader of *American Artist*. However, he does define some of those terms. What do these definitions suggest about readers of *American Artist?*

2. What evidence is there that Feit's intended audience consists of novice artists or art collectors rather than accomplished artists? In other words, would Harrington himself be a part of the intended audience for this essay?

3. Harrington has strong opinions about art supplies, painting techniques, and compositional strategies. To what extent does Feit seem to be siding with Harrington and to what extent does he seem to be a fairly neutral reporter?

4. What response do you think Feit is hoping for? Does he want readers to buy Harrington's paintings? Does he want them to seek out these paintings in galleries? Does he hope to change the readers' own painting techniques? Does he hope to expand their knowledge about painting or about one specific painter?

QUESTIONS ABOUT THE ESSAY'S VOICE

1. About what topic has Feit made himself an authority? What interpretations or generalizations does he offer that establish him as an authority?

2. Feit relies more on paraphrase than McNutt or Oliver did in their essays in this chapter. Why? Is his strategy a good one?

3. How effective are the quotations used by Feit? Do any in particular create a vivid picture of the painter? How?

4. Feit quite often interrupts Harrington's quotations in the middle by adding the phrase "Harrington explains." How would these quotations sound different if the tag phrase appeared either before or after the quotation instead of in the middle? Based on your observations of Feit's use of this technique, can you form any generalizations about when you can use it effectively?

5. In the middle of several paragraphs recounting Harrington's life, Feit inserts ¶4 about Harrington's fascination with paint. How effective a place is this for this paragraph? Can you find any other place in the essay where it might fit more effectively? Explain your answers.

6. What organizational pattern does Feit use in ¶10–16? How does this organization help to give the essay the voice of authority?

7. In ¶17, Feit appears to have changed subjects completely, yet no transition appears to link this paragraph to what has preceded it. Does he need a transition here? If so, what might it be? If not, why not?

8. This interview essay concludes with a final comment by the interviewee
   also. How effective a final quotation is this? (You might compare it to the
   concluding quotations in McNutt's and Oliver's essays.)

TOPICS TO WRITE ABOUT

1. Interview an artist or craftsperson about his or her art or craft. (Remember that Harrington himself describes bricklaying as a creative profession.) POTENTIAL AUDIENCES: beginners in the same art or craft field/
   readers who had not thought of the craft as creative. POTENTIAL PURPOSES:
   to offer instruction in how to begin or how to improve in the craft/to explain to such readers that the craft is indeed creative by describing how
   the craftsperson works.
2. Interview someone who has traveled to the Louvre in France or to the
   Prado in Spain or to the Rodin Museum in Philadelphia or to any famous
   art museum. POTENTIAL AUDIENCES: readers of a travel magazine/the students in your class. POTENTIAL PURPOSE: to depict vividly what such a trip
   might be like.

Roach Fever

Ann Hornaday

Ann Hornaday, who lives in New York City, is a contributing editor to *Ms.*
magazine. This interview first appeared in *Ms.* in 1986. *Ms.* was first published in the early 1970s and was intended to provide women with their own
magazine, one not focused on the traditional domestic roles of women. A recent typical issue of the magazine included articles on a woman sailor, a
woman singer, women and Mayan culture, national political conventions, and
health problems specific to women. However, the issue also included articles
on sports, books, technology, psychology, and finances. This interview was
part of a series of interviews with women in professions not considered traditionally female.

QUESTIONS ABOUT IDEAS

1. Betty Faber herself confesses to having serious doubts at times about the
   value of her unusual work. What value does such scientific study have?
   What value need it have to justify government funding? Should scientists

be funded to study roaches? Would your answer be different if the species being studied were different? Gorillas? Dogs? Minnows?

2. How do you explain the very strong negative reactions toward insects and spiders on the part of many people? Do you know anyone who has such strong aversions? Why do they feel the way they do? Do you know anyone, on the other hand, who is quite interested in insects (beekeepers, butterfly collectors, for instance)? What would be the appeal of these species?

3. Can you relate to Faber's patience in studying roaches? Have you or people you know ever exhibited similar patience when involved in a hobby or pastime or job (such as building doll furniture or making jewelry or knitting)? Is there any parallel between the two situations?

For the last ten years, on any given night of the week, shortly before 1
sunset, one could find Betty Lane Faber arriving at the American Museum of Natural History on New York's Upper West Side. As she entered the museum's baroque lobby and walked to the bank of elevators, the darkened, cavernous corridors would be nearly deserted. Exiting at the fifth floor, Faber would climb a tiny circular staircase, and yet another narrow stair to her office, where she checked and loaded batteries into her infrared equipment, prepared her camera, and tested the microphone of her tape recorder. As night descended, she walked next door to the museum's greenhouse, where she would spend the next five to six hours tracking, observing, and compiling meticulous records on cockroaches.

Betty is an entomologist—a specialist in the study of insects—and over 2
the last decade she has trained her professional curiosity almost entirely on cockroaches. If this seems an unlikely choice for exhaustive study, Faber is undaunted. The fact that most people consider cockroaches worthy only of squashing, not studying, seems to be lost on her—she speaks of her subjects as any other scientist would, with a combination of professional detachment, grudging respect, and dedicated affection.

Lay people's most common assumption about entomologists is that 3
they are the types who always liked bugs—the kids who constantly poked around puddles and peered under stones with intrepid wonder. But Betty Faber was never a member of this curious society. She grew up in Biloxi, Mississippi, where they know from cockroaches—in Biloxi the roaches are big, and they fly. Faber engaged in typical adolescent pursuits—sailing, swimming off the Gulf coast, playing her violin—that did not include an inordinate interest in the insect world; in fact, bugs had always made Betty Faber, as she puts it, "squirmy."

But during her course of study in biology at William and Mary College, in Williamsburg, Virginia, Faber became fascinated with circadian 4
rhythms—the way that animals tell time without clocks or exposure to

light—and decided to pursue a graduate degree at New Jersey's Rutgers
University. There she read a definitive project on circadian rhythms using
cockroaches and came to the sobering conclusion that "if I wanted to go on
in this type of research, I really had to get used to roaches."

It took Faber the next four years to conquer completely her fear of   5
roaches: "When I started to identify particular species of roaches *within* my
nightmares, I knew I was getting better," she says with a laugh.

Today she shares her office—a cramped, colorful sanctum in the mu-   6
seum's animal behavior department—with a menagerie of white mice, rats, a
boa constrictor, and several thousand cockroaches (housed in five aquari-
ums), which she handles with almost disconcerting nonchalance.

Smiling, she reaches into an aquarium and lifts out a three-inch,   7
mahogany-brown cockroach (if Hollywood ever does Kafka's *The Metamor-
phosis*, she's got their Gregor Samsa). The bug curls around Faber's index
finger and begins to hiss loudly. "This one is from Madagascar—he's hissing
because he thinks I'm a predator. He's saying, 'Please don't eat me.'" She
puts the roach back tenderly, and it commences to munch on a piece of apple.

Faber is now one of the nation's leading experts on roach behavior.   8
Pesticide companies are especially interested in her discoveries regarding the
minutiae of cockroach behavior; the more they know about the habits of
cockroaches, the more effectively they can kill them. "It's really important
to understand animals if you want to control them. You have to know what
they do in a natural environment—what they like and what they don't like,"
says Faber.

Last year she was asked by American Cyanamid, the manufacturers of   9
Combat Roach Control Systems, to brief lay people on roach behavior as
part of its marketing effort. Faber was under no obligation to boost the
product, but it turns out that Combat may well be the state-of-the-art answer
to over-the-counter roach control. The secret is its delayed action: when
cockroaches eat the poison, they don't die on the spot, so other insects aren't
"warned off" by their death. And it stays potent for months, not leaving
their system, so that the roaches that don't die the first time will eventually
die of the poison's buildup. Faber uses Combat in her own office, to control
her escapees.

Faber is pleased to share her expertise where it is most needed, but in   10
hearing her describe her work, it becomes clear that the cornerstone of her
research is the time she spends observing the wild roaches of the museum's
greenhouse. ("Wild" roaches are simply those that are not caged in a lab.)
Here, what roaches "like and what they don't like" is demonstrated with
every subtle antennae curl or tentative six-legged step.

Watches usually begin as soon as the sun sets and run until midnight   11
or 1 A.M.—long, uneventful hours during which Faber is on constant alert.
Once the sun goes down, the cockroaches emerge for their four-hour feed-

ing, eating the greenhouse plants and an occasional dead fish. Almost immediately after feeding, the females disappear, but the males hang around, doing nothing or grooming themselves. Eventually, the males disappear as well, and by the end of a watch there might be as few as ten roaches in sight. During that time Faber talks into her tape recorder, observing the roaches' habits and noting any "weird" behavior. She has been rewarded for her vigilance and patience with a few adventures.

She recalls: "The most fascinating event I've seen was a centipede am- 12 bushing a cockroach. I was almost finished with an unusually late three A.M. watch when I came across a centipede. In about five minutes, a cockroach—number 191 female, to be precise—lumbered toward the centipede. Finally her antennae came in contact with the appendages on the centipede's rear.

"For an instant, the centipede mimicked the familiar cockroach greet- 13 ing by fencing with its rear legs as though they were the antennae of another cockroach. The roach paused, the centipede pounced, and they fought. The cockroach managed to shrug the centipede off and lumbered away. Nobody was fatally injured."

Faber has also been witness to the rarely observed courtship dance of 14 the greenhouse's wild cockroach ("It consists of a lot of wing flapping, erratic running, and backing into things"), but she is still waiting to see a newly molted cockroach—pure white, before the eight-hour "tanning" process, when the shell hardens and the roach becomes that familiar shade of brown.

Such diversions are rare, however, and cockroach behaviors are usually 15 mundane. Faber's challenge these last eleven years, aside from discovering and honing her hitherto unknown reserves of patience, has been in perfecting the art of roach watching itself—recording what she sees in such a way that she will be able to understand it later, tease out consistencies, and draw conclusions. Every movement that the greenhouse cockroaches make—feeding, grooming, interacting with other roaches—is spotted and recorded, time after time. It is a long, arduous, and demanding process: in five years of painstaking surveillance, Faber has documented the behavior and habits of more than 2,000 roaches. Her study is thought to be one of the most extensive collections of data in the field.

Although Faber started by focusing on circadian rhythms, and then 16 later, feeding habits, recently she has become fascinated by the differences between male and female cockroaches' behaviors.

"Males tend to stay out at night a lot later, and tend to be much more 17 obvious and vulnerable, probably because a male that has mated—while maybe not worthless—isn't as useful as a female cockroach. The female continually produces eggs, so she is, in that way, a more valuable member of the community.

"Females also eat a lot more, because they're producing eggs, and they 18 spend a lot more time looking for food.

"It's hard to say who's more aggressive," Faber muses. "It might be 19 more a question of size than of gender. I've been studying food carrying—if you put food out, which will be the first ones to come out and get it? They're almost always the little ones. Once they get it back to the hiding place, a big one will come out and grab it. I don't know if it means anything or not, but I think it's interesting."

Faber is currently writing up all the data she has collected since she 20 arrived at the museum—an endeavor that will result in a study of cockroach behavior that will be among the most comprehensive in the entomological field. Although her midnight watches have come to an end (in fact, the museum is planning to tear down the rooftop greenhouse), Faber intends to continue her wild-roach observations, perhaps in the building's appropriately dank basement. She welcomes the change of scenery. "Roaches behave differently in different locations," she explains. "Adding another roach population to my data will make the information more accurate in the long run."

In addition to her work at the museum, Faber teaches biology at New 21 York's Baruch College two days a week. In May of 1985, she gave birth to a baby boy, Joshua, whose care is shared by Marcel Faber, Betty's husband of seventeen years. As a biotechnologist, he is able to do much of his work in the house, and when Betty is teaching all day, the brunt of the household duties fall on him. "We don't have any of those kinds of divisions where there's one task that's always mine or always his," Faber says. "He's done everything I've done—except breast-feeding."

If the mainstay of Faber's research has consisted of the hours she 22 spends waiting and watching in the greenhouse, then the romance of her career—and the reason she has persevered—derives from field study. In the last five years, Faber has received grants to observe the wild roaches of Trinidad, whose jungles spawn about 200 species for her to track, compared to about twenty-five species indigenous to the United States.

In the wild, the scientist becomes an intrepid explorer and cockroaches 23 take on an exotic, almost romantic patina. "It's sort of like science fiction," says Faber. "If I were going to Mars, and I was looking at some creature I didn't understand, where would I start? That's how I try to treat cockroaches. That way at least I'm thinking of them as not being too closely related to me."

The flip side of the fierce independence Faber enjoys in the field is the 24 profound loneliness she has also known there. "It can be horrible work, and sometimes it's very depressing," she admits. "When you're doing fieldwork, and you're all alone and there's no one there to talk to who's doing the same thing you are, sometimes it's overwhelming. Then, after you've collected the data and you're writing it up and it doesn't seem as if anybody's doing the kind of work you are, you *really* wonder about the value of it."

Faber plans to return to Trinidad as soon as her son is old enough to go 25 with her, and she is beckoned by other alluring climes. "I'd really like to get to Peru one of these days—in parts of South America there are roaches that are *huge,* and I've never seen a live one. There's a beautiful, beautiful roach that's red, yellow, and blue, and there are polka-dotted ones in Africa." Her mellow southern drawl rises slightly in anticipation. "And New Guinea! New Guinea has *fabulous* roaches..."

QUESTIONS ABOUT THE RHETORICAL SITUATION

1. Hornaday's essay was published in *Ms.* magazine, not a magazine likely to have a large percentage of scientists as readers. How has Hornaday adapted her essay to her audience so that her readers can understand what she has written?
2. Are there any parts of this essay that seem to be included specifically for the readers of *Ms.?* If you think so, what would be the effect of omitting this material?
3. While Faber is quite comfortable with roaches and, in fact, seems to like them, Hornaday herself is not an entomologist. Is there any indication in the essay of how Hornaday feels about the cockroaches? How does she feel about Faber?
4. How are Hornaday's attitude and her objectives in this essay different from the attitude and objectives of Alexander Petrunkevitch, the entomologist who wrote "The Spider and the Wasp" (Chapter 11)?

QUESTIONS ABOUT THE ESSAY'S VOICE

1. Late in the essay, Hornaday refers to Faber's southern drawl. Why hasn't she been more consistent in depicting that aspect of Faber's speech? What technique does she use to give her readers some idea of the sound of Faber's speech? Is the technique successful?
2. Hornaday does not very often describe *how* Faber speaks. Should she do so more frequently? How effective is the essay in presenting Faber's personality to us?
3. Hornaday does not quote Faber very much in the opening six paragraphs or so. Why not? How do these paragraphs establish the essay's voice? She uses the pronoun "one" in ¶1, suggesting a rather formal approach to the essay. Later, however, she refers to Dr. Faber as "Betty." How consistent is Hornaday in keeping to the formal voice established early in the essay? Is she consistent enough? Why or why not?
4. Hornaday uses longer quotations from her interviewee than did the writers of the earlier essays in this chapter. Examine these long quotations. What is the effect on the essay's voice of these lengthy passages? Should Hornaday have used more indirect quotation or paraphrase? Explain.

5. In ¶15, Hornaday writes about Faber's study that it "is thought to be one of the most extensive collections of data in the field." Why has Hornaday used the passive voice here? Is this an effective use of the passive voice?
6. What evidence is there that Hornaday asked Faber the question "Such as?" Why was this an important question for Hornaday to be asking?
7. In ¶23, Hornaday uses the word *patina,* a term also used by the painter in Edward Feit's essay "James Harrington." How is the word used similarly/differently in the the two essays?
8. As the other essays in this chapter have done, "Roach Fever" concludes by quoting the interview subject. How effective is the conclusion of this essay? Why does the final quotation end with an ellipsis?

TOPICS TO WRITE ABOUT

1. Interview someone who is actively engaged in a research project. POTENTIAL AUDIENCES: others in the same field of expertise/readers who do not understand the technical aspects of the field being researched. POTENTIAL PURPOSE: to explain in clear terms the significance of the research.
2. Interview someone with an unusual hobby. POTENTIAL AUDIENCES: readers of a magazine entitled *Hobbies and Pastimes*/the general reading public. POTENTIAL PURPOSES: to explain one of the less-known hobbies/to make the readers understand why someone might pursue such an unusual hobby.

Living after Dying
Lynn Sawyer

Lynn Sawyer has been an R.N. in New York, Maryland, and Ohio for more than sixteen years, working in critical care units for more than eight of those years. Currently a Ph.D. candidate in nursing, Sawyer has published extensively in nursing journals on her research and on nursing care issues. Recently Sawyer has researched the effects on families of near death experiences and the resulting implications for critical care nurses caring for people who have had near death experiences and their families. "Living after Dying," written for *Model Voices,* is an outgrowth of that research. (Note: Tom Sawyer, the subject of this interview is no relation to Lynn Sawyer, the interviewer.)

QUESTIONS ABOUT IDEAS

1. How do you think family members and loved ones of a person who has undergone a near-death experience (NDE) might be affected by the NDE and its aftermath?

2. How does a near-death experience compare to the experience of Lazarus in the New Testament, who was raised from the dead by Jesus? Are there significant similarities or differences between the story of Lazarus and the near-death experience described in "Living after Dying"?
3. Which theories mentioned in the essay seem most convincing to you in explaining the phenomenon of the near-death experience?

> I saw blotches of colors, all the colors of the rainbow, some that I
> have never been able to duplicate, fluorescences, phosphorescences,
> and fuschia-type colors. It was very beautiful. I had the sensation
> of waking up in absolute darkness. It was absolutely opaque
> blackness—there was no light at all or no identifiable objects, but I
> knew that I was awake. As it got darker, I had the feeling of
> forward motion.

So begins Tom Sawyer when he describes his Near-Death experience 1
(NDE), an experience that changed a self-described "all-American brat" and fistfighting "class comedian" into a student of quantum physics and a lecturer who has spoken to audiences across the U.S.

NDE is a series of vivid events that survivors of a life-threatening 2
accident or illness describe once they regain consciousness. More than one theory has been developed to explain the NDE phenomenon. A psychological explanation might suggest that the NDE occurs as a coping mechanism, allowing an individual to deal with a catastrophic illness or accident. Lack of oxygen to the brain, natural hormonal secretions such as endorphins, and changes in body chemistries can cause alterations in thought processes or even hallucinations and offer possible scientific explanations for NDE. Some religious groups, however, theorize that the NDE is a spiritual phenomenon, a glimpse of afterlife, even proof of God's existence. Whatever NDE may be, it was very real to Tom Sawyer on that spring morning in 1978. Although not all victims of catastrophic experiences tell of an NDE, Tom has detailed memories of the episode, which only took eight minutes according to clock time but lasted long enough in Tom's mind for him to review his entire life. The after-effects of the NDE have given him a sense of urgency to share his new-found knowledge with others, which Tom accomplishes through his lectures at colleges and universities, participation in research studies, and interviews such as this one.

Although he claims he had not read a complete book cover-to-cover 3
throughout his high school education, Tom is a captivating speaker with a vocabulary drawn from the literature of physics, religion, philosophy, and the Far East. As he explains his experience, he becomes emotionally caught up in the description, at times hesitant, his head bowed and his voice husky, and at other times his body leaning forward, his voice excited and persuasive.

Tom Sawyer had never heard of an NDE on what he terms a "typical **4**
suburban American" morning in 1978 when he and his son began repairing
his truck in the Sawyer driveway. Quite knowledgeable about the safety
principles of automobile repair, Tom placed his truck on jack stands with
the wheels blocked for safety. But as he was teaching his son how to repair
the truck, the driveway collapsed because of air pockets underneath the asphalt, and the truck fell across Tom's chest, crushing his ribs, liver, and
lungs.

After several minutes, Tom lost consciousness and had neither heart **5**
beat nor respiration. He then saw the array of fluorescent and phosphores-
cent colors that signalled the beginning of his NDE. Typically, according to
those who have undergone a near-death experience, NDE often begins with
the separation of the mind and body, known as an "out-of-body" experience. The mind moves away from and above the body, and the individual
starts to move through a dark tunnel toward a light, the forward motion
Tom mentioned earlier.

Even now, Tom still recalls his experience vividly. After seeing the **6**
colors, he started to move down a tunnel, a tunnel, he says, that "was like
if you took a tornado, stretched it out straight, and looked down the center of it. It was cylindrical. It was very vast, as compared to small and
confining. It ranged anywhere from a thousand feet wide to ten thousand
miles wide." The movement continued, Tom says. "I was either floating
or traveling in the very center of the tunnel. There was no walkway.
There was nothing around me other than indescribable air. There was no
wind. There was no sound at all. There was no vibration. It was absolutely comfortable." Tom remembers the tunnel as a very desirable place
to be.

During Tom's journey through the tunnel, he experienced a review of **7**
his entire life. "The reminiscence of the life review allowed me to remember
events in such unbelievable detail from the first thirty-three years of my
life." Not only did the review provide information of specific events, but
Tom was actually able to feel the emotions of others and better understand
the reasons for their behavior.

For example, Tom's life review included a situation that had oc- **8**
curred when Tom was a teenager. He had gotten into a fight with a
drunken pedestrian who darted out in front of Tom's "hot rod," causing
Tom to slam on the brakes. Tom then rolled down the window of the car
and said sarcastically, "You know, next time you really ought to use the
crosswalk." The pedestrian reached through the window and slapped
Tom, calling him a "young whipper snapper." Tom immediately stepped
out of the truck and punched the man, who fell backward and struck his
head on the pavement. During his life review, Tom relived this incident,
but this time he actually understood how the pedestrian felt in the situation. "I can feel the total degradation, the humiliation, the drunken

state of that man. I'm aware of his devastated state, his uncontrollable bereavement which put him in that frame of mind since his wife had passed on two years prior."

For the first time in his life, Tom truly felt the pain of others, and 9 learned a great deal about himself as well. He describes this acquisition of knowledge as a humiliating and humbling experience. The life review taught Tom a number of such important lessons about himself and others.

As Tom continued to move forward, a speck of light appeared at the 10 end of the tunnel, and Tom's interaction with this light became the pivotal moment in his NDE. At the end of the tunnel he became motionless. He describes the light as "brighter than anything imaginable or than a million anythings imaginable. And yet paradoxically it didn't hurt my eyes at all. In fact the feeling of peace and contentment is indescribable, absolutely indescribable." Tom pauses in his narrative. "The right phrase is 'ineffable.'"

In spite of describing himself as an agnostic, Tom, in a voice thick 11 with emotion, explains that the light was "The Light of Jesus Christ. It was God. It was Heaven. It was the Light of Buddah enlightened. It was the Essence of the very pure Khrishna. It was all of those things. It was absolutely everything. It was even me. It equalled absolute pure unconditional love."

When Tom became a part of the light, he had the opportunity to com- 12 municate with the light, to ask questions, questions to which he was instantaneously given the correct answer. Tom also had to choose whether to return to a normal life or to stay and remain part of the light. His voice still choked with tears, Tom explains that he was told that he had the opportunity to return to normal life. In other words, by deciding to return, Tom would "instantaneously survive this death situation. No conditions. No strings attached. There were no conditions at all. Just my decision and my desire." But it was a choice, Tom notes. "I also had the choice to stay and become part of this light."

Because the light was perfection, Tom chose to stay. Hesitatingly, he 13 describes his sorrow in leaving the light and returning to a normal life. "In other words I'm actually feeling sorry for myself that I'm here right now. I'm loving this, and this is okay, but it can't even begin to compare with perfection." After his interaction with the light, Tom found himself moving back through the tunnel and regained consciousness as he slammed back into his body "like a tremendous electrical shock." The return to his body marked a common conclusion to an NDE.

Tom's interaction with the light changed him forever. The former hot- 14 rodder who once got into a fistfight in the street now reads physics texts and the literature of many religions, and works with troubled teenagers. "So many things are a priority in my life now. If anything it enhanced my love for my family and my wife." Because his life review enabled him to see from an outsider's view all the events of his life up to that point, Tom learned to accept others as they are. He learned to love them for themselves, experiencing what he refers to as "unconditional love" for all humans, an outlook that has since become a way of life for Tom Sawyer.

Tom does not question why or how his NDE occurred, believing that 15 he was destined on that particular day in May to have a spiritual awakening. How does he feel about it now, almost a decade later? "How do I feel about it? It's something that happened to me. It is something that I was given. I do consider it a loving gift from God." Still thinking about his own reactions, Tom goes on to say that the NDE "has both positive aspects and negative aspects. There are burdens to bear as a result which I didn't have to put up with before. Gee, I guess I'm kind of neutral in deciding is it all good or all bad." But Tom's final word about his NDE is clear when he concludes, "I think I'm personally much better off."

Whether the NDE occurred because of lack of oxygen or as an hallu- 16 cination or as proof of God is not significant; the significance to Tom Sawyer is the burning reality of his near experience with death and his burning need to communicate his new way of looking at living after so very nearly dying.

QUESTIONS ABOUT THE RHETORICAL SITUATION

1. "Living after Dying" was written specifically for *Model Voices*. Much of the same material, however, has been written about in a more scientific way for nursing science publications. In what ways does this essay demonstrate that it has been adapted to its audience: students enrolled in a college writing course?
2. What is the author's own attitude toward the phenomenon of the near death experience? To what extent can you determine which of the two theories offered in the text as explanations of NDE is more convincing to Lynn Sawyer? To what extent does she take a side in the controversy?
3. The research study out of which this essay grew was designed to assist critical care nurses to plan suitably to care for patients and their families after a near death experience. What is this essay's purpose?

QUESTIONS ABOUT THE ESSAY'S VOICE

1. Would this essay fit into the chapter on the persuasive voice? Why or why not? If not, how might it be changed in order to fit in that chapter?
2. The author herself never appears in this essay at all. How does that decision affect the interviewer's voice in this piece?
3. Examine the use of direct and indirect quotations in the essay. How effectively has the author used each form of quotation? Find a specific use of either a direct or indirect quotation that seems particularly effective to

you. Explain why. Find a specific use of either a direct or indirect quotation that seems particularly ineffective to you. Explain why.

4. Sawyer chooses not to conclude her essay with a quotation from her subject. How effective is her conclusion? Do you see any quotations that she might have used to conclude the essay?

5. The longest quotation used in the essay occurs at its very beginning. How effective was this quotation in getting your attention? In establishing what the essay would be about? In establishing the interviewer's voice?

6. In ¶8, the essay focuses on a single anecdote from Tom Sawyer's life review. How effective is this anecdote in illustrating the life review's significance to Sawyer?

7. In ¶11, Tom Sawyer tries to explain the light at the end of the tunnel. What does this explanation illustrate about his personality?

8. Most of the essays in Chapter 2 focus on people we have never heard of. Oliver's interview with a movie star focuses on someone we may know a little about. How is the voice in that essay different from the voices in the other essays, including Lynn Sawyer's voice in this essay?

TOPICS TO WRITE ABOUT

1. Interview someone who has undergone and recovered from a serious illness or a major operation. POTENTIAL AUDIENCES: the medical personnel who treated the patient you have interviewed/those readers facing similar treatment. POTENTIAL PURPOSES: to provide a patient's view of the experiece to the health care providers/to help prepare the readers for what lies ahead for them.

2. Interview a psychologist, a nurse, a physician, or a member of the clergy about the phenomenon of the near-death experience. POTENTIAL AUDIENCES: your classmates who have read Lynn Sawyer's "Living after Dying"/the general reading public. POTENTIAL PURPOSES: to provide them with an expert's views on the NDE phenomenon that will illuminate the experiences recounted by Tom Sawyer in "Living after Dying"/to provide them with an expert's views on the phenomenon of NDE.

THE WRITING PROCESS: REVISION

The essay you have just read was a fourth draft. Lynn Sawyer's main problem in writing "Living after Dying" was to find a focus for all of the interview material she had accumulated from her conversations with Tom Sawyer. She had over three and a half hours of interviews on tape, but she needed to discover a focus that would enable her to select useful information from the large amount of material available to her, quite a common problem for writers working with interview material. The first thing Lynn Sawyer did was to jot down possibilities in a quick list. Here is her first attempt to deal with the material.

Focus: (1) attitude change following the NDE or (2) simply the description of the NDE?

Start: description of the movement through the tunnel toward the light; paraphrased for effect as attention getter?

(2) Background information: what is it?

when does it happen?

how often does it happen?

Not culturally or religiously related.

(1) attitude changes: quotes illustrating

"unconditional love"

predestination

urgency to communicate knowledge

preciousness of life

(2) description of event: quotes illustrating

out of body

movement through tunnel

light

interaction with light

return to body

How to end??

quotes from NDEr or wife on changes in lives?

quote discussing neither positive or negative experience?

Following these preliminary thoughts, she wrote two drafts. These drafts relied very heavily on the interview subject's description of what had happened to him during and after the experience. Finally, Lynn Sawyer decided that her focus needed to be on the attitude change in her interview subject, requiring her to provide some background of what the experience itself was like but stressing Tom Sawyer's perceptions of the event more than the facts of what happened. Having solved her major problem, she then wrote a third draft. Take a look at that third draft, which includes the author's handwritten revisions.

Third Draft

I saw blotches of colors, all the colors of the rainbow, some that I

have never been able to duplicate, fluorescences, phosphorescences,

and fuschia-type colors. It was very beautiful. I had the sensation of waking up in absolute darkness. It was absolutely opaque blackness—

there was no light at all or no identifiable objects, but I knew that I

was awake. As it got darker, I had the feeling of forward motion.

So begins Tom Sawyer's ~~description of~~ *when he describes* his Near-Death Experience   1

(NDE), an experience that changed a self-described "all-American brat" and

fistfighting "class comedian" into a student of quantum physics and a

~~nation-wide~~ lecturer, *who has spoken to audiences across the U.S.*

~~The~~ NDE is a series of vivid events that survivors of a life-threatening   2

accident or illness describe once they regain consciousness. *(insert A) whatever NDE maybe,* ~~Not all victims of~~

It was real to Tom Sawyer on that spring morning *Although* *in 1978.*

catastrophic experiences tell of an NDE, ~~however,~~ Tom has detailed mem-

ories of the ~~experience that~~ *episode, which only* lasted eight minutes according to clock time, but

lasted long enough in Tom's mind for ~~a~~ *him to* review ~~of~~ his entire life. The after-

effects of the NDE have given him a sense of urgency to share *his* new-found

knowledge with others, which Tom accomplishes ~~by~~ *through his* lectures at colleges and ①

universities, ~~interviews for magazines, and~~ participation in research studies, ②

③ *and interviews such as this one,*

Although he claims he had not read a complete book cover-to-cover   3

throughout his high school education, Tom is a captivating speaker, *with a* ~~His~~ vo-

cabulary ~~is~~ drawn from the literature of physics, religion, philosophy, and

the Far East. As he explains his experience, he becomes emotionally caught

up in the description, at times, *hesitant,* his head bowed and his voice husky, ~~hesitant~~

his body and at other times, leaning forward, *his voice* excited and persuasive.

¶ *More than one theory has been developed to explain phenomenon.*

~~Several theories exist as to why~~ the NDE ~~occurs.~~ *Psychological theo-*   4

A medical point of view might ~~ries~~ suggest that the NDE occurs as a coping mechanism, *allowing an individual* to deal with ~~the~~ *a* catastrophic illness or accident. ~~Physiological influences such as lack~~ of [*Lack*]

oxygen to the brain, ~~the presence of~~ natural hormonal secretions such as

endorphins, ~~of~~ changes in body chemistries ~~are known to~~ cause alter- [*and* ... *can*]

ations in thought processes or even hallucinations‸ Some religious groups, [*and offer one possible explanation for NDE.*]

‸~~claim~~ that the NDE is‸ ~~proof of~~ afterlife, ~~and proof of God.~~ [*however, theorize*] [*a spiritual phenomenon, a glimpse of*] [*even proof of God's existance.*]

Tom Sawyer had ~~never heard of an NDE in 1978~~ when he and his son   5 [*on that typical suburban morning*]

began repairing his truck in the Sawyer driveway. ~~Tom, with obvious~~ [*Quite*]

knowledge‸ ~~of~~ safety principles of automobile repair,‸ placed his truck on jack [*able about the*] [*Tom*]

stands with the wheels blocked for safety. ~~As~~ he was teaching his son how to [*But as*]

repair the truck, the driveway collapsed because of air pockets underneath

the asphalt, and the truck fell across Tom's chest, crushing his ribs, liver,

and lungs.

After several minutes, Tom lost consciousness, ~~probably~~ had ~~no~~   6 [*and   neither ~~heart~~*]

heart beat ~~and breathing, and~~ saw the array of fluorescent and phospho- [*nor respiration. He then*]

rescent colors that signalled the beginning of his NDE. ~~What events are~~ [*Typically, according to*]

~~common to an NDE? The experience~~ often begins with the separation of [*those who have undergone a Near-Death Experience,*] [*NDE*]

the mind and body, ~~called~~ an "out-of-body" experience. ~~as~~ the mind [*known as*]

moves away from and above the body, ~~Near-Death Experieneers describe~~ [*and the individual starts to move*]

~~movement~~ through a dark tunnel toward a light, ~~a total life review of past~~ [*the foward motion Tom*]

~~events, meeting escorts and family members who have died previously,~~ [*mentioned earlier.*]

~~and a return to the body.~~

~~Tom's experience paralleled these common NDE themes. Tom's de-~~   7 [*Even now, Tom still recalls his experience vividly. After*]

Seeing the colors, he started to move down a tunnel, a tunnel,
~~scription, given almost ten years after the event occurred, demonstrates~~
he says, that
~~vivid imagery:~~

~~Now so onwardly I go and I had this feeling of forward motion and~~

~~then visually this darkness or void or abyss that took that shape of a~~

~~tunnel. The description of the tunnel can best be described as saying~~

" it was like if you took a tornado, stretched it out straight, and looked

down the center of it. It was cylindrical. It was very vast, as compared

to small and confining. It ranged anywhere from a thousand feet wide
" The moment continued.
to ten thousand miles wide." I was either floating or traveling in the
the tunnel
very center of it. There was no walkway. There was nothing around me

other than indescribable air. There was no wind; there was no sound
" Tom
at all, there was no vibration. It was absolutely comfortable ~~and very~~
remembers the tunnel as a very desirable place to be.
~~very desirous to be in this condition.~~

During Tom's journey through the tunnel, he experienced a life re- 8
of his entire life.
view, ~~a very detailed visual description of all events in his life since birth. He~~

~~explains the life review:~~ "The reminiscence of the life review allowed me to

remember events in such unbelievable detail from the first thirty-three years

of my life." Not only did the review provide information of specific events,
was able to feel   better understand   their
but Tom actually ~~felt~~ the emotions of others and ~~saw~~ the reasons for ~~other~~

~~individual's~~ behavior.
¶ For example,
                    that had
∧ The life review included a situation ~~which~~ occurred when Tom was a 9
He had gotten   drunken
teenager. ~~Tom got~~ into a fight with a pedestrian who darted out in front of

Tom's "hot rod," causing Tom to slam on the brakes. ~~Although he did not~~

~~hit the pedestrian with his truck;~~ Tom than rolled down the window of the car and said sarcastically, "You know, next time you really ought to use the cross walk." The pedestrian reached through the window and slapped Tom, calling him a "young whipper snapper." Tom immediately stepped out of the truck and punched the man ~~pedestrian~~, who fell backward and struck his head on the pavement. During ~~the~~ his life review, Tom ~~relived the~~ this *stet* incident, but this time he actually understood how the pedestrian felt in the situation:

> "I can feel the total degradation, the humiliation, the drunken state of that man. I'm aware of his devastated state, his uncontrollable bereavement which put him in that frame of mind, since his wife had passed on two years prior." ~~Now if you don't learn a lot of things in a hurry. One minor event, actually, and I learned many things about that one man that were impossible to find out.~~

For the first time in his life, Tom truly felt the pain of others, and learned a 10 great deal about himself as well. He describes this acquisition of knowledge as a humiliating and humbling experience. ~~Other events in the NDE also~~ The life review taught Tom a number of such important ~~information~~ lessons about himself and others.

Tom continued to move foward

As ~~he moved through the tunnel,~~ a speck of light appeared at the end 11 of the tunnel, and Tom's interaction with this light became the pivotal moment in his NDE. At the end of the tunnel he became motionless. He describes The light ~~was~~ as "brighter than anything imaginable or than a millions anythings imaginable. And yet paradoxically it didn't hurt my eyes at all. In fact the feeling of

Tom pauses in his narrative. —————— "

peace and contentment is indescribable, absolutely indescribable. The right

phrase is ineffable."

~~Tom describes the light as being outside the tunnel, and~~ In spite of de-   12

Tom,   *thick with emotion,*

scribing himself as an agnostic, ~~in a husky~~ voice explains that the light was "The

Light of Jesus Christ. It was God. It was Heaven. It was the Light of Buddah

enlightened. It was the Essence of the very pure Khrishna. It was all of those

things. It was absolutely everything. It was even me. It equalled absolute pure

unconditional love."

had

When Tom became a part of the light, he ~~was given~~ the opportunity to   13

communicate with the light, ~~He was given the opportunity~~ to ask questions,

questions to which he was   *had to choose*

~~and~~ instantaneously ~~was~~ given the correct answer. Tom ~~was~~ also ~~given the~~

~~choice~~ whether to return to a normal life or to stay and remain part of the

light. His voice still choked with tears ~~and emotion,~~ Tom explains, *that he*

that he had

~~I~~ was told, "~~Tom, you have~~ the opportunity to return to normal life." 14

In other words, by deciding to return, Tom would

~~Now what that meant was~~ instantaneously ~~upon my desire it would be facil-~~

~~itated that I would~~ survive this death situation. No conditions. No strings

attached. There were no conditions at all. Just my decision and my desire."

But it was a choice, Tom notes.

~~However,~~ I also had the choice to stay and become part of this light. "

Tom chose to stay. ~~with the light,~~ Because the light was perfection, ~~with~~ 15

Hesitatingly,

~~great emotion~~ he describes his sorrow in leaving the light and returning to a

normal life. "In other words I'm actually feeling sorry for myself that I'm here right now. I'm loving this, and this is okay, but it can't even begin to

compare with perfection." After his interaction with the light, ~~he~~ *Tom* found

himself moving back through the tunnel, and regained consciousness as he

slammed back into his body "like a tremendous electrical shock." *The return to his body marked a common conclusion to an NDE.*

Tom's interaction with the light changed him forever. The former ~~fist~~ *hot-* 16
rodder who once got into a fist fight in the street, now
~~wielding, All-American brat~~ reads physics texts, ~~the~~ *and* literature of many reli-

gions, and works with troubled teenagers. "So many things are a priority in

my life now. If anything, it enhanced my love for my family and my wife."

~~Mainly~~ Because *his* ~~as part of my~~ life review ~~I was able~~ *enabled him* to see from an outsider's

view ~~of from an unconditional love point of view~~ all the events of ~~my~~ *his* life up

to that point. *Tom learned to accept* ~~Unconditional love, the acceptance of~~ others as they are, ~~and~~ *He learned how*
to love ~~experiencing~~ experiencing what he calls "unconditional love," an outlook that has
~~loving~~ them for themselves, ~~because~~ a way of life for Tom Sawyer. *since become*

~~When Tom Sawyer was asked about his feelings about the NDE, he~~ 17

~~was somewhat puzzled.~~

INSERT B "How do I feel about it? It's something that happened to me. It is

something that I was given. I do consider it a loving gift from God." ~~It~~

INSERT C has both positive aspects and negative aspects. There are burdens to

bear as a result which I didn't have to put up with before. Gee, I

guess I'm kind of neutral in deciding is it all good or all bad." "I think **INSERT D**

I'm personally much better off."

Tom does not question why or how the NDE occurred, *believing that* ~~He believes~~ he 18

was destined on that particular day in May to have a spiritual awakening.
How does he feel almost a decade later? **INSERT B** *still thinking*

about his own reactions, Tom goes on to say that the NDE [Insert C] Tom's final word about his NDE is clear when he concludes [INSERT D]

¶ Whether the NDE occurred because of lack of oxygen, or as an hallucination, or as proof of God is not significant; the significance to Tom is the burning reality of his experience ~~at~~ [near] [with] [his] death, and ~~the~~ burning need to communicate ~~a~~ [his] new way of looking at living after [so very nearly] dying.

QUESTIONS ABOUT THE REVISING PROCESS

1. Why did Sawyer move insert A from ¶4 to ¶2?
2. This earlier draft has more direct quotations from the interview subject than does the final draft. Why has Sawyer reduced the length and number of quotations? How effective a strategy is this?
3. One of the most frequent locations for revisions in this draft is at the beginning of paragraphs. What is Sawyer trying to accomplish by such changes? How effective are these changes?
4. In ¶6, Sawyer cuts out one of the few questions she has included in her draft. She also cuts out some information at the end of the paragraph. What are her reasons for doing so?
5. Which revisions has Sawyer made in her text that surprise you? In other words, what might you have expected her to leave unchanged? Why? Do you agree with what she has done? What would you have changed that she has chosen not to change? Why would you make such changes?
6. In what ways is her final draft an improvement over her third draft? Why?
7. In what ways has Sawyer's revision process resembled your own revision process? In what ways has it differed?

13

The Research Voice

WHY DO RESEARCH?

Suppose you read *Oliver Twist* in an English class and discover that you are interested in its author, Charles Dickens. In fact, suppose that you are interested enough in Dickens to want to write about him. However, you realize that all you know about Dickens is the little bit that appeared in the introduction to the novel you have just read and a few anecdotes about the writer that you have heard over the years. What would you do?

Obviously, you would have to seek out the information you needed, most likely by visiting your campus library. You might read more of Dickens' novels, but you might also read a biography of him, perhaps some books by literary critics offering their own theories about his writing, perhaps a magazine photo essay about Dickens' various homes and travels. You might track down a filmstrip about Dickens' career as a public speaker or a collected edition of his letters. Perhaps you would listen to a recorded dramatization of one of his books. With some effort you might be able to examine a few of Dickens' manuscripts, the actual pages on which he wrote out his novels in longhand.

At that point you would be ready to begin thinking about writing an essay about Dickens. But what would you write? You could write a condensed biography of the writer, focusing on those events of his life that turn up most memorably in his novels. Or you might examine one of his novels in great detail, offering your own interpretations of its themes, contrasting your opinions with those of other literary critics. You might explain the strengths and weaknesses of the many film versions made of his novels, including *Oliver Twist* and the film musical *Oliver!* You might try to explain how a specific novel developed through examining the manuscripts.

All these potential essays would require you to adopt the voice of the expert. But even more specifically, you would be adopting a special form of the expert's voice—the research voice. It would be readily apparent to your

428

readers that you had become an authority by virtue of your hard work in researching your topic, and, in fairness to the published work of other experts whom you had consulted, you would be sure to indicate just which information you had borrowed and from which source.

The research process and the voice it produces are obviously not limited to literary subjects. In Chapter 13 you will read essays that use the research voice in writing about nurses, Arctic ice fields, Indian folklore, and trial by jury, in addition to literary subjects.

ACADEMIC WRITING

As I mentioned in the introduction to this section of *Model Voices*, the voice of authority may be the most common voice in the writing of college students and teachers. And perhaps the research voice is the most common variety of the voice of authority used by those writers. Certainly, you will write research papers during your time as a college student, but you will also undoubtedly write essay exam answers, and they too, in a special sense, are products of research, research in the form of the reading and note taking you have done during the term.

So this chapter focuses on a familiar and important voice. The most common form taken by essays in the research voice is a familiar one also: *exposition.*

If a writer wished to write a vivid narrative or a vivid description, he would most likely write it in such a way that readers would almost feel as if they were a part of the narrative or description. Writing secondhand about someone else's vivid experience, however, would not be a very good way to create that feeling of vicariousness, of actually living through the experiences oneself. I might write an essay about someone else's vivid description of a coral reef so that I could make comments about her writing or about the conclusions she draws about coral reefs, but if I wanted to make my readers live the experience, I would have to quote her entire piece of writing. Not much point in that.

Narrative writing and descriptive writing are far more likely to occur in the voice of firsthand experience or even the interview voice than the research voice. The research voice, on the other hand, is more compatible with the goal of explaining or informing. Using data gathered from a variety of sources, the research writer may be able to explain to readers how the methods for selecting American juries have evolved in the past several decades, and why one method of jury selection is better than another. Or the writer, through research, might convince readers that the two-year college experience simply does not appear very often in short stories and novels by contemporary writers.

A COMMON PITFALL

The reason why writing in the research voice so frequently takes the form of exposition is easy to see: facts and details are necessary for explaining, and facts and details are often what research uncovers; however, by themselves facts and details do not explain. The research voice, remember, is a variety of the voice of authority, and authorities or experts, as we have seen, *not only report facts but also connect and interpret them.* So too do writers who effectively use the research voice, and therefore it is important for writers to avoid the common pitfall of mistaking a compendium of facts for an essay. There must be a point to the research, a reason for presenting the material to the reader. Indeed, the purpose of conducting the research is to allow the writer to become expert enough to begin *making connections and interpretations for his own readers.*

Some of the connections such writers make are between research and firsthand experience, as you will see in a number of the essays in this chapter. While the essays in Chapters 10 and 11 work quite effectively by relying entirely upon firsthand experience, the essays in this chapter could work just as effectively without any firsthand experience at all. It is the research—the facts, the details, the borrowed ideas—that make the research voice a distinctive form of the voice of authority.

A Sample

Here is an excerpt from an essay entitled "Extinction: An Historical Perspective," written by a freshman zoology major named Christopher Hockett. Chris wanted to publish this essay in our campus newspaper in hopes that other students would read it and learn something important. Notice how Chris uses the many details and facts he has researched to make a point; there's more to his essay than just a collection of facts.

Profit was also an indirect cause of extinction among many other animal species. Many countries in the Old World were sending explorers to search out new lands and waterways to the east. Many times these explorers would become shipwrecked and would have to rely upon local wildlife for subsistence. In 1742 Russian explorers off the coast of Alaska suffered such a wreck and came to depend on the Stellars Sea Cow for food. The giant, whale-like animal was unafraid of man and was easily hooked and pulled ashore. The Stellars Sea Cow also lived in close-knit communities along the shore line, so it was fairly easy to hook as many as desired. A Russian sailor noted that after a sea cow had been hooked and pulled ashore, its mate stayed in the same area for two days until it was also killed. Since the Stellars Sea Cow was so easy to catch, it took the sailors and explorers just twenty-seven years from 1742–1769 to kill off this species. Similarly the cormorant was eaten into extinction by explorers in the Bering Sea from 1741–1800, as was the Great Auk of the North Atlantic between the years of 1534 to 1844.

DOCUMENTING YOUR SOURCES

Perhaps the most distinctive feature of writing that displays the research voice is its use of *documentation. Documentation occurs when a writer carefully informs his readers of the original source of a piece of researched information, information that may take the form of a direct quotation; a statistic; a chart, graph, or illustration; or an idea, even an idea restated in the research writer's own words.* Notice how Chris Hockett identifies a Russian sailor as the source for an anecdote he relates.

Documentation is unnecessary in essays that create the voice of first-hand experience because the reader understands that all the information presented has come directly from the writer's own lived experience. Documentation of an informal sort occurs in essays using the interview voice whenever the writer identifies a quotation and attributes it to the interview subject. But documentation of the sort used in research writing is generally a bit more formal and may take several forms. Standard documentation approaches are explained in the following publications:

Publication Manual of the American Psychological Association. 3d ed., Washington, D.C.: American Psychological Association, 1983.
A Manual for Writers of Term Papers, Theses, and Dissertations. Kate Turabian, 5th ed., Chicago: University of Chicago Press, 1987.
Modern Language Association Handbook for Writers of Research Papers. Joseph Gibaldi and Walter S. Achtert, 2d ed., New York: The Modern Language Association of America, 1984.

Footnotes/Endnotes

Footnotes and endnotes serve a similar purpose in that they identify for the reader a specific bit of information as having come from a specific source. The bit of borrowed information is marked in the text either by a superscript numeral or by a reference in parentheses. Somewhere else in the text, the source is identified more fully; usually the note provides information on the author and publisher of the source. Footnotes appear at the foot, or bottom, of each page; endnotes appear cumulatively at the end of the piece of writing. As with many of the other documentation features I will be describing, there are a number of styles used to incorporate notes effectively into a piece of writing. You probably will need to ask your instructor which style she prefers.

Bibliography/List of Works Consulted

Another method of documentation, generally used in conjunction with either footnotes or endnotes, is to provide readers with a list of research sources appended to the essay. A bibliography or list of works consulted is an alphabetic listing of the books and research sources that a writer has used in writing an essay; such a listing may well include sources that the writer has read although he does not choose to include any specific piece of information from them in the essay. This listing provides the readers with enough information to be able to locate the same source for further individual research.

List of Works Cited

Another method of documenting sources embodies features of both the other methods already discussed. The writer using this approach lists, in alphabetical order, only those materials from which specific information has been taken and used in the essay. Thus the list of works cited will probably be shorter than a list of works consulted would be for the same essay. Instead of using footnotes or endnotes, the writer documents the information by mentioning the name of the writer whose work is being cited, sometimes inserting in parentheses the specific page number of the book or article used as a source for that specific information. The list of works cited at the conclusion of the piece provides the rest of the information for the reference. The MLA style now works in this manner as part of an effort to simplify documentation (which is why few documentation authorities still recommend the use of the old-fashioned *ibid.* and *op. cit.* so popular years ago in research writing).

AN ILLUSTRATION

Let me illustrate how documentation works. Let's suppose that you are writing your essay about Charles Dickens, and you wish to include a photograph of his home at Gad's Hill. Unless you plan to travel to England to snap the photo yourself, you will have to document the source of the borrowed photo. If you wish to quote from one of Dickens' letters in which he discusses his home at Gad's Hill, you will have to document the source of that quotation. If you have found a literary scholar who argues that the Gad's Hill years were not among Dickens' best as a writer, you will need to document the source of that idea even if you do not quote it but only paraphrase it in your own words. If, however, you wish to mention the specific dates in which Dickens resided at Gad's Hill, you need not document your source because that type of historical fact is readily obtained in any number of sources.

To change my example for a moment, you would not need to cite your source for claiming that Columbus sailed to the new world in 1492, a well-known fact. But if you find a naval historian whose opinion is that Columbus was "overrated" as a sailor, you will need to document your source. And if you reproduce a map of Columbus' route, you will need to document its source, while if you create your own map based on your research into the history of his travels, you will not have to document.

THE BASIC PRINCIPLE

This all sounds somewhat tricky, but documentation is based on an easy-to-understand principle: no one has the right to borrow another person's property without permission—that's theft—and ideas are property. The custom among those who conduct research is that when a writer documents his sources appropriately, he has obtained permission to use someone else's property, or ideas. Most facts, like the dates of Columbus' travels or Dickens' period of residency, are no one person's property and thus do not need documentation (although some facts—such as statistics derived by social scientists as part of a scientific study—may well be viewed as private property.)

LEVELS OF FORMALITY

Another factor to consider in documentation is the *level of formality* of the piece of writing. In a research paper for a college or high school course, the convention, or understanding, is that generally the writing is very formal. Documentation, in whichever forms are acceptable to the instructor, is required. Similarly, when professors, regardless of their field of study, publish in scholarly journals, they are engaged in a very formal kind of writing; principles of documentation must be followed scrupulously. Some forms of school writing, however, may be less formal, and the documentation may be similarly less formal. For instance, essay exam answers are certainly the product of research, but generally no footnoting or bibliography is expected by the professor. Some essays may require footnotes but not bibliographies, depending on the instructor. Sometimes in some literature courses where all readers of an essay have the same textbook, simple page references in parentheses are used to indicate the source of direct quotations from stories and poems rather than using footnotes.

Other forms of research writing may be more informal and may rely on different forms of documentation. For instance, magazine articles that are the product of research both of secondary sources (information obtained by reading biographies and books of interpretation by experts) and primary sources (information obtained by conducting interviews or surveys, or by reading diaries, manuscripts, letters written from first-hand experience) frequently omit all documentation. Chris Hockett's essay on extinction used a very informal approach to documentation because his readers could easily see that he had done research into historical documents in order to write his essay. He did not include footnotes or bibliography, however, because they would have been inappropriate in the school newspaper, his intended place of publication.

Some books, if intended for a general audience rather than a specialized academic one, also omit documentation, sometimes including a bibliography but no footnotes. In these cases, the writers and editors and publishers involved are placing a premium on readability of the essays. It is more distracting to read an essay with footnotes frequently interspersed in the text, and since nonacademic readers are not usually as concerned with the source of the information as with the information itself, the decision is often made to reduce the amount of documentation. These essays that downplay documentation often sound closer to the voice of firsthand experience than do the more formal research essays, for the use of documentation itself helps create the research voice.

WHAT TO LOOK FOR

You will see a variety of approaches to the question of proper documentation in this chapter. As you read the selections in Chapter 13, consider the audience for each piece of writing and then ask yourself if the writer has met that audience's expectations in a fair way or not. Consider the sound of the voice you are hearing: does it sound like the product of research or the product of firsthand experience? The topic may be a clue, but I could certainly write an essay on Charles Dickens at this point that would not rely upon my research. I have read enough of his novels to write an essay about them—perhaps explaining why I prefer *Great Expectations* to *David Copperfield* or arguing that *Oliver Twist* is a superior film to *Oliver!*—and I probably would not need to footnote anything at all. See, however, if you don't hear the same voice in these essays that I do, a voice of authority but one that could only be the end product of an active process of research.

Who Shall Judge Me?
Seymour Wishman

Seymour Wishman has practiced criminal law as both a defense attorney and a prosecutor. Author of the novel *Nothing Personal* and the autobiographical *Confessions of a Criminal Lawyer*, Wishmans has published articles in *Newsweek*, the *New York Times*, and the *Village Voice*.

"Who Shall Judge Me?" is an excerpt from Chapter 1 of *Anatomy of a Jury: The System on Trial* (1986). In this book, Wishman examines the jury system by focusing on a single case, "a composite case, most of which is derived from a single trial. All the characters are real, but a few have been drawn from different cases," he explains in his preface. His decision to use a narrative approach was an effort to avoid writing "a dissertation full of legal abstractions." Nevertheless, Wishman has drawn upon his research and does informally append endnotes to his piece although he does not number his references in the text; I have done that for increased ease in reading.

In Wishman's composite case, Leander Rafshoon is a black man on trial for murder in Essex County, New Jersey. Jurors mentioned in the excerpt from Chapter 1 include Leonard Klein and Maureen Whalen, both middle-aged, white, and middle-class; Alex Butler, a young would-be novelist; Julius Solars, a retired workingman; and Carl Copco, a man with a minor criminal record.

QUESTIONS ABOUT IDEAS

1. Wishman's article focuses on issues surrounding the carrying out of the constitutional guarantee to a trial by a jury of peers. How fair do the various Supreme Court rulings Wishman discusses seem to you?
2. How much did you know about jury selection processes prior to reading this essay? How important is it that the public understand how juries are selected?
3. At the end of the essay, Wishman suggests that no attorney really desires a random jury. To what degree then are attorneys struggling against the system itself as well as the constitutional principle of trial by a jury of peers?
4. How important a civic responsibility is it to serve jury duty when one is summoned?

And where do the people come from who are considered qualified to judge their neighbor, Leander Rafshoon? Under our Constitution a defendant's fate is supposed to be decided by people randomly drawn from a "fair cross section of the community." The compilation of jury rolls, as for example the gathering of bits of encoded information on computer tapes in Essex

County, is the beginning of an elaborate process that ends with a group of twelve who constitute a "jury of peers."

As Leonard Klein realized from the material in the questionnaire, the rules make *almost* every adult American citizen eligible. But is a system of drawing by chance from an all-inclusive pool the best way to come up with the most reliable jurors to judge Leander Rafshoon?

Sixteen states in New England and the South use the once more popular "key-man" system to assemble "better-than-average" jurors: jury commissioners ask prominent members of the community—the head of the Kiwanis, the chamber of commerce, or other community organizations, for example—to supply the names of people they think would make good jurors.[1] Seems simple enough.

The "key-man" method has often produced white, comparatively affluent, better-educated jurors who very much resembled the profiles of the key men making the selections. In the South the key-man method managed for years to virtually eliminate blacks from serving as jurors.[2]

In 1968 federal legislation replaced key men with voter lists.[3] Today the federal courts and thirty-four states put their faith in the common sense of the randomly selected "average" citizens over the community leaders' subjective judgments of who might be the "best" jurors. Under the key-man method, perhaps Leonard Klein and Maureen Whalen would have been included; Alex Butler and Julius Solars might not have been; and if it worked properly, Carl Copco would have been excluded.

Unfortunately, reliance on voter lists creates its own biases. Less than three quarters of the people eligible to vote in 1984 were registered; in some states the level was below 60 percent.[4] And those who do register are not a random group: whites, the middle-aged, and the better educated are overrepresented, while nonwhites, the poor, the young, the old, and the less educated are underrepresented.

Ironically, some people (a *Los Angeles Times* survey in 1977 found 6 percent, and a Rutgers University poll in 1980 found 5 percent) do not vote in order to avoid jury duty, but in some twenty states, like New Jersey, these people still wind up being called as jurors because other lists such as those of licensed drivers or taxpayers are added to voter registrants to constitute the jury rolls.[5]

When Maureen Whalen headed to the courthouse to begin her service as a juror, she was one of over three million people summoned every year in America, one of 137,000 people called in New Jersey for the court year of 1983–84[6], to determine a neighbor's guilt or innocence.

If the process of selecting the people to be summoned to jury duty is not truly random, the profile of the jury picked for a particular case can be distorted. If more people, for example, are called from a Jewish neighborhood than other neighborhoods, or Hispanic or Italian names are overlooked, the jury panel will favor one group of people over another. In a more heavy-handed example of stacking the deck at this stage of the process, until 1955 the names of white potential jurors in Georgia were put on white cards and the names of blacks were put on yellow cards; when the names were "randomly" drawn to determine who would be summoned, few blacks were called. A Georgia trial court and the Georgia Supreme Court found nothing wrong with the procedure; it took the United States Supreme Court to stop the charade.[7] The use of a computer such as the one in Essex County can avoid this kind of obstacle in arriving at a fair jury.

It is interesting to speculate what differences result when a particular 10 group in our society is absent from juries. The Supreme Court has referred to the underrepresentation of women on juries as the loss of "a flavor, a distinct quality,"[8] and the absence of the young or old has a similar impact on jury deliberations.

Different age groups differ in a variety of ways. Older people differ 11 sharply from younger in many of their attitudes about such basic aspects of life as health, personal problems, and death. The old also tend to be more intolerant of political and social nonconformists than the young and more inclined toward favoring tougher law enforcement.[9]

Prosecutors and defense lawyers should be wary of using stereotypes 12 and statistics in picking juries because there is no way to be sure whether the individual juror is typical of the class to which he might belong. Though young, Alex Butler, for example, wrote sympathetically in his first novel about a teen-ager driven to revenge because legal technicalities had prevented the prosecution of the man who had killed his father. A lawyer would be mistaken to pigeonhole Alex as a juror who fell into the category of "young people."

On the other hand, while it is impossible to be sure that an individual 13 is representative of his group, a lawyer must make decisions on probabilities. And a lawyer defending someone accused of murder should be interested to know that 44 percent of those between eighteen and twenty-four opposed the death penalty, while only 27 percent of those over fifty opposed it.[10]

Should our concept of a jury of peers require that Leander Rafshoon 14 be tried by young, urban blacks? Most people would agree that a brilliant professor is not entitled to a jury composed entirely of brilliant professors, but should he be allowed to be judged only by college graduates, or at least high school graduates? Most people would also agree that a dangerous felon is not entitled to a jury of dangerous felons. Does a young Korean have a right to expect a jury of young Koreans, or a percentage of young people, or of Koreans corresponding to the percentage in the community? If not Koreans, is it fair to confront him with a jury composed predominantly of white, middle-class, average-educated, native-born Americans?

Foreigners have not always been denied the right to jurors from their 15 own countries. The issue of where jurors come from is at the heart of the very concept of a jury of peers. On April 10, 1201, in England, King John signed a charter giving Jews on trial the right to have juries composed of equal numbers of Jews and Christians. King John adopted this charter to protect Jews from the loss of their property, which was being jeopardized in trials because of prejudice against them. This special treatment was afforded less as a favor to Jews than out of self-interest, since the king regarded the property of Jews as belonging to him.[11] Later statutes granted foreign merchants this same right to "mixed juries" in order to encourage merchants to continue doing business in England.

These mixed juries, also called juries *de medietate linguae*, composed [16] half of native jurors and half of jurors speaking the defendant's native language, were allowed, as it was put in the 1880 Supreme Court ruling in *Virginia* v. *Rives*, "probably as much because of the difference of language and customs between the foreigner and Englishmen, and the greater probability of his defense being more fully understood, as because it would be heard in a more friendly spirit by jurors of his own country and language."[12]

Mixed juries were used on several occasions in previous centuries in [17] America.[13] Four Italians charged with murder in Pennsylvania requested and received a mixed jury in 1783. In 1807 an alien in New York received a mixed jury in his trial for murder. An alien charged with piracy was tried in 1823 by a mixed jury (he was convicted and sentenced to death). In 1841 an Englishman requested a mixed jury from the Virginia court that was about to try him for perjury. His request was granted, but only three Englishmen responded to the summons to court. One of the Englishmen was excused for legal reasons, and the judge went on with the trial, with the two remaining jurors representing only one sixth of the jury of twelve. The defendant's conviction was upheld after he appealed on the grounds that he had not had his proper "half-English" jury.

The basic issue raised by mixed juries was considered by the Supreme [18] Court as recently as 1961. The Court rejected the arguments of a woman convicted of murdering her husband when she claimed that she had been denied a fair trial because her jury had been all male. The defendant had argued that women jurors would have been more understanding than men in assessing her behavior. The right to an impartially selected jury, said the Court, "does not entitle one accused of crime to a jury tailored to the circumstances of the particular case, whether relating to the sex or other condition of the defendant, or to the nature of the charges to be tried."[14]

Legal scholars continue to debate endlessly the merits of the various [19] methods of constituting our juries. Civil rights lawyers have succeeded in changing the way some of the state systems compile lists or select panels from them. But the average criminal lawyer has never challenged the jury lists, and while he may have tried hundreds of cases, it is likely that he barely knows how all those people have turned up in the courtroom waiting to be selected as the final twelve to decide a specific case.

While there may be biases built into the system, their significance is [20] minimal when compared with the kind of distortions accomplished at the voir dire, that part of the selection process in which the lawyers choose the particular twelve they want for their trial. The last thing the prosecutor and the defense lawyer in a case like that of Leander Rafshoon would want would be a truly random jury. Both would want jurors they thought favored their side.

Notes

[1] Sixteen states in New England and the South use the once more popular "key-man" system. H. Dogin and D. Tevelin, "Jury Selection in the Eighties: Toward a Fairer Cross Section and Increased Efficiency," 11 *University of Toledo Law Review* 939 (1980).

[2] The "key-man method has often produced social peers of the commissioners." I. Kaufman, "A Fair Trial—The Essence of Justice," 51 *Judicature* 88 (1967).

[3] The 1968 federal legislation that replaced key men with voter lists is called the Jury Selection and Service Act, which was passed to guarantee a trial by a fair and impartial jury in the federal district courts. The Act prohibits discrimination in jury service on the basis of race, color, religion, sex, national origin, or economic status. The Act also specifies how a random jury is to be chosen. Each federal district court is to compose its own plan under the guidelines set forth in the Act. The basic source of names for jurors must be either a voter registration list or actual voting list. If there is any reason to believe that these lists are not sufficiently representative, they must be supplemented from other sources. Names must be selected randomly from these lists and put in a master jury wheel from which names are randomly drawn for jury service. The wheel itself must be refilled at least every four years.

[4] Less than three quarters of eligible voters in 1984 were registered—in some states the level was below 60 percent. *1985 Statistical Abstract of the United States*, U.S. Government Printing Office. "And those who do register are not a random group: whites, the middle-aged, and the better educated are overrepresented, while nonwhites, the poor, the young, the old, and the less educated are underrepresented." Dogin and Tevelin, p. 939.

[5] The studies showing the percentages of people who do not vote in order to avoid jury duty are cited in "The Constitutionality of Calling Jurors Exclusively From Voter Registration Lists," 55 *New York University Law Review* 1266, 168–9 (1980), and are referring to a survey published on January 9, 1977, in the *Los Angeles Times* of 253 unregistered voters and a 1980 Eagleton Institute of Rutgers University survey of 118 unregistered voters.

[6] "We, the Jury, Find...", *Time* magazine, September 28, 1981, p. 44.

[7] The United States Supreme Court stopped the Georgia practice of placing the names of white potential jurors on white cards and the names of blacks on yellow cards in 1953. *Avery* v. *Georgia*, 345 U.S. 559 (1953).

[8] The Supreme Court referred to the absence of women on juries as the loss of "a flavor, a distinct quality," in *Ballard* v. *United States*, 319 U.S. 187, 193 (1943).

[9] A thorough discussion of how the various age groups differ in important attitudes

can be found in D. Ziegler, "Young Adults as a Cognizable Group in Jury Selection," 76 *Michigan Law Review* 1045, 1075 (1978).

[10] According to a 1972 Gallup poll 44 percent of those between 18 and 24 opposed the death penalty, while only 27 percent of those over 50 opposed it. J. Van Dyke, *Jury Selection Procedures: Our Uncertain Commitment to Representative Panels.* Cambridge, Massachusetts: Ballantine Publishing Company, 1977, p. 38.

[11] On April 10, 1201, King John signed a charter giving Jews on trial the right to have juries composed of equal numbers of Jews and Christians. L. LaRue, "A Jury of One's Peers," 33 *Washington and Lee Law Review*, 841 (1976).

[12] The Supreme Court case that discussed mixed juries was *Virginia* v. *Rives,* 100 U.S. 313 (1880).

[13] The various cases in which mixed juries were involved is discussed in LaRue (1976).

[14] The Supreme Court rejected the arguments of a woman convicted of murdering her husband that she had been denied a fair trial because her jury had been all male in the case of *Hoyt* v. *Florida,* 368 U.S. 57 (1961).

QUESTIONS ABOUT THE RHETORICAL SITUATION

1. Wishman's book was sold in retail book stores, suggesting that he saw the general public as his audience. What evidence can you find that Wishman has deliberately avoided writing in "legalese" more appropriate to readers who are themselves attorneys? How consistent is he in addressing his essay to the general reading public?
2. What is Wishman's purpose in this essay? Is he trying to create doubt about our jury system? Is he trying to inspire reform in jury selection processes?
3. Clearly Wishman takes his subject seriously, yet he says in his preface that he does not want to write "a dissertation full of legal abstractions." Does Wishman sound detached and distant from the subject, as he might if he were writing a "dissertation"? To what extent does he get involved forcefully enough in the material to create a persuasive-sounding voice?

QUESTIONS ABOUT THE ESSAY'S VOICE

1. Wishman is an authority on the subject of juries both through research and firsthand experience. So not every paragraph of his selection requires a footnote—because much of what he writes comes from his own prior knowledge. What kinds of information did he need to seek out and what kinds of information did he already know? What conclusions can you reach about the role played in Wishman's essay by his research?
2. Why do you think Wishman, an experienced trial attorney, has chosen to write in a formal-sounding researcher's voice, using endnotes, rather than

relying upon his own extensive personal experiences to write about the same topic in the voice of firsthand experience? How would the selection be improved or harmed by his adopting a first-person point of view?

3. Wishman relies very sparingly upon quotations from his sources. How effective is his use of quotations? Are there places where a quotation might have worked more effectively than his usual paraphrased approach? If so, where?

4. Wishman does make fairly frequent use of statistics from his research. How do the statistics affect the voice? How do they affect your reading experience? How clearly does Wishman explain and integrate into his selection the statistics?

5. One of the noteworthy strategies used by Wishman is to make use of a number of characters associated with the fictionalized trial of Leander Rafshoon. What is the effect on the voice of his references to these characters (see ¶2 and ¶5, for example)?

6. Research writing can easily deteriorate into a compilation of research findings: a pasted-together scrapbook of quotations, facts, and statistics. One way to avoid that scrapbook approach is to form generalizations based on the researched information. What are the main generalizations made by Wishman? How successfully does he avoid the "scrapbook" approach?

TOPICS TO WRITE ABOUT

1. Write a research paper that continues from where Wishman leaves off: investigate the *voir dire* portion of jury selection or how juries deliberate or the history of the size of juries or the principle of unanimous verdicts. POTENTIAL AUDIENCES: your classmates who have read "Who Shall Judge Me?"/the general public. POTENTIAL PURPOSES: to help place Wishman's selection about the beginning of a trial into the larger context of an entire trial/to raise some issues about our jury system, perhaps focusing on problems that need public attention.

2. Write a research paper about some other governmental institution. For example, you might examine the military draft over the past century or the development of the Internal Revenue Service. POTENTIAL AUDIENCE: college students. POTENTIAL PURPOSE: to explain how this governmental institution might affect citizens their age.

3. Research some important recent historical moment and then write a letter to the editor as if you were living through that moment. For example, you might do research on the Nazi invasion of Poland in September 1939 and write to your local newspaper arguing that the United States should or should not assist the Polish army in fighting Hitler. POTENTIAL AUDIENCES: readers of your local newspaper/readers of your campus newspa-

per. POTENTIAL PURPOSES: to persuade them to support your position/to argue for what you feel to be an appropriate position to take on the issue for a college newspaper.

The Missing Majority: The Community College in American Fiction
Nancy LaPaglia

Nancy LaPaglia has been a professor in the Department of Art, Humanities, Language, and Music at Daley College in Chicago since 1967. Professor LaPaglia received a B.A. in liberal arts from the University of Illinois in 1957 and an M.A. in history from Illinois in 1958. Her academic interests include women artists; with a grant from the City College of Chicago, she sought to improve the presentation of women artists, architects, and composers in humanities survey courses at Daley College. She has given papers on women artists of the eighteenth century at several conferences. Currently, LaPaglia does monthly art and architecture reviews on a local classical music radio station in Chicago.

This essay was originally presented in a workshop at the 1986 "Literature Across the Disciplines" conference sponsored by the City Colleges of Chicago. It was later published in *City: A Journal of the City Colleges of Chicago.*

QUESTIONS ABOUT IDEAS

1. What should be the proper role of the two-year college in American education? What purpose does the two-year college serve that is not served by other institutions of higher education?
2. To what extent do college students select colleges based on the prestige of the institution? Is too much, too little, or the right emphasis placed on reputation and prestige when choosing a college? To what extent does society itself emphasize reputation and prestige?
3. What literary works have you read that focus on the more traditional four-year campus? With what other depictions of college life in the media, such as film or television, are you familiar? In what respects do these books, films, television shows accurately depict life on a college campus? In what respects are they inaccurate?

Norma Jean Moffitt is working on her pectorals in a body-building   1
class (Mason 1982). She is also learning to write paragraphs at Paducah Community College. This thirty-four year old student is strengthening her

mind and body in order to leave Leroy and Mabel, her truck-driver husband and her domineering mother. She is typical of many characters in contemporary American fiction. Her story is told in the present tense, and it concerns an uneducated, working-class person whose life just sort of happens. The tone is comic much of the time. But in one way she is a rarity. Norma Jean may be taking only one composition course at night, but she is one of the very few characters in American fiction that has any connection to a two-year college.

This is not an accurate reflection of our cultural pattern. More than   2 half of all college students in this country are enrolled in two-year colleges, and nearly half of all college faculty members teach in two-year colleges. I am one of those two-year college teachers, and I also spent my freshman year in a junior college, so I find the problem of the missing majority interesting. In addition to questioning many friends and colleagues, I sent a survey to almost one hundred people who read widely, most of them community college faculty, asking for any examples in American fiction of characters, however peripheral, who attend or teach in two-year colleges. This request turned up three novels, one of them listed by two respondents, and an unpublished short story by a colleague who has published several novels. I already knew of three short stories, and I later found a recently published novel with a narrator who is a community college dropout.

Two librarian friends polled colleagues at the Chicago Public Library,   3 especially those whose job it is to review new works, and a writer friend took my survey to the Iowa Writer's Workshop this summer. No results in either place. Two respondents suggested I contact people who went on themselves from a two-year college to become well-known as writers or in some related field. I wrote to Sidney Harris, the columnist, and Gwendolyn Brooks, the poet, both of whom attended a city college in Chicago, and Roger Ebert, the film critic, who taught at Daley College, my own school, early in his career. No luck here, either. Brooks wrote a poem for a Crane Junior College yearbook in 1968, but it is an all-purpose celebration of a student who struggled to succeed, with no specific indication that the school is a two-year college, or even urban or black. A reader of June Brindel's "Sartre is a Cold Fish" who did not know she taught for some years in a Chicago City College would never make the connection.

Someone suggested I look through the short stories of Raymond   4 Carver, and a friend thought John Barth's *The End of the Road* was set in a community college. Both Carver and Barth turned up characters at state colleges, not at community college. In a third example of misdirection, Roger Ebert's assistant came up with the movie *Educating Rita*. It is set in Dublin at Trinity College, but features an uneducated, working-class, part-time, re-

turning woman student. In each of these cases, my informant made a connection between lack of status and the two-year college.

This leaves four novels and two short stories. The characters in them   5
who are students are non-intellectual, often shallow, and perhaps comic.
They are sometimes sympathetic. All but one of them are women, and all
but one of their creators are women. Three of the novels depict two-year
college faculty members as well as students, and they are mostly male. The
teachers themselves are not always non-intellectual, shallow or comic, but
their jobs are seen this way. The job of teaching in a two-year school may
have some positive qualities, but it is not a job for a responsible adult.
Maybe as a temporary or part-time job, but full-time it is a ridiculous thing
to do with your life.

In Susan Fromberg Schaeffer's *Falling*, Elizabeth, the central charac-   6
ter, is in much-needed therapy. She takes a job in the English Department
of a Chicago City College, along the way to getting well. When she is more
normal she will move on to a four-year institute of technology, and then to a
New York university. Her experience with us is grim, and often very funny.
The building looks like a penitentiary, everything is painted Ex-Lax brown,
and the department chairman has, of course, no future. The students are
morons. At best, one can enjoy watching them become semi-morons. The
morons like Elizabeth, and they improve under her teaching. She and the
only other teacher worth considering form what they call an aristocracy of
disgust. There are no academic standards, and there is no scholarship. A faculty member who long ago published one article is there because he lacks
self-respect and he has six children. The surrounding working-class neighborhood is filled with pasteboard houses covered with plastic reindeer whose
noses light up.

In June, however, at the end of the semester, she realizes she is sorry   7
to leave. She may have changed some lives for the better, and she sees that
she has not seen all that was going on in front of her. Her students become
sympathetic characters.

Maureen, the central character in Joyce Carol Oates's *Them*, lives a life   8
filled with unrelieved grimness and uncontrolled violence. She comes from a
working-class Detroit neighborhood filled with tired and helpless people.
Near the end of this longish novel, twenty-six year old Maureen attempts
some control of her future by enrolling in a night class at squalid Highland
Park Junior College. She has heard that this school is easier than the University of Detroit, where she flunked out of her night classes some years earlier. She determines to marry her English instructor as part of her life-
improvement plan, although he is already married and has three children.
She accomplishes her goal. Jim, the part-time junior college instructor she
chooses, is thirty-four, is described by others as kind, loves his first wife of

nine years, and dreams of escaping from Detroit. A graduate student at Wayne State University, he is short of money and shabby. He wants Maureen, as if in a dream. They marry. Their life together is very much like his former life, but for Maureen it is the step up that enables her to turn her back on her terrible past and her dismal family.

The only black writer on my short list is Gloria Naylor, although a 9 high percentage of black college students are enrolled in two-year schools. *The Women of Brewster Place* live, desperate and abused, in the underclass of a dying city neighborhood. One who is an exception is young Kiswana Browne, formerly Melanie Browne, who has dropped out of college and moved to Brewster Place deliberately in order to bring political consciousness to the downtrodden and trouble her middle-class family at the same time. Near the end of the book, as she is coming to terms with who she is, she enrolls part-time in a community college, studying there precisely because a community college has no status. She need not apologize as much for her change in behavior—towards the upwardly mobile.

Ella Leffland's "Last Courtesies" barely qualifies for my list. Jody, a 10 gum-snapping, stereo-blasting young hooker who lives upstairs of Lillian, the central character, is taking macrame and World Lit. at the jay cee. Lillian is told this by Jody's boyfriend, a serial murderer known as the Rain Man. For a better idea of Leffland's ability as a writer, try her fine novel *Rumors of Peace*, instead.

I use Bobbie Ann Mason's "Shiloh," Norma Jean's story, in a human- 11 ities course, with interesting results. Many of the students find it strange to read about a character that in so many ways is like themselves. Those who seem closest to this Paducah Community College student are often those who try to distance themselves from her the most. A class discussion can bring out the similarities and lessen the distance. Norma Jean, like many of the fictional characters we have discussed, and like many of our students, is trying to gain some control of her life. She and they see the community college as one place to get help.

The last work on my list, which is also the newest, is T. Glen Cough- 12 lin's *The Hero of New York*. It differs from the others in that both writer and student character are male. Charlie, the nineteen year old narrator, drops out of a Long Island community college that is one hour from New York City. The school and area are one step up from the Brooklyn working-class neighborhood from which his family moved. Charlie is a bored and failing business administration major. He is interested only in his waitress girlfriend and the troubles of his policeman father, the hero of the title.

We meet one of his instructors briefly, a carefully dressed corporation 13 accountant, who teaches part-time. Charlie refers to him as a little turd. Charlie himself is on his way to being a violent alcoholic like his father. He is in Rinky-Dink College, as he calls it, instead of a state university, because his father convinced him to stay at home. He fantasizes transferring to Prince-

ton, as a former good friend of his did when they graduated, but this is unlikely. At the end of the novel, Charlie is unsure of his direction, and the
girlfriend, who dropped him for a rich dope dealer, is taking a community
college course in hair cutting.

Those of us connected to two-year colleges probably recognize Charlie, **14**
and maybe we know his accounting teacher. We know the women students
in some of the other works, certainly. But why don't they appear more often
in American fiction, and where are the others? Ones who are not seen as
comic failures, at least not by themselves and their families, and perhaps not
by some faculty. The ones who do not feel that life just happens to them,
mostly for the worse. Graduation at Daley, for example, is both humorous
and moving. Our gym is packed with grandmas in Slavic babushkas and
Arab gowns, parents in suits and in working clothes, and a lot of kids, including the grown children of our graduates. Black women wearing outfits
out of MGM musicals arrive late, carrying long-stemmed roses for their
nieces and daughters. It's wonderful theater, and these people have not
come to see losers. They have come to applaud winners, often the first family member to attend college, on her or his way up.

I would like to suggest reasons for our near invisibility, and why, when **15**
we do show up, it may be as comic relief. I offer three possibilities: 1) the
relative newness of the two-year college as a mass cultural pattern, 2) the
social status of the major groups who enroll, particularly in the urban community college, and 3) intellectual elitism.

Although the two-year college was established much earlier, attending **16**
one did not become an American pattern for large numbers of people until
the 1960's, when, during some years, the federal money tree sprouted a new
campus at the rate of one per week. Every book discussed here was published after that, many of them around 1980. Like Vietnam, the experience
may take a decade or longer to emerge. Or unlike Vietnam, two-year colleges
are considered so colorless, beneath even satire, as one of my respondents
wrote, that we will not emerge, even with more time. Community colleges
could at least turn up in popular culture, but there are no movies or TV
situation comedies about them.

The social status of the major groups enrolled in two-year schools, es- **17**
pecially in large cities, is low. A decided majority of students are women,
many of them older than the traditional college age. Hispanic and black students are more likely to be in a community college, along with any group,
like recent immigrants, that has a large percentage of its members who are
working-class or underclass.

Writers from these groups who are familiar with community colleges **18**
do not use the experience overtly, even though they may write about other
low-status activities. I could find very little from feminist or Hispanic or
black or working-class writers. Having a past that includes attending a community college seems to be something like having played the accordion. It is

not only low status; there is something embarrassing about it that makes people want to forget it ever happened. I don't intend to argue the actual intellectual merits of two-year colleges versus other undergraduate schools. Community colleges are not elite. Intellectual elitism, or snobbery, as several respondents called it, is another matter. After more than two decades of teaching, I can think of only two male faculty members who actually say they feel that they belong in a community college. Many others give the impression that they are stooping; they have somehow been sidetracked from their true destinies at major universities or businesses. Women faculty members are less likely to feel this way, perhaps because we have not been taught as thoroughly to have higher ambitions. It is not accidental that all but one of the books I found were written by women.

Even authors who are also teachers at a two-year school do not write   19 about the experience, although, as a respondent wrote from Boston, "It's such a natural for autobiographical whining." Several of the faculty members I questioned told me they always intended to write a novel set in a two-year college, but no one has actually done so. Short biographies, on book covers, for instance, or even resumes, do not mention attendance at or teaching in a community college. I know that such experience may have been only a stepping stone to a college degree, or a temporary job on the way to another, but this remains still another aspect of our invisibility. I admit that before writing, on the first page, that I attended a junior college as a freshman, I hesitated a moment, feeling, rightly or wrongly, that anything I said thereafter would be devalued, filtered through that piece of information.

A colleague from an English Department who answered the survey   20 supposes that we will remain unstoried and unsung. On the other hand, June Brindel, whose short story was mentioned earlier, predicts that at least some more fiction will appear after this paper, including a story that she herself is thinking of writing. I hope she is right. It's time we are sung, whatever the voice, however inarticulate the non-intellectual croak.

Since submitting this essay, Nancy LaPaglia has come across three addi-   21 *tional novels with major characters who are either community college teachers or students: Clyde Edgerton,* Raney, *Algonquin, 1985; Lorrie Moore,* Anagrams. Knopf, *1986, Lee Smith,* Oral History. Putnam, *1983; Ballantine paperback, 1984.*

Works Cited

Barth, John. *The End of the Road.* New York: Doubleday, 1967.

Brindel, June Rachuy. "Sartre is a Cold Fish." *Nobody is Ever Missing.* Chicago: Story Press, 1984.

Coughlin, T. Glen. *The Hero of New York.* New York: Norton, 1986.

Leffland, Ella. "Last Courtesies." *Last Courtesies and Other Stories.* New York: Harper & Row, 1980.

Mason, Bobbie Ann. "Shiloh." *Shiloh and Other Stories.* New York: Harper & Row, 1982.

Naylor, Gloria. *The Women of Brewster Place.* New York: Viking Press, 1982.

Oates, Joyce Carol. *Them.* New York: Fawcett Crest, 1969.

Schaeffer, Susan Fromberg. *Falling.* New York: Avon Books, 1973.

QUESTIONS ABOUT THE RHETORICAL SITUATION

1. LaPaglia's essay uses the first-person plural pronoun *we*. Whom is she addressing? How else can you identify her audience in this essay? How might the essay have to be changed if your class, including your teacher, were the intended audience?

2. What purposes has LaPaglia in this essay? Is she primarily interested in informing her audience about a situation? Explaining a situation? Presenting an argument about what must be done about a situation? A combination of these purposes? Why did you answer as you did?

3. How important is this subject to LaPaglia? How can you tell? (For example, note that in ¶18, LaPaglia makes a joke about an accordion. What does the joke suggest about her feelings about her subject?)

QUESTIONS ABOUT THE ESSAY'S VOICE

1. There are many methods of conducting research beside visiting the library. What other means has LaPaglia used in gathering information for her essay? How effective did you find these other means of researching?

2. The first half of LaPaglia's essay is primarily concerned with summarizing the plots of the novels and stories she has located that deal with community college teachers and students. How consistently does she offer these summaries in a neutral, objective manner? (For example, is her voice the same in ¶5 as in ¶6?)

3. Contrast the voice you hear in ¶14 with the voice you have heard in the preceding paragraphs. What is the cause of the difference?

4. What other voices that we have heard in *Model Voices* might LaPaglia have used in writing this paper? Why has she written instead in the researcher's voice?

5. In ¶19, LaPaglia speaks honestly about her own feelings about her community college background. What was your reaction to this paragraph? Should she have included it or not?

6. What argument could you make that this essay belongs in Chapter 11, The Voice of Firsthand Experience? How does this essay's voice mark it as a research essay?

7. LaPaglia's essay is full of information acquired through her research; however, to establish her voice as that of an authority, she needs to go beyond reporting information and must make generalizations. Where in her essay does she do so? How convincing an expert is she?
8. How does LaPaglia's voice in this essay compare with Karen Stubbs' voice in her essay "Mark Twain and Bret Harte: Social Critics" in Chapter 11? With Kathleen Cox's essay "Symbol of Humanity" in this chapter?

TOPICS TO WRITE ABOUT

1. Read a group of short stories about a similar topic: high school life, an organized religion, a war, a sporting event, an election, a public protest, a labor strike, a natural disaster. Write a research paper in which you reach some conclusions about the way this particular topic has been presented by the writers you have read. POTENTIAL AUDIENCES: other readers who have read the same stories/readers who have not yet read the literary works. POTENTIAL PURPOSES: to offer them a new insight into the manner in which these literary works treat a common topic/to introduce them to these literary works and their treatment of a common topic.
2. Write a research paper based in large part upon a survey that you create and administer. Your questionnaire might focus on opinions of local or campus issues; you might include questions about the backgrounds of your respondents, such as year in school, hometown, age, gender. Form conclusions based on the data you collect. (Of course, your essay will not really be statistically valid, but it should prove interesting nonetheless.) POTENTIAL AUDIENCES: your class/those who responded to the survey. POTENTIAL PURPOSE: to explain and interpret the information you have acquired.
3. Write a research paper about the history of your campus. POTENTIAL AUDIENCE: your class. POTENTIAL PURPOSE: to provide your readers with a better understanding of your university or college.

A Symbol of Humanity
Kathleen Cox

Kathleen Cox was a first-year student at Miami University when she wrote "A Symbol of Humanity." She wrote the essay as part of an honors course in literature and writing. She remembers that the purpose of the assignment was to "draw together several of the works we had read and discussed in class. It was also partly a research paper and we were expected to use and cite a certain number of outside works." The research process proved to be a positive experience for her. "I remember...the more I read about the characteristics of a tragic hero, the more similarities I saw. I remember being fascinated by the fact that even though these plays are from different times under drastically different circumstances, they follow the same pattern."

Since writing "A Symbol of Humanity," Cox has held a summer internship as a reporter for the Richmond, Indiana, *Palladium-Item* and has published in a number of campus periodicals. Cox became a chemistry major with plans to become a science writer for a major newspaper, magazine, or corporation.

QUESTIONS ABOUT IDEAS

1. Cox analyzes two tragic figures from two classic dramas, both written many centuries ago. What more recent literary figures fit the definition offered in this essay of a tragic hero or heroine? Are there such figures in contemporary literature? Explain your answer.
2. Sophocles and Shakespeare were separated by geography and time, yet both, according to Kathleen Cox, have created tragic characters who fit the same definition. What conclusions can you draw about the nature of tragedy from that fact?
3. Oedipus and Othello are fictional characters. What historical or contemporary figures also fit the definition offered in this essay of a tragic hero or heroine?

Aristotle defines a tragic hero as "a man, not preeminently virtuous   1
and just, whose misfortune, however, is brought upon him not by vice
and depravity, but by some error of judgement."[1] He should be "better
than the ordinary man,"[2] act consistently and appropriately within his
character, and his situation should be believable. He must go through
three main stages—"purpose, passion, and perception,"[3] but his transformations must appear both probable in the course of the play and natural to his character. Arthur Miller adds to this "list" of criteria for the
tragic hero. He says that a "tragedy is the consequence of man's total
compulsion to evaluate himself justly,"[4] and a tragic hero is "a character
who is ready to lay down his life, if need be, to secure one thing—his
sense of personal dignity."[5] This certainly is a long list of detailed descriptions of the qualities of a tragic hero, and it does not even encompass
them all. It seems as though it would be extremely difficult to create a
character who satisfies all of these requirements and still make the tragedy itself meaningful. Yet, it can be done. Both Sophocles' Oedipus, and
Shakespeare's Othello meet all of these requirements and more, and the
tragedies themselves have survived the test of time.

Sophocles and Shakespeare lived in two very different times and cul-   2
tures, so it is understandable that their plays would have different settings
and different themes. Sophocles' *Oedipus Rex* takes place in the ancient city
of Thebes where the people believe that the events of their lives are all predetermined by the gods. Shakespeare's *Othello*, on the other hand, takes
place in the much more modern city of Venice where the people believe that
man himself controls his own destiny. Likewise, the two heroes, Oedipus
and Othello, are caught in two very different situations, yet they both possess all the qualities of a tragic hero, and the emotions they portray are
present in all men regardless of where they live or how they change with the
passage of time.

A tragic hero should be a man who is better off than the ordinary man,   3
in his social standing as well as in his virtues, so that his fall is indeed a tragedy. Yet, he cannot be placed so high that the common man cannot understand his suffering. Oedipus is the king of Thebes, yet he does not inherit
that position. He earns his rank by being clever enough to outwit the
Sphinx. He is a good king who is loved and trusted by his people. When the
city itself is in trouble, the people come to Oedipus "to make our prayer as
to the man of all men best in adversity and wisest in the ways of God."[6] The
audience is able to admire and respect Oedipus, but because he was not always the king, his character is not so high that the common man cannot
sympathize with his plight.

Likewise, Othello had to work very hard for his position in Venice. He   4
is a black man in a white society, and he had to overcome a lot of resentment
before he could gain the respect of his peers. We do not see this directly, but
Othello tells Desdemona of being "taken into slavery, and of my redemption
thence."[7] Iago also makes derogatory comments in reference to Othello's
heritage throughout the play. He tells Brabantio that "you think we are ruf-
fians, yet you'll have your daughter covered with a Barbary horse."[8] Othello, like Oedipus, is a man who has achieved his position only by using his
exemplary virtues and skills. The audience respects him but can still feel
pity at his fall.

Sophocles felt that it was essential to the tragedy "that we should see   5
the hero as complex, not single minded."[9] We cannot understand his tragedy until we have seen how his character changes throughout the course of
the play. He must go through the three different stages of mind: purpose,
passion, and perception.

Oedipus begins as "hero, monarch, helmsman of the state; the solver   6
of the Sphinx's riddle, the triumphant being."[10] Yet, he seems almost over-
confident in his abilities to rule Thebes. He calls the people of Thebes "poor
children,"[11] and treats them as such. He takes it upon himself to find the
murderer of Laios and punish him so that the disease will be lifted from the
city. He proclaims that

If any man knows by whose hand Laios, son of Labdakos, met his

death, I direct that man to tell me everything, no matter what he fears
for having so long withheld it.[12]

Thus, Oedipus has entered the first stage. He has a purpose.

His trusted friend Creon brings the blind prophet to Oedipus with the   7
hope that he might be able to solve the mystery. Oedipus is patient and kind
to him and begs him to tell the secret that he is hiding. As soon as Teiresias
tells Oedipus that "you yourself are the pollution of this country,"[13] Oedipus enters the second stage: passion. He understandably flies into a rage at
Teiresias' accusation, but then he goes too far. He accuses the blind old man
of plotting with Creon to take over Thebes. This accusation is entirely un-
founded, but Oedipus is beyond reason. He lashes out at anyone who brings
further support of Teiresias' claim, and denies all proof that he did, in fact,
kill his father, Laios, and marry his mother. He is no longer the benevolent
king from whom the people had nothing to fear.

Finally, the evidence is too overwhelming, and Oedipus is forced to   8
face the truth. He stops fighting, and once again his character changes as he
enters the final stage: perception. As he punishes himself for the sins he has
committed by gouging out his eyes and banishing himself from Thebes, his
thoughts turn inward.

Although Othello's situation is very different from Oedipus', he still   9
goes through the same fundamental stages. Othello is introduced as

> A great man, naturally modest, but conscious of his worth...secure, it
> would seem against all dangers from without and all rebellion from
> within."[14]

When Brabantio wants to fight with him for stealing Desdemona away,   10
Othello says, "keep up your bright swords for the dew will rust them."[15] He
does not want to fight, not only because he knows that it is unnecessary, but
also because he knows that he could easily defeat the men, and the swords
would rust before they ever touched him. This single scene shows us that
Othello is not one to act rashly, and also that he is a little bit arrogant. These
qualities are shown again when Iago tells him that Desdemona is having an
affair with Cassio. Othello refuses to believe it because he knows that Desdemona loves him, so he demands proof of her infidelity. Thus, his purpose
has been established.

As soon as Iago presents Othello with the "proof" that Desdemona has   11
been seeing Cassio, Othello becomes inconsolable. His arrogance is still
there, but now Iago controls his emotions, and Othello's mind is filled only
with thoughts of jealousy and revenge. He has lost the ability to think rationally and even strikes Desdemona out of anger. An old friend wonders, "Is
this the nature whom passion could not shake?"[16] Othello is now driven totally by passion.

He does not realize his mistake until after he has murdered Desde-   12
mona, and Emilia forces him to listen to the truth. Once again his character

changes. He has lost all of his arrogance and self-righteous pride. He begs
Cassio's forgiveness and acknowledges himself as "one that loved not wisely,
but too well."[17] As soon as he has fully perceived his mistakes, he punishes
himself by taking his own life.

Perhaps the most important characteristic of the tragic hero is his fatal 13
flaw. It is this part of the hero's character which forces him to be driven by
an all-consuming passion and eventually causes him to fall.

Oedipus's fatal flaw is his excessive pride. He believes himself to be as 14
good or better than the gods themselves; therefore he has to be punished. In
contrast to *Othello*, all the events which cause the tragedy in *Oedipus Rex*
have already occurred and there is nothing that Oedipus can do to stop his
fall. Yet, it is his fierce pride which will not let him accept his fate. Only
when he loses his pride can he face the truth and receive retribution. This is
his "fall." Although we pity Oedipus, we still admire him because he accepts
the responsibility for his actions and says, "Of all men, I alone can bear this
guilt."[18] He suffers for all humanity, and in his sacrifice, we feel atonement.

Although the events in *Othello* are not predetermined, Iago is, to a cer- 15
tain extent, controlling Othello's actions. Othello's main flaw is that he
trusts too much. "His trust, where he trusts, is absolute."[19] Iago takes advantage of this part of Othello's nature to destroy him. Othello flies into a
rage because he trusts Desdemona, and he thinks she has betrayed him.
When he realizes that it was Iago who has in fact betrayed him, Othello takes
all of the blame upon himself. Although we feel pity for Othello's suffering,
we cannot help but admire his heroic character. He feels as though he has
been betrayed by the whole universe and there is nothing else that he can
believe in. He is suffering for all of humanity, and with his death, he has
absolved all of our guilt and all that remains is the memory of his dignity and
courage.

A tragic hero is made up of many different aspects, but most of all, he 16
is humanity personified. He is introduced as the kind of person we would
like to be. Yet, he is not perfect, as none of us are. Oedipus and Othello are
two tragic heroes caught in circumstances beyond their control, and we
watch them react in the same way we would had we been in their situation.
Each hero aims toward finding an answer, and he refuses the horrible truth
for as long as he can, yet the truth cannot be denied forever. When he does
finally fall, the hero accepts his fate with dignity and courage. With his
death, only his flaw and our pity for him die, leaving us cleansed, and filled
only with love and admiration.

Notes

[1] Denniston, J. D., *Greek Literary Criticism* (Aristotle, *The Poetics*, "Definition of
    Tragedy") (London: J. M. Dent and Sons, Ltd., 1924), pp. 127–128.
[2] *Ibid.*, p. 132.

[3] Fergusson, Francis, *The Idea of a Theater* ("Oedipus Rex") (London: Princeton University Press, 1940), p. 37.

[4] Miller, Arthur, "Tragedy and the Common Man," in Kennedy's *Literature: An Introduction to Fiction, Poetry, and Drama* (Boston and Toronto: Little, Brown, and Co., 1983), p. 1341.

[5] *Ibid.*

[6] Sophocles, *Oedipus Rex*, translated by Dudley Fitts and Robert Fitzgerald, in Kennedy, *op. cit.*, p. 832.

[7] Shakespeare, *The Tragedy of Othello*, in Kennedy, *op. cit.*, p. 887.

[8] *Ibid.*, p. 878.

[9] Kitto, H. D. F., *Greek Tragedy: A Literary Study* ("The Dramatic Art of Sophocles") (London: Methuen and Company, Ltd., 1939) p. 148.

[10] Fergusson, *op. cit.*, p. 19.

[11] Sophocles, *op. cit.*, p. 833.

[12] *Ibid.*, p. 837.

[13] *Ibid.*, p. 840.

[14] Bradley, A. C., *Shakespeare Tragedy* ("Othello"—Lecture V) (London: Macmillan and Company, Ltd., 1950) p. 189.

[15] Shakespeare, *op. cit.*, p. 882.

[16] *Ibid.*, p. 935.

[17] *Ibid.*, p. 957.

[18] Sophocles, *op. cit.*, p. 857.

[19] Bradley, *op. cit.*, p. 191.

Bibliography

Auden, W. H. *The Dyer's Hand and Other Essays* ("The Joker in the Pack"), New York: Random House, 1956.

Bradley, A. C. *Shakespearean Tragedy* ("Othello"—Lecture V), London: Macmillan and Company Ltd., 1950.

Denniston, J. D. *Greek Literary Criticism* (Aristotle, *The Poetics*, "Definition of Tragedy"), London: J. M. Dent and Sons Ltd., 1924.

Fergusson, Francis. *The Idea of a Theater* ("Oedipus Rex"), London: Princeton University Press, 1940.

Kitto, H. D. F. *Greek Tragedy: A Literary Study* ("The Dramatic Art of Sophocles"), London: Methuen and Company Ltd., 1939.

Miller, Arthur. "Tragedy and the Common Man" in Kennedy, X. J., *Literature: An Introduction to Fiction, Poetry, and Drama,* Boston and Toronto: Little, Brown and Company, 1983. pp. 1340–1343.

Rossier, A. P. "Shakespearean Tragedy" in Michel, Laurence and Richard B. Sewall's *Tragedy: Modern Essays in Criticism,* New Jersey: Prentice-Hall, Inc., 1963.

Shakespeare, William. *The Tragedy of Othello* in Kennedy's *Literature: An Introduction to Fiction, Poetry, and Drama,* Boston and Toronto: Little, Brown and Company, 1983. pp. 875–958.

Sophocles, *Oedipus Rex,* translated by Dudley Fitts and Robert Fitzgerald in Kennedy's *Literature: An Introduction to Fiction, Poetry, and Drama,* Boston and Toronto: Little, Brown and Company, 1983, pp. 831–870.

QUESTIONS ABOUT THE RHETORICAL SITUATION

1. To what degree is Cox writing for an audience of readers who are familiar with *Oedipus* and *Othello*?
2. What is Cox's purpose in writing this essay? What are her readers supposed to "get out of" reading "A Symbol of Humanity"? How are Cox's intentions in this essay different from Pauline Kael's intentions in her review of *The Color Purple*? (See Chapter 11.)
3. How does Cox feel about Othello and Oedipus as characters? Does she express any preference for one character or one play over the other? How does Cox's attitude toward her subject differ from Pauline Kael's attitude toward *The Color Purple* in her review of that movie?

QUESTIONS ABOUT THE ESSAY'S VOICE

1. In her opening paragraph, Cox relies very heavily upon her research to set up her discussion. Do you hear enough of her voice in this opening paragraph? How might she have written this paragraph so that her readers heard more of her and a bit less of her sources?
2. One reason that Cox's essay is so effective is that she juggles a number of subjects at the same time: her working definition of the tragic hero, *Oedipus*, *Othello*. Examine her organization closely. What is the pattern she has used to keep her materials under control? Notice her use of transitions in particular.
3. Cox uses very brief quotations from the two tragedies and from her other sources. How effectively has she integrated these quoted materials into the rest of her essay?
4. A number of Cox's paragraphs appear to be summaries of the action of the two tragedies. What else is she doing in these paragraphs, however, that makes them more significant than a mere review of the plot would be?
5. Notice that in the final paragraph, Cox does not use any footnoted material. Why has she constructed her essay in this way? Why is it important to her that in her final paragraph, only *her* voice be heard? Notice how authoritative Cox sounds in that final paragraph. Why is it appropriate that she end her essay in such a way?
6. How consistently does Cox's essay have the sound of the voice of an authority? How does she create that voice? Does she make generalizations as experts do? If so, where?
7. In Chapter 7, an essay by James Pokas, also a student writer, appears as a sample of the persuasive voice. Pokas makes use of research, including footnotes, in his essay. What argument could you make that his essay really belongs in this chapter on the research voice?

TOPICS TO WRITE ABOUT

1. Write a research paper that examines the classical definition of comedy and then applies that definition to one or more plays you have read. PO-TENTIAL AUDIENCE: readers who have read the plays. POTENTIAL PURPOSE: to explain how some basic principles of comedy apply to specific plays.
2. Write a research paper about the relationship between leaders of govern-ments and the people they govern, trying to reach some conclusions about what makes people follow some leaders and not others. POTENTIAL AUDIENCE: students majoring in political science. POTENTIAL PURPOSE: to explain your theory about how governments lead.
3. Write a research paper about Sophocles or Shakespeare. POTENTIAL AUDI-ENCES: students who are not majoring in literature/high school students in a literature class. POTENTIAL PURPOSE: to provide useful historical and bio-graphical background on the two writers that might help them in reading *Oedipus* or *Othello* or any of the other dramas written by these two play-wrights.

Why Nurses Leave Nursing

Jane Wilson

Jane Wilson is a registered nurse. She is also a self-employed freelance editor and writer, living in Ottawa. Her essay was originally published in *The Cana-dian Nurse* in March 1987 and addresses an issue of real concern to the nursing profession. Staffing hospitals to provide adequate nursing care has become a problem of major proportions with organizations such as the American Nurses' Association and the American Medical Association seeking solutions. Wilson's essay focuses on one of the contributing causes of the problem—nurses who leave the profession.

QUESTIONS ABOUT IDEAS

1. What is your perception of nursing as a career? Are you at all surprised by Wilson's descriptions (see ¶2, ¶21) of the nursing profession? How are doctors viewed differently by the public? Why?
2. To what extent are the problems faced by nurses the result of nursing being seen as a woman's profession?
3. What are your own priorities in your future career? How will the career you are pointing toward meet these priorities? What problems do you foresee in meeting your own priorities?

It's nearly twenty years now since nurses and students clipped the car- 1
toon strip *Miss Peach* from the newspaper and, smiling, hung it up on their
nursing station walls or refrigerator doors. The simple line drawing depicted
a group of rather earnest looking nursing students sitting before a blackboard on which was written, "Nurses of America." They were seen repeat-
ing their motto, "Never before have so beautiful gotten so clean to do so
many dirty jobs."

These days, nursing is rarely described as a "dirty job"—although to 2
be sure, there are elements of the work that would make many people uncomfortable. It is more often characterized as a very demanding profession.

Nurses have been a respected segment of society for decades; jobs are 3
virtually secure, as long as one is willing to relocate to areas of need, and
salary levels are at least reasonable compared to what nurses were paid before the 1970s. Why then, when you see respected elders in other professions, is it uncommon to see a nurse over the age of 40 still practicing full-
time? Why is it that nurses seem to choose another career path after having
paid their nursing dues early in their twenties? Why do nurses leave nursing?

For Canadian hospitals, especially those in large urban centers, that's a 4
serious question. Late last year, newspapers regularly featured stories on an
acute shortage of nurses. Toronto General Hospital was so short of trained
operating room and critical care nurses, it was reported, that administrators
were travelling to the Maritimes to woo less well-paid Eastern nurses to the
big city. While new staff was being sought, operating schedules were
trimmed and part-time "relief" nurses were much in demand.

There was another story behind the headlines, however. Administra- 5
tors said that the shortage was simply the natural result of the ebb and flow
in demand for nurses. But that explanation had nurses shaking their heads.
"If they'd only do something about the working conditions," sighed a Toronto nurse assigned to a busy surgical unit, "they wouldn't have people leaving in droves. But no, they'll go and hire these new nurses and in a year, or
two, those nurses will quit, too. It's easier to just go and find some more
bodies."

Not all the nurses who quit full-time work in hospitals leave the pro- 6
fession entirely, of course. It has long been recognized that having a family
and a nursing career is a difficult if not impossible combination and many
nurses (the females, that is) opt for a part-time career once they begin to
have children, fitting their nursing schedules around school hours and husbands' work hours. The advantage of part-time work, too, is that the nurse,
perhaps for the first time, has control over which hours she will work.

For other nurses who leave, however, the decision is a more dramatic 7
one: the nurse who leaves her nursing career behind her acknowledges that
the profession she chose is no longer right for her. It may be the perception
that the work ethic has failed; for the average hospital nurse, all his or her

hard work gets *is more* hard work. The real opportunities for advancement
and promotion are few and far between, and salary levels stop rising after a
mere seven years' service in most cases. The money is an important issue,
but for most of the nurses who leave nursing, it isn't the most important
issue.

"Nursing isn't a career," says Pam Haslam, a former nurse educator   8
who is now a systems analyst, "it's just a job. There is so little relationship
between the responsibility and the authority in the work, it's quite unfair
and, frankly, very frustrating." Haslam was a kind of nurse's nurse for many
years; she has a degree in nursing and has experience both in Canada and the
United States. For a time she was deeply involved in cardiovascular nursing—so much that she wrote a book for nursing students on how to read
electrocardiograms, a book that is still in use at some learning centers. Computers became her life when she worked on a project to analyze data on cardiac patients at the University of Ottawa Heart Institute. After she completed a program in computer science, she took a position at Health and
Welfare Canada as a systems analyst. There, her nursing knowledge has
been a boon for her employers: she has a deeper understanding of the use of
the data she is organizing, and has been able to serve on and contribute to
the work of several government committees.

The nurses who seem to abandon nursing don't feel the years they   9
spent in the profession were a total loss; like Pam Haslam, they carry their
knowledge with them and use it to their advantage. Unlike Haslam, however, some nurses choose careers that are completely unrelated to health and
health care. Most experienced nurses have developed very valuable skills and
have knowledge that can easily—and profitably—be applied to other careers.
Their skill and ease in dealing with people aids them in careers such as sales,
public relations, and teaching.

It's an interesting fact that a significant number of women real estate   10
agents are nurses (teachers are also strongly represented). Real estate is a career which draws heavily on "people skills" but which also demands that a
person be able to organize herself well and set priorities quickly. It's also a
job for which the formal preparation is a scant (but gruelling) six weeks; the
most successful agents work from personal strength and energy, not a set of
letters after their names.

There is a wide variety of choices open to nurses now but there are   11
other reasons behind that final decision to leave the career nurses spent years
preparing for. Working conditions seem to be top of the list for most, but
contrary to what outsiders think, it isn't "burnout" that finally drives nurses
away. It's the day-in, day-out drudgery they face, in a job they feel is without thanks or just reward. "Things have just gotten worse over the years,"
says a nurse who works in a large general hospital. "Now there are no or-
derlies or ward aides to help us, even on neurosurgery where the patients are
sick and heavy and need frequent turning. We have so much more work to

do, the patient assignments are getting heavier, and now we even have to do all the little jobs that used to be done by a lot of other people. Worse, our liability, our responsibility hasn't changed, but there just isn't time to do it all, never mind do it the way you'd like to."

Nurses in Ontario, and perhaps across Canada, trace some of their dis- 12 content to two signal events in Canadian nursing history. The first was the case of the intensive care unit nurses at the Mount Sinai Hospital in Toronto. Three nurses, on night shift in the ICU, refused to admit a critically ill patient one night several years ago on the grounds that the unit was already overloaded and, since the new patient would require one-to-one care, they informed the admitting doctor and their nursing supervisor that they would not accept the patient because they felt they could not be responsible for him. The hospital suspended the nurses without pay for three days as a disciplinary action, but they took their case to court. They lost. Nurses are to obey first and grieve later, was the judgement, but that's a sentence most nurses find impossible to accept. For all the talk among the profession as to nurses' accountability, it was clear that the court and the hospital saw nurses simply as employees who must do as they are told.

The second event was the arrest of Susan Nelles for the murders of 13 four infants at The Hospital for Sick Children, also in Toronto. It was not so much the arrest of a nurse that sickened and appalled Nelles' fellow nurses, but the clear conviction of the police that the culprit simply *had* to be a nurse. Moreover, during the inquiry, which was televised, the treatment given to nurses and physicians was dramatically different: doctors, the few who were publicly questioned, were treated with deference and respect, while the nurses were questioned in an atmosphere of suspicion. It was as if the police assumed, if it wasn't *this* nurse who committed the crime, which nurse was it?

The lesson that nurses learned from these two events (and, of course, 14 there have been others, less publicized) was that nursing is a profession like no other: when trouble comes, no one—not your employer, not your supervisors, perhaps not even your colleagues—will stand behind you. And that's a terrifying thought, particularly these days when nurses' workload and responsibility are increasing and the general public is becoming more litigious.

For many hospital-based nurses, the loss of the old fashioned head 15 nurse figure has been another factor in their discontent. The head nurse of old, who knew each and every patient, who oversaw patient care and acted as interface between physicians and nurses, tended to "take care" of the staff nurses and assumed some of the enormous responsibility nurses have. Primary care is a system that looks good on paper documented in professional journals, but the reality of primary care in a busy medical or surgical unit of a huge big-city hospital, is that the nurse manager sits in an office somewhere poring over budgets, while the staff nurses are virtually alone in their decision making and their accountability.

Nurses still do not like to talk about money—if a high salary were im- 16
portant, they might not have chosen nursing in the first place—but after
years of hard work the dissonance becomes painfully apparent: people who
don't work as hard as nurses do get paid the same, or more, money. In addition, diploma nurses realize that if they want to advance in the profession,
they must go to university and get a nursing degree. But their employers are
not always accommodating in granting time off for studies (or even a regular
time plan so that a nurse could arrange part-time classes); the universities do
not appear to think much of the diploma nurse's education and experience
(many institutions offer "challenge" exams but others require the diploma
nurse to start virtually at "square one"), and for all the effort, there is no
difference in pay or work assignment. "I figured if I had to go to university
anyway," says one nurse, "I might as well go and do something worthwhile,
and get out of nursing."

The recent shortage of nurses was most acute in specialty areas of care 17
such as the operating room and in critical or intensive care units. The nurses
who work in these areas have additional preparation and education, and
work under a great deal of stress, yet receive no extra financial compensation
and have no better chance at advancement than does any other nurse. After
a few years, some decide it's simply not worth it any longer and leave. Here,
nurses really do burn out under the constant pressure of dealing with critically ill people. "There's no gratification," explains one ICU nurse. "We see
people when they're very ill and then when the crisis is over, they go upstairs
and other nurses get to see them get well and go home. We never see the
good times, it's just one crisis after another."

"I'm not surprised nurses leave," says one senior nurse who is a coor- 18
dinator with a community health agency, who has seen friends leave the profession and whose own daughter, aged 27, plans to work "a few more years"
and then get out. "These are vibrant, intelligent women who have a lot of
knowledge, a lot of skill, and tremendous energy. It's only natural that they
should turn to something where all those attributes can be put to use."

An Ottawa nurse who decided to give up working nights in a nursing 19
home to sell life insurance became one of her company's top
salespeople...in just one year. Although her friends disapproved of her decision to leave nursing, she is unapologetic: "Nurses are always made to feel
guilty for wanting a little something for themselves, and I don't think that's
right. I'll tell you, when I was working as a nurse I wasn't feeling particularly productive or worthwhile. I feel like I'm doing as much for people now
as when I was a practicing RN."

It is also interesting to note that the nurses who are over age 35 and 20
have chosen to leave their profession, or perhaps scale down their involvement to as little as a few days a month (which means they are counted among
the nurses still employed in nursing in government statistics) are those
women graduating from high school in the 1960s for whom the career

choices were very limited. In those days, if you were an intelligent young woman, your choice was to be a nurse or a teacher, now the choices are much broader, and it appears it isn't too late for these nurses to change their direction in life. Nursing is no longer the ideal profession for women; in 1986, *Working Woman* magazine named nursing as one of 10 "dead-end" occupations.

In the end, the answer to the question, why do nurses leave nursing, 21 might seem to be "the working conditions." Nurses are educated to become independent-thinking professionals, accountable for their own practice, but the real life workaday world does not accommodate such lofty views of the profession. To the public, nursing remains something of a vocation: nurses are supposed to nurse because of a desire to help people, not to advance in a career or to make money. Doctors and hospitals feel nurses are just there to carry out orders, to get the job done, no matter what.

"The worm has turned," declares a Toronto nurse. Nursing jobs are 22 vacant in British Columbia, Quebec, Ontario and the North, and although schools of nursing report an increase in enrollment for 1986, it is unlikely that the current shortage will ever be resolved. Moreover, if the only nurses left practicing are those who have their eyes on the day they can get out, or who have just entered practice, surely the profession itself will suffer.

Who will want to be a nurse in the year 2000? 23

References

Hospitals alarmed as disgruntled nurses flee profession, *The Globe and Mail*, Dec. 6, 1986.
New beginnings—changing career in midstream, *Ottawa Magazine*, May 1986.
Nursing shortage a growing problem in Canada, *The Toronto Star*, Sept. 25, 1986.
Toronto looking east for nurses, *The Globe and Mail*, Nov. 28, 1986.

QUESTIONS ABOUT THE RHETORICAL SITUATION

1. Wilson's essay was published in *The Canadian Nurse*. To what extent is the essay difficult to follow for people who are not nurses or for non-Canadian readers? To what extent is Wilson's essay one that should be of concern to the general reading public?
2. Would you describe Wilson as optimistic, pessimistic, or neutral about her subject? She herself is a nurse. Can you tell how she feels about her profession and its problems? Do you think she herself will stay with a nursing career? Why or why not?
3. Wilson's nurse readers are probably familiar with much of what she says here. What then is her purpose in writing about a familiar subject?

QUESTIONS ABOUT THE ESSAY'S VOICE

1. Wilson quotes a number of nurses in her essay, yet her essay does not convey the interview voice. What makes this essay's voice different from the essays in Chapter 12, The Interview Voice?
2. Why does Wilson only identify one of her interview subjects? Is this an effective strategy? Should she identify more of them?
3. All of those nurses quoted have left or are about to leave nursing. Should Wilson have spoken to older nurses who have not left nursing? Explain your answer.
4. Wilson concludes ¶2 by raising several questions. What purposes does this strategy serve?
5. Wilson lists four published "references," yet she does not document specific portions of her essay as being derived from these sources. How appropriate is her decision regarding documentation of sources? Why?
6. In ¶12 and ¶13, Wilson tells two stories that she describes as "signal events in Canadian nursing history." Why are these stories so important? How convincing do you find Wilson's interpretations of their significance (to be found at the end of each paragraph)?
7. In which parts of her essay does Wilson sound most knowledgeable about her subject? Why? How does her voice on a medical topic differ from Lewis Grizzard's voice on a different medical topic (see Chapter 2)?
8. How effective is Wilson's conclusion (¶21–23)?

TOPICS TO WRITE ABOUT

1. Write a research paper on job satisfaction in your chosen career or on problems faced in that career both currently and in the decades to come or on the public's image of workers in your chosen profession. Pay particular attention to mass media depictions (television, films, paperback books). You might interview several professionals as well as researching in the library. POTENTIAL AUDIENCES: other majors in your field/the general public. POTENTIAL PURPOSES: to warn them about some of the obstacles or difficulties they may face in the future/to inform the public more fully about your chosen field.
2. Write a research paper about a medical or health-care or related subject: for example, training of nurses, physicians, paramedics; medical ethics; technology and its impact on medical costs; gene-splicing research. POTENTIAL AUDIENCES: college students with nonscience majors/premed or nursing students. POTENTIAL PURPOSES: to explain in everyday terms some of the major concerns in the fields of medicine and health care/to make them more aware of important issues in their chosen field of study.

Ice and Light

Barry Lopez

Barry Lopez is a writer whose books focus on the natural world. He has written about deserts, rivers, and wolves in books such as *Desert Notes, River Notes,* and *Of Wolves and Men.* "Ice and Light" is a selection from a chapter of his 1986 book *Arctic Dreams: Imagination and Desire in a Northern Landscape.*

Arctic Dreams is a book that grew out of Lopez's years of travel throughout the Arctic region. He mentions two incidents in particular that gave birth to this book, one involving an evening walk when he was moved by the variety of astonishing birds he observed while camping in western Alaska and one involving the burial place of an Arctic explorer who died while camped near the North Pole. "I remember looking out the back window of the car that evening and seeing Israel's grave in the falling light. What had this man hoped to find? What sort of place did he think lay out there before him...?"

In "Ice and Light" Lopez explains in vivid terms the dangerous and powerful, yet beautiful, ice packs of the Arctic Ocean.

QUESTIONS ABOUT IDEAS

1. Why do some people, such as the whalers described in this essay, choose dangerous professions?
2. Examine closely the behavior of the different sailors who are trapped by the ice. Were you surprised at some of their reactions? What conclusions can you draw about human behavior under adverse conditions?
3. Earlier in his book, Lopez compares the Arctic region to a desert. What similarities do you see between the Arctic as described in this essay and a desert?

Shorefast ice, embayed ice, or sea ice that has formed in regions where   1
there are no appreciable currents can offer a serene and dependable surface over which to travel, even at night. Pack ice, the ice beyond the flaw lead, holds a different sort of attraction because of its constant motion, varied topography, and the access it provides to certain animals. But to venture out there on foot is, to put it simply, to court death. Pack ice moves irregularly before the wind, and the change in orientation of an individual piece of ice is unpredictable. Commonly, especially on larger pieces of ice, there is no sensation at all of movement or change. A person might discover suddenly that he was far from shore, or realize he had no idea of his position. In every coastal village from Inglefield Fiord to Saint Lawrence Island there is a story of someone who got caught out there by mistake, often pursuing a polar bear, and who was never seen again.

The crushing power of moving pack ice is not a great threat to people   2
traveling with dogs or on foot. They can usually move nimbly enough over
its surface. To be at its mercy in a boat or small ship, however, is to know an
exhausting, nerve-wracking vulnerability. In May 1814, with his whaling
ship beset off the east coast of Greenland, William Scoresby set out on foot
to reconnoiter the final mile of maneuvering that he hoped would set him
free. Like many men caught in such circumstances, Scoresby was terrified.
But he was mesmerized as well by the ice, by its sheer power, its daunting
scale, the inexorability of its movement. The sound of its constant adjustment before the wind was like "complicated machinery, or distant thunder,"
he wrote. Even as he sought a way out, he marveled at the way it distracted
him. He lost the sense of plight that spurred him, the pleading whining that
came from his ship's pinched hull; he became a mere "careless spectator." It
was as though he were walking over the back of some enormous and me-
thodical beast.

The sea ice was a more perilous environment in the era of wood ships   3
than it seems today from the bridge of a steel-hulled icebreaker, but no arctic sailor was or is ever at ease in it. The whalers forced their way in with
poorly fitted ships and lived for months at the extreme limits of their ability
to cope. To get through a stretch of ice and out to open water, or to survive
in a stream of ice driven down on them in a storm, nineteenth-century sailors had to employ several operations. With a favorable wind and an ice-
strengthened prow, they could "bore" their way through, following the
shouted directions of a lookout in the crow's nest. But a sail ship has no re-
verse, no reliable "dead slow," no instant "hard-to-port" response. More often they had to take the ship in tow behind their whaleboats and row
through the ice. Or "warp" it forward, winching from the windlass against
anchors set in the ice ahead. Or "mill-doll," by dropping a boat with three
or four men from the bowsprit, to fracture ice in advance of the prow.

In the shifting pack, even a 250-ton ship could conceivably be crushed   4
in two or three minutes, forced up in the air with an explosion of its oak ribs
and driven under with a grunt, like a grand piano caught in an industrial
press. To protect it during a storm in the ice front, or at night when they
could not find open water, the crews sawed temporary docks in the floes. As
often as not they lost that protection and had to begin all over again the wea-
rying task of cutting and removing blocks of ice. In heavy weather the pack
moved like a jigsaw puzzle; loose ice hit them repeatedly, "hard enough to
knock the ship's brains out." Officers tried to mete out a crew's strength
over the course of a storm, or until they got out of the ice. But any situation
could change instantly—ice at rest one minute was moving the next. Officers
felt the strain of unceasing responsibility and vigilance. "During that time,"
wrote one captain of a harrowing seventeen hours he spent running a shore
lead, "I did the heaviest smoking of my life. I smoked twenty-two cigars and
numerous pipes, and I had coffee brought to me every hour. I don't know

whether it was the tobacco or the coffee that brought us through, but we made it with no damage."

Damage was routine, some of it serious. "Relays of men at the pumps   5 and others working with buckets," wrote a captain of his stove ship, "succeeded in raising seven to eight tons of water per minute, [but] the sea came in quicker than it could be thrown out." And the sea was a frigid 30°F. They fothered their broken hulls with wads of sail and filled the cracks as well as they could with cordage and oakum. They sought a desperate protection up-current of icebergs. *But the icebergs sometimes disintegrated and the ships were swamped or crushed. Once a storm passed and the menacing ice was still, they no longer had to lie in their bunks and listen to the "rending, crashing, tearing noise," the screech and detonation of a ship's timbers. But until they were clear of it, its capricious and unappeasable nature preyed on their imaginations.

If it got very cold, as often happened toward the end of the whaling   6 season, ice might congeal around a ship, creating in only a few hours "a crystal pavement by the breath of Heaven cemented firm." When a man stood on the deck in such stillness, he could hear his watch ticking in his pocket. Men who had collapsed at the pumps or lost their appetites when ice peeled the copper sheathing off the ship's bottom now went out on the ice for a stroll and flew kites or tossed a ball, as though they were on a commons.

When a ship was seriously beset, the crew packed their belongings, set   7 them on deck, and waited. The slow compression of the ship could go on for weeks before the keel finally broke or the holds flooded. When a ship was lost, however, it rarely sank right away—the men had time to step overboard and walk away, if they were lucky, to another ship. In the fall of 1777, more than 350 such shipwrecked men, whalers and sealers, were to be found hiking over the ice off the southeast coast of Greenland. About 140, given food and clothing at native settlements, eventually reached Danish villages on the west coast. The others perished. In 1830, so many ships were destroyed in Melville Bay (the place they called "the breaking-up yard") that at one point nearly 1000 men were camped on the ice. Legally under the command of no captain, they set fire to the broken ships and milled about for weeks in drunken celebration. (Not a man was lost in this weird catastrophe.)

Five years later an isolated group of British ships, fishing too late, be-   8 came for the first time irrevocably beset in Baffin Bay. The men had neither proper clothing nor food enough to see them through the winter. Most died of starvation, exposure, and despair during the four months they were carried passively south in the Canadian Current. The ships' logs are poignant. On November 11, 1835, an officer of the *Viewforth* wrote: "Weather milder.

---

*Icebergs, because of their deep keels, move with the current, while sea ice moves before the wind. An iceberg can therefore plow a course through oncoming sea ice, providing shelter for a ship in its wake.

A great many fish have been playing around the ship to-day, amongst which we observed unicorns and white whales. We are now to the southward of Cape Searle, a sublime object. The moon has been in sight all day—it never sets—a thing I never saw before." On November 13 a mate aboard the *Jane* wrote: "Strong breezes with snow; heavy press, ship suffering greatly, how she can bear it God only knows. It's awful work; long dark nights, no hope for us if she goes. May God preserve our shelter."

When they reached the ice front in February, the floes opened and ⁹ then closed, opened and then closed on them. Each day they built up their hope from scratch. One of the whalers sank. When the others were finally released, too few men were still alive aboard some of the ships to hoist sail. They drifted aimlessly in weather so foul that for days on end they could not take a bearing or fix their position. Some were met by outwardbound whalers; miraculously, every ship eventually reached England. The following year, a dozen vessels froze in again. Half these ships sank, and the loss of life was extensive—forty-four of fifty-eight aboard the *Dee*, forty-two of forty-nine aboard the *Advice*.

Sometimes it was over very quickly. At 3:30 A.M. on the 26th of April 10 1832, the whaler *Shannon* of Hull, running before a southeast gale, slammed bow first into an iceberg. The captain ran forward in the darkness and laid his hands to the wall of ice even as it continued past them, ripping open the ship's starboard side. They were awash in minutes. Sixteen men and three boys were swept away. The survivors clung to each other beneath a sail, on a part of the ship kept afloat by trapped air. They were without food or fresh water. They survived, with the death of but three more, by bleeding each other and drinking the blood from a shoe. A man who left their deck shelter to commit suicide spotted two Danish brigs on the 2nd of May. The survivors, save the captain, were all frostbitten. "The rescue," writes a historian of the arctic whale fisheries, "was one of those providential affairs of which many instances could be related."

I think of a final image of devastation: the remnant of several whaling 11 crews found in a frozen stupor behind a sea wall of dead bodies, stacked up to protect them from the worst of the heavy seas in which their small floe rolled and pitched.

The horror and loss of life are remote from us now. Our assessment of 12 arctic seas is today more often made from an airplane, amid the crackle of constant radio contact, or from the warm bridge of an icebreaker, guided by the lugubrious movement of a gyrocompass and the deep-space silence of satellite navigation systems. This machinery compresses time and space, and comforts us because of the authority with which it keeps danger at bay. From these quarters, its scale reduced, we appraise the landscape very differently.

Few men in northern ships today, however, are without regard for the 13 human history that preceded their own in those waters. And no arctic ship's master, his Lloyd's of London Ice Class IA Super ship boring through four feet of sea ice at a steady five knots, sleeps free of the stories that have been passed down. They are ignored only by men for whom the recalcitrance of the land is but a distraction, a disturbance to be quelled by machinery.

The frozen ocean itself still turns in its winter sleep like a dragon.   14

QUESTIONS ABOUT THE RHETORICAL SITUATION

1. Is Lopez writing for a general reading public or does he appear to have a more specific readership in mind? Explain your answer.
2. This selection comes from Chapter 6 of *Arctic Dreams*. Is there any indication that reading the first five chapters is necessary to a fuller appreciation of this selection? How well does it stand on its own as a piece of writing?
3. How does Lopez seem to feel about the Arctic ice packs? about modern ice-breaking nautical equipment?
4. Given your answer to question number 3 above, what do you see as Lopez's purpose in writing this selection? How does he want you as a reader to respond? How did you respond?

QUESTIONS ABOUT THE ESSAY'S VOICE

1. Lopez quotes a number of primary sources (documents written by actual participants in the events described). How effective are these quotations in conveying what sailing in the Arctic Ocean was like in the days of sailing ships? Does Lopez rely too heavily upon such material?
2. Lopez does not identify his sources either by footnoting them or listing them in a systematic way. Although his book does include a bibliography, it is not clear which books were the sources for the quoted diaries and ship's logs. Why do you think Lopez does not provide documentation? What is the effect on his voice of his decision? How clear is it when he is reporting his research and when he is speaking out of firsthand experience? Is his documentation sufficient? (See ¶10 for an example of Lopez's very informal sort of documentation.)
3. Notice Lopez's use of similes (¶4, ¶14). What is the effect created by each? Why is ¶14 set off as a separate paragraph?
4. Although Lopez's anecdotes involve several deaths, the voice remains somewhat distant, uninvolved in these deaths. (For example, he refers to the ships' logs of several doomed British ships as "poignant" in ¶8, yet he remains rather distant in his reporting of these deaths as well as several others.) Why has Lopez chosen such a voice? How would the impact change if his voice were to be more emotional?

5. In ¶5, Lopez uses a footnote to make a further point about icebergs. Why does he do so in a footnote instead of in the body of the paragraph itself?
6. Aside from the many stories and facts Lopez includes, what generalizations does he make that give his voice the sound of authority?

TOPICS TO WRITE ABOUT

1. Write a research paper based on diaries and letters written by people who have undergone interesting experiences of some sort: fought in a battle, were imprisoned, traveled extensively, survived an accident or illness, trained for an athletic event, created a major work of art, explored an unfamiliar territory. POTENTIAL AUDIENCES: readers with interests similar to the diarists' interests/your history class. POTENTIAL PURPOSES: to inform and entertain them with stories about the subject that appeals to them/to bring an individual perspective to an historical event.
2. Write a research paper about an interesting geographical location. For example, one of my students researched the history of the 100-year-old house in which she lived. POTENTIAL AUDIENCES: people who live in that location/your geography class. POTENTIAL PURPOSES: to give them an historical perspective on their own hometown/to show how past influences have created current conditions in a specific location.

Something Whistling in the Night
Richard Erdoes and Alfonso Ortiz

"Something Whistling in the Night" was originally published in *American Indian Myths and Legends,* an anthology of more than 150 American Indian stories collected, as the authors explain in their preface, over a period of twenty-five years. The stories have been translated by Erdoes and Ortiz, often from taped accounts given by Indian storytellers. Other stories, Erdoes and Ortiz explain, "are classic accounts" and appear in their original form—while still others come from published accounts of the nineteenth century. This selection serves as the introduction to a section of folk stories and legends focusing on ghosts and the spirit world: twelve tales in all from nine different Indian tribes.

QUESTIONS ABOUT IDEAS

1. How does our modern society view ghosts and the spirit world? To what influences can you attribute the differences between our modern views

and those Indian views described by Erdoes and Ortiz in "Something Whistling in the Night"?

2. What does a society's view of death reveal about that society's view of life?

3. Why are people so fascinated with ghosts and spirits? Why are ghosts and spirits so reliable a source of entertainment? In other words, why is the "horror" genre—novels, films, and television shows—so popular?

Ghost stories and tales of the dead are essential parts of almost every 1 people's folklore, and American Indians are no exception. The ghosts here, however, are not necessarily always evil or threatening; the dead don't automatically become ghosts, either, so all haunting visions are not necessarily spirits of the departed. Among some tribes there are only vague ideas of the existence of an afterlife. Death was the end, and that was that. At the other extreme of the cultural spectrum were the burial-mound builders like the Natchez, who practiced an elaborate death cult with pyramids for the dead. The ruler was buried with treasures of copper, mica, shell, and pearls, as well as a host of women and retainers, dispatched to serve him in the next world.

In between are the cultures that envision the souls of the dead living in 2 the spirit land in much the same way that they lived on earth—the men hunting buffalo, gathering crops, or fishing; the women tending the home or tipi. The Mandans believed that people had four souls, and the sage and meadowlark souls merged to form the spirit that went on to another world. The third soul remained in its old lodge, and the fourth appeared from time to time simply to frighten people.

In variations on the classical Orpheus theme, the tales here recount 3 several voyages made by the living into the land of the departed, from either curiosity or devotion to a dead relative. While the Greek hero follows his beloved to a world underground, his Indian counterpart may find himself traveling to the bottom of a lake, across the Milky Way, or over mountains and plains similar to those inhabited by the living, although the road is usually strewn with traps for the cowardly or careless.

Exchanges between the dead and the living are common—men or 4 women suddenly find out that they have married a ghost, a discovery that puts an interesting twist in romance. The lives of the dead and the living are not generally compatible over the long run, it would seem; each must return to his or her own kind eventually, so that order may be reestablished.

Relations with the departed continue, however, through ritual. Among 5 many tribes a warrior must purify himself, fast, and abstain from sex in order to propitiate the ghost of an enemy he has killed. When a Sioux died, his *wanagi,* his ghost or soul, left the body but stayed near for four days. "You'd better please this spirit," Lame Deer said, "or it might make trouble."

> With every meal, you leave a morsel aside for the spirits. When I drink some *mni-sha,* wine, or some *suta,* hard liquor, I always spill a little bit for an old wino friend, saying, "Here, *kola,* is something for you to enjoy." A good man could take his horse along to the Happy Hunting Grounds. That's why a great chief's or fighter's best horse was sometimes killed after his death, and the horse's head and tail were tied to the funeral scaffold. We didn't believe in burying people in the earth. No, the body of our dead were put on scaffolds or in trees, where the birds, the wind, and the rain could take care of them. The soul went on to the spirit land through the sky, and on the trail sat Owl-Woman, Hihan-Kaha, who would not let them pass unless they had the right signs on their foreheads, or chins, or wrists. When a child died, sometimes the father could not stand parting from it. Then he took some hair from the body and put it into a bundle which he placed in a special tipi. There he kept the child's soul. Soul keeping was hard. It might go on for a year, and during this time the father could not touch his wife, his gun, his weapons; he could not go out and hunt. At the end, the soul was released with a great giveaway feast.

Among the Navajo and some other Southwestern tribes, the dwelling 6 in which a person had died was abandoned or destroyed, and his corpse, the token of lifelessness, greatly feared. People not related to the departed would offer to bury or cover the body as a gesture of good will. They believed that ghosts come out only after dark, and their appearance often betokens the imminent death of a close relative. In tribes the name of a dead person was never mentioned again.

Some ghosts are harmlessly funny, prompting (or getting caught in) a 7 string of comic episodes among the living. They have also been known to play tricks on people, making a man's mouth crooked or bringing illness. Parents invoke them as bogeymen to scare children—"If you don't behave, Siyoko will take you away," a Sioux mother might threaten. Other ghosts may bless a person in his dreams, or warn of approaching dangers.

A whistling sound behind a tipi usually announces the arrival of a 8 ghostly messenger. Ghosts are generally dark and indistinct in shape; they nourish themselves only on the smell, not the substance, of food. However, they have also been known to appear in the guise of coyotes, mice, and sparks of fire. The Crow believe that certain ghosts haunt graves, hoot like owls, and manifest themselves as whirlwinds.

Among the Tewa Pueblos, the newly dead soul wanders about in the 9 world of the living, in the company of his ancestors, for four days, during which time the village remains generally uneasy. Relatives fear that the soul will become lonely and return to take one of them with him. The house itself must not be left unoccupied at any time during these four days, in order to keep the soul from reoccupying it. The soul is eventually released when the head elder utters a short prayer and reveals the purpose of the symbolic acts the relatives have performed.

> We have muddied the water for you (the smoke)
> We have cast shadows between us (the charcoal)
> We have made deep gullies between us (the lines)
> Do not, therefore, reach for even a hair on our heads
> Rather, help us attain that which we are always seeking
> Long life, that our children may grow
> Abundant game, the raising of crops
> And in all the works of man
> Ask for these things for all, and do no more
> And now you must go, for you are now free.

When Incarnacion Peña, the last sacred clown of San Ildefonso Pueblo, 10 had been dead four days, one of his friends remarked, "He is already up there in the mountains, making rain for us."

QUESTIONS ABOUT THE RHETORICAL SITUATION

1. What suggestions are there in this essay that the authors are writing for an audience not very familiar with Indian ways or folklore?
2. What is the authors' intention in writing this essay? What did you "get out of" reading this essay?
3. The authors are anthropologists/sociologists. How scientific is their attitude towards their material in this essay? How judgmental are they about what they describe? How are these two questions related to one another?

QUESTIONS ABOUT THE ESSAY'S VOICE

1. What is the purpose of ¶1 of the essay? How effectively does it achieve this purpose? How does ¶1 also help to establish the essay's voice?
2. Paragraph 3 makes links with Orpheus and Greek mythology. What is the significance of these links? Why do the authors make this connection?
3. What purpose do Erdoes and Ortiz have in including the two lengthy quotations in ¶5 and ¶9? How effective are these quotations?
4. How does ¶8 help establish the authors as experts in this subject?
5. What is the source of the authors' expertise? Why does this essay belong in this chapter on the research voice, when there is neither documentation nor bibliography?

6. How effective a conclusion is ¶10? In what other ways might the authors have concluded this selection?
7. What holds "Something Whistling in the Night" together as an essay? Do the authors make extensive use of transitions? What seems to be the organizing principle behind the essay?

TOPICS TO WRITE ABOUT

1. Write a research paper about ghosts, death, or the spirit world in contemporary American life. (You might read such books as Jessica Mitford's *The American Way of Death*, Elisabeth Kübler-Ross' *On Death and Dying*, Shirley MacLaine's *Out on a Limb*.) POTENTIAL AUDIENCES: your classmates/your sociology class. POTENTIAL PURPOSES: to offer a contrast between contemporary American beliefs and those outlined in the Erdoes and Ortiz essay/to explain the sociological implications of the subject you have researched.
2. Write a research paper about the folklore or mythology of a particular national or ethnic group; the paper should focus on a specific subject. (For example, you might investigate the folklore of China on a subject such as death, courtship, marriage, childrearing, the legal system, natural disasters). POTENTIAL AUDIENCES: readers of an American magazine with an interest in the same subject you are researching/readers planning to travel to the country in question. POTENTIAL PURPOSES: to offer an insight into a foreign culture's attitudes toward a subject of mutual interest/to offer an insight into a foreign culture's attitudes.
3. Write a research on an aspect of the American Indian way of life. POTENTIAL AUDIENCES: your history call/your sociology or anthropology class. POTENTIAL PURPOSE: to offer a deeper and more comprehensive examination of one specific aspect of the Indian way of life.
4. Write a research paper based on oral history. (For example, you might interview a number of people with a common historical background to see what generalizations you can form about their history. You could speak with a number of people who have lived in the local community for more than fifty years about the educational system of the 1920s and 1930s. You could interview retired workers about the changes in local industries over the past fifty or sixty years.) POTENTIAL AUDIENCES: readers of your local newspaper's Sunday magazine section/the local historical society. POTENTIAL PURPOSES: to interest readers in their local history/to provide a deeper insight into the past events that have shaped current local conditions.

SECTION FIVE

Other Voices

Throughout the course of a day we all hear any number of voices: conversations with family, friends, classmates, teachers, librarians, coworkers, servers in restaurants and at stores, and so forth. We also *overhear* just as many voices, voices we really are not attending to but that form part of the background of our environment: students at the next table in the cafeteria conversing, disk jockeys blabbing on a radio turned up too loud in the car next to us at the traffic light, pedestrians on the sidewalk, the person in front of us at the dry cleaner's cash register, the manager and cashier at the fast food restaurant, the woman on the telephone in the lobby of the library that we hear as we walk in.

So it is with written voices also. Throughout *Model Voices*, you have been listening to writers' voices, the voices of authors whose objective was to speak to you, the reader. But there are other written voices also, voices you encounter every day but perhaps don't notice: the written voices in letters; the voices you hear in public speeches and later find in written form in newspapers or history books; and more personal voices such as those found in memoirs, diaries, journals.

WHAT YOU WILL FIND

In Section Five of *Model Voices* I have included a number of readings that did not fit neatly into any of the earlier sections of the book. You may find that, with some imagination, you might be able to place these selections in one or more of the earlier chapters, but they still seem different enough to me to be included here, in a sort of potpourri of different voices.

In Section Five you will find

• Selections from two diaries

- A series of personal letters
- An open letter
- Two oral histories
- A sermon
- A short story
- A famous political speech
- A commencement address

Notice as you read that, whether the text was originally spoken rather than written, whether it was written to be read only by the writer herself, whether you do not even know who the writer is, the considerations of the rhetorical situation—the audience, the purpose, the writer's attitude toward her subject matter—still help to create the voice you are hearing. These pieces provide a fascinating variety of interesting reading, interesting in large part because they possess distinctive and memorable voices.

DIARIES

The Diary of Helen Marnie Stewart

Helen Marnie Stewart lived from 1835 to 1873. Stewart traveled with her parents and siblings from their home in Pennsylvania to Oregon in 1853 as part of a wagon train. In this excerpt from her diary she describes her encounters with the Sioux Indians near Fort Laramie.

   The excerpt was published in *A Day at a Time: The Diary Literature of American Women from 1764 to the Present,* edited by Margo Cullen. The original diary is at the University of Oregon in Eugene, Oregon, where it belongs to the Lane County Historical Society.

[*June* 1853]   1

fry 17   2

   we started this morning at the usual time   we got to court house rock   3
we eat dinner neerly opisite to it and in site of chimney rock

   to day we hear great word of the indians   they say that there is five   4
hundred of them going to fight   we hear that they have laid down blankets   that is the sine for the emigrants not dare govern them   we shall see
when we come up to the place whether it is true or not and that they have
sent over the river to gether up more

   there was one old bachlier poor old fellow that was dreadful afraid   5

   he looked as if he wished his eyes might go ahead a peace to se if it was   6
true or not   I had to laugh at him   while his legs were running backward
for he said that if the emigrants was stopt untill more would come up he
thought it would be best just to have enough men with the wagons to mind
them and the rest to go and kill every one men weamon and children and he
would kill little sucking baby so he would for if they could not fight not they
would kill white peoples babys when they got big enough so they would by
G   swearing all the time at a great rate   poor little soul   he has a toleable
big body but a very little soul but old bachaliars ought to be excused a little
all ways for they are not always accountable

   but the great army that frightened him so proved to be an Indian camp   7
and in deed they were very friendly with us for they was one come first and
shuck hands with us all showed us a peace of paper that had the name of
evry thing he wanted such as tobacco flower coffe and whole lot of other
things   he told to that his was the best family among them and that he had
ten children   I saw some of the prittyist girls to and they ware drest so nice
after their own fashion of course though I do not know wether old John has
got over his panic yet or not

Sat 18   8

we have had good luck so far   one of our oxen was sick last night but   9
better this morning   the indians followed us so far today   oh it is beautiful   there is such romantic sereneary   we can see scots bluffs and a rang
on the opste side that is far more beautiful   o deare me it is so warm the
dust is flying in a cloud

sabeth 19   10

it is a fine day extremely windy   the dust is flying   the poor oxen I do   11
pity them so   I wish they had goggles   we come to an exslent spring of water but required some diging out   it i[s] runing out   of a very mountain-
neer this spring is the hill that if you go up on it you can larimie peak   I
went up but it was such a dull dusty day we could not see any distance

mon 20   12

it is warm   the cattle is travling with there toungs hanging out there   13
are so warm and tiard   there is a storm comeing up

tews 21   14

this morning is a beautiful after the rain   the road is leavel and   15
good   we past three dead oxen no a great distance apart   what death they
died I know not poor things   we are nearing for laramie   it is about five
miles to it yet there is so many that is there before us waiting to get across
that there is no grass neer it so we have to wait here awhile

wed 22   16

this is my birthday   my eighteenth birthday   I feel myself geting   17
older but not any wiser   it is a cold bleak day   the wind blows extremely
hard;   we are washing and bakeing and fixing ma[n]y little things   there
is lots of camps all around us   some is moveing on and others are moveing
in ther places   we had some what of snow storm on my birthday the 22 of
June 1853

thirs 23   18

we start to the ford and stops awhile on the above it   there is some   19
wagons there yet   Mary Ag and I took a walk up some of the high hills and
as we was comeing back we met in two Indians one of them was dressed fine
he had a brod stripe of beads sowd in the middle of his blanket and his
shoulders was just covered with them   he had two peaces of some kind of
fur and a long plated consurne it looked like a whip fastened to the back of
his head and a black bird on the place where they ware fasend   he had a
small loocking glass set in wood string round his neck   some thing to smell

also it had a very pleasant smell   I cannot begin to describe all the fixings
he had on   the other one had nothing nice only his legins and shoes   ther
ware just covered with beads   the drest one was very talktive and wanted
me to get on his horse behind him and wride to where the wagons was

---

The Diary of a Young Girl
Anne Frank

Anne Frank and her family were Jews who hid from the Nazis during World
War II in the attic of a sympathetic friend in Amsterdam. The only surviving
member of the Frank family, Anne's father Otto, had Anne's diary published
after the war. The excerpt reprinted here is the third entry in the diary, which
was translated by B. M. Mooyaart from its original Dutch.

1   I haven't written for a few days, because I wanted first of all to think
about my diary. It's an odd idea for someone like me to keep a diary; not
only because I have never done so before, but because it seems to me that
neither I—nor for that matter anyone else—will be interested in the unbo-
somings of a thirteen-year-old schoolgirl. Still, what does that matter? I want
to write, but more than that, I want to bring out all kinds of things that lie
buried deep in my heart.

2   There is a saying that "paper is more patient than man"; it came back
to me on one of my slightly melancholy days, while I sat chin in hand, feeling too bored and limp even to make up my mind whether to go out or stay
at home. Yes, there is no doubt that paper is patient and as I don't intend to
show this cardboard-covered notebook, bearing the proud name of "diary,"
to anyone, unless I find a real friend, boy or girl, probably nobody cares.
And now I come to the root of the matter, the reason for my starting a diary:
it is that I have no such real friend.

3   Let me put it more clearly, since no one will believe that a girl of thirteen feels herself quite alone in the world, nor is it so. I have darling parents
and a sister of sixteen. I know about thirty people whom one might call
friends—I have strings of boy friends, anxious to catch a glimpse of me and
who, failing that, peep at me through mirrors in class. I have relations, aunts
and uncles, who are darlings too, a good home, no—I don't seem to lack
anything. But it's the same with all my friends, just fun and joking, nothing
more. I can never bring myself to talk of anything outside the common
round. We don't seem to be able to get any closer, that is the root of the
trouble. Perhaps I lack confidence, but anyway, there it is, a stubborn fact
and I don't seem to be able to do anything about it.

Hence, this diary. In order to enhance in my mind's eye the picture of 4
the friend for whom I have waited so long, I don't want to set down a series
of bald facts in a diary like most people do, but I want this diary itself to be
my friend, and I shall call my friend Kitty. No one will grasp what I'm talking about if I begin my letters to Kitty just out of the blue, so albeit unwill-
ingly, so I will start by sketching in brief the story of my life.

My father was thirty-six when he married my mother, who was then 5
twenty-five. My sister Margot was born in 1926 in Frankfort-on-Main, I followed on June 12, 1929, and, as we are Jewish, we emigrated to Holland in
1933, where my father was appointed Managing Director of Travies N.V.
This firm is in close relationship with the firm of Kolen & Co. in the same
building, of which my father is a partner.

The rest of our family, however, felt the full impact of Hitler's anti- 6
Jewish laws, so life was filled with anxiety. In 1938 after the pogroms, my
two uncles (my mother's brothers) escaped to the U.S.A. My old grandmother came to us, she was then seventy-three. After May 1940 good times
rapidly fled: first the war, then the capitulation, followed by the arrival of
the Germans, which is when the sufferings of us Jews really began. Anti-
Jewish decrees followed each other in quick succession. Jews must wear a
yellow star, Jews must hand in their bicycles, Jews are banned from trains
and are forbidden to drive. Jews are only allowed to do their shopping between three and five o'clock and then only in shops which bear the placard
"Jewish shop." Jews must be indoors by eight o'clock and cannot even sit in
their own gardens after that hour. Jews are forbidden to visit theaters, cin-
emas, and other places of entertainment. Jews may not take part in public
sports. Swimming baths, tennis courts, hockey fields, and other sports
grounds are all prohibited to them. Jews may not visit Christians. Jews must
go to Jewish schools, and many more restrictions of a similar kind.

So we could not do this and were forbidden to do that. But life went on 7
in spite of it all. Jopie used to say to me, "You're scared to do anything,
because it may be forbidden." Our freedom was strictly limited. Yet things
were still bearable.

Granny died in January 1942; no one will ever know how much she is 8
present in my thoughts and how much I love her still.

In 1934 I went to school at the Montessori Kindergarten and continued 9
there. It was at the end of the school year, I was in form 6B, when I had to
say good-by to Mrs. K. We both wept, it was very sad. In 1941 I went, with
my sister Margot, to the Jewish Secondary School, she into the fourth form
and I into the first.

So far everything is all right with the four of us and here I come to the 10
present day.

LETTERS

A Family's Personal Letters

This selection of three letters includes a letter from a daughter to her parents, her mother's response, and a note from her father in response to her letter. The letters first appeared in *Between Ourselves: Letters Between Mothers and Daughters 1750–1982*, edited by Karen Payne.

1 August 1972   1

Dear Mom and Dad,   2
...I'm not moving back home after I graduate. There is really nothing   3
for me there (aside from being with the family). I am contented, happy, and settled down in a place where I don't mind living. What would you rather have: me as a mature adult, handling my own affairs and making my own decisions...or me as a 'child' depending on you for everything? I want to be able to handle my own financial matters after I graduate. It is time for me to stop accepting money from you and start supporting myself. I don't want to limit my world to one thing or one place or one set of ideals.

My roommate is moving out at the end of this term. There is a possi-   4
bility that Tony will move in. We have talked about it and it seems like the logical thing to do since we might as well be living together anyway. I hope you have realized by now that I am not a little girl any more. I firmly believe we have made the right decision and so does Tony. We are happy together and we have much to learn and gain, and much to experience by doing this. Also, if I am living with a man I will feel safer living in an area where rapes and robberies are a common occurrence.

I assume you think that living together is morally wrong as opposed to   5
marriage which is morally 'right'. I feel that two people can be just as close and happy living together, and they do not need a marriage contract to make theirs a 'legal' partnership. If marriage is a form of 'security', then I don't want that form of security. Security alone is not a valid reason for two people to be together. This is what I believe and I want you to be able to accept it and be aware that this is what I really am.

Much love,   6
your daughter, Pat   7

8 August 1972   1

Dear Pat,   2
I don't know what reaction you expected from us after reading your   3
Air Mail letter to us this week. Naturally we are disappointed at your apparent lack of appreciation and respect for us, as well as respect for yourself. We did the best we could for both our girls, and expected to see you grad-

uate, as did Sharon [*Pat's sister*], knowing where you were going and with both feet on the ground. As it is, you seem to be in a confused state, changing your major for the third time and not knowing exactly what you want or where you are going.

When you gave us the snow job several months ago, convincing us that 4 you wanted to move from the dorm into an apartment, even though we had a few misgivings as to the advisability of it, our trust and confidence in you overruled our doubts and we gave our consent. At that time you seemed to be acting with mature judgement with goals firmly set. We are now convinced that you weren't as prepared as we thought you were to handle the outside world.

You always prided yourself on dating fellows who respected you. 5 What happened along the way that you can no longer demand such respect? Aren't you able to look ahead and visualize what may be in store for you in two, five, or ten years? When this fellow has finished with you and moves on to someone else, and when you meet THE ONE you will want to spend the rest of your life with, will he want to settle for second-hand, used merchandise?

No Pat, we didn't expect you to move here after graduation. You had 6 wanted to go to grad school, and we had made plans to see you thru after your graduation. We wanted to give you every opportunity to fit yourself for self-support. If you are willing to throw all this away, there is nothing we can do about it since you are now an adult and must make your own decisions. If you believe Tony is THE ONE in your life, then he will be willing to wait for you to attain your goals. You have your whole life ahead of you and one more year or less shouldn't make any difference.

Naturally we are disappointed that you do not want to spend your 7 quarter break with us, but you know what is best so far as your studies are concerned. We do want you to be able to retain your good grades and graduate when you planned, and hope that you will reconsider what you proposed in your letter so that we will want to put you through this last quarter. Of course you realize that would be impossible if you should go through with it.

How about Tony's sweet mother, the one who mailed the violin to 8 you? Are you a girl whom he would like to take home to meet his mother? Would she condone such an arrangement? Is he considering her feelings? I'm leaving the remainder to be said by your daddy.

Your loving 9
Mom 10

P.S. Whatever will I do with the pretty blue print corduroy bedspread 11 I have just made for you?

Honey, anytime you want to come home for a visit, your room will be 12 waiting for you. Your husband, if and when you get one, will also be welcome. Here is a picture of the happy family that once was [*family snapshot enclosed*].

[*Note from her father, attached:*]   13

Pat, as you can well understand from what your mother has written, 14 you know we do not condone your proposal to shack up with Tony. You stated in your letter that you wanted to be independent and make your own decisions. We have let you do just that. However, if you decide to go through with your proposal, God pity you. Here are some of my proposals:

1. Be sure and get some insurance.
2. Get acquainted with income tax rules and regulations.
3. Don't expect any more financial assistance from us.
4. Straighten up and fly right. You will be all the better off if you do.

If you are going to live with a man I will expect him to support you. I 15 pray that you will give this matter some serious thought. Let us know your decision so we can know where we stand financially.

Daddy 16

Letter from Birmingham Jail
Martin Luther King, Jr.

Martin Luther King, Jr., was the best-known and best-loved civil rights leader of the 1960s, tragically assassinated in 1968. Here is his author's note to "Letter from Birmingham Jail":

> This response to a published statement by eight fellow clergymen from
> Alabama...was composed under somewhat constricting circumstances.
> Begun on the margins of the newspaper in which the statement
> appeared while I was in jail, the letter was continued on scraps of
> writing paper supplied by a friendly Negro trusty, and concluded on a
> pad my attorneys were eventually permitted to leave me. Although the
> text remains in substance unaltered, I have indulged in the author's
> prerogative of polishing it for publication.

April 16, 1963 1

My Dear Fellow Clergymen: 2

While confined here in the Birmingham city jail, I came across your 3 recent statement calling my present activities "unwise and untimely." Seldom do I pause to answer criticism of my work and ideas. If I sought to answer all the criticisms that cross my desk, my secretaries would have little time for anything other than such correspondence in the course of the day, and I would have no time for constructive work. But since I feel that you are men of genuine good will and that your criticisms are sincerely set forth, I want to try to answer your statement in what I hope will be patient and reasonable terms.

I think I should indicate why I am here in Birmingham, since you have 4 been influenced by the view which argues against "outsiders coming in." I have the honor of serving as president of the Southern Christian Leadership Conference, an organization operating in every southern state, with headquarters in Atlanta, Georgia. We have some eighty-five affiliated organizations across the South, and one of them is the Alabama Christian Movement for Human Rights. Frequently we share staff, educational and financial resources with our affiliates. Several months ago the affiliate here in Birmingham asked us to be on call to engage in a nonviolent direct-action program if such were deemed necessary. We readily consented, and when the hour came we lived up to our promise. So I, along with several members of my staff, am here because I was invited here. I am here because I have organizational ties here.

But more basically, I am in Birmingham because injustice is here. Just 5 as the prophets of the eighth century B.C. left their villages and carried their "thus saith the Lord" far beyond the boundaries of their home towns, and just as the Apostle Paul left his village of Tarsus and carried the gospel of Jesus Christ to the far corners of the Greco-Roman world, so am I compelled to carry the gospel of freedom beyond my own home town. Like Paul, I must constantly respond to the Macedonian call for aid.

Moreover, I am cognizant of the interrelatedness of all communities 6 and states. I cannot sit idly by in Atlanta and not be concerned about what happens in Birmingham. Injustice anywhere is a threat to justice everywhere. We are caught in an inescapable network of mutuality, tied in a single garment of destiny. Whatever affects one directly, affects all indirectly. Never again can we afford to live with the narrow, provincial "outside agitator" idea. Anyone who lives inside the United States can never be considered an outsider anywhere within its bounds.

You deplore the demonstrations taking place in Birmingham. But your 7 statement, I am sorry to say, fails to express a similar concern for the conditions that brought about the demonstrations. I am sure that none of you would want to rest content with the superficial kind of social analysis that deals merely with effects and does not grapple with underlying causes. It is unfortunate that demonstrations are taking place in Birmingham, but it is even more unfortunate that the city's white power structure left the Negro community with no alternative.

In any nonviolent campaign there are four basic steps: collection of the 8 facts to determine whether injustices exist; negotiation; self-purification; and direct action. We have gone through all these steps in Birmingham. There can be no gainsaying the fact that racial injustice engulfs this community. Birmingham is probably the most thoroughly segregated city in the United States. Its ugly record of brutality is widely known. Negroes have experienced grossly unjust treatment in the courts. There have been more unsolved bombings of Negro homes and churches in Birmingham than in any other city in the nation. These are the hard, brutal facts of the case. On the basis of these conditions, Negro leaders sought to negotiate with the city fathers. But the latter consistently refused to engage in good-faith negotiation.

Then, last September, came the opportunity to talk with leaders of 9 Birmingham's economic community. In the course of the negotiations, certain promises were made by the merchants—for example, to remove the stores' humiliating racial signs. On the basis of these promises, the Reverend Fred Shuttlesworth and the leaders of the Alabama Christian Movement for Human Rights agreed to a moratorium on all demonstrations. As the weeks and months went by, we realized that we were the victims of a broken promise. A few signs, briefly removed, returned; the others remained.

As in so many past experiences, our hopes had been blasted, and the 10 shadow of deep disappointment settled upon us. We had no alternative except to prepare for direct action, whereby we would present our very bodies as a means of laying our case before the conscience of the local and the national community. Mindful of the difficulties involved, we decided to undertake a process of self-purification. We began a series of workshops on nonviolence, and we repeatedly asked ourselves: "Are you able to accept blows without retaliating?" "Are you able to endure the ordeal of jail?" We decided to schedule our direct-action program for the Easter season, realizing that except for Christmas, this is the main shopping period of the year. Knowing that a strong economic-withdrawal program would be the by-product of direct action, we felt that this would be the best time to bring pressure to bear on the merchants for the needed change.

Then it occurred to us that Birmingham's mayoralty election was com- 11 ing up in March, and we speedily decided to postpone action until after election day. When we discovered that the Commissioner of Public Safety, Eugene "Bull" Connor, had piled up enough votes to be in the run-off, we decided again to postpone action until the day after the run-off so that the demonstrations could not be used to cloud the issues. Like many others, we waited to see Mr. Connor defeated, and to this end we endured postponement after postponement. Having aided in this community need, we felt that our direct-action program could be delayed no longer.

You may well ask: "Why direct action? Why sit-ins, marches and so 12 forth? Isn't negotiation a better path?" You are quite right in calling for negotiation. Indeed, this is the very purpose of direct action. Nonviolent direct action seeks to create such a crisis and foster such a tension that a community which has constantly refused to negotiate is forced to confront the issue. It seeks so to dramatize the issue that it can no longer be ignored. My citing

the creation of tension as part of the work of the nonviolent-resister may
sound rather shocking. But I must confess that I am not afraid of the word
"tension." I have earnestly opposed violent tension, but there is a type of
constructive, nonviolent tension which is necessary for growth. Just as
Socrates felt that it was necessary to create a tension in the mind so that individuals could rise from the bondage of myths and half-truths to the unfet-
tered realm of creative analysis and objective appraisal, so must we see the
need for nonviolent gadflies to create the kind of tension in society that will
help men rise from the dark depths of prejudice and racism to the majestic
heights of understanding and brotherhood.

The purpose of our direct-action program is to create a situation so 13
crisis-packed that it will inevitably open the door to negotiation. I therefore
concur with you in your call for negotiation. Too long has our beloved
Southland been bogged down in a tragic effort to live in monologue rather
than dialogue.

One of the basic points in your statement is that the action that I and 14
my associates have taken in Birmingham is untimely. Some have asked:
"Why didn't you give the new city administration time to act?" The only
answer that I can give to this query is that the new Birmingham administration must be prodded about as much as the outgoing one, before it will act.
We are sadly mistaken if we feel that the election of Albert Boutwell as
mayor will bring the millennium to Birmingham. While Mr. Boutwell is a
much more gentle person than Mr. Connor, they are both segregationists,
dedicated to maintenance of the status quo. I have hope that Mr. Boutwell
will be reasonable enough to see the futility of massive resistance to desegregation. But he will not see this without pressure from devotees of civil
rights. My friends, I must say to you that we have not made a single gain in
civil rights without determined legal and nonviolent pressure. Lamentably,
it is an historical fact that privileged groups seldom give up their privileges
voluntarily. Individuals may see the moral light and voluntarily give up their
unjust posture; but, as Reinhold Niebuhr has reminded us, groups tend to
be more immoral than individuals.

We know through painful experience that freedom is never voluntarily 15
given by the oppressor; it must be demanded by the oppressed. Frankly, I
have yet to engage in a direct-action campaign that was "well timed" in the
view of those who have not suffered unduly from the disease of segregation.
For years now I have heard the word "Wait!" It rings in the ear of every
Negro with piercing familiarity. This "Wait" has almost always meant
"Never." We must come to see, with one of our distinguished jurists, that
"justice too long delayed is justice denied."

We have waited for more than 340 years for our constitutional and 16
God-given rights. The nations of Asia and Africa are moving with jetlike
speed toward gaining political independence, but we still creep at horse-and-
buggy pace toward gaining a cup of coffee at a lunch counter. Perhaps it is

easy for those who have never felt the stinging darts of segregation to say, "Wait." But when you have seen vicious mobs lynch your mothers and fathers at will and drown your sisters and brothers at whim; when you have seen hate-filled policemen curse, kick and even kill your black brothers and sisters; when you see the vast majority of your twenty million Negro brothers smothering in an airtight cage of poverty in the midst of an affluent society; when you suddenly find your tongue twisted and your speech stammering as you seek to explain to your six-year-old daughter why she can't go to the public amusement park that has just been advertised on television, and see tears welling up in her eyes when she is told that Funtown is closed to colored children, and see ominous clouds of inferiority beginning to form in her little mental sky, and see her beginning to distort her personality by developing an unconscious bitterness toward white people; when you have to concoct an answer for a five-year-old son who is asking: "Daddy, why do white people treat colored people so mean?"; when you take a cross-country drive and find it necessary to sleep night after night in the uncomfortable corners of your automobile because no motel will accept you; when you are humiliated day in and day out by nagging signs reading "white" and "colored"; when your first name becomes "nigger," your middle name becomes "boy" (however old you are) and your last name becomes "John," and your wife and mother are never given the respected title "Mrs."; when you are harried by day and haunted by night by the fact that you are a Negro, living constantly at tiptoe stance, never quite knowing what to expect next, and are plagued with inner fears and outer resentments; when you are forever fighting a degenerating sense of "nobodiness"—then you will understand why we find it difficult to wait. There comes a time when the cup of endurance runs over, and men are no longer willing to be plunged into the abyss of despair. I hope, sirs, you can understand our legitimate and unavoidable impatience.

You express a great deal of anxiety over our willingness to break laws. 17 This is certainly a legitimate concern. Since we so diligently urge people to obey the Supreme Court's decision of 1954 outlawing segregation in the public schools, at first glance it may seem rather paradoxical for us consciously to break laws. One may well ask: "How can you advocate breaking some laws and obeying others?" The answer lies in the fact that there are two types of laws: just and unjust. I would be the first to advocate obeying just laws. One has not only a legal but a moral responsibility to obey just laws. Conversely, one has a moral responsibility to disobey unjust laws. I would agree with St. Augustine that "an unjust law is no law at all."

Now, what is the difference between the two? How does one determine 18 whether a law is just or unjust? A just law is a man-made code that squares with the moral law or the law of God. An unjust law is a code that is out of harmony with the moral law. To put it in the terms of St. Thomas Aquinas: An unjust law is a human law that is not rooted in eternal law and natural law. Any law that uplifts human personality is just. Any law that degrades human personality is unjust. All segregation statutes are unjust because segregation distorts the soul and damages the personality. It gives the segregator a false sense of superiority and the segregated a false sense of inferiority. Segregation, to use the terminology of the Jewish philosopher Martin Buber, substitutes an "I—it" relationship for an "I—thou" relationship and ends up relegating persons to the status of things. Hence segregation is not only politically, economically and sociologically unsound, it is morally wrong and sinful. Paul Tillich has said that sin is separation. Is not segregation an existential expression of man's tragic separation, his awful estrangement, his terrible sinfulness? Thus it is that I can urge men to obey the 1954 decision of the Supreme Court, for it is morally right; and I can urge them to disobey segregation ordinances, for they are morally wrong.

Let us consider a more concrete example of just and unjust laws. An 19 unjust law is a code that a numerical or power majority group compels a minority group to obey but does not make binding on itself. This is *difference* made legal. By the same token, a just law is a code that a majority compels a minority to follow and that it is willing to follow itself. This is *sameness* made legal.

Let me give another explanation. A law is unjust if it is inflicted on a 20 minority that, as a result of being denied the right to vote, had no part in enacting or devising the law. Who can say that the legislature of Alabama which set up that state's segregation laws was democratically elected? Throughout Alabama all sorts of devious methods are used to prevent Negroes from becoming registered voters, and there are some counties in which, even though Negroes constitute a majority of the population, not a single Negro is registered. Can any law enacted under such circumstances be considered democratically structured?

Sometimes a law is just on its face and unjust in its application. For 21 instance, I have been arrested on a charge of parading without a permit. Now, there is nothing wrong in having an ordinance which requires a permit for a parade. But such an ordinance becomes unjust when it is used to maintain segregation and to deny citizens the First-Amendment privilege of peaceful assembly and protest.

I hope you are able to see the distinction I am trying to point out. In no 22 sense do I advocate evading or defying the law, as would the rabid segregationist. That would lead to anarchy. One who breaks an unjust law must do so openly, lovingly, and with a willingness to accept the penalty. I submit that an individual who breaks a law that conscience tells him is unjust, and who willingly accepts the penalty of imprisonment in order to arouse the conscience of the community over its injustice, is in reality expressing the highest respect for law.

Of course, there is nothing new about this kind of civil disobedience. It 23 was evidenced sublimely in the refusal of Shadrach, Meshach and Abednego to obey the laws of Nebuchadnezzar, on the ground that a higher moral law was at stake. It was practiced superbly by the early Christians, who were willing to face hungry lions and the excruciating pain of chopping blocks rather than submit to certain unjust laws of the Roman Empire. To a degree, academic freedom is a reality today because Socrates practiced civil disobedience. In our own nation, the Boston Tea Party represented a massive act of civil disobedience.

We should never forget that everything Adolf Hitler did in Germany 24 was "legal" and everything the Hungarian freedom fighters did in Hungary was "illegal." It was "illegal" to aid and comfort a Jew in Hitler's Germany. Even so, I am sure that, had I lived in Germany at the time, I would have aided and comforted my Jewish brothers. If today I lived in a Communist country where certain principles dear to the Christian faith are suppressed, I would openly advocate disobeying that country's antireligious laws.

I must make two honest confessions to you, my Christian and Jewish 25 brothers. First, I must confess that over the past few years I have been gravely disappointed with the white moderate. I have almost reached the regrettable conclusion that the Negro's great stumbling block in his stride toward freedom is not the White Citizen's Counciler or the Ku Klux Klanner, but the white moderate, who is more devoted to "order" than to justice; who prefers a negative peace which is the absence of tension to a positive peace which is the presence of justice; who constantly says: "I agree with you in the goal you seek, but I cannot agree with your methods of direct action"; who paternalistically believes he can set the timetable for another man's freedom; who lives by a mythical concept of time and who constantly advises the Negro to wait for a "more convenient season." Shallow understanding from people of good will is more frustrating than absolute misunderstanding from people of ill will. Lukewarm acceptance is much more bewildering than outright rejection.

I had hoped that the white moderate would understand that law and 26 order exist for the purpose of establishing justice and that when they fail in this purpose they become the dangerously structured dams that block the flow of social progress. I had hoped that the white moderate would understand that the present tension in the South is a necessary phase of the transition from an obnoxious negative peace, in which the Negro passively accepted his unjust plight, to a substantive and positive peace, in which all men will respect the dignity and worth of human personality. Actually, we who engage in nonviolent direct action are not the creators of tension. We merely bring to the surface the hidden tension that is already alive. We bring it out in the open, where it can be seen and dealt with. Like a boil that can never be cured so long as it is covered up but must be opened with all its ugliness to the natural medicines of air and light, injustice must be exposed, with all the tension its exposure creates, to the light of human conscience and the air of national opinion before it can be cured.

In your statement you assert that our actions, even though peaceful, 27 must be condemned because they precipitate violence. But is this a logical assertion? Isn't this like condemning a robbed man because his possession of money precipitated the evil act of robbery? Isn't this like condemning Socrates because his unswerving commitment to truth and his philosophical inquiries precipitated the act by the misguided populace in which they made him drink hemlock? Isn't this like condemning Jesus because his unique God-consciousness and never-ceasing devotion to God's will precipitated the evil act of crucifixion? We must come to see that, as the federal courts have consistently affirmed, it is wrong to urge an individual to cease his efforts to gain his basic constitutional rights because the quest may precipitate violence. Society must protect the robbed and punish the robber.

I had also hoped that the white moderate would reject the myth concerning time in relation to the struggle for freedom. I have just received a letter from a white brother in Texas. He writes: "All Christians know that the colored people will receive equal rights eventually, but it is possible that you are in too great a religious hurry. It has taken Christianity almost two thousand years to accomplish what it has. The teachings of Christ take time to come to earth." Such an attitude stems from a tragic misconception of time, from the strangely irrational notion that there is something in the very flow of time that will inevitably cure all ills. Actually, time itself is neutral; it can be used either destructively or constructively. More and more I feel that the people of ill will have used time much more effectively than have the people of good will. We will have to repent in this generation not merely for the hateful words and actions of the bad people but for the appalling silence of the good people. Human progress never rolls in on wheels of inevitability; it comes through the tireless efforts of men willing to be co-workers with God, and without this hard work, time itself becomes an ally of the forces of social stagnation. We must use time creatively, in the knowledge that the time is always ripe to do right. Now is the time to make real the promise of democracy and transform our pending national elegy into a creative psalm of brotherhood. Now is the time to lift our national policy from the quicksand of racial injustice to the solid rock of human dignity. 28

You speak of our activity in Birmingham as extreme. At first I was rather disappointed that fellow clergymen would see my nonviolent efforts as those of an extremist. I began thinking about the fact that I stand in the middle of two opposing forces in the Negro community. One is a force of complacency, made up in part of Negroes who, as a result of long years of oppression, are so drained of self-respect and a sense of "somebodiness" that they have adjusted to segregation; and in part of a few middleclass Negroes who, because of a degree of academic and economic security and because in some ways they profit by segregation, have become insensitive to the problems of the masses. The other force is one of bitterness and hatred, and it comes perilously close to advocating violence. It is expressed in the various black nationalist groups that are springing up across the nation, the largest and best-known being Elijah Muhammad's Muslim movement. Nourished by the Negro's frustration over the continued existence of racial discrimina- 29 tion, this movement is made up of people who have lost faith in America, who have absolutely repudiated Christianity, and who have concluded that the white man is an incorrigible "devil."

I have tried to stand between these two forces, saying that we need em- 30 ulate neither the "do-nothingism" of the complacent nor the hatred and despair of the black nationalist. For there is the more excellent way of love and nonviolent protest. I am grateful to God that, through the influence of the Negro church, the way of nonviolence became an integral part of our struggle.

If this philosophy had not emerged, by now many streets of the South 31 would, I am convinced, be flowing with blood. And I am further convinced that if our white brothers dismiss as "rabble-rousers" and "outside agitators" those of us who employ nonviolent direct action, and if they refuse to support our nonviolent efforts, millions of Negroes will, out of frustration and despair, seek solace and security in black-nationalist ideologies—a development that would inevitably lead to a frightening racial nightmare.

Oppressed people cannot remain oppressed forever. The yearning for 32 freedom eventually manifests itself, and that is what has happened to the American Negro. Something within has reminded him of his birthright of freedom, and something without has reminded him that it can be gained. Consciously or unconsciously, he has been caught up by the Zeitgeist, and with his black brothers of Africa and his brown and yellow brothers of Asia, South America and the Caribbean, the United States Negro is moving with a sense of great urgency toward the promised land of racial justice. If one recognizes this vital urge that has engulfed the Negro community, one should readily understand why public demonstrations are taking place. The Negro has many pent-up resentments and latent frustrations, and he must release them. So let him march; let him make prayer pilgrimages to the city hall; let him go on freedom rides—and try to understand why he must do so. If his repressed emotions are not released in nonviolent ways, they will seek expression through violence; this is not a threat but a fact of history. So I have not said to my people: "Get rid of your discontent." Rather, I have tried to say that this normal and healthy discontent can be channeled into the creative outlet of nonviolent direct action. And now this approach is being termed extremist.

But though I was initially disappointed at being categorized as an ex- 33 tremist, as I continued to think about the matter I gradually gained a measure of satisfaction from the label. Was not Jesus an extremist for love: "Love your enemies, bless them that curse you, do good to them that hate you, and pray for them which despitefully use you, and persecute you." Was not Amos an extremist for justice: "Let justice roll down like waters and righteousness like an ever-flowing stream." Was not Paul an extremist for the Christian gospel: "I bear in my body the marks of the Lord Jesus." Was not Martin Luther an extremist: "Here I stand; I cannot do otherwise, so help me God." And John Bunyan: "I will stay in jail to the end of my days before I make a butchery of my conscience." And Abraham Lincoln: "This nation cannot survive half slave and half free." And Thomas Jefferson: "We hold these truths to be self-evident, that all men are created equal..." So the question is not whether we will be extremists, but what kind of extremists we will be. Will we be extremists for hate or for love? Will we be extremists for the preservation of injustice or for the extension of justice? In that dramatic scene on Calvary's hill three men were crucified. We must never forget that all three were crucified for the same crime—the crime of extremism. Two were extremists for immorality, and thus fell below their environment. The other, Jesus Christ, was an extremist for love, truth and goodness, and thereby rose above his environment. Perhaps the South, the nation and the world are in dire need of creative extremists.

I had hoped that the white moderate would see this need. Perhaps I 34 was too optimistic; perhaps I expected too much. I suppose I should have realized that few members of the oppressor race can understand the deep groans and passionate yearnings of the oppressed race, and still fewer have the vision to see that injustice must be rooted out by strong, persistent and determined action. I am thankful, however, that some of our white brothers in the South have grasped the meaning of this social revolution and committed themselves to it. They are still all too few in quantity, but they are big in quality. Some—such as Ralph McGill, Lillian Smith, Harry Golden, James McBride Dabbs, Ann Braden and Sarah Patton Boyle—have written about our struggle in eloquent and prophetic terms. Others have marched with us down nameless streets of the South. They have languished in filthy, roach-infested jails, suffering the abuse and brutality of policemen who view them as "dirty nigger-lovers." Unlike so many of their moderate brothers and sisters, they have recognized the urgency of the moment and sensed the need for powerful "action" antidotes to combat the disease of segregation.

Let me take note of my other major disappointment. I have been so 35 greatly disappointed with the white church and its leadership. Of course, there are some notable exceptions. I am not unmindful of the fact that each of you has taken some significant stands on this issue. I commend you, Reverend Stallings, for your Christian stand on this past Sunday, in welcoming Negroes to your worship service on a nonsegregated basis. I commend the Catholic leaders of this state for integrating Spring Hill College several years ago.

But despite these notable exceptions, I must honestly reiterate that I 36 have been disappointed with the church. I do not say this as one of those negative critics who can always find something wrong with the church. I say this as a minister of the gospel, who loves the church; who was nurtured in its bosom; who has been sustained by its spiritual blessings and who will remain true to it as long as the cord of life shall lengthen.

When I was suddenly catapulted into the leadership of the bus protest 37 in Montgomery, Alabama, a few years ago, I felt we would be supported by the white church. I felt that the white ministers, priests and rabbis of the South would be among our strongest allies. Instead, some have been outright opponents, refusing to understand the freedom movement and misrepresenting its leaders; all too many others have been more cautious than courageous and have remained silent behind the anesthetizing security of stained-glass windows.

In spite of my shattered dreams, I came to Birmingham with the hope 38 that the white religious leadership of this community would see the justice of our cause and, with deep moral concern, would serve as the channel through which our just grievances could reach the power structure. I had hoped that each of you would understand. But again I have been disappointed.

I have heard numerous southern religious leaders admonish their wor- 39 shipers to comply with a desegregation decision because it is the law, but I have longed to hear white ministers declare: "Follow this decree because integration is morally right and because the Negro is your brother." In the midst of blatant injustices inflicted upon the Negro, I have watched white churchmen stand on the sideline and mouth pious irrelevancies and sanctimonious trivialities. In the midst of a mighty struggle to rid our nation of social and economic injustice, I have heard many ministers say: "Those are social issues, with which the gospel has no real concern." And I have watched many churches commit themselves to a completely other-worldly religion which makes a strange, un-Biblical distinction between body and soul, between the sacred and the secular.

I have traveled the length and breadth of Alabama, Mississippi and all 40 the other southern states. On sweltering summer days and crisp autumn mornings I have looked at the South's beautiful churches with their lofty spires pointing heavenward. I have beheld the impressive outlines of her massive religious-education buildings. Over and over I have found myself asking: "What kind of people worship here? Who is their God? Where were their voices when the lips of Governor Barnett dripped with words of interposition and nullification? Where were they when Governor Wallace gave a clarion call for defiance and hatred? Where were their voices of support when bruised and weary Negro men and women decided to rise from the dark dungeons of complacency to the bright hills of creative protest?"

Yes, these questions are still in my mind. In deep disappointment I 41 have wept over the laxity of the church. But be assured that my tears have been tears of love. There can be no deep disappointment where there is not deep love. Yes, I love the church. How could I do otherwise? I am in the rather unique position of being the son, the grandson and the great-grandson of preachers. Yes, I see the church as the body of Christ. But, oh! How we have blemished and scarred that body through social neglect and through fear of being nonconformists.

There was a time when the church was very powerful—in the time 42 when the early Christians rejoiced at being deemed worthy to suffer for what they believed. In those days the church was not merely a thermometer that recorded the ideas and principles of popular opinion; it was a thermostat that transformed the mores of society. Whenever the early Christians entered a town, the people in power became disturbed and immediately sought to convict the Christians for being "disturbers of the peace" and "outside agitators." But the Christians pressed on, in the conviction that they were "a colony of heaven," called to obey God rather than man. Small in number, they were big in commitment. They were too God-intoxicated to be "astronomically intimidated." By their effort and example they brought an end to such ancient evils as infanticide and gladiatorial contests.

Things are different now. So often the contemporary church is a weak, 43 ineffectual voice with an uncertain sound. So often it is an archdefender of the status quo. Far from being disturbed by the presence of the church, the power structure of the average community is consoled by the church's silent—and often even vocal—sanction of things as they are.

But the judgment of God is upon the church as never before. If today's 44 church does not recapture the sacrificial spirit of the early church, it will lose its authenticity, forfeit the loyalty of millions, and be dismissed as an irrelevant social club with no meaning for the twentieth century. Every day I meet young people whose disappointment with the church has turned into outright disgust.

Perhaps I have once again been too optimistic. Is organized religion too 45 inextricably bound to the status quo to save our nation and the world? Perhaps I must turn my faith to the inner spiritual church, the church within the church, as the true *ekklesia* and the hope of the world. But again I am thankful to God that some noble souls from the ranks of organized religion have broken loose from the paralyzing chains of conformity and joined us as active partners in the struggle for freedom. They have left their secure congregations and walked the streets of Albany, Georgia, with us. They have gone down the highways of the South on tortuous rides for freedom. Yes, they have gone to jail with us. Some have been dismissed from their churches, have lost the support of their bishops and fellow ministers. But they have acted in the faith that right defeated is stronger than evil triumphant. Their witness has been the spiritual salt that has preserved the true meaning of the gospel in these troubled times. They have carved a tunnel of hope through the dark mountain of disappointment.

I hope the church as a whole will meet the challenge of this decisive 46 hour. But even if the church does not come to the aid of justice, I have no despair about the future. I have no fear about the outcome of our struggle in Birmingham, even if our motives are at present misunderstood. We will reach the goal of freedom in Birmingham and all over the nation, because the goal of America is freedom. Abused and scorned though we may be, our destiny is tied up with America's destiny. Before the pilgrims landed at Plymouth, we were here. Before the pen of Jefferson etched the majestic words of the Declaration of Independence across the pages of history, we were here. For more than two centuries our forebears labored in this country without wages; they made cotton king; they built the homes of their masters while suffering gross injustice and shameful humiliation—and yet out of a bottomless vitality they continued to thrive and develop. If the inexpressible cruelties of slavery could not stop us, the opposition we now face will surely fail. We will win our freedom because the sacred heritage of our nation and the eternal will of God are embodied in our echoing demands.

Before closing I feel impelled to mention one other point in your state-   47
ment that has troubled me profoundly. You warmly commended the Bir-mingham police force for keeping "order" and "preventing violence." I doubt that you would have so warmly commended the police force if you had seen its dogs sinking their teeth into unarmed, nonviolent Negroes. I doubt that you would so quickly commend the policemen if you were to ob-serve their ugly and inhumane treatment of Negroes here in the city jail; if you were to watch them push and curse old Negro women and young Negro girls; if you were to see them slap and kick old Negro men and young boys; if you were to observe them, as they did on two occasions, refuse to give us food because we wanted to sing our grace together. I cannot join you in your praise of the Birmingham police department.

It is true that the police have exercised a degree of discipline in han-   48
dling the demonstrators. In this sense they have conducted themselves rather "nonviolently" in public. But for what purpose? To preserve the evil system of segregation. Over the past few years I have consistently preached that nonviolence demands that the means we use must be as pure as the ends we seek. I have tried to make clear that it is wrong to use immoral means to attain moral ends. But now I must affirm that it is just as wrong, or perhaps even more so, to use moral means to preserve immoral ends. Perhaps Mr. Connor and his policemen have been rather nonviolent in public, as was Chief Pritchett in Albany, Georgia, but they have used the moral means of nonviolence to maintain the immoral end of racial injustice. As T. S. Eliot has said: "The last temptation is the greatest treason: To do the right deed for the wrong reason."

I wish you had commended the Negro sit-inners and demonstrators of   49
Birmingham for their sublime courage, their willingness to suffer and their amazing discipline in the midst of great provocation. One day the South will recognize its real heroes. They will be the James Merediths, with the noble sense of purpose that enables them to face jeering and hostile mobs, and with the agonizing loneliness that characterizes the life of the pioneer. They will be old, oppressed, battered Negro women, symbolized in a seventy-two-year-old woman in Montgomery, Alabama, who rose up with a sense of dig-nity and with her people decided not to ride segregated buses, and who re-sponded with ungrammatical profundity to one who inquired about her weariness: "My feets is tired, but my soul is at rest." They will be the young high school and college students, the young ministers of the gospel and a

host of their elders, courageously and nonviolently sitting in at lunch counters and willingly going to jail for conscience' sake. One day the South will know that when these disinherited children of God sat down at lunch counters, they were in reality standing up for what is best in the American dream and for the most sacred values in our Judaeo-Christian heritage, thereby bringing our nation back to those great wells of democracy which were dug deep by the founding fathers in their formulation of the Constitution and the Declaration of Independence.

Never before have I written so long a letter. I'm afraid it is much too 50 long to take your precious time. I can assure you that it would have been much shorter if I had been writing from a comfortable desk, but what else can one do when he is alone in a narrow jail cell, other than write long letters, think long thoughts and pray long prayers?

If I have said anything in this letter that overstates the truth and indicates 51 an unreasonable impatience, I beg you to forgive me. If I have said anything that understates the truth and indicates my having a patience that allows me to settle for anything less than brotherhood, I beg God to forgive me.

I hope this letter finds you strong in the faith. I also hope that circum- 52 stances will soon make it possible for me to meet each of you, not as an integrationist or a civil rights leader but as a fellow clergyman and a Christian brother. Let us all hope that the dark clouds of racial prejudice will soon pass away and the deep fog of misunderstanding will be lifted from our fear-drenched communities, and in some not too distant tomorrow the radiant stars of love and brotherhood will shine over our great nation with all their scintillating beauty.

Yours for the cause of Peace and Brotherhood, 53
Martin Luther King, Jr. 54

ORAL HISTORY

Specialist 4 Charles Strong

Wallace Terry's oral history of the Vietnam War, *Bloods* (1984), includes interviews with twenty black soldiers and officers who fought in Vietnam. Rather than rewriting his interviews into a book, Terry decided to capture the exact words of these men with firsthand experience. Although these oral histories did not start out as written pieces, Terry's intention all along was to publish them. Charles Strong, from Pompano Beach, Florida, was a machine gunner in the American Division of the U.S. Army; Strong served at Chu Lai from July 1969 to July 1970.

I got out in December 1972. The longest day I lived was the day I got   1
out. When I got home, I figured I would lay around a couple of months. I
was drinking beer, wine, any kind of alcoholic beverage. That time, too, I
started messin' around with some THC. But I really didn't mess around
with it for that long, because it makes you feel unsure of yourself. I decided
to marry this young lady I was going with for seven years. I wanted to show
her I really loved her. That's when the effects of Vietnam really had their toll
on me.

I started having flashbacks. When I would lay down and dream at   2
night, my mind would play tricks on me. I still had my jungle boots and
fatigues. And when it would rain real hard, I would put them on and go
wherever I wanted to go. I would be ducking around in the bushes, crawling
around just like you do in actual combat. And I would do silly stuff like
breaking out the street lamps, and they put me in jail a couple of times for
being disorderly.

But I did a really strange thing. I had this little .22. Something   3
prompted me to turn it into the police department. It was a good thing, too.
Because I got real mad at my wife one day. I put on my fatigues, and put this
ice pick at my side. When I couldn't find her, I just totally demolished the
house. People called the police, but they couldn't find me. I just lightly
eased out of the house and went across the street, where there were some
high bushes. It was dark and stuff, and I moved just like I learned in Vietnam. I thought I could keep running forever. But after 30 minutes, I cooled
off and got out of the bushes and went back over the house. The neighbors
said they didn't know what was wrong with me. The police didn't take me to
jail but to the hospital, where they put me in the psychiatric ward for four
days. And the psychiatrist told me I loved my wife too much. Nothing about
Vietnam.

I decided to go live with my mother, because I didn't want to hear my   4
wife nag. I worked at welding for a while, but I kept getting a lot of burns.
So I tried construction work, but it got real bad because the housing business went down. So this VA counselor told me to try to enter school, and I
started going to Broward Community College to get computers one day like
I wanted back before 'Nam.

But the real thing that happened to me was the Lord touched my vi-   5
sion. I found out that I was just not existing. Now I done fell into the real
life that I am living. I'm living 24 hours a day, no matter how rough the
situation. Within my body I maintain peace and tranquillity. I see I have all
I need. I can cope with anything. I lost my fear of death, because I have
really accepted life. Although I live in a merchandise society, I don't try to
keep up with it. I don't even watch TV unless it is a live sports event or
something happening right then. When you watch someone pretend to live
life, you wasting your time. And I see many people back here stateside kill-

ing as many people as they were killing in Vietnam. Vietnam really gave me
a respect for human life. I value people. People make me happy now. And I
don't feel inferior anymore. When I was six or seven, I used to wonder why
I was born black; I should have been born white. See, I found out from
reading about my past before slavery—my ancestors built the pyramids that
still stand today. They omitted the small things like the Caesars of Rome
studied in a university in Africa before they became Caesars. I learned that
as a black man the only problem I had was that I wasn't exposed to things.
I feel equal to everyone, and I walk humbly among men. I'm studying to be
a computer programmer, but that doesn't make me better than a garbage
man.

Most of the nightmares are gone. Except one.   6

I still think about this North Vietnamese soldier. We took two hours to   7
kill him. This was a brave dude. I'll never forget him. It took a whole platoon to kill him.

He was held up in a tunnel. He knew he had no possible chance of   8
winning whatsoever. And he wasn't really expecting no help. But this was
the bravest dude I had ever seen. And I respect this dude.

The "rabbits," they were so crazy they didn't understand nothing, see.   9
We had interpreters to rap to him to give up. If he give up, they would re-
habilitate him and shit like that. And he would fight for the regular South
Vietnamese army. They rapped and rapped to him. And we started shooting
and throwing frags and Willie Peter rounds—white phosphorous grenades
that burn through metal and shit.

But the only way we got him was this crazy rabbit jumped down in the   10
hole and beat him to the punch. With a shotgun right through his neck. So
when they pulled him out, he was hit badder than an ol' boy. He had a hunk
of meat out of his leg, big as that. He had shrapnel all over his body. He had
a hole in his side. But he wouldn't give up. Because he really believed in
something. This man was willing to die for what he believed in. That was
the first time I ran into contact with a real man. I will never forget him.

When I was in Vietnam, it was not important to me where I died. Now   11
it is very important to me. I made a promise in 'Nam that I would never risk
my life or limb to protect anybody else's property. I will protect my own. So
this country is not going to tell me to go out again to stop the spread of communism. In Germany we were buying beef for the GIs that came from Communist countries. They telling us to fight the spread of Communism, but
they be helping the Communist economy. I don't walk around blind anymore. If another war breaks out and they want me to go, I'd rather die. I'll
fight anyone here in America. But if they come and get me to send to some
other country, I'm going to have my gun ready for them.

From *Part of My Soul Went with Him*
Winnie Mandela

Winnie Mandela is the wife of Nelson Mandela, a black politician jailed for
many years by the South African government for his antiapartheid activities. Mrs. Mandela herself has been under government supervision for a
number of years. This excerpt is from Winnie Mandela's oral autobiography, the only kind of autobiography she can compose since she is forbidden
to write by the government. *Part of My Soul Went with Him* was originally
published in 1984.

1   I never had a reference book all these years; I couldn't be registered
in any job, that's another reason why I lost so many jobs. And in 1965
they said: 'You have applied to see your husband? You won't see him
without a pass.' They came and picked me up from home and took me to
the pass office; they filled out the forms themselves. So that's how I came
to get it.

2   I have to apply to the local magistrate for a permit to leave the district
each time I visit Nelson. I am barred from using trains and I am not allowed
to use the car to get there, so I have to fly at tremendous cost. A lot of
friends have spent a fortune on my trips.

3   The permit prescribes that I must take the shortest route from the airport to Caledon Square, the police station where I report my arrival, and
from there take the shortest route to my friends' house in Elsie's River.
There I remain confined to the house. I cannot even go outside the gate.
From the time I arrive I find police cars waiting, parked outside the house
right through twenty-four hours. They actually take shifts. When Nelson
was on Robben Island I had to go from that house direct to the embarkation
office, where I joined the queue of visitors from all over the country, coming
directly from the trains.

4   I had to sign the same book I had been signing for the last twenty
years. You are not allowed to bring cameras, no cats, no dogs, no children
under sixteen, and already, there, you are warned to limit your conversation
to family affairs. The permit for the journey is 50c. Then you walk ten steps
down to the quay where you enter a little boat. Sometimes when the sea is
rough, they just cancel the trip—you are at the mercy of these officers. That
means all the visitors have taken the long journey to Cape Town in vain. The
journey to the island takes forty-five minutes. In the past they used to put a
special chair for me in a special corner of the boat. Of course I ignored that.
Really, to be confined in a prison ferry on a chair was lunatic. So I just sat
where everybody else was sitting.

5   When you arrive at the island you are met by prison officials who ac-

company you. On the left is a high grey stone wall which shuts the island off and on the right is the open sea.

You walk straight to a big door; the entrance to the waiting-room, 6 which has a few chairs. I remember a big shell ashtray on the windowsill, always full of cigarette butts, and I always wondered who was there before me. The two toilets were always filthy. Three officers would parade up and down while one stood at the door, making you feel you were part of the prison population. The whole atmosphere was cold and brutal.

Then some senior officer calls out your name: 'Mrs Mandela, you can 7 come now.' But before that he reminds you each time—I must be extremely dumb—for nearly twenty years: 'By the way, you must talk about your family and the children and that's all. Nothing political; if we feel there is something we don't understand in your conversation, we shall cut your visit.'

Sometimes they put additional restrictions on our conversation: for in- 8 stance, when one of our children was arrested and when there were attempts on my life, which were mentioned in the local press, or when heads of state from all over the world had sent telegrams for Nelson's birthday to my address—all this was not allowed.

I was always called in last to a little room at the end of a passage.   9

There were three warders behind me and three behind him. The light- 10 ing was very bad and the glass partition so thick—I could never see a clear picture of him, just a silhouette really. I think he has a better view of me. He jocularly used to say I must stand back so that he could see what I was wearing. We had to talk through earphones which they could switch off any time. And of course we were once again reminded not to talk about anything but the family. If, for instance, I mentioned a name they didn't know—grandchildren, we call them by all kinds of names—they disconnected the phone and politely asked me what we were talking about. It used to be very bad. Visits were stopped altogether on some occasions. We used to have violent exchanges with the officers; he would address them as the boys they are.

When you have been a prisoner as long as I have, there is a certain 11 communicating language just known between the two of you. I think that's the case with every one of us. This develops on its own, so you are able to convey quite a lot.

The warders have come to treat him very respectfully. His attitude is 12 somehow as if they are his Praetorian guard. He has maintained his role within prison itself; he has continued looking after his family of black people even in there. He does so much welfare work, exactly as he did outside.

On the island he used to spend half the time discussing family prob- 13 lems of the prisoners. I gathered that he'd got special permission throughout the years to do that because they were not part of the family. Some of the prisoners who had been there for, say, ten years, without having had any contacts with their families, he would give me instructions about them. We have a lot of broken homes in our society, children who land up in prison,

and he would ask me to raise funds for their education which he would channel to them.

I would sit there like a little girl. I sometimes think, for him I am a   14
continuation of his children. He cannot imagine that I've grown up. When
he wants me to do something, sometimes I feel like saying: don't you think
that this is a bit difficult? But then he says it again, he repeats it a bit slower,
and you just can't say no.

Zindzi is the only one who dares to interrupt him occasionally, if she   15
feels he is not right or that he is demanding too much. But it usually ends up
the same way. 'Darling,' he would say gently, 'just think about it again,' and
she would go and do it. When Nelson asks you to do something, you do it.
Arguing you can start later. He is not authoritative as such, but he commu-
nicates with you in such a way that you can't question what he says. For
instance, when there was something important I wanted to tell him, I'd rehearse it before I would talk to him. (*Laughs.*) Sometimes I would even write
it down to hear how it sounds.

After forty-five minutes they would say: 'Time is up!' We kissed fare-   16
well through the glass partition.

Except for the little I can gather from his letters, I have no idea what   17
Nelson does with himself through the day. When his study facilities were
withdrawn for four years, that was really bad. He was supposed to have
abused his study facilities. He told me that they claimed to have found memoirs he was supposed to have written somewhere in prison. He had asked
them to bring those memoirs to him. After a year he was still waiting for
them. I don't know what actually happened.

So I sent him the *Reader's Digest* guide-book of South Africa—it is re-   18
ally meant for tourists. It was sent back. I sent him *The Boer War*—surely
that should show him how strong the powers he was trying to fight are;
that's the type of thing that should deflate his spirit, if anything, and the
prison authorities would be happy for him to see the might of this land. It
was sent back.

Until recently even gifts of food were returned. What harm would it   19
have done if you'd sent a box of chocolates to a man doing life imprisonment! We weren't allowed to give him a watch for his birthday. He can only
see and touch the presents before they are taken away. The only thing that is
allowed is money.

There have always been speculations about his health. In 1981 Harry   20
Pitman—a white politician!—said publicly that Nelson had cancer. I don't
know where he got it from and why he said such a cruel thing and why he
thought he was the Mandela family spokesman. Supposing it had been true,
it would have been the responsibility of the family to release that to the public. It's this master-servant relationship, they think they know everything
better about us! So to counter this silly claim by Harry Pitman, the authorities brought me all the medical files on Nelson from the day he entered

prison. It was such a wonderful feeling to see all these little things he had suffered from, the colds, how he had Disprins prescribed—I told you he doesn't believe in tablets, he believes in exercise! The last entry was a conversation between him and a senior physician, in which he said that he was worried about his weight, from 77kg it was now 80. The doctor prescribed a high-protein diet. So now he has fish for supper. It was the first time I heard what my husband eats, from prison records!

All he lives for—besides of course the knowledge that he'll come out   21 one day—is the letters and family visits that have played an extremely important role in his life, and one of the things he enjoys most is visits from his children. (Children's visits are prohibited from the age of two up to sixteen.) He didn't bring them up, they had to be introduced to him—one of the most traumatic experiences for all of us. It is not easy for a mother to say: 'Look, your father, he is doing life in prison.' It is not easy for a child to go and see that father she has heard so much about in those conditions, in that atmosphere. Psychologically, it's a fifty-fifty sort of thing. You never know what the child's reaction is going to be: either break-down or the child emerges solid as a rock from the experience, and proud of seeing father.

Because, how do you bring up a child in this kind of society—you can't   22 have any sense of crime in this country if you have brought up a child to be proud of parents behind bars. In a child's mind a criminal is in fact somebody who fights for liberation—how can you teach children otherwise?

SERMON

Sinners in the Hands of an Angry God
Jonathan Edwards

Jonathan Edwards (1703–1758) was born in Connecticut and educated at Yale. He became a Congregational minister. "Sinners in the Hands of an Angry God," perhaps one of the best-known pieces of religious prose written in the United States, was first delivered in 1741 at Enfield, Massachusetts, and published that same year.

The use may be of *awakening* to unconverted persons in this congre-   1 gation. This that you have heard is the case of every one of you that are out of Christ. That world of misery, that lake of burning brimstone is extended abroad under you. *There* is the dreadful pit of the glowing flames of the wrath of God; there is Hell's wide gaping mouth open; and you have nothing to stand upon, nor any thing to take hold of: there is nothing between you and Hell but the air; 'tis only the power and mere pleasure of God that holds you up.

You probably are not sensible of this; you find you are kept out of 2 Hell, but don't see the hand of God in it, but look at other things, as the good state of your bodily constitution, your care of your own life, and the means you use for your own preservation. But indeed these things are nothing; if God should withdraw his hand, they would avail no more to keep you from falling, than the thin air to hold up a person that is suspended in it.

Your wickedness makes you as it were heavy as lead, and to tend 3 downwards with great weight and pressure towards Hell; and if God should let you go, you would immediately sink and swiftly descend and plunge into the bottomless gulf, and your healthy constitution, and your own care and prudence, and best contrivance, and all your righteousness, would have no more influence to uphold you and keep you out of Hell, than a spider's web would have to stop a falling rock. Were it not that so is the sovereign pleasure of God, the earth would not bear you one moment; for you are a burden to it; the creation groans with you; the creature is made subject to the bondage of your corruption, not willingly; the sun don't willingly shine upon you to give you light to serve sin and Satan; the earth don't willingly yield her increase to satisfy your lusts; nor is it willingly a stage for your wickedness to be acted upon; the air don't willingly serve you for breath to maintain the flame of life in your vitals, while you spend your life in the service of God's enemies. God's creatures are good, and were made for men to serve God with, and don't willingly subserve to any other purpose, and groan when they are abused to purposes so directly contrary to their nature and end. And the world would spue you out, were it not for the sovereign hand of him who hath subjected it in hope. There are the black clouds of God's wrath now hanging directly over your heads, full of the dreadful storm, and big with thunder; and were it not for the restraining hand of God it would immediately burst forth upon you. The sovereign pleasure of God for the present stays his rough wind; otherwise it would come with fury, and your destruction would come like a whirlwind, and you would be like the chaff of the summer threshing floor.

The wrath of God is like great waters that are dammed for the present; 4 they increase more and more, and rise higher and higher, till an outlet is given, and the longer the stream is stopped, the more rapid and mighty is its course, when once it is let loose. 'Tis true, that judgment against your evil works has not been executed hitherto; the floods of God's vengeance have been withheld; but your guilt in the meantime is constantly increasing, and you are every day treasuring up more wrath; the waters are continually rising and waxing more and more mighty; and there is nothing but the mere pleasure of God that holds the waters back that are unwilling to be stopped, and press hard to go forward; if God should only withdraw his hand from the flood-gate, it would immediately fly open, and the fiery floods of the fierceness and wrath of God would rush forth with inconceivable fury, and would come upon you with omnipotent power; and if your strength were ten thousand times greater than it is, yea ten thousand times greater than the strength of the stoutest, sturdiest devil in Hell, it would be nothing to withstand or endure it.

The bow of God's wrath is bent, and the arrow made ready on the string, and justice bends the arrow at your heart, and strains the bow, and it is nothing but the mere pleasure of God, and that of an angry God, without any promise or obligation at all, that keeps the arrow one moment from being made drunk with your blood. 5

Thus are all you that never passed under a great change of heart, by the mighty power of the spirit of God upon your souls; all that were never born again, and made new creatures, and raised from being dead in sin, to a state of new, and before altogether unexperienced light and life, (however you may have reformed your life in many things, and may have had religious affections, and may keep up a form of religion in your families and closets, and in the house of God, and may be strict in it,) you are thus in the hands of an angry God; 'tis nothing but his mere pleasure that keeps you from being this moment swallowed up in everlasting destruction. 6

However unconvinced you may now be of the truth of what you hear, by and by you will be fully convinced of it. Those that are gone from being in the like circumstances with you, see that it was so with them; for destruction came suddenly upon most of them, when they expected nothing of it, and while they were saying, *peace and safety:* Now they see, that those things that they depended on for peace and safety, were nothing but thin air and empty shadows. 7

The God that holds you over the pit of Hell, much as one holds a spider, or some loathsome insect, over the fire, abhors you, and is dreadfully provoked; his wrath towards you burns like fire; he looks upon you as worthy of nothing else, but to be cast into the fire; he is of purer eyes than to bear to have you in his sight; you are ten thousand times so abominable in his eyes as the most hateful venomous serpent is in ours. You have offended him infinitely more than ever a stubborn rebel did his prince: and yet 'tis nothing but his hand that holds you from falling into the fire every moment: 'tis to be ascribed to nothing else, that you did not go to Hell the last night; that you was suffered to awake again in this world, after you closed your eyes to sleep: and there is no other reason to be given why you have not dropped into Hell since you arose in the morning, but that God's hand has held you up: there is no other reason to be given why you have not gone to Hell since you have sat here in the house of God, provoking his pure eyes by your sinful wicked manner of attending his solemn worship: yea, there is nothing else that is to be given as a reason why you don't this very moment drop down into Hell. 8

O sinner! Consider the fearful danger you are in: 'tis a great furnace   9
of wrath, a wide and bottomless pit, full of the fire of wrath, that you are
held over in the hand of that God, whose wrath is provoked and incensed
as much against you as against many of the damned in Hell: you hang by
a slender thread, with the flames of divine wrath flashing about it, and
ready every moment to singe it, and burn it asunder; and you have no
interest in any mediator, and nothing to lay hold of to save yourself,
nothing to keep off the flames of wrath, nothing of your own, nothing
that you ever have done, nothing that you can do, to induce God to spare
you one moment.

FICTION

The Outcasts of Poker Flat
Bret Harte

Bret Harte (1836–1902) was a journalist in San Francisco in the 1860s. His
sketches of life in the west in books like *The Luck of Roaring Camp* and *The
Outcasts of Poker Flat* soon made him famous. He is still read as one of the
significant "local colorists," writers of the nineteenth century whose depictions
of regional life in the United States have helped preserve detailed glimpses of
bygone eras. (See Karen Stubbs' essay, "Mark Twain and Bret Harte: Social
Critics," in Chapter 11, in which Stubbs discusses "The Outcasts of Poker
Flat.")

As Mr. John Oakhurst, gambler, stepped into the main street of Poker   1
Flat on the morning of the twenty-third of November, 1850, he was conscious of a change in its moral atmosphere from the preceding night. Two or
three men, conversing earnestly together, ceased as he approached, and exchanged significant glances. There was a Sabbath lull in the air, which, in a
settlement unused to Sabbath influences, looked ominous.

Mr. Oakhurst's calm, handsome face betrayed small concern of these   2
indications. Whether he was conscious of any predisposing cause, was another question. "I reckon they're after somebody," he reflected; "likely it's
me." He returned to his pocket the handkerchief with which he had been
whipping away the red dust of Poker Flat from his neat boots, and quietly
discharged his mind of any further conjecture.

In point of fact, Poker Flat was "after somebody." It had lately suf-   3
fered the loss of several thousand dollars, two valuable horses, and a prominent citizen. It was experiencing a spasm of virtuous reaction, quite as lawless and ungovernable as any of the acts that had provoked it. A secret
committee had determined to rid the town of all improper persons. This was
done permanently in regard of two men who were then hanging from the

boughs of a sycamore in the gulch, and temporarily in the banishment of certain other objectionable characters. I regret to say that some of these were ladies. It is but due to the sex, however, to state that their impropriety was professional, and it was only in such easily established standards of evil that Poker Flat ventured to sit in judgment.

Mr. Oakhurst was right in supposing that he was included in this cat- **4** egory. A few of the committee had urged hanging him as a possible example, and a sure method of reimbursing themselves from his pockets of the sums he had won from them. "It's agin justice," said Jim Wheeler, "to let this yer young man from Roaring Camp—an entire stranger—carry away our money." But a crude sentiment of equity residing in the breasts of those who had been fortunate enough to win from Mr. Oakhurst, overruled this narrower local prejudice.

Mr. Oakhurst received his sentence with philosophic calmness, none **5** the less coolly, that he was aware of the hesitation of his judges. He was too much of a gambler not to accept Fate. With him life was at best an uncertain game, and he recognized the usual percentage in favor of the dealer.

A body of armed men accompanied the deported wickedness of Poker **6** Flat to the outskirts of the settlement. Besides Mr. Oakhurst, who was known to be a coolly desperate man, and for whose intimidation the armed escort was intended, the expatriated party consisted of a young woman familiarly known as "The Duchess;" another, who had gained the infelicitous title of "Mother Shipton," and "Uncle Billy," a suspected sluice-robber and confirmed drunkard. The cavalcade provoked no comments from the spectators, nor was any word uttered by the escort. Only when the gulch which marked the uttermost limit of Poker Flat was reached, the leader spoke briefly and to the point. The exiles were forbidden to return at the peril of their lives.

As the escort disappeared, their pent-up feelings found vent in a few **7** hysterical tears from "The Duchess," some bad language from Mother Shipton, and a Partheian volley of expletives from Uncle Billy. The philosophic Oakhurst alone remained silent. He listened calmly to Mother Shipton's desire to cut somebody's heart out, to the repeated statements of "The Duchess" that she would die in the road, and to the alarming oaths that seemed to be bumped out of Uncle Billy as he rode forward. With the easy good-humor characteristic of his class, he insisted upon exchanging his own ridinghorse, "Five Spot," for the sorry mule which the Duchess rode. But even this act did not draw the party into any closer sympathy. The young woman readjusted her somewhat draggled plumes with a feeble, faded coquetry; Mother Shipton eyed the possessor of "Five Spot" with malevolence, and Uncle Billy included the whole party in one sweeping anathema.

The road to Sandy Bar—a camp that not having as yet experienced the **8** regenerating influences of Poker Flat, consequently seemed to offer some invitation to the emigrants—lay over a steep mountain range. It was distant a day's severe journey. In that advanced season, the party soon passed out of the moist, temperate regions of the foot-hills, into the dry, cold, bracing air of the Sierras. The trail was narrow and difficult. At noon the Duchess, rolling out of her saddle upon the ground, declared her intention of going no further, and the party halted.

The spot was singularly wild and impressive. A wooded amphitheatre, 9 surrounded on three sides by precipitous cliffs of naked granite, sloped gently toward the crest of another precipice that overlooked the valley. It was undoubtedly the most suitable spot for a camp, had camping been advisable. But Mr. Oakhurst knew that scarcely half the journey to Sandy Bar was accomplished, and the party were not equipped or provisioned for delay. This fact he pointed out to his companions curtly, with a philosophic commentary on the folly of "throwing up their hand before the game was played out." But they were furnished with liquor, which in this emergency stood them in place of food, fuel, rest and prescience. In spite of his remonstrances, it was not long before they were more or less under its influence. Uncle Billy passed rapidly from a bellicose state into one of stupor, the Duchess became maudlin, and Mother Shipton snored. Mr. Oakhurst alone remained erect, leaning against a rock, calmly surveying them.

Mr. Oakhurst did not drink. It interfered with a profession which re- 10 quired coolness, impassiveness and presence of mind, and, in his own language, he "couldn't afford it." As he gazed at his recumbent fellow-exiles, the loneliness begotten of his pariah-trade, his habits of life, his very vices, for the first time seriously oppressed him. He bestirred himself in dusting his black clothes, washing his hands and face, and other acts characteristic of his studiously neat habits, and for a moment forgot his annoyance. The thought of deserting his weaker and more pitiable companions never perhaps occurred to him. Yet he could not help feeling the want of that excitement, which singularly enough was most conducive to that calm equanimity for which he was notorious. He looked at the gloomy walls that rose a thousand feet sheer above the circling pines around him; at the sky, ominously clouded; at the valley below, already deepening into shadow. And doing so, suddenly he heard his own name called.

A horseman slowly ascended the trail. In the fresh, open face of the new- 11 comer, Mr. Oakhurst recognized Tom Simson, otherwise known as "The Innocent" of Sandy Bar. He had met him some months before over a "little game," and had, with perfect equanimity, won the entire fortune—amounting to some forty dollars—of that guileless youth. After the game was finished, Mr. Oakhurst drew the youthful speculator behind the door and thus addressed him: "Tommy, you're a good little man, but you can't gamble worth a cent. Don't try it over again." He then handed him his money back, pushed him gently from the room, and so made a devoted slave of Tom Simson.

There was a remembrance of this in his boyish and enthusiastic greet- 12 ing of Mr. Oakhurst. He had started, he said, to go to Poker Flat to seek his fortune. "Alone?" No, not exactly alone; in fact—a giggle—he had run away with Piney Woods. Didn't Mr. Oakhurst remember Piney? She that used to wait on the table at the Temperance House? They had been engaged a long time, but old Jake Woods had objected, and so they had run away, and were going to Poker Flat to be married, and here they were. And they were tired out, and how lucky it was they had found a place to camp and company. All this The Innocent delivered rapidly, while Piney—a stout, comely damsel of fifteen—emerged from behind the pine tree, where she had been blushing unseen, and rode to the side of her lover.

Mr. Oakhurst seldom troubled himself with sentiment. Still less with   13
propriety. But he had a vague idea that the situation was not felicitous. He retained, however, his presence of mind sufficiently to kick Uncle Billy, who was about to say something, and Uncle Billy was sober enough to recognize in Mr. Oakhurst's kick a superior power that would not bear trifling. He then endeavored to dissuade Tom Simson from delaying further, but in vain. He even pointed out the fact that there was no provision, nor means of making a camp. But, unluckily, "The Innocent" met this objection by assuring the party that he was provided with an extra mule loaded with provisions, and by the discovery of a rude attempt at a log-house near the trail. "Piney can stay with Mrs. Oakhurst," said The Innocent, pointing to the Duchess, "and I can shift for myself."

Nothing but Mr. Oakhurst's admonishing foot saved Uncle Billy from   14
bursting into a roar of laughter. As it was, he felt compelled to retire up the cañon until he could recover his gravity. There he confided the joke to the tall pine trees, with many slaps of his leg, contortions of his face, and the usual profanity. But when he returned to the party, he found them seated by a fire—for the air had grown strangely chill and the sky overcast—in apparently amicable conversation. Piney was actually talking in an impulsive, girlish fashion to the Duchess, who was listening with an interest and animation she had not shown for many days. The Innocent was holding forth, apparently with equal effect, to Mr. Oakhurst and Mother Shipton, who was actually relaxing into amiability. "Is this yer a d——d picnic?" said Uncle Billy, with inward scorn, as he surveyed the sylvan group, the glancing firelight and the tethered animals in the foreground. Suddenly an idea mingled with the alcoholic fumes that disturbed his brain. It was apparently of a jocular nature, for he felt impelled to slap his leg again and cram his fist into his mouth.

As the shadows crept slowly up the mountain, a slight breeze rocked   15
the tops of the pine trees, and moaned through their long and gloomy aisles. The ruined cabin, patched and covered with pine boughs, was set apart for the ladies. As the lovers parted, they unaffectedly exchanged a parting kiss, so honest and sincere that it might have been heard above the swaying pines. The frail Duchess and the malevolent Mother Shipton were probably too stunned to remark upon this last evidence of simplicity, and so turned with-

out a word to the hut. The fire was replenished, the men lay down before the door, and in a few minutes were asleep.

Mr. Oakhurst was a light sleeper. Toward morning he awoke be- 16 numbed and cold. As he stirred the dying fire, the wind, which was now blowing strongly, brought to his cheek that which caused the blood to leave it—snow!

He started to his feet with the intention of awakening the sleepers, for 17 there was not time to lose. But turning to where Uncle Billy had been lying he found him gone. A suspicion leaped to his brain and a curse to his lips. He ran to the spot where the mules had been tethered; they were no longer there. The tracks were already rapidly disappearing in the snow.

The momentary excitement brought Mr. Oakhurst back to the fire 18 with his usual calm. He did not waken the sleepers. The Innocent slumbered peacefully, with a smile on his good-humored, freckled face; the virgin Piney slept beside her frailer sisters as sweetly as though attended by celestial guardians, and Mr. Oakhurst, drawing his blanket over his shoulders, stroked his mustachios and waited for the dawn. It came slowly in a whirling mist of snowflakes, that dazzled and confused the eye. What could be seen of the landscape appeared magically changed. He looked over the valley, and summed up the present and future in two words—"Snowed in!"

A careful inventory of the provisions, which, fortunately for the party, 19 had been stored within the hut, and so escaped the felonious fingers of Uncle Billy, disclosed the fact that with care and prudence they might last ten days longer. "That is," said Mr. Oakhurst, *sotto voce* to The Innocent, "if you're willing to board us. If you ain't—and perhaps you'd better not—you can wait till Uncle Billy gets back with provisions." For some occult reason, Mr. Oakhurst could not bring himself to disclose Uncle Billy's rascality, and so offered the hypothesis that he had wandered from the camp and had accidentally stampeded the animals. He dropped a warning to the Duchess and Mother Shipton, who of course knew the facts of their associate's defection. "They'll find out the truth about us *all*, when they find out anything," he added, significantly, "and there's no good frightening them now."

Tom Simson not only put all his worldly store at the disposal of Mr. 20 Oakhurst, but seemed to enjoy the prospect of their enforced seclusion. "We'll have a good camp for a week, and then the snow'll melt, and we'll all go back together." The cheerful gayety of the young man and Mr. Oakhurst's calm infected the others. The Innocent, with the aid of pine boughs, extemporized a thatch for the roofless cabin, and the Duchess directed Piney in the reärrangement of the interior with a taste and tact that opened the blue eyes of that provincial maiden to their fullest extent. "I reckon now you're used to fine things at Poker Flat," said Piney. The Duchess turned away sharply to conceal something that reddened her cheeks

through its professional tint, and Mother Shipton requested Piney not to
"chatter." But when Mr. Oakhurst returned from a weary search for the
trail, he heard the sound of happy laughter echoed from the rocks. He
stopped in some alarm, and his thoughts first naturally reverted to the whiskey—which he had prudently *cachéd*. "And yet it don't somehow sound like
whiskey," said the gambler. It was not until he caught sight of the blazing
fire through the still blinding storm, and the group around it, that he settled
to the conviction that it was "square fun."

Whether Mr. Oakhurst had *cachéd* his cards with the whiskey as some- 21
thing debarred the free access of the community, I cannot say. It was certain
that, in Mother Shipton's words, he "didn't say cards once" during that
evening. Haply the time was beguiled by an accordeon, produced somewhat
ostentatiously by Tom Simson, from his pack. Notwithstanding some difficulties attending the manipulation of this instrument, Piney Woods managed to pluck several reluctant melodies from its keys, to an accompaniment
by The Innocent on a pair of bone castinets. But the crowning festivity of
the evening was reached in a rude camp-meeting hymn, which the lovers,
joining hands, sang with great earnestness and vociferation. I fear that a certain defiant tone and Covenanter's swing to its chorus, rather than any de-
votional quality, caused it to speedily infect the others, who at last joined in
the refrain:

"I'm proud to live in the service of the Lord,
And I'm bound to die in His army."

The pines rocked, the storm eddied and whirled above the miserable 22
group, and the flames of their altar leaped heavenward, as if in token of the
vow.

At midnight the storm abated, the rolling clouds parted, and the stars 23
glittered keenly above the sleeping camp. Mr. Oakhurst, whose professional
habits had enabled him to live on the smallest possible amount of sleep, in
dividing the watch with Tom Simson, somehow managed to take upon himself the greater part of that duty. He excused himself to The Innocent, by
saying that he had "often been a week without sleep." "Doing what?" asked
Tom. "Poker!" replied Oakhurst, sententiously; "when a man gets a streak
of luck—nigger-luck—he don't get tired. The luck gives in first. Luck,"
continued the gambler, reflectively, "is a mighty queer thing. All you know
about it for certain is that it's bound to change. And it's finding out when
it's going to change that makes you. We've had a streak of bad luck since we
left Poker Flat—you come along and slap you get into it, too. If you can hold
your cards right along you're all right. For," added the gambler, with cheerful irrelevance,

"I'm proud to live in the service of the Lord,
And I'm bound to die in His army."

The third day came, and the sun, looking through the white-curtained 24 valley, saw the outcasts divide their slowly decreasing store of provisions for the morning meal. It was one of the peculiarities of that mountain climate that its rays diffused a kindly warmth over the wintry landscape, as if in regretful commiseration of the past. But it revealed drift on drift of snow piled high around the hut; a hopeless, uncharted, trackless sea of white lying below the rocky shores to which the castaways still clung. Through the marvellously clear air, the smoke of the pastoral village of Poker Flat rose miles away. Mother Shipton saw it, and from a remote pinnacle of her rocky fastness, hurled in that direction a final malediction. It was her last vituperative attempt, and perhaps for that reason was invested with a certain degree of sublimity. It did her good, she privately informed the Duchess. "Just you go out there and cuss, and see." She then set herself to the task of amusing 'the child,'" as she and the Duchess were pleased to call Piney. Piney was no chicken, but it was a soothing and ingenious theory of the pair to thus account for the fact that she didn't swear and wasn't improper.

When night crept up again through the gorges, the reedy notes of the 25 accordeon rose and fell in fitful spasms and long-drawn gasps by the flickering camp-fire. But music failed to fill entirely the aching void left by insufficient food, and a new diversion was proposed by Piney—story-telling. Neither Mr. Oakhurst nor his female companions caring to relate their personal experiences, this plan would have failed, too, but for The Innocent. Some months before he had chanced upon a stray copy of Mr. Pope's ingenious translation of the Iliad. He now proposed to narrate the principal incidents of that poem—having thoroughly mastered the argument and fairly forgotten the words—in the current vernacular of Sandy Bar. And so for the rest of that night the Homeric demi-gods again walked the earth. Trojan bully and wily Greek wrestled in the winds, and the great pines in the cañon seemed to bow to the wrath of the son of Peleus. Mr. Oakhurst listened with quiet satisfaction. Most especially was he interested in the fate of "Ash-heels," as The Innocent persisted in denominating the "swift-footed Achilles."

So with small food and much of Homer and the accordeon, a week 26 passed over the heads of the outcasts. The sun again forsook them, and again from leaden skies the snow-flakes were sifted over the land. Day by day closer around them drew the snowy circle, until at last they looked from their prison over drifted walls of dazzling white, that towered twenty feet above their heads. It became more and more difficult to replenish their fires, even from the fallen trees beside them, now half-hidden in the drifts. And yet no one complained. The lovers turned from the dreary prospect and looked into each other's eyes, and were happy. Mr. Oakhurst settled himself coolly to the losing game before him. The Duchess, more cheerful than she had been, assumed the care of Piney. Only Mother Shipton—once the strongest of the party—seemed to sicken and fade. At midnight on the tenth day she called Oakhurst to her side. "I'm going," she said, in a voice of querulous weakness, "but don't say anything about it. Don't waken the kids. Take the bundle from under my head and open it." Mr. Oakhurst did so. It contained Mother Shipton's rations for the last week, untouched. "Give 'em to the child," she said, pointing to the sleeping Piney. "You've starved yourself," said the gambler. "That's what they call it," said the woman querulously, as she lay down again, and turning her face to the wall, passed quietly away.

The accordeon and the bones were put aside that day, and Homer was   27 forgotten. When the body of Mother Shipton had been committed to the snow, Mr. Oakhurst took The Innocent aside, and showed him a pair of snow-shoes, which he had fashioned from the old pack-saddle. "There's one chance in a hundred to save her yet," he said, pointing to Piney; "but it's there," he added, pointing toward Poker Flat. "If you can reach there in two days she's safe." "And you?" asked Tom Simson. "I'll stay here," was the curt reply.

The lovers parted with a long embrace. "You are not going, too," said   28 the Duchess, as she saw Mr. Oakhurst apparently waiting to accompany him. "As far as the cañon," he replied. He turned suddenly, and kissed the Duchess, leaving her pallid face aflame, and her trembling limbs rigid with amazement.

Night came, but not Mr. Oakhurst. It brought the storm again and the   29 whirling snow. Then the Duchess, feeding the fire, found that some one had quietly piled beside the hut enough fuel to last a few days longer. The tears rose to her eyes, but she hid them from Piney.

The women slept but little. In the morning, looking into each other's   30 faces, they read their fate. Neither spoke; but Piney, accepting the position of the stronger, drew near and placed her arm around the Duchess's waist. They kept this attitude for the rest of the day. That night the storm reached its greatest fury, and rending asunder the protecting pines, invaded the very hut.

Toward morning they found themselves unable to feed the fire, which   31 gradually died away. As the embers slowly blackened, the Duchess crept closer to Piney, and broke the silence of many hours: "Piney, can you pray?" "No, dear," said Piney, simply. The Duchess, without knowing exactly why, felt relieved, and putting her head upon Piney's shoulder, spoke no more. And so reclining, the younger and purer pillowing the head of her soiled sister upon her virgin breast, they fell asleep.

The wind lulled as if it feared to waken them. Feathery drifts of snow,   32 shaken from the long pine boughs, flew like white-winged birds, and settled about them as they slept. The moon through the rifted clouds looked down upon what had been the camp. But all human stain, all trace of earthly travail, was hidden beneath the spotless mantle mercifully flung from above.

They slept all that day and the next, nor did they waken when voices   33 and footsteps broke the silence of the camp. And when pitying fingers brushed the snow from their wan faces, you could scarcely have told from the equal peace that dwelt upon them, which was she that had sinned. Even the Law of Poker Flat recognized this, and turned away, leaving them still locked in each other's arms.

But at the head of the gulch, on one of the largest pine trees, they 34 found the deuce of clubs pinned to the bark with a bowie knife. It bore the following, written in pencil, in a firm hand:

BENEATH THIS TREE

LIES THE BODY

OF

JOHN OAKHURST,

WHO STRUCK A STREAK OF BAD LUCK

ON THE 23D OF NOVEMBER, 1850,

AND

HANDED IN HIS CHECKS

ON THE 7TH DECEMBER, 1850

And pulseless and cold, with a Derringer by his side and a bullet in his 35 heart, though still calm as in life, beneath the snow, lay he who was at once the strongest and yet the weakest of the outcasts of Poker Flat.

SPEECH

The Gettysburg Address
Abraham Lincoln

Abraham Lincoln, sixteenth President of the United States, delivered this famous eulogy at a ceremony commemorating the Civil War Battle of Gettysburg. Lincoln, whose speech did not cause a great stir at the time of his delivering it, gave The Gettysburg Address on November 19, 1863.

Four score and seven years ago our fathers brought forth on this con- 1
tinent, a new nation, conceived in Liberty, and dedicated to the proposition that all men are created equal.

Now we are engaged in a great civil war, testing whether that nation or 2
any nation so conceived and so dedicated, can long endure. We are met on a great battle-field of that war. We have come to dedicate a portion of that field, as a final resting place for those who here gave their lives that that nation might live. It is altogether fitting and proper that we should do this.

But, in a larger sense, we can not dedicate—we can not consecrate—we   3
can not hallow—this ground. The brave men, living and dead, who struggled here, have consecrated it, far above our poor power to add or detract.
The world will little note, nor long remember what we say here, but it can
never forget what they did here. It is for us the living, rather, to be dedicated here to the unfinished work which they who fought here have thus far
so nobly advanced. It is rather for us to be here dedicated to the great task
remaining before us—that from these honored dead we take increased devotion to that cause for which they gave the last full measure of devotion—that
we here highly resolve that these dead shall not have died in vain—that this
nation, under God, shall have a new birth of freedom—and that government
of the people, by the people, for the people, shall not perish from the earth.

COMMENCEMENT ADDRESS

What Every Girl Should Know
Robertson Davies

Robertson Davies is one of Canada's most important writers, publishing plays,
criticism, and novels, including *Fifth Business* and *The Manticore*. Here is his
own introduction to "What Every Girl Should Know."
"As a schoolboy I listened to many speeches on Prize Days from older persons whose good intentions were impeccable, but whose manner and matter
were tediously patronizing and stuff. When my own turn came I determined to
be as honest as possible, not to talk down, and if possible to say something that
was not usually said in schools. This is what I said to the girls of the Bishop
Strachan School in June 1973."

During the years when my own daughters were pupils in this school I   1
attended many of these gatherings, and heard many speeches made by men
who stood where I stand at this moment. They said all sorts of things. I recall one speaker who said that as he looked out at the girls who were assembled to receive prizes, and to pay their last respects to their school, he felt as
though he were looking over a garden of exquisite flowers. He was drunk,
poor man, and it would be absurd to treat his remark as though he were
speaking on oath. I am not drunk, although I have lunched elegantly at the
table of the Chairman of your Board of Governors; I have had enough of his
excellent wine to be philosophical, but with me philosophy does not take the
form of paying extravagant and manifestly untruthful compliments. Let me
put myself on record as saying that I do *not* feel as though I were looking
over a garden of exquisite flowers.

On the contrary, I feel as though I were looking into the past. You look   2
uncommonly as the girls of this school looked when my daughters were of

your number. And in those days I used to think how much you looked like the girls who were in this school when I was myself a schoolboy, just down the road, at Upper Canada College.

I remember that boy very well. He was a romantic boy, and he thought   3
that girls were quite the most wonderful objects of God's creation. In these liberated days, when it is possible for anyone to say anything on any occasion, I may perhaps make a confession to you, and this is it: I never liked anything but girls. Nowadays it is accepted as gospel that everybody goes through a homosexual period of life. I cannot recall any such thing: I always regarded other boys as rivals, or nuisances, or—very occasionally—friends. I am rather sorry about it now, because in the eyes of modern psychologists and sociologists it marks me as a stunted personality. Nowadays it appears that there is something warped about a man who never had a homosexual period. But there it is. I stand before you with all my imperfections weighing heavily upon me. I always liked girls, and simply because of geography, the girls I liked best were the girls of B.S.S.

I have recovered from this folly. I have myself achieved some knowl-   4
edge of psychology and sociology, and it tells me significant but not always complimentary things about you. I don't know how many of you are here today, but statistically I know that during the next ten years 58.7 per cent of you will marry, and that of that number 43.4 per cent will have two and a half children apiece, and that 15.3 per cent will be divorced. Of the remainder, 3.9 per cent will be dead, 14.5 per cent will have been deserted, 24.2 per cent will have spent some time in jail. One hundred per cent of those who have married will have given up splendid careers in order to do so, and of this number 98.5 per cent will have mentioned the fact, at some time, to their husbands. These statistics were compiled for me by a graduate student at OISE, and if you doubt them, you must quarrel with her, and not with me. I accept no responsibility for statistics, which are a kind of magic beyond my comprehension.

I have said that when I was a boy I entertained a lofty, uncritical ad-   5
miration for the girls of this school. Our romantic approach in those days was more delicate than it is today, when sexual fervour has achieved almost cannibalistic exuberance, and I thought I was lucky when I had a chance simply to talk to one of the girls from this school. I never had enough of that pleasure; I yearned for more. Now here I offer my first piece of good advice to you: be very careful of what you greatly desire, in your inmost heart, because the chances are very strong that you will get it, in one form or another. But it will never be just the way you expected. You see what has happened? As a boy I wanted to talk to the girls of B.S.S., and I always thought of doing this to one girl at a time, in shaded light, with music playing in the distance. And here I am today, talking to all of you, in broad daylight. The things I planned to say when I was a boy would be embarrassingly inappropriate if I were to say them now. Indeed, I don't want to say them; they have

ceased to be true or relevant for you or for me. I know too much about you
to compliment you, and in your eyes I am not a romantic object. Or if I am,
you had better put yourself under the treatment of some wise psychiatrist.

Here I am, after all these years, and Fate has granted one of my   6
wishes, in the way Fate so often does—at the wrong time and in wholesale
quantity. What am I to say to you?

The hallowed custom, at such times as these, is that I should offer you   7
some good advice. But what about? It was easier in the days when girls like
yourselves thought chiefly about marriage. Nowadays when little girls play

Rich man, poor man, beggar man, thief,
Doctor, lawyer, Indian chief

they are trying to discover their own careers, not those of their husbands.   8
Quite recently a very young girl told me that she did not intend to bother
with a husband; she would be content with affairs, because they would interfere less with her career. That remark showed how much she knew about
it. A girl who thinks love affairs are less trouble than a marriage is probably
also the kind of girl who thinks that picnics are simpler than dinner-parties.
A first-class picnic, which has to be planned to the last detail, but which
must also pretend to be wholly impromptu, is a vastly more complicated un-
dertaking than a formal dinner for twenty guests, which moves according to
a well-understood pattern. Personally I have always greatly liked dinner-
parties, and hated picnics. But then I am a classicist by temperament, and I
think the formality and the pattern, either in love or in entertaining, is half
the fun.

But you may have different views, so we won't talk about that. Let us   9
talk about something that will be applicable to your life, whether the love
aspect of it takes the dinner-party or the picnic form. Let us talk about enjoying life.

Don't imagine for a moment that I am going to talk about that foolish   10
thing happiness. I meet all kinds of people who think that happiness is a
condition that can be achieved, and maintained, indefinitely, and that the
quality of life is determined by the number of hours of happiness you can
clock up. I hope you won't bother your heads about happiness. It is a cat-
like emotion; if you try to coax it, happiness will avoid you, but if you pay
no attention to it it will rub against your legs and spring unbidden into your
lap. Forget happiness, and pin your hopes on understanding.

Many people, and especially many young people, think that variety of   11
sensation is what gives spice to life. They want to do everything, go everywhere, meet everybody, and drink from every bottle. It can't be done. Whoever you are, your energies and your opportunities are limited. Of course
you want to try several alternatives in order to find out what suits you, but
I hope that ten years from today you will agree with me that the good life is

lived not widely, but deeply. It is not doing things, but understanding what you do, that brings real excitement and lasting pleasure.

You should start now. It is dangerously easy to get into a pattern of 12 life, and if you live shallowly until you are thirty, it will not be easy to begin living deeply. Whatever your own desires may be, the people around you won't put up with it. They know you as one sort of person, and they will be resentful if you show signs of becoming somebody else. Live shallowly, and you will find yourself surrounded by shallow people.

How are you to avoid that fate? I can tell you, but it is not a magic 13 secret which will transform your life. It is very, very difficult. What you must do is to spend twenty-three hours of every day of your life doing whatever falls in your way, whether it be duty or pleasure or necessary for your health and physical well-being. But—and this is the difficult thing—you must set aside one hour of your life every day for yourself, in which you attempt to understand what you are doing.

Do you think it sounds easy? Try it, and find out. All kinds of things 14 will interfere. People—husbands, lovers, friends, children, employers, teachers, enemies, and all the multifarious army of mankind will want that hour, and they will have all sorts of blandishments to persuade you to yield it to them. And the worst enemy of all—yourself—will find so many things that seem attractive upon which the hour can be spent. It is extremely difficult to claim that hour solely for the task of understanding, questioning, and deciding.

It used to be somewhat easier, because people used to be religious, or 15 pretended they were. If you went to the chapel, or the church, or a praying-chamber in your own house, and fell on your knees and buried your face in your hands, they might—not always, but quite often—leave you alone. Not now. 'Why are you sitting there, staring into space?' they will say. Or 'What are you mooning about now?' If you say 'I am thinking' they may perhaps hoot with laughter, or they will go away and tell everybody that you are intolerably pretentious. But you are doing very much what you would have been doing if you were your great-grandmother, and said that you were praying. Because you would be trying your hardest to unravel the tangles of your life, and seek the aid of the greatest thing you know—whatever you may call it—in making sense of what will often seem utterly senseless.

I am not going to advise you to pray, because I am not an expert on 16 that subject. But I do know that it is rather the fashion among many people who do pray to think that it is pretentious to pray too much for yourself; you are supposed to pray for others, who obviously need Divine assistance more than you do. But when I was a boy at the school down the road, we were taught that prayer has three modes—petition, which is for yourself; intercession, which is for others; and contemplation, which is listening to what is said to *you*. If I might be permitted to advise you on this delicate subject, I would suggest that you skip intercession until you are a little more certain what other people need; stick to petition, in the form of self-examination, and to contemplation, which is waiting for suggestions from the deepest part of you.

If I embarrass you by talking about praying, don't think of it that way. 17 Call it 'pondering' instead. I don't know if you still learn any Latin in this school, but if you do, you know that the word ponder comes from the Latin *ponderare,* which means 'to weigh'. Weigh up your life, and do it every day. If you find you are getting short weight, attend to the matter at once. The remedy usually lies in your own hands. And in that direction the true enjoyment of life is to be found.

There you are. I promised your Headmaster I would not speak for too 18 long. But I have done what a speaker on such occasions as this ought to do. I have given you good advice. It is often and carelessly said that nobody ever takes advice. It is not true. I have taken an enormous amount of advice myself, and some of it was extraordinarily helpful to me. I have passed on some of the best of it to you this afternoon, and I have enjoyed doing so. Because, as I told you, it was my ambition for years to have a chance to talk to every girl in B.S.S. and today I have achieved it. Not quite as I had hoped, but then, in this uncertain world, whatever comes about quite as one hopes? I have enjoyed myself, and for what I have received from you I am truly thankful.

Acknowledgments

Asimov, Isaac, "What Do You Call a Platypus?" published in *National Wildlife Magazine*, March/April 1972. Reprinted by permission of author.

Attenborough, David, excerpts from *Life on Earth*. Copyright 1979, by David Attenborough Productions Limited. Reprinted by permission of Little, Brown and Company.

Atwood, Margaret, "Just Like a Woman" excerpted from *Open Places*, Spring 1985, by permission of publisher.

Barrett, Steve, "Private and Public Writer," reprinted by permission of author.

Barry, Dave, "For The Birds." Copyright © 1981, reprinted by permission of author.

Blakely, Mary Kay, column reprinted from *Hers: Through Women's Eyes*, edited by Nancy Newhouse, Villard Books, 1986. Copyright ©1981 by Mary Kay Blakely. Originally appeared in The New York Times. Reprinted by permission of Rosenstone/Wender.

Bradley, David, "The Star Who Went Astray." Reprinted by permission of The Wendy Weil Agency Inc. Copyright 1983 by David Bradley. Originally published in *Esquire* as "My Hero, Malcolm X."

Brown, Robert McAfee, "They Could Do No Other," from *The Courage to Care*. Copyright ©1986, New York University Press. Reprinted by permission of The Elie Wiesel Foundation for Humanity and the New York University Press.

Caputo, Philip, "Prologue to A Rumor of War," from *A Rumor of War* by Philip Caputo. Copyright ©1977 by Philip Caputo. Reprinted by permission of Henry Holt and Company, Inc.

Cosby, Bill, "No Hope on a Rope," excerpts from *Fatherhood* by Bill Cosby. Copyright ©1986 by William H. Cosby, Jr. Reprinted by permission of Doubleday, a Division of Bantam, Doubleday, Dell Publishing Group, Inc.

Cox, Kathleen, "A Symbol of Humanity," reprinted by permission of author.

Davies, Robertson, "What Every Girl Should Know," from *One Half of Robertson Davies*. Copyright ©1977 by Robertson Davies. All rights reserved. Reprinted by permission of Viking Penguin, Inc.

Dillard, Annie, "Strangers to Darkness," from *Pilgrim at Tinker Creek*, by Annie Dillard. Copyright ©1974 by Annie Dillard. Reprinted by permission of Harper & Row.

517

Eastman, Tracy, "Is the Brown on My Nose Showing?" reprinted by permission of author.

Ephron, Delia, "Ex-Husbands for Sale," *Funny Sauce* by Delia Ephron. Copyright ©1982, 1983, 1986 by Delia Ephron. All rights reserved. Reprinted with permission of Viking Penguin, Inc.

Erdoes, Richard, and Alfonso Ortiz, "Something Whistling in the Night," from *American Indian Myths and Legends.* Copyright ©1984 by Richard Erdoes and Alfonso Ortiz. Reprinted by permission of Pantheon Books, a Division of Random House, Inc.

Feit, Edward, "James Harrington," from *The American Artist,* July 1, 1987. Reprinted by permission of *The American Artist* magazine.

Frank, Anne, excerpts from *Anne Frank: The Diary of a Young Girl* by Anne Frank. Copyright ©1952 by Otto H. Frank. Reprinted by permission of Doubleday, a Division of Bantam, Doubleday, Dell Publishing Group, Inc.

Friedrich, Otto, "A Small Moral Quandary." Copyright ©1987 by TIME Inc. All rights reserved. Reprinted by permission of TIME.

Greenfield, Jeff, "A Simpler Life for Consumers." Copyright ©1987 by Jeff Greenfield. Reprinted by permission of Sterling Lord Literistic Inc.

Grizzard, Lewis, "This Might Sting a Little," from *They Tore Out My Heart and Stomped that Sucker Flat,* Warner Books Edition, copyright ©1982, Peachtree Publishing Ltd. Reprinted by permission of publisher.

Hirshey, Gerri, "Sympathy for the Devil," from *Nowhere to Run.* Copyright ©1984 by Gerri Hirshey. Reprinted by permission of Times Books, a Division of Random House, Inc.

Hockett, Christopher, "Extinction" reprinted by permission of author.

Hornaday, Ann, "Roach Fever," reprinted by permission of author.

Jacobs, De'Lois, "In Our Own Image," *Essence,* June 1986. Reprinted by permission of author.

Jenkins, Dan, "The P.G.A. Plays Through," *Playboy,* May 1986. Reproduced by special permission of Playboy Magazine. Copyright ©1986 by PLAYBOY.

Kael, Pauline, "Review of *The Color Purple*" excerpted from "Sacred Monsters." Reprinted by permission of author. Copyright ©1985 by Pauline Kael. Originally appeared in The New Yorker.

King, Dr. Martin Luther, Jr., "Letter from a Birmingham Jail" by Dr. Martin Luther King, Jr. from the book *Why We Can't Wait.* Copyright 1963, 1964 by Dr. Martin Luther King, Jr. Reprinted by permission of Harper & Row.

Kocol, Cleo, "The Rent-a-Womb Dilemma." This article appeared in *The Humanist* issue of July/August 1987 and is reprinted by permission.

Krents, Harold, "Darkness at Noon." Copyright ©1976 by The New York Times Company. Reprinted by permission.

LaPaglia, Nancy, "The Missing Majority: The Community College in American Fiction," from *City: A Journal of the City Colleges of Chicago,* pp. 67–70. Reprinted by permission of author and the City Colleges of Chicago.

Leacock, Stephen, "Index: There Is No Index." Reprinted by permission of Dodd, Mead, & Company, Inc. from *My Remarkable Uncle* by Stephen Leacock. Copyright 1942 by Dodd, Mead, & Company, Inc. Copyright renewed 1970 by Stephen L. Leacock.

Lehrter, Laurie, "Who's Afraid?" reprinted by permission of author.

Leopold, Aldo, "Goose Music" from *Sand County Almanac with Other Essays on Conservation from Round River* by Aldo Leopold. Copyright ©1949, 1953, 1966. Renewed 1977, 1981 by Oxford University Press, Inc. Reprinted by permission.

Lopez, Barry, excerpted from "Ice and Light" in *Arctic Dreams.* Copyright ©1986 Barry Holstun Lopez. Reprinted with the permission of Charles Scribner's Sons, an imprint of MacMillan Publishing Company.

Ly, Kieu K., "A Taste of Reality" reprinted by permission of author.

Mandela, Winnie, "From *Part of My Soul Went with Him.*" Reprinted from *Part of My Soul Went with Him* by Winnie Mandela, edited by Anne Benjamin and adapted by Mary Benson, with the permission of W. W. Norton & Company, Inc. Copyright ©1984 by Rowohlt Taschenbuch Verlag GmbH, Reinbek bei Hamburg. All rights reserved. First American Edition 1985.

Markham, Beryl, "Royal Exile" excerpted from *West with the Night.* Copyright ©1942, 1983 by Beryl Markham. Published by North Point Press and reprinted by permission.

McNutt, Randy, "Foot Soldiers in the War on Imports," Cincinnati *Enquirer,* June 1, 1987. Reprinted by permission of the Cincinnati *Enquirer.*

McWhirter, Nickie, "Glory, Those Shoes of Imelda Marcos," published in Detroit *Free Press,* March 16, 1986 (Metro Final Edition). Reprinted with permission of Detroit *Free Press.*

Moon, William Least Heat, excerpts from *Blue Highways: A Journey into America* by William Least Heat Moon. Copyright ©1982 by William Least Heat Moon. Reprinted by permission of Little, Brown and Company in association with the Atlantic Monthly Press.

Mowat, Farley, "To Kill a Wolf" from *Never Cry Wolf.* Copyright 1963 by Farley Mowat Limited. Reprinted by permission of Little, Brown, and Company.

Neruda, Pablo, "The Odors of Homecoming" from *Passions and Impressions* by Pablo Neruda. English translation copyright 1980, 1981, 1983 by Farrar, Straus and Girous, Inc. Reprinted by permission of Farrar, Straus, and Girous, Inc.Reprinted by permission of Farrar, Straus, and Girous, Inc.

Olds, Sally Wendkos, "America's Grandmother Fixation" reprinted by permission of author.

Oliver, Stephanie Stokes, "Beyond *The Color Purple,*" *Essence,* September 1986, pp. 119–121. Reprinted by permission of the author.

O'Connor, Kathryn, Susan Glueck, and Stephanie Turner, "Aack!" reprinted by permission of authors.

Painter, Nell Irvin, column from *Hers: Through Women's Eyes,* Villard Books, 1986, pp. 269–272, edited by Nancy Newhouse. Reprinted by permission of the author.

Parker, Jo Goodwin, "What Is Poverty?" from *America's Other Children: Public Schools Outside Suburbia,* edited by George Henderson. Copyright 1971 by The University of Oklahoma Press. Reprinted with permission of The University of Oklahoma Press.

Payne, Karen, A Family's Personal Letters from *Between Ourselves: Letters Between Mothers and Daughters, 1750–1982,* edited by Karen Payne, Michael Joseph LTD. Reprinted by permission of Michael Joseph LTD.

Petrunkevitch, Alexander, "The Spider and the Wasp," *Scientific American.* Copyright 1952, by Scientific American, Inc. All rights reserved. Reprinted by permission of the publisher.

Pfeifer, Jackie, "Grandma's Veranda" reprinted by permission of author.

Pokas, James, "When Thou Prayest, Enter into Thy Closet" reprinted by permission of author.

Quammen, David, "The Tree People: A Man, A Storm, A Magnolia," excerpted from *Natural Acts* by permission of Nick Lyons Books. Copyright 1985 by David Quammen.

Rawlings, Diane, "Reflections," copyright 1987. Reprinted by permission of author.

Reed, Ishmael, "Real Democrats Don't Eat Quiche," *The Nation,* April 6, 1985. Copyright 1985. The Nation Company, Inc. Reprinted with permission.

Rodriquez, Richard, excerpts from *Hunger of Memory* by Richard Rodriquez. Copyright 1981 by Richard Rodriquez. Reprinted by permission of David R. Godine, Publisher.

Rowntree, Derek, "What Is Statistics?" excerpted from *Statistics without Tears.* Copyright 1981 by Derek Rowntree. Reprinted with the permission of Charles Scribner's Sons, an imprint of MacMillan Publishing Company and Penguin Books, Ltd.

Sawyer, Lynn, "Living after Dying" (essay, drafts, notes, handwritten emendations). Reprinted by permission of author.

Schramm, Pamela, "Interview with James Lehman" reprinted by permission of author.

Slater, Beverly and Frances Spatz Leighton, "Waking Up." Copyright 1984 by Beverly Slater and Frances Spatz Leighton. Reprinted by permission of William Morrow and Company, Inc.

Sommers, Jeffrey, "Training for the Magic Kingdon," reprinted by permission of the author.

Staples, Brent, "Black Men, Public Spaces" *Ms.,* September 1986. Reprinted by permission of author.

Steward, Helen Marnie, "The Diary of Helen Marnie Steward" from *A Day at a Time* (entries from Friday, June 17, 1853 through Thursday, June 23, 1853) edited by Margo Culley (Feminist Press Edition, 1985). Reprinted by permission of Lake County Historical Society.

Stubbs, Karen, "Mark Twain and Bret Harte: Social Critics," reprinted by permission of author.

Syfers, Judy, "Why I Want a Wife," *Ms.,* 1971. Reprinted by permission of author.

Terry, Wallace, from *Bloods: An Oral History of the Vietnam War by Black Veterans.* Copyright 1984 by Wallace Terry. Reprinted by permission of Random House, Inc.

Thurber, James, "University Days" copyright 1933, 1961 by James Thurber. From *My Life and Hard Times,* published by Harper & Row. Reprinted by permission.

Tuchman, Barbara W., "A Letter to the House of Representatives" from *Practicing History.* Copyright 1981 by Alma Tuchman, Lucy T. Eisenberg, and Jessica Tuchman Matthews. Reprinted by permission of Alfred A. Knopf, Inc.

Verquer, Timothy, "The Rough Life" reprinted by permission of author.

Weber, Vikki, "Two Letters about a Sorority Pledging Prank" reprinted by permission of author.

White, E. B., "Once More to the Lake," by E. B. White. Copyright 1941 by E. B. White from the book *Essays of E. B. White.* Reprinted by permission of Harper & Row.

Wiesel, Elie, "Was He Normal? Human? Poor Humanity." Copyright 1987 TIME Inc. All rights reserved. Reprinted by permission of TIME.

Wilson, Cindy, "Fast Food Drive Thrus" reprinted by permission of author.

Wilson, Jane, "Why Nurses Leave Nursing," *Canadian Nurse/L'Infirmiere Canadienne,* vol. 83, number 3. Reprinted by permission of the Canadian Nurses Association.

Wishman, Seymour, "Who Shall Judge Me?" from *Anatomy of a Jury.* Copyright 1986 by Seymour Wishman. Reprinted by permission of Times Books, a Division of Random House, Inc.

Wylie, Philip, "Common Women," from *A Generation of Vipers,* copyright 1942 by Philip Wylie, renewed. Reprinted by permission of Harold Ober Associates.